The
L/L Research
Channeling Archives

Transcripts of
the Meditation Sessions

Volume 14
September 3, 1995 to December 20, 1998

Don
Elkins

Jim
McCarty

Carla L.
Rueckert

Copyright © 2009 L/L Research

All rights reserved. No part of this book may be reproduced or used in any form or by any means—graphic, electronic or mechanical, including photocopying or information storage and retrieval systems—without written permission from the copyright holder.

ISBN: 978-0-945007-88-3

Published by L/L Research
Box 5195
Louisville, Kentucky 40255-0195

E-mail: contact@llresearch.org
www.llresearch.org

About the cover photo: *This photograph of Jim McCarty and Carla L. Rueckert was taken during an L/L Research channeling session on August 4, 2009, in the living room of their Louisville, Kentucky home. Jim always holds hands with Carla when she channels, following the Ra group's advice on how she can avoid any possibility of astral travel.*

Dedication

These archive volumes are dedicated to Hal and Jo Price, who faithfully and lovingly hosted this group's weekly meditation meetings from 1962 to 1975,

to Walt Rogers, whose work with the research group Man, Consciousness and Understanding of Detroit offered the information needed to begin this ongoing channeling experiment,

and to the Confederation of Angels and Planets in the Service of the Infinite Creator, for sharing their love and wisdom with us so generously through the years.

Table of Contents

Introduction 7
Year 1995 9
    September 3, 1995 10
    September 10, 1995 13
    September 17, 1995 17
    September 24, 1995 21
    October 1, 1995 27
    October 6, 1995 32
    October 7, 1995 34
    October 15, 1995 37
    October 22, 1995 43
    October 29, 1995 48
    November 5, 1995 51
    November 12, 1995 54
    November 17, 1995 58
    November 18, 1995 64
    November 18, 1995 72
    November 19, 1995 80
    December 10, 1995 87
    December 17, 1995 90
Year 1996 97
    January 14, 1996 98
    January 21, 1996 101
    February 4, 1996 106
    February 11, 1996 109
    February 18, 1996 113
    March 3, 1996 119
    March 10, 1996 124
    March 17, 1996 127
    March 24, 1996 130
    March 31, 1996 134
    April 7, 1996 140
    April 14, 1996 143
    April 21, 1996 149
    April 28, 1996 153
    May 12, 1996 159
    May 26, 1996 163
    August 25, 1996 165
    September 8, 1996 168

September 15, 1996	172
October 6, 1996	178
October 20, 1996	182
October 27, 1996	185
November 3, 1996	188
November 10, 1996	192
November 22, 1996	195
November 23, 1996	202
November 24, 1996	212
December 15, 1996	222
December 22, 1996	227

Year 1997 .... **231**

January 5, 1997	232
January 12, 1997	237
January 19, 1997	241
February 2, 1997	246
February 9, 1997	253
February 23, 1997	258
March 16, 1997	263
March 23, 1997	268
March 30, 1997	273
April 6, 1997	276
April 13, 1997	281
April 20, 1997	285
April 26, 1997	289
May 18, 1997	292
May 25, 1997	298
August 3, 1997	302
November 19, 1997	310
December 29, 1997	313

Year 1998 .... **318**

January 11, 1998	319
January 18, 1998	324
February 15, 1998	329
March 1, 1998	333
March 15, 1998	338
April 4, 1998	342
April 19, 1998	346
May 3, 1998	351
May 24, 1998	355
September 11, 1998	360
September 20, 1998	364

October 4, 1998	369
October 18, 1998	375
November 1, 1998	380
November 15, 1998	383
November 29, 1998	388
December 20, 1998	392

Introduction

Welcome to this volume of the *L/L Research Channeling Archives*. This series of publications represents the collection of channeling sessions recorded by L/L Research during the period from the early seventies to the present day. The sessions are also available on the L/L Research website, www.llresearch.org.

Starting in the mid-1950s, Don Elkins, a professor of physics and engineering at Speed Scientific School, had begun researching the paranormal in general and UFOs in particular. Elkins was a pilot as well as a professor and he flew his small plane to meet with many of the UFO contactees of the period.

Hal Price had been a part of a UFO-contactee channeling circle in Detroit called "The Detroit Group." When Price was transferred from Detroit's Ford plant to its Louisville truck plant, mutual friends discovered that Price also was a UFO researcher and put the two men together. Hal introduced Elkins to material called *The Brown Notebook* which contained instructions on how to create a group and receive UFO contactee information. In January of 1962 they decided to put the instructions to use and began holding silent meditation meetings on Sunday nights just across the Ohio River in the southern Indiana home of Hal and his wife, Jo. This was the beginning of what was called the "Louisville Group."

I was an original member of that group, along with a dozen of Elkins' physics students. However, I did not learn to channel until 1974. Before that date, almost none of our weekly channeling sessions were recorded or transcribed. After I began improving as a channel, Elkins decided for the first time to record all the sessions and transcribe them.

During the first eighteen months or so of my studying channeling and producing material, we tended to reuse the tapes as soon as the transcriptions were finished. Since those were typewriter days, we had no record of the work that could be reopened and used again, as we do now with computers. And I used up the original and the carbon copy of my transcriptions putting together a manuscript, *Voices of the Gods*, which has not yet been published. It remains as almost the only record of Don Elkins' and my channeling of that period.

We learned from this experience to retain the original tapes of all of our sessions, and during the remainder of the seventies and through the eighties, our "Louisville Group" was prolific. The "Louisville Group" became "L/L Research" after Elkins and I published a book in 1976, *Secrets of the UFO*, using that publishing name. At first we met almost every night. In later years, we met gradually less often, and the number of sessions recorded by our group in a year accordingly went down. Eventually, the group began taking three months off from channeling during the summer. And after 2000, we began having channeling meditations only twice a month. The volume of sessions dropped to its present output of eighteen or so each year.

These sessions feature channeling from sources which call themselves members of the Confederation of Planets in the Service of the Infinite Creator. At first we enjoyed hearing from many different voices: Hatonn, Laitos, Oxal, L/Leema and Yadda being just a few of them. As I improved my tuning techniques, and became the sole senior channel in L/L Research, the number of contacts dwindled. When I began asking for "the highest and best contact which I can receive of Jesus the Christ's vibration of unconditional love in a conscious and stable manner," the entity offering its thoughts through our group was almost always Q'uo. This remains true as our group continues to channel on an ongoing basis.

The channelings are always about love and unity, enunciating "The Law of One" in one aspect or another. Seekers who are working with spiritual principles often find the material a good resource. We hope that you will as well. As time has gone on the questions have shifted somewhat, but in general the content of the channeling is metaphysical and focused on helping seekers find the love in the moment and the Creator in the love.

At first, I transcribed our channeling sessions. I got busier, as our little group became more widely known, and got hopelessly behind on transcribing. Two early transcribers who took that job off my hands were Kim

Howard and Judy Dunn, both of whom masterfully transcribed literally hundreds of sessions through the eighties and early nineties.

Then Ian Jaffray volunteered to create a web site for these transcriptions, and single-handedly unified the many different formats that the transcripts were in at that time and made them available online. This additional exposure prompted more volunteers to join the ranks of our transcribers, and now there are a dozen or so who help with this. Our thanks go out to all of these kind volunteers, early and late, who have made it possible for our webguy to make these archives available.

Around the turn of the millennium, I decided to commit to editing each session after it had been transcribed. So the later transcripts have fewer errata than the earlier ones, which are quite imperfect in places. One day, perhaps, those earlier sessions will be revisited and corrections will be made to the transcripts. It would be a large task, since there are well over 1500 channeling sessions as of this date, and counting. We apologize for the imperfections in those transcripts, and trust that you can ascertain the sense of them regardless of a mistake here and there.

Blessings, dear reader! Enjoy these "humble thoughts" from the Confederation of Planets. May they prove good companions to your spiritual seeking. ♣

For all of us at L/L Research,

Carla L. Rueckert

Louisville, Kentucky

July 16, 2009

Year 1995
September 3, 1995 to December 17, 1995

L/L Research

L/L Research is a subsidiary of Rock Creek Research & Development Laboratories, Inc.

P.O. Box 5195
Louisville, KY 40255-0195

www.llresearch.org

Rock Creek is a non-profit corporation dedicated to discovering and sharing information which may aid in the spiritual evolution of humankind.

ABOUT THE CONTENTS OF THIS TRANSCRIPT: This telepathic channeling has been taken from transcriptions of the weekly study and meditation meetings of the Rock Creek Research & Development Laboratories and L/L Research. It is offered in the hope that it may be useful to you. As the Confederation entities always make a point of saying, please use your discrimination and judgment in assessing this material. If something rings true to you, fine. If something does not resonate, please leave it behind, for neither we nor those of the Confederation would wish to be a stumbling block for any.

CAVEAT: This transcript is being published by L/L Research in a not yet final form. It has, however, been edited and any obvious errors have been corrected. When it is in a final form, this caveat will be removed.

© 2009 L/L Research

Sunday Meditation
September 3, 1995

Group question: We would like to know if when we try to be of service to others are we doing anything other than working on ourselves? Are we really being of service to others? Is there any way of being of service to others other than by providing catalyst that could be provided to that person almost in any way. That person is going to go through that catalyst with or without us. So, what is our role other than working on ourselves?

(Carla channeling)

We are those of the principle of Q'uo, and we greet you in the love and in the light of the one infinite Creator. May we say how happy we are to speak to this group this day. It has been some time since we have spoken with you and your presence delights us. We thank you for the privilege of being a part of this circle. We bear greetings also from those of Hatonn and those of Oxal, for they wish, as well as we, to thank each who has asked us to meditate with them in the period during which there were no formal meetings held. This also is a great privilege for us and we count it as a substantial part of that service which we have come here to offer you.

This day you ask us whether teaching has any value other than that of working upon the self. You will notice here the paradox that is endless. How can one serve another since all that one does to serve another serves the self? This paradox is only apparent. It is not authentic or genuine, yet it is to be noted that paradox seems an essential and necessary part of any spiritual question or line of questioning. And when one runs head on into a paradox, an enigma, a riddle, one has a kind of sign that, yes, this is spiritual work. There is nothing more baffling or more complete than the mystery that is the Creator.

The difficulty with teaching among your peoples is that difficulty which one finds in the use of words. Were teachers silent, were there no concepts traded from one to another, yet still the teacher would teach and that teaching slowly absorbed would be that which hewed closer to truth. We point this out because it is apart from the main thrust of what we wish to say. However, it is a problem that weighs heavily upon both teacher and student, this relationship both have to the words they speak and the words they hear.

We would turn to the main thrust of this query with the statement that we are here as a kind of obvious symbol of our own opinion that teaching is possible and that one is doing more than teaching the self. Wise is the teacher who waits for the student to ask to indicate interest in a subject, a concept or a train of thought, for what the teacher essentially is for the student is a kind of catalyst that bears a weight, a heaviness, a bottom which balances and makes stable for that student the point of delivery for the catalyst given. All are teaching each other. Sometimes intentionally. Often unintentionally. But when the entity teaching is not self-perceived as a teacher the teaching that comes to the other is interpreted for the most part by the other as having no weight. It is not a kind of teaching that attracts because it is completely random, each person responding to the other and each teaching each.

When the student perceives that an entity is a teacher, when the student then gives weight and respect to and for that teacher's opinions, then there has been made a stable connection. The student becomes ready to open. The teacher, likewise, becomes ready to share, and that which is offered is offered in a stable and careful manner. This is the advantage of intending to teach. The disadvantage of intending to teach is that there are expectations upon the part of the teacher and upon the part of the student and these expectations, while benign for the most part, sometimes block the student or the teacher from paying attention or being completely aware of all that is transpiring and all that is being communicated. Directions can be missed by teacher and by student.

Perhaps we would say that the ideal between teacher and student is a union wherein each shares what each has brought and the other listens in a way that does not distort and together there is the plaiting of one strand of thought with another and another and another in a rope or string of new connections and new facets to the subject that both are focused upon. This is the kind of teaching which gives both new strength and a new awareness and a continuing desire for more.

At the same time we need to look at the fact that is so well known to this instrument and to each of you and that is that there is only one self. There is only one Creator and insofar as the deepest levels of truth that we know may go, the basic truth is that all centers of consciousness alike work upon the self, for what is not the self?

Let us turn back now to the teacher for a moment. Let us gaze at this structure, this place or position and the ramifications of it. What does the teacher teach? Within third density it is popularly and generally perceived that the teacher teaches a subject. "What do you teach?" is the response to discovering that an entity is a teacher. However, students are well aware, whether teachers are or not, that a great deal, sometimes a majority, of what a teacher brings to teaching is not on the subject that is being taught, for teachers teach first of all by who they are and how they allow entities to come within their gates of acceptance. Those whose teachings affect students most are those who allow the students to learn the teacher [as a being] as well as the teaching, for each is a teacher in that each presents a certain complex of vibrations to the world. And those fundamental vibrations are as clearly perceived by a student as are the words spoken. So that the teacher who has truly been called to be a teacher has a store of being that it is willing to share. This beingness, this way of living and of presenting the self is a catalyst to the student on a deeper level, shall we say, than the actual subject matter which has been discussed.

And this is each entity's gift to give to the world, this way of living that allows the world to see into the self. This is a way of each teaching each that is unparalleled in its ability to transform and rejuvenate those who receive such unspoken instructions.

Within third density talking, communicating, expressing the self and even the arguing, the disputes, the dynamics of difference are the meat and drink of those who wish to learn and those who wish to seek the truth. We encourage each to know within the self that the way of being, the way of living, is a great offering, we feel, the greatest offering and the first job, shall we say, of those who wish to serve. Everything springs from your beingness, so the first career of any seeker is that career of one who seeks to live devotionally throughout a lifetime. In terms of students and teachers this dedication to a life of devotion and faith makes one the eternal student and the eternal teacher. Again, the paradox.

In the end there is not a great deal of activity that does not teach and certainly that which is worthwhile, that which is worthy of being taught has many, many witnesses and needs many, many more. The condition of mortality is one which encourages some illusions more than others. One illusion that being within incarnation does create well is that sense of beginning and ending which is exemplified by each birth and each death of a being that comes into incarnation and then leaves it again. In this context it is easy to question the value of teachers that are teaching that which will not put bread upon the table, give the worker the job, or present to the society one who is capable of fulfilling the mundane requirements of one position or another. Yet that kind of teaching which looks to a life well lived rather than a job well done is the teaching that will open for the student the greater amount of life and give the teacher's eyes to the student on a deeper level.

Before we leave this instrument we would like to say again how pleased we are that this group continues and seeks new life, new learning, new catalyst for contemplation. We feel that truth is new every day and that there is always the way that has not been found that waits for the one who wishes to sing a new song. Truth is never exhausted and teachers shall never be unemployed.

This student and teacher reminds us that we need to be aware of time and so we would transfer to the one known as Jim at this time, feeling that we have made a beginning on this interesting question. We thank this instrument and leave it in love and in light. We are those of Q'uo.

(Jim channeling)

I am Q'uo, and greet each again in love and in light through this instrument. Again, may we say that we are full of gratitude to be able to utilize each of these instruments this day and would ask those gathered about if there might be any further queries at this time?

Carla: There was something that you were offering me that I didn't quite get at one point and it had to do with the students teaching and the teachers learning. If you can comment on this I would appreciate it.

I am Q'uo, and we are aware of your query but are not quite certain as to the portion which you did not understand so we shall attempt to speak thusly.

The student, when considering instructions of the teacher, takes that which is the self which it is at its heart with it upon a journey that the teacher offers by presenting the concepts and considerations which are just beyond the student's current level of understanding and integration within its *(inaudible)*. As the student walks with the teacher on this mutual journey of teaching and learning the teacher becomes aware of the student's response according to its own observation of the student's feedback and the intuition that develops in any relationship that involves energy exchange. Thus, the teacher is being taught how to teach as the student learns what is given. The teacher finds new areas *(inaudible)* so that there is no possibility of teaching without learning or learning without teaching for those engaged in this process of changing the self. All change is learning. All learning is change.

Is there a further query, my sister?

Carla: No, I think I hear what you are saying …

(Rest of recording is inaudible.) ✒

L/L Research

L/L Research is a subsidiary of Rock Creek Research & Development Laboratories, Inc.

P.O. Box 5195
Louisville, KY 40255-0195

www.llresearch.org

Rock Creek is a non-profit corporation dedicated to discovering and sharing information which may aid in the spiritual evolution of humankind.

ABOUT THE CONTENTS OF THIS TRANSCRIPT: This telepathic channeling has been taken from transcriptions of the weekly study and meditation meetings of the Rock Creek Research & Development Laboratories and L/L Research. It is offered in the hope that it may be useful to you. As the Confederation entities always make a point of saying, please use your discrimination and judgment in assessing this material. If something rings true to you, fine. If something does not resonate, please leave it behind, for neither we nor those of the Confederation would wish to be a stumbling block for any.

CAVEAT: This transcript is being published by L/L Research in a not yet final form. It has, however, been edited and any obvious errors have been corrected. When it is in a final form, this caveat will be removed.

© 2009 L/L Research

Sunday Meditation
September 10, 1995

Group question: We would like to know more about worry and fear in their relation to faith. Can one create faith, or must one wait for a gift of faith, like grace? Does worry or fear ever help us by giving us the motivation to protect ourselves from injury?

(Carla channeling)

We are those of Q'uo. Greetings in the love and in the light of the one infinite Creator. May we say what a blessing it is to be with you at this time, to share our thoughts with you and to blend our vibrations with your own. That which you ask this day is a question of much substance, for in learning the lessons of love the development of the faculty of faith plays a central role. The worry and fear which move through the awareness of those who seek is not so much that which is a mistake or error as that which reacts rather than responds and in developing the faculty called faith the lesson learned of responding rather than reacting is key.

You also ask if there are any positive aspects to worry and we say that, of course, that which is loosely termed worry can be foolish and mean nothing but it can also be wisdom or intuition which senses the need for concern. The entity who worries that the house has not been shut properly before leaving will turn off the light, will check the locks, will secure the dwelling in as many ways as is necessary. Worry gets the bad name because entities do not always focus upon the central question of whether there is in the concern any area or portion of that concern which lies within the purview or control of the one who is concerned. When there is no avenue open for action which can address a concern the worry has no function within the physical illusion. Its function in the inner life then becomes that of moving the entity off center, removing the peace which lies within the one whose heart is clear, and sets up catalyst. This function is useful. It is a way by which the mind focuses itself upon that point of inner distress. Over this inner universe, unlike the outer manifestation, the seeker does have resources to which he may turn.

The question was asked during your study period—this instrument needs a moment to deepen the tuning and we pause that this may be done.

(Pause)

We are again with this instrument. The question that was asked earlier was what is there to choose to do instead of worrying, and we suggest to you that worry is disorganized and random prayer. The deepest inner dialogue is with the great Self that overarches and undergirds all that is. Worries and fears not only stew and seethe within the mind, they also register with the infinite One as cries of distress. However, the energy used in worrying is tangled and mazed and the Creator, although reaching within always to comfort, simply cannot move through that tangle that has stopped the inner hearing, the inner vision, the inner sensing, of that peaceful, creative and wise self.

Thusly, when the seeker sees itself in a muddle, worrying and fretting, we suggest that one resource that may aid is the memory, the remembrance of the fact that one who worries may also be one who prays and enters into conversation with the infinite Creator, that greater Self of which each is an ineffable and unique portion.

Now, each knows within the heart that worry founded or unfounded is only effective when there is an option open, something that can be adjusted or controlled. The one thing over which the seeker has constant control is the will, and it is the function of the will to aid in the establishment of a life in faith, for worry may be contractive to faith. So we come to the question of what can be done to increase faith.

Now, the faith, when taken hold of by the seeker, creates an area of control in all situations within this or your illusion, indeed, within any that we know of. How to lay hold upon that natural function? How to encourage it? We have often said that faith, when first chosen as a way of living, is nothing more than a leap into space. Faith creates itself in the mid-air, when the will of the seeker has been surrendered. That first so-called leap of faith is a beginning. It could be nothing more than the conscious decision, the promise to the self, "I will live by faith." This is a good beginning.

The will is invoked by such an affirmation. Each time the seeker subsequently [finds] itself mired in useless and cyclical worry the affirmation may be repeated, "I will live by faith." Sooner or later there comes a moment when the repetition has bred a new and positive habit of mind and in that moment the seeker finds that she has skipped the usual habit of worry and been inspired spontaneously to affirm, "I will live by faith." That moment of peace is as precious as your rare metals and should be stored carefully in a special part of the memory, that memory that lies just behind the surface of things.

Now, the faculty called faith stems from an infinite sureness, a knowledge of self that rests deep within the roots of mind. All that the seeker does when invoking faith is to reach towards the root of mind where that faculty lies waiting to be encouraged to grow. Eventually, faith does become a habit, and during periods of the incarnation when an entity is experiencing those things which are perceived as pleasant, she may rest and experience the peace which passes understanding. Yet there shall, in the natural cycle of light and dark that is your illusion, be times when there is no comfort. There is no spontaneous feeling of faith. And then it is that the wise seeker is content to live upon the bare memory of those winsome, glad times when the spirit is high and the faith flowed like water. These memories are true and they are as the talisman that protects the entity suffering through change and transformation even though no sense of faith remains.

Faith is indeed a gift in that some entities have a clearer line or connection with their own unconscious mind. Faith is also a built-in, inherent and native portion of the deep mind and thusly it can be developed and pulled up into the conscious existence by one who works to form the habit of turning to faith and faith's ability to give one the opportunity to create that area of control which changes the fear and fret of daily worry into an occasion to invoke faith. Once that feeling has been experienced of the support given by faith, then it becomes more and more natural to turn from the small circle of worry to the upreaching of prayer, intercession, praise and thanksgiving.

Those things which aid in connecting the faith deep within to the conscious mind include first of all the regular meditation, for in the silence of meditation connections from within the deep mind are being made and information is flowing. Also, we suggest the encouragement within the self of praise and thanksgiving for all, large and small, or the ephemeral world that may meet the senses. Prayer, praise and thanksgiving are three resources that add and strengthen the connection to faith.

We feel that this is a good beginning upon this interesting subject and would ask at this time for any questions that you may have. Is there a query at this time?

R: This instrument has a new computer. Is there something that the instrument can do to make sure that the computer keeps working, or is there some effect she has on it that we should know about?

We are those of Q'uo. We feel that the instrument and the instrument are compatible. The energy which creates disturbance within sound-producing equipment does not produce the same distortion with the computer. Indeed, the instrument has, shall we say, a beneficial effect upon the computer.

Is there another query?

R: To be sure, then, the computer would not have any deleterious effect upon the instrument as far as using hands is concerned?

We are those of Q'uo, and if we grasped your query correctly it is the instrument's choice to martyr the self in some degree that lies prior to any handling of any equipment that requires fine motor motion.

May we respond further, my brother?

R: To restate: might the computer emit any harmful energy fields for the instrument, since she is sensitive?

We are those of Q'uo, and we grasp your query now. We do not see a deleterious effect upon the instrument from the electromagnetic field of the computer.

Is there another query?

P: Two. First is a personal question. I am having a child and I want to know how the development of this child affects the energy centers of the mother?

We are those of Q'uo. As a woman accepts within the physical body the new physical entity she finds the energies within the self to be moving into harmony with the nascent and developing energies of the child within. This creates, at first, a dimming or lessening throughout the energy centers of the mother as the system adapts to and balances with the incoming entity's energies. Because of the fundamental nature of conception and gestation the mother will often find the red or root ray energy center becoming stronger. During this strengthening it is easy to experience imbalance within that center because of the relative rapidity with which this process affects both child and mother.

So the energies involved in living, breathing, eating, sleeping, those creature comforts, those natural sexual functions, may seem to be very strong but confused or muddied. Likewise the green ray energy center tends to run very hot, shall we say, for the natural faculties within the mother are opened as a flower to the sun by the process of nurturing and creating the life and all that that great opportunity brings with it. The remaining energy centers have a tendency to be dim and not particularly well balanced due to the immense amount of energy which is being devoted on the red ray and green ray levels by the mother.

Therefore, it is helpful in attempting to balance the energy centers to use the visualization of that more balanced and even flow of energy, visualizing this, even speaking of it aloud to the self in affirmative sentences may do much to even out those energies and create more vitality and sense of comfort to the mother.

May we answer you further?

P: When do the energy centers of the child develop?

The energy centers of the child are already developed. The energy centers of the physical vehicle are in an inchoate state until the entity decides to come into the physical vehicle. When that melding of spirit and flesh takes place the physical body then takes on the basic energy balances of the entity taking advantage of the incarnational opportunity. As the entity settles into the physical vehicle the physical energy centers are invested with the entity's energies which are as a complex of vibrations expressing the self and its personality. The resulting harmonies of spirit and physical vehicle create the energy centers in the configuration which the child begins the incarnation with.

We may say also that the child whose mother consciously seeks cooperation and balance between her energies and the incoming spirit's energies creates the better atmosphere for the child to be in. The function of the thinking about or brooding about the child to come is that it creates a more and more comfortable pathway for the child as it is welcomed into physical existence.

May we answer further?

P: You spoke of the melding of spirit and body. A certain time?

The incoming spirit chooses its unique moment to enter. It may be very early in the pregnancy. It may be almost identical to the moment of birth. Some life paths need to begin with catalyst within the womb and some therefore choose to dwell within that environment and experience suffering. Others may choose to come in early because there is a tremendous attraction between mother and child. And such a child experiences great communion and unconditional love during this time so that an entity begins life perhaps already burdened with sorrow or with unreasoning optimism and joy. These are very individual choices and there is not one selected moment for all but, rather, each chooses for the self.

Is there another query?

P: Is there a sign or indication that the mother would know when the spirit begins to interact?

I am Q'uo. Often there is indeed that moment of recognition, that moment when the mother knows the child within. The more tuned in to the self and its true feelings the mother is the more sensitive and vulnerable to such contact that person is. We would suggest that it will always have a beneficial effect to the child when the mother communicates with that entity; whether that is talking out loud to it or simply thinking to it, such efforts at sharing and communicating are often rewarded.

Further queries?

P: Would you be able to suggest any method of meditation for the mother that is helpful to the child? Thinking and talking are good. Should she refrain from certain activities that may be harmful to the child?

We are those of Q'uo. To the entity coming into incarnation the world is at first a disorienting place. It picks up and takes as its own any strong emotion or state which is the mother's. If the mother's life is that which creates a deep unhappiness this has a tremendous effect upon the child within. Similarly, the child will drink in joy and peace and love to the fullest extent, finding this gift as natural as the mother's blood which flows through its veins. As the physical fetus develops the child begins to have independent feelings, but this is not marked until after the birth.

May we answer you further?

P: No, thanks.

My sister, we thank you also. We do find that the instrument is tiring and so we would at this time leave our blessing, our love, and our faith with you, and take leave of this instrument and this group. We leave you in the love and in the light of the One Who is All. We are those of the principle known to you as Q'uo. Go forth with joy. Adonai. Adonai. ✣

Sunday Meditation
September 17, 1995

Group question: What part does wisdom play in our lives as seekers of truth attempting to learn compassion, forgiveness and mercy? Is there anything that we can do to inform our actions with wisdom? What is wisdom in this density?

(Carla channeling)

We are those of Q'uo, and we greet you in the love and in the light of the one infinite Creator. It is such a blessing for us to be called to address your circle. We thank you and assure you that the honor is much prized and appreciated by us. We have come to feel a kinship with those of this group and this privilege rests in our hearts.

As we speak, as always we ask that each recall that our truth is opinion, not fact, and though we offer those truths which we have learned carefully, yet these may not be those truths of your heart which you must lay claim upon. Each thought that we offer is as a gift. Place those aside that you do not respond to with recognition and a feeling of remembrance, and take those that may fit you and your circumstances. We thank you for reserving your own powers of discrimination. This enables us to speak freely and share with you those opinions which we have earned.

We might begin by saying that there is a sense in which wisdom is a term describing an illusion within your density, for the concept of wisdom implies that there is a right or correct way of thinking or acting. And while in things of your third-density illusion there are a nearly endlessly supply of right or correct answers, within the spiritual search, within that world which is walked within the heart and within the mind by those who seek to accelerate the rate of their spiritual evolution, there is often no correct solution to a perceived situation or difficulty. As this instrument was saying earlier, the tendency of the rational mind to search for a correct solution and to think in terms of solutions can sometimes lead the seeker astray.

Let us look, if you will, at the wisdom of your world. Its structure, through your recorded history, has been that logical structure which so arranges and subdivides the multitudinous phenomena absorbable in daily life in such a way that the mind may contain a working picture, if you will, of the contents of the environment around the thinker. Wisdom is seen to be a structure of logic and thought into which one may place the various learnings and systems of learning that comprise the well-rounded mental atmosphere. One might almost think of wisdom as the housekeeper of the house of light, each kind of thought and area of endeavor having its own room, shelf, or closet. The wise man can be seen to be one whose house stands befor the blast of random circumstances, able to take new information and fit that within that logical structure which has these thoughts in that room, those thoughts in the other.

In the eyes of your world, then, the wiser man is he who, when faced with new and challenging information, is able to restructure or, shall we say, remodel the house of thought so that the new furniture fits with the old. It is, however, the case that wise as the wisdom of your world is, it reaches to the limits of the spiritual walk and not beyond them. We wish, however, to make a point of saying that. A seeker whose worldly house of logic and thought is untended and unkempt shall have unnecessary difficulties in the spiritual seeking. Perhaps the wisdom of the world is greatly limited, but the physical being that carries your consciousness around is well served by one who takes the time and energy to develop that worldly kind of wisdom which is mostly the application of logical analysis to the constant stream of in-coming sense impressions that gives that hungry mind fodder to eat.

The seeker whose house is in order, then, has the inner sense of freedom to address that spiritual walk which is so dear and so necessary to those who have awakened to that hunger for truth that marks the seeker in a metaphysical sense. We see the sadness and the reluctance that this instrument feels when it gazes upon the turning of the season from warmth to cold, and we would compare the wisdom of the world to the experience of the physical vehicle in summer. The world invades and encroaches upon the self. It curls about one. There is a feeling of abundance and richness, and as this instrument would say, "the living is easy." Hard as the decisions the world asks of you are in a worldly sense, they are of great comfort and ease compared to the often chilly choices and challenges facing the metaphysical seeker, for in the world of spirit there is a far colder kind of wisdom. It is the wisdom of one who gazes upon illusion and is able to see through the illusion to the mystery.

Thusly, the spiritual wise man is first the world's fool. That ability to gaze at the richness and fullness of life and see its vanity is infinite is that ability which reaches into the beginnings of spiritual wisdom. Perhaps each is familiar with the concept of the sight which sees that which is becoming that which is not and, finally, becoming again that which is yet known more fully, [and] will be able to move up a step or two; each time the realization turns itself inside out and then reverts once again.

Let us look at the reflection of the wisdom of the spirit. One reflection is the activity chosen by the seeker known as inner listening, practicing the presence of the one infinite Creator, meditation or prayer. One may see that an entity has laid claim to wisdom as that one surrenders the mind that is so capable in the worldly sense and takes up instead the silent mystery that speaks the one great original Thought. There is a reflection of wisdom in one who opens the hand and releases some necessity, some urgency, letting it go, releasing worry and concern, placing the feet solidly in the mid-air of faith alone.

One may see the reflection of wisdom in the one who leaves the presence of good times and good company in order to be of service to one who is lost and has asked for aid. One may see the reflection of wisdom shining from the face of one who is laying hold of some infinite virtue, [who] stands unafraid and submits to whatever the world wishes to do regardless of the inconvenience of the outcome. One may see the reflection of wisdom in one who lays down the life for the cause of another. The key to spiritual wisdom is a kind of seeing.

Now, the physical sight is beautifully created and gives to a seeker windows upon an incredible and amazing physical universe, full of beauty and rhythms and perfect harmony. Each seeker has nascent, often inchoate inner vision as well. One may think of this faculty as the eyes of the spiritual body. These eyes, too, are wonderfully created, yet they lie dormant within the physical illusion until the seeker awakes to that clarion call of the spiritual walk. Then it is as if the worldly self has birthed the spirit within and as with all infants that eyesight of the inner spiritual entity is unfocused, untaught and very, very limited in its ability to see.

As the seeker begins to gain experience it discovers that the worldly sight, excellent as it is for the things of the physical universe, can tell lies if the physical sight is taken to equal spiritual sight as well. The spiritual self will look at the situation where all the things of the world are had in plenty and be able to see those imbalances, lacks and hungers that lie just below the surface of the illusion and that greatly change the truth that is seen. The spiritual self sees the riches of the world as poverty and sees the naked and vulnerable spirit in all its poverty as riches. To the spiritual eye the concepts such as death, limitation, emergency, catastrophe, fear and terror are not necessarily bad things. The riches for the spiritual self lie in every circumstance, those perceived as negative perhaps more than those perceived as positive by the physical self.

Strictly speaking, wisdom is a null word within third density. If it is striven for the result is a greater and greater ability to see the truth of the physical existence. That is, the man counted as wise is the one who seems to see most clearly, yet we say to you that the utmost clarity of awareness of [an] entity's true motives and so forth is still that which contain great distortion.

In a non-relative sense we may say that wisdom is to be embodied rather than contained within the mind. A great amount of work is done within the density of wisdom to improve the spiritual eyesight. Foreshadowings of this density of wisdom fall across the seeker's path in third density daily, and the seeker does well to give a good effort to striving to attain a measure of wisdom even though that effort is doomed to certain failure, because the desire to seek wisdom in itself contains the wisdom of third density. If you burn to be truly wise then focus upon that burning, that yearning desire. Seek to penetrate the mystery. Ache and reach for the heart of truth. The result is that to the extent you have purified that desire you have embodied wisdom such as it can be in your present illusion. The prelude to spiritual wisdom is surrender.

When we greet you in love and in light we greet you in love or compassion and light or wisdom. Wisdom is concerned with the structure that tells its story within your awareness in such a way that you are best equipped to consider the mystery in all its stunning totality. If you seek to be spiritually wise then know that love and light, compassion and wisdom, are the substance and form of the Creator and the Creator's universe. Wisdom builds the house of thought within which one may think upon the mystery. Love is the only solitary quality that can fill that form and create out of emptiness all that there is in its rejoicing, exulting splendor.

This is a stunning universe. This is an amazing mystery. We cannot express our excitement and our joy at the simple contemplation of the Creator. And beyond all seeking for light and knowledge there lies the golden, living, powerful and ever-penetrating fact of love. Your form is spun of light, your nature of love.

We leave this instrument in that love and light and would transfer at this time to the one known as Jim. We are those of the principle of Q'uo.

(Jim channeling)

I am Q'uo, and greet each again in love and in light through this instrument. At this time we would ask if we may speak to any further queries which those present may have for us?

R: *(Inaudible).*

I am Q'uo, and, my brother, we grasp that your query is clear yet we would suggest that there are mysteries aplenty and that each entity will find the appropriate response to all catalyst.

(Side one of tape ends.)

(Jim channeling)

I am Q'uo, and am again with this instrument. Is there any further query, my brother?

R: No, Q'uo. Thank you.

I am Q'uo, and it is our great honor and privilege to share with you the catalyst of words, of thoughts, of desires and of the path of the seeker.

Is there another query at this time?

P: *(Inaudible).*

I am Q'uo, and am aware of your query. The one known as Chocolate Bar, as all things in this illusion, has utilized its catalyst well and now approaches the removing of the garment of this incarnational experience, the physical vehicle which begins to deteriorate and to indicate to all who observe the ending of the incarnation. The giving of love to this entity and the rejoicing in its presence is that which is always most helpful, whether the entity chooses to remain or to go further upon its path.

Is there any further query?

P: *(Inaudible).*

I am Q'uo, and we are aware of your query, my sister, and may speak in the affirmative in that this entity has through its many years of devotion to those about it been able to gain that ability, to give and to receive love in a manner which will allow it to choose whether it shall go forward into the third-density experience or whether it shall return once again as a second-density being so that it might dwell with those with whom it now shares its incarnational experience.

Is there a further query, my sister?

P: No, thank you.

I am Q'uo, and again we thank you. Is there another query?

Carla: Is it possible to answer whether Chocolate Bar is the reincarnation of Jim's dog, Trixie, from his childhood?

I am Q'uo, and am aware of your query, my sister. We find that it is best, in our opinion, to leave this possibility as a possibility.

Is there any further query, my sister?

Carla: No, thank you.

I am Q'uo, and we thank you, my sister. Is there another query?

(Pause)

I am Q'uo, and we feel that we have spoken to those concerns which those present have offered to us and we are most grateful for this opportunity to be with each of you, and we further affirm to each that we are with you at any time at which you request our presence. We walk with light and gladsome feet and move where we are called, rejoicing at each calling and each journey of movement and we thank those present for offering us the possibility of service. Though we are never certain of service, we are always certain of the desire to serve and it is with a whole heart that we answer your call.

At this time we shall take our leave of this instrument and this group, rejoicing in the presence of each, feeling great joy for the One who shines forth in all. We are known to you as those of Q'uo. Adonai, my friends. Adonai. ☙

L/L Research

Sunday Meditation
September 24, 1995

Group question: The question this afternoon concerns the topic discussed this afternoon. Many religions and philosophies have as one of the basic tenets the dropping of all desires, because the desire is seen as that which ties us to this world, and if we wish to transcend this world and go to the next, better world, or a better state of mind, then we need to drop the desires that are tying us here.

Don said many times that it was a good idea to release the dedication to an outcome for any action we were undertaking, to simply do whatever it was we wish to do or thought best to do but to not be dedicated to however it came out except whatever it was that was the result, without great joy or sorrow.

Ra speaks of balancing distortions or desires, so that you allow them their spontaneous action; you do everything that is a natural part of the situation, and then later on, without imposing anything on the situation, you attempt to balance the situation so that you have a full range of experience. Many of the Confederation have said over the years that is a good idea to accept that which is, to accept those failings in ourselves and others and the world around us and to attempt to give love, compassion and forgiveness and mercy instead. Yet, if we continue to accept everything that is we would be accepting what would seem to be a lot of injustices and difficulties that are putting people at a disadvantage … disease, and a lot of difficulty.

So, we would like for Q'uo to comment about this entire range of dropping desire, reducing the dedication to an outcome, or loving, accepting and yet working for a change so that we continue to strive for an ideal, and to improve, to grow in mind, body and spirit … and if that's too long Q'uo, you can just pick any question you want.

(Carla channeling)

We are those of the principle of Q'uo, and we greet you in love and in light in the name of the one infinite Creator. As always, we express a great appreciation to those who diligently seek from day to day, from week to week, from year to year, walking the way one foot at a time in front of the other, steadily, faithfully, hewing to that which is held in the heart the way that truth lives. We share those footsteps with you and as we speak with you concerning desire we assure you that our desire to serve is both deep and pure. The opportunity your desire for truth gives us is a great treasure for us …

(Carla asks for a drink.)

We are those of Q'uo, and we apologize for the pause while this instrument wets her whistle.

Gazing at the nature of your density we may safely remark that desire is the fuel that runs the engine of your illusion, both the portion which is shadow and that portion which is form. That is to say, that desire is intrinsic to the awareness of being individuated. Desire is inherent in a consciousness of the self and the not-self. Whether it be wise or foolish, profitable or unfortunate to desire, those enjoying incarnation within your density will experience the proceeding and issuing forth of desires. One desires, for instance, oxygen, because that is the food for the blood that gives life to your organism. Not to desire oxygen is from the bodily point of view nearly unthinkable and certainly were one to achieve the cessation of a desire to breathe that entity's life as a non-desiring being would be short. It is not, then, unwise to desire food for the physical vehicle, or the mental, emotional, spiritual vehicles, all of which bodies have natural functions and desires.

However, hidden from the first glance amongst rightful desires lies the exercise of what we have sometimes called the will. Each surely has experienced that energy of willing something to be so or not to be so. The personal will can take a part in desire which distorts desire from natural and even functioning into skewed values and incorrect or incorrectly perceived ways of thinking and processing information. Now, we say that we have called the faculty the will or the self-will. We might also call such distortion in natural desires the function—we correct this instrument—the action of prideful will or simple pride, for pride over and above the natural feelings connected with desire is that—we search this instrument's mind for an appropriate word—and find none. Therefore we shall begin again.

Pride as it interacts with natural desires is as the cancer which takes over natural cells and begins multiplying them without stint. Growth, desire is considered an excellent thing but prideful growth in the form of the cancerous tumor can kill the organism which experiences it. So we would say that perhaps it might be useful to think of the desires that one has, asking oneself whether the pride is stirred up in the expressing of this desire, whichever one that the seeker is considering

This is subtle work, but as each desire comes forward the mind may entertain it, gazing at it to find those places where prideful will has puffed up the importance of obtaining that which one desires. To desire to be in the presence of the one infinite Creator is in our opinion the most basic and true of desires. Nor would we suggest that any discourages the hunger and thirst for the life-giving presence of love. We would not suggest that any relinquish the desire to be of service, for the purity of that desire is what works to accentuate the polarity of the seeker and that which will give the seeker continuing and helpful catalyst which acts to feed back support into that desire to be united with the infinite One.

As we look over the many instances that you mentioned in your query where various religious and philosophical systems have encouraged the cessation of desire as being wise we can certainly understand the feelings which prompt such wise advice, for truly to relinquish desire is to relinquish discomfort. There is a valid path towards the Creator, following this simple advice. However, the choice of path does not stop with this, shall we say, simplistic a solution to the question of desire. While this relinquishing of desires seems all one, there are an infinity of alternate paths, paths which are more complex but which do lead to the same one original and central Logos. Within third density the likelihood is that one within the cultural nexus within which this group finds itself will not find the path of self-effacement to be as helpful or available as paths in which desire is not shunned but rather dealt with in a way which enables the seeker to strip from desire that pride of self which would puff up. Each is seeking, as it were, to refine those things which are natural.

The skin, for example, is cleansed and the lotion placed on it to alleviate dryness; the desire for friends and companionship is refined and subjected to enough examination and to the journey towards finding the ways to refine that need for company so that the desire is not for the company that feeds the self but rather the desire becomes purely the hope to serve a beloved other self. To the increasingly quiet mind from which pride is systematically being discouraged, little by little the pride becomes easier to spot. The emotions associated with impure desire become more transparent to the eye and to the ear and to the heart.

It is very likely, we feel, that which you call desire is implicit within the process which the Creator is engaged in this present moment. That sensing of the self which is the Creator's relationship with all of its parts is a relationship full of desire. The desire to know the self is that which launched the universe in all of its infinity. Without this freely chosen desire on the part of the Creator there would be all that there is but there would be no awareness of it. The

Creator Itself, then, is expressing desire—else we, you, and all would not exist. Every tiny mote of consciousness in the infinite creation is loved, desired and manifested because of that desire.

Now, we cannot say that all those systems are wrong to encourage the removal of desire, for truly much of life as you experience it, as it responds to unconscious and deep desires runs directly counter to one's conscious desires. The instinct of the seeker is often to [fight] against the way the experience is going, to desire a change, whereas the deeper desire of the self may well be to experience loss, limitation or some difficulty. We would ask you then to think of your desires as those things which are natural and good in their essence.

However, because the illusion is thick and because there is the veil drawn between the conscious mind and the unconscious mind many times it seems impossible to embrace that which is occurring, even though the deep mind does indeed embrace this seemingly negative situation. The task of the seeker is simply to place the self within the fire and allow the catalyst to burn away that pride of self which suggests that the desirerer knows the way to purify desire. You have within you the capacity for great faith and we may suggest that one way to exercise this capacity and so enlarge it is to reflect, when faced with that which one does not desire, with the quiet mind which is willing to open the hand and say "Here is all I feel. Teach me what is the pure desire and what is the husk and chaff of pride."

Now let us step back and gaze at the unity of creation and know the sweetness of perfect harmony, harmony that is not still but which carries desire in its arms, but in a rhythmic and graceful fashion. To desire love and light is an instinct in the human blooming just as it is instinct which turns flower to the sun. There are words that aid in the gradual working away at that pride which says "I know better." Words such as "surrender," "allow," "accept." These are words of health when used carefully. We suggest that a great tool to use in working with pride is kindness towards the self. You are within an illusion which insists that you begin with impure and cluttered emotions.

All the wisdom and passion that there is lies within, yet because the spiritual child is young it is clumsy and awkward. It feels so much love and yearning and wishes so much to be more comfortable, more light and spirit-filled. Yet we say to you that the path that is appropriate for each, no matter how wise, who comes into incarnation is the path of impure and confusing desires and it is within this puzzling atmosphere of emotion and thought within which each is intended to do the work and find the learning within the incarnation. The Creator to be found is found here, within that sea of confusion and prideful desire that mask the rightful and pure emotion that is hunger and thirst for truth, love, and for beauty.

This is not an easy topic to discuss, for as you pointed out in your discussion earlier, even the desire not to have desires is a desire. So we say to you—desire! Go ahead with that emotion but subject that emotion to self-examination, seeking always to prick the puffed up pride of self that insists it is the holder of the keys to righteousness. And meanwhile, expend time comforting and supporting that spiritual child within, whose yearnings are the breath of life itself for the evolving spirit. Comfort, succor and cherish this being within that is stirring and growing and beginning to see within this illusion through your eyes, that spiritual self, the one child each shall have regardless of the sex or the age. Love and support that evolving self and look for ways to purify the emotions that drive and teach and give opportunity for learning within this life, this incarnational experience which you now so briefly enjoy. There is peace in purified emotion, there is comfort at least, and the home within the clear and lucid desire.

We would at this time transfer the contact to the one known as Jim. We leave this instrument in love and in light. We are those of Q'uo.

(Jim channeling)

I am Q'uo, and greet each again in love and in light through this instrument. We would ask at this time if there may be any further queries to which we may speak for the service of those in this circle?

Questioner: I have a question. I have been experiencing difficulties in my relationship with an acquaintance who is trying to serve the Creator with me. I find it difficult to deal with her because she is not reasonable and I wonder if there are thoughts that you could give me to work with as I try to be part of the good in her life while retaining my own peace of mind.

We are those of Q'uo, and are aware of your query, my sister. We scan your mind in order to get a fuller background on this situation and are aware that you are desirous of being of service of not only the Creator and to this entity but to the many who will be served by you and by this entity and we feel this is most important point, that is that you desire to serve without imposing your will on any, even though another or others may attempt to do that to you.

It is a difficult situation for those who wish to serve to see that there are others whose desire to serve may be as strong and yet these may find that their desires are overlaid by personal concerns and the details of the day that are seen as paramount at the moment. We can only recommend that you hew to the higher road, if you will, and maintain the desire to serve the Creator as the first and strongest desire within you. Seek to the best of your ability to give love and understanding to those who demonstrate the need for such in their own difficulties and wrangling. It is often the case that work of an important nature can be done in such situations where one who seeks to serve gives of the self without knowing any particular outcome, casts the self-bread upon the water, as it is stated in your holy works, knowing that the heart is full of love and gives this love freely …

(Side one of tape ends.)

(Jim channeling)

I am Q'uo, and am again with this instrument. Is there another query?

Questioner: Q'uo, I have a question. You spoke of pride early on, through the other instrument. Is it possible to say pride is the same thing as ego, and do you distinguish it?

I am Q'uo, and am aware of your query, my sister, and we would agree that these two terms are basically interchangeable, for each is an illustration of an entity who wishes to impose its own will or desires on those about it in some fashion, not seeing that there is a larger picture, if you will, into which the entity fits as a much needed portion yet a portion which is not to be placed everywhere, for there must be room made for others within the thinking of entities who truly wish to be of service, and to serve in whatever way is asked without judging whether the means is dignified enough, important enough, interesting enough, or any quality enough to fit one as important as the self.

The focus upon the self in the means of balancing distortions and looking for ways to understand more of what is occurring within the self is an activity that may seem to some to be full of pride and ego, yet we would suggest that such a concentration of an entity's attention upon its own self in that manner is a means by which a seeker grows, for it needs to be aware of the activity of intellect, of emotion, and of the spirit that moves within one's own being. Yet that information is used only to temper the steel, shall we say, the character of the entity, and not to impose this character upon another.

Is there another query, my sister?

Questioner: Yes, another concept from an earlier channeling was the difference between a smaller self, the personality, and the deeper or what is called the higher self. You spoke of a deeper desire of the self, the unconscious desire. My understanding is that perhaps one way that a seeker should be aware of is the distinction between the smaller self and the higher self, try to follow the voice of the higher self. Am I right in this concept?

I am Q'uo, and am aware of your query, my sister. We would suggest that you have a correct appraisal of the relationship between that personality which inhabits one particular incarnation and the deeper portion of the self that is often called the higher self, the oversoul, shall we say, that oversees each incarnation and sends into each incarnation a portion of itself which develops its own personality for its own purpose of learning and serving.

Is there another question?

Questioner: Well, my next question is rather personal and if you cannot comment on it, I understand. I wonder if you would be able to say anything about a friend of mine who just left his physical body, incarnation, this morning. Would it be possible for you to tell me if this person fulfilled its life's purpose, in this lifetime. Had he suffered a premature death?

I am Q'uo, and we are aware of your query, my sister. Though we are desirous of aiding you by giving you the information which you seek we have a difficulty in the type of instrument we use and its access to information of this kind. However, we shall attempt to give something of that which we perceive.

In this entity's case, as in the case of a great majority of those who pass through the doors of what you see as death from this life, there are indeed no mistakes or premature leavings of the incarnation, though it may seem so to those who remain behind, as it were. This entity has striven to meet the pre-incarnational choices and has done so in a manner which is to the design of the entity, in that those challenges desired were met with the kind of attitude that was hoped for before the incarnation began, for it was the choice of this entity to balance certain aspects of its overall identity or soul-self that it felt were somewhat lacking and in the incarnation just completed was able to achieve the kind of response to life, if you will, that was planned.

Is there a further query, my sister?

Questioner: No, thank you.

I am Q'uo, and we thank you once again, my sister. Is there another query at this time?

Questioner: I have one query Q'uo. I am working with the desire for companionship and I wonder if you could suggest some thoughts for me to work with, as I try to strip the ego out of the desire and see with more clarity.

I am Q'uo, and am aware of your query, my brother. This instrument has difficulty speaking the first line, however we shall give it again … we know a nice little Jewish girl …

(Laughter)

We are Q'uo, and wish to speak seriously now …

(More laughter.)

We are glad that we can partake in your mirth, and we would recommend that this kind of attitude, that which takes the self lightly, is that which is most helpful in such an endeavor, for the feeling that you have in your heart and in your mind, that is, one of lightness, is a feeling which is seen and felt by all about you, and when there is the opportunity for the meeting of those who may fulfill your desire the perception of yourself as the one who takes the life in a lighter sense and can find humor in many situations is a vibration or attitude that is most attractive to those who you would desire to share your time and energies with.

Thus, our only suggestion to you is that which sees the self as whole and perfect and attempts to expand upon that perception with the experiences such as you are undertaking at this time, those which expand your range of activities and the people possible to meet, and to do this with the light and gladsome heart.

Is there another query, my brother?

Questioner: No, thank you, Q'uo, that is a nice answer.

I am Q'uo, and we thank you, my brother. Is there another query?

Questioner: I do have a question. Actually I am not sure if it is appropriate to ask. I'd like to ask about catalyst that I am experiencing with my parents. Would it be possible for you to offer any insights, suggestions, comments on what would be the best way for me to approach the situation, on the desire of a person who seeks to live the truth, to seek truth, and what would be the best way for me to approach such a situation?

I am Q'uo, and we are aware of your query, my sister. We shall comment in the following way. We would suggest that it is well not to plan or scheme in a manner in which one would hope would be successful in winning over the approval and support of those who you call your parents or friends but to speak that which is true for you and to speak it with a strength that is built upon love, to give freely of your thoughts and your self in a manner which speaks as close to the heart of this experience as you can. If you build upon truth and love then your foundation is strong and it will be apparent to those about you.

Is there any further query, my sister?

Questioner: That was a very good answer, Q'uo. I really appreciate it. Thank you.

I am Q'uo, and again we thank you, my sister. Is there another query?

(Pause)

I am Q'uo, and we would take this opportunity to thank those present for allowing us to join with you on this day in which you seek the One within the beauty and joy and love in the One all about you, for we are aware that your seasons change now and that [the] light becomes bright and the days grow short. The desire to seek burns strongly, and all about each are challenges that await. We walk with you as you meet each challenge and are happy to lend our conditioning vibration of love to you whether you are meditating or mediating, shall we say.

We shall take our leave of this instrument and this group at this time, leaving each, as always, in the love and the light of the one infinite Creator. We are known to you as Q'uo. Adonai, my friends. Adonai. ♣

Sunday Meditation
October 1, 1995

Group question: We would like to know how to balance having the light touch with ourselves with being a serious student in using our catalyst. What quality is there in laughter that is healing and helpful in the metaphysical sense?

(Carla channeling)

We are those of Q'uo. Greetings to you in the love and in the light of the one infinite Creator. We find our dear gathered group in the country this day with the birds and trees and stream running wild and yet moving along in the routine of their ways. We are most happy to speak with you concerning the question of the light touch and as we speak we would ask that each of you realize that we are your neighbors and your friends but we are not infallible. So although we are sharing with you our heartfelt opinion we ask that you realize that it is just that, and that you take what resonates to you and leave the rest behind. We thank you for this privilege of sharing these thoughts. It means a lot to us to be able to offer this service and we humbly thank you.

In the life of one who is seeking to live a spiritually directed life the opportunities to move from the periphery of a life lived in the spirit more towards the center of that desire are many. Indeed, each diurnal period is bursting with windows of opportunity for the experience of resonating with the heart of all things. This is because the universe is the Creator as well as the creation and whether one's milieu is that of people and relationship or that of nature and those relationships, all of these experiences of relating beyond the inner self are as glimpses in a changeable mirror. For one who does not pay the attention the mirror simply reflects a flat image. For the one who by a lucky or careful coincidence is paying attention that mirror of otherness can become that through which one sees the Creator. And so in the life of a seeker there is always the pressure to remember, to focus, and to center the self upon that firm rock of deity, that mystery which we call the one great original Thought of Love.

This being so, it is no wonder that the seeker can become so absorbed in improving his ability to center the self upon the Creator that he may lose sight of the fact that this center that is sought is not only within the small self but is echoed and iterated redundantly throughout all of the experiences of your illusion. Because so much of the creation is perceived as otherness the tendency within the illusion is to stay firmly within one's own self. This tendency is that which is instinctual to the second-density creature which functions as your physical vehicle. The physical vehicle wishes at all times to establish and maintain boundaries within which lie safety and comfort. This agenda works upon the seeker in an unconscious or subconscious manner, and that seeking for safety and comfort quite often adds to the tendency of the seeker to turn more and more inward.

As this occurs—and it is, we repeat, a natural occurrence—the seeker finds itself within a trap of its own making, for it has used that instinctual tendency to create a zone of safety to think about the spiritual and to act upon those thoughts. Consequently, even though the seeker knows it is doing spiritual work, yet still the seeker considers this the kind of work which entails labor, time and intensity.

Now, let us look at the way a student begins to learn the craft [that] contains the infinite. Let us, for instance, gaze at the student who begins to learn how to play the piano. The beginning student must focus and concentrate intensely in order to begin to master the fundamentals of piano playing. The beginner does the scales and does them over and over and over. This is effortful, heavy work to all but the very gifted, yet it is necessary in order to make the unfamiliar into the familiar and the impossible into the possible.

As the piano student moves through the years of apprenticeship of its craft it gradually begins to get a sense of what lies beyond the finite notes that it has been reading off the page of the music score. The student begins to hear in a different way, a way which has an expanded awareness of the whole. Armed with this hard won resource the student at last opens the door to mastery of its craft, for the true instrumentalist plays not the notes but the music. Even the best must play the scales to warm up, but there is that moment when the instrumentalist realizes the shape of its craft and sees how it may serve as an instrument to pour forth the heart of the composer. Then the instrument knows how to make music.

Now, the seeker has a craft to learn and there are the scales that must be played again and again and again. There are scales which teach the notes of patience. There are scales which teach the notes of devotion. There are other exercises that teach the spareness and the reserve of true service. And these exercises must be repeated, and certainly for the seeker to become inward and inwardly focused and moving in a small circle is completely understandable and acceptable. And we say to those who feel they are indeed too serious, too solemn, too earnest, we say that this is the stage that the student does the basic work to learn its craft, for seekers are artisans and artists of a certain kind. The closest perhaps we might come to expressing the nature of this craft is that of aesthetics, for in the philosophical tradition known as aesthetics the goal is to discover what true beauty is and what the seeker wishes to discover is what the deepest and truest beauty, truth and love is, for it wishes to clothe itself in that armor, and then it wishes to sally forth in service and in love.

So we ask that you think of the earnest self as a lovable, respectable, acceptable self and to see that there is a stage in spiritual seeking where effort is made, and it seems heavy, lonely, and sometimes empty. And we say that this naturally will yield in time as the seeker himself begins to hear that which silence tells so well and begins to sense the shape of things, the form of that undergirding reality, the true nature of love, and once this occurs the universe changes. And it begins to spark into a life that was hitherto unseen, for the soul and the heart are expanding and the center is not only that place in the heart of the self where one has opened the door to love but also is expanded to make a center of the whole creation, with all included and nothing omitted, nothing irrelevant, nothing wrong, but all, all one shade or shadow or another of infinite love.

Now, while the student is playing the scales of daily meditation, daily contemplation, while the student is seeking earnestly, it may if it chooses open a window to larger awareness. How may that occur? That occurs when the student drops whatever is upon the mind and asks the self, as this instrument is fond of saying, "Will this matter in ten thousand years?" There are things within your incarnations that will matter, no matter how many millennia pass. These things are precious. These things do not comprise a large percentage of what is in the perceived sea of confusion within which all of you paddle about at this time. It is most likely that when the student is tightest and most weary and most disturbed the issues will not matter in ten millennia and this is the key that unlocks that corset of tightness and allows the weary student to expand its consciousness beyond the perceived, opening simply to enjoy the breeze, expanding as a flower in sunlight, turning to the sun.

It does take, for most entities, a conscious decision to choose the larger perspective. But we say to you that it is worth the effort it takes when one perceives that one has become straightened, closed, and narrowed simply to affirm the enormous breadth and depth of the possibilities of any and all situations. The energy that is moving when there is laughter, when there is the light touch, is a mixture of the green-ray energy center being full and open, the blue-ray energy center working within its center at self-expression and communication and the lower three energy centers agreeing to lessen or cease their demands.

This is not something which one should do to the denigration of the lower energy centers. It is always important to affirm, to trust, and to do all one can to balance these all-important energy centers. But within these three energy centers there does not exist a light touch. It takes a mixture of the agreement of the lower centers to rest and allow the heart to open and allow the self to communicate with the creation, with the mystery which is the one Creator, and with that Creator within the self.

There are some who have a gift for the light touch. These are the entities you will find saying just the right thing to break the ice to make people laugh and find comfort in each other's company. But for most this skill of asking the self to stop and open to a larger view must be learned as any habit must be learned. Now you "oof" and "grunt" and try, and find it hard to do, but we say to you simply continue to "oof" and "grunt." This is good work. At some point, your own self will begin to yearn for and to seek the stoppage of that earnestness and will begin to hunger for the music behind the notes of the devotional life. Trust yourself through these practice periods, for cyclically, as lessons are learned, each seeker will go through learning periods which seem quite adverse. One cannot gain a certain amount of wisdom and then coast for the rest of the incarnation, for the Creator and your higher self hope to learn as many depths and resonances of the lessons you came to learn as time permits. So you will find seemingly the same material coming in again to cramp your style and make life hard and earnest, yet you are not repeating but rather learning at another level of subtlety and profundity.

We hope you can take the perpendicular route out of that little circle walked by the earnest soul and that you choose to take time out for a laugh or a smile, with all compassion for the self, for that earnest toiler who truly wishes to learn and to be better, wiser and more loving than before. Yet these things are reflections of something within that are so precious that there are no words to express the gemlike quality of this crystalline heart of self that is the Creator.

So know that the human experience is driven by instinct and at the same time there are opportunities every instant to grow into a spiritual body and a spiritual instinct and when this begins to occur you shall find meditation and contemplation flowing easily and quietly in natural ways throughout the life pattern, and the muscles of spirit will have learned these notes so that now they can work subconsciously, naturally, so that one does not have to think about the process but can enjoy the music of spiritual consciousness and can turn that consciousness upon a world that is all too short on love and laughter. Each of you can be of service to others in this respect, of lightening other's loads, of offering that light and caring touch, sharing that laugh, and spending time together easing each other's burdens.

We would at this time transfer this contact to the one known as Jim. We are those of Q'uo.

(Jim channeling)

I am Q'uo, and greet each again in love and in light. We are, again, privileged to be able to utilize both of these instruments this day and would thank all gathered for inviting us to speak our thoughts and opinions. We would ask if we may speak to any further queries at this time?

P: When you are dealing with intense bodily catalyst life seems to overtake the entity. How can she keep the light touch and remember the spiritual path that she is walking while everything else seems to be consumed with just the maintenance of the body?

I am Q'uo, and am aware of your query, my sister. And being aware as we are of the situation in which you find yourself, that is where your physical vehicle prepares to bring forth new life, we are well aware that the catalyst which you face is much more intense than that which is normally faced, for the experience that your physical vehicle and, indeed, the intellectual and emotional aspects as well, now undergoes is one which is more challenging in that the affirmations that could normally affect an entity are now less able to have sway, for the changes in your body's functioning are so basic to its nature and fundamentally overpowering that you will find that there is great difficulty in programming an alteration from this experience.

There is much of metaphysical value in attempting to do so, however. Much catalyst of this illusion is of that nature, although most within this circle do not experience it as a day-to-day experience. There are those experiences within your illusion such as this one which you now encounter that will require the simple persistence of the exercise of your will and your faith on a daily basis. The one known as Carla has had many of these experiences as its physical vehicle was malfunctioning. Your vehicle is not malfunctioning, but is functioning in a manner that is so far deviated from the normal functioning that you experience much of the same difficulties as the one known as Carla has experienced in her past.

And we would recommend, as in the case of the one known as Carla, that you find those small pleasures that feed you in any way that you find helpful, whether these are certain foods, certain music, inspirational readings, the company of certain entities or whatever means is available to you, that you utilize them to feed yourself that which is nourishing on whatever level you may find nourishment. And remember always that this process is one which is holy. Give praise and thanksgiving for it and find within each of your days a means whereby you may give this praise and thanksgiving so that it might build a kind of momentum in your life experience and begin to have an effect upon the mental, emotional and physical aspects of this process which your body now is undergoing.

May we speak in any further way, my sister?

P: Should one entertain moments of depression or should one try to fight against it?

I am Q'uo, and am aware of your query, my sister. We would recommend that all such moments, whether up or down, be experienced as spontaneously as is possible for the length of the emotion if this is possible, for to battle against the feelings of depression, the feelings of hopelessness, the feelings of loneliness and the feelings of despair is to deny another portion of your experience which has value to you, for it deepens your ability to experience in general. It is as though a deep hole or well is dug even deeper, yet when this is dug by the emotions there is made within you both the ability to experience that which is difficult and that which is joyous. All of this together shall create the tapestry of this particular experience. The difficult, the joyous, the hard, the soft, the light, the heavy, the bright, the dark—these experiences may be difficult, some of them, in what you may call the short run, the moment …

(Side one of tape ends.)

(Jim channeling)

I am Q'uo, and am again with this instrument. May we speak in any further way?

P: No. Thank you.

I am Q'uo, and we thank you, my sister. Is there another query?

Carla: I have a comment. I would have answered P's question differently. I would have talked about faith and I was surprised when the channeling went as it did. Why did you not say more about the faculty of faith and its perspective?

I am Q'uo, and am aware of your query within the comment, my sister. As we spoke of the quality of perseverance we were beginning that avenue of which you speak, that being of faith, though not clearly stated. You are quite correct about the quality of faith. The quality of faith is that which when joined with the quality of will are the two most helpful aspects of the attitude that a student may exercise at any point within this illusion, for all that you see before you and all that you see about you is born of mystery, much in the pain of birth and much must be taken on faith, for there is no other quality which may sustain one through the difficulties which any seeker will encounter within the incarnation, and we thank you, my sister, for clarifying the necessity for relying upon faith, for indeed it is a great ally for any seeker.

Is there another query?

Carla: I wondered whether the reason you did not go that route is that it is easy for people to feel that they do not have faith or do not believe in a system that includes faith. Was that the reason that you did not go into faith?

I am Q'uo, and am aware of your query, my sister. We would simply claim an omission. This instrument does not always pick up that which is given. Is there another query?

Carla: No, thank you.

I am Q'uo. Again we thank you, my sister. Is there another query?

R: Just a comment. I enjoyed your view of the subject. As I read through the channelings from Yadda and Latwii, [they] always bring forth a light touch on a serious subject for me and I just want to thank you all for that.

I am Q'uo, and we appreciate your comments and are grateful that we and our friends of Yadda have been able to add a certain light touch.

Is there a final query at this time?

(Pause)

I am Q'uo, and we are aware that we have spoken to those queries which are available at this time, and we are grateful for each, my friends. We listen to the sounds of the wind in the trees through this instrument's ears and this sound gives us a great feeling of peace, for the revolutions of your planet about the sun body move in a cyclical fashion and as your Earth revolves those entities upon its surface are subject to the movement of the planet, of the seasons, of the sun, and of the quality of compassion and love that is evident in the one Creator Who makes all move in this motion that is as a dance for those of us who are witnessing the experience of the one Creator moving in all.

The wind, as it moves freely through the leaves, through the field, and through the hair upon the head of those upon the planet, is a reminder of the freedom of movement of thought, the movement of thought of the One as It moves ceaselessly throughout the one creation. We are thankful that we are able to share this with you.

We would at this time take our leave of this group, moving about you as the wind, leaving each in the love and in the light of the one Creator. We are known to you as those of Q'uo. Adonai, my friends. Adonai.

Intensive Meditation
October 6, 1995

(Jim channeling)

I am Laitos, and greet you, my friends, in the love and in the light of our infinite Creator. It is our privilege to join your group again for the purpose of working with the new instrument known as K. We were, before contacting this instrument, attempting to initiate a contact through the one known as K. From time to time we use this technique with an instrument who has progressed to the point of being able to speak a phrase or two after identifying our contact. It is always helpful to be able to make one more step upon this journey by expanding the abilities whenever possible. We do not wish to rush any new instrument past the point of confidence, yet we shall always provide the opportunity for a new instrument to continue to expand its abilities.

This is true for all instruments, in fact, for even with an instrument which has practiced its art for many of your years, there is the constant opportunity to expand such an instrument's capabilities by presenting concepts of greater scope and, shall we say, intricacy, though we do not mean to suggest complexity.

At this time we would attempt to transfer our contact to the one known as K, and when this new instrument is comfortable with the conditioning vibration which we offer, we would then speak a few words through this new instrument. Again, we would remind the one known as K that we are happy to adjust our conditioning vibration if it is not comfortable to begin with. As always, we remind that new instrument that refraining from analysis is most helpful in speaking those concepts which appear within the mind. We would transfer this contact at this time. I am Laitos.

(K channeling)

I am Laitos, and greet you, my friends, in the love and the light of the one infinite Creator. *(Inaudible)* for the purpose of transmitting our thoughts to you at this time. We do not wish to see you [hurried] *(inaudible)*. It is our wish to convey as much as possible through this instrument. At this time *(inaudible)*. I am Laitos.

(Jim channeling)

I am Laitos, and greet each of you again in love and light through this instrument. We are very pleased with the progress which the one known as K has made since our last session together, and we continue to applaud this new instrument's efforts and willingness to take one further step and to move yet further upon the limb which continues to hold this instrument firmly.

At this time we would pause for the opportunity to respond to any queries which those present may find value in asking. May we attempt any query at this time?

K: I don't think I have any questions now, thank you.

Carla: Nor I, thank you.

I am Laitos, and we thank each of you for affirming that which we had discovered ourselves. We are always happy when there are queries, for this allows us the opportunity to discover how the progress in the new instrument's learning of vocal channeling is taking form, for queries are those gifts which we honor due to the new avenues of thought which they open. We are also pleased when there are no such queries, for in that situation we may assume that what we have offered has been utilized to its fullest and is ready for further expansion, shall we say.

At this time we would make one final contact with the one known as K in order that she might perhaps discover another facet of this ability. We transfer this contact at this time. I am Laitos.

(Kim channeling)

I am Laitos, and I greet you again in the love of the Creator. We wish to make known to you that there is progress being made even though you may not feel it at this time. We also wish to say that we thank you for your presence here, for it provides us with an opportunity to be of service with you. We ask now that you put aside your own thoughts of analysis *(inaudible)* and take [part] in [the] continuing adventure which is *(inaudible)* is [of] the Creator. We ask you to rejoice with us, for it is a merry life if you choose it to be, and we wish you happiness in your in *(inaudible)* difficulties and hardships. *(Inaudible)* understand [that]. We perhaps have more perspective [on] things that are happening to you [than you]. *(Inaudible)* journey *(inaudible)*.

[Undertaking of this adventure] which you are on. It is not easy to understand and in fact you are [not asked to do so] but only to love, for in this way *(inaudible)* for *(inaudible)* together it is wise lending cohesiveness to all [that you do] *(inaudible)* for what you are and do. Love is the connector to *(inaudible)*. [Such as we consider it to be] and *(inaudible)* the action that one may take.

At this time we leave you loved ones rejoicing in the love and in the light of the one infinite Creator. We are [pleased] for having two *(inaudible)*. I am Laitos. Adonai.

(Tape ends.) ♣

Intensive Meditation
October 7, 1995

(K channeling)

[I am Laitos,] and I greet you, my friends, in the love and in the light of the one infinite Creator. It is a great pleasure to be here with you this evening and *(inaudible)* working with this new instrument. We are quite pleased with the progress that she has made since yesterday. We thank her for her friends, and are glad for the opportunity to be here again. [At this] time we will say a few words through the one known as Jim. We transfer this contact at this time. I am Laitos.

(Jim channeling)

I am Laitos, and greet each of you once again in love and light. We look upon this opportunity to speak to this group as one which offers great possibilities of service, for we see each instrument likened to a seed when planted within the consciousness of the peoples of your planet. Each of you as you serve as vocal channels begin a kind of growth that may be likened unto one of your trees.

The trees that you call "oak" begin modestly, as any other seed. When planted within fertile ground and when there is the proper nourishment of the water, the sunlight and those nutrients of the soil, the seed sprouts and begins its growth that will culminate in a great, spreading oak. Many are the travelers that may pass beneath such an oak, and if the day is hot and the journey has been long, perhaps the traveler shall take the time to rest beneath the tree, to recline at the base of the trunk, and to relax in the shade provided by the great spreading limbs and leaves. Thus does one of your trees provide a service to those who travel in its vicinity, it being the traveler's choice to seek shade and rest beneath the arms of the oak.

So each of you as a vocal instrument may be likened to the oak, providing a rest, and more, perhaps an inspiration to travelers upon the spiritual journey who come within the reach of your branches. Such travelers make their own choices as to where they shall seek shelter. Your service is to be there when shelter is sought and to share what is within your ability to share. The oak does not provide oranges or apples, but provides shade and rest and a calming effect that is its own to provide.

Many times in your services as vocal instruments you will be asked to provide services which lie outside of your abilities. Be not concerned when this occurs—and it shall—but rejoice in your ability to give what you have to give and to give it freely. This is the essence of the vocal channeling experience, that the desire to serve others is strong and that [there is] the ability to hollow oneself out sufficiently enough to allow concepts and inspiration to move through one's instrument in a free and flowing fashion. This is what is yours to share with others, and your sharing of serving of others is most efficient when you give away that which you have to make room for more to follow.

At this time it our desire that we ask if there be any queries to which we may reply in order to aid in the intellectual grasp of the process of learning to be a vocal channel. Are there any queries at this time?

Carla: I have a query. I wonder if you could enlighten me in any way about the relationship between performing spiritually oriented services for others and the accepting of money? I've been pondering that problem because of writing the book on channeling.

I am Laitos. We see in this instance that the query points toward the heart of the polarity of service to others, and includes in this direction the necessity of viewing the metaphysical journey as a whole as well. One who seeks to serve in the positive sense is one who engages in a practice which many who have not chosen their polarity would think quite foolish, for to be of the most efficient polarity in the positive sense one must be willing and able to give freely enough of the self that one is not concerned whether there be a return for what is given. One rather seeks to share that which is greater with the self with all those who are equal to the self, and in this service the one so serving trusts in that which is greater than the self to sustain the small self in its daily round of activities that it might be nourished and supported in a fashion that will allow its service to continue.

This is not to say that one would refuse gifts which are freely given, even if those gifts be given in response to that which one has shared with another or others. The salient point in our humble opinion is that such gifts are not sought. To be able to give without expectation of return is the essence of the positive polarity. To be able to receive freely offered gifts without feeling the necessity to reciprocate points more toward the essence of the metaphysical journey itself.

For when one sees the universe and all that populates it, including the self, as portions of one being, then one begins to see that boundaries between entities, and systems of dealing in a fair manner with portions of one entity are illusions that aid each portion of the one Creator to gather experience that will glorify that one Creator, and to become aware that all is a portion of the one Creator, the self and each other self with whom one may share experience.

May we answer further, my sister?

Carla: Only if you can indicate to me anything helpful I might say to people whose question is not whether they should charge, but how much?

I am Laitos, and given the assumption that some to whom you speak will be asking this query, having already decided that the charge shall be made, it is, we feel, a difficult matter to determine the price, shall we say, for how much does one value the service when they offer another? Could it be sold for any price? How much does one value the ability to serve another? If the information which is freely given through the instrument is heeded or not, is the price the same? We cannot answer this query, my sister—we can only respond to it with further queries, for it is a difficult thing to put a price and a limit upon that which has no price and is infinite.

May we answer further, my sister?

Carla: No, Laitos. You sound as confused as anyone. Thank you.

I am Laitos, and, indeed, my sister, it would be a confusing thing to have to make this choice and to assume that one would indeed make such a choice. Thus, we apologize for not being able to guide you in a more coherent fashion.

Carla: Don't think anything of it. I haven't been able to figure out what to say either. Thank you.

I am Laitos, and we thank you again, my sister. Is there another query?

Carla: I will say you outlined the question real well. Exactly the problem [as I see it]. You don't have to respond. I have no other question.

K: I have no questions.

I am Laitos, and we thank you for those queries which were offered as gifts to us. We would at this time attempt to speak a few final words through the one known as K. We feel that the progress that this new instrument has shown from one session to the next is exemplary, and we are overjoyed that we have had the opportunity and shall continue to have the opportunity to work with this new instrument. We would transfer this contact at this time to the one known as K. I am Laitos.

(K channeling)

(The recording is mostly inaudible because of a recording problem.)

I am Laitos. I am with this instrument again. We wish to thank you again for your presence here for it is an opportunity for service for you and for us, and we appreciate it.

(Inaudible) cause to rejoice [with you. For this is the] time of thanksgiving with us, and we wish to share it [with you]. At this time we wish to [say] this instrument is progressing well, just like a [computer]. We ask *(inaudible)* again. *(Inaudible)* continue this work *(inaudible)*.

(Inaudible) attempting services which are not always clear to *(inaudible)* we continue to *(inaudible)* for the purpose of service. In spite of the confusions we may feel …

(Side one of tape ends.)

(K channeling)

I am Laitos, and am again with this instrument. To continue with [this] to rejoice *(inaudible)* service. We are *(inaudible)* as you lead your [lives] *(inaudible)* until our journey into the light is complete and [whole]. In the meantime, my friends, we offer ourselves as best we know how with what capabilities we have to offer. We rejoice that *(inaudible)*. We thank you once again for all you are the opportunity to *(inaudible)* you again *(inaudible)*.

(Tape ends.)

L/L Research

L/L Research is a subsidiary of Rock Creek Research & Development Laboratories, Inc.

P.O. Box 5195
Louisville, KY 40255-0195

www.llresearch.org

Rock Creek is a non-profit corporation dedicated to discovering and sharing information which may aid in the spiritual evolution of humankind.

ABOUT THE CONTENTS OF THIS TRANSCRIPT: This telepathic channeling has been taken from transcriptions of the weekly study and meditation meetings of the Rock Creek Research & Development Laboratories and L/L Research. It is offered in the hope that it may be useful to you. As the Confederation entities always make a point of saying, please use your discrimination and judgment in assessing this material. If something rings true to you, fine. If something does not resonate, please leave it behind, for neither we nor those of the Confederation would wish to be a stumbling block for any.

CAVEAT: This transcript is being published by L/L Research in a not yet final form. It has, however, been edited and any obvious errors have been corrected. When it is in a final form, this caveat will be removed.

© 2009 L/L Research

Sunday Meditation
October 15, 1995

Group question: We were talking about changes that occur through synchronistic events. Is there a way to prepare oneself for such synchronistic events or is one wildly and wonderfully taken by it and at its mercy when it comes? And the other thing we were talking about was how our growth seems to be enhanced when we gather together in groups, whether just to talk or to meditate or worship, and we are wondering how that works, its value, etc.

(Carla channeling)

We are those of the principle known to you as Q'uo. We greet you in the love and the light of the one infinite Creator. It is distinctly our privilege and our blessing to be sharing in your circle of seeking and in your communal vibration. We are so thankful and appreciative that you wish to consider our thoughts on these interesting matters. We ask only one thing of you as we speak and that is to realize that we are not final authorities, for we make many errors. Therefore, we ask you to take those thoughts which ring a bell—as this instrument would say—with you and to leave the rest behind without a second thought, for each person has a path that is unique as the person is unique, and upon each unique path there is a line of logic that can be called personal truth. This truth is unique. Some personal truths are long-lasting, through many lifetimes and densities. Others are less permanent, but each has its place in your unique path.

Thusly, to best cooperate with the destiny you have set for yourself it is very helpful to use the feelings associated with hearing that which is instinctively known from the heart to be true and keeping that truth special. This way will encourage a speedier process of change and transformation. The discrimination is all in this wise. So we greatly thank each for using his and her own personal discrimination, for each has the knowledge within, and when it resonates the effect is unmistakable. Wait for that resonance and take no authority without question. If you would do this for us then we are free to serve with the best of our humble ability.

We must remark before going further at the beauty of your combined vibrations. This is truly a good group and we are most happy to be here. We greet each who has not been with this group in the flesh, shall we say, before with especial delight. But each brings to us a special delight, new and old alike. Indeed, the harmonies within this circle are very beautiful, which brings us to your questions concerning synchronicity and change and groups such as this one.

Let us begin by setting a few basic suppositions. One supposition which we use is the feeling that the incarnation, the experience of having a life in your density even though the illusion is very thick, is a magical experience. This magical depth or side of incarnative life is for many among your peoples unknown. It is as though they were asleep too deeply to be aware of this potential. What awakens entities to this magic is in one form or another the awakening of awareness that the deeper self is not what it seems to be, but rather than being a creature of flesh, blood, sinew and limitation is instead a creature of infinity, eternity and unity with all that there is. This can be a dim sense at first, but it is that sense of being other than in the illusion, of having a reality that cannot be seen, that is the key factor in awakening the magical potential of life even within the best and most thick illusion.

As entities stretch and yawn their spirit selves awake within incarnation there is within your culture a decided bias towards discouraging further awareness of the magical type. This is not deliberate but is rather an artifact of the sustaining strength of the illusion and of those whose sleep has been undisturbed and who wish all things to remain as they are. Many of these entities are perhaps in your religious groups, yet the magical side does not open because such entities are focused upon absolute truth, absolute faith, absolute adherence, whereas the creation which lives beyond this illusion is various, indeed, infinite in its potentials and its possibilities.

To the world of humankind these considerations are null for they cannot be tracted, measured or reproduced, and so many so-called religious groups do not experience the intensifying of magic. On the other hand, to be anthropomorphic, many of your spiritually oriented groups are aware of the delicious and pervasive magicalness that can be experienced within this illusion. And it is within groups such as yours and many others that entities can come together and more surely seek, more lovingly find, more intensely knock at the door of further—we look for a word—further development, we shall say. Yet it is more of a flowering, a blooming that takes place when entities of like mind seek together, for within such groups each is a mirror which shows the Creator to the self and the self to the self. Each face that is seen has the wonderful capacity to surprise us with a side of truth that we had not guessed before.

As we gaze into each other's eyes, as we touch each other's hearts, whether we are in incarnation as are you or are speaking from other levels of manifestation as are we, we bloom together and that blossom is taken away by all, strength added to strength, weakness shared with weakness, and love in all things found and felt in ways that do not harm, but rather support. These gifts you can hardly help giving around such a circle such as this, and this is a gift that you give yourself, to come together.

The reason that synchronicity seems to occur more in groups is simply that as more and more entities who are spiritually awake come together each individual's path being synchronous with its own destiny, when the group joins and shares its thoughts and experiences the commonality of synchronicities becomes remarkable. The strength of a group as opposed to an individual or a couple who work together is that the group universalizes each entity's unique path so that instead of being caught within the biases created by the long path which has lead the individual to this moment, each individual remains free of the limitations of self and of the dynamic betwixt one and another of a couple, so that each has wisdom that becomes available to all, and in this atmosphere each can somehow gain light and strength. This is a completely natural and highly-to-be-encouraged event or process and we do feel strongly that the awareness of each is nurtured by regular dwelling within a group of those like-minded. Blessed indeed is the entity whose path has brought her to a place where this option is available.

Now, the individual who does not have the luxury of a spiritually oriented supporting group may still accelerate the pace of his own advancement upon the path of spiritual evolution, but may we say that companions make the way merrier and the stones smaller and certainly the smiles more frequent, for that exhaustion which each may feel within the self over issues which it has been working upon for as long as it can remember does not have these biases where other's troubles are concerned. The fresh ear, the new perspective is what can be expected from a group. This is most helpful.

Perhaps the most important thing which the individual does, in our humble opinion, is to become completely aware of itself being itself. This essence of self is your gift, moment by moment to the infinite Creator, and are you not most yourself when among those who see you and care for you as yourself? When those whose lives have become spiritually based arrive at a common meeting place the one thing that is so isolating is not present. That isolating factor in terms of the general environment of your culture is that many entities are asleep to the true nature of their own consciousness. In a group such as this each is aware of the common basis of spirituality or metaphysical reality and each gives that a credence without thinking or concerning the self with such thoughts. It is taken, shall we say, for granted that the basis of the living is the spirit and the basis for striving is to know that great truth that is the one great original Thought which is the Logos which is Love.

So each comes to this group dwelling in love, seeking tools and resources that will help us learn how to love, how to accept love, and each wishes to learn these intangible and inexpressible skills: loving and being loved. You see how the environment becomes charged and magical simply by the unspoken assumptions or biases which each brings to this circle.

We come to share one simple, basic thought; that thought is love. We are not terribly clever, but we simply use instruments such as this one to find within each instrument's nexus of thoughts, experiences and emotions those things which we can use to say in a slightly different way that all is love. The ramifications of that simple statement, as far as we know, are infinite. We do not see the end of our path. So there is no reason for us to tell you that there is an end or a place of achievement to your path. But we can say that in our opinion as one strives to become more of that mystery that cannot be expressed it is well to choose your companions [with care], for these companions will help you to suffer that which you have wished to suffer in a more acceptable, comfortable and pleasant way.

The illusion promises the suffering and we feel that those who are attempting to block out or repress or run from the suffering are missing the point. You did not work so hard to gain this incarnative experience in order to become all spirit. You came into this opportunity in order to be refined and that refining or purifying or distilling of the essence of self is necessarily a rough business from time to time as all change is difficult and goes against the second-density instincts of your physical and mental vehicles. So in this group or in any group spiritually oriented you have the capacity to embrace transformation more easily, more comfortably, and more pleasantly while still doing the work on the refining of the self's personality that you have wishes to complete.

Now, the reason that each came to this particular planetary sphere is for service to that sphere at this time of transition. But you also each did come with a personal agenda, so we encourage each to relish the process of suffering and to know that it is this very seemingly difficult experience that you so wished before in order to make vivid to the self those lessons of love which you felt you could learn better. When it comes to the service each came to perform, this service is one simple to speak of but very difficult to make sense of, for each who came to this particular place at this particular time came to aid in lightening the consciousness of your planet.

You do this by being here, not by doing any service such as healing or channeling as this instrument is doing but rather by living. Being is your great gift and your first occupation. It is the hardest job you shall have within your incarnational experience and again the group together aids each in that process of individuation. Here are hearts that wish for you to be who you most deeply are. Here is where there is a lack of fear for the you that may emerge as transformations occur. Here is a home which one needs not to be at in order to feel at home. The spirit of a spiritual group is enormously powerful, metaphysically speaking, and each senses this. As this instrument has often said, no individual is the reason that a light group such as this offers a magical place, a metaphysical home that works and functions, but rather the faith of all who have come to such a place, the knowledge within those that come that this is a safe place. This is what makes the power of such a light center.

The entities who dwell here simply keep the doors open. Each of you has brought the magic with you, and each shall find solutions, tools and resources here because you have already known about the magic of this place. It is a mystery as faith is always a mystery. How did faith in something called L/L Research begin? How has it grown? Person by person by person by person, a net of gold, that gold being love, faith, the desire for that which is higher and more lovely. The open heart of each has given this particular center its character, person by person by person. And each has then gone out into the larger world and has touched person by person by person and so the net spreads and other centers hear about this center and communicate and another link has been established.

This process of what many call networking is radically changing the basic consciousness of your planet. We are happy to see this take place, for it has been our concern that the transition this planet is already moving through would be far more difficult than it is being. We can only thank each individual whom we have the pleasure of meeting, as we have met each of you, for the love and care you give to the cause of love.

Remember as you touch each other's lives and as you go forth and continue this process, that the magic of life is much more obvious when each finds the groups or the new people that have a commonality of attitude and interest in the metaphysical. Be able to reach out in faith to those who are new …

(Side one of tape ends.)

(Carla channeling)

… for this is truly a path in which companions are the most help and the least difficulty.

This instrument is telling me that we have once again spoken too long, and we are not sorry but we should be, so we shall muzzle ourselves to transfer this contact to the one known as Jim. We are those of Q'uo.

(Jim channeling)

I am Q'uo, and greet each again in love and in light through this instrument. It is our privilege at this time to offer ourselves in the attempt to speak to any further queries which those present may have for us. May we ask if there is a query with which we may begin?

K: I really enjoy being here again. Over the past several months I have encountered several sources of information coming onto the planet. It's all helping. There seem to be several different sources. This group, to my knowledge, primarily receives information from the Confederation of Planets in the Service of the Infinite Creator. I have also gotten information from a source called the Essansani channeled to us from an entity known as Bashar, from that relatively small group of Pleaidians channeled through Barbara Marciniak and through an entity known as the Kyron. The Essansani state that they are part of a group called the Association of Worlds. It is very clear to me that all of these are positively oriented entities who have answered the call of those requesting help with the transition. I am curious if all of these work together. Do those of the Confederation work with those of the Association or others, or are these various groups doing their own thing in answering the calls of those needing help?

I am Q'uo, and am aware of your query, my sister. And may we say that we are most grateful to be able to share your vibrations once again, my sister, though we can assure you that we are always available to you upon your request as we have been numerous times.

The many sources of information are in truth, and from that truth we begin. Each source, entity or group has the desire to be of service to others, to serve the one Creator in many or any of Its manifestations. Thus is the path of all made clear by the heart of the desire of each. And many times do these paths intertwine with each other so that there is not so much a need to consciously coordinate the giving of information, the serving of *(inaudible)*, as it is what you may call, as you did before this group began, a celestial synchronicity of service.

We have passed the way of service many times, meeting others upon this path, finding that as the threads of this group have woven a beautiful and loving tapestry, just so is such a tapestry woven by all those who seek to serve the one Creator. If one could see the metaphysical reality of these paths of service, planets such as yours would seem to be bathed in light as many tracings and trails of light converge at this point that you call Earth. We and our brothers and sisters of the Confederation of Planets in the Service of the One Creator feel the kinship in our hearts with all others who serve as do we and those who serve in ways which may not be easily comprehensible by those who observe, yet there are many who are enriched and nourished by service which is as unique as each entity which seeks. Thus, the fabric of creation is one and is traveled by each portion of the one Creator, from density to density, from home to home.

Is there another query, my sister?

K: That's all for now, and I want to say that I have been aware of your presence many times and have appreciated it.

I am Q'uo, and we thank you, my sister. Is there another query at this time?

B: It has been my dream to sit here in a session for many years, and I offer my gratitude for being here.

Many do not have the luxury of seeking in such a group and how might such an individual continue his advancement in awareness by one's self even though we are all one?

I am Q'uo, and am aware of your query, my brother, and we are as gratified and humbled to be in your presence as you are to be in ours. We share with you the great joy of the blending of our vibrations, and we can assure you that all seekers of truth are able to pursue the path that their desire opens for them, for it is always the case that an entity will find about it that which it seeks and that which it needs for the next step on this infinite journey of seeking. It may take some effort of recognition, some facing of inner truths, yet when a seeker utilizes the daily round of activities as a focus for thought, prayer or contemplation, then this entity opens wider the door of opportunity, of possibility before it that the teacher, the fellow seeker which it needs will be presented to it whether in a physical form such as a person, a book, a program, [or as] a thought, an experience, a coincidence of events.

Just so, each seeker will find that the day which it has lived is fruitful in the catalyst presented for possible growth. The simple desire to seek, the opening of the self to new experience, is all that is necessary. Groups such as this, of course, aid that process by providing the support necessary to encourage continual seeking, and the mirroring effect where entities may speak in terms understood by fellow seekers to be helpful as means of seeing the self in new ways. But all who seek shall find, for what is sought is a deeper, greater portion of the self within [each] seeker *(inaudible)* the outer or personality self with as much desire as the small self which seeks the One.

Is there a further query, my brother?

B: Not at this time. Thank you.

I am Q'uo, and we thank you, my brother. Is there another query?

P: Today is an election in Iraq, and the population there has one choice to choose from. I wonder about the social structure of our societies in the face of a major transition from this reality to a larger one, from the third to the fourth. How much would it help in the direction of social liberation to raise awareness in consciousness in such a milieu?

I am Q'uo, and believe that we are aware of your query, my sister. We would suggest that the events within this third-density illusion are meant to serve as a kind of catalyst, a kind of motivator so that entities may begin to think and be in terms greater than this third-density illusion. There is, of course, a path of service through each level of experience, including the social awareness, the political rights, the democratic freedoms, and many there are who serve with shining brilliance in these areas doing that which they feel strongly is their part in this dance together with the One.

However, we have also suggested previously that those who are most helpful in any regard or manifestation are those who seek first to love and to give in that attitude of love that which is theirs to give, seeing beyond the illusion of limits and the seeming prison that many upon your planet inhabit in systems of governing that do not allow certain freedoms. These boundaries can serve as the cell within the prison that causes the entity to move within itself even more deeply that true freedom might be found as the shackles of the mind are dropped one by one, the thought for such being the seeming chains surrounding the entity everywhere.

Is there a further query, my sister?

P: Yes, but I will need time to develop them. Thank you.

I am Q'uo, and we thank you, my sister. We would ask if there is a final query at this time for we know that we have spoken for a great portion of your time and do not wish to overtire.

V: For several years I wished to get here to this group and it is difficult for me to express my gratitude at being here. My understanding is that as we move closer to fourth density there will be a higher frequency of visual and personal or physical contact with extraterrestrial entities, and I myself have searched the skies almost nightly and daily to recognize some visual contact with those of Q'uo or any other extraterrestrial entity. Will the frequency increase with contact with humans on this planet and will you be part of that contact in the near or distant future?

I am Q'uo, and am aware of your query, my sister. We would suggest that this enhancement of the frequency of contacts with those of your planet has been in effect for some of your time as you measure it, and this may be expected to continue apace, yet perhaps in a manner that is less obvious than the actual sighting of one of our physical craft, for each seeker is approached in a manner which is most comfortable to that entity, many occurring in a meditative or the sleep and dreaming stages, to be remembered at a future time, much as the laying of a trail or the signaling of the lights as the one known as R spoke of previous to this session's beginning.

We do not deny that there may indeed be further extensive sightings of craft in your skies and messages delivered through instruments such as this one, but would also suggest that the contacts which are most helpful to entities will be less visibly noticed and will have their effect upon the level of the soul, shall we say, so that those who have prepared themselves for service to others and the growth that this implies on a physical level will find the avenues of their expression of this service and growth to be enhanced in ways that are touched by, shall we say, unseen hands. There shall indeed be a greater and greater contact, and it shall be from heart to heart.

Is there a further query, my sister?

Carla: She wanted to know if you were going to be one of those who will show themselves on this Earth physically.

I am Q'uo, and we are aware of this portion of this query and when replying as we did implied that we would be those who speak as we do. We are not those who move about at this time in a craft in your skies, though that may become a possibility, though it is a contact of hearts that is of paramount importance to us at this time.

We are those of Q'uo, and would again thank those present for inviting our presence in your circle of seeking. We are greatly filled with joy at this opportunity and cannot begin to express our great gratitude, for by inviting our opinions and thoughts upon your queries we are able to respond in a fashion which gives us beingness in your illusion and the opportunity to experience yet another facet of the jewel of the one Creator.

At this time we shall take our leave of this instrument and this group, leaving each in the love and in the light of the one infinite Creator. We are known to you as those of Q'uo. Adonai. ✣

L/L Research

L/L Research is a subsidiary of Rock Creek Research & Development Laboratories, Inc.

P.O. Box 5195
Louisville, KY 40255-0195

www.llresearch.org

Rock Creek is a non-profit corporation dedicated to discovering and sharing information which may aid in the spiritual evolution of humankind.

ABOUT THE CONTENTS OF THIS TRANSCRIPT: This telepathic channeling has been taken from transcriptions of the weekly study and meditation meetings of the Rock Creek Research & Development Laboratories and L/L Research. It is offered in the hope that it may be useful to you. As the Confederation entities always make a point of saying, please use your discrimination and judgment in assessing this material. If something rings true to you, fine. If something does not resonate, please leave it behind, for neither we nor those of the Confederation would wish to be a stumbling block for any.

CAVEAT: This transcript is being published by L/L Research in a not yet final form. It has, however, been edited and any obvious errors have been corrected. When it is in a final form, this caveat will be removed.

© 2009 L/L Research

Sunday Meditation
October 22, 1995

Group question: We have been talking about two concepts, the preincarnative programming that allows us to learn the lessons we have chosen and the free will of the incarnation that blends with the supposed predestination of the preincarnative choices. The other question concerns the blending of the planet's religions, cultures and philosophies and we wonder how these can be reconciled to achieve peace. We would like Q'uo's comments on whatever seems to be of value to our evolution in these areas.

(Carla channeling)

We are those of Q'uo. We greet you in the love and in the light of the one infinite Creator. We are most pleased and happy to be with you this day and we greet and bless each of you. We thank you for calling us to your circle.

It is our privilege to serve by offering you our thoughts and we ask only that you take the thoughts that ring true to you and leave the rest behind, for each has his own path to follow and each path is correct for the one person that is following it, and each has discrimination and knows what is true and right for him. If you will do that we then feel free to offer our honest opinions. They are not infallible; we ask you to realize that. We are the Brothers and Sisters of Sorrow. We come when there is a call. Your planet has a great call at this time. We feel that we have good news and we share it with you with a whole heart and a humble spirit.

Your queries this day are most interesting. We shall attempt to speak on this subject to some extent but we ask you to realize that this is a large subject and one which can be explored certainly further than we will this day.

Perhaps we shall begin by looking at the way that entities come into being in your density. Your density is the culmination of the first two densities, those being the density of elemental awareness known by your rocks and earth, your sea and sky, and the second density of animal and vegetable growth with its turning to the light and feeding from the light. In your third density you come into third density fresh from the creation of the Father as a flower or a tree or an animal. Consciousness is one, both the consciousness of the species and the consciousness of the place and the creation and the nature of creation. There is a tremendous intercooperation, even to the killing of the weak and diseased of one species by another while the others are allowed to escape. There is an intimate and instinctual awareness of the Creator, yet there is no awareness of the self.

The second-density entity gradually becomes aware of love because of human energy invested in the second-density creatures such as your pets. The awareness of self and the inward-turning gaze are the hallmarks of third density. As each density has its lessons, so the lesson of third density is that lesson of finding ways to love and to be loved, not only in relationships of one person to another but also in relationship of groups of people to other groups. Yours is a density that begins with primitive, small and scattered communities and by the end of the cycle becomes an environment of great, clearly defined and very conscious groups of entities.

The energies that are being worked on in third density are potentially all energies, from the basic red-ray or sexual energy center through that rainbow of energies. However, it is the function of third density to complete work on that orange ray of personal relationships and to study and attempt to absorb ways of learning to love within the yellow-ray energy center, that ray which is involved when group-oriented energies are shared between individuals. The instinct to gather together in groups is deep. The instinct to include some and exclude others is very deep. And it is extremely easy for the seeker to become quite lost in the sea of confusion in which all of these energies are experienced, for your world is indeed a sea of confusion.

Now, if it is understood that the primary work of third density is in tuning and balancing those lower three energy centers of red, orange and yellow and then of opening and finding ways to maintain an openness and fullness of the heart, then it may be seen that those energies are not instinctual. The refinement has begun, for you stand as a third-density entity as a kind of rough diamond with unpolished edges and without sparkling facets, and through lifetime after lifetime within your third-density experience the self that is inherent within, that crystalline entity that you truly are, begins to become visible as the friction of everyday living works to smooth and refine that crystalline self.

Certainly, some of the abrasive and cleansing experiences of your illusion seem unlucky and unfortunate, yet it is precisely that friction that does the work of exposing the crystal that sparkles within, and the work that is done by the seeker is work upon the self. The seeker wishes to balance red ray, for that is the basic and very important beginning of energies, and that which is not freed and flowing within that root energy center constitutes a primal blockage that will slow and distort the pure light energy which you are receiving from the Creator.

Then it is that you work upon the relationship chakra by working within the self to come into more awareness of what you are feeling and thinking concerning the self in relationship to the self and to other selves. Often it is that an entity that truly does not wish to advance or finds it too painful to advance further will turn from yellow-ray work and move back into orange-ray work, that which is strictly between one entity and another or between the self and the self, in order to be more comfortable.

However, at this end time of your present third-density cycle it is entirely appropriate that each set the self the task of finding new ways of coming into harmony with other cultures, other races and other structures of thought, logic and being. The end result of this planetary effort to come into spiritual convergence shall be that social memory complex that is the basic structure for fourth-density work. You are attempting to learn how to be one people, sharing each other's thoughts, hopes and fears, carrying each other's burdens as naturally as breathing, sharing each other's joys as if they are your own.

There is much work in fourth density, but once one has become able to be able to be part of a social memory complex one is no longer veiled from that which is most true. Each of you, then, is in the situation of coming close to the ability to merge with all other people. And so there is a yearning and a desire to go further, to become more spirit than flesh, to cease striving after the way of third density. Yet the fact that you are within incarnation is sufficient to justify the opinion that this is precisely where you think you should be, for places within your world for incarnation are very rare compared to the number of entities who wish to come into the Earth plane at this time in order to aid in the transformation of your planetary sphere.

You are the one who chose this foggy, barren landscape, metaphysically speaking. It was your desire to place the self within this thick and dim illusion that is the Earth world in order that you might forget that which you know instinctively, for one cannot learn as one does in third density unless there is the physical stimulus, the emotional battering and so forth that constitutes catalyst for the individual as it goes through its daily round. So no matter how difficult things may seem, it is our opinion that the situation remains perfect, for it is the outworking of the self's plan for this incarnation that is being experienced.

Let us look at this plan. The entity who gets the opportunity to incarnate within your density upon your sphere first goes through the process of creating the scenario or the screenplay, shall we say, for your personal movie of life. You choose the cast. You choose who shall play mother, father, spouse, lover, friend, enemy and so forth. You make agreements with these entities, not within the Earth plane, but within the finer world which this instrument calls the inner planes. No matter how difficult the relationships seems or how much pain has been experienced, this was part of your own choice. It may be difficult to believe or to understand how you would wish to choose to ask yourself to suffer, yet we can only say that when one is outside of the illusion that you now enjoy it seems like child's play, and a good kind of playing at that, to plunge into the sea of confusion and to swim about in its waters.

Perhaps you have had the experience of thinking something was going to be fun until you have done it, and discovered that that was not fun, that [it] was horrible, scary, or some other negative feeling. This is the situation of man on Earth. He cannot believe that he has done it to himself. Yet, my friends, you have. You have asked for personal lessons and you have asked for the chance to serve. Perhaps it may aid you in dealing with these difficulties simply to remind yourself that this is a part of the play, or as this instrument would say, the situation comedy of life. If you can find faith within yourself, faith that believes and knows that no matter what occurs that you are on track and the deeper goals are being met, perhaps that may alleviate and soften the harshness of lessons.

As your third density further draws towards its conclusion you shall experience more and more of the yellow-ray or group-to-group catalyst. That solar plexus chakra comes in for much use and abuse in working with these lessons. This is the time when one discovers what it feels like to be pulled at emotionally, mentally and spiritually. These are the times when you find out how to cut the cord that develops between two people or two groups that limits their freedom. If you can approach dealing with groups with faith then we feel it is not so long away until you can observe the dynamics of the various groups of entities upon your planet and see all peoples as one.

One thing that greatly disturbs and puzzles seekers is the persistent friction betwixt races and peoples. This is not a reflection upon any civilizations' or individual's integrity, maturity or honor. The reasons for this instinctively felt friction lie in the fact that there is more than one race of entities populating your sphere. Your planet in this third-density cycle has been a place which has accepted many other planetary third-density entities who graduated into third density or were in third density yet were not able to dwell upon their home planet.

Now, each civilization or race throughout your galaxy, shall we say, has a slightly different archetypical consciousness, for it is the work of each sun or Logos to add the details to the basic plan of the one infinite Creator. When an entity or a people move from the heart, then, they are moving from an archetypical environment that is other than that archetypical environment enjoyed by those who have come here from places other than the one you have come from. Because of the thick illusion it seems that one way of experiencing or perceiving incoming sense data must drive out another way of seeing or perceiving sense data. As the times roll on and as each entity gains maturity these differences in archetypal mind will begin not to repel but to fascinate entities. And as they lose fear, having become more secure in their own individual self, they will be able more and more to embrace those distinctly unlike themselves in appearance, in manner and in thinking.

Mostly to be remembered in this regard is one simple rule: you are here to learn to love. Find within the self at any time where the love is, where it can shine. Open the self to that opportunity and you shall have acted well indeed, for each is a spark of the one infinite Creator, capable of healing, forgiving, embracing and transforming each other. The one known to you as Jesus said to you, "Love one another." As you love one another you are loving the one infinite Creator, for this spark is the basic essence of all conscious entities. You are love. There is just a very heavy coat of flesh upon that lightening spirit born of love that is you.

As you have your daily periods of meditation and contemplation, spend a moment reaching out to embrace all of the self's catalyst, all that the world has to offer, both war and peace, both heat and cold in so many ways. Be or practice to be unafraid of trouble. Find ways to be serene while you are not understanding, for this lack of understanding will continue and is irrelevant to the process of spiritual evolution. When the heart is opening a tremendous strength fills the spirit. Whenever this is not felt and you become aware that the heart is closed we ask that you touch in to your own faith, to the guidance that surrounds you, to the love that overshadows you, the mystery that made you and claims you for its own, and rise refreshed and peaceful.

You have much to learn. You will make mistakes, but they are not metaphysical mistakes. The mistakes are part of your learning, part of the illusion, part of being human. Forgive yourself, for in forgiving the self you become able to forgive all and the redemption in the eyes of a peaceful person is a blessing indeed to those who behold it, and to the planet in general, for love lightens the planetary vibrations. This love does not come from you. We would not ask you to attempt to develop such a thing as infinite love. We ask only that you open the self, allow pain to hollow you out and make you a beautiful and transparent instrument through which infinite love can flow. You are a vessel, a precious, precious vessel. What shall you hold? What shall you offer?

We would at this time transfer to the one known as Jim. We thank this instrument and leave it in love and light.

(Jim channeling)

I am Q'uo, and greet each again in love and light through this instrument. At this time it is our privilege to offer ourselves in the attempt to speak to any other query which those present may have for us. Is there another query?

B: My question concerns Bosnia-Herzegovina. What are the karmic patterns of the groups involved?

I am Q'uo, and am aware of your query, my brother, and we would begin by offering our great gratitude and thanks to you for allowing us to speak our thoughts to you. We also feel great joy at this privilege. We feel that it is appropriate …

(Side one of tape ends.)

(Jim channeling)

We shall continue. We feel it appropriate to speak in a general fashion about the entities of which you speak but are not able to give specific information about their particular development and the forces which have them as they are, for in truth, my brother, all peoples of this planet and indeed all entities within this creation, share the formative powers of love. These creative forces have made these entities individualized as they are, for these forces have included not only the love of the Creator and the light of the creation but the free will of entities working as races, as groups of entities that have for many incarnative episodes chosen to move along a certain path that would make them unique, that would give them identity, that would give them purpose, that would give them direction, that would give them inspiration to continue upon this infinite journey of seeking, of learning and of sharing that all portions of the Creator has chosen as means whereby each portion shall glorify the Creator by that which it is, by that which it becomes.

Thus, each race, each culture, each religion offers to the entities that are grouped within it an identification that makes them who they are and what they are. In order to become individualized from the larger realms of creation and of consciousness more and more specific choices are made, much as the sculptor removes a portion of stone in such and such a fashion so that in the end there remains that which began in the eye of the artist. And this which remains is only that which remains and no other. That it is so identified gives a certain strength, a pride, a power and purpose to the entities. This enlivens the group as a whole and each individual as a portion of this group, so that it is helpful in the individuation process for such choices to be made, for the choices to be vivid, colorful, much likened to the peacock's tail when spread, revealing colors that are very, very bright and individualized.

However, this great strength can also become like unto a weakness when those who are within the particular grouping are unable, for a portion of experience, to move beyond these boundaries and see a larger identity that is shared with others who in the smaller identification seem quite separate and perhaps even at odds with the original grouping. There are, however, within each culture, each religion, each philosophy, those far-seeing individuals who are like unto the hero in any journey or story, that can open up new possibilities to the people by their far-seeing vision.

Thus, within each grouping is seeded the potential for the expansion of the vision that includes a larger definition of the identity so that the evolutionary process may continue upon a new level of experience and understanding. It is the struggle of each culture and grouping to break free of that which makes them what they are or what they were and to become more than that. It is like unto the chick inside the egg pecking at the shell that it might break free and become a greater being. This is often a painful process in terms of your third-density illusion as this breaking free and breaking through the shell of identity occurs. Thus, there is much opportunity for reconciliation, for forgiveness, for mercy and indeed for compassion.

The great healing power of love, then, is that which aids all in this process and those which are far-seeing in each grouping will become aware of that healing power, for all spring from it. Some see it and feel it and experience it before others, and these are the way-showers.

Is there another query, my brother?

B: Not at this time, thank you.

I am Q'uo, and we thank you, my brother. Is there another query?

P: To follow up, is the emergence of a new identity a portion of the fighting that is going on in the Balkan states?

I am Q'uo, and am aware of your query, my sister. It is our opinion, and we offer it as opinion, that the emergence of a new identity is most important for all cultures of this planet at this time, for it is the divisions between entities that fuels the animosity that one grouping feels for another as one grouping holds its religion, its philosophy, its history, its experience against another which it has opposed for a great portion of time. When entities can move beyond the boundaries of previous identity and see themselves similar to others in a larger grouping then the lines which divide are removed and the environment which all inhabit is seen as home to all.

Is there another query, my sister?

P: Many groups do not wish to share histories or experiences. Do entities reincarnate within the same groups?

I am Q'uo, and we speak now in generalities as there are always exceptions to each rule and situation. But in the main, we may agree that entities tend to remain with those whose beginnings they share, for there are families or clans or groups who have had shared origins upon other planetary influences with experiences that are distinct from those who have reached your particular planetary influence from yet another planetary influence and these energies are appropriate to be worked out together so that the evolution of each individual entity aids the evolution of the group and the evolution of the group aids the evolution of the individual. Thus is the great plan of evolution undertaken as a means whereby these groups may evolve and aid the evolution of others as well.

(Tape ends.) ☙

Sunday Meditation
October 29, 1995

Group question: Our question today deals with the foundation self that we attempt to know, to build a path to, to solidify with faith throughout our lives. It seems that catalyst either peels away layers of our being so that we get closer to this foundation self or an adding unto the various experiences and personalities that we have so that we approximate this ideal or core self, whether it is faith or soul essence that comes with us from incarnation to incarnation. We would like information about how we work to know this core of self, how we balance various aspects of this self that seem at odds with each other, how we get to know mysterious parts of this self that make themselves known from time to time, how we find messages from that core self in our dreams that come in archetypical images.

(Carla channeling)

Greetings in the love and in the light of the one infinite Creator. We are those of the principle known to you as Q'uo, and may we say what a privilege and blessing it is for us to share in your meditation and in your seeking for your own truth.

We are within your planetary sphere specifically to aid those who would wish to ask us for our thoughts and we only ask that you evaluate our opinions using your own discrimination, for each seeker has an unique path to the one infinite Creator and therefore each has an unique point of view which creates personal truths that you hear and resonate to. Keep those that resonate within your own being and leave the rest behind. This favor allows us to share our humble and often incorrect opinions with you without infringing upon your free will and we appreciate your understanding this, for we do not come to teach, but rather to share. We are those upon that same path of seeking as you but a few steps further on. We know not the mystery. We yearn for it as do you.

As we gaze at the subject of the core being and how within incarnation to find access to it to know the self we ponder which tack to take in discussing this seminal and interesting question, for in one sense the core being of all that exists is the one great original Thought, that unit vibration, shall we say, known as Love. Indeed, this love is your essential self. Due to the Creator's adopting free will, the original Thought created that which you know as light and those photons, as you call them, which are the particles, shall we say, of light have built all that you are aware of and all that exists in manifestation, either in the inner or time/space planes of existence, or the outer or space/time planes of existence.

To be transparent is the most apt skill that can be created within your practice in terms of becoming aware of the ultimate essence of who you are. This transparency is, shall we say, not a state of being which is primary on the agenda of lessons learned within your density. However, those who seek the one infinite Mystery often yearn to be transparent to the surrounding illusion and wish mightily to experience that lightness in transparency of being which is associated with being pure spirit. The most calm and the most busy of times alike offer moments or windows of opportunity wherein suddenly the illusion crystallizes and shimmers, and the transparency of being can be felt. When these moments occur, find time to give praise and thanks for these experiences of a truth that lies within you.

We, however, would not choose this level of core beingness to discuss primarily with you at this working because it is our opinion that each density has its purpose. Now, we would preface this line of thinking by pointing out that the seeming progression of densities is an artifact of time and space and is not the deepest truth of the cosmos and its makeup. In a deeper reality, or shall we say, a more shallow illusion, all time and space is one and as an entity, therefore each seeker is working simultaneously upon all densities and sub-densities. However, within incarnation there is time, there is space and there is progression. Therefore, we use the concept of densities to indicate which lessons are learned first, which lessons are the foundation for further lessons.

In first density the lesson is simply consciousness. In second density the lesson involves the turning to the light, the beginning of choices. In third density, which you now enjoy, the lesson is in learning how to love and how to accept love. These lessons are two sides of the one coin of love. You have entered into this incarnative experience because you felt that there was room for improvement in your understanding of love. Now, there are other reasons which cause you to wish to come at this time having to do with service to this planet and its peoples in this time of transformation on a planetary scale. But each also has lessons to learn, and so we would focus upon the core beingness of the self as it can in a stable manner be experienced helpfully within incarnation.

You have heard us speak of meditation, not once—except for the one known as J—but again and again. We use this term meditation because it is what this instrument is used to calling it, but often in meditation people visualize, pray and contemplate. However, the core of being within incarnation, we feel, can perhaps most purely be sought within the concept of listening. Each is aware when someone physical speaks and the sound vibrations carry to the physical ear. Even if the language is foreign the entity knows that communication is being attempted. There is within each seeker an instinct for hearing within. However, this instinct is latent in most entities within incarnation, and it needs to be encouraged over time on a regular basis.

Your holy work known as the Bible talks of the "still, small voice." We would characterize this voice as that of what this instrument would call Christ consciousness, or the spirit within. Within each entity there lies a country that is a holy high place. You spoke earlier of geography of the self and we would say that this high place exists within a dark continent of the subconscious mind. Into this place comes the seeker who opens the inner ear and in this place dwells the Creator in fullness and in mystery, and the silent speech of this mystery is food and drink to the eternal self within. Each condemns the self for not meditating well and yet we say to you that the attempt is all. Each experiences usually the subjective feeling that a meditation could have been purer or less cluttered with the errant thoughts of a foolish and shallow personality that seem to drift and rush through the calm and silent chamber within with undue rudeness and haste. Yet we ask you to be very patient and compassionate when looking at the performance of meditation or silent listening.

You see, within incarnation, within the progression of youth to age and day-to-day, each has learned to value performance and production. Each has the internal checklist of things to do and there is an uncanny delight in crossing off those never-ending things to do, and yet your beingness depends not one whit upon your crossing off the items on your list. Rather, your value depends upon your vibration. If you are in love with life, if you embrace the present moment, then your core vibration is expressing at its best, shall we say, at its most harmonious, at its clearest and most lucid. And this is what people receive from you louder and more impressively often than what you are doing at the time. This nexus of vibratory patterns is that which you came to share with this planet so beloved to each of you. This is the gift you have to give to your fellow beings at this time—yourself.

Are you thinking that you are not good enough? Let us square away and tackle that thought, for the self-judgment, while useful in Earthly pursuits, is peculiarly disadvantageous to one who seeks to give the self in love. There is a sense of proportion that comes to one who has touched that core being which is tabernacling with the one infinite Creator. Beyond words, beyond actions, this essence is your gift and it is worthy. How beaten down each entity is when he attempts to judge the self against the yardsticks so eagerly accepted.

Now, we are not suggesting that good behavior is not appropriate. Indeed, each action and each thought can be examined and each can profitably learn about the self as she contemplates the actions of the day and sees ways to do things more as she would wish to have done them. This learning is legitimate and is part of why you are here. But in judging one's own value it is very easy to spend time tearing the self down, which could better be spent in holding that dear human self in the arms of the love within and comforting and being with that dear child of Earth that tries so hard and fails so often. It is appropriate for each of you to fail often, to fall down and to pick the self up.

This is why you came into such a heavy, chemical illusion. You wanted to fall down and go boom, as this instrument would say. You wanted to be a baby and to learn in the illusion, of the illusion, for the illusion because within this thick illusion the forgetting of who the true self is can take place so that each entity feels alone and each entity has the chance using nothing but free will and faith to choose to come face to face with that core self you all seek, and to within that self make the decision of how to serve the infinite Creator. Each within this room has chosen to serve along the path of service to others. And so you seek by will and faith alone to make choices that place you to the best of your judgment and ability increasingly in mental and physical states where you are dwelling within the love of the moment and are able to serve others.

Were you not dwelling behind this veil of forgetting these choices would be easily made. Within this illusion, however, the choice to give, the choice to make expressions of love, especially in the face of a perceived not-love is precious, for choices made in the darkness, in the absence of knowledge, go very deep. You are working upon that core vibration more efficiently, shall we say, within this illusion than you ever will in all of the illusions that follow, for once you have graduated from this third density the veil of forgetting shall be lifted and you will know that you are one with the infinite One but that all others are one with that infinite One and with you, and there will be the strength of the group who together seek that shall aid greatly in the basic awareness of a more solid illusion, shall we say, one more filled with light.

Never again shall you build the foundation of all that is to come. This is a short and intense experience during which you have marvelous opportunities to transform the self. These chances shall come in a cyclical fashion. Just as you have learned one lesson and are feeling secure, as the one known as B was speaking earlier, the next lesson shall come forward and all shall be out of kilter again, and in the initiation into that next level of the lesson of the incarnation much will seem disjointed and difficult. And then the lesson begins to be learned. The experience smoothes out, perhaps, for a time and then another time of learning begins.

Each portion of this cycle is equally useful and we encourage each to appreciate the easy times and the difficult ones, for in each state of mind there are many, many lessons that can be worked upon. It, for instance, is easier to work on thanksgiving when all seems to be rosy. However, there is equal work in thanksgiving when things seem difficult. This is a chance you worked hard for, this chance to dwell in dimness of perception and challenge the self to find the light. When you are listening, know that you are at your most precious time, that listening within is as the key that unlocks the door to that holy ground which is, in truth, in all places, in all times, and in all things.

We would at this time transfer this contact to the one known as Jim. We would thank this instrument and leave it in love and in light. We are known to you as those of Q'uo.

(Tape ends.)

L/L Research

L/L Research is a subsidiary of Rock Creek Research & Development Laboratories, Inc.

P.O. Box 5195
Louisville, KY 40255-0195

www.llresearch.org

Rock Creek is a non-profit corporation dedicated to discovering and sharing information which may aid in the spiritual evolution of humankind.

ABOUT THE CONTENTS OF THIS TRANSCRIPT: This telepathic channeling has been taken from transcriptions of the weekly study and meditation meetings of the Rock Creek Research & Development Laboratories and L/L Research. It is offered in the hope that it may be useful to you. As the Confederation entities always make a point of saying, please use your discrimination and judgment in assessing this material. If something rings true to you, fine. If something does not resonate, please leave it behind, for neither we nor those of the Confederation would wish to be a stumbling block for any.

CAVEAT: This transcript is being published by L/L Research in a not yet final form. It has, however, been edited and any obvious errors have been corrected. When it is in a final form, this caveat will be removed.

© 2009 L/L Research

Sunday Meditation
November 5, 1995

Group question: We are wondering how change and new growth seem to come from confusion, pain, anger and all sorts of negative emotions frequently. How can we open ourselves up to such difficult circumstances to aid positive change?

(Carla channeling)

We are those of Q'uo. Greetings in the love and in the limitless light of the one infinite Creator. It is a great privilege to be called to your circle of seeking at this time and we wish to extend to each of you our thanks and our blessing. As we share our thoughts with you we would ask each to remain very able to discriminate in those thoughts which you wish to take and those you wish to leave behind, for we are fallible and are not those who speak with great authority, but rather those who care deeply to be of service to those of your planet who would wish to know what we have to say at this time. We trust you to use that discrimination which is your unshakable gift.

Your third-density Earth experience could be said to be of a certain nature or kind. Basic to that nature is duality. Your illusion is rich and redundant in its dualities and opposites. This two-sidedness is the result of the very kind of illusion which has been prepared for you. It was prepared thusly for a purpose. That purpose is the using of individual free will to make choices concerning how each wishes to progress along the lines of spiritual evolution. As each comes into the incarnative experience upon this Earth plane …

We apologize for this instrument who says she has a frog in her throat. We do not find any such creature to be inhabiting this part of her anatomy. However, if you will bear with us we will bear with her.

Even the infant begins to differentiate and choose who shall best supply its needs. And as that young spirit becomes familiarized with the illusion, and as the veil of forgetting drops, that infant soul prepares for what we might call a long school year, for your incarnative experience takes place in a beautiful and plenteous classroom, that orb upon which you dwell. At the heart of the new experiences lies a consciousness. This consciousness has many parts. There is a great range of awareness to which each of you is privy and the number of choices that is made by you in even one hour of your existence is vast, for as each dwells in this moment, for example, the senses are being bombarded by the noises the ear can hear, by that light or darkness and the images which the eye can see. There are several different sorts of odors which make up that which can be smelled or sniffed in the domicile which each now enjoys. There are literally unlimited numbers of impressions which enter into the nexus of your physical, emotional, mental and spiritual being all the time, and far below the threshold of consciousness about ninety percent of that which is taken in does not come into the consciousness mind.

The young soul upon your planet works upon the surface of experience. This surface experience fills the being completely, for everything is new. But very quickly the choices begin being made, and by the time the youngster has become even a young adult the choices have become solidified into a structure of personality and character which preordains or biases the way sense impressions are taken into the being and used. Along the way in this continuing learn[ing] process the experiences of love and of fear have gone deep, penetrating the surface of the personality, penetrating eventually even the deeper character traits. Those experiences when one has experienced love have provided each with times of transcendent joy, and this is the gift of love, that when experienced purely it brings with it a freedom and a lightness that is ineffable and that is precious and to be trusted as a real experience.

Those experiences wherein one has sounded the depths of fear have also shaped the life experience. This experiencing of fear is what we would look at at this time, for it serves a great and useful purpose and yet it is also that which solidifies and weights experience with what we would term unnecessary poundage. Now, when one looks at fear one first needs to express that there is an appropriate reaction to many hazards which can be called fear. Fear is not always the bogey man or the villain. Often fear is wisdom, but also quite often the action of fear is counterproductive. So let us gaze at the way fear works.

The child touches the stove and receives a burn. Thereafter the child sees the stove and still finds it attractive but the mind and the emotions contract about that seeing and keep the child from hurting itself. However good fear can be, it also is that dark side of the self in its more subtle expressions and as that shadow self it serves the seeker ill. Now, we would not ask you to extirpate this fear. We do not suggest that you become full of fearlessness, ignoring the environment in which you find yourselves. We do, however, encourage each to spend the time each day to reflect upon those times when you have felt that contracting which fear invokes, for often that reaction of fear, that contracting, creates a knot, a tangle of the beingness so that the consciousness is narrowed and straightened and limited unnecessarily. It is good, then, we think, to reflect upon whether you have used fear well in the day or whether in the events of the day fear has used you, for what you were describing in your question was the way fears create pain.

Now, the basic nature of your illusion, that duality of which we spoke, is as it is in order to provide a structure within which the student of truth may work upon itself in the refining and the disciplining of the personality. Basically, you are attempting, through the choices you make, to become more aware of who you really are and what your personal truth consists in. When you are moving from an attitude that is free and relaxed you have the capacity to be more aware in a conscious way of the rhythm of life than when you are contracted through various kinds of fear. When one is unsure, uncertain, tentative and holding back cautiously these contracting feelings create a friction and this friction makes the seeking so vastly uncomfortable. And since there are so many ways in which a sensitive consciousness can be hurt it is no wonder that the experiences of living seem to have much pain in them.

But you see, as you came into this incarnational experience you were looking forward to the opportunity to enter into the transforming of the self alchemically with great enthusiasm and gusto, for the veil of forgetting was not yet in place and you saw the incredible opportunity to learn and to serve in the name of love. And like all those who are not in the thick of things you thought it would be easier than it turned out to be and this is inevitable, for does any of us have the strength of imagination that is capable of becoming fully aware of a situation never experienced?

And so it seems that the times of suffering are those times which give us the gifts of learning. Now, the amount of pain and suffering, emotionally speaking, that a seeker must carry is entirely up to that seeker, for that seeker has set for itself, and this is true of each, certain goals. Each came into this incarnation determined to learn certain lessons. These lessons were chosen uniquely by you and address those areas in which you felt you could become clearer, purer and finer, and you wished to work upon the consciousness. And you chose to come here not only to help this dear planet as its consciousness is transformed but you came also for your own agenda. And this agenda [is] always to do with love, for you see this is not the density of wisdom. This is the density of love. And you seek, when you think you are seeking wisdom, confusedly.

We must share with you that it is our perception that one within your density will not become wise, for the illusion was created specifically to confound wisdom. Perhaps we may say that your journey is the journey from the head to the heart, from reason to feeling, from rigid structure to rhythmic and flowing structure, from holding to letting go. And, paradoxically, as you allow each strand you hold so tightly to be released you do become more wise as you release fear, release undue concern about those things which are to come.

One can feel a victim very easily as one seeks to live spiritually. One can feel the weight of all that has been given up. One can drown in the hopes that have not happened. One can be deafened by one's doubts. And we say to you that all this is satisfactory. All this is acceptable. For truly you did not come here to be happy. You did not come here to be satisfied. But, rather, you came here to work, and to learn, and to serve.

So we encourage you to go on, day by day, and hour by hour, not asking yourself to be wise, but asking yourself to be loving to yourself, to the world around you, and to your other selves which [are] the very essence of your being. We ask you to allow yourself to be foolish. We ask you to get to know yourself in all of your impulses and little eccentric ways, to have a childlike feeling of exploration as you find yourself responding to the catalyst that the world brings to your senses. We ask you to put your arms around yourself within and to give love and support to that pilgrim soul which sails the seas of life, seeking hungrily, yearningly, constantly for that which beckons, that which calls.

Your heart is already full of all that you seek. All that you wish is possible, and yet it shall always come unexpectedly, sideways, as you have not prefigured it. And it shall come in uncomfortable ways, for when anything changes there is the adjustment to be made, and this, perhaps, is the heart of what we wish to say, that it is your desire in coming here to change, and change means movement. And if you have ever attempted to stop something that has momentum you know that there must be force applied in order to make that momentum cease and another vector begin.

This is what you have asked of yourself: to change. Each wishes to accelerate the rate of her own spiritual evolution and this involves change. And the natural reaction to this change is contraction and resistance, and this friction hurts. Can you learn to allow change without contraction and concern? Perhaps, on a good day. Not on a bad day. And this is acceptable. The less you worry about how foolishly you worry the less you condemn yourself for fearing that which turns out not to be scary, the less in the end you shall have suffered.

We encourage each to be patient with the self. It is not a characteristic of your illusion that things be clear, and yet there lies within each a heart that is full and fair and perfect. And there is a door into that holy place that is within. We encourage each to knock upon that door each day and say, "Good morning. Today I am with the infinite Creator. Today I am love made visible. Today I am. I am. I am."

We would at this time transfer this contact to the one known as Jim. We thank this instrument and leave it in love and in light.

(Tape ends.)

Sunday Meditation
November 12, 1995

Group question: We are taking potluck today.

(Carla channeling)

We greet you in the love and in the light of the one infinite Creator. We are known to you as the principle of Q'uo. Thank you for calling us to your meeting on this day. It is a great privilege to have offered to us the opportunity to share our views with you. As always, we ask that you use your discrimination, for we are fallible creatures as are you.

The vibrations that this group has, in its melding together, are heavy with the weariness that is of the spirit rather than of the body, although each here also has some degree of physical weariness as well. And this being the case in a group which is often very high in energy we would take some time to work with the concept of having the lower spiritual and emotional energies, for as in all conditions or estates of living such a situation has much to offer in the way of learning and in increasing the capacity for personal compassion.

Energy is the most fundamental of ideated structures within your physical illusion. The shapes and forms of manifestation are illusory, they being instead fields of energy. Even your physical body can usefully be viewed as a field of energy which contains multiple energy fields which work in cooperation with each other within the structure of the shell energy of the physical body. So that when the seeker experiences low energy it is experiencing a symptom which points deeply into the structure of the manifested being. If the energy of the field becomes untenably weak the physical vehicle simply ceases to function. A breath is expelled and another is not taken. Even if there is nothing physically wrong with the physical vehicle it is possible to cease viability strictly because of the disintegration of the energy field.

This is quite rare among your peoples as a cause of death, but it can be seen to occur in the case of the entity who has lost a mate after having a long and mutually beneficial experience together. When one leaves the physical plane the remaining mate not infrequently chooses to turn the whole being towards the day when he or she may be reunited with the loved partner and this affects the energy levels within the physical vehicle to the point where any illness which is encountered is embraced and used to effect the ending of the experience which is desired.

When the kind of weariness that a seeker feels is spiritual in nature it often signifies a time in which the experience of incarnative life will seem very difficult. Small matters seem to take on a larger aspect, and therefore any small change or unexpected occurrence triggers catalyst far in excess of what the seeker would usually expect of itself. It is a condition of vulnerability because weariness sensitizes the perceptive web which alters the level of information given to the physical mind and to the consciousness within. Small efforts seem to become major. The mind turns from tasks that normally would be accomplished easily, for it sees these tasks with the jaundiced eye and the discontented heart of the weary seeker.

The sense of self is disturbed and the level of comfort of mind drops. Into this weakened web of perception can come extremely helpful—this instrument is not able to find a word for the essences that are available within the deeper mind. But the state of low energy, because it increases sensitivity, offers the opportunity to go more deeply within the self, reaching towards those essences that can be called archetypical, those essences which this instrument would call hope, faith and charity.

So we ask each to gaze upon the weakened self, not with impatience but with, as far as possible, an undismayed peace of mind, for you have come into this illusion to be affected by it. Yours is not the path of evenness and spiritual perfection. Yours is a path that is full of dimness, confusion and perceived difficulty and suffering. Above all things we would ask you to retain the concept of what is fundamental, spiritually speaking, in this experience. That which is fundamental is the one original Thought which is Love. In a weakened state one has difficulty in reaching out to others in love, reaching to the self in love, and reaching to the Creator in love. However, in this weakened state one is more able to allow the self to be ministered unto by these essences which dwell, irregardless of the surface consciousness within, deeply seated within the unconscious mind.

The instinct sometimes is to thrash about mentally attempting to affect the energy state, to bring it into what is seen as a more advanced or acceptable state. Insofar as you can be aware of this tendency, we encourage you to say to the self, "Peace, be still and stay where you are. Abide. Rest. Release the effort to better or improve your situation," and allow the deep self to open into the consciousness. Allow that essence that is the Creator, that is love itself, to minister unto you. There is no need to thrash or wrestle. There is no need to give sermons to the self. There is no need, in fact, to alter the state you experience. The need is simply to remember love, for all things shall pass but love. Moods shall come and go. Incarnations bloom, wither and die. Love remains.

Those who strive each day, each moment, walk a razor's edge. On the one side of such intentional living lies a golden land of ideals and promises, dreams and heartfelt emotion. Your garden of Eden, your Elysium, and your heaven lie within those broad expanses of psychic energy. On the other side of the razor lies the bleakness of despair, the darkness of midnight and the hopelessness of those lost within the sea of confusion, rudderless, suffering, questioning and doubting. Is it any wonder with two such contrasting experiences available moment by moment that an even, steady life is difficult to arrange? And yet we ask you to gaze at your ups and downs and see that you did not come here to walk the razor without falling, but rather to see that balance and aim towards it.

Give it your best effort and when you perceive yourself falling off of that evenness into rosy idealism or bleak despair allow those emotions and know that all states of mind alike have as their basis, love. See the self, the consciousness that dwells deep within as a kind of tree of life. Or perhaps we should give it as a vine, for the vine itself, root and branch, is the Creator, and you, each, are a branch off of that vine. By your own free will you choose to graft various other plants, shall we say, other kinds of vine onto that vine and so your experience is a kind of hybrid.

Some grafts take the self towards the ideal and seem most fair and beautiful. Some grafts do not take well at all and the vine that issues from that graft is sour and bitter and difficult to digest when that fruit is plucked. And when the mouth is bitter with the taste of despair it is difficult to remember that the basic vine is love and that one needs only to travel back down to the roots to ground the self in the Creator. In times of difficulty, goading oneself towards enthusiasm and inspiration is not our suggestion. We indeed would suggest that you avoid pushing the self around except when it is deemed absolutely necessary. Rather, attempt to come into a relationship with the momentary self in which that self that is suffering is seen as a child, a child that you can take within the embrace of your own heart and rock and comfort and strengthen.

You can take that child and open the doors of your attention to love and let that love dwell, beaming, radiating that one great original Thought until that child within is permeated and completely saturated with that love that dwells so perfectly at the center of your being.

As you learn to work with your own moods without judgment, without reproach, but with love and patience, so you shall begin to learn peace, for peace is not the removal of all that is not peaceful. Peace within is a fruit of regular, repeated, consistent and thoroughgoing willingness to experience the self as the self and to regard it with love, for all things in their time shall certainly occur within you. The best and the hardest of experiences alike shall come to you and flow through you and recede at last. And so the surface shall always be confused to some extent, but it is in the grounds of your being that the work you wish to do shall be done. Be patient in that work. Be quiet when you try to judge. Remember, and refrain. And as you find charity for yourself, so shall you be able to be part of the good in other people's experience. The peace begins within.

We would at this time transfer this contact to the one known as Jim, thanking this instrument and leaving it in love and in light. We are those of Q'uo.

(Jim channeling)

I am Q'uo, and greet you again in the love and in the light through this instrument. At this time we would offer ourselves to any further queries which those gathered here may have to offer us. Is there another query at this time?

K: I would like to ask about the original Thought. This is a product of the Logos that created the universe? How do we experience this one original Thought at this time?

I am Q'uo, and am aware of your query, my brother. The one great original Thought that has set all into motion is the creation itself, that which you experience at this time and that which is beyond your current ability to perceive but which shall become more and more available to you as you progress in your own evolutionary journey. To say that the one great original Thought is the Logos is to somewhat misapply the term "Logos," for the one Thought of the Creator was the thought that It would know Itself. This is the concept of free will as you know it.

The means by which the Creator decided to know Itself was to employ the great creative energy and power of infinite numbers of Logoi so that each Logos is as a star or sun body and is an entity of completeness with all densities represented within it. Each Logos has within its care some form of planetary system that also offers the opportunity for what you know as life to be created and supported therein and to move upon the evolutionary path utilizing the free will embedded within all creation by the Creator in Its one great original Thought.

Is there another query, my brother?

K: How were you able to perceive the nature of the one great original Thought if it was in the mind of the Creator or within the Creator?

I am Q'uo, and am aware of your query, my brother. As we all are a portion of this one Creator, cells within the one great body of Being, each may through the process of meditation retire in a single-pointed fashion to that sacred room within and in those special moments of illumination become aware of the nature of the self and the nature of the Creator and the nature of the creation as being One.

Is there a further query, my brother?

K: You speak of yourself as the principle of Q'uo. Are you not a collection of unified souls—what I would call souls—in your present state?

I am Q'uo, and am aware of your query, my brother. As a principle, in our particular experience, we are a blending of two of what you would call social memory complexes that have united their efforts to be of service by offering our contact to this group. Thus, the blending is as a principle.

Is there a further query, my brother?

K: I would like to clarify. Was there a single Logos that created the multiple Logoi of which you speak to make the Big Bang theory of the universe? Is the Big Bang theory correct, and what the Creator used to make the creation?

I am Q'uo, and am aware of your query, my brother. We would suggest that this one Logos was indeed the one Creator who then created the infinite number of Logoi that you may see in your night sky as a representation of infinity. Each Logos, then, has a various strength or capacity for creation, some having created a solar system, others having created an entire galaxy, each being one of an infinite number of Logoi.

Is there a further query, my brother?

K: Some spirits say that they can travel by thought between galaxies. Is there a medium required to travel between galaxies by thought, or is this a consciousness or mind that would allow that?

I am Q'uo, and am aware of your query, my brother. We would call this a discipline of the personality that would reflect what you would call the level of one's spiritual understanding that would allow entities to move throughout the one Creation in thought and in what you would call zero time. Most entities of the third and the fourth density vibrations move with the aid of mechanical devices that allow the physical vehicle to be transported in time through space. As these entities continue upon the evolutionary journey and improve their means by which they seek union with the one Creator then are opened to them the disciplines of the personality that allow movement without the necessity of mechanical devices.

Is there a further query, my brother?

K: What happened in Roswell, New Mexico in 1947? Was there one flying saucer in Soccoro, New Mexico, or were there two? Were they from the psychic dimension, fourth density?

I am Q'uo, and am aware of your query, my brother. And though we find this is an area of great interest, especially at this time, among many of your peoples, we must refrain from working this riddle, for it is of importance to many to find this answer for the self and we would not take from them the fruits of this endeavor.

Is there any other query?

K: No, thank you, Q'uo.

I am Q'uo, and again we thank you, my brother. Is there any other query at this time?

R: No question, but could you say "Hi" for us to Hatonn?

I am Q'uo, and we are pleased to report that those of Hatonn are always with this group in spirit and lend their aid and love to each.

Is there a final query at this time?

(Pause)

I am Q'uo, and we are greatly filled with joy at the opportunity of joining our vibrations with this group once again. At this time we shall take our leave of this entity and this group, leaving each in the love and in the light of the one infinite Creator. Adonai, my friends. Adonai. ☥

L/L Research

L/L Research is a subsidiary of Rock Creek Research & Development Laboratories, Inc.

P.O. Box 5195
Louisville, KY 40255-0195

www.llresearch.org

Rock Creek is a non-profit corporation dedicated to discovering and sharing information which may aid in the spiritual evolution of humankind.

ABOUT THE CONTENTS OF THIS TRANSCRIPT: This telepathic channeling has been taken from transcriptions of the weekly study and meditation meetings of the Rock Creek Research & Development Laboratories and L/L Research. It is offered in the hope that it may be useful to you. As the Confederation entities always make a point of saying, please use your discrimination and judgment in assessing this material. If something rings true to you, fine. If something does not resonate, please leave it behind, for neither we nor those of the Confederation would wish to be a stumbling block for any.

CAVEAT: This transcript is being published by L/L Research in a not yet final form. It has, however, been edited and any obvious errors have been corrected. When it is in a final form, this caveat will be removed.

© 2009 L/L Research

The Aaron/Q'uo Dialogues, Session 27
November 17, 1995

(This session was preceded by a period of tuning and meditation.)

Group discussion: *(The group agreed upon the topic of living the devotional life in all of its variety and dimension. Thoughts from the group are presented below.)*

We had originally thought that we would talk about living the devotional life.

R says he is thinking about the fact that he takes himself too seriously.

G is thinking about the oneness of all and yet feeling different as well.

Barbara said that many in her group were feeling the "two by four" between the eyes to learn lessons, and I. says that this is not always the case.

Carla says that just deciding to live the devotional life is the only way to do it.

Incarnation as the devotional body is a statement that I. would like either Aaron or Q'uo to speak on. This life, this job, is devotional, no matter what we are doing. Do we have information on being too hard on ourselves, or could we focus more on that as well? The devotional life is not so much what you try to do as what you are able to do; and we get angry with ourselves for failing time after time.

G enjoys reading what Barbara has to say about living her normal life, because that is practical.

Q'uo: We are those of Q'uo. Greetings in the love and in the light of the one infinite Creator. It is both a blessing and a great privilege to greet each of you this evening. We are humbly privileged to be called to share our opinions and thoughts with you. We would ask, as always, that you use your discrimination as you hear what we have to offer. If the thoughts ring within your resonant heart then we offer them freely. If they do not ring true, then simply leave them, put them aside and move on; for truth is a personal and intimate matter. And each person will recognize her own truth.

We are blending our vibrations with yours; and as we weave our way through the ribbons of your thoughts we sense the energy of birth and transformation within each who sits in this circle of seeking. Each seeker sincerely wishes nothing more than to find truth in the self, in the environment, in the thoughts, and in each other. Each has a burden that is carried at some cost, and each has a yearning that cries within and yet is deeper than tears can express: to love, to be loved, and to be of true service.

Each may well and justly consider himself a devotee, an adorer of that which is of ultimate truth. The level of anguish that has been experienced as each walks along the path of seeking is sometimes quite high. And as we speak concerning the living of a life in faith—that is, the devotional life—we cannot promise that any of you will find in our words or in any others the goal that you so desire. For within the classroom of earthly life the questions are far, far more important than the answers. And the desire, the emotions of yearning and hope, are in themselves more highly to be regarded than any knowledge that can be expressed in words for the life of the seeker within your density's journey from the head to the heart, from knowing to loving; nevertheless, much in the way of tools and resources that may aid in seeking can be expressed. But as we move through many considerations and details, please remember that your keen thirst for an inner reality that pierces the illusions of earthly life holds within their invisible field a strength and a truth that shall, one day, be a revelation. And in that day, knowing no more than you do now, you shall yet be satisfied.

At this time we turn the microphone over to our beloved brother Aaron. We leave this instrument in love and light. We are those of the principle of Q'uo.

Aaron: I am Aaron. My greetings and love to you all. I ask your forgiveness for my intrusion on your planning session. Of course, this is your human choice, because this concerns your human experience to which we properly respond.

There are many of you with slightly different needs. I will attempt to extract from the expressed needs, the commonality of need. You all wish to lead your life in love; and yet sometimes incomprehensibly to you, you end up living parts of it in fear. Sometimes you judge that fear and say, "I am no longer living the devotional life. How do I get rid of my fear and return to love?" Others of you understand that both the love and the fear are expressions of devotion. But still your strong choice is to live your life in love, and there may or may not be subtle judgments about fear.

I do not want to go too far here, only to express that my perspective is that simply to incarnate is a devotional act. It takes tremendous love and courage to move into incarnation. To live the devotional life is not to be rid of fear; but to even offer that fear is part of the devotion—to learn that everything is an expression of God so that the love is found within the fear, for fear is merely a distortion of love.

My brothers and sisters, if it feels appropriate to you, my brother/sister Q'uo and myself would choose to focus on this question: "What does it mean to live the devotional life?" And how do you run askew of that meaning when fear prevents you from seeing the truth of fear and you find yourself moving into a stance of self-contempt for the fear-based actions or need to get rid of fear?

I make this statement in an attempt to pull together those threads of commonality, not only in your verbal questions but in your thinking. Please feel free to redefine the question and put aside my suggestions if they do not feel appropriate. I thank you. That is all.

Aaron: I am Aaron. Please take my words and consider them within your own heart. I am not omniscient. I can only speak to you from my own perspective, which I offer to you lovingly. If my words ring true to you, please use them. If they do not ring true, discard them. If any words that are offered to you do not help you to live your life with more faith, more skill, more love, you must always put them aside.

I wish to speak about living the devotional life. First we need to ask *who* wishes to live the devotional life, because there are many aspects of your self. The soul knows that it always lives the devotional life. It does not live behind a veil, so it sees clearly. But once you walk into human awareness, it is a struggle to live the devotional life. You struggle with that which seems inconsistent with that life.

I wish to offer you an example. Be a fish with me, twenty yards down under water. Feel the heaviness of the water, the darkness below you. Look up and see the light. Seen through the density of water and then through the atmosphere is the sun. It is hard to see this orb. Certainly there is something called light, but there is no clear perception of the source of that light. Now please emerge from the water; and when you arrive at those last inches, suddenly, "Ah! There it is! The sun! This has been the source of light."

This act of looking through the surface, this moment, is akin to the spiritual awakening that each of you have experienced in your lives. Some of you clearly perceived the spirit realm as children, so there was no moment of awakening to the truth of the spirit realm. But even for those of you who experienced that realm as children, there was a time when suddenly you understood, "This isn't concept; this is real. This is the deepest root of my being." There are some of you who were further under water and had the precise experience of looking through the surface, seeing the sun, and coming into the belief, "Now I am seeing clearly."

But my dear ones, what about Earth's atmosphere? You still do not have a direct experience of the sun. Your meditation and other inner work bring you into that space where finally there is nothing to distort the direct experience of the sun; but still you are seeing at a distance. Then you must go into the heart of the sun. "I will be burned up, destroyed," you say. Yes, "I" will be destroyed. The self cannot exist except as concept in the brilliance of that sun. Self is seen only as the tool, having no other existence other than as the tool; and yet it must be cherished because it is the tool of the incarnation and you need it. But you wear it only as a cloak; there is no identity with it. It is a tool!

When you come to the readiness to release even ego self, then you are ready to dive into the heart of the sun—no water, no atmosphere, no distance. Here, at last, is the direct experience of the sun. And what do you find there? One has to laugh as one enters that moment because you find that you have always been there, that you have never left, that the rest was all illusion.

The soul knows that it always lives the devotional life, because it knows the reality of itself as spirit. Those who live in the heaviness of Earth's atmosphere (never mind those under water who are not yet aware of the sun) become caught in thinking there is something they need to do to experience the sun. And from the relative perspective, indeed, there is. Here is where confusion lies.

The doing is not to wage war with the ego, which solidifies the illusion of relative reality. The work is to bring even the ego self into the Divine, to the divine Self. You cannot transcend ego until you accept ego. The work is not to wage war with ego self until the Higher Self wins, for that is an impossible task, self-defeating from the start. The work is to embrace the ego self so that it becomes transparent, becomes seen as a serviceable tool of the incarnation.

You, as human, have a challenge, which is to move in both places at once: within the relative structure in which ego seems solid; and within the ultimate structure, which sees with absolute clarity. Relative reality lies within ultimate reality.

My friends, think of a carton. Set yourself down inside it. The lid is closed. Here is your relative reality. You think that is all there is. May I ask you to take a finger and poke up the lid. Slowly raise the head just enough so that the eyes can peer out. Aha! There are a thousand; no, a million; no, ten million or far more cartons which beings inhabit. And around them is this infinitive space which we call ultimate reality.

You can never leave ultimate reality, and so you can never cease living the devotional life. And yet the relative human must, in part, give its effort to the living of the devotional life, not because that effort is needed for the devotional life to be lived but because the offering of effort is part of the teaching tool of the incarnation. I wish to turn the microphone over to my beloved brother/sister/friend Q'uo. That is all.

Q'uo: We are those of Q'uo. We wished to wait until the competition for sound value went a little more towards our favor, as the sound of sirens somewhat overmasters the human voice.

It is just such moments when the pilgrim soul identifies the sound of a passing siren and thinks, "What an intrusion it is into my peace," and yet you also dwell within that siren's wail. You are the entity in the ambulance. You are the child trapped in the fire. And the siren may be equally, justly, seen as the aid, the tocsin which rings, to remind the heart of the love it bears for that portion of the self caught in pain, in fire, or in the ceaseless athanor of the alchemist's lore.

"Who seeks the devotional life?" asked our brother Aaron. Who, indeed, should stand up and say, "I am the real person"? What portion of self can represent that seeker? We ask each to look within and estimate how much the self has been included as an object worthy of devotion. Those who seek along the path of service to others can more easily see and recognize those efforts poured out upon friend and stranger far more so than they can look within and see there, those portions of the self that need support, comfort, reassurance, and that ineffable quality you often call mercy.

Why is the self so often not an object of devotion? Perhaps in part it is because the seeker hears its own thoughts and sniffs the dark side some dark thoughts suggest or even reveal. And how righteous is the self in judging that dark side, that "hue-manity"? Now, it is our perception that it is entirely appropriate for the self to be more and more aware as it goes through the incarnational experience that this dark side of self exists. We ask you not to flinch away from that portion of your human nature you perceive as dark.

You are a whole and completed entity bearing all that there is within the mystery of your consciousness. The illusion that you enjoy presents the night and the day, the dark side and the light side, as the entire globe of your Earth turns again and again … light following dark, following light, following dark … This is the nature of the dance you now are enjoying to a greater or lesser extent.

Perhaps the greatest single stumbling block to the self's perception of how to live devotionally is this vein of judgment that the human lode contains. As in all ore, you are miners digging through useless rock as well as precious. Do you judge the material surrounding a vein of valuable metal because it is not that valuable substance? Or do you simply process the ore to refine it and to purify it?

Truly, as that precious metal within you—that pure consciousness—is refined in the furnace of incarnation, it is very helpful for the self to learn to minister to the self within that is undergoing transformation. What age are you within? What age is the shadow side of self? Is not your isolation—your feelings of alienation, this whole constellation of painful lacks and perceived limitations—the product of a young child's agony as it attempts to grow into that which it was not? We suggest to you that when you begin to turn to self-judgment that you perhaps turn again and take up that self within that you perceive as misbehaving and embrace that being, showering it with compassion, for it does no more than express its nature.

You judge not the slag, the dross. It simply does not make it into the ring, the ornament, the coin … Just so, love all of the self. This seemingly imperfect instrument is in fact perfectly created to give the seeker the maximum degree of potential for learning. Sometimes lessons come hard, but it is precisely your confusion and perceived lack of understanding that place you in so exquisite a rightness of position to meet and to learn to embrace and cooperate with the destiny that you have planned for yourself within this incarnative experience.

We would at this time turn the microphone back to our beloved brother. We leave this instrument in love and in light. We are those of Q'uo.

Aaron: I am Aaron. Q'uo picked up the words, "What aspect of the self is the real self?" Have you seen a small child playing in costumes? Perhaps it picks up its mother's briefcase and pretends to be a businessperson, or picks up a cooking spoon and apron and pretends to be a cook. It is very easy to see that each masquerade the child moves into is an expression of the true Self.

Just so, in incarnation you wear many masks. Is one the true Self? They are all expressions of the true Self. Which true Self is that which is no self at all, but empty of ego identification, the transcended Self which rests fully in its own Pure Awareness, in its own divinity?

You are familiar, of course, with the lines in your scripture known as the Bible that God created man in his/her image. I beg your pardon. I ask that you look for a moment at that sentence. This which we might call God is infinite love, infinite wisdom and intelligence, always thinking to expand itself and to express itself. The individuated awareness is one expression and furtherance of the Divine. It also moves into myriad experience as the child that masquerades. It is all part of its coming to know itself.

My brother/sister/friend of Q'uo has spoken eloquently of what happens when that which is being expressed in the self is that upon which judgment arises. For example, when that which has arisen is anger or fear or greed, Q'uo has suggested that you are pulled out of the experience that you are living the devotional life. When fear solidifies as judgment and in effect closes you into that box which I described earlier, from which place you lose perception of your divinity, then you cease to see the larger Self which is no self and how self is offered these myriad expressions as part of its learning opportunity. And instead, you move into a pattern of fixation on what arose in experience and into a relationship with that expression in which you must either call it good or bad, to be kept or to be gotten rid of.

There is nothing wrong with discriminating mind. In fact, you need such mind for the incarnation. The judgment that flagellates the self is unnecessary to discriminating mind. Discriminating mind can simply observe, "This is unskillful." But the energy field need not contract around that discernment. It is made from a place of Pure Awareness which sees the human slipping into fear. *What* slips into fear? Fear slips into fear. Do not go with it! It is only a problem when there is no awareness that one is slipping into fear. Then the energy field contracts and it is as if the box lid were shut. Then you forget who you are. You begin to believe the masquerade, to believe, "I am the bad one who's feeling cheap, who's been cruel," or whatever else may have arisen. You forget that there is a soul out there, and this moment of feeling fear is simply one expression.

Fear is not to bind you in a box of hatred. Fear is to teach you compassion. That was the whole reason for your incarnation: to move into a situation where you find the catalysts which help to open your heart. You do not have to get rid of anything. When you do not need it, it will go. As long as there is an attack on what has arisen in the human self, there is separation from the self and from the Divine of which that self is expression.

I want to ask that you begin to observe this contraction of the energy field. When a fear arises—anger, desire, impatience, pride—then, as Q'uo pointed out, judgment arises that says, "I shouldn't be feeling this," and with that judgment you move into a space of strong self-condemnation: "Fix it. Get rid of what's broken." But, my dear ones, nothing was ever broken.

Does a mathematics teacher put a hard problem on the board to convince you that you are inadequate or to help you learn how to solve the problem? Does incarnation hand you the heavy emotions which give rise to judgment in order to confirm your inadequacy or to teach you compassion? The question is not that these heavy emotions arise, but rather is wherein identification lies.

With the emotion and the clarity that can observe the emotion arising without ownership of it, here is the hole poked through the box so you can see the space, see the angel that you are. "Ah, yes. I am here experiencing this heaviness for a reason. I don't have to hate myself for experiencing it, only love and respect the experiencer of it. My aversion, then, is against the unpleasantness of the experience; but I don't have to attack myself that it came into me. Instead can there be greater compassion for this one?" This clarity is one essence of living the devotional life.

On the ultimate plane you are always living the devotional life; but on the relative plane, in order to live that life there must be a willingness to stay in touch with the divine aspect of the self, to create that spaciousness whereby the true Self can be seen through the clouds of delusion.

To live the devotional life is to be willing not to attach to fixing the self, but rather, to aspire to loving the self. There is effort involved. It is the effort to learn that the box is transparent. As long as the box seems solid, it provides both barrier and safety—barrier to protect the small self and safety to that which is "outside" and may seem threatened by the negative thoughts of the ego self. And so you hide in the box.

To live the devotional life is to love the Divine so much that you are willing to put holes in that armor, to give up your fear or at least your ownership of that fear. When you poke holes in the box you cannot help but see the brilliance of the light that shines beyond, shines through even into this expression that we call small self. Can you love this small self that falls into mud puddles? It is easy to love God; but can you love this that quakes in fear, that sometimes lies, grasps or abuses as expression of that fear?

Q'uo: We are those of Q'uo and are again with this instrument.

In closing we would ask that as you lay your frail barque of flesh down between the soft, cool sheets of your bed, think on all your attributes and shower them with your affection. "Ah, sweet feet and legs that have carried me where I chose to go this day … ah, dear back, strong, bent under the burdens of the day … kindly stomach, hard-working heart, sweet tongue spouting such folly … ah, dear, dear pride, lovely vanity, elegant sloth …" Do not fear these attributes. They are yours to command, to use in understanding more. They all are yours—precious, precious gifts. Without all of your attributes you could not swim so well in the sea of confusion that is breeding new life within you.

Tuck yourself in with love this night, and cast all your burdens into the powerful and compassionate arms of the Creator, whose nature is love and whose love is nearer than your breathing. The Creator does not care that you perceive yourself as imperfect, for the Creator knows your heart and dwells therein in perfect contentment.

Good night, each weary spirit. Our joy at being given this opportunity to share with you this weekend is too great to express. We love and bless each of you, and for now leave this instrument and you in the ineffable Mystery of the love and the light of the one infinite Creator. Adonai. We are those of Q'uo.

Aaron: I am Aaron. You are weary and I will be brief. No more words or thoughts; but I want to bring your bodies into this because you learn with these bodies. Both Q'uo and I have raised the question, "What do you do with this judgment? What about these contractions of self-condemnation or of heavy emotion?"

There is an exercise drawn from Tai Chi called "pushing hands." In this exercise, two people stand face to face, one foot behind the other and arms resting, forearm against forearm. A pushes sharply. B's usual reaction to that push is that its body's energy contracts. If it is deeply aware, it may go only as far as that contraction; otherwise, it will push back or resist.[1]

A is not just another person. A is all of those conditions of life which push at you. When life pushes you, you have two choices. The traditional choice is to push back, but you can also learn to dance with that force, to absorb it; and when the force releases itself, take it back. It is quite powerful to practice this and watch that which wants to resist arising, to see, "I can't just will that the resistance fall away. I can wish it would go, but I can't make it go. I can pretend it's not there, but that doesn't mean that it no longer exists. But when I soften around that resistance, not trying to make it go away any longer and not acting it out, but just making space for it, then I become able to dance with that which pushes at me, be it internal or external. And with the worst hailstorm falling on my head or an emotion arising, I give it more space and become able to dance with it."

I want Barbara to demonstrate this to you that you might practice it tonight and in the morning, so that we may talk a bit about the exercise and what it means to dance with life.

It is such joy to rest here in this circle of sincere and loving seekers. I express a gratitude that you have invited me into your circle. I love you all and wish you a good night. Barbara will show you this exercise when my words are concluded. That is all. ☙

---

[1] Aaron is using the letters A and B to refer to two individuals in relationship.

L/L Research

L/L Research is a subsidiary of Rock Creek Research & Development Laboratories, Inc.

P.O. Box 5195
Louisville, KY 40255-0195

www.llresearch.org

Rock Creek is a non-profit corporation dedicated to discovering and sharing information which may aid in the spiritual evolution of humankind.

ABOUT THE CONTENTS OF THIS TRANSCRIPT: This telepathic channeling has been taken from transcriptions of the weekly study and meditation meetings of the Rock Creek Research & Development Laboratories and L/L Research. It is offered in the hope that it may be useful to you. As the Confederation entities always make a point of saying, please use your discrimination and judgment in assessing this material. If something rings true to you, fine. If something does not resonate, please leave it behind, for neither we nor those of the Confederation would wish to be a stumbling block for any.

CAVEAT: This transcript is being published by L/L Research in a not yet final form. It has, however, been edited and any obvious errors have been corrected. When it is in a final form, this caveat will be removed.

© 2009 L/L Research

The Aaron/Q'uo Dialogues, Session 28
November 18, 1995

(This session was preceded by a period of tuning and meditation.)

Aaron: I am Aaron. Good morning and my love to you all. I hope you have had a restful night. A few of you are aware of dreams in which you were observant of the movement between contraction and opposition to it, and to dancing with that catalyst and the resultant contraction about which we spoke last night. We have been talking about this balance between the ultimate being—which is whole and knows its wholeness, which experiences no veil separating itself from the reality of its wholeness—and the relative being which perceives itself to be less than whole and is struggling to become whole.

You are not incarnated to get rid of that struggle, but to live it out and learn from it. You must cherish the experience of the incarnation without getting lost in it. This, to me, is another aspect of the devotional life: the willingness to work in an ongoing way to keep both doors open, cherishing and living the incarnation from a perspective that sees it clearly.

You are the mother tying the child's shoes before it leaves to march in the parade, straightening its collar, adjusting the outfit, smoothing its hair. And you are simultaneously on the tenth-floor balcony observing not only the whole parade but the infinite landscape through which the parade marches. From that perspective you cannot see whether the child's shoe is still tied; but if it is not tied, if you had not given that care on the relative plane, then it might stumble and fall, disrupting the entire parade behind it. And that disruption you would see from your balcony.

So, you must attend to both, attend with infinite care to the details of relative existence. And that attendance is what I name as devotion—attending but without fixation, with the spaciousness which sets you up on that balcony. You might even move to the sixtieth floor where you can see all the neighboring villages and all the other parades.

I want to invite you to do a small inner exercise with me. Walk into a bathroom with me. Turn on the faucet and observe the water filling the sink. Suddenly it threatens to overflow and the faucet that turned it on does not turn off. It seems to turn in only one direction. The water is up to the top lip now and here it comes over the top, running down onto the floor. Try to turn it off again; it will not turn. Feel the tension building in you. It is streaming over the top now, a literal waterfall, and you know that this bathroom is directly above the living room. It will leak through. Quick, gather towels. Mop up the water. Toss the saturated towel into the bathtub and take another and another. If you go fast you can keep up. Can you feel the tension of that? "Me against this water." This is the relative human. And now I walk into the bathroom and pull the plug. *Whoosh!* The water goes down the drain. Feel the tension relax?

Life constantly hands you its barrage of overflowing sinks, of problems to be solved; and your energy contracts into a self that will handle those problems. This, my dear ones, is not devotion. This is control. This is fear.

Even if that sink was above not your own but your neighbor's living room in an apartment, and if your desire to stop the water was so that no harm would come to your neighbor, implying focus on service to another—when you are meeting the issue with that contraction of fear, you are simply moving into a perpetuation of an old pattern which believes that the ego self must be in control. If it must be in control, then there is something "other than" out there of which it must be in control.

So, you move into the myth of strengthening the self, being the powerful or capable or good one. There is nothing "other than." In the moment when you symbolically pull the plug, you shift tracks from the fear track to the love track. You come back into harmony. The universe is not throwing mud on you in order to make you feel small or inadequate. If the universe does fling mud on you, in some way you have invited participation in that experience because the soul sought the experience—that 4X4 beat over the head that we talk about—sought the experience because there was a higher area of learning which it sought, and it did not know how to open to that area of learning.

I want to offer a brief example of Barbara's experience here. She did not ask for the tendonitis in her shoulder or the hernia in her belly. The conscious self did not want these distortions. The conscious self wanted to be healthy and free of pain. The higher wisdom sought the experience of moving into full harmony with the universe and was aware of the use to draw to itself the catalyst needed to make evident the areas of delusion, so as to allow the fullest possible expression of this intended harmony. The personal self agreed, without knowing the details, "This learning is the highest priority. Whatever it takes, I agree." It was offered milder lessons of the truth of harmony and was unable to pay attention to those. It truly needed something either life-threatening or physically painful to catch its attention.

And so, the body began to manifest these symptoms, these symptoms rather than other symptoms, because they grew out of a karmic stream, because there had been past injuries to the body in these areas and there is a cellular level of memory which perpetuates that distortion until it is released. My intention here this morning is not to explain how karma works in depth, so I will leave off that particular track and be glad to answer any questions about it at another time.

Simply put, here was the human frantically mopping up the floor, and it needed to be reminded that the water is not "other than." You need not attack it. Instead of perpetuating the practice in which you find yourself in opposition to it, stop. Use whatever practices are necessary or useful to release the tension of these old patterns in the ways that you practiced in the dance last night. That is one type of practice for coming back into this sixth-floor perspective; and then you see all of the other possibilities, nothing in opposition to you. Pull the plug or open your heart or whatever is appropriate in that circumstance—"Nothing against me."

To do this over and over and over is to live the devotional life. This is coming back to the memory, "I am divine and everything is divine, and I do not need to live my life in fear and disharmony." To do this is so difficult because the personal self is so attached to its fear, attached to its perpetuation of its mythical separation. It has felt safe, albeit alone, in that separation. And you are constantly asked to give up that mythical separation which has held you alone but safe, to offer your fear of the Divine—not getting rid of it, just releasing it/offering it—to offer your unworthiness, another illusion; to offer the myth that you are bad or broken.

My dear ones, all of those myths served a purpose to the personal self. You come to one and then another and you ask, "This one, too? Must I let go of this?" Yes, all of it. With each letting-go there is resistance. When you learn to greet that resistance with a gentle kindness, it is not so hard.

After some time, you find that you can be observant of the parade on the ground level from a basement window that watches the feet go by and sees all of the untied shoes. And you can watch the parade from the sixtieth floor at the same time—a spaciousness which reaches out and ties each shoe as it passes by, but without any fixation on any of this passing parade as "self," without any self to protect, just love which comes up to the highest floor and watches the whole process.

At this time I would like to pass the microphone to my brother/sister/friend Q'uo. I want to state here that it brings much joy (I speak for myself here but I know that Q'uo would echo my words). It brings me much joy to share with you in this dialogue pattern, each adding the richness of our own perspective. We speak as two souls speaking to this gathering of souls, all of us gathered together. I thank you with loving and grateful heart for wanting to share with this circle in this way. That is all.

Q'uo: We are those of Q'uo. And we, too, greet you with love, light, and joy in the infinite Creator.

How pleased we are to be exploring that great Mystery which is the ground of being with you. To us it remains an inimitable and ineffable Mystery; and at the same time, as we become more ripened as spirits, we become ever more deeply in love with this Mystery. We know not at what point we shall move beyond distortion, but we care not; for the delight of consciousness is like the odor of remembered flowers, a scent of supernal beauty that stays with utmost clarity in the memory.

We have been talking about the core of the art of living well, shall we say. That core being the establishment of a truly peaceful and non-judgmental attitude with regard to the self in all of its human vagaries. We have encouraged you to have mercy on yourselves and to allow healing, to touch the jagged edges of the wounds that the self's reaction to catalyst have caused. But how to do that? We are not speaking of releasing the self from the processes of self-determined ethics. We do not discourage the seeker from creating personal standards or from attempting with a whole heart to fulfill and honor these ethical commitments; but rather, our concern is that the sense of self not be diminished in the self's regard by the straying from the subjective structure of perceived righteousness or justice.

This work is important to the emerging metaphysical being. To enter into these processes with healing is for many difficult due to the self's disappointment with itself. We might suggest as a tool to be used in moments of self-judgment, the visualizing of a scene upon the stage of consciousness in which the Creator's hand is downstretched, open, palm upward—that hand being as tall as you, you being just able to reach into the palm to give to this outstretched hand of love the gifts of your humanity; for we assure you that the Creator finds these gifts precious. Here is the thing not done. Here is the thing done in error, omissions and commissions that you perceive as erroneous. Give them up. One by one let them tumble into that palm, one upon the other. Here, envy and pride ... all the sorry gifts of the undisciplined self.

Now look upon these bits of colored stone that are the form of these metaphysical gifts. To you, when you gave them, they were gray, ugly, broken pieces of self, fit only for the trash. Look now and see the beautiful colors of these shards of a life broken as they gleam and shine—blessed, accepted, and transfigured by the love of the infinite One. These are gifts indeed.

When these gifts have been given, when you see these colors, retreat a step at a time from the visualization and come back to the self—forgiven, blessed, renewed. You are loved in every tiny iota of the fullness of your being. There is, then, the opportunity to begin anew; and truly this chance is always real, not a mirage. For metaphysically speaking, the one who turns over its perceived errors is doing substantial and blessed labor. Take the deep breaths of the light that dwells as plenum in all that there is and know that you are made new.

We would at this time turn the working over to our beloved cohort, that prince in monk's robes, our Aaron. We leave this instrument in love and light for the moment. We are those of Q'uo.

Aaron: I am Aaron. As there will be a fourth session, my choice is to keep the next body of material separate and offer it this afternoon, and to focus our attention here for now. One of you has spoken to me of the questions of the human as teacher and learner. Each of you is always a teacher to other. At times, that which it teaches is the personal ego self. At times, that which it teaches is the Pure-Awareness Self. She states that it would be ideal if all who taught could teach from that highest level, but of course you cannot. Thus, your teaching of another is a process of discovering and analyzing that highest awareness in yourself.

For many of you, because you are aware that the teaching comes from the ego self, you become frozen, afraid to offer that because of your abhorrence that you will offer distortion and thereby defile another. I bring this up as one area about which we would like to hear your concerns. Please offer any other questions that come to your minds and to which you would have us speak.

M: In the exercise that Aaron described last night, is there a way to do this without anyone else with us?

Aaron: I am Aaron. I hear your question. You may constantly do this. There is always a partner, although often not a human partner. There is the sink that overflows.

This instrument showered this morning and found some water on the floor. Immediately her energy contracted against the water. Then you must offer that small, whispered, "Dance with it. The water on the floor is not my enemy." If you stub your toe and there is pain, you can fight with that pain or embrace the pain and soften your energy field around it. If the letter which you sought was not in the mailbox in the incoming mail, feel the contraction—wanting, wanting, grasping—and remind yourself, "I am not in opposition to the universe nor the universe in opposition to me. That letter not coming is the catalyst … this is the water on the floor by the tub …"

What is your relation to the catalyst? You will see it constantly at every red light, at every wait in the supermarket line. Noting the contraction, you make the skillful and loving decision to move back into harmony, to observe the contraction with a certain spaciousness and kindness. You are not getting rid of the contraction. If you are late getting across town and hit a string of red lights, you may note at each one that there is contraction.

If you walked across a graveled driveway strewn with rocks and your feet were bare, many of them would prick your feet and there would be pain and contraction. You would not say, "There should not be contraction," but you, out of kindness to the body, might feel anger towards the driveway. "Why does it have to have sharp rocks?" You might think, "Next time I will bring shoes to cross this road," but you do not think, "I shouldn't feel pain." You do not think, "My body should not contract. My body should like the pain." There is kindness to the body.

With emotional catalyst—the red lights as you drive across town—the energy contracts in the same way. Just come back to, "What is tense?" Come back to harmony with the universe. "The universe is handing me precisely the catalyst that I need. Can I sit here with each light, on the ground floor with the human squirming, wanting the light to change, while from the top floor, awareness is observing how much tension this human is feeling and offering it love?"

As you nurture that higher perspective, you begin to keep the door open so that you can come into painful catalyst, observe the painful contraction, and not fixate on doing anything about the contraction—not getting rid of it or flinging your anger about it on another, but just noting, "Here is contraction," and dancing with it.

As Q'uo just pointed out, this does not stop you, for example, from putting on shoes and going out and removing the sharpest rocks from the driveway. You learn to act skillfully from a place of love; to relate to the world in ways harmonious to the human's value system; to bring about change, but from a place of love and not from a place of fear. May we hear others of your questions directed either to Q'uo or to myself, or else simply thrown out loosely for us to decide who will answer?

Carla: Usually when I channel I can feel that the energy of the circle is upholding me perfectly. Occasionally I can tell that in addition to this energy, my essence is somehow being tapped and I am spending a lot of my own energy. Can you give me any insight into whether this is random or whether this is as it should be?

Aaron: I believe we would both like to speak to this question. May I speak first? This is not random. It is the place where the ego self has become more solid, where there is tension—perhaps internal tension about the answer or some thought that the self should know the answer, so that the self ceases for that moment to be a perfectly clear instrument and offers also its own opinion or need or fear into the workings. And this is fine, although uncomfortable and certainly less clear in the resultant channel. But it is your catalyst, your opportunity for learning.

There is a level of mind present in you which is observing this tension. My sister, may I suggest that when you experience this tension, you simply begin to note it as "Tension, tension …" I would suggest that you use a very non-judgmental label. To say, "Ego is present," becomes a judgment. Your observance of this situation in yourself simply points out the presence of some tension within you about the question or about the receiving of the answer. And as you note it, "Tension, tension …" you find an infinite spaciousness opening to that tension and you find yourself coming back to the clarity which is your preferred way of channeling, both for the clarity of the answer and to not drain your self's energy. I believe Q'uo would like also to speak to this. I pause.

Q'uo: We are with this instrument. We are those of Q'uo.

We would say to this instrument: My child, you remember the parable of Peter in the boat at night on the Sea of Galilee[2], how Peter saw his teacher walking upon the waters to him. Recall how Peter leapt from the boat and walked to meet his beloved rabbi. Only when Peter became aware that he was doing an impossible thing did he begin to sink. And then Peter remembered to reach out his hand to grasp his teacher's. Always your beloved's hand awaits your reach. Always the turning to trust will not be in vain.

We are those of Q'uo. May Aaron and we have the next query, please?

I: When Barbara and I danced a bit last evening, there seemed to be several stages of release as we did. The final stage caused a different sort of contraction because I seemed to perceive flashes of some immense, bright space. But the sense of personal me couldn't find itself there, so it kept retreating. Is it so that there is perceived these stages of release?

Aaron: I am Aaron. I hear your question, my brother. It is hard to think of it as stages so much as continuum from utmost involvement in the personal ego self with no notion of the expanded self to total resting in the expanded self. There lies a vast continuum. Because the mind cannot experience the subtleties of that continuum, it may see it in terms of plateaus. But in the reaching of each plateau, there is a continuum.

Ultimately you open into that space of light. There is no personal self there and there need not be a personal self there. But that does not mean the personal self has ceased to exist. On the ultimate level it never did exist, but was simply one expression of the Divine. But on a relative plane it does not and will not cease to exist.

If you have a screw to set in a hole and you go to your toolbox and get the screwdriver, turn the screw, and then put the screwdriver down—five minutes later has the screwdriver ceased to exist? It does not exist in that space/time, but it still exists. When you reach that place of infinite spaciousness and innate clarity, the personal self simply has no need to exist in that space/time. You will come back to it when you need it.

There are very valuable meditation practices which teach you to rest stably in this infinite space and Pure-Awareness Mind, to rest in the divine Self, and to reopen skillfully to the personal self when you have need to do so. You cannot take out the garbage merely from the soul self. Your humanity is needed. I would pass the microphone at this time to Q'uo. I pause.

Q'uo: We are those of Q'uo. My brother, we ask: What now remains as the direction of your seeking upon this planet within this pattern?

(Pause)

We are those of Q'uo. And in your silence lies a gift that you give yourself. For skill can wane and heart can fail. Yet upon the sea of consciousness there is that spirit which abides, moving over the water to create and alike to destroy. It is in the opening to and allowing of this overarching energy that the seeker will find answers that have no words, but only open the door into that purity of emotion within which lies personal truth.

We are those of Q'uo.

I: Thank you, Q'uo and Aaron.

Q'uo: Is there a further query at this time?

G: I have been working with anger in my partner. I understand his pain and why he lashes out at me, and yet am hurt by this. I don't understand why, if I can see with compassion that his road is different and I can learn from him … how can I be hurt? When I think about this it makes me sad and teary. That's my question.

Q'uo: We are those of Q'uo. My sister, was it the immortal bard which asked, "If you prick me, do I not bleed?" It is appropriate to hurt or to be hurt when there are negative emotions directed upon

---

[2] *Holy Bible*, Matthew 14:26-32.

your hapless head. This is his gift to you. To the world it is a kind of abuse to be tolerated. To the spirit it represents, as do all catalysts, an opportunity to respond rather than react, to allow the self to feel mourning, grieving, returning anger and resentment, and every iota of reaction. And at the same time it remains a viable option to decide to create a response that bears feeling from the heart and that turns from pity of self to peace in the end, and from anger to the sender of these errors to an embrace of the arrows that wound and the anger that smites. Until that entire energy is seen as the self, confusedly striking out at its own self, this friction seems hot and very physical; yet the issues underlying this catalyst are old and cold as stone. The challenge is to warm—with your allowing—that system of karmic friction, by your honoring of pain and your utter willingness to suffer until all is balanced.

We are those of Q'uo.

Aaron: I am Aaron. I would also speak to this question. Amongst those of you who place high value on offering your energy lovingly to others and who look with abhorrence on the possibility of offering your energy in ways that will hurt another, there is popular misconception that when you are abused, you must be doormat to that abuse.

The partner offers its anger in seemingly inappropriate ways. There is indeed real compassion seeing the fear, the pain, and tightness out of which the partner's hateful words have grown. There is the understanding that the partner's highest intention is not to hurt you but to defend itself, and that it simply does not know how to defend itself without hurting you. As Q'uo has clearly stated, of course there is hurt, especially as you grow in understanding and in ability to control that which would fling out of yourself in harm to others. The hurt is that the partner is not willing or able to grow in that way and so perpetuates its own pattern of offering hurt to you.

There may even be compassion about that, seeing that this partner is stuck there. So, there you are with your compassion and your sense of hurt, and a stoicism which says, "I will abide. I will tolerate." And, as Q'uo has said, to be willing to suffer as the karmic threads work themselves out is an essential part of this.

But also, there is a time to speak your own truth, not from a place of fear which would defend in the same pattern that the partner defends, but from a loving place to both of you which says, "This is enough." The statement is not offered in condemnation of the partner, but offered in the same way that a loving parent picks up the crying two-year-old who is having a temper tantrum and who has begun to pick up items, such as pots, and fling them. The parent does not condemn the two-year-old; it understands that the child is exhausted. But it wraps it in its loving embrace and prevents it from doing further damage. It holds it lovingly until its energy has quieted.

It is important that the parent does not say, "You are only a two-year-old." It respects the force that is moving through the other, but recognizes that it is not skillful nor appropriate to allow that force to fling itself out at the world. Sometimes the two-year-old will cry all the harder for a bit.

When you say to your partner, "I understand that you are angry, but your statements do cause pain. Is that what you want to do? Is your priority here to defend yourself and cause pain in me, or is your priority to help us learn to communicate better? But you see that neither of us knows how best to allow that communication at this time. If your real wish is to communicate, can we wait until your anger settles itself a bit? And can we then attempt that communication?"

In such a way you begin to allow the partner the right to its anger, the right to its fear. There is a certain respect for its processes. But there is a clear statement, "While you have a right to your own processes, you do not have the right to pour the energy of those processes on me in hurtful ways."

Of course, it is more complex because sometimes the partner does not seem to be ready to hear that statement. I do not pinpoint the question here; but in certain circumstances you will find that the other wants to perpetuate the pattern of its fear and cannot tolerate your invitation to move beyond its fear, and so it becomes necessary that you part ways. In that situation you will have to ask yourself, "Am I willing to allow the continuance of this pattern of fear and continue to participate in it in order to have that which I value from this other person, or am I no longer willing to allow the perpetuation of those patterns?"

Most often if you are patient … it will not happen all at once, but if you are patient through weeks, or months, or even years, the other will open to your invitation. When I say patient, it is not that you will have to wait years for the beginning of opening, but for the fruition.

Both instruments are becoming a bit tired. May we ask for just one more question? And we'll continue your questions in the afternoon session. I pause here.

I: In the bathroom meditation Aaron was speaking about, he said that when we move from a place of control, we contract into a self that can handle an overflowing sink. He also called this moving from a fear track and not a love track. Obviously this is not truly effective; but there is the habitual thought that to be effective in a situation that we find overwhelming, we do have to take personal control. Love is unlimited. Why don't we find it easy to trust that?

Aaron: I am Aaron. I hear your question. You say there is a habit that, from a place of fear, you do have to take personal control. What does personal control mean? The small ego self is one piece of personal control. The higher self is a different aspect of personal control. This is partway on that progression from enclosure in the small ego self to resting in the Pure Heart/Mind, the Pure Spirit Body that is the ultimate level of your understanding, and unrelated to the personal. The higher self includes the mental body, but it is a place that is free of fear.

My friends, you like your problems, even though you claim to dislike them. You invite them back over and over and over. If you do not have a problem in yourself, you go out and find a comrade whose problem you can solve. To be a problem-solver helps you to feel strong, safe. You repeat the same patterns over and over and over.

If indeed there are infinite solutions, if in fact there has never been a problem, only a situation that needs loving attention, then you must begin to ask yourself why these "myriad solutions" elude you. What is there that does not want to find the solution, because to do so is to give up being the problem-solver, to give up studying the problem?

I would ask you to begin to work from a very different place. Here you are in the bathroom with the sink water rushing over the sides of the sink. Your final goal is a dry floor. You had a stack of a hundred towels, but now there are only four or five left. Clearly this is not going to work. What if you stop this mad rush to be in control and begin instead to visualize just what it is that you want to have happen?

What if G were to begin to visualize a loving and harmonious relationship with her husband? What if she sees how that experience of mutual fear can become two people treating each other with respect? Several things may happen. She may begin to have insight into why she is attached at some level to the perpetuation of the pattern of disrespect, the ways that this pattern keeps the ego safe even though the heart-self longs for communication and light. As she comes into awareness of the ways she has perpetuated the pattern, the heart's deepest wisdom intuitively will provide the pathways leading into harmony. I said before and I repeat, you must be willing to offer up that which holds to disharmony for ego-centered or defended reasons.

As Q'uo pointed out, you must be willing to take that hand which offers to you the strength, the courage, the love to follow in the path. It is not easy. But within those two movements—to offer up that which has so long been held and to seek the Divine without and within—within those two movements is the doorway to growth, to healing, to peace.

At this time I would pass this microphone to my beloved friend Q'uo for final thoughts and the conclusion of this session. I thank you all deeply for allowing me into your circle; and also, on behalf of all who live for the greater opening of love in the universe, my thanks to you for the courage with which you continue to seek those openings of love in yourself. That is all.

Q'uo: We are those of Q'uo. Dear ones, vampires and vampiric energies, those spears which assail and wound, seem to come from the enemy. Yet you are always wounded by your very self. You cannot go around such energy. You cannot escape from this energy, for like an ill wind, it will blow where it will. Yet you can enfold such wounding energy in an embrace which accepts the energy, honors it, and takes it in without fear. Love does abide—not your love, but the Creator's love.

You cannot overspend the love that comes through you. The task lies in allowing the self to become transparent so that the love flowing through creates that glow that recreates the face of the earth. You tremble on the brink of miracles. Lift high your hopes and live by faith. We shall speak again soon. Meanwhile we leave each of you with great thanks in the love and in the light of the one infinite Creator. We are those of the principle known to you as Q'uo. Adonai. Adonai.

L/L Research

L/L Research is a subsidiary of Rock Creek Research & Development Laboratories, Inc.

P.O. Box 5195
Louisville, KY 40255-0195

www.llresearch.org

Rock Creek is a non-profit corporation dedicated to discovering and sharing information which may aid in the spiritual evolution of humankind.

ABOUT THE CONTENTS OF THIS TRANSCRIPT: This telepathic channeling has been taken from transcriptions of the weekly study and meditation meetings of the Rock Creek Research & Development Laboratories and L/L Research. It is offered in the hope that it may be useful to you. As the Confederation entities always make a point of saying, please use your discrimination and judgment in assessing this material. If something rings true to you, fine. If something does not resonate, please leave it behind, for neither we nor those of the Confederation would wish to be a stumbling block for any.

CAVEAT: This transcript is being published by L/L Research in a not yet final form. It has, however, been edited and any obvious errors have been corrected. When it is in a final form, this caveat will be removed.

© 2009 L/L Research

The Aaron/Q'uo Dialogues, Session 29
November 18, 1995

Session 29

(This session was preceded by a period of tuning and meditation.)

Aaron: Good evening and my love to you all. I am Aaron. With much joy I rejoin this circle of light. We have been speaking of different aspects of the devotional life. We come to a large aspect, which is ego's desire to blame. Somehow this that recognizes itself as entity may have experienced pain or felt a sense of humiliation or experienced a heavy emotion. Any of these arisings are uncomfortable and make ego squirm.

If there is perceived threat, there is desire to pinpoint the cause of that threat so as to feel safe. If there is blame, there is desire to explain the self and cast blame elsewhere. If there is hurt which has come to the self through another's words or actions, there is desire to raise the shielding of anger. These are all natural responses of the human. They are not necessary responses, such as the response of the body to bleed if the skin is punctured, but still they are natural accompaniments of the emotional body.

To feel anger is not the same as to hold on to that anger. To wish to defend is not the same as to attack another as enactment of that defense. To hold another out of your heart insures the continuance of the karma around which the issue revolved. To live in devotion is to be willing to reflect upon your fear, your anger, your pain, and the ways that the holding of these have served to solidify the ego self and allow it to feel safe.

To reflect upon the attachment of maintaining the anger is the beginning of the consideration that anger or blame might be released. To release that blame and anger is to forgive. To live the devotional life is to learn how to forgive. Forgiveness cuts karma, dissolves it entirely.

At the place where that karma was formed, we find always an energy contraction. The karma is not about "A did this to me," but it is about the way self solidifies around "A did this to me." It is about the misunderstandings that "I must angrily confront A or be doormat to A."[3]

G. spoke earlier about the arising of compassion for her husband. She spoke about seeing deeply into his fears and into what drives him to rage. She spoke of the fact that, although she understands the roots of his rage and feels compassion, she still feels pain. When we feel pain, there is natural desire to return to safety by moving into the illusion of control over the catalyst for that pain. To forgive is to become willing to suffer that hurt, to acknowledge, "I am

---

[3] As in previous sessions, Aaron is using the letters A and B to refer to two individuals in relationship.

human. I will feel hurt, but I do not have to hold myself separate because of that hurt."

Then you change your relationship with the entire catalyst. Compassion is there; the ability to skillfully say no to abuse is there. And the compassion touches your own condition, your own hurt, as well as the pain and fear which encompass the catalyst. It is not your compassion to him for his pain nor your compassion to yourself for your own pain. Your pain is a part of each other, and compassion is just compassion. It opens your heart and allows the possibility of forgiveness.

Ultimately, with deepening compassion, there is no need for forgiveness, for there is nothing left to forgive. But until that point, forgiveness is a very powerful practice. And, as I have said, it cuts through karma by totally changing your relationship with the catalyst.

Forgiveness is a process and not an event. You enter lightly into the forgiveness. Liken it to the way you enter the cold lake on the first hot day of spring. The air is warm, giving rise to desire to swim; but when that toe touches the water, it is still frigid from the winter's ice. In just such a way, the heart may still be frigid from winter's ice. Kindness does not ask you to go to the end of the dock and leap in. Wade in slowly. If it feels good or even possible, go in. At the point where the feet are numb and there is discomfort, it is time to get out and wait until the water may be warmer. Tomorrow the heart may have thawed just a bit more. So, forgiveness is a process.

To consider the possibility of forgiveness is to touch the deepest hurt places in the self with an honesty which acknowledges the wish to enact pain in return for pain, acknowledges the enormity of the desire to be safe and comfortable. And it is not enough to acknowledge these forces, but one must do so without judgment. Thus, the process of forgiveness begins with the self.

Fear is an illusion. It is an illusion to which the small ego self has become attached. It is a habit. To live the devotional life is to love the Divine enough to take that hand that is offered, to offer up those brown stones that Q'uo spoke of and allow the Divine to turn them into shining gems; to release fear, to observe and release attachment to fear. It is to look deeply at the ways in which the illusion of fear has been used as protection.

You then come to the truth of your being: that the divine Self has no need of protection. You may cut yourself loose from this illusion of fear and have the love and faith to come back and rest in that divine truth of your being, which is fearless. This is not a statement of condemnation of fear. It is simply a statement of a higher truth.

When you practice forgiveness, it must come from a place of opening in the heart which aspires to approach ever closer to that truth, and not from a place of judgment which says, "I should not fear. I should not blame." To do this takes much practice, practice at noting judgment as it arises, practice of simply opening the heart in the myriad of small ways the universe invites you to open the heart.

At this time, I wish to pass this session to my dear friend of Q'uo. Later this evening I would like to lead you in what I term a forgiveness meditation. I thank you for your attention. That is all.

Q'uo: We are those of the principle of Q'uo. Greetings once again in the love and in the light of the one infinite Creator.

Perhaps you have noticed that we have not given you a set of instructions, a doctrine of things to do in order to live the spiritually directed life. This is because it is our opinion that there are as many ways to live a spiritually directed life as there are people who wish to do so. We cannot tell you to spend this number of hours in meditation or that number of hours in prayer, because for one seeker two minutes would be the conservative estimate of how much is necessary to maintain the attitude desired, whereas for another the time would be twenty or thirty or sixty minutes. Indeed, we offer you our thought that there is a very real danger to those who go overboard, as this instrument would say, with spiritual disciplines.

The Creator is not tame. The love that ignited creation is also that which destroys. Intimate contact with Deity can be fatal. And there are those mythical and also very physical and real entities throughout your history whose difficulties and deaths tell their own story. The custom of coming together in order to worship and to focus upon Deity is a most practical safeguard; for the dynamics of the conversation between the Mystery and the group is universal, touching each unique psyche gently, the energy of contact buffered by the group of like-minded seekers. We do not wish to frighten you but only to express to you our bias that it is well to be moderate in spiritual discipline and to make haste slowly. For you have an infinite amount of time to progress, whereas you have only minutes, hours, just a few million days, and then you are through the experience. We correct this instrument. It would indeed be a long-lived entity who had millions of days! Our sense in this was that this life experience is precious, and it was not any entity's intention to come to this illusion in order to ignore it or to preserve itself from social contact.

Work in consciousness is something which the spiritual seeker tends to think of as working with the higher energies, and certainly this can be true. However, the most common mistake of the spiritual seeker is that, in its eagerness, it moves into the higher energy centers to do its perceived tasks without maintaining the health and balance of the all-important lower energies.

Faced with weakness, blockage, or stress in the energies which are involved in the self's dealing with the self and with others, the spirit rushes headlong into communication and work upon the inner planes. It is as if the owner of a house with cracks in its foundation set about building another story onto the house. The foundation not being secure, the loftier and heavier weight might very possibly crack the foundation further and the entire structure might end up in pieces.

We would encourage each of you to view the work within these lower energy centers—and this does include work with those close to you in relationship—with great respect and with the awareness of what this instrument has called the one-hundred-and-eighty-degree rule; that is, that if something feels or seems right to the wisdom of the world, it very probably is wrong. If you yearn to back away from dealing with something, it very well may be time to deal with it. If the seeker cannot wait to have an outcome occur, the wise seeker may take that heady desire as a sign that more time is required to evaluate the situation in spiritual terms.

The core of devotional living is an attitude of mind and heart. One way we could describe this attitude is remembrance; for the one who remembers who the self is—that is, a child of the infinite Creator—will respond to catalyst within the structure of that identity. To the one who has the attitude of devotion, all moments alike are moments that take place upon holy ground.

The hundred-and-eighty-degree rule applies also to those things which the world feels are important. The world does not value the laborer who washes dishes, but rather, values the surgeon who successfully excises diseased flesh from a patient, thereby prolonging life. And yet if the surgeon has not a love within its touch, there will be curing but no healing. Whereas if the seeker who does the dishes has that remembrance of the holy nature of all life, it shall be lightening the consciousness of the planet as it lovingly cleanses, rinses, and appreciates each dish; and the very dishes themselves shall lift their tiny voices in praise.

It is the small things of everyday, as this instrument would say—the *chop wood/carry water* of life, the chores, the repeated tasks—that hold the most potential for being part of the training wheels for the seeker who is striving to learn to ride the bicycle of devotional life[4]. Things that are done daily are those things which the seeker can practice daily. And it is the nature of the human mind to form habits; that which is done daily becomes habitual, and through repetition over your years such homely routines can become permanent.

This instrument is having trouble voicing our concept. The closest word we can find is *ganglia* or *node* which acts as a memory jogger, bringing that remembrance before the attention many times in each day. Each of you has had much mental enjoyment contemplating times when the life can be made simpler, and we would encourage such thoughts; for what this instrument has called the little life, the life of obscurity and modest attainments, is that life in which the quality of daily remembrance is more possible, whereas the seemingly brilliant life can often be the husk with no seed within.

The world thinks in large terms and is ambitious for gain, for power, and for authority, whereas the most fruitful path for the seeker does not contain the great ambitions. Those things which create the large or brilliant life sometimes are that which one has incarnated to do. But in the case of the well-oriented spiritual seeker, such a worldly success will simply

---

[4] *Chop Wood, Carry Water: A Guide to Finding Spiritual Fulfillment in Everyday Life.* Rick Fields with Peggy Taylor, Rex Weyler and Rick Ingrasci. New York: St. Martin's Press, 1984.

blossom, developing naturally and without the contraction and push inherent in ambition; for ambition in the worldly sense and desire to seek the Creator are polar opposites. For one who seeks the Creator, the refrain of all the facets of living is, "not my will, but thine …"[5]

It is into the heart that is not being shoved about by ambition that the consciousness finds itself bubbling up with joy. We do not mean to suggest that any run away from success of a worldly nature, for it is not success but the drive towards success which influences the attitude. You have often heard the phrase, "in the world but not of it."[6] Brothers and sisters, this is each and every Earth-person's situation. Many feel that they are wanderers from another planet; but we say to you that you are all natives of eternity, and you have all wandered to this place to be together and to help each other to see the Creator in the self, in others, and in each and every mote of manifestation. The living flora of your planet sings in everlasting rhythms the songs of its seasons. As we speak, your great tree creatures lift their skeletal arms to the night sky about your dwelling. As the energies within them tuck themselves away for the winter's sleep, there is the evensong of praise and thanksgiving. It is possible to touch into this energy simply by remembering that all things are alive and aware and loved by the infinite One.

We would at this time hand the microphone to our dear brother Aaron. We leave this instrument in love and in light. We are those of Q'uo.

Aaron: I am Aaron. My dear friend has made many important observations. Especially I would emphasize the importance of the strong foundation before you build. He also spoke of living the simple life and not grasping at attainment, if one would live a life in spiritual consciousness. I want to expand a bit on this statement and also on Q'uo's statement that intimate contact with Deity can be fatal.

I would precede my remarks with this statement that on fundamental issues we speak from identical voice; but of course we each do have our own bias. We are not afraid of that bias, but we rejoice in our diversity. Where diversity exists in our biases, it does not lead us into irreconcilable difference but rather into expanding, each of us moving also to encompass each other's bias as understanding deepens. Finally, neither of us ever has a need to be right, because we know we are not speaking here of wrong or right but of interpretation of experience.

Q'uo says intimate contact with Deity can be fatal. Yes, it can. But I would expand this statement with the observation that intimate contact with Deity can be fatal if there is not the foundation laid, because the high frequency vibration resultant of that contact must have foundation to support. And that foundation is established by the daily workings of your life, as Q'uo pointed out—the working with the lower energy centers, with relationships, with the physical body, and so on.

Intimate contact with Deity, or any grasping at spiritual enlightenment, lays a fatal crack in the foundation when such grasping at contact or enlightenment is grasping from a place of fear rather than opening from a place of love. When the foundation is strong, when the homework has been attended and the opening to the Deity is a natural opening of the loving heart from a place of no fear or grasping—then it is never fatal, but expanding and wondrous. However, you are still in the incarnation. You cannot sustain the intensity of that contact. To seek to do so is to encourage another fatal crack. There must be willingness to come back into the relative human.

I spoke some moments ago about a difference in bias. I speak from the bias of a being who has worked its way through the lower densities on the earth plane. I am quite in agreement with Q'uo that there is no rush. And I know that Q'uo is quite in agreement with me that each moment of incarnation is a precious gift and not to be wasted. And yet from my human experience, I do feel an intensity which Q'uo does not feel. Neither of us is wrong or right. We merely each speak from our own perspective.

That intensity must be handled with caution. If it becomes the grasping of which Q'uo spoke, then you have the fatal crack. When the intensity derives from a loving heart that so deeply aspires to purify its energy, so deeply aspires to move itself into harmony, then that intensity becomes a powerful lifting device, moving the seeker forward on its path. When the intensity derives from the voice of fear that would fix that in itself which it sees as defective,

---

[5] *Holy Bible*, Luke 22:42.
[6] *Table Talk: On Living to One's Self.* William Hazlitt, 1821 - 1822.

then it is striving to build that third floor over the cracked foundation.

And so, there must be deepening awareness of which voice is predominant. Usually both voices will blend. It is rare for the human to act solely on one voice or another. But that motivation comes both from the heart of love and from places of fear. You do not need to get rid of fear in order not to be reactive to fear. You do not need to get rid of fear to speak and move from a place of love. But you need to be honest about fear's presence and learn to make space for it so that it does not control you.

A wise man in your nation's history said, "We have nothing to fear except fear itself"[7] … to fear *fear*, to fear falling blindly into the grip of fear. But when we learn to relate lovingly even to our fear, then it no longer controls. It does not need to go away; simply, it no longer controls. It no longer has the power to urge you to build that third story. It allows you to tend to the foundation.

Here I would pass the microphone to my dear brother/sister/friend of Q'uo. That is all.

Q'uo: We are again with this instrument. We are those of Q'uo.

We have spoken of several challenging concepts and would at this time pause to ask if there are questions concerning those things that the ones known as Aaron and we have offered. Is there a query at this time which we or our brother Aaron might answer to make our concepts more lucid or more in focus?

R: Are you saying that we should strive for the best effort but not for the best result?

Q'uo: We are Q'uo. My brother, we are saying that when one is striving to be one's best, there is skill in taking the self lightly. And when there is the lack of striving, then there is the opposite possibility that not enough effort is being made to live that moment to its utmost. The tendency is to strive for the visible or substantial goal and to gaze at the small homely details of life as that which keeps one from the business of living spiritually, whereas it is precisely in those time-consuming, personal chores that the greatest opportunity for spiritual work comes. For each action, each relationship, each detail and nicety of the day, is ripe with the blossoms of love, beauty, and truth.

One who can see the holy in the homely has the greater life than one whose accomplishments are brilliant to the world but whose personal orientation towards large portions of the humble side of life is to get them done in order to get to the important things.

May we answer you further, my brother?

R: I think I need to wait and look for the light side. Thank you.

Q'uo: We are Q'uo, and we thank you, my brother. Is there a further query at this time?

I: You mentioned high frequency vibration with the spirit coming into contact with the mundane mind. I would like to understand that analogy better. Higher frequency in what respects?

Q'uo: We are those of Q'uo. My brother, are you familiar with the concept of octaves? The entire gamut of densities and sub-densities is as the keys upon the piano, equally beautiful and worthy to be praised; but some notes are low, others high. The various energy centers of the physical vehicle and its attendant finer bodies are as the piano in that there are octaves of resonance between the so-called higher and so-called lower energies.

When the trine of lower energies is being attended to, then it is simple and natural to move up to the next octave and the next and so forth. When the lower energies are out of tune, it is as though the musician took the string to touch the half to make the octave. That octave also is out of tune with the creation, having become distorted at the base. Thus, all of the spiritual realm rings badly out of tune unless the foundation is first tuned.

May we answer you further, my brother?

I: The image I get is that we in a way are participating in the building of a home for the spirit, and that the building of the foundation firmly allows that home to be well laid. There also seems though to be a point of raising the point of habitation to a higher level of comfort. The cracks that might appear with incorrect placement or perception are really cracks of kindness as opposed to flaws. I'm sorry, Q'uo, I can't formulate a further question. Thank you.

---

[7] *First Inaugural Address* by Franklin D. Roosevelt; March 4, 1933.

Q'uo: We are those of Q'uo. Perhaps it is a clearer analogy to compare the housekeeping of the house that the vehicle of flesh inhabits. The upper rooms are delightful; but there is no dining room, no kitchen there, so that the inhabitant of the house must first cleanse and make acceptable that lower floor, stocking the refrigerator, having the appliances which create your cooked food in order, tidying and sweeping and dusting and making the windows shine. When that lower story is peaceful and in order, then it is the time to ascend the staircase and to enjoy the den, the room of rest, the gazing with the higher and longer point of view out the windows that give so much broader a view.

We mean simply to suggest that the humble and earthly things in your experience are precious, and that this is far too often not realized; and in the lack of this concept, the unskillful soul can make itself rather uncomfortable. Then the self thinks, "How can I fix this? I shall meditate more. I shall contemplate more. I shall read improving works." But the actual point of departure instead lies often in going back to those simple things and giving them the honor and respect that you give to that which is obviously spirit.

There is a great shift of attitude that we are encouraging each to consider at this time. In the metaphysical world, thoughts are things; and this truth, being of the higher octave, overarches the smaller truth. You perhaps have heard the old maxim, "As above, so below."[8] The humble details of life are Deity, many octaves lower; but touch those lower notes and all the octaves resonate.

Is there another question for Aaron or ourselves at this time?

K: Q'uo and Aaron, can you speak to the topic of the coming Earth harvest and any purpose we may have towards care in that future harvest? Or does this interfere with free will? And is there presently on the Earth or affecting the Earth a greater proportion of opposing force because of the harvest (or whatever that may be) interfering, or that may make it more difficult for us to be balanced and stay in tune?

Aaron: I am Aaron. May I speak to your question, my sister? Yes, there is indeed a greater opposing force. This is not a problem. This is not bad/negative. When you lift weights, if you practice with increasingly heavier weights, you develop stronger muscles. When you practice returning love to increasingly heavy catalyst, you strengthen the ability to love. And it is the strengthening of that ability to love which will offer the universe the ability to move into its potential of light.

The darkness is not your foe; it is your teacher. In the approaching harvest, the universe has the potential to arrive at a new balance. Please remember that not only positive polarity but also negative polarity is harvested. But please also remember that at a certain place within sixth density, negativity becomes a dead end.

The concern is that between third and sixth density, negativity can be force for much suffering and so much harm. Therefore, your increasing ability to return love to negativity and not to heed it is one major force that will shift the balance. Negativity that cannot engender fear has no place left to go. This is your work. This truly is the core reason for this harvest: to bring all of the mature, loving, and wise energy into as strong play as possible—saying no to negativity, not with fear, but with love.

My friend of Q'uo would like to speak further to this question. I pause. This instrument returns to a deeper tuning. Please start the tape.

Q'uo: We are those of Q'uo and are with this instrument. The … we must pause, for this instrument needs to retune somewhat. We are Q'uo.

(Pause)

We would ask that you revibrate the query.

K: I required deeper understanding of the urgency that I and my partner and many others around us are feeling presently with respect to our service, our purpose, towards the coming harvest.

Q'uo: We thank you, my sister. The vibration allowed this entity to come fully back into the tuning that it was seeking.

Perhaps you have heard the phrase, "The fields are white with harvest, but where are the laborers to make the harvest?"[9] The field of your planet has become ripe with harvest, and the time of change has begun. It is a process which will take quite some of your years, perhaps as much as two centuries to fully express.

---

[8] *The Kybalion*, Anonymous.

[9] *Holy Bible*, Matthew 9:37, Luke 10:2.

Those who have come here to aid in this harvest are activated if they are sensitive to the beating of their own heart. By this time there is the sensation often that there is some specific task to accomplish as a harvester. And sometimes there is. But the primary task of each who has come to serve is to be who you are; for this essence of being is your greatest gift to this planet at harvest. As more and more harvesters are activated, there is the acceleration of the cumulative effect so that it is as if one touches two, and two four, and four eight and so forth.

By being yourself, by seeking to be more authentic and more that unique entity that you are, you are working in the field. For this harvest is a metaphysical one; and as the planetary vibration lightens, the strength of the positive orientation grows. The one known as M. who sits within this circle recently said to this instrument that after a long struggle to know what was its service, it finally realized that it was in the spiritual reserve and was content to wait until its activation notice.

May we answer you further, my sister?

K: Thank you.

Q'uo: We thank you, my sister, most truly, and encourage you to wear that crown which lies heavy upon your head.

We would leave this instrument for this evening and transfer the microphone to the one known as Aaron, only pausing long enough to thank each for the beauty that you share, as you share your essence with us.

We are overwhelmed. For now, we are those of Q'uo. Adonai. We leave you in the love and in the light of the Mystery that created all and is all.

Aaron: I am Aaron. We pause while this instrument returns to a deeper tuning.

(Pause)

Aaron: I am Aaron. I had earlier requested the opportunity to lead you in a meditation into the opening to the practice of forgiveness. I invite you here to join me. I know you are weary and I will be brief.

Please bring to your heart and mind the image or presence of one whom you love and who loves you. No matter how much love there may be between you, there are times when this one has hurt you and there are times when you have hurt this one.

We begin by asking forgiveness, speaking with open heart to this loved one. Can you offer the words, "I have hurt you, whether intentionally or unintentionally, through something I said or did or even thought. I have hurt you. I love you and do not wish to hurt you. It was my fear speaking. I am responsible for the speech of my fear and sorry that my reactivity to my fear led me to hurt you. I ask your forgiveness. Through the depth of your compassion, your kindness, can you forgive me?"

As much as is possible, relax and feel the forgiveness offered to you. Feel yourself allowed back into this one's heart. It may say to you, "Yes, for the ways you have hurt me or what you said or did or even thought. Yes, I forgive you and I welcome you back into my heart."

And he will ask you for the same opening. Think of the ways that this being has hurt you, intentionally or unintentionally. You might wish to tell him or her, "Love has been there between us, but also pain. Through something you said or did or even thought, you have hurt me. I forgive you. I understand the depth of your pain and I forgive you. I invite you back into my heart."

Can you feel the wonder of the healing when that wall between you comes down? There is so much space in forgiveness. We now turn to someone harder to forgive, which is the self. Please look at the self as you just looked at this loved one. What needs to be forgiven: the manifestations of fear as need to control, as anger, as greed, as pride? Observe the way the fearful self has moved on the basis of that fear and caused pain, not only to others but to the self. Observe the ways that self has hurt itself by not manifesting the fullness of self, but hiding instead in a small place.

Here I would ask you to say your own name to the self and bring into the heart that which has been done that seemed difficult to forgive. "How have I abused myself? In what ways have I condemned myself or pushed myself so hard that I could not stably endure? These movements were prompted by fear's voice."

Saying your own name to yourself, state, "I invite you in. You have been afraid and have acted on that fear. I love you. I hear you. I forgive you." It is difficult to say those words to the self. "I love you. I forgive you." Yet, these words become the basis for laying a firm foundation. They become the basis for the eventual dissolution of the myth of fear, like wading into that icy water on a warm day.

Enter this water of forgiveness and feel the peace in it. Say your own name to yourself, "I love you. I embrace you. I forgive you, and I will explore the further depths of forgiveness that I may open my heart ever deeper to myself and to all beings."

My friends your energy is low, so I will conclude. There is a third part in this process which I would ask you to experiment with on your own. As you become able to extend forgiveness to the loved one who has hurt you, to receive forgiveness from that loved one, and to extend forgiveness to the self for its seeming imperfections, can you then reach out even further into the icy water to one with whom there has been deep pain? Can you ask for forgiveness from this being? And then, if only for experiment's sake, can you breathe in and try the words, "I forgive you"?

Remember, it is a process. You are touching the possibility of forgiveness as you open your heart to the immensity of your pain and the infinite nature of your love:

May all beings everywhere love and be loved.

(Bell)

May all beings know the infinite spaciousness and joy of the forgiving heart.

(Bell)

May all beings follow this path of letting go into the deepest truth of their own being and therein find perfect peace.

(Bell)

I thank all of you for inviting us into your circle. I love you all and wish you a good night. That is all. ❧

The Aaron/Q'uo Dialogues, Session 30
November 19, 1995

(This session was preceded by a period of tuning and meditation.)

Group discussion: The group suggested a question and answer session with possibly more discussion regarding the forgiveness meditation.

Q'uo: We are those of the principle known to you as Q'uo, and with a light and merry heart we greet you in the love and in the light of the one infinite Creator. It has been such a blessing to spend these few hours with you in seeking together a more lucid distortion of the one great original Thought, which is Love.

It has been such a pleasure to speak about living a life in faith and devotion. The one known as Aaron speaks for us when he says that he could discuss this subject at almost infinite length, for living devotionally is as much our hope as it is yours. And as the logicians have it, we keep getting halfway to the goal, then halfway to the goal, then halfway to the goal, closer and closer; yet still the goal is before us, surrounded in sublime mystery.

There are relatively easy spiritual practices such as meditation, prayer, contemplation and the reading of inspired works, the listening to inspired music, and the sharing of worship in groups such as this that light up your planet especially on this Sabbath day. And there are relatively difficult spiritual practices such as standing in the checkout line at the grocer's and scrubbing the toilet bowl. The life of devotion is lived where you are or not at all. It is a common hope of those upon your earth plane someday to retire to a pleasant and secluded place where finally you can devote yourself to worship; but we suggest to you that the life of devotion is lived now, wherever you may be. It is the confidence and focus within that turns bare earth into holy ground, blazing with the incandescent light of love supernal, limitless, and whole.

It is your challenge to find ways to open the heart to the present moment and the love therein. You shall fail according to your cruel judgment, again and again. We ask you to know deeply and surely that each mistake, each error, each missed opportunity, is a gift to the infinite One just as much as each moment when you judge yourselves to be, as this instrument would say, "on the beam/in the groove." Clumsy or graceful, awkward or flowing, your spirit is utterly beloved.

Begin to allow yourself to feel that you are never alone, never isolated, never alienated, in the world within that is as real to each of you as the world without. In that world you have many companions: those unseen which you call angels, those such as we who accompany those with the desire to ask for us as they sit in meditation or as they go about the small business of the everyday life. May you encourage yourselves when you forget where your center is.

May you rest in contentment and praise those sublime moments when you can feel the rhythm of creation and the rightness of all that there is.

You are the universe in little, and as a holograph you are as whole and complete as the infinite illusion in which you and we dwell. Know that as you serve either by disciplining and refining yourself or by being a part of the good in another's life, you serve the light.

Thank you for this great privilege. The one known as Aaron and we can never express adequately our love for your pilgrim souls. Blessings. Blessings. Blessings. How reluctantly we come to the end of our time on the soapbox. Ah, the soapbox, the pedestal. We spout truth and then we come down and roll down the hill with you into the warmth of the water, splashing, playing in the sunlight. May you play together like otters. May you be merry with each other. May you share each other's burdens and joys. May you know that you are about the Creator's business.

We now open the working to your questions. As our beloved Aaron says, simply express which of us you wish to respond, and we shall go from there. May we have the first query, please?

I: I have one I would like to ask Aaron. This is a statement of my understanding of something he spoke about last evening. I will read it and ask for his enhancement to my understanding. For the incarnate self, forgiveness is a process; but forgiveness radiates as an aspect of the whole Self, so the process of forgiveness is part of the movement from a thought-point to a known space, a going nowhere. Could Aaron comment?

Aaron: I am Aaron. Does the right hand need to forgive the left hand? If the baby, the fetus, is kicking in the night and wakes the mother, does the mother need to forgive the fetus? In the first example, the right and left hands are clearly a part of the same being. The mother and fetus still experience that state of non-separation.

The angel aspect of yourself knows it is not separate and never has been separate. It knows the crystal clarity of its oneness, which could never become tarnished. To move into incarnation is to accept the illusion of separation, to agree to this veil of forgetting of your true being. Thus, you move into the illusion that there are spots on the wings, that the body and the mind are unclean in some way.

You have all heard me call you angels in earthsuits. Yes, I, from the human perspective, you practice forgiveness because there has been the experience of pain for the human and the practice of forgiveness opens the heart. It is not just bringing you back to where you were; you are then Love. And there is no limit to the amount of love that you can express. If there were a limit, there would be no reason to move into incarnation. As you are aware, the universe does not run on linear time; there is no rush, no schedule. So, you would rest in the astral planes, picking up those lessons of love easily as they came until you had reached that point where you could say, "I've learned it."

As Q'uo just expressed, that shining light is always ahead. One has never finished, even in sixth density. I am not finished. There is always more to learn about love. You have entered incarnation in faith that this is a tool that will help you to learn about love, not to a finished point, but to continually enhance the process of loving.

We find that the wonder and beauty is that those that have graduated through the earth plane teach love and compassion to the rest of the universe. Truly, the masters of love in our universe are amongst those who have moved through Earth's catalyst. It is a very powerful teacher. Yes, I like your image: the spot expands.

There was never anything to forgive, but from the human perspective you have practiced forgiveness. And that practice expands you out of the small ego self and into the heart we all share, into that place where there is no individuated self taken as real, but only the illusion of individuated self, as you are learning, too. Thus, you practice forgiveness not so much to forgive, although that is the idea within the relative mind, but to stretch the heart, to move out of your illusions of separation.

You are unbalanced. I said to some of you this morning, you come into incarnation and you immediately pick up thick glasses that serve as microscope. They allow you to tie and untie the knots, to see what you do. But they close you off to the vast perspective that you had before you came into incarnation.

If somebody lifts these microscope glasses for a moment, you look out and say, "Wow! There is all that space." Then the glasses slip back. How quickly you forget that space. When you practice entering that space regularly through any spiritual practice, you learn to rest very stably; but the knots still need to be tied and untied. If someone has stepped on you and asked your pardon, you still need to work with the pain and hurt and come to the place where the human can offer forgiveness, can let go of its fear, anger, and separation.

The practice of forgiveness leads you repeatedly back to the angel. But the practice of forgiveness is also what allows the human to put back on its microscope glasses and work with the knots of incarnation in a much more skillful and loving way.

Does this answer your question, I, or may I speak further to it? I pause.

I: There are some new ideas. I have the feeling that I am substituting the idea of the angel state to erase the incarnate-self idea, and I don't believe it's correct. Aaron is speaking about a partnership, a balance.

Barbara: A balance between the relative and ultimate self. Aaron says a partnership is a perfect word.

I: I am currently walking between the two.

Barbara: Aaron says (I am paraphrasing Aaron), at first one tends to leap back and forth. He says picture yourself alone on the seesaw trying to get it to balance. First you run from one end to the other, and then you begin to understand how to keep your weight balanced equally on both ends. He asks you to also remember his image of the box in the infinitely spacious room. The relative rests in the ultimate. You cannot leave the ultimate, only forget about it for awhile.

Aaron: I am Aaron. Of course, for the angel there can be nothing to forgive. How could there be? Of course, for the human, caught deeply in its own small ego self, forgiveness is almost impossible. You are living in a balance, a partnership between, so that the human does not hear there is nothing to forgive, because for the human there is something to forgive. But forgiveness is possible because you recognize that the angel exists and that you are both sides through from human to angel, the balance always changing slightly depending on the needs and clarity of the moment. I pause.

I: I like the idea of forgiveness as a spiritual practice.

Aaron: I am Aaron. Only watch for pride and self-righteousness, which are apt to crop up when you become the one who is forgiving. And if they do crop up, then shift the forgiveness practice to find forgiveness for the human who has found pride in its path. I pause.

May we hear your further questions? I pause.

K: Please Aaron and Q'uo, speak to us further with more depth regarding pride. We are angels. When we discover this, how can we also not be clothed in pride?

Aaron: I am Aaron. I hear your question, my sister. To be clothed in pride is just to be clothed in pride, just as to feel anger arise is just to feel anger arise, just as to step on a tack until the blood flows from your foot is just to step on a tack and have blood flow. Certain conditions give rise to certain inner circumstances. Yes, eventually you will reach a point where anger and pride do not arise, at least not nearly so often or forcefully, but this is not done through will power.

There is a deep humility and understanding that you are human; and as you realize your angelness, pride has arisen: "Here I am being the angel; and suddenly here's pride. So what else is new? I do not need to act upon that pride nor to get rid of it, only to note, here is pride."

Pride is part of the distortion of fear, part of that which wants to be somebody, to be safe and in control. How can the loving heart not open to the human who wants to feel safe and in control? When you embrace the fearful self that does not feel safe, the circumstances that gave rise to pride begin to diminish. And in that way, pride begins to dissolve. When there is nobody left who feels unsafe, then pride and anger and other such emotions will cease to arise. May I pass this further to Q'uo? I pause.

Q'uo: We are those of Q'uo. My sister, perhaps you recall the parable of the teacher known to you as Jesus concerning the Pharisee and the tax collector. The parable goes that there were two men in the temple. One was a Pharisee, the other a tax collector, which in those days was tantamount to the dishonest, greedy, and altogether undesirable. The Pharisee prayed thusly, "Lord I thank thee that I am not as other men are: robbers, thieves, hypocrites. I fast two times a week. I tithe to the temple." The publican on the other hand was on his knees, praying, "Lord, have mercy on me, for I am a sinner."[10] Which of the two prayed well?

The issue of pride is going to be yours and every seeker's intimate companion for the foreseeable future. We ask you simply to view the self as if you were a rough, huge planetoid with deep ridges and valleys—an elephantine chunk of jagged roundness, tiny in the infinite reaches of space. The influences and essences of the cosmos beam and radiate in a refining fire, lamentably playing over those mountains of pride and all the associated errors of the soul in manifestation. In the fullness of time, to use the least distorted word, those ridges shall be smooth; and through eons of lifetimes, with painstaking thoroughness, the path or orbit of your consciousness shall become smooth and then smoother until at last the mantle of rock that covers your surface as flesh covers the living being within shall finally be polished away, and the immense jewel that your consciousness is shall emerge and become as the sun. And this sun body at last will have no pride, for it shall simply be. Do not hurry towards that destiny. Enjoy your crust of imperfections. They shall not harm your spirit, but only give it the catalyst that your consciousness seeks in order to buff and polish and slowly erode the parts of your self that are least true.

Know that all things are acceptable. Each entity sees its own shadows; and the more the spirit wishes and longs to be free of humanness, the more that humanness shall be unable to serve you and teach you what you came to learn. We suggest you simply stop resisting these untoward and wayward tendencies. These are the shadows made dark because you are beginning to shine. The taking of the spiritual temperature is judgment; and as you find yourself caught in pride and judgment, smile. Take those broken shards of your being and hand them on up to the infinite One. They shall be transformed in that mighty hand and return a hundred blessings as you yield them up with an honest and contrite heart. Meanwhile this is the very creation and the exact moment into which you came to find your Creator. Drinking your coffee, you bring the world into balance.

May we answer you further, my sister?

---

[10] *Holy Bible, Luke 18:10-13.*

K: In this painstaking thoroughness we find ourselves entering into perfectionist behaviors, striving to reach what we already know we are. And knowing seems not to help very much. We become frustrated with this awful veil. We cannot be perfect, and yet we know we are. What a struggle!

Aaron: I am Aaron. I hear your pain. Yet, if you were already perfect in human terms, why would you have incarnated? The veil is not burden to you but is a gift, not a very pleasant gift at times; but it is precisely the catalyst that you need.

I ask this instrument to move deeper into a trance state. There is a story told about the spiritual teacher, Gurdjieff. There lived in his community a man who was rude. He did not do his share of the work. He even smelled badly because he did not bathe. He became tired of others' negativity toward him and he left. Gurdjieff went after him and asked him to come back. While others paid to live in the community, Gurdjieff said to him, "If you will come back, I will pay you." The man was reluctant at first, but he was greedy; and since Gurdjieff offered to pay him, he agreed and returned.

Those in the community were aghast. They said, "How could you invite him back? How could you pay him to come back?" Gurdjieff said, "He is the yeast for the bread. Here in this place where everyone is kind and generous with one another, how else will you learn compassion?"

Child, this yearning for perfection in you, this self-striving to become what it already is, the fears, the patterns of reactivity, pride, all of it—these are the yeast for your bread. In the astral plane and beyond, you will practice discarnate skills, practice your perfection. Why seek to practice that perfection within the incarnation? This does not mean that you do not aspire to perfection. But understand that the human is perfect in its imperfection.

I would speak also to the strength to your aspiring. There is such pain in many of your hearts because you see this brilliant light of the Divine and you see the shadow in the self and feel, "I can never be worthy of that." You then wish so badly to be rid of the shadow. This is a piece of every seeker's path, that dark night of the soul. But when you pass through the dark night, you begin to see the truth of what Q'uo just said—that the shadows are seen only because of the inherent luminousness of your being. The brighter you shine, the starker are the shadows.

Just let the light shine. Be the light and give kindness instead of contempt to this being who has agreed to also carry shadow. May I further answer your question or is this sufficient? I pause.

K: Is loving more deeply one way to move out of perfectionism?

Aaron: I am Aaron. It is the only way. I pause.

Q'uo: We are those of Q'uo. My sister, you shall progress. You shall not know in this your present illusion how or because of what stimuli. In fact, the whole point of this illusion is to so confuse and addle and aggravate the sentient self that eventually you stop attempting to make sense of it all and move from head to heart. We ask that you employ that which you have in abundance: your sense of humor. Is your life not a marvelous situation comedy? In music you have many times experienced that when the conductor calls for the hush of singing quietly, the chorus begins to be heavy and instinctively begins singing more slowly and losing the pulse. The effort of creating the pleasant piano sound weights down that sense of rhythm. The answer to perceived error is not adding wisdom, but rather lifting away into the rhythm. Lift when you experience this frustration and pain. Lift and laugh at the well-termed human comedy. There is great humor in the infinite Creator.

May we speak further, dear friend?

Aaron: I wish to inject something here. When I said love is the only way, I do not mean that you must find a love switch and flick it from off to on. The offer of love is a dimmer switch. You have found the switch. You keep nudging it up through many of the practices we have spoken of this weekend—through prayer and meditation, through the practice of generosity, through mindful awareness of how negative and harmful emotions arise, through reaching that hand up to Divinity and taking the help that is offered to lift you, through cultivating faith and patience.

Like the one who has walked a long path in the dark night without clear sense of where she has walked, but at dawn she finds herself higher in the mountain looking back and able to say, "Ah! There's the ravine where I stumbled, there's the steep place, there's the place where there was mud; and I have come through them all." And then you turn and look, and notice that the mountain goes up and up and up. You are in process.

The love that is inherent to you cannot help but manifest itself if you give it the opportunity to do so. May we speak further or is this sufficient? I pause.

K: I thank you both.

Q'uo: We are those of Q'uo, and we seem to linger on this issue with you my sister; but we simply have such a love of talking. We have one last suggestion in this regard, and that is that you adopt for yourself the motto, "God bless this mess." We are those of Q'uo and are open to further queries at this time.

K: I have a recurring dream of being in a situation where people are all standing around a huge trough of slop, and I find that it is mandatory that I dive into this trough. I have no choice. And as I go through this slop I feel no pain; and I suddenly arrive in an L-shaped, white room with those around me robed in white. I am feeling grateful, as these are my brothers and sisters, perhaps colleagues and teachers. Is this the school in which we learn while we're sleeping and not in the Earth?

Aaron: I am Aaron. I hear your question, K. First, may I state that this dream is as perfect an illustration of the process of incarnation as I have ever heard. A pile of slop … yes, as Q'uo said, "Bless this mess."

There are two different types of dreams: that which is symbolic and that which we call a teaching dream. This would seem to have portion of both—the diving into the trough of slop being the symbolic part; and the awareness that only when you move through the messiness of incarnation, the messiness of a body and emotions, do you emerge into the angel that you are.

You stated that they seem to be teachers, but perhaps also colleagues. K, likely these are teachers, but teachers are also colleagues. One cannot teach without learning. It is a mutual participation.

The dream does not seem to me to represent only a wish to arrive in this room, but also a statement of readiness. We on the upper planes use teaching dreams when the meditation practice is not sufficiently developed to allow you to hear us in a more conscious state, so we bypass that conscious state into the dream. It is a very effective way of reaching you. The only problem with it is that often there is not the practice to retain the dream after, so it is not as clearly integrated into the incarnate state as it would be in meditation. Those who have further developed the ability to hear their teachers while the body is in the state we call awake as opposed to asleep find that teaching dreams seem to slacken off.

What I hear from you, K, is that there is a readiness to enter this realm. I would like to suggest that if this is a repeated dream or in meditation itself, you allow yourself to open to the experience of that room and then you make the very firm statement, "What do I need to learn? I am open. Please teach me," and just see what you hear. May I please pass this question now to Q'uo? I pause.

Q'uo: We are those of Q'uo and have little to add to what our brother has said, except to say that the kindest thing that you can do as the white-robed one who has taken on the mantle of earth is to trust in and cooperate with the rhythms of your unfolding destiny. Allow the falling away of things in their own time. Allow the contradictions, opposites, and riddles that characterize spiritual matters to tangle you up and to be untangled in the natural way.

We fear the hour grows late. We would ask for a final query at this time. We are those of Q'uo.

(No further queries.)

Aaron: I am Aaron. In the process of moving through your incarnation, there are many times when there is simply pain in yourself and in others. And I am often asked, "What helps? What allows me to touch that pain with more kindness?"

There is a very powerful practice taken from Tibetan Buddhism. It is called *Tonglen* or "giving/receiving practice." I find it a very powerful tool to use in case of suffering within the self or without. I would like to teach it to you.

I ask you to bring into your heart and mind the image of someone who is suffering. They do not have to be mired down by suffering, but someone who's experiencing pain. It could be someone in this room, someone in your family or your circle of friends, even someone whose face you have seen on your television screen, a victim of a disaster of one sort or another. Normally, before we do this practice we ask the person, the Higher Self of the person, "May I do this practice with you?" We do not impose our need to serve another on the person.

So, the first step is to invite this person into your heart and mind and ask, "May I do this practice with you?" Visualize or feel yourself sitting within a cylinder of light. This is not something you need to imagine since you are already sitting in a cylinder of light. Simply open yourself in whatever way is appropriate to the experience of that light. If imagination is what works, that is fine. But remember, you are not creating by your imagination, you are merely allowing yourself into a different level of reality.

Breathing in, allow that light to come through the crown chakra and down to the heart center. Breathing out, feel it centered in the heart. Breathing in, intention to send it out to where there is suffering … and exhale, sending it out either as a ray coming from the heart or you may feel it as a ray coming through the third eye or even with the breath; wherever it feels most natural to you, send it out. Breathing in, light coming into the heart center … breathing out, let it stabilize … breathing in, intention to release … out, release … in, light … out, stabilize … in, intention … out, release … in … out … in, release.

Now we are going to add the second part of the practice. With this next exhale, note the suffering as a heavy, black, tar-like mass. Breathe it in, taking it into the heart center. Notice any resistance to allowing that suffering into the self. Out, feeling the heaviness of it. You do not need to carry this. You are merely the vehicle through whom it passes. In, intention to release … out, release it up through the upper chakras and crown chakra and back up to the Divine, letting it go … out … Again from the beginning … in, light … out, feeling it fill the heart … in, intention to release … out, release … in, the big, black mass … out, feeling the weight of it … in, intention to release … out, release …

You may do this practice at this speed, at double, or at half speed. In other words, in light and send it out … in blackness and send it out. That is double speed. Or: In, light … exhale … in, feeling that light filling, and exhale … in, noting the intention to release … exhale … in and then releasing it with the exhale … in, drawing that heavy blackness into yourself … exhale … in, feeling the heaviness of it … exhale … in and out with the intention to release … in, feeling it gathering from the heart center and rising … and out, send it out.

I am going to be silent for several minutes. Please work at the speed that feels best to you. Please choose one and stay with it for the duration of these few minutes. Now, I will be silent.

(Pause)

(Bell)

May the love and light within this room shine itself out into the universe.

(Bell)

Everywhere in this universe may all beings come to know their own infinite capacity as instrument for light.

(Bell)

With the continued expansion of that capacity may all beings find their way into the light and come to know their true being and thereby find perfect peace.

There are no words for my boundless love and appreciation of you. As you walk this path and sometimes feel alone, please remember how deeply you are cherished and be aware of all the hands that extend themselves in love to accompany you on the path. I pass this to Q'uo to have the opportunity also to say farewell for a while, because, of course, there is never a good-bye when one soul speaks to another. That is all.

Q'uo: We are those of the principle of Q'uo. Bon voyage. We are with you on the waves. Adonai.

We leave this instrument and you in the love and in the light of the one infinite Creator. We are known to you as Q'uo. Adonai. Adonai. ☙

Sunday Meditation
December 10, 1995

Group question: For the group question this week we are taking pot luck and will be glad to listen to whatever words of inspiration Q'uo has to offer.

(Carla channeling)

We are those of the principle of Q'uo. We greet you in the light, the clarity and the love of the one infinite Creator. We are pleased indeed that you have chosen to call us to your circle this evening, and we are most grateful for the privilege of sharing our thoughts. As always, we ask that you evaluate these thoughts as you would any other person's thoughts, taking what you feel is worth your attention and leaving the rest behind, for we are not infallible but seekers like yourself.

As we merge with your vibrations at this time we can feel much of the yearning of all of those present for the light that is so absent from your days as the planet you now enjoy moves towards its farthest from the sun. These dark days that weigh upon the spirit are challenges for all who enjoy your density of existence. Those who have distortions towards physical weakness find it harder to shake off those difficulties and enjoy life. Those who have sorrows find the sorrow is greater as the days grow shorter. The physical instrument which you call your body is carefully aligned and attuned to light, and just as do plants, the spirit needs the light for its health.

There is also a spiritual difficulty as the days grow short, and that is that when one is less comfortable, huddled in upon the self and responding to the increased darkness, one is also apt to become hungry for the food of spirit, for the light that appears as love itself, warmth within the heart, secure openness to the being. These things are more difficult to achieve. The balance is more difficult to find. And as we paint this picture we are hoping that you can see yourself in this picture and see in better context those concerns which you have brought to this circle. When spirit is turned in upon itself as darkness urges you to do, there is within the self that turning to the shadows of uncertainty and hesitation. Those energies which create the shadow that always follows faith, that shadow is inextinguishable, for the light that casts that shadow is consciousness itself, and that sun does not go down. And yet in dark days it feels as though the inner sun itself has set.

In this atmosphere it is easy indeed to wonder, "Who am I," and, "Where am I going?" Hopes and dreams seem somehow frivolous, for the energies are heavy and quiet. All this is as it should be, and we do not intend to suggest that the questions of identity and the path of the future are questions that have any negative import, for these are the questions into which you took incarnation to address. Indeed, all the knowledge of self was deliberately laid aside by you before the beginning of this incarnation, for you wished to be affected by the light and the dark. You desired to come among the people of this planet as one of them to experience all that you could and to ask yourself those things which sprang up in the course of the daily life. You had hopes of this bold venture called incarnation. You hoped to serve in the name of love. You hoped to learn those lessons of love which you felt were worth refining and emphasizing in your deep personality. You wished to form relationships with those with whom you have worked before to enjoy companionship with them, to learn with them, to share catalyst together. And each of you is doing all those things.

So, from the standpoint of the work of the spirit all is well. The doubts and inner discords are not only acceptable but also of value. Only the self can dig so deeply into the substrata of a busy and complex personality. Only the self can ask the self these questions with such desire to know. This is, then, a positive and a necessary portion of the rhythm of living an incarnation—the questioning and probing, the lifting up and gazing and putting down again and then lifting and looking from another angle. These things are well. This is good work.

Perhaps you hear our reserve in saying this. Yes, there is also another side to be considered in this issue. And that is that the Creator has placed humankind within the paradox that affects the deep personality and that is that the self sees the process of learning about the self as one of delving into and clarifying what the self really thinks and feels, thereby adding unto the beingness a higher degree of self-knowledge, while at the same time the Creator has so arranged the processes of learning so that the path to self-knowledge is actually the path of turning the gaze beyond the self and being able to allow the falling away of self. And in spiritual terms this losing of self is also a positive and wise effort to enjoy.

It is not logical that the way to self-knowledge is the allowing of that which may fall away. Yet that entity who knows itself most deeply is the entity who has given much of the personality away. We do not suggest a solution to this paradox of addition and subtraction. The self remains unlimited, being part of all, positive and negative, existing before time and space and existing within time and space so that there is wisdom in working upon the self by addition, by naming the characteristics of the self. And when the rhythm of life is such that the mood is one of peace and relaxation of the personality, that work also is good.

We would ask you to think about who the self is in relation to the teacher known to you as Jesus. This entity's sense of self was such that when the entity was but a child it studied and learned from its teachers and by the time it was a teenager, as this instrument would say, it was already considered a teacher. This entity had a sense of self that enabled it simply to do what it must, even when those about him did not understand. That sense of self carried this entity through a wandering ministry that was remarkable for the purity of its teaching. And yet when the one known as Jesus was asked to describe the self he said that "He who sees me sees not me but the Father." This entity had learned subtraction as well as addition and he was content to be impersonal and to relinquish much of the Earthly personality. Yet there can be no more sure-footed identity than that attitude which the one known as Jesus had.

We would perhaps encourage, more than working one way or another. Rather, encourage the seeker to flow freely and gladly along with those currents and rhythms of life which put one in a certain mood or state of receptivity. We encourage each to trust the intuition of self, that feeling that says, "go here," or "go there." We would encourage the sense of proportion, the sense of humor so that one takes oneself seriously but also finds the light touch. The entity that each is is the one infinite creation and the one Creator. Due to the illusions of time and space those fields of energy which comprise each entity vibrate, not perfectly in tune with the vibration of that one great original Thought, but rather in some distorted fashion; that is, distorted from perfection. This is as it should be. However, if we were to discuss our own idea of who the entity truly is we simply would look at the vibration, for each self has a vibratory complex which is as distinctive as your finger print. You are, before you can think about who you are. You are not inventing yourself, but you are asking yourself to become more than you were. And it is right and good to seek to progress.

We hope that we can aid in some small way as each goes through that eternal cycle of questioning and resting in faith, moving and being still that yields to you a life well-lived and service well done. We would continue through the instrument known as Jim. We leave this instrument in love and in light. We are those of Q'uo.

(Jim channeling)

I am Q'uo, and greet each again through this instrument in the love and the light of the one Creator. At this time we would ask if we may speak to any other queries that are present among those in this circle?

Carla: I sensed some kind of sadness in the contact, Q'uo. Could you speak to that?

I am Q'uo, and am aware of your query, my sister. The topic itself, which deals with the condition of entities upon your planet, is one which feels to be somewhat heavy in that it speaks of beings of light lost, it would seem, in the darkness of the illusion and the confusion that this illusion generates. And this particular aspect of existence is one which has resonance, shall we say, with each in this circle of seeking and therefore there is the feeling/tone of what you would call a certain sadness.

Is there another query, my sister?

Carla: No. Thank you. I was just curious about that.

I am Q'uo, and we thank you again, my sister. Is there another query?

R: I just wanted to say that you are helping me much with your words of inspiration and for others I am sure, too. Knowing that you are there somewhere in the background when things are bearing down heavily is also a comfort to me as a seeker. So I just wanted to say thanks.

I am Q'uo, and we receive your kind words with a great joy in our hearts, for these words are a confirmation to us that we have made an effort which has born fruit, and for this we are grateful.

Is there any further query at this time?

(Pause)

I am Q'uo, and as it appears that we have exhausted the queries for this time of working together we would again express our great appreciation for the invitation that is so freely and consistently offered to us to blend our vibrations with yours and to walk for the moment with you upon your journey of seeking. This is always an opportunity and occasion of great happiness and joy for us, for it gives us the opportunity to exercise our great desire to serve and to work with those such as yourselves whose desire to serve is also great. We cannot begin to thank you enough for this privilege and our humble words and thoughts are mere tokens of the great and bounteous appreciation which exists within our being and resonates with the harmony in this circle of seeking at each working.

We would take our leave at this time of this instrument and this group, and yet we do not truly leave, for all who are of like mind and heart in the seeking and the service of the One are always together in that seeking and in that service. Thus, we only leave in an apparent fashion, and in that leaving we leave in the love and in the light of the one infinite Creator. We are known to you as those of Q'uo. Adonai, my friends. Adonai. ✺

L/L Research

L/L Research is a subsidiary of Rock Creek Research & Development Laboratories, Inc.

P.O. Box 5195
Louisville, KY 40255-0195

www.llresearch.org

Rock Creek is a non-profit corporation dedicated to discovering and sharing information which may aid in the spiritual evolution of humankind.

ABOUT THE CONTENTS OF THIS TRANSCRIPT: This telepathic channeling has been taken from transcriptions of the weekly study and meditation meetings of the Rock Creek Research & Development Laboratories and L/L Research. It is offered in the hope that it may be useful to you. As the Confederation entities always make a point of saying, please use your discrimination and judgment in assessing this material. If something rings true to you, fine. If something does not resonate, please leave it behind, for neither we nor those of the Confederation would wish to be a stumbling block for any.

CAVEAT: This transcript is being published by L/L Research in a not yet final form. It has, however, been edited and any obvious errors have been corrected. When it is in a final form, this caveat will be removed.

© 2009 L/L Research

Sunday Meditation
December 17, 1995

Group question: We're talking about grace and where it might come from: the Holy Spirit, the Creator, the intelligent energy that enters through our feet and base chakras, to guides, spiritual teachers, etc. And we are wondering if the expression of grace is some means of communication from the metaphysical life that we live to the physical life that we live? Is this a way by which we are given a gift? Is this something that is with us always? Is it with us only at particular moments? How can we interpret the experiences of grace that come our way? Is there any way to use grace consciously in our spiritual lives? Is there a way of responding to it appropriately, or is it something that we are simply caught up in?

(Carla channeling)

We are those of the principle known to you as Q'uo. Greetings in the love and in the light of the one infinite Creator. It is our distinct privilege to be called to your group and we greet and bless each who sits in this circle of seeking. We greet you as your fellow pilgrims who have traveled your path and who are still traveling, seeking still the one Mystery Who created us, in whom we have our being, and to whom we now return, step by step by step. We ask only that you regard us as your brothers and sisters rather than as authorities. We gladly share our opinions with you. We do not claim them to be infallible. And so we ask that you use your discrimination, choosing those thoughts that you would further consider and leaving the rest behind.

You have asked for us to speak on the concept of grace. We find often when presented with a topic that much of the energy connected with the topic is baffled or biased because the words of your language are imprecise. One person means one thing by such a word as grace. Another person has another related but somewhat different idea. And, consequently, there is some difficulty is speaking to the heart of this concept. Perhaps we may discover a more precise way of describing what we see as the concept of grace.

We see grace as a state of mind, a state of mind that is natural to the self-conscious entity who is in balance, whose energies are moving freely and in a balanced manner. This state is a kind of level which is natural to each entity. For each entity, then, grace is a vibratory level which reflects a lack of movement in attitude away from that state of nature with which the entity is blessed. On a computer, then, grace would become the default setting for being in good form.

Now, the mind of the self-conscious entity tends to cause this state to become unavailable because the mind has the tendency to leave its natural balance because it is not aware of a natural state and instead is seeking something which is outside of and not controlled by the self. To sound the archetypal roots of grace we could say that the state of grace can equal that Garden of Eden or that ideal state of nature into which humankind is naturally born.

The training of the young entity in your culture tends to develop a state of mind or an attitude which is geared towards the accomplishment of mental and physical goals and the attempting to fit into the various ways of thinking, acting and being which are regarded as appropriate by your culture. The young child is taught to be civil, to share, to obey the direction of authority, and on and on. And as the young child grows, virtue is seen and taught to be coming into accord or compliance with an ever-growing set of standards to be met, of behaviors to pay attention to and to offer when appropriate.

And consequently the growing entity does not have a way to come into the concept of that state of mind or attitude which is that entity's natural gift. Rather, the entity tends to drift further and further away from a feeling of wholeness and appropriateness which comes from the heart outward. And most entities move through the incarnative experience only becoming aware of that state of grace in which the universe is kindly and in which all things which are needed appear from time to time. Thusly, most entities see grace as that which occurs episodically, now here, now there, and then again elsewhere.

In actuality, these times when grace seems to come near and touch the entity are those times when the individual has been able involuntarily or consciously to allow the self to be completely natural, to rest in the center of being and to allow the natural flow of energy. It is as though the self were a receiver that only intermittently worked. In simplistic terms, then, the way towards maximizing the experience of grace in the incarnative experience is to attempt to come to a feeling within of balance. We would encourage seekers to think upon and ponder the concept of self with regard to the nature of the basic attitude that is given as a natural gift by the Creator to each entity, for the maximizing of the experience of grace can be accomplished by increasing the allowing of the self to rest in the natural balance.

This requires that the entity gradually uncover within itself an awareness and a growing familiarity with a kind of trust in the self and in that part of self that goes beyond self and connects with all that there is that is not commonly taught among your peoples.

The young child is repeatedly taught what it must do to obtain the approval and the satisfaction of those whom it wishes to please and of the self, for each entity talks to the self and communicates with the deeper self as if it were another person. Thusly, when one talks with another person one is talking to the projection of the self.

Many things will attempt to unbalance the natural poise of a seeker throughout the daily round of activity. There is the constant ebb and flow of the personal and individual rhythms of self, and we are not suggesting that it is easy to become aware of the deep and unchanging portion of the self that is perhaps best described in emotional terms, or rather in terms of emotion. Emotions are given short shrift by your peoples. Those who are emotional or considered to be emotional are those who seem unbalanced and out of control, whereas from our point of view we would say that those who feel emotion are moving into truth as they begin to purify and refine those emotions. The entity who becomes able through the discipline of the life and the personality to express and manifest pure emotions is the one who shall be closer to balance and nearer to the constant awareness of that state of grace which abides for each entity below the level of confusion which clutters the surface of life and of the mind of each seeker.

Grace, then, is seen by your peoples as a visitation that occurs from time to time. It is seen in various cultures as coming from various outside agencies—angels that come into the life pattern as messengers of grace, personal guides, entities such as we, many, many different ways of thinking about the experience of coming into a state of balance and harmony with the outworking of personal destiny. And this is as it should be, for within each culture there are somewhat different ways of perceiving the same states of mind, but we would ask you to consider the vagaries of language, the limited nature of words, and the deeply illusory environment in which third density finds itself living, for this is a concept that, more than most, asks the entity to open up the mind and to empty it of concept. Grace is that which is beneath the superstructures of conscious thought, and indeed all the structure of metaphysical thought may be seen to be structure of a mechanical nature in which logical connections are made which enable people to think about spiritual things.

We are part of a logical structure by which you as a conscious individual attempt to address the deeper metaphysical questions. Are we real? Do we come from a physical planet to you? Are we a portion of this instrument's deeper mind? Are all things outside this instrument's mind illusions? All of these questions can be answered positively. It is difficult for your minds to grasp. Nevertheless, it is deeply true, in our opinion, that all spiritual circumstance is simply aimed at by word and concept. The truth, the reality, of who we are, who you are, and what your basic nature is is beyond mental acquisition. Those who seek the truth of being are those who are destined to follow a mystery, and much is gained by the entity who simply decides to trust that mystery, to trust the basic nature of the self, and to ask not to become something he is not, but rather to become that which he most truly is, for each of you has the pure and perfect light within. Each of you dwells in a state of grace at a very deep level at all times in all places whatsoever.

Can you by thought or conscious action increase the experiences of grace? We find this a difficult question to answer for each entity will have its own way of dealing with deep illusion. Each entity has a unique natural balance and each has an unique nature which causes the experiences of grace to be gotten to or arrived at in a unique way. Meditation is always helpful, but we might suggest also the conscious attempt to experience thanksgiving when all is going unexceptionally, for this is that blessed state that is so often missed by the spiritual seeker, the state of doing and being that flows throughout a normal day. Within this quiet flow of energy dwells tremendous power, joy, and deep emotion.

Always these rivers run through the depths of being. When the conscious mind turns and gives thanksgiving for this normality, this normal day, this thankful, grateful opening of the heart causes the balance within to strengthen and to normalize. Beyond this practice of thanksgiving we cannot say that there is a way reliably to achieve the awareness of the state of grace, for the illusion in which you dwell was designed not to give one the experience of balance but rather to give one the feeling of imbalance, bafflement and confusion so that the self has material against which to push and from which to learn.

This instrument is suggesting to us that we allow more time than usual for questions and answers, and so at this time we would transfer this contact to the one known as Jim, thanking this instrument and leaving it in love and in light. We are those of Q'uo.

(Jim channeling)

We are those of Q'uo, and we greet each again in love and in light through this instrument. At this time it is our privilege to offer ourselves to the possibility of speaking to further queries. Is there a query with which we may begin?

K: I would ask first of all, the state of grace existed in us prior to our incarnation and was not enough in times past to make a choice to serve others or to serve ourselves because in this state of grace we were feeling oneness with the Creator, and this caused us not to do work? Is this correct?

I am Q'uo, and am aware of your query, my brother. We would compliment the clarity, for this is a perception which is quite correct.

Is there a further query, my brother?

K: I am interested in the origination of souls. How did our souls first originate and what is your view of them?

I am Q'uo, and am aware of your query, my brother. The origination of souls is the story of the evolutionary process whereby the one Creator has utilized the beginning or basic densities of this octave of creation to bring about that which you call the mind, that which you call the body and that which you call the spirit, that together these complexes will form that which may be called the soul, the essence of the entity which has become individualized enough from the one Creator to be able to pursue what would seem to be a quite individualized path of spiritual evolution.

The mind portion is formed in the large extent within the first-density experience where the awareness, the very simple awareness of all being, is the salient feature associated with earth, wind, fire and water.

As this process of spiraling light leading upward continues, the second density offers the mind complex a more individualized focus in the form of second-density creatures of the plant and then the animal nature. This provides a more individualized experience as the consciousness that is moving forward moves towards the light ever more certainly in the grouping known in second density as the flocks of birds, the schools of fish, the swarms of bees, and so forth.

As the line of light continues to move upward, the spirit complex is added to those individualized portions of the one Creator which have been able to give and receive the concept that you know of as love in sufficient degree to so individualize the entity that it is ready to add the spirit complex and thus have the completion of complexes available for the free will choice of third density as to the positive or negative—so-called—paths of continued evolution. At this point within third density, in most cases, the soul then comes into being in its fullness.

Is there a further query, my brother?

K: So you are saying then that the soul does not come out as a living, conscious, thinking entity from the Creator, that it has to develop through the processes of the densities in order to become an actual soul?

I am Q'uo, and this is basically correct, my brother, for the process begins with total unity, moves into seeming separation to the point of seeming complete separation in the third density and then begins the movement back into the unity of all things.

Is there a further query?

K: Yes. Then the soul is a type of consciousness? Is it a type of spiritual material would you [say] that separates from the one Creator and then becomes available for the densities' experience? Just what is that nature that first comes out of the one Creator?

I am Q'uo, and am aware of your query, but aware of no sure means of describing the nature of the soul with words that can be understood, for the nature of each soul is the essence of each soul is the essence of the one Creator and this essence at its heart is mystery. There is energy. There is intelligence. There is infinity. There is unity. All these are a portion of this soul essence.

Is there a further query?

K: One more. In thinking of evolution and the development of third-density bodies on this planet from the second-density prototypes, I am wondering why every third-density body developed the same, with the same features. This is universal on our planet. How did it happen that all third-density bodies developed the same?

I am Q'uo, and am aware of your query, my brother, and again we must remind each that the answer to most queries with depth such as this query is mystery. Why the one Creator chose the bipedal, opposable thumb, ape-like creature to enspirit is truly a mystery, but we can surmise that the one Creator felt that in this instance this form was the most liable to allow the expression of those energies of third density that would lead to the continued evolution of this consciousness. This form is universal upon this planetary sphere and upon a number of others as well, yet within the One Creation, to our knowledge, it is but one of many forms chosen.

Is there a further query, my brother?

K: Just a quick one. Do we have extraterrestrials who helped to engineer the human form in our distant past to help create what we know it as today?

I am Q'uo, and am aware of your query, my brother, and must respond in the affirmative for there have been in distant and ancient times of your species' evolution such involvement by entities who were seeking to aid in the evolutionary process of the species with whom they felt responsibility.

Is there a further query, my brother?

K: No. Thank you. P, you had some.

P: As we were sitting here and listening to you I noticed activity in the child that I am carrying. I just wondered if this activity is random or if the child is responding to the energy of the group? I have noticed this at other times when I thought it was responding to my thoughts, but I could not say whether this was random or is really a response. Could you comment on this?

I am Q'uo, and am aware of your query, my sister. We would respond by suggesting that this young entity is one which is sensitive to the vibratory frequencies of the environment which surrounds it, not only the immediate environment of your physical vehicle but the environment of what we would call the feeling-tone or, less accurately, the emotional environment of this circle of seeking.

Is there a further query, my sister?

P: Thank you. That was reassuring. My questions concern the history of Islam. Would you be able to comment on the origin of the Koran?

I am Q'uo, and am aware of your query, my sister. We are working with this instrument to give it the image of the answer, shall we say. The means of transmission and point of origin of this holy work is the inspiration that the one known as Mohammed was able to open itself to receive at various times during its life experience which it had offered to the one Creator as a gift or glorification, for this entity had many experiences of the unity of all things and was desirous in a great extent to bring back this inspiration that those of its peoples might also be blessed as it was blessed.

Thus, the information that has been gathered in this holy work was that which was divinely inspired and though difficult to describe in the languages of the time, yet this entity set itself to this purpose and was single-minded in its pursuit of this mission, shall we say.

Is there a further query, my sister?

P: Yes. In the book itself it says Mohammed was inspired and that the message came through Gabriel, that the work itself is the word of God Itself and was absolute and had no flaw. Could you tell me the density of Gabriel and the identity of Gabriel? And what do they mean really when they say this is the word of God and is absolute?

I am Q'uo, and am aware of your query, my sister. We will attempt to respond. The entity, Gabriel, was one of a number of entities that assisted in this transmission, being the focus of the effort, was one which worked with the entity known as Mohammed as this entity had dedicated its life purpose previous to the incarnation to working with those of its own kind, shall we say. Thus, the effort was put forth by those of the density of love and light in balance, that being six, working with those of the same vibratory level who had taken incarnation for the purpose of such a mission.

Is there a further query, my sister?

P: When you say those of the same vibratory level do you mean then that Mohammed was a sixth-density entity who incarnated as a third-density entity?

I am Q'uo, and this is correct, my sister.

Is there a further query?

P: Could you comment on the amount of negative or Orion influence in the book itself?

I am Q'uo, and am aware of your query, my sister. As with all such efforts of light and service to others the power of the polarity puts forth an attraction and is, shall we say, noticed by those in the vicinity. There is often notice by those of the so-called Orion Empire that they be able to utilize the balancing efforts of this planet's quarantine system to offer some form of their own information wherever possible and to make this offering to appear as the same as that which first attracted their notice.

Thus, with all such efforts there is some infiltration of the signal with other information at odd moments or targets of opportunity that exist in all entities that are mortal. Thus, all such inspirational information has this feature whereby there is attracted to it the balancing efforts by those of the so-called loyal opposition.

Is there a further query, my sister?

P: I wonder where in the Koran it says that the book is the absolute truth and should be followed absolutely instead of giving a way for self-transcendence to the work. I wonder if that part particularly is Orion work?

I am Q'uo, and am aware of your query, my sister. But with this query we find that the response lies beyond the Law of Confusion, for it is at this point that all entities must look at that which is offered and choose for the self that which is at the heart of the work.

Is there a further query, my sister?

P: After Mohammed received the inspirations and came to be of service and delivered the Koran and left the work and left the incarnation would you be able to estimate the balance in the struggle between light forces and the dark, shall we say? In the history of the development of Islam is there a way of saying which force had the upper hand or currently would it be possible for you to estimate the power of the two forces? Which is stronger?

I am Q'uo, and am aware of your query, my sister. And again we find a difficulty in a specific response for this points to the heart of the matter of discrimination and we can only suggest that when even the most holy and pure work of divine inspiration falls to the mortals below there will be human error entered at some point, whether it be by chance or by design, as the various levels of relationship and interrelationship work to bring entities with personal incarnational lessons into touch with that which is divine. Thus, there is opportunity for distortion and the use of the inspiration for purposes other than the original intentions. As the cycles of human reincarnation occur from time to time and culture to culture there are overriding issues of relationships of groups and their purpose for incarnation. Thus, there is always the opportunity for interpretation.

Is there a further query, my sister?

P: If an entity wants to be of service helping those in Islamic cultures and has to deal with such fixed influence such as the Koran and its history which has been crystallized in the society as a set structure, and one wants to offer a way for people to realize or live the truth, freedom and happiness and joy in that way, what is the best way to go about working in such a society where you cannot challenge the authority of a work such as the Koran? What is the best way to deal with the distortions and keep one's own clarity and be of service?

I am Q'uo, and am aware of your query, my sister. We would recommend the path that moves to the heart of the matter. Look to that which is the integrity of the work. The one known as Jesus replaced the many laws of Moses with but two: to love the Lord, the God, with all the heart, the mind and the soul, and to love one's neighbor as oneself. This entity moved to the heart of the work and gave itself in completeness in this effort and allowed itself to be used as a vessel or an instrument—not its will, but the will of the Father, the one Creator.

If you will give yourself in such dedication and move to the heart of all creation and to the work which you revere then you will be moving in harmony with all that is and will offer yourself as purely as possible.

Is there a further query, my sister?

P: You see moving to the heart of the matter and I see that as coming from the heart and Jesus' statement is one which comes from the heart. There also needs to be a balance in working from the heart and working from the mind as well. Could you comment on the balance between working from the heart and from the mind? I guess it's really a balance between wisdom and compassion.

I am Q'uo, and an aware of your query, my sister. We would again recommend that you begin in the heart and end in the heart. That is, do all that you do because you love. Consider with your mind how you shall do, what you shall do, when you shall do, with whom you shall do. Make those plans. Do what you can. Then give over any dedication to an outcome by the surrendering of your will to the will of the One and receive that which comes with as much joy as you would any other gift.

Is there any further query, my sister?

P: I think I have two. From what I understood from what you just said that the way of the heart is the way that we are traveling and the mind seems to be an instrument much like the stick that the Fool in the Tarot carries to distinguish. Is this analogy correct?

I am Q'uo, and am aware of your query, and would suggest that the analogy is a good analogy, for the mind in its intellectual capabilities is able to refine the great outpouring of love from the heart in a manner which may be more effective in serving others as it takes into account that which they ask.

Is there a further query, my sister?

P: The next question has to do with the earlier concept of grace. The first state of grace is like the Garden of Eden, you said. I had the image of the Tarot card, the Sun, where the male and female entity are facing each other in a circle and holding hands. Is there a relation between this card and the concept of grace being much like the Garden of Eden?

I am Q'uo, and this is so, my sister. We would suggest that you have found a correlation that is of significance in precisely the manner described.

Is there another question, my sister?

P: Thank you so much, and thanks to the group for all the inspiration, help and clarity.

I am Q'uo, and we would echo your gratitude for the very same reasons. The aid that you and each in the circle give us by asking those queries which are heavy or important upon the heart and the mind is a gift for which we are most grateful.

At this time we would ask if there is a final query for this session?

K: One thing about fourth density. When Ra says that in the fourth density we are every experience and every feeling, everything, if we are everything and every thought why would it be necessary to form a social memory complex …

(Tape ends.) ❧

Year 1996
January 14, 1996 to December 22, 1996

Sunday Meditation
January 14, 1996

Group question: *(No group question.)*

(Carla channeling)

We are those of Q'uo. We greet each of you in the love and in the light of the one infinite Creator. It is a great privilege to be called to your group and we thank each for seeking the truth and for being willing to allow us to share some thoughts with you at this time.

We are not those who speak with perfect authority. We are souls such as yourself. We make mistakes and still are learning and truly know very little. But that which we have thought and learned we gladly offer to you with the understanding that you use your discrimination. Accept those thoughts which ring true to you and leave the rest behind.

As you have given us permission to speak in any way we choose, we turn towards the heart of that which we came to share with your people. We come to encourage each who seeks the truth to open the doors of your attention, to behold the present moment. It is our opinion that the physical body which you now enjoy and the world which you now live in is a passing thing. In time it was created and in time it shall disappear, changed into that which was not. Yet there is that which was before the worlds were made and which shall be long after your sun has gone nova.

There are many words among your peoples to describe this basic inalterable reality from which all things spring. Among those words we choose love. The love of the one infinite Creator is a vibration, a logos, if you will, and that pure love has generated that which you call light in order to create a manifested world. You are made of light which has been regularized and built upon. Within your essence, unchanged and unchangeable, resides this vibration, this logos. This is your true self. That true self peeks up into the passing days like the tip of a great iceberg, barely clearing the water, yet being a mighty mass below the surface. Indeed, all that your people's tend to think of as their identity, all were created and will cease to be.

When we say open to the present moment, we speak of that present moment which is eternal. Within time the attempt to grasp the present moment is constantly doomed to failure for your mind—that is, your earthly intelligence—and the illusion itself were created so that things would occur in an order. In the eternal present moment, all things exist simultaneously. That which is, is, and in this fullness of being resides the peace that is so eagerly sought by those who weary of the passing scene.

How can one find this present moment? We suggest often the practice of regular contemplation or meditation, for within silence there is that key which unlocks the doors of attention. And into that sanctum sanctorum of the open heart, silent and listening, there resides the Creator whose name is Love.

We encourage each to form the habit of silence on a regular basis, for that voice which speaks in silence is that which gives life and peace. We do not say that it gives wisdom. Rather, we suggest that it works little by little to open the heart and the awareness to the presence of love. There are other ways to find love. If you gaze into another's eyes, truly looking into those remarkable depths, you may see the Creator. Even if you look within the mirror at your own eyes and look *into* them, you shall see that which you do not know or recognize as personal, for you carry within you a consciousness which is love. It is a matter of uncovering and recognizing that which has always been there, that presence which is closer than your breathing, more intimate than your hands and your feet. It is that which abides. And if you may find that center for just a moment in each day, the passing scene changes in its appearance, for the heart has changed, and so the eyes change.

We are here within your inner planes at this time because there is a time of harvest approaching. Indeed, this harvest has begun. There is a time when entities may choose how to continue in fellowship with each other. Your creation is expanding and changing as your entire solar system moves into a new area of space and time. Your scientists have begun to study many new subatomic particles which are native to this new area of space. Within the instreamings of light into this particular portion of the infinite creation, the physical illusion which you enjoy as your life, your incarnation, will change. The physical vehicle will become lighter. The experience of dwelling in a physical reality will be quite a bit easier, for within these new vibrations there lies the opportunity for sharing of thoughts and experiences which is now, within your illusion, not possible.

Not all entities, however, will move into this new vibration because some there are who do not find themselves at all weary of the present world scene. Those who are pleased with this present world scene shall continue to work on the lessons of love that your illusion provides so generously. Those who wish to accelerate the process of their spiritual evolution will find that they wish to make a fundamental choice. This choice is the choice of how to manifest that love. The two paths of manifesting love we have often called "service to others" and "service to self," for if one looks into another's eyes and sees the Creator, if one can gaze in the mirror and see the Creator, then to serve the self is to serve the Creator and to serve others is to serve the Creator. We are those who have chosen the service-to-others path. This is what we know and what we share.

We encourage each to spend some time contemplating the implications of service to others and service to self, for in one path there is the giving up of the energy of the self to others. In the other path there is the attracting and magnetic pulling of others' energies so that they may serve you. The ability to chose is the hallmark of the Creator. This Creator loves each spark that It has flung from Itself. You are loved in a way far deeper than you can imagine, and whatever path you chose, the Creator abides with you. There is no time limit upon this process of evolution, so we encourage you to rest and gain confidence and from the practicing of that centering presence, you may find at any moment the door opening to the present moment. And we are with you as you go.

We would at this time transfer this contact to the one known as Jim. We thank this instrument and leave it in love and in light. We are those of Q'uo.

(Jim channeling)

I am Q'uo, and greet each again in love and in light through this instrument. At this time it is our privilege to ask if there may be further queries to which we may speak. Is there a query at this time?

Carla: I'm going in the hospital in about a week and a half and I wondered if you could comment on anything I might do to prepare for that experience that would enhance it.

I am Q'uo, and am aware of your query, my sister. We can only recommend that you see yourself and those about you as the Creator that is experiencing Itself and enter into this work upon your wrist area with the quiet confidence that the plan of the One is being worked out well and that you shall again be available for service to those who request your assistance.

Is there a further query, my sister?

Carla: No, thank you, Q'uo.

I am Q'uo, and again we thank you, my sister. Is there another query?

Questioner: I have a question, Q'uo. I have noticed that my meditations have changed. I seem to be having reluctance to continue meditating the way I have been. I wonder if you could speak to the ebb and flow of finding the moment of silence. If you can generalize about how it works, I'd appreciate it.

I am Q'uo, and am aware of your query, my brother. Each seeker of truth will find that the path it travels is one which has those places which are wide and through which passage is easy and those places which are more narrow, making passage difficult. When you find your practice of seeking in the way of meditation beginning to flag, you may be aware that the faith and will, which are the rod and staff of each seeker, may need reinforcing, for there is much to distract an entity from completing the practices that it has set for itself, and these distractions are also a part of your journey. As you are able to see afield and redirect the changing energies of your own commitment, your own faith, and your will to persevere in the face of distractions and difficulties, you will be learning the kind of perseverance that will give you that peace which passes understanding at some point in your seeking, for if the journey were always easy then the pearl of great price would be much devalued and easily acquired by all.

The continuing beyond confusion, beyond distraction, beyond the difficulties, is much likened to the tempering of the metal in a tool that gives it strength, burnishing it that it might shine brightly and continue in its service with a renewed strength because of the difficulty, confusion and so forth. Thus, as you see the difficulty in motivating yourself to complete your meditations, this in itself is likened to a meditation where the focus falters and moves from the one point so that it must again be returned with patience and love to that one point. As you continue to accept the difficult portions of your journey and of your practices you will find that there is an underlying strength that you build. To persevere and persevere and persevere is perhaps the most common and at times difficult portion of any seeker's journey, yet to be aware that such is occurring within your own experience is an illustration of your own dedication upon another level. Thus, we can only recommend that you continue as you are with faith, with forgiveness, with acceptance.

Is there a further query, my brother?

Questioner: No, thank you.

I am Q'uo, and we thank you. Is there another query at this time?

(Pause)

I am Q'uo, and as it appears that we have exhausted those queries which you have for us, we shall again take this opportunity to thank those present for inviting our presence in your circle of seeking this day. We are always overjoyed at the opportunity to blend our vibrations with yours and to walk but a few steps upon your journey with you. You are not alone, my friends, even when you may feel great isolation, for there are those such as ourselves and many, many others who walk with you and rejoice at your every step of seeking the light, the love, and the truth of the one Creator.

At this time we shall take our leave of this group and this instrument, leaving each, as always, in the love and in the light of the one Creator. We are known to you as those of Q'uo. Adonai, my friends. Adonai. ❧

L/L Research

L/L Research is a subsidiary of Rock Creek Research & Development Laboratories, Inc.

P.O. Box 5195
Louisville, KY 40255-0195

www.llresearch.org

Rock Creek is a non-profit corporation dedicated to discovering and sharing information which may aid in the spiritual evolution of humankind.

ABOUT THE CONTENTS OF THIS TRANSCRIPT: This telepathic channeling has been taken from transcriptions of the weekly study and meditation meetings of the Rock Creek Research & Development Laboratories and L/L Research. It is offered in the hope that it may be useful to you. As the Confederation entities always make a point of saying, please use your discrimination and judgment in assessing this material. If something rings true to you, fine. If something does not resonate, please leave it behind, for neither we nor those of the Confederation would wish to be a stumbling block for any.

CAVEAT: This transcript is being published by L/L Research in a not yet final form. It has, however, been edited and any obvious errors have been corrected. When it is in a final form, this caveat will be removed.

© 2009 L/L Research

Sunday Meditation
January 21, 1996

Group question: Our question this week concerns the affiliation between the Yahweh entities and the Mars population that rendered their planet unlivable. Yahweh became like a shepherd or god and this seemed to open the door for negative balancing opportunities. A negative entity from Orion claimed to be the original Yahweh and made a covenant with them so if they obeyed his laws their enemies would be laid low by Yahweh and they would prosper.

We are wondering if this covenant made with the Jewish race, and perhaps the Arabs too, was why Jesus made a new covenant focusing on love rather than the eye-for-an-eye nature of the old covenant, and we are wondering what Q'uo might have to say about that subject.

(Carla channeling)

We are those of Q'uo. We greet you in the love and in the light of the one infinite Creator. We thank you for calling us to your circle for this working, and we bless and greet each who sits within your circle. There is a heavenly light that shines from groups such as yours, not only because of the people that are there in person but also because of those who link up with these meditations. Each center which gathers for the purpose of seeking the truth and finding light and love is a kind of lamp that turns the darkness into dawn. This is a service that you perform for your peoples as well as for yourselves, and certainly this is a service for us, for it allows us to use instruments such as this one in order to communicate with you concerning principles that we hold dear and opinions which we have to share. As always, we ask that you take nothing from this meeting that is not truly your own, recognized, remembered and fitting with those things which you seek at this time.

We are aware of the many questions that those at this meeting do have, and as you have requested information on that entity that you call Yahweh we shall attempt to speak along these lines to your satisfaction. When we finish that which we have to say there shall be time for more detailed follow-up questions.

Your question concerns history, the history of your people. And yet this history is also a mythology and the one function is as important as the other. Because of these historical and mythological coincidences of meaning and value it takes a careful and subtle intelligence to find one's true and clarified way through the many by-lanes of cultural detail and distortion. We say this because your query concerns that which your peoples see as a god or the God. Within another mythological system—that being the extraterrestrial model—this entity is a Guardian. The god-like qualities of each entity are precisely those of the entity, Yahweh. The qualities of Creator within all beings are the same. When the intelligence of consciousness attempts to grasp that which lies beyond rational, physical, Euclidean models of space/time, facts become ladders and thoughts become structures, structures of logic upon which the entities which dwell in the darkness of flesh attempt to use with those imprecise items you call words to express the relationship between the self and the Creator.

All of those within the Confederation of Planets in the Service of the Infinite Creator are those who are people of this mythology and people of this history. Yet time and space are not as they are in space/time when one attempts to delve beneath the surface of the story of the race of humanity upon Earth. Thusly, while we are real we are also metaphysical as opposed to physical, just as your thoughts have no flesh but are as they are. So are we within your space/time continuum.

That which the entity Jehovah or Yahweh did among your peoples was within history and yet also of the quality of the thought that has no place within history. We say this in order to deflect the intellectual desire of the seeker of truth from aiming directly into this matter as though it were logical or linear. That which has to do with the relationship of consciousness in the personal sense with consciousness in the creative sense or the sense of being the Creator will always fly before any gust of wind that attempts to chase it and the more words that are thrown at it, the faster it will flee.

So, at the very beginning of anything that we say at this time, we ask that you understand that we are using analogy, and we are mixing mythology and historicity because that is the way the creation is melded within your illusion.

The entity, Yahweh, as the one known as Jim surmised within his question, was indeed one who had the plan of enabling those who wished to transfer to your planet with that move. The concept seemed to them fairly direct; that is, to improve the intelligence and the curiosity and the physical and emotional strength of the type of physical vehicle which had been the native physical vehicle for those within the Martian sphere. And as was surmised, this entity discovered, to its discomfiture, that it had caused great distortion, worse distortion, shall we say, than the distortions would have been without the aid.

This kind of situation occurs at all levels of consciousness. The mistake is made. There it is. One cannot go back. One simply learns and moves forward. However, this people indeed did crave and wish for a continuing source of, shall we say, God-given help. Its expectations were very high because there had been interaction betwixt a god-like being and humans. The remarkable nature of this history speaks for itself.

The entity which succeeded the first Yahweh—calling itself by the same name and using the same frequency of light to express—simply continued to offer aid and comfort when it wished but with the ever increasing distortions towards belligerency and aggressiveness that is the hallmark of a negatively oriented being or culture. The echoes of this action which was transmitted long ago redounds even now and shall continue to echo and re-echo as long as there are those within third density within this sphere who wish to claim power and who seek a god of power.

Now, let us look at the promise first made and the promise that took its place. The hunger which many among your peoples have had revolves around knowing what is right. It is instinctive within your physical vehicle to watch out for the safety and the comfort of the body, the mind and the spirit. The continual proclamations and greatly detailed taboos, prohibitions and schedules of sacrifice that characterized the relationship of your so-called Old Testament God constituted an order, a structure, a logic within which entities felt comfortable living. Through this structure they knew what was right. The tendency was to enunciate finer and finer points of law until all possible actions with ethical consequences or consequences of safety and health were covered and the entities within this system were safe.

We ask you to look about you within your present world scene and see the entities about you looking for a way to be safe. Look upon your leaders who wish to prohibit freedom in order to guarantee safety. The spirit of Yahweh is strong and it survives. It is part of that mixture of light and dark which makes up all that is. In other words, we are saying that entities continue to have a choice between the many laws of moral rectitude in such a logic as Yahweh's. They can also choose a logic and a path which is not rational or linear, which does not hold, which does not insist, and which is not aggressive.

This spirit was before the one known as Jesus the Christ. It exists, as does Yahweh, within each entity, for each of you is the universe. You are looking out at a world that is actually interior. Such is the illusion created by flesh.

In the testament of the one known as Jesus the place of the law is simply turned upon its head, as the one known as Jesus is quoted as saying, "Man was not made for the Sabbath, but the Sabbath for man." The direction to love the one infinite Creator and to love each other self as the self is not a detailed, closed or encapsulated direction. It is specifically open-ended, and the one known as Jesus goes to some pains in the body of teaching that survives to impress upon those whom he taught that there is never an end to love. There is never the need to return to the old prescriptions and old taboos. These are not either/or situations but rather either/or processes, and as each student works upon its personal polarity perhaps it will aid the student to ponder and remember these two kinds of promises, these two kinds of ways of thinking. And perhaps this can be instructive in showing the way, the balance, when that way seems unclear.

We wish to tell you that your model of the universe is very, very limited. The attempt to nail down a history which is replete with metaphysical subject matter shall always be unending and full of lacunae, holes, gaps and spaces where there is no logic, there are no words, there is no road, there is no structure. Not that there is no structure, just that there is beyond all structure, love. The illusion is so very, very deep, for you are a dream, yet when you leave the flesh and enter a larger life you will still be a dream, for we also are but illusions and ahead we see illusion. Yet always that siren call which beckons you and beckons us calls us all forward.

And yet are we forward-going? We do not think so. We feel at this point the comfortable awareness that we do not know what is occurring. We only know how to be faithful to love. When it is accepted within the heart that nothing can be known and that a sea of confusion will always surround love, then the mind and the heart are better armed to take up the walk of the pilgrim who seeks truth, peace and love.

That call has come to many who wander within this world of yours at this time, listening for a sound, a tone, a letter from home, waiting, hardly hoping at some times, yet holding onto the faith that that which is within, that which is so hungrily sought, does exist. And we say to you, "Yes, love exists. Love is before, after and around all that is." You do not seek after ephemera. You seek that which is and that which exists perfectly. We encourage all lines of thinking which fascinate your minds, and we hope that we can, within your meditative periods, be with you as strengtheners of your own vibration. But we do continue to remark that the ways of seeking which are scholarly and of the mind yield a limited harvest. This is acceptable to us. We can look at what is possible within your world and see that it will be helpful and useful. And we encourage those who are drawn to this material, to this subject, to continue that process of thinking, meditating and reflecting, for these are helpful things not simply to the self, but in terms of service to others as well.

Let those truths that you seek remain small enough for you to remember that beyond all that can be understood or discussed is the truth, and that is a vibration which has created all that is and into which we hunger and yearn to move again. That should keep your intelligence and your heart on a sturdy road that has good perspective.

We would at this time transfer this contact to the one known as Jim. We do thank this instrument and leave it in love and in light. We are those known to you as Q'uo.

(Jim channeling)

I am Q'uo, and we greet each again in love and in light through this instrument. It is our privilege at this time to offer ourselves in the attempt to speak to any further queries. Is there another query at this time?

K: I understand you to say that there were two Yahwehs? The original who brought the entities from Mars to Earth and then a second entity using his vibration?

I am Q'uo, and am aware of your query, my brother. This is correct, with the second entity being of a negative orientation and utilizing the name of the first as a means of gaining control of the entities to whom the first Yahweh had spoken.

Is there a further query, my brother?

K: The second Yahweh then gave the Laws of Moses to the people as well as the curses that attended them?

I am Q'uo, and this is correct, my brother. Is there a further query?

K: Ra said that the first Yahweh gave the Law of One in a very simple form to Moses. Is this the saying, "I am that I am," or was this the Ten Commandments, or something else? What was this exactly that he was talking about?

I am Q'uo, and am aware of your query, my brother. The entity, Yahweh, from the Confederation of Planets in Service to the Infinite Creator, was one who spoke with those entities from the Mars influence in a manner that reflected the unity of all creation and the attempt to be of service to others. Through this speaking and intermingling, shall we say, the attempt was formed or fashioned in a way or in a philosophy that attempted to weave all experience, desires and expenditures of energy as portions of one great tapestry of energy, love and unity. All communications were based upon this simple recognition of the unified nature of all creation. It was the foundation upon which the interrelationship was built.

Is there a further query?

K: The Ten Commandments were given by the second, negative Yahweh? Is that correct?

I am Q'uo, and am aware of your query, my brother. This is basically correct, for these commandments were seen as the pillars upon which would rest the many laws that would protect and guide the chosen people in a manner that was in accordance with the desires of the Orion-based Yahweh. These commandments included previous concepts given by the first Yahweh contact and then there was added unto those concepts a turning or twisting toward the negative orientation so that the commandments were, shall we say, then restrictions upon entities more than inspiration to affirmative or positive action and imaging of concepts.

Is there a further query, my brother?

K: In the Old Testament we have this record of Yahweh speaking. It is a strong personality. Can we take this strong personality to be the creation of later editors or writers, or is this a faithful reproduction of the negative Yahweh?

I am Q'uo, and am aware of your query, my brother. We find in most instances there is, as you have surmised, the faithful reproduction of words spoken and recorded carefully. However, as in all recording by human hand there is the possibility of coloration or distortion which has occurred in some instances.

Is there a further query?

K: Was the negative Yahweh responsible for the miracles on the journey out of Egypt such as the parting of the Red Sea, the manna from heaven, or the water from the rock? Or did these not happen at all?

I am Q'uo, and am aware of your query, my brother. We find here that there is some mixture of influence and there is some difficulty in interpretation although much is carefully recorded and in a reasonably accurate manner. We would take this opportunity to remind each entity present that though the details of such an interaction are quite interesting upon many levels, that it is well to remember that the process of the evolution of the entities involved is one which is at its heart in accordance with the free will choices of the peoples of this time who, though laboring under dual influences, did have enough previous understanding of the heart of the evolutionary process being love and compassion that this positively oriented source of information was for the most part ignored by the majority of these entities who were evolving according to the energies set in motion …

(Side one of tape ends.)

(Jim channeling)

I am Q'uo, and am again with this instrument. As we mentioned previously, these entities had access to information of a positive nature but chose through their own free will to move with those energies which had originated with their experience on the red planet known to you as Mars, and there was indeed much interaction and influence offered to these entities by both positively and negatively oriented entities who were interested in the evolution of these Mars entities.

Is there a final query at this time?

K: I would ask about what Ra said about giving some visionary information to some philosophers of ancient Greece about 600 BC. Can you tell me what this information pertained to and how it showed up in Greek philosophy?

I am Q'uo, and am aware of your query, my brother. And we would answer by suggesting that the Law of One was the primary information given in the distortion of the ways of love and understanding, so that there were those philosophers within the Greek culture and experience which made this assumption the foundation of their philosophy and their view of the nature of creation, its purpose, direction and ultimate conclusion.

Is there any further query?

K: Do we have time for some more?

I am Q'uo, and we would entertain one final query, my brother.

K: I am interested in Jesus of Nazareth. He often had the term, "Son of God," attributed to him. Is this to be taken literally or was this a reference to the Logos of Philo Judeas of Alexandria, who often used that term for his Logos?

I am Q'uo, and am aware of your query, my brother. The phrase, "Son of God," or the phrase, "The Christed One," are means of expressing the kind of consciousness available to those who have been able to open the green-ray energy center in sufficient degree to feel and experience this creative force of love that has made all that there is. This quality of consciousness or attitude of beingness is the goal or opportunity which is offered each third-density entity as a means of passing from this illusion to the fourth density where the study of this creative power of love is that which is the focus of all energy expenditure. Thus, the one known as Jesus was able to offer itself as a model or pattern by which entities could move their own consciousness to a larger view in which the acceptance of self and others as one being was far more easily facilitated.

We are those of Q'uo and we would take this opportunity to thank again those who have gathered in this circle of seeking this day and who have graciously offered us the opportunity to speak our words and to share our thoughts in those areas that are of interest to you. We are always most grateful for this opportunity to walk with you upon this journey which all make together. At this time we shall take our leave of this instrument and this group, leaving each, as always, in the love and in the light of the infinite Creator. Adonai. Adonai. ✦

L/L Research

L/L Research is a subsidiary of Rock Creek Research & Development Laboratories, Inc.

P.O. Box 5195
Louisville, KY 40255-0195

www.llresearch.org

Rock Creek is a non-profit corporation dedicated to discovering and sharing information which may aid in the spiritual evolution of humankind.

ABOUT THE CONTENTS OF THIS TRANSCRIPT: This telepathic channeling has been taken from transcriptions of the weekly study and meditation meetings of the Rock Creek Research & Development Laboratories and L/L Research. It is offered in the hope that it may be useful to you. As the Confederation entities always make a point of saying, please use your discrimination and judgment in assessing this material. If something rings true to you, fine. If something does not resonate, please leave it behind, for neither we nor those of the Confederation would wish to be a stumbling block for any.

CAVEAT: This transcript is being published by L/L Research in a not yet final form. It has, however, been edited and any obvious errors have been corrected. When it is in a final form, this caveat will be removed.

© 2009 L/L Research

Sunday Meditation
February 4, 1996

Group question: The question this week has to do with the possibility that it might be as hard for service-to-others oriented people to accept the love offerings of others as it is to give love in service to others. In fact, many of us have the feeling that we like to be able to reciprocate in kind as soon as possible when somebody helps us out and gives us a helping hand because we want to be sure that we give more than we receive, that what we really want to do is to give. So, we would like to have some comments from Q'uo or anyone from the Confederation on giving and receiving and the importance of each, the difficulties of each, the advantages and anything you would care to say.

(Carla channeling)

We are those of the principle known to you as Q'uo and we greet you warmly after a winter's holiday. We have enjoyed gazing at the scene among your peoples as the gift-giving and resolution-making of your culture's ways had their merry rhythms and rippled outward through the deep mind of your, shall we say, racial and planetary minds, creating light and space and leavening the whole with good vibrations. Your peoples are capable of the greatest degree of love and kindness and we rejoice in seeing that in that season when those things are hoped for, they also occur.

As we come to you we bring many thanks, as always, for your careful asking of us. The opportunity to share our opinions with you is an enormously profitable one for us, for we are able to be of service to you and we truly do give that service with a whole heart and an unreserved love for each of you and for the light that each comes to and yet brings within him or her to this circle of seeking. We ask you only one thing and that is not to take our advice as gospel, for it is only the thoughts of your neighbors, and we are glad to share them, but we must tell you that we often err, and when in error we do not know it, else we would have not done it. So take those thoughts from us that ring with the peculiar inner ring of recognition that is reserved for your own personal truth and leave the rest behind.

This instrument just told me that she felt like W. C. Fields in getting a drink from her inside jacket pocket. We thought that was worthy, so we passed it on. This instrument is saying to us, "Hello, Laitos," and we say, "Hello, dear one." We also say from Hatonn, "Hello, dear ones."

Now to your topic of the day, which is receiving the love offerings of others. Ah, my children, how you will laugh when you rise from the safe confusion in which you now play and amuse yourselves and look back upon the giving and the receiving that you have done within this Earth world that you call your home. It will surprise you to some extent, but perhaps not, for perhaps you already suspect that things are not as they seem.

We invoke the one known as Don's "180 degree rule." Receiving the love offerings of others is the greatest gift you can give and is won by giving in service to others. When you reach the point at which there is no difference between receiving and giving absolute and unreserved love, then shall you be ready to learn the ways of wisdom. Until then, you must learn these lessons that seem so opposite: how to serve others, how to accept service from others. Yet are you not looking in a mirror when you gaze upon another? Is that entity not looking at the Creator when he gazes back at you? Is this not the essence of your being?

Now, let us look at the values of your culture. The emphasis is always upon that which carries what this instrument calls the green energy of money. Some have more; some have less. Needless to say, this is an illusion, for all things belong to the one infinite Creator, and as you give and as you receive, you are simply moving the energy around.

This instrument is fond of saying, "Keep the energy flowing; don't resist." This is an excellent piece of advice. When it is time to accept love, learn, my children, to say, "thank you" with an open heart and a clear mind. The reciprocity is in accepting love without reservation or any evasion that would create an invulnerability between you and the other self.

Similarly, when you give, give wholeheartedly and you shall experience that event as if you were being fed by heavenly food. You see, it is not money, or places, or times, or any event, or object, or any occurrence whatever that is given or received, for what is actually occurring [is], you are a thought. That thought is love unreserved, complete, utter and whole. This love chose to manifest itself and created light. That light in all of its rotations and degrees has built the universe in its infinity, and all that you see and all that you are is light. All manifestation is light in heavier and heavier outer garments.

Yes, but always each iota carries the signature of the one original Thought, which is love. All you give is love. All you receive is love. The rest is masks, symbols and placeholders. So, gird your loins to accept with joy when it is time to accept and to give with equal joy when it is time to give and know that what you give, you give to yourself and what you receive is what you have given away. All is balanced in the one infinite Moment which is all that there is in reality.

Because this instrument has somewhat low energy due to inconveniences of the physical type, we would at this time terminate this part of the working and request perhaps two or three short queries, that the energy not drop too low. We thank this instrument as we leave it in love and in light. We are those of Q'uo.

(Jim channeling)

I am Q'uo, and greet each again in love and in light through this instrument. We would at this time offer ourselves for those queries that may be present upon your minds. May we begin with a query?

Carla: I would like to ask if you have any advice to give me as I go into a mode which is not my natural mode, for I don't want to use my right hand for absolutely anything. I'm having real problems with that.

I am Q'uo, and am aware of your query, my sister. The choice which you have made to have the surgical procedure upon the right hand is one which has the hoped-for result of aiding the further functioning of this appendage and it is quite understandable that the desire to serve and to function as a servant would continue even though the hand would be incapacitated and wisdom lies on the side of its rest rather than any use. So, our first suggestion is that you see yourself and your response as one of normalcy.

Secondly, we would suggest that you provide for yourself a reminder that this hand is to remain inactive. Perhaps you could carry a pencil in this hand and let that pencil remind you upon any attempted use of this appendage that it is to remain at rest. Any reminder would be helpful; one that you carry with you continually would be most helpful.

Is there any further query?

Carla: *(Inaudible).*

We are Q'uo, and we again thank you, my sister. Is there another query at this time?

Questioner: I just noticed that you sound a little different today. The image that came to me usually feels like a brother or sister in the circle and today it was more like an old, kind uncle sitting next to the fireplace with kids around it, with a beard, speaking, and I wonder if it is my perception or it there is some different energy mixed into it.

I am Q'uo, and am aware of your query, my brother. We of Q'uo offer our vibrations as a blending of your own, so that each in the circle adds to that which is the shared vibration of our work as all entities change and move. As their own seasons change and move there is a blend between us that, though familiar from session to session, also has alternating characteristics, if you will, so that that which we experience is a function of the totality of ourselves. This being, as all beings, changes and grows according to its own rhythms. There are times when each within the circle is perhaps more sensitive to these changes, to the basic nature of the sharing that we undertake, each with the other at these workings.

Thus, the experience of this session of working is likened to a microcosmic view of that which is the larger experience of the incarnation. Each incarnation has its own rhythms and is affected by all that one experiences. Each entity will have the opportunity to open itself to new experiences of itself experiencing all experience. Thus, upon the river of consciousness each of us ride and share that which is uniquely ours to give and to receive that which is uniquely another's. We are always honored to partake in this sharing.

Is there a final query at this time?

Questioner: I have expressed to the members of this circle of seeking how I feel that this is an entirely new life, my coming up here and the way I feel within myself and what I experience, etc. I feel that I have been given a great gift, if you will, almost as if I'm starting all over in thinking. And I was wondering if you'd care to comment on that or if you have any advice?

I am Q'uo, and am aware of your query, my brother. It is said among your peoples that each day is a new beginning. And indeed this is so, yet some beginnings are larger than others, for as we spoke previously, each entity has cycles and seasons of growth, of harvest, of quiet time, of renewal, of beginning again this great cycle of experiencing the one Creator in many forms and yet seeing how all dissolves to one concept or quality called love.

As you begin this, which for you has been an obvious new beginning, our only suggestion is the suggestion which we would make to all entities at all times—that is to give praise and thanksgiving, for that which is all seasons and all cycles, all experience, whether that which you call good or that which you call bad, difficult or easy, happy or sad, will pass away. And yet all will dissolve into this quality of love. And it is this unifying energy of love which seeks to express itself at all times and in all guises.

Thus, for one who begins a new journey, there is love. For one who ends a long journey, there is love. For one who feels confusion in the midst of what seems like a difficult journey, there is love. To be able to accept that which is in one's incarnation at the time of the experience is love revealed.

May we speak in any further way, my brother?

Questioner: *(Inaudible).*

I am Q'uo, and we are most honored and filled with joy at the opportunity of [talking] with you and welcoming you in this circle of seeking, for we are always glad to welcome what may seem to be a new friend and yet what may be an old friend to our common circle of seeking.

At this time we will take our leave of this group and of this instrument, for we do not wish to overextend the one known as Carla, leaving each, as always, in the love and in the light of the one infinite Creator. We are known to you as those of Q'uo. Adonai, my friends. Adonai. ✧

L/L Research

L/L Research is a subsidiary of Rock Creek Research & Development Laboratories, Inc.

P.O. Box 5195
Louisville, KY 40255-0195

www.llresearch.org

Rock Creek is a non-profit corporation dedicated to discovering and sharing information which may aid in the spiritual evolution of humankind.

ABOUT THE CONTENTS OF THIS TRANSCRIPT: This telepathic channeling has been taken from transcriptions of the weekly study and meditation meetings of the Rock Creek Research & Development Laboratories and L/L Research. It is offered in the hope that it may be useful to you. As the Confederation entities always make a point of saying, please use your discrimination and judgment in assessing this material. If something rings true to you, fine. If something does not resonate, please leave it behind, for neither we nor those of the Confederation would wish to be a stumbling block for any.

CAVEAT: This transcript is being published by L/L Research in a not yet final form. It has, however, been edited and any obvious errors have been corrected. When it is in a final form, this caveat will be removed.

© 2009 L/L RESEARCH

Sunday Meditation
February 11, 1996

Group question: We have a two part question. First, why Hatonn has been overshadowing our group and why Carla felt the need to challenge Hatonn a few sessions ago, and, secondly, could you give us the principle why the seniority of incarnation by vibration is in effect? It rewards those who have done spiritual work successfully but makes it more difficult for those who have not been successful. Even that which they have is taken away, and the lessons become more difficult. If you can't do the first set of lessons well then it seems unlikely that more difficult lessons will be done well either. When we feel eager to grow and yet there are restrictions around us does that mean blockages from other lives or is that the nature of this illusion to have restrictions around one even when ready and eager to grow?

(Carla channeling)

We are those of the principle of Q'uo. We greet you in the love and in the light of the one infinite Creator. It is a privilege and a blessing, as always, to move among the harmonizing energies of your circle and to share with you in the desire to seek the truth. We happily share our opinions with you with the one request that each keep the powers of personal discrimination sharp and allow only those of our thoughts which find an answering recognition in your hearts to stay with you and to allow the rest to float away on the wind.

We shall deal with these several questions in part separately. We shall speak concerning the instrument's question about those known to you as Hatonn. The principle which speaks through this instrument, as each knows, is a created collaboration between those of the social memory complex known to you as Ra and that known to you as Latwii. This combined fifth and sixth-density vibration was that which was called to your group at the time of this instrument's reception of our signal. However, as the one known as B made a decision to establish the residence in order to be a part of this group, week by week, there was a call for the compassion and loving attention which the ones of Hatonn so beautifully personify.

This is the adjusted balance which we feel shall be the appropriate mixing of information and that which you have no real word for in your language that we can find but that this instrument would call the emotional tone. The call for the one known as Hatonn had been such that it was always, shall we say, aware of these transmissions, for it has a long established contact with this group. However, we have been pleased with the way the new blending of energies matches the call of your particular group as it is made up at this time. The portion of this collaboration which speaks through this instrument is the voice of Latwii. However, both those of Hatonn and those of Ra are able to share in the process of creating that which we offer this instrument.

The perception that this instrument has had of the ones known as Hatonn is, in our opinion, a sign of this instrument's fastidiousness. We are pleased that this instrument is careful and does challenge those energies and essences which she perceives, whether or not she grasps the reason for their approaching your circle of seeking. We would commend this instrument for its care in attempting to retain a precise tuning. This is greatly appreciated by us.

This instrument requests that we move on to the other topics at this time and so we shall. The subject of seniority by vibration is a concept which is easily misperceived by one who is attempting to think upon it in a logical manner. This is due to the improper emphasis which your culture places upon the direction of catalytic energy. The principle of seniority of incarnation by vibration is simply that as an entity takes hold of those gifts, talents and resources with which it entered the incarnational experience and works to maximize the giving of those gifts through the manner of living the efforts and intentions to serve and to offer the perceived gifts as fully as possible, it creates a rhythm of learning, changing, consolidating and preparing for more learning. This cycle, once perceived by an entity, can be cooperated with by that entity, thereby doubling and redoubling the polarity of the incarnational experience and the efficiency of processing the catalyst received.

This process has virtually nothing to do with the Earthly values. That is, the lessons given for which the gifts are prepared are lessons in loving, in becoming more able to accept love, in the patience that is love's steely center, and so forth. These are Earthly gifts but in spiritual terms they move towards the metaphysical processes of spiritual evolution so that the entity which gazes at the world scene and attempts to make sense of the gifts that it has been given with regard to the world scene will surely be confused and stymied, for those things which are accomplished in the career, the working of the daily job, and so forth, are those actions which take place upon the surface of the illusion, whereas the spiritual work is being done through these everyday experiences but tending towards the building not of a worldly success but of the what the one known as B called the discipline of the personality.

So, one who has gained seniority by vibration is one who has taken those gifts that it was given and has attempted wholeheartedly to use them in order to work upon those inner lessons of love, patience, mercy and compassion. These are the actual riches to be gleaned from the Earthly illusion. The purifying of emotion, the cleansing of the processes of perception—these are the work that tends towards seniority by vibration. These gifts may seem to express in many manifestations, many fruits of labor, many accomplishments, yet the actual vibration of the entity experiencing these processes is the thing at question.

For instance, the one known as B pointed out that while inwardly this entity is experiencing a fairly rapid expansion of the array of tools consciously realized and recognized, its outer experience has been one of needing to be the youngest, the least experienced, and so forth. In Earthly terms the atmosphere of work conducted under these restrictions seems completely against the rhythm of the expansion of consciousness and yet it is in working with the guise of humility while remaining able to keep the expanded viewpoint that shall make a difference in the entity's vibration, not any success of an outer nature [that] could change that vibration, but rather the work done while the outer illusion dances merrily by. This is the heart of the work.

So, gazing upon the outer circumstances and making judgments is guaranteed to be an exercise in folly, metaphysically speaking, for the illusion is designed specifically to confuse and trap the intellect in such a way that eventually it must give up the attempt to make sense of the illusion.

We are aware that this group is desirous of serving to the very, very best of its capacity and we feel that this is the intention to be encouraged, that the attempt personally and the attempt as a group to share in love and service is the heart of that which shall indeed speed the processes of the spiritual evolution of each. For when there is the group that gathers together there is the additional energy generated by the combination of the entities which, as each in this group is already aware, is an energy that is doubled and redoubled far beyond simply the addition of one entity to another.

We are pleased with this group that offers itself in service at this time in terms of its sincere and honest attempt to be the best it can be. We can assure each that the world scene offers a story that has its most helpful points fairly well hidden in the folds of many and various details. It is almost impossible to dwell within the dream and know what lies beyond that dream. This is your situation at this time. This is not a situation we encourage you to escape. This is your appropriate position, not to know or to understand why destiny has offered this lesson or that but rather to gaze at that moment that is the present and to look with complete attention at the wonder, the depth, the infinity of that moment. Love lies within each and every moment of this infinite creation. If the seeking soul can keep its eyes upon that love, if the fainting heart and the overtired brain can remember that love, then the work which will encourage seniority is being done to the best of your capacity.

We encourage each to love, respect and enjoy the dream life that is the incarnation in the shadow world of Earthly life, yet not to expect it necessarily to make sense. We suggest that each not be fooled by what the world view may think in terms of the station you hold in life or what is actually going on. We encourage instead that living desire to seek, to love, to serve. Taste the keenness of hope. Rest in the fullness of faith, and keep the eyes upon the goal, and that goal is the realization of love.

We would at this time continue this transmission through the one known as Jim. We leave this instrument with thanks in the love and the light. We are Q'uo.

(Jim channeling)

I am Q'uo, and greet each again in love and in light through this instrument. At this time, as is our custom with this group, we would offer ourselves to those who may yet have a query for us. Is there a query at this time?

Carla: At the meeting last week I experienced great flows of energy which just [went] storming up my spine and falling like cascades of water off my head, my fingers and toes. It went on for most of the night and it was delightful. I couldn't actually do anything with it, and I felt it was coming from B. I feel better when he is around. Could you say anything about it? Is there something you can say as to why it occurs? How can we offer it in a balanced way?

I am Q'uo, and am aware of your query, my sister. We have some difficulty in speaking directly to this query, for there is the experience which is unusual that has a significance for the growth of at least one entity within this circle of seeking. The experience of the energy moving through your physical vehicle is the experience that has been made available both by the receptivity of your vehicle, its ability to respond to the desire you have shown for a new beginning, and the energies in this circle that have been opened to you through this desire.

There has been the choice upon your part to restrict certain activities and to adopt a new attitude. You, by this choice, have made available the opportunity for assistance, shall we say, from in your estimation any source which offers itself in service. Thus, the one known as B has been available for adding his own energies to this circle of seeking by his own choice and through this mutual making of choices has come the opportunity for each to be available for the further energizing of this group's seeking in these meditations, each choosing to give and receive that which is most appropriate for each at this time.

We find that beyond this point of our speaking lies information which must at this time remain unspoken due to our desire to maintain the free will of all.

Is there any further query to which we may speak, my sister?

Carla: Yes. I'll ask Aaron about previous lifetimes and I imagine that he will be glad to speak about that. I had some feelings that I probably, if this was a balanced energy exchange, then B was probably getting energy also but it was of a different type and this was probably the inspirational kind of energy—or "new motherboard," as he called it—being set up. Am I thinking along balanced lines here?

I am Q'uo, and am aware of your query, my sister. As we spoke previously there is interesting information available which is of somewhat the nature you have mentioned and does include the feeling of the one known as B that there is a new foundation, shall we say, upon which to build the remaining incarnation and this new beginning has aided in your own energizing as well. Beyond this point we find a difficulty in speaking further for the aforementioned reasons.

Carla: Yes, let me ask in a slightly different way and see if I can get an answer. Are we doing everything that we can to offer this energy clearly and in a balanced manner?

I am Q'uo, and am aware of your query, my sister. We feel that you have been most conscientious in attempting to balance and use these newfound energies, and will find further refinements available.

Is there any further query, my sister?

Carla: No, I am done. Thank you very much.

I am Q'uo, and again we thank you, my sister. Is there another query at this time?

B: I am curious about Hatonn's calling to this particular group. I am curious as to the origination of the call. Was it a call resulting from the blending of the energies of this particular group?

I am Q'uo, and am aware of your query, my brother. The call was the addition of your presence to this circle in a more, shall we say, stabilized manner. It is those of Hatonn's estimation that the compassion that they have to offer by their very nature is a quality which would be helpful to your own beingness. Thus, they have responded with their presence.

Is there any further query, my brother?

B: No, not at this time. Thank you.

I am Q'uo, and we thank you, my brother. Is there another query?

R: Was it the same when I joined the circle? I am curious.

I am Q'uo, and am aware of your query, my brother. It is the case, my brother, that when entities who seek the ability to give and receive that quality of love that is most closely aligned with compassion that the entities of Hatonn respond, for it is their hallmark that is able to meet most sufficiently the desire of a new member to feel the inspiration and the compassion together in the kind and quality of messages offered by Confederation contacts in this group, this call which was indeed offered by your presence in this circle some time previously and which those of Hatonn were happy to offer.

Is there a further query, my brother?

R: No. Thank you. I greet the brothers and sisters of Hatonn.

I am Q'uo, and we thank you as well, my brother. Is there another query at this time?

(Side one of tape ends.)

B: *(Question not recorded.)*

I am Q'uo, and we are gratified, my brother, that you have found a home within this circle of seeking, for we and those of Hatonn value beyond measure each entity which chooses to work in a conscious fashion in a group such as this one, for it is by such combined efforts that each progresses most rapidly in the gaining of the service-to-others polarity. Thus, we join you in the feeling of gratitude.

Is there any further query at this time?

B: No, not from me. Thank you.

I am Q'uo. In closing, then, we would thank each entity present for blending their vibrations into this circle of seeking, for the energies of each present, though at this circle somewhat lower than usual, are yet a glorious sight to behold from our point of view. Such energies may be seen for their variety, their intensity and their brilliance.

At this time we shall take our leave of this instrument and this group, leaving each, as always, in the love and the light of the one infinite Creator. We are known to you as those of Q'uo. Adonai, my friends. Adonai. ✣

L/L Research

Sunday Meditation
February 18, 1996

Group question: Concerns red-ray energy transfers and how they are accomplished, whether by sexual energy transfer or just by being in people's presence. Does it differ from second to third density? What would the lack or abundance of red-ray energy look like in a person?

(Carla channeling)

We are those of Q'uo. We greet you in the love and in the light of the one infinite Creator in whom there is no variation or shadow. We thank you for calling us to speak with you this afternoon, for it is indeed a great privilege for us to join this circle of seekers of truth. We, too, are seekers of truth, and yet we do not have the final answers ourselves, so as always, we ask that each listen and take from those things which we say only those ideas and conceptions that ring true for you personally, for we would not want to put a stumbling block in your way. We wish only to aid. Please know that you are aiding us, for allowing us to perform this service for you is great generosity on your part. We have only one reason to be here, and you are allowing us to further that hope of ours to lend what aid we can to those upon your sphere at this time who seek those lessons of love which lie beyond the present Earth world.

You have elected this day to focus upon a very, literally, basic portion of the energy distortions which form the structure of your mind/body/spirit complex, as this instrument would call it—those rays that feed and inform the physical bodies, the mental bodies, the emotional bodies, and the spiritual. And so let us look at that first incoming port of call within your personal energy field, for there is a field about that entity which is you.

It is the kind of field that holds together. If you see it on the top of a liquid you would call this field a meniscus. It is that which holds the surface and allows it to form a shape. Such are the complex of fields that contain your consciousness and allow it to manifest within that world of shadows in which you live at this time. The energy which is received by the physical body is infinite and perfect and without distortion. It moves into the body, rushing in from the earth, from the air, from the sky, in through the feet and at the root of the spine. And the welcome that it finds at that base chakra or energy center at the root of the spine places the limit upon the energy that can be transformed as it moves through the remaining energy centers of your body, your mind and your spirit.

When entities wish to think about what you have called red ray it is natural that the consideration tends towards that of identifying red-ray energy with sexual energy. And certainly sexual energy is a manifestation of red-ray energy, just as the functions of the parasympathetic nervous system are functions of red-ray energy. As you have suspected there is a scope, a range of ways that the pure base chakra energy may be distorted, and the sexual expression is only one of those ways.

Perhaps the most skillful expression of strong red-ray energy is the allowing of the self to rejoice in the feeling of health and life, to feel the vivid energy of the blood moving through the physical body, of the organs doing their balanced working, and of the nervous system opening and relaxing and turning towards the light of the physical world or that world of entities in which the expression of light, perhaps the lamp in the window or the smile that lights up the face, can express, for the red ray is in its pure form the energy that created all things, moving in its first expression into the individual splinter of the love and the light of the one infinite Creator that is each of you.

Certainly the expression of red-ray energy in sexual activity is an appropriate and helpful expenditure of this valuable energy and the transfer of energy which can be exchanged in the sexual act does create what this instrument would call the Holy Eucharist of this energy, that expression of unified praise and thanksgiving that in uniting two bodies unites also the adoration of the one infinite Creator and becomes a hymn of praise. And yet, as this instrument has suspected for some time, because of its own experiences at receiving such energy from others, it is entirely possible and natural and certainly helpful when entities which have good polarity meet to allow the free exchange of red-ray energy.

Depending upon the polarities involved, one entity in such an energy exchange is able to fall into an open circuit which allows the two entities who are polarized to circulate the shared energy back and forth, around and around. In this expression one of the polarities will be sharing physical energy. The other will be sharing its excess of spiritual/emotional energy. Although it is most often true that the biological female will share the emotional and spiritual energies whereas the male will share its excess of physical energy, this is not always the polarity which two entities will discover, for many biological males have the excess of spiritual energy. Many biological females have an excess of physical energy.

When two females or two males find the energy exchange opening to link their fields, one will have the polarity of the opposite sex. This does not mean that the biological male is actually a female if it has spiritual rather than physical distortions of excess energy. It simply means that each entity, whether biologically male or female is both, has been both, many times, and contains within the self the entire range of expressions, emotions and feelings. So there is not a state of complete blindness which separates the two kinds of energies which are transferred, but rather there is the great desire of the everyday culture to keep things simple, and to that world view which expresses within your people's culture, the man is the man and the woman is the woman, and the two natures are irretrievably opposite.

It is our opinion that this is an immensely overstated truth. There is the tendency, rather, for the sexual biases to be as the culture thinks them. The truth is that each has all of the available distortions within a vast memory that lies deep within the mind complex, and within this deep memory lie recollections of being many, many things, many plants, many animals, many minerals, elements and states, for this protean, plastic, endlessly reforming material that houses the energy that is consciousness is that which, like the various parts of the sea, may seem to split into this wave and that, this bubble and that froth, and yet it is all one. It is all the one water, and there is in truth no differentiation, and yet you have come out of that sea of consciousness. You have dressed yourself in a body of flesh and you have deliberately come into the land of the shadows, there to face the choices that a person of energy can make, for this energy comes to each as a gift of the one infinite Creator.

The energy that gives life is also the energy that can limit and kill. It is up to each individual so to mold the thinking and the attitude and the processes of perception that this perfect, precious, infinite energy may flow through all the energy centers unimpeded, unforced, spiraling upward naturally and back to the infinite Creator as it leaves the physical top of the body, the head, the face, and the fingers.

In order to best allow the free passage of energy through the red ray it is well to sit with the self and contemplate to one's satisfaction what it is to have life, what it is to have the beating heart, and the in-taken breath. What it is to be caught between the Creator and nothingness, what it is to have the eyes open upon the present moment. That gift of life, if perceived for one instant as the infinite gift that it is is stunning, breathtaking, miraculous, unbelievable. And yet it is yours, each one of you. This energy, this indrawn breath, this moment in space and time to form as you will, to express just as you choose to do.

As you contemplate this energy of life know that it is but a shadow of something that is within each of you that is even closer to the Creator than the light that you welcome into your energy field. For light is a manifested thing, yet that which lies closer than your breathing, nearer than your hands, is that which you are: the great original Thought of Love. One may identify with the body, or one may identify with the consciousness that is the one infinite Creator. And depending upon whether the person identifies itself as body or as consciousness much may be affected. We encourage each of you, while loving the body, to see it as the shadow of the true self, that true self that took this second-density physical vehicle to be its home within the Earth world, that consciousness that shall drop the garment of the body, lovingly, gently and with thanks when it is time to move on through the door of death.

You are love, and you have chosen to come into the builded universe, that land of light and dark, and to enter into a vast round of experience, from the primeval blackness through the dim forms of earth and fire, through all the ways of the life stream moving through vegetable and animal and now you stand at the threshold of self-knowledge, self-awareness, self-consciousness. And it is your precious task to take these gifts that you have been given and to offer them back up to the infinite Creator with as much increase of love and service, compassion and caring, as you can. The second-density red ray which is the environment which your body enjoys selects those entities which may aid it in promulgating the species and in creating a safe place in which to bring up young. The third-density red-ray energy adds to that the energies of self-conscious love which opens this energy up to embrace all, male and female, which takes that red ray and chooses to allow it to flow naturally, not only in the act of sex but in the act of living.

Perhaps a good model for this would be the boomerang. As you release this energy of selfhood, this energy of basic health, as this instrument would call it, there is the comfortable confidence that this energy shall return with gifts in its arms from a universe which has all the polarities possible within it. Any two entities may share third-density red-ray energy to the extent of their dynamic. It will always be that certain pairs of entities will happen to have particularly good dynamics and thus will experience a more remarkable stream of energy transfer. But the open sharing of this energy with all is certainly that which aids the red ray in the remaining open, powerful and pure, thus ensuring that the maximum amount of energy moves through red ray and into the next.

We find this to be a good stopping place and would continue this transmission through the one known as Jim. We are those of Q'uo, and we thank this instrument as we leave it in light and love. We are those of Q'uo.

(Jim channeling)

I am Q'uo, and I greet you once again through this instrument. At this time it is our privilege to ask if we may speak to further queries which those present may have for us. Is there another query at this time?

K: You mentioned that we are on the threshold of self-consciousness. As third-density people is it true that we are only on the threshold of self-consciousness and have not attained it? What is your concept of self-consciousness that we have yet to attain?

I am Q'uo, and am aware of your query, my brother. The self-consciousness of which we spoke is that consciousness of the greater self which may be likened unto the higher self, revealing itself in stages, shall we say. This is that kind of compassion which includes the universe about one and not just those other selves which are in close proximity or in an interactive relationship with the self. The self-consciousness of which third-density entities are so proud is that self-consciousness which each feels as an individualized portion of the one Creator. That is the great achievement of this density's work: to give the individualization a chance to work its transformative ways upon the consciousness of the second density which has much in common with that greater awareness whose threshold you now begin to pass through, for each is partaking of the great consciousness of all that is—the second-density entity moving from it into an individualized awareness available in third density, the third-density entity moving from this individualized awareness into a consciousness which partakes more of the one Creator once again, yet does so in an informed manner, one which has chosen for itself the path to this threshold.

Is there a further query, my brother?

K: The energy that you spoke of coming through the feet and the red-ray chakra, is this light energy or another kind of energy? If it is light energy, how is it changed from the light that we know so that it may enter the chakra and the consciousness that is enclosed in the plastic matter that you mentioned. Is there a relationship between the energy that enters the chakra and this consciousness that is the soul?

I am Q'uo, and believe that we are aware of your query, my brother. The energy which enters the feet and base of the spine is an intelligent kind of energy that is most likened to what you would call love, that creative energy which enlivens all creation. It is the enlivener, the energizer, and is the daily gift of the Logos to all within its care. A kind of manna, shall we say, which each entity will use in an individualized fashion. This is a tool of the soul, as you have called it. The soul essence of each entity is that focus of consciousness which exists from time immemorial and moves into the evolutionary process as a portion of the one Creator. It utilizes the various densities and incarnations within each density to achieve certain levels of awareness and expressions of energy within them.

Thus, the intelligent energy or prana of the Logos is that which propels the creation. The soul is that portion of consciousness which can use this universal energy for personal evolution.

Is there a further query, my brother?

K: Does this love energy come from the sun as a Logos or from the one infinite Creator as Logos?

I am Q'uo, and am aware of your query, my brother. It comes from the One as does all come from the One, for there is only the one infinite Creator. This infinite, universal, cosmic mind of the one Creator is refined and varied in infinite ways by each Logos as means by which to glorify the one Creator and give It the opportunity to know Itself that would not be present without the individual refinements by each Logos to this cosmic mind or energy.

Is there a further query, my brother?

K: How is the harvest brought about as a mechanism? What determines the time for the harvest to occur? Does the harvest depend on a certain point of the zodiac transiting the center of the galaxy and, if so, what is the exact mechanism by which that harvest takes place?

I am Q'uo, and am aware of your query, my brother, though perhaps somewhat less able to express it in the precise terms which you request, for though such precision would be possible with other instruments we must content ourselves with the general statement that there is a clock-like mechanism, indeed, that is the cause, shall we say, for the harvest to occur as it does. For each energy focus, be it planetary, be it that of the Logos or any entity which exists as an individualized portion of the one Creator, will move in a spiraling fashion towards the light and the love of the one Creator. This movement is a progression of increasing awareness and expression of this awareness by the entities undertaking this process.

For those within your third-density illusion, the planetary progress, as this sphere which you call Earth moves through its own unfolding and position in the cosmic web of creation, will have those times during which the entities upon its surface and within its care will have the opportunity to demonstrate the level of apprehension of the unity of all things. Within this illusion the lessons of love and the ability to open the green-ray energy center to the experience about one and the identity, indeed, of oneself is the kind of energy expression that will find the opportunity to be harvested at regular intervals that are determined, as we stated, in a general fashion by this planet's own progress and position and will be offered as well as each entity is able to become more consciously aware of the evolutionary process. So, for the entity which has been more successful in untangling the illusory nature of its own existence in this third density there is always the opportunity to harvest the self at any point within this density's progress. Such entities are most likely, in the positive polarity, to remain with the planetary sphere until all of those of its kind are also harvestable …

(Side one of tape ends.)

(Jim channeling)

I am Q'uo, and am once again with this instrument. Is there another query at this time?

K: I have one more. What is the nature of the fifth-density body that can be materialized into our third-density illusion? Does it have any physical substance to it? Or is it a manipulation of light in some way?

I am Q'uo, and am aware of your query, my brother. Though there are few instruments within your third-density illusion that could measure any physical qualities of the light body of fifth density there would be, to the most sensitive, some small register of that which could be called matter, or could be called energy within a field.

However, the light body is indeed constructed of that which is light and can be manipulated in any fashion that an entity of fifth density or above desires, for it is the ability of light to be formed in such and such a fashion that allows the creation to exist, and as an entity moves into more and more harmony with the unity of all creation there comes the ability to be co-Creator and to move into the light, and become the light, and form the light as the will directs.

Is there a further query, my brother?

K: The light from the being in fifth density could be changed into physical matter here in third density so that we could see the entity?

I am Q'uo, and am aware of your query, my brother. This is correct, although the matter formed would not be that which could be expected to exist for a lengthy portion of your time measurement, for the focus necessary to maintain the third-density illusion of matter is one which is quite concentrated and requires a certain grounding and dedication to this density which entities of fifth density or above would not have as their native makeup, as their illusion at this time is of a much finer quality.

Is there a further query, my brother?

K: Thank you.

I am Q'uo, and we thank you again, my brother. Is there another query at this time?

Carla: I would like to ask three things. What was going on when last week I first got energy from B? It spilled over and B said he would just send it around the circle. What was that? After that I seemed to have good energy when B was around. It didn't build up and I didn't feel extra energy around. Third, is there something about my vital energy that makes me able to use pure red-ray energy better than most people?

I am Q'uo, and am aware of your query, my sister. The one known as B has a natural ability, the nature of which he is beginning to discover. The discovering of this nature allowed the modifying of the experience. The connection between your spiritual expression of red-ray energy is that which enhances your ability to receive that which the one known as B is beginning to understand how to modify.

Is there another query?

Carla: No, thank you.

I am Q'uo, and again we thank you, my sister. Is there another query?

B: I was wondering if there is a difference between a second-density yellow-ray expression and a third-density yellow-ray expression?

I am Q'uo, and am aware of your query, my brother. There is a range of expression for each of the rays or centers of energy. For the second density to express the beginning grasp of yellow ray is to become enough individualized that the entity can give and receive that quality known as love. A primary example of such would be the pets which many within this culture enjoy, each pet becoming more individualized with the loving care of the third-density entity.

The third-density expression of the yellow-ray energy, taken to the more advanced end of the scale, would see entities working harmoniously with each other in the groupings of the daily round of activities, each moving into more and more harmony, compassion and understanding of those with whom the illusion is shared, this done in a more and more conscious fashion.

Is there a further query, my brother?

B: Not at this time.

Carla: Would the second-density animal finding its place in the pecking order be an example of second-density yellow ray, or is that part of third density?

I am Q'uo, and am aware of your query, my sister. There are many expressions of energy and behavior patterns within the second-density illusion which may be seen as being of the orange rays expression even though the observer within third density can see great similarities between those actions which you mentioned and the third-density experience which sees entities doing much the same under similar circumstances. Yet, within each illusion there is also the undergirding quality of the experience that shades it towards the orange ray for the second-density creature and the yellow ray for the third-density entity, even though there may be instances within the second-density illusion where second-density entities may indeed be demonstrating more behavior toward the yellow-ray spectrum within their orange-ray environment. This is the natural progression of the second density towards third so that at most times in the evolution of second-density entities there is the preponderance of orange-ray activity with the movement toward the yellow ray of individualized behavior.

Is there another query, my sister?

Carla: No. Thank you.

I am Q'uo, and we thank you again, my sister. Is there another query at this time?

(Pause)

I am Q'uo, and as it appears that we have evolved in this session to a lack of queries we shall thank each for walking with us for these few brief moments this day. It has been, as it always is, our great privilege and pleasure to be with you and to be allowed to speak our thoughts through these instruments. We hope that you will always remember to take only those thoughts which have value for you and leave all others behind. We are known to you as those of Q'uo, and we would leave this instrument and this group at this time. Adonai, my friends. Adonai. ✦

Sunday Meditation
March 3, 1996

Group question: Today we will have a session of questions and answers from those in the circle.

(Carla channeling)

We are those of the principle known to you as Q'uo. Greetings in the love and in the light of the one infinite Creator. It is a vast pleasure and a doughty privilege to share in this circle of seeking and to share our thoughts with you at this time. We thank each of you for coming together to seek truth and we only hope that our thoughts may prove to be a resource that has a way of being helpful. If there are thoughts that we share that do not seem valuable at this time we do ask that you leave them behind and do not take them with you to worry them over as though you should believe or think in the ways that we offer, for this is not our grasp of our relationship with you. We do not see ourselves as being wiser than those within third density but merely in a somewhat different illusion, and, therefore, in somewhat different circumstances. Yet we, as you, seek to know and yet do not know. We simply have come to hold fairly settled opinions, and as is the way of things spiritual our truths move constantly into the unknown, as do your own. Thusly, there is always the contradiction, the tangle, the knot of attempting to understand that which can only be embodied.

As this is a question and answer session, we will save our philosophizing for the queries themselves and would ask at this time if there is a beginning question?

B: Yes. I have noticed recently and periodically throughout my life that I have been absolutely full of energy and there is a floating in and out of a semi-lucid state wherein in my daily activities I am going through the motions but my consciousness is in a different state of mind, if you will. Can you comment on this experience in terms of what its nature is to myself and to seekers in general?

We are Q'uo, and would be glad to comment upon this thoughtful question. There are ways in which we must avoid speaking in order to preserve for you the free will of your own learning. However, we may comment upon two phenomena which often occur when those who work metaphysically make contact with new people who are the so-called birds of a feather that flock together, as this instrument would say.

The first phenomenon is that of the energizing by situation; that is, when a seeker moves into an environment in which it perceives spiritual power, that perceived power functions not only as a blessing of a place but can also set up resonance within the individual seeking so that which energizes the location energizes also those within that location.

This is quite common to those of your people as they begin what this instrument would call the conversion or the beginning of new fundamental concepts used to enhance the personal spiritual journey.

The second phenomenon which is also fairly common is that of the awakening of and flow of energy which is energized by contact with entities with which one has a particularly good dynamic. The energizing, for instance, of this instrument about which we spoke at another of your workings occurred immediately within this instrument when it opened to the energy of the group. It is not always so that the energy which moves from one to another is successful in moving circularly from that other back to the original sender which creates the open circuit between two such individuals. When the level of dynamic is sufficient this phenomenon continues to occur; that is, the circuit continues to be open. As long as this circulation or mutual transfer of energy is found to be a useful tool or resource each for the other, then the experience of feeling the energizing is well. If such a feeling seems to be too intense to be useful then there is simply the matter of moving back into the meditative state and asking within that state for the higher self or the guidance that you may think of as your own to adjust and stabilize such energy flow. It is not the place of this energy to lead the seeker, but rather it is the seeker's place to accept and to attempt to regularize those energies which are incoming.

May we answer further, my brother?

B: That was very enlightening. Thank you. Related to this I have noted prior to today that when we offer a group question you respond in the framework of those gathered. The thoughts seem to be specifically fashioned to include the personal experiences that we have shared as a group. Is there a reason that you respond in this way, if my observation is correct? Is the preservation of free will related to this?

We are those of Q'uo and believe that we grasp your query. That which we give this instrument is given based upon that which lies deeper than words within the group or circle that is asking the question. That is, when there is a group question it is our hope to be able to, for want of a better term, understand that question with as many nuances and layers of depth as resides not only in the words of the question but also within those complexes of thought which each present proceeded through in order to arrive at just that query.

Thusly, we are responding to emotional/mental configurations of energy and this colors, shall we say, the bare words the instrument offers as it processes the concepts received. There is further coloration as to the specific individuals within the group due to the instrument's own mind complex which she plunders in order to, as she would say, nail together the structure of words which she uses to contain the concepts which we offer, for we do not offer words usually. Most usually we offer concepts and these concepts are then clothed in words which the instrument chooses. The instrument thusly may use examples from its own experiences or thoughts which have been flowing through the mind prior to the contact. On these two levels the distortion increases from universal wisdom to that which is received from a particular essence or source through a particular instrument at a particular nexus in space and time.

May we answer you further, my brother?

B: Thank you. Two weeks ago in one of these sessions as you responded to the query you responded very specifically to a question that had been on my mind which had to do with Hatonn's presence in the group responding to a call from the group. My thoughts had to do with feeling gratitude and wishing to offer service in return to Hatonn but I did not verbalize that question, but you responded to it anyway. The only reason that I ask is that I am becoming aware of my gifts which I seem to have; that is, thoughts having power such as wishing to send energy to Carla and it occurred. I ask that question because I would like to become aware of this gift so I might be more responsible with it. Could you comment, please?

We are those of Q'uo, and we fear that we have missed the thrust of your query. Could you restate its essence quickly, my brother?

B: Were you aware of the question that I did not speak, and, if so, how were you aware of it?

We are those of Q'uo, and grasp your query at this time. We thank you for being patient with us. As we said before, what we respond to is not just those words which are brought to meetings such as this one but also those things which are upon the mind, spoken or unspoken. It is not that we read the mind, for the mind is not a book, but rather that we sense the gradations of desire and when desire has a vector we can sense that which it aims at, shall we say.

These desires are that which we call "the call." When we thank the circle for calling us to a meeting we are speaking as those who dwell within a certain vibrational range and broadcast within a certain range. And that which we pick up is that which is aimed at our range, not that one number on a dial is more advanced or better than another, but that there is a range of possible contact that is quite broad. When a new dynamic enters a group—and this is not difficult to see in a group that numbers less than ten—that new element then creates a new summation of call, and as the one known as Bob moved into harmony with this particular group that which it blended was a desire whose coloration included that of our brothers and sisters of Hatonn so this call was heard just as a radio that was set to a certain number on the dial would pick up broadcasts from that number.

The difference between hearing the desires and emotions of the group and reading the mind is that we are able to pick up that which is of the emotion without infringement upon the privacy of one's thoughts. We do not move into the phenomena of mentation that go on within the mind and simply read them off.

Does this answer your query, my brother?

B: Yes. When I find myself in these semi-lucid states there are times that I find myself in a flow of information that deals with everything from things going on in my personal life to people around me, and in some instances to flashes of supposedly past life experiences and how they affect what is occurring today. Can you tell me what the source of this information is? Am I establishing contact with my higher self?

We are Q'uo, and believe we grasp your query, my brother. We give this instrument the picture of the starfish who reaches out and touches the sandy bottom of the sea this way and this way and this way, each tentacle or point of the starfish reaching in a different direction. The starfish may be thought to consider itself as reaching out into all parts of the universe, for it reaches in a complete circle. The consciousness that each entity carries about during each incarnative experience is that consciousness which has points that reach out in all directions on one level and then on the next, and then on the next, and then on the next, so that there are universes within universes within universes which dwell within that which you are.

Indeed, not only does the entity carry within those understandings of the incarnation with all of that depth and breadth of experience within incarnation there is also carried within memory of all that has been experienced and this memory is contained in progressively deeper and more spacious containments or structures which hold one level of information. There is the high subconscious, that which feeds the dreams and so forth, that is the easiest to touch into while at the conscious state.

The phenomena which you experience at this time is to a great extent coming from that high subconscious level. There are some who consider that there dwells within this level of mind that higher self or guidance which can move from the subconscious up through the threshold of consciousness into the living day of conscious mind. This is a process to be encouraged. Further, there are levels of mind progressively more profound and progressively more spacious in terms of the amount of light which illuminates and fills consciousness. These levels are of the lower subconscious and contain that racial history which is the consciousness of the second-density physical vehicle which supports and carries your consciousness. There are inner guides within these darker and more obscure levels of consciousness. There in the deep portions of mind exist the mind of the archetypes, and, indeed, ultimately the ground of consciousness becomes that which is and that which is is the Creator Itself.

Thusly, it is as though within the mind there lie temples whose doors are carefully guarded, and as one moves into the process of seeking the truth in a persistent and sacrificial manner one begins to trigger or put the key into some of those temple doors. It is, we feel, helpful to experience such flows of the information which lies within and to keep some record of such trains of thought when they occur. For the most part these trains of thought are subconscious material which the practices of meditation and contemplative analysis are encouraging and enhancing.

May we answer further, my brother?

B: No. Thank you for your answers and your patience with me as I attempt to ask these questions that are often hard to phrase.

We are Q'uo. My brother, we have the same difficulty with our answers and we throw ourselves upon your mercy as well.

Is there a further query at this time?

R: Greetings in the love and light. Could you restate what you said earlier about trying to learn the truth that can only be embodied in another way, and perhaps add to it?

We are Q'uo, and are glad to speak more upon this concept. There are many ways to think about the spirit, the life of the spirit, and its evolution. Because of the condition of physical incarnation it is only natural to look at any process of learning as a process of gathering facts, making inferences, proving postulates, and then using these new axioms to create further knowledge. However, the world of spirit is specifically and thoroughly non-rational. It does not build from one fact to two and from two to three. Rather, it exists and those sparks of it which are walking about differentiated by energy fields which are called bodies …

We find we have started a sentence we cannot finish through this instrument, so we shall drop back and try again.

Those who seek tend to put a great emphasis upon learning the truth. However, that which is true lies already as the heart and soul of all that depends therefrom, including the energy field which is each seeker's location or body in space and time. Thusly, one may add fact upon fact upon fact, all in the name of spiritual seeking, and become an entity whose head is filled with many, many facts. However, the journey of spirit is a journey from head to heart and that which comes from or through the consciousness of an entity in the way of the basic vibration, the basic way of perceiving, that is the clearest indication and gift of self to spirit which seekers are capable of offering.

Far more high, if you will, or exalted are the puzzled, confusing thoughts of one who loves with the whole heart than those words, however wonderful, which build an intellectual house for truth or have a central place for the heart. It is the heart that holds truth. It is the heart that can be disciplined to show those truths which now seem murky to the mind. It is the heart from which will, hope and faith journey into expression. It is the heart that gives meaning to the whole. The function of the intellect is the prosecution of that which needs to be done in order to make the physical being comfortable and happy within the world.

We do not denigrate the use of the intellect. We were simply affirming our opinion, which is that the truth embodied by the seeker is a far more whole and full truth than any words, however brilliant.

May we answer further, my brother?

R: Could you express in another way the comment to discipline the heart will show the truth that is already in there?

We are those of Q'uo, and shall attempt to do so, my brother. Picture, if you will, the color and energy of anger. Not anger at an object, but that emotion. Perhaps you might even see within a certain color—or complement of the color—this is the coloration which you as an entity at present give to a truth which is called emotion. Picture, then, that color and texture which is the shape of love, of joy, of healing, of grief, and so forth. These deep feelings, shall we call them, are truths. And they are not in their pure state either limited in any way, or of negative connotation, or positive connotation.

Much of metaphysical thought has been given to creating logical structures which explain spiritual concepts throughout the history of your peoples, and this is a universal bias in favor of that which can be seen and measured. It is difficult for entities to perceive of their own emotions as pure, and indeed they are not normally experienced purely. Normally, the experience of emotion has strong moral, mental and emotional reservations, limitations and colorations.

As the seeker grows in experience throughout the incarnation, it may choose to begin to look at that which is being experienced as it is being experienced with an eye to lessening the emotional biases which are coloring and often creating pain through that emotion, for once such coloration can be perceived by the seeker it can be grasped and gradually laid aside so that we experience, for example, grief and can move from [it] being a rending and tearing inner experience to an experience of channeling, as this instrument would say, a purer and less limited form of that emotion.

Once one takes the bars down that hold perceived emotion in one particular structure, that emotion can begin to express more purely, and as the seeker grows in self-knowledge more and more those imposed limitations can be dropped away and the deeper emotions can then be channeled through the functioning, living mechanism in less and less difficult ways and more and more deeply true ways.

May we answer further, my brother?

R: This is difficult for me to grasp. Are you saying to encourage the heart to work with each coloration of emotion to distill it to more pure and universal light of truth as you work through it, and in the process dissolve the contractions and blockages associated with it?

We are those of Q'uo, and you grasp the gist of our answer, my brother.

R: Thank you for that answer. It is very interesting. It would be great to hold hands and run from star to star and jump all over the place.

We are Q'uo, and thank you, my brother. We shall meet you as you dream and explore.

We are those of Q'uo. Is there a final query at this time?

(Pause)

We are those of Q'uo. What a thing it is, dear ones, to open the heart. What great adventures lie before each. What great puzzlement, bewilderment, as well as joy await each. We thank you once again that of all the places upon your Earth you chose to come together to share with us hope and love and the desire to know the truth. You enable us to serve and we most humbly thank you.

At this time we would take our leave of this instrument and this group, leaving each in the love and the light of that which is wonderful, the one infinite Creator, that Thought of love that created all that there is. We are those of Q'uo, and we bid you adonai. ❧

Sunday Meditation
March 10, 1996

Group question: We would like some information about the darker self, or side, of our self. What is the shadow and how should we relate to it? What is the most positive way to deal with it?

(Carla channeling)

We are those of Q'uo. Greetings in the love and in the light of the one infinite Creator. It is, as always, a great honor to be called to come among you at this time. We cannot emphasize enough how much we appreciate your kindness in asking us to share our thought with you, for by doing so you enable us to serve the infinite One, and in the garden of the Father there is always great pleasure in the budding new leaves that spring forth from thoughts of things heavenly. We are so happy to be a small part of that process for each. We do request that our information be regarded as opinion rather than fact, for we are often incorrect.

This day you wish to speak about the shadow self. Each seeker comes to a point where it decides what path it shall follow. Sometimes the choices seem shallow. Sometimes they seem profound. The choice is always between the perceived light and the perceived dark, that which is the higher road as opposed to that which seems less honorable. And in the making of these choices the seeker hopes to bring forth the light and to dismiss the dark. The hope is to become light itself, all that is good and correct and of the spirit. This is not a hope that bears fruit, for the light and dark are the two sides of one coin, that coin being the very essence of that seeker.

As the process of graduation from third density continues each shall walk the stairs of light with each its own dark side firmly integrated into that self which walks for eternity. Therefore, the paradox that is the sign of all spiritual truth is laid bare. The challenge is so to acknowledge, accept and balance the shadow self that the total being is ready to gaze into that light which blesses fourth-density existence, for you can leave not one whit of self behind. Now, how can this be done? How can that blackness within which expresses within the self in ways of hurt and pain ever be a part of the love and light of the one infinite Creator?

Each entity walks upon two legs. When the spirit finds its legs, one is the light, one is the dark. Together they make one holograph which is identical to the infinite Creator. The shadow self is to be related to, then, as one of the two legs which cause the spirit to stand within the illusion in which each finds itself. One relates to the shadow self as to the musculature, the connective tissue, the power and the strength which enable the spiritual seeker to stand fast through times of difficulty and woe. The shadow that seems so heavy and dark is also that which grounds and sustains and makes secure. The will is part of the shadow self. This will animates, informs and vivifies those ideals, hopes and dreams which the light portion of being so loves to dream. The shadow side is that which persists until all has been accomplished.

If your shadow self could be objectified, what animal would you choose to represent it? Perhaps we might suggest that to the naked eye, to the uninformed person, the dark side might be seen as a dangerous wolf, ready to savage and to tear those treasures which the seeker would protect. To the more informed eye, the dark side might perhaps have become half wolf and half dog and well-trained. That which feels like the dark side has tremendous, infinite vitality. It blesses the spiritual seeker with that night which envelopes as an eggshell does an egg, the newborn spirit, velvet, soft and black as midnight. It couches and sustains eternity and gives its gift to time by allowing the separation of light from dark. The evolution of spirit takes place within that night and as graduation dawns, so dawns that spiritual night at last.

We are aware that the demands of the physical vehicle may seem to be dark and inconvenient. The belly calls for food. Sexuality calls for the mate. The body demands to breed, and chaos threatens if these needs are not met. Then it is often that the seeker must deal with the shadow. May we suggest the taming of the wolf, the learning of discipline for the dog, and the love of master for a faithful companion and servant.

We feel that this is sufficient for the main query and since the one known as Jim is quite involved in attempting to record that which is being channeled through this instrument, [may we] ask if there are any further queries at this time?

B: I have a question with respect to a concept having to do with darkness and would ask you to comment on this. Is darkness from a positive entity's perspective simply the lack of awareness of the one infinite Creator?

We are those of Q'uo. My brother, we were using the image of darkness not as an absence of anything but rather as that fertile blackness of night wherein the spirit has its birth.

May we answer you further, my brother?

B: I am a little confused about something that you said early in the session. It had to do with pursuing or seeking the shadow as not bearing fruit. Could you please elaborate on that concept?

We are Q'uo. We were speaking of the desire to lose the darkness of the nature as not bearing fruit. We were suggesting that the seeker does not need to remove the dark side of the nature in order to progress. Rather, the seeker needs to come to an inner understanding of its particular workings, looking for ways to achieve such a discipline of the character and personality that the darker images are disciplined and allowed to move through appropriate channels. We are suggesting that once the dark nature of the will is grasped, the positively oriented seeker can then begin to see that shadow self as an asset rather than viewing it as an enemy.

The processes by which one becomes able to discipline this dark side is individual and each seeker shall wrestle with those dark angels as each continues to discover, accept and discipline new aspects or newly perceived aspects of that dark genius. We are asking each seeker, then, to take into the heart the full spectrum of self and to love each and every aspect and yet to find ways to express only those things which are intended. We do not wish you to run away from what is one of the great strengths of the self.

May we answer you further, my brother?

B: Thank you. In my present experience there are two characters on the stage with whom I interact daily. I look at them now after this last week of exploring various memories and I see blackness around them. I do not feel any ill will towards them. I simply see the blackness and know that they're there to teach as I am to teach them. I would ask for your opinion on an appropriate way to deal with these two souls.

We are those of Q'uo. My brother, we would suggest that you see each soul as the one infinite Creator.

May we answer you further, my brother?

B: No, thank you.

Is there another query?

R: I noticed that I would ask questions often as I joined this group. And now I observe that the desire to ask questions faded. And I am curious about the process. Would you comment please?

We are those of Q'uo. My brother, when one first climbs into the boat one determines to row very quickly to the opposite shore. After one has rowed the boat for a while one becomes more calm. Each stroke is no longer brand new. In time one has rowed all over the lake. Just when the scenery becomes familiar, just when the questions are beginning to be less, something occurs, some critical mass within and the seeker realizes that he has no oars, that there is no shore and that faith alone shall move the barque within which he sits. How can one ask questions of the ocean?

May we answer you further, my brother?

R: I have no further question. I will say that it is a great joy to know that you sit in that rowboat for those who ask.

We are those of Q'uo, and we thank you for your thoughts. We and you, my brother, are bubbles upon the sea.

We would at this time ask if there is a final query?

B: If there is anything that we in this circle may do that we are not already doing to assist the instrument with her current physical pain?

We are those of Q'uo. My brother, the sending of love to this instrument is already being done and there is no greater gift or help for this instrument than that. We thank you for your concern and thank each within this group for supporting this instrument.

As we take our leave of you we encourage each to feel that balance point within which holds all the illusion of light and dark in calm and peaceful equilibrium. Third density, and fourth as well, move deeply within the ways of polarity and duality. There are many lessons the dark and light alike can teach. We ask each to rest in the essential and eternal goodness of that foundation which is the one infinite Creator. Light and dark alike find their source and ending in love. Know that you are loved, and allow that truth to sink deep within. Each entity is fragile. Each life is tender. Be tender with [each] other. Share love. Share burdens. Share encouragement. And we shall take our leave of you in love, in light, in the service of the one infinite Creator. Adonai. Adonai. We are Q'uo. ✣

Sunday Meditation
March 17, 1996

Group question: This week we are going to take pot luck.

(Carla channeling)

We are those of Q'uo. We greet you in the love and in the light of the one infinite Creator. We come to you as you call us. We are most privileged to be called and we thank you very much for this service that you give us in allowing us to serve you. As always, we ask that you use your discrimination, for we are error-prone, as are you.

And yet, though we are prone to error and though each of you is prone to error, though our experience is illusion and our thoughts are those which are about the illusion, there is that which binds us together. There is that which makes us one. And that is the nature of each of us, of each of you. Many things seem apparent and *prima facie* and these generally take that which they can see and construct the structure about which you were speaking earlier, that house of life which is created by the everyday and ordinary things that, in toto, add up to an incarnation.

It is interesting that those who seek, to the point of knowing clearly and lucidly that all is an illusion still continue to process the catalyst and to be affected. It is interesting and it is valuable that the desire to understand, the desire to figure it out, creates the continuing sense of insecurity and causes us each to dig deeper, to look further, even though we know that all is illusion. Yet, do we truly know, especially do we know what our illusion, and do you know what your illusion, is? We seek to move beyond self, yet we have not moved beyond self, and this is your situation. The thought of moving on to higher densities is that there will be a surcease of gaining catalyst, being affected, and changing. Yet this is not so. But the alterations and changes that each of us hopes for and desires with the greatest of purity is that which is between the lines, in the margins of life.

We seek. We yearn. And we desire to move beyond self, and yet that to which we move is self, that great Self that is the Creator. Indeed, moving up the ladder of evolution can, from one standpoint, seem like a process of things falling away that we thought we knew rather than our learning more things to hold onto, for each and every thing that you can hold onto will fail you. The only thing that does not fail is love itself. Love remains, passes each test, and waits for the weary to finish the current round of tests and questions, wonderings and murmurings, waits patiently, waits with all the love, literally, in the world. Our self awaits us between each word, between each breath, between each bone within your bodies, between each synapse in your nerves and brains. Love awaits.

Are you in the desert? Love will find you there and will hover about you with living water, waiting for you to open the door to the present moment. Are you in the garden, the oasis of life, where blessings abound? Then love is everywhere. Then it is easy to forget that the feelings, the emotions that run high are not those deep emotions that are the tide of the heart, for when times are good it is easy to be lazy and to move away from that holy of holies again, for all is so beautiful and so lovely and so pleasant. It is easy to be content with playing in the garden.

Yet, the love that awaits is not that full sunshine of noon, is not that fountain of water that satisfies physical thirst, is not even those emotional structures, if you will, that accompany that blessed state of contentment. Love gives life and yet also it is a call for more remembrance. Love calls to itself from within the good times and bad as experienced by you. It remains the same in bad times and good. It can be perceived only fitfully by the incarnate spirit and yet those moments of inner awareness, of holiness, of that presence of self in its wholeness are enough and more than enough to exalt and strengthen and inspire.

We encourage each to move into remembrance as often as it can be thought. The remembrance shall be of love. That love, in its power and strength, in its grace and beauty, has created the harmony of all the illusions that there are, an infinite and infinitely complex system of fields of energy, an illusion created by a Self that wishes to know Itself. It loves each field of energy that It has born within Its mind. It nurtures moment by moment that infinite and eternal consciousness that is Itself within each of you. We call you to a deeper awareness, the awareness that is in the grounds of being, beneath the surface of good times and bad. We call you to remembrance of love.

Ask yourself to remember, to give thanks and praise. We ask this, knowing that it is nearly impossible in the midst of the illusion to have a constant and faithful memory, yet if a desire is honed and sharpened day by day that faculty will create a rhythm of evolution that is accelerated, for that within you which is deep enough to remember moment by moment is that self towards which you yearn, that slightly more aware and then slightly more aware self that is opening its consciousness up to the infinite depths of the love of the one infinite Creator. When this love is realized in memory within it is as always when one is in love, the outer illusion becomes extraordinary and each and every trick of the weather and happenstance of the day can be seen to shine with excellence and beauty.

We know that you seek to deepen the self and your awareness of self. Let that energy have its ground in remembrance of the one infinite Creator, that original Thought which is and which all else is becoming.

We would at this time transfer this contact to the one known as Jim in order that he may speak to the ending of this session of working. We are those of Q'uo. We leave this instrument in love and in light.

(Jim channeling)

I am Q'uo, and greet each again in love and in light. We are at this time honored to offer ourselves in the attempt to speak to any further queries which those present may have for us. At this time we would ask if there is a query with which we may deal?

Carla: I have been thinking lately that I am just massaging my ego with these channeled messages. I know that you say each time that you come what a privilege it is for you and how much we are helping you. I wonder if you could give me some things to think about in seeing myself as being of the same use that I have been before. It just seems like by now have we not covered everything by now?

I am Q'uo, and am aware of your query, my sister. Over the years of your time during which this group's efforts have been offered in the form of service to others in the channeling there has indeed been a great array of topics covered, for there are many, many ways by which love may be approached and it is our great privilege to assist any who wishes to know more of this power of love and the one great original Thought that produced love in all its infinite forms. Though the sharing of this information in many forms so that the mind may consider and the heart embrace more fully the concept of love is a great service to offer, it is not the heart, for the heart of this blending of our vibrations with yours at each working is the seeking of love and the sharing of love, the birthing of love that did not exist before the blending occurred.

Each time that we are able to utilize instruments such as these present we are able to give and receive not only information and inspiration but the essence of love, the seeking to know, the seeking to share.

The seeking, this is that which is most fundamental to our times together. This is much like the carrier wave of the radio stations that infuse messages upon this primary wave of energy. Thus, at each working we, with you, are able to create another form, if you will, which love may take in the attempt of entities to apprehend it. It is a joy and a pleasure to see what interesting and intricate forms we and you create. Yet it is a blessing that each is made of love. Through the opportunity that you offer to us and we offer to you, thus the treasure is the time together. We thank you for each such opportunity and bless you as you sit and ponder the possibilities of your purpose and your gifts.

Is there a further query, my sister?

Carla: Would you, from your standpoint, rank both silent meditation and channeled meditations as equal as ways of sharing the presence of love?

I am Q'uo, and am aware of your query, my sister. And it is a difficult distinction to make as to whether there is more or better love created through one form of meditation or another, for each is potentially full of that quality that we call love. Some entities are more biased, shall we say, or appreciate the silent meditation, for it speaks not to the mind but more directly to the heart and the foundation of one's being. Whereas with other entities it is necessary to go through the doorway of the mind, shall we say, in order to reach the heart in a fashion which is appreciated by that entity, though the heart may be reached without the entity's appreciation in silent meditation. Thus, the choice is yours. We could suggest trying each and assessing your own appreciation.

Is there another query, my sister?

Carla: To tell you the truth, I have been continuing on with the channeling because the people around me are still wanting it. Do you think this is a way of thinking that is accurate as far as my motivations are concerned or should I spend some time examining this? I have no feeling one way or the other.

I am Q'uo, and am aware of your query, my sister. We would comment thusly. It is oftentimes that the most helpful information comes through an instrument that has little desire to be an instrument at that time but answers a call. We answer your call. You answer the call of others. This is the way of service.

Is there a further query?

Carla: No, that pretty well does it. I was hung up on that because I really *(inaudible)* being able to help these people. OK.

I am Q'uo, and we again thank you, my sister, and would suggest that true cause for concern could come about if you experienced that experience of the Maytag repairman with no call.

Is there a further query?

Carla: Not from me. You know that I have always been a reluctant channel but I do answer a call.

I am Q'uo. We are most grateful for your efforts at questioning the channeling and most especially at living the life.

Is there another query at this time?

(Pause)

I am Q'uo, and we are aware that we have exhausted those queries which have been offered to us so carefully and lovingly and [which move] to the center of our being for we feel that they come from the center of your being. We thank you for your dedication. We thank you for the care with which you enter these sessions of working and the honest effort that each makes at offering the self in service to others. We are known to you as those of Q'uo and shall take our leave of this instrument and this group at this time, leaving each in the love and in the light of the one infinite Creator. Adonai, my friends. Adonai. ❧

L/L Research

L/L Research is a subsidiary of Rock Creek Research & Development Laboratories, Inc.

P.O. Box 5195
Louisville, KY 40255-0195

www.llresearch.org

Rock Creek is a non-profit corporation dedicated to discovering and sharing information which may aid in the spiritual evolution of humankind.

ABOUT THE CONTENTS OF THIS TRANSCRIPT: This telepathic channeling has been taken from transcriptions of the weekly study and meditation meetings of the Rock Creek Research & Development Laboratories and L/L Research. It is offered in the hope that it may be useful to you. As the Confederation entities always make a point of saying, please use your discrimination and judgment in assessing this material. If something rings true to you, fine. If something does not resonate, please leave it behind, for neither we nor those of the Confederation would wish to be a stumbling block for any.

CAVEAT: This transcript is being published by L/L Research in a not yet final form. It has, however, been edited and any obvious errors have been corrected. When it is in a final form, this caveat will be removed.

© 2009 L/L Research

Sunday Meditation
March 24, 1996

Group question: We would like to know about [how] the balancing process works. Should we be spontaneous in each experience to reflect who we are, or should we try to bring light consciously into each situation so that we affect it more positively? How can we use the catalyst of each situation to partake in the balancing process? How can we be the best mirrors to people?

(Carla channeling)

We are those of Q'uo. We send greetings through this instrument in the love and the light of the one infinite Creator. We are most happy to be with you this evening, and thank you for calling us to this blessed assembly of souls.

As always, we ask that each take from those things we say that which seems helpful and disregard those things which do not seem so. In this way we feel more able to share our humble opinions with you, knowing that you can discriminate between that which is your personal truth and that which is not.

You ask concerning the processes of balancing. There is much to say concerning this interesting topic. Perhaps we should begin by stating some assumptions which we are making. The primary assumption that we use as the basis for balancing is that there is a center to things, that there is a sense to be made of the universe. This ground of being is difficult to talk about because its mode of being is that which is in process. The living processes of self relating to self and other self cannot be pinned like the butterfly on the collector's exhibit. It cannot be stopped, for when it is halted it ceases being living. So the basic picture, shall we say, that we have of the illusion is that it does make sense. It does add up to a unified and complete whole, but that sense is not linear and that whole or totality holds each pair of opposites in a dynamic balance.

Our second assumption is that it is the business of humankind to experience and to bear witness to that experience. This is confusing to those who desire to become perfect, for it is not our way to hunger after perfection. Rather, it is our feeling that it is the depth and quality of perception that is the desirable quality. The seeker of truth can be seen as that witness which makes the fallen tree make a sound. It is the tenuous, half-grasped witness of the imperfect entity that is precious to the infinite Creator, not the polished conclusion of a scholar or aesthete, but, rather, the diamond in the rough, if you will, of the person as it is, bearing witness to that catalyst which has struck it.

Therefore, it is not important to create perfect responses. Rather, it is important to allow the most deep felt truth of one's being to thrive.

Now, there is a kind of understanding which we have shared before many times within this group that there are successively more light-filled kingdoms of thought, if you will, each reality comprising a truth, yet each succeeding density of truth being higher. This instrument is familiar with this concept from its reading of cabalistic literature and the phrase with which it is familiar with, "as above, so below." In terms of a point of view for the seeker what this means is that a catalyst can be perceived truly on successively more lucid or profound levels.

One can see this, for instance, in the physical act of movement. When one is very, very close to an elephant it is possible only to see a portion of dark leathery skin. If one were able to pull oneself up and back, as if being taken into the atmosphere by a helicopter, one could move a very few feet back and see, not a patch of skin, but an animal recognizable as an elephant. And this is a truth which does not contradict or deny the first truth, but adds to it and clarifies it.

Now, if one continued moving up and back from this elephant one would see the elephant become a small dot surrounded by the myriad truths and dwelling places of your peoples. And this truth, not contradicting or denying the elephant, yet adds the context within which that animal abides. Now, if one continued pulling away from this scene one eventually would see the planet upon which dwelt that elephant, spinning in space with the precision of clockwork. And, again, this would be a setting of the elephant in its larger context. If one continued to pull away one would eventually see empty space and stars. And this too would be the greater truth.

When one seeks to balance the self a great deal of the necessary work is a learning of and a claiming of the larger point of view, not a specifically larger or a specific point of view, but rather a point of view which has pulled back from the previous view. In this, as in all things a spiritual seeker does, truth is relative. Progress is relative, and to judge the self's balance by gazing at another is only to confuse the processes of spiritual evolution, for each entity truly has an unique path and on that path is where that seeker is. Each seeker must needs wrestle continuously with those angels which show the face of the Creator to the seeking self.

The skill with which one handles situations involving other selves is a good resource to encourage in the self, for one who seeks to serve others naturally and organically wishes to be helpful and positive in the effect one has upon others. And we congratulate each when each has treated an entity with compassion and kindness in excess of what one may be feeling internally, for it is well to treat others kindly and with love. Yet this activity of social intercourse needs to be seen as one which does not demand a balance but rather demands the most—this instrument would say—Christ-like response or rejoinder. Being true to the self by being kind even when one does not feel kindly is a polarizing and positive choice. Yet, if this unbalanced action is not taken into the self in some way and balanced or assimilated it will drain the entity of energy for the entity will be speaking a lie. In order for the self to gather its energy anew there must be the process of looking for and seeking the truth of that imperfect and polarizing experience within the illusion.

Much of health is involved in this process of balancing, for the self is as the soldier at the line of battle. Often there is incoming fire that wounds the self. This wound needs to be attended to. The wounded self needs healing. The healing takes place due to the seeker's willingness to open the self and its imperfections to the centering influence of the largest perspective. Now, the largest perspective is that of love. In love the opposites are reconciled. This love is the seed of each of you, the truth at the center of you. It can be realized, not by taking it, but by releasing self so that that self which has suffered during the unbalanced actions of self can be bathed in the living water of truth.

It is easy for humankind to perceive spiritual evolution as a building process, going higher and higher and building one's intelligence and wisdom so that greater and greater things are understood. Yet, it is our perception that it is somewhat the opposite that is the case. That is, that as the seeker evolves the seeker becomes more and more able to release self, to let go, to surrender that part of self which wishes to be perfect or better or wiser.

What then is balance and how can one balance? This group has received information concerning exercises for balancing having to do with the technique of reviewing the day's perceptions, noting when the self has been swayed positively or negatively. Each point of experience then is felt, intensified and then held while the mind allows that which has been felt to take its place within the range of that feeling and its opposite. This reconnects the distorted self with that truer self which contains the entire range of each and every emotion.

To be truest to the self it is well to reckon with that self and doing so on a daily basis is recommended. The key in balancing is the remembrance of the larger viewpoint and it is a skill which is good to work on to develop the ability to see the self from that higher perspective which sees the whole range of the human comedy, as this instrument would say. Now, this large viewpoint does not come easily to most, and that is the challenge to each: to so live that one is bearing witness to one's truth, knowing that that truth is in process and will not stay the same, for each entity will grow along the lines desired most deeply.

There is certainly one thing which is helpful and that is the sense of humor, for the use of this gift can take the sting from difficult experiences, not by denying pain, but rather by seeing the pain of living in its larger context of sorrow and joy.

To those in third density the intellect seems the higher faculty within the human consciousness and the stirrings and feelings that arise making little logical sense or offering little structure seem to be less useful. Yet the balance which each seeks is a balance within the open heart, not an intellectually precise balance between two intellectual concepts, for wisdom is not an aspect of your density. There is little use seeking wisdom. There is a great deal of wisdom seeking that center of feeling which is absolute.

Let us pause to allow each present to open the heart to that center which is the Creator: love. We pause for a moment.

(Pause)

Now, as we speak keep this center, this heart of self visualized, see it as the glowing ball of perfectly white light that is dwelling within the darkness of flesh, as the sacrament within the cathedral which, within its place upon the altar, expresses and identifies that huge structure [though] it is only a small wafer of bread. This perfect light cannot be brought into your illusion, but it can be distorted by each heart that bears witness to it imperfectly. Love abides within each. Light dwells in the very heart of each. This is your truth. All else is language.

The way to pursue being a witness to the light is to live today. The hopes for tomorrow, the regrets or memories of yesterday, aid in many things but do not aid in bearing witness to the love and the light within. By the time the impulse has reached the manifested expression it no longer bears witness to truth but to the judgment of the individual who is editing the self. Therefore, go ahead and edit the self, for such is the way of service to others. But allow the self to heal from these expressions by spending time and attention just letting go of and releasing the pains and joys alike to the infinite One. These are the harvests that the Creator desires. These are the expressions of love that the Creator appreciates. Just as you are, you are loved, and this is the thing of the moment, for each moment, each instant is as that point from which a universe of possibility depends. Each moment is a moment of choice. Each moment is an opportunity for witness. Each moment is infinite.

We trust we have confused you, and to celebrate this fact we shall leave this somewhat befuddled instrument and transfer the contact to the one known as Jim. We leave this instrument in love and light. We are Q'uo.

(Jim channeling)

I am Q'uo, and greet each again in love and in light through this instrument. It is now our privilege to ask if there might be any further queries from this group to which we may speak?

Carla: Earlier this week I was conscious of feeling energy within identical to the energy transfers from B when he is here. Are there any suggestions you could make as to how I could regularize this kind of energy or any comments you could make at all?

I am Q'uo, and am aware of your query, my sister. We find in this instance that there is a sympathetic connection which has been set up between the one known as B and yourself that operates upon the metaphysical level and allows you to feel the essence of energy, shall we say, that is offered to you by the one known as B in its desire to be of service. This desire is that which allows the transfer of energy as well as does your own need for it. The nature of the connection is that which is preincarnatively chosen, as there are many who offer themselves in such a fashion. The means of affecting this opportunity for transfer is that which must remain within the realm of your free will choice and experimentation.

Is there a further query, my sister?

Carla: Yes. In a way. My hope is that if I am receiving a transfer of energy that B is also receiving a transfer of my kind of energy. Also, that it not be depleting either of us but being like a completed circuit. Would you have any comments about this?

I am Q'uo, and am aware of your query, my sister. In the large part, as you would say, this is correct. However, it is the closed or closing circuit with which you deal, for when this circuit is completed there is the possibility of mutual transfer.

Is there a further query, my sister?

Carla: So what you are saying is that I could not even receive that energy as I am were it not mutual. Is that correct?

I am Q'uo, and this is correct, my sister.

Is there another query?

Carla: No. Thank you.

Is there another query at this time from any other source?

B: In my recent experiences I have felt some very distinctive physical effects. Is it of any value to the seeker of truth to make note of these physical effects? Spiritual value, that is?

I am Q'uo, and am aware of your query, my brother. It is helpful for the pilgrim upon the path to make notes of the nature of the journey in order that some glimpse of a larger reality be made available to it. There is not the need for great detail but to make note of the salient features that accompany those experiences that are felt to be of a metaphysical nature.

Is there a further query, my brother?

B: Yes. But I forgot it!

I am Q'uo, and we are not at liberty to remember for you.

Is there a final query at this time?

B: Words seem to mean less in my interactions with others now and an energy seems to be becoming more prevalent. Could you help me with this a little?

I am Q'uo, and am aware of your query, my brother. We may comment by suggesting that this experience is an enhancement of your ability to perceive the world not only about you but more importantly that world within you, the lens through which you experience that which is your incarnation. As you begin to allow more impressions to arise within your own being it becomes somewhat more difficult to describe with any hope of accuracy that which grows within, yet the desire to do so grows as well. Thus, one is frequently left with the feeling and few words to describe it. This is not to be concerned about for there will come in its own time the ability to put into words more accurately the experience which continues to increase.

The entire effect is one much like exploring new terrain for the pilgrim on the path of moving into the lands which are more exotic and mysterious than those through which the entity has previously moved. Thus, there is a time of acclimation which is of necessity experienced at the beginning of this feeling and arising of more impressions internally. We would simply counsel patience and the honing of the desire to understand into a kind of awaiting with joy.

Is there a further query, my brother?

B: How might I cooperate with this more fully?

I am Q'uo, and am aware of your query, my brother. Our only suggestion is that one may profit greatly from learning to accept not only the self but the new territories through which the self moves and the responses from the self without feeling overly whelmed or insignificant to the point of inaction, allowing the experience to develop as it will. Patience, tolerance and the light touch are always good allies upon such a journey.

Is there any further query, my brother?

B: No. Thank you.

I am Q'uo. Is there a final query?

(Pause)

I am Q'uo. We again thank each for inviting our presence in this circle of working this day. We are most honored to have been able to join you and remind you that we speak that which is but our opinions. Take that which is helpful to you and leave all else behind.

At this time we shall bid each a fond farewell for the nonce. We are known to you as those of Q'uo. Adonai, my friends. Adonai.

L/L Research

L/L Research is a subsidiary of Rock Creek Research & Development Laboratories, Inc.

P.O. Box 5195
Louisville, KY 40255-0195

www.llresearch.org

Rock Creek is a non-profit corporation dedicated to discovering and sharing information which may aid in the spiritual evolution of humankind.

ABOUT THE CONTENTS OF THIS TRANSCRIPT: This telepathic channeling has been taken from transcriptions of the weekly study and meditation meetings of the Rock Creek Research & Development Laboratories and L/L Research. It is offered in the hope that it may be useful to you. As the Confederation entities always make a point of saying, please use your discrimination and judgment in assessing this material. If something rings true to you, fine. If something does not resonate, please leave it behind, for neither we nor those of the Confederation would wish to be a stumbling block for any.

CAVEAT: This transcript is being published by L/L Research in a not yet final form. It has, however, been edited and any obvious errors have been corrected. When it is in a final form, this caveat will be removed.

© 2009 L/L Research

Sunday Meditation
March 31, 1996

Group question: Our question this afternoon has to do with our tapes, our individual behavior patterns that we notice, hopefully, at some point in the life experience. They, we think, have something to do with what we are here to learn. And we were wondering if Q'uo could give us some sort of idea about how these behavior patterns work, how we set them up. Most importantly, how do we recognize them? And how do we begin to change them if we feel that change is a good thing to do?

(Carla channeling)

We are those of the principle known to you as Q'uo. Greetings in the love and in the ineffable light of the one infinite Creator. It is such a pleasure to respond to your call for our thoughts at this working and we thank you most gratefully for this privilege. To blend our vibrations with yours is a precious experience and to be able to share our opinions with those who seek the truth is a great privilege and you offer us great service allowing us to attempt to serve you. As always, we ask that your powers of discrimination guide your intake of our thoughts or any thoughts. Listen to no man's truth except your own, for, for each seeker, there is but one path. That path is ready, prepared and waiting, but it is an individual path. It may be in concert with others, in harmony [with] others, or quite different than others, yet it is unique. And we encourage each to listen to the promptings of that inner recognition that is almost like remembering something already known. Thoughts that do not have this ring of personal truth we ask each to lay aside.

This day you wish to discuss the tapes that play in the mind when things occur in the outer manifestation. You wish to know where these tapes come from and how to deal with them. Before we move into detail, we wish to establish our picture of the third-density experience because there are two sorts of ways we wish to discuss which can work on these tapes. Each has value, but each is a separate resource from the other.

Our model of the experience of humankind upon third-density Earth is that of the second density physical vehicle with an instinctual life of its own which carries a consciousness that preceded the first spark of life within that physical vehicle and that lives on into infinity after the expiration of the physical vehicle's second-density life. This image of the so-called naked ape carrying truth, love and infinite values is a useful model because it offers a way in which to think about the human experience of the self that is in the world but not of the world.

This is the spiritual truth for all within third density. These physical vehicles you now enjoy are native to a particular time and a particular place. The consciousness they carry has no address and is a citizen of the universe and a child of the infinite

Creator. This being said, we may gaze first at the way in which the so-called tapes are prepared and have their being.

When the physical vehicle emerges from the womb, the consciousness within it is mature, responsible and has a fair degree of crystallization. However, the infant physical vehicle is helpless, helpless to communicate its thoughts and concepts, helpless to take care of itself. This infant being is utterly dependent upon others for its survival. And when the tapes are made, they are made by very young entities who perceive that the way to more healthy survival is to heed and to react to certain key stimuli that are repeated again and again in the small life experience of the young one.

The world of this young being considers those who provide the necessity of life to be, shall we say, titanic or god-like. Therefore, instinctively, the young mind stores information of things that have aided comfort and continued survival. Often perceiving difficulties where none actually exist and not perceiving where the difficulties are coming from in reality, the young self begins more and more to distort the incoming data and sense impressions because triggers, as it were, have been laid into certain thought and speech patterns. The mind of second density files away all information concerning survival and keeps it at the ready in order to enhance each opportunity to respond in a timely manner to that which affects survival.

The consciousness that this struggling young physical vehicle carries may have almost no relationship to the self that is attempting to survive, or the consciousness and the second-density mind may be very close. Various entities bring various characters and what you call the personality with them. However close or distant that relationship is, in general, it is not feasible to the younger entity to ask the consciousness within to affect the second-density mind. The work of that path is considerably different from the first way of working with these crystallizations or tapes. The way of the mind from second density, then, is our first target for finding a resource. That resource is locked within memory. Whatever the distortion, whatever the tape that is being played, observation will gradually inform the entity who seeks the solution to these discordant tapes.

There is a specific beginning to each crystallization, a certain trigger, if you will, that begins the tape. What triggers the distorted reaction may be usefully noted and over a period of your time you may build intelligence concerning each tape or crystallization. Then the goal of this second-density mind is simply to move back and further back until the original experience which started the distortion at the young and tender age is exposed. When the root of the distortion is uncovered, it will often have a phrase or a sentence that the seeker gradually learns to identify. These are the triggers and by moving back into those first experiences, those crystallizing, tightening, hardening, shielding reactions, it is possible to encapsulate those distortion roots, and by mechanical redirection of thought when the triggers are recognized, gradually remove the distortion from the interior tape library, if you will.

This form of work is exacting, largely intellectual and often very useful. Even though the work requires intellectual analysis and would seem to remain upon the surface, it is possible to move into an aura or atmosphere within which the brain chooses to move into the untying of knots, the releasing of strictures, and when these are done even intellectually, the emotional release is often great.

So, there are these things which the seeker can do, simply by sharing with another or with the self, those moments of unguarded reaction that tell the tale of where this crystallized, fear-driven tightness has its roots, and from where it distorts experience.

This is painstaking work and work often better done under some direction from another, for the intellect is almost inevitably blind-sided by the depth of self-awareness. It is difficult to stand outside the self and see that self whole. Thusly, we encourage those contemplations when it is desired to work upon a particular tape, spending time and attention looking into what is felt and what is thought, as well as what is heard on that tape. We suggest working with another simply to regularize the process of following the truth within these examinations. One outside the self may quite often speak very little, but move a wandering thought back into the path that will lead to a greater grasp of what survival issue drove the self to build this distortion system in the first place.

This is one resource and it works at that level which is conscious and full of mind. There is a way to work upon these same experiences from the standpoint of consciousness, that consciousness which is your infinite and eternal Self which has only adopted a manifested symbol of self for a little while. That self that is truly you connects into the deep mind of the second-density mind, that perfectly good bio-computer which makes the choices that improve chances of survival.

The entry into individual expression of love that is each questing itself is that which can be trusted. There is a true engagement of consciousness to this spark of flesh that houses it. It is secure, and it represents a vast foray of awareness that is not thought-driven, but is rather driven by love, with love, to love, for love's sake. Unlike the individual with the delineated face and body and ways of speaking, there are no set limits to self at the level of consciousness. The program, shall we say, of that infinite self is non-logical, nonintellectual, nonphysical. It is as that which sings the tune. It is that bell which is struck, and when struck rings in a certain combination of tones that is unique to the self, that has evolved itself within your infinite consciousness. Unlike the mind of second density which accretes knowledge and holds it against further need, the self's infinite mind simply moves between the various—the closest word you have is "emotions." There are true states of emotions that have purity and clarity and the self that is the citizen of the stars swims within this infinite sea of feeling and that which is felt is automatically seen with thanksgiving for this is the way of love itself.

This consciousness does not work upon a particular tape or a particular problem. One could look at this consciousness that is infinite as a metaprogram that the computer that is the living mind can access by opening certain doors between the conscious and deep mind. Each is familiar with our constant recommendations for periods of meditation and contemplation within each daily period. Within those times of silence within, the Creator speaks those words that have no words, those thoughts that have no concept. And yet, because they move from love itself, when invited they come into the interior conscious life with healing in their hands.

We cannot say enough about silence. The silence within is a precious gift that you give yourself. When you open to the presence of the one infinite Creator, wonderful life-enhancing energies can flow into the sore and aching cracks and crevices of the conscious life, offering that strength that is love, offering that higher and deeper truth that is love, offering a larger and yet again larger perspective, for that is the way of love.

We hope you are very charitable to yourself and do give yourself that wonderful endowment of time to be still and know that the place whereon you stand is truly holy ground.

We would at this time transfer this contact to the one known as Jim. We thank this instrument and leave it in love and in light. We are Q'uo.

(Jim channeling)

I am Q'uo, and greet each again in love and in light through this instrument. It is our privilege at this time to offer ourselves in the attempt to speak to you for any further queries which those present may have to offer us. Is there a query at this time?

B: Hi, Q'uo. I have a question related to a *(inaudible)* experience. I would ask that you provide some insight into *(inaudible)*. I've noticed in my experience working with an individual who seems to have an effect upon me *(inaudible)* to the point where I feel physically. I was wondering if you could comment on this experience?

I am Q'uo, and am aware of your query, my brother. There are those comments which we may make and those which we must refrain from making in order to assure the integrity of your free will. Firstly, your ability to give and to receive the energy-filled love is that which you have begun to discover in your own experience. There is the necessity upon your part to continue to investigate the nature of this ability, for it is at present functioning at a level which far exceeds your grasp of it and this is something that does have an effect upon you. We may also suggest that the suggestions that have been made to you previous to this session's beginning may prove of assistance in a practical manner.

Yet, to these suggestions we would add that any action taken needs to have two prerequisites, shall we say, that the desire to seek be honed in your meditations, that you seek within your meditation to understand not with the mind alone, but also with the heart, the nature of this experience which you share with another. The second suggestion follows closely upon the first, that being that any action be built upon the foundation of heart-felt love, for this is not only the greatest protection for any entity, but is also the greatest healing effect that one can provide for the self or another. It is helpful in all third-density experiences to attempt to grasp the parameters of the experience and to contemplate and consider carefully the experience which you share, and this we also suggest, but in a role which is subservient to both the meditation and the imbuing with love of all actions considered.

Is there a further query, my brother?

B: No, thank you, Q'uo. I feel enormous [gratitude].

I am Q'uo, and we also feel the same gratitude for you and your concerns, my brother. Is there another query at this time?

Questioner: Q'uo, I have a question. It's regarding a problem I have with insomnia. Would you comment on this, I guess, and what causes the problem, what I might do to correct it?

I am Q'uo, and am aware of your query, my brother, and in the same vein as that which we have just shared with the one known as B, there are those comments which we may make and those which we may not. Firstly, we would recommend that you consider in the meditative state the components, shall we say, that comprise the problem of being unable to sleep, that is …

(Side one of tape ends.)

(Jim channeling)

I am Q'uo, and am again with this instrument. We shall continue.

That you attempt to discover during the periods where this difficulty in sleeping is most active. What are the components or experiences that accompany and precede the difficulty? Is there a pattern that you can discover that will give an indication of the origin of this difficulty? As a simple and potentially helpful suggestion, we might recommend that, in the short run, while you are investigating the underlying features of this experience, that it might be helpful to include a program of exercise that would bring you to a true physical weariness, to be included at some point in your daily round of activities. That would help the physical vehicle be pointed, shall we say, in the right direction, for in a portion of this problem we see that there is the storing of a certain kind of energy that needs expression so that it does not cause an overactivation of the wakefulness of the mind and body complexes.

Is there a further query, my brother?

Questioner: Thank you, Q'uo. I think that will be helpful.

I am Q'uo, and we thank you, my brother. Is there another query?

Questioner: I wonder if I could follow K's question. I've heard recently that there's a switch inside our brain, a sleep switch, and if it's not switched, you can't go to sleep regardless of how tired you are. But if it's switched, you can. I was wondering, why is this valuable? Why is this a part of our nature? Do you have any insight into this, Q'uo?

I am Q'uo, and am aware of your query, my sister. It is valuable for entities of your density and others as well to be able to rest the physical vehicle that it might be recharged, shall we say. And in this resting and all other physical functions, there are physical features that are operated, not so much physically perhaps, but by the mental and emotional intentions of each entity. These mental impulses and intentions, however, have the ability to be affected by many different energies and patterns of thinking that make a direct ratio or relationship difficult to describe with precision. Thus, it is helpful to explore those forces that move within one's being in order that one have a grasp of how the mental, emotional and physical complexes are interrelated.

Is there a further query, my sister?

Questioner: No, thank you, Q'uo.

I am Q'uo. Again, we thank you, my sister. Is there another query?

Questioner: Q'uo, I have one. Q'uo, I have this feeling, impression that *(inaudible)* I've been thinking about asking the question for three weeks *(inaudible)* meditation group. I wonder if there is some sort of balance achieved when there are a similar number of males and females? If there is … let me back up. Does the number of males imbalance the group *(inaudible)*.

I am Q'uo, and am aware of your query, my brother. Firstly, those of Hatonn are always with this group and send their greetings to each, for they are a part of this group. Secondly, the makeup of this group in the male and female energies present is, indeed, affected by the biological nature of the entities present in most cases. However, there are those of the biological male in nature that are also able to offer the female energies, for each entity is working upon an inner balance which will be able to reflect both the male and female energies, that which reaches and that which awaits the reaching.

There are in your culture those forces and habits which are dependably able to cause the biological male to focus primarily on male energies and the biological female to focus primarily on female energies. Thus, the present configuration of this group is indeed swayed in a large extent toward the male energies. This tends to operate in an unseen fashion where metaphysical energies are concerned and not so much in the actual or practical operation and functioning of this group.

Thus, we find that each group presents its own kind of balance of energies and each is unique in its composition, its interests, desires, and tensions.

Is there a further query, my brother?

Questioner: *(Inaudible)* this question, it appears that perhaps *(inaudible)* strike a balance by trying to somehow balance the males and females, because I have a feeling from what you said, it is the [intention] of the group coming together that counts more than the actual makeup. I'm not very clear on this subject, so if you comment on this, that's all right, if not *(inaudible)*.

I am Q'uo, and am aware of your query, my brother. We do not feel a necessity for there to be an actual balance between the either biological or the metaphysical energies regarding male and female. It is, as you have observed, more important that those who are here are desirous of seeking that which you call the truth and offer themselves in a clear and open fashion in this seeking. In such an environment there is the opportunity for all energies to be nourished in their development, in their movement, and in their ability to blend the personalities of each present into one seeking entity that offers itself in service to others and calls for those such as ourselves to aid in this effort.

Is there a further query, my brother?

Questioner: *(Inaudible)*.

I am Q'uo, and we do indeed smile when we speak to this group, my brother, for we feel that there is underlying each entity's experience a great joy of being, and we are honored and happy to blend our vibrations with yours in the same seeking.

Is there another query at this time?

Questioner: Q'uo, I'll venture this question. I've written a manuscript. I've done a great deal of work. I'm wondering, from your perspective what would you comment about it? Do you see anything that I should reconsider? Is there anything else that should be done with this book? Can you say anything about this?

I am Q'uo, and am aware of your query, my brother. We would not choose to play the part of the technician that would turn one dial up and another down in order to achieve a certain sound. It is rather our estimation of the effort which you have put forth that it has been put forth with a great deal of love and attention to the desire to be of service. This is the critical feature. You have done the equivalent of planting the seed and providing it with water and the appropriate environment in which to grow. We are of the opinion that this is all any can do. That which you have done has been done with an whole heart and is in itself its own reward as far as you are concerned. That it may also be of service to others is a possibility which will become a reality in its own way and in its own time, for there are unseen hands which work to aid each in the service that has been chosen, and the ways of the assistance being put forth are many and mysterious.

Is there a further query, my brother?

Questioner: Would you suggest a publisher that I should try to send the manuscript to or would this be *(inaudible)*?

I am Q'uo, and am aware of your query, my brother. We are not able to make such recommendations due to our desire to preserve the free will of not only yourself but of others as well. Thus, we can only recommend that the effort is good.

Is there a further query, my brother?

Questioner: I appreciate that Q'uo. I'm wondering if … in our recent talks we were mentioning first density and second density. I was wondering if there was a [quantum] change of the Earth between first density and second density, or is this one process that grows out of another due to the necessity to have a new sphere around the Earth? Is there a separate sphere that is formed around the Earth to facilitate second density from first?

I am Q'uo, and am aware of your query, my brother. There are in truth seven different densities of Earth that are present at all times, though at this time only one through four are in activation, the fourth beginning its activation in a fashion which is perceived by those who are sensitive to these changes in a gradual or step by step fashion, so that there are small indications that are notable as each stage builds upon the last to move the planet itself into a new vibrational frequency.

Is there a final query at this time?

Questioner: If you would, Q'uo, I'd like you to comment on Jesus Christ and why his death is considered a martyrdom. In what exact way was Jesus' death a service to humanity so that it could be called upon?

I am Q'uo, and am aware of your query, my brother. We shall attempt to respond to this most thoughtful query by suggesting that the one known as Jesus or Jehoshua was an entity which was able to gain a great deal of understanding of the nature of this illusion in which all which an entity has of a physical, mental and emotional nature is sacrificed in order that the entity of third density might be reborn to a new level of being. This density was seen by this entity as that which offers itself in sacrifice to all who move through it. All the illusions, the experience and the very fabric of this density exist in order that each entity which moves through it might be able to become transformed by the experience.

Thus, the one known as Jesus wished to offer itself as one who provided a pattern or model of beingness that delineated the nature of sacrifice and transformation, that there was indeed no death which would end the experience of consciousness in this illusion, that there was the possibility of using the illusion about one as a means by which one could give and receive love from all other entities according to the desire or choice made within one's own being, no matter the circumstances without the self.

Thus, the one known as Jesus was able to offer its own life as an example of the kind of transformation possible for each entity within this illusion. Thus, this entity used the illusion for a greater purpose than becoming any kind of king or power within the illusion. This entity offered a means through the illusion and beyond the illusion as it explored and shared the love of the one Creator in a pure and undistorted fashion.

At this time we feel that we have spoken long enough for the patience and comfort of those present and would thank those present for inviting us to your group once again in your circle of your seeking. We are always honored to do so and would, at this time, take our leave of this instrument, leaving each, as always, in the love and in the ineffable light of the one Creator. We are known to you as those of Q'uo. Adonai, my friends. Adonai. ✥

Sunday Meditation
April 7, 1996

(The beginning of this transcript is missing.)
(Carla channeling)

… To that which one has hoped he would be. Yet, each daily dying is simultaneously the day of resurrection. As within the curtain of flesh, each capitulates in the daily cycle and in the yearly cycles of light and darkness the seasons of spirit. There is a revolving wheel of being that moves the planets in their courses and the hearts of men within its daily cycles and seasons; always moving, never still. Life and death tumble like puppies with each other, experiencing endlessly limitation, expansion, darkness, light, sadness, joy. And each emotion is a truth. How often have you met the resurrected Christ consciousness upon the road and not known that it was Creator.

We encourage each to lift those blinders as often as possible to lift the self into faith, into hope, into peace, by thinking upon these things. Thinking upon the concept of sacrifice, concept of a love that would give itself and spent itself to the point of death. Each has known great heroes and read of mighty deeds, but each is a hero within his own creation. In one season, it is easy to see the self as together, efficient, able.

Each has many, many times, perhaps sometimes overwhelmingly so, [judged the self] as unworthy, inadequate, not coming up to the expectation of self.

We ask that you seek again and again [self-forgiveness and self-worth] whenever in the course of the daily activities you remember to move in mind to that tune that is the Earthly heart.

There if you have the eyes to see, you will find that the stone has been rolled away and that the light has claimed the tomb for its own.

My dear ones, you are the light of the world. It is from hearts such as yours that the light of your planet comes. It is from lives such as yours that the great procession of life and death is [imbued] in the passion play of life on earth with honor, dignity, compassion and deep caring. You have within you every [force of death] and every [force of light]. Nothing has been left out of your makeup. It is the way of the spiritual sojourner to live that uncomfortable life that is aware of these matters, that is aware of the great wheel of evolution working through time and space to bring consciousness to that infinite present moment, where that great love that created all that there is suddenly explodes into light infinite and indivisible.

We would at this time transfer the contact to the one known as Jim. We leave this instrument in love and in light. We are those of Q'uo.

(Jim channeling)

I am Q'uo, and greet each again in love and in light through this instrument. It is our privilege at this time to ask if we may speak to any further queries. Is there another query at this time?

Questioner: Yes, Q'uo, could you describe please the Law of Responsibility, how does *(inaudible)* that all *(inaudible)* on a spiritual *(inaudible)*?

I am Q'uo, and I am aware of your query, my brother. Each seeker in the process of seeking will find those resources that are of assistance in the revealing of the heart of love and the nature of truth to the seeker. As the seeker becomes aware of more principles, shall we say, that are applicable to the life pattern the seeker has the responsibility of utilizing these resources in the service to others and in the enhancing of the life pattern. If the seeker is unable or unwilling to use that which it has learned, then it will find greater difficulty in its future seeking in discovering further principles and resources that will assist in this process. Thus, the Law of Responsibility simply asks each seeker to use that which is learned to the best of its ability in the life pattern, in revealing love to self, love for self, love to others, love for others.

Is there a further query, my brother?

Questioner: You spoke once previously about if a catalyst were not processed, or something along those lines, that it ended up draining the entity. Does this relate to what you have just spoken of?

I am Q'uo, and I am aware of your query, my brother. And this is correct. For if the entity has a catalyst which is yet to be processed, and if the entity is aware that that which has been given to it it is capable of processing, then the entity will find itself in a situation of what you may call inner turmoil or confusion, until it utilizes those principles which it has gathered thus far in the processing of the catalyst which is before it.

Is there any further query, my brother?

Questioner: Not from me, thank you, Q'uo.

I am Q'uo, and we are grateful to you as well, my brother, for your heartfelt queries. Is there another query at this time?

Questioner: Yes, Q'uo, I do have one other question. Prior to our beginning this meditation we had a group dynamic issue specifically focused on my own feelings, that rose rather sharply, based on a comment that was made, and I was wondering if you could tell me—tell us the condition of the group energy dynamic effect that our discussions had on that?

I am Q'uo, and I am aware of your query, my brother. We were observing this experience and were pleased to find that the group dynamics, as you have called them, were greatly enhanced by the discussion which ensued concerning the difficulties which you were feeling and appreciating [regarding] your own experiences. It is not the presence of difficult feelings that causes a problem for the group energy, it is the lack of attention given to them that can cause holes, shall we say, in the wall of light that surrounds this group. Thus, we were greatly pleased that each present was willing to share what each had available at that time, which is the fruit of one's being in the service of others. This is a greatly blessed event, when the vision of sorrow is replaced by the vision of hope as a result of the efforts of those present to support each other in any situation, especially those which are difficult.

Is there a further query, my brother?

Questioner: I don't think so, thank you, Q'uo. I feel relief hearing your words on that subject and great joy *(inaudible)*.

I am Q'uo, and we also feel great joy, my brother, and are greatly appreciative for your efforts this day. Is there another query?

Carla: I'd just like to follow up and ask if there is anything that Jim and I can do to help make this place a safe place to be *(inaudible)*?

I am Q'uo, and I am aware of your query, my sister. We observe the efforts of each present and can only commend each within this circle for offering all that each has. There will always be more that can be done, for the journey which you travel is one which is infinite in nature. If you choose to look at that which is not yet done and judge the self accordingly, you will always come up short, shall we say, and the estimation of the self will seem small. If, instead, you will look at that which has been accomplished, and each has done much, then there is reason for rejoicing and we recommend rejoicing, my sister.

Is there any further query?

Carla: That's all.

I am Q'uo, and we thank you once again, my sister. Is there another query at this time?

(Pause)

I am Q'uo, and we are most grateful to each for the offering of those questions which have been given to us in love and in true desire to know the truth, and we again thank each for the being which each brings into this circle of working, for it is your being which is of inestimable value, though most are unaware of the value or the being, for it is that which is at one's center of heart, and this is the journey my friends, to move to the center of the heart, which would seem to be a quick and easy journey. For do you not carry it with you? Oh, but, my friends, this is the infinite journey, for are you not all things and are you not the one Creator? So when you seek the heart of love, you seek the heart of self and you contain and express the heart of self in ways which even you do not begin to understand. Have faith, my brothers and sisters, for this is a journey that you each are well set upon. There shall be difficulties. There shall be challenges. How else shall you learn that which you do not know? But if you have faith and continue with a strong will, you shall find the heart of yourself and the heart of the one Creator in the same place.

At this time we shall take our leave of this group, leaving each, as always, in the love and in the light of the one infinite Creator. We are known to you as those of Q'uo. Adonai, my friends, Adonai. ✣

L/L Research

L/L Research is a subsidiary of Rock Creek Research & Development Laboratories, Inc.

P.O. Box 5195
Louisville, KY 40255-0195

www.llresearch.org

Rock Creek is a non-profit corporation dedicated to discovering and sharing information which may aid in the spiritual evolution of humankind.

ABOUT THE CONTENTS OF THIS TRANSCRIPT: This telepathic channeling has been taken from transcriptions of the weekly study and meditation meetings of the Rock Creek Research & Development Laboratories and L/L Research. It is offered in the hope that it may be useful to you. As the Confederation entities always make a point of saying, please use your discrimination and judgment in assessing this material. If something rings true to you, fine. If something does not resonate, please leave it behind, for neither we nor those of the Confederation would wish to be a stumbling block for any.

CAVEAT: This transcript is being published by L/L Research in a not yet final form. It has, however, been edited and any obvious errors have been corrected. When it is in a final form, this caveat will be removed.

© 2009 L/L Research

Sunday Meditation
April 14, 1996

Group question: Each of us here is a seeker and we would like to do whatever is necessary to make the harvest by being of service to others in whatever way necessary. We would like to know what the steps or stages are that are necessary to make the harvest and for walking the path of the seeker of truth. And where does this desire to walk the path and be a seeker of truth come from?

(Carla channeling)

We are those of the principle of Q'uo. Greetings to each of you in the love and in the light of the one infinite Creator. It is our privilege and our blessing to be called to this circle of seeking, and we thank each who has allowed us to come to share our thoughts with you at this time. As always, we ask that it be remembered that we are not infallible, that we are not all-wise, that we are not authorities, but travelers on that path with no steps that is the spiritual path. And so we ask that each respect his and her personal truth and take those thoughts of ours which seem good to you, leaving the rest behind without a second thought, for each seeker has within that compass that tells when the direction is right and we ask each to use that discrimination and that guidance and to trust that feeling within, not any authority, for each is the authority of his own path. Each is truly the captain of her own ship in an ocean whose tides are not known and upon which there is no land. Each spiritual seeker sets out upon a voyage of discovery. And yet each island of truth, each continent of discovery, is within the seeker. The journey across perilous waters is an illusion necessary because all within third density dwell within a heavy illusion and the way to grasp the nature of that illusion and to use it is also illusion, for is not all the shadow of one great original Truth: Love—that which is ever unmanifest, invisible, ungraspable, unprovable. Such is the nature of the spiritual journey.

This day you have asked for our thoughts on what are the steps for achieving harvest, the harvest of third density, those specks of light which we have talked about. How can seekers learn to bear the intensity and fullness of the light that illumines fourth-density illusion, for you see all within our grasp is illusion, yet each harvest delivers the seeker into an illusion that is fuller of light, that light which is the first manifestation of love.

So when we say that all is illusion this is not to suggest that there is a way out of illusion. No, rather we suggest and encourage each to contemplate the seeking of that illusion which contains that fullness of light which can be accepted and borne through the circumstances of each day, each hour, and each moment.

This instrument was saying earlier that none is worthy, and the one known as Tom suggested that all are worthy. And we say to you that as with all paradoxes this is the mark of the spiritual, this is a sign of the metaphysical: paradox and puzzlement—for each statement is quite true to the best of our knowledge. No one is "worthy" if worthy means that one has accomplished a certain number of understandings so that one is able to pass the final test. None, by learning, no matter how abstruse, shall be able to accept fullness of light through knowledge. None is worthy to enter into fuller experience and larger life by what striving that entity has done. It is also very important that each realize that beyond and throughout all illusions that each entity is perfect. Each entity is loved by the Creator. Every iota of flesh, every thought, every emotion is loved, accepted and forgiven by Love Itself. So there the human experience balances between complete unworth and complete worth. Between is that pathless path which each seeker treads.

As we speak to this instrument we ask each to breath deeply, feeling that inspiration, that life that dwells in each breath. And as each breathes out, let that life that is given back be felt. As each breathes in each breathes that which the trees and the plants have given, and as each breathes out each is giving to the atmosphere that which feeds second density plants, trees and so forth. There is a depth of interconnectedness between third and second density, and in between all second density entities that articulates without words the way of service.

Indeed, do plants consider themselves other than trees? Do trees consider themselves other than animals? And so forth. Indeed, these entities for the most part know only that all is well and that all will be well. And instinct, growth and desire for the light lead each into the paths of living and of releasing that light. It can be, although it is not [often], the same for third-density entities, and for a lucky few the instinct to serve and live by faith [is such] that there is not the need or the use of the so-called spiritual seeking. But for the great, great majority of those who enter third density there is a tremendous need to find the path that is one's own, that speaks to the feelings within.

We said earlier that your density is one of illusion, and indeed each has that garment of flesh that carries about the consciousness that is infinite and eternal. While this consciousness dwells within the physical vehicle each has one great gift which overshadows all other gifts and that is the gift of what has been called presence. Each is aware that he or she is conscious. This self-awareness opens a door which, once opened, cannot be traversed in reversed; the door shuts upon those who have been awakened to the call of their deeper nature.

Now, not all entities are on a consciously spiritual sojourn. Not all entities are ready to awaken into the responsibility of knowing that they are spiritual beings and that they wish to accelerate the rate of their spiritual learning or evolution. For those who are asleep we ask each to rest easy. There is a time and a season for each entity and when that time comes that entity shall awaken. That entity shall begin to investigate what is true, what is real, where he is, and where he is going.

For those who have come to this realization, for those who have embarked upon that journey from which there is no return, we say to you that your greatest gift, your most precious gift, is your incarnation. Each of you has chosen to be in this illusion at this time in order to learn and in order to serve. These two are interconnected, two sides of one coin, the being and the doing. The attention so often is on what one is doing, where is the ministry? What do I do to be more spiritual? And yet, it is the sheer identity of each that is the great gift each has to offer this dear planet upon which you enjoy incarnation at this time.

Let us look at what we mean by consciousness, what we mean by presence. Consciousness is, in truth, consciousness of love, for love and the distortions of love is all that there is. Each then has a native vibration that is completely congruent with the Logos that created and formed all the millions of infinite universes. And each, through the process of taking on an incarnation, have, shall we say, signed up for a difficult yet rewarding term of service.

That consciousness, then, that some have called Christ consciousness or cosmic consciousness, dwells within that vessel of skin and bones, muscles and thoughts. Each rattles around in this somewhat alien configuration, a spirit trapped, or just visiting. Most entities spend some time feeling very trapped, and yet this is an opportunity you wished for very much. This was a trip you planned for, setting up for yourself relationships that would help to focus your own heart and mind upon those lessons of love you yourself deemed to be the most telling and critical for you at this point. And so the basic vibration of each is love itself, distorted, contracted, controlled, shall we say, by the various ways which, by free will, the entity has chosen to limit or shape consciousness.

The way to climb the steps of light to a fullness that is fourth density is actually not to take on learning but to release learning, to release those strictures of contraction which you have placed upon consciousness in order to defend the self. When entities pull themselves away from the fully open heart it is usually not from a motive of anger, bitterness or offense but rather it is a move to defend the vulnerable self within. Little by little, then, the path towards graduation into fourth density involves discovering, balancing and releasing those things from which one pulls back and contracts the self in order to survive.

You see, each is as the note, tone or complex of tones which makes up an harmonic. Each is a perfect yet unique jewel, a gem with facets that have been cleaned and polished and shaped by the tempering of those furnaces which consume distortion. These furnaces burn brightest during times of initiation into lessons, when all seems dark and there is challenge and struggle within. In these times we say to you, "Rejoice, for you have joined forces with your destiny. You have come to a time of transformation. Take courage and know that sorrow, sadness, suffering and grief, anger, rage, disappointment and all the negative emotions that are felt are gifts which hold in their hands hours of despair, days, months, even years of isolation and pain and tempering." The oven of the alchemist is one designed to refine gold, to cleanse from it those things which are not gold. You may see the alchemical process working with consciousness as that refining fire in which dross is burned away, leaving that precious original Thought, pure, shining and untouched. You carry within you the sea of consciousness. All that there is within you. All that you seek lies waiting to be rediscovered.

Now, the third density lessons are lessons in love, lessons in connecting with other entities in loving ways. When one has spiritually awakened one becomes aware of a world suffering, an enormous cry of pain that is all about one, that not only exists within the self but is found whenever the entity reaches out here or there. Touch that place. Gaze into that interest and you will find that the human heart has suffered there too, and in this suffering all are one, just as all are one in the perfect joy and peace of love. And so each seeker dances amid distortions, choosing whenever possible to find the love that is there.

Each hopes to serve and we assure you that this is both simple and nearly impossible. It is simple in that simply by being who you are you are expressing love, for that is all that [can] be expressed. The question is always, "How shall I give love?" And we say to you that if you attempt to give love of yourself with your own energies you shall quickly run out of love, for it is in short supply within your illusion. However, it is not necessary for any to give love from the self. It is only necessary that the one who seeks to serve move the self out of the way of that love which comes in infinite supply from the one Creator.

That love can be poured through the instrument that is open and empty, and the world shall feel that light and shall not know whence it comes. Yet the one who is able to be a witness of light, the one who is able, if you will, to be a channel of love, that effort and that desire to serve has reached its greatest apex. If one wishes then to accelerate the speed or rate at which one evolves spiritually then one simply attempts to spend time and attention on love in daily meditation, listening to the silence within. One enters the inner sanctum of one's own heart, and one feeds there on that life-giving water that ends thirst. And as one becomes able to, one attempts more and more to see each moment as a moment in the silence, to see that all is perfect beneath that surface noise and confusion that characterize mortal, human kind.

We find that this instrument wishes to be politically correct and so we are attempting to remember both sexes in what we say but we must say that your language is not very well formed for this, so please pardon our many stumblings as we attempt to find a word that indicates that male and female alike are one with the infinite Creator.

Now, service to others is, again, as always, paradoxical, for if one serves others is not one serving the self, and vice versa? Perhaps one way to think about serving others is to ask the self to wait, to listen and to become aware in more and more fullness of what that other entity desires. And when one wishes to serve that entity then one asks the self, "How can I express love in serving this entity?" There are many times when the only way to express love is to be silent, and in that situation that is the most loving thing to do. Where there is perhaps a request from another, then one simply responds to that request as best as one can.

This willingness to take time to listen to another is in itself a service and we encourage each to open those inward ears that hear what that consciousness is saying upon the level of depth at which the self and the other are most truly expressing, for some request those things which seem fair but which, within the self, are found to be wanting and in those situations one serves best by turning to prayer to find acceptance and love.

We give this instrument the vision of the starry skies in midsummer on a clear, clear night. As you breath in, you breath in the universe, and as you breathe out, you create it again. Each is so precious. Each so beloved. Feel that rightness, that perfection that is the basis of consciousness. Breathe in and feel the heart expand. Breathe out and feel that love pour through. You are the light of the world. You are the Creator's hands, the Creator's voices.

We would, at this time, transfer this contact to the one known as Jim. We thank this instrument and leave it in love and in light. We are those of the principle of Q'uo.

(Jim channeling)

I am Q'uo, and greet each again in the love and the light through this instrument. At this time it is our privilege to attempt to speak to any further queries which those present may have for us. Is there a query at this time?

Carla: I have two questions from P. She would like to know if she and the child will be all right, and what she should do regarding waiting for the natural birth of the child and risk her own health, or whether she should do as the doctors suggest and give birth now by C-section and reduce the risk to both her and her child. She is grateful for anything that you can tell her.

I am Q'uo, and am aware of your query, my sister. We send our love and our greetings to the one known as P and to the life that grows within her and readies its entrance into this illusion. It will not be a surprise to any that we cannot directly address this query with a specific response concerning the choices that the one known as P is faced with making, for to so choose for another would be to learn for another and affect that entity's discrimination and future in a fashion which is not truly of service when seen from the metaphysical point of view.

From this same point of view it may be said with certainty that the one known as P and her child are well and will be well for all is truly of the one Creator and the will of the one Creator works its way into each entity's incarnation in a fashion which is appropriate for that entity and which is in accordance with that entity's choices, both previous to the incarnation and made during the incarnation.

The one known as P faces a great challenge in her incarnation, one which is at the core of her very being. The blending of one's vibrations with another to the point of bringing a new life into this illusion and becoming the guiding force in this new life's experience—this is never an easy choice for any, for the responsibility is great. Yet with such great responsibility come also those rewards which are beyond enumeration.

We would recommend that all who feel concern and love for the one known as P send this love upon the wings of thought which binds all things together as one being to this entity that she might be inspired by this support. We encourage the one known as P to retire within itself to that sacred room in meditation where she can feel and experience the presence of the one Creator, that she may rest within this presence and be nourished by it in her time of need. That after resting there, that she ask the questions of her heart within this sacred presence and feel the response growing within her as certainly as does the life force grows within the child that grows within her now.

Each entity may take refuge in this sacred room and feel the presence of the one Creator there. Within this sacred room there is protection, there is love, there is light, there is unity, and there is direction through the maze of choices that this illusion offers that both confuses and illuminates, that opens doors and shuts doors. Within this sacred room there is the clear inspiration of the one Creator which moves through each entity's life patterns, for the most part unnoticed because ignored. If entities seek regularly within this place of unity there is support and direction.

We cannot speak more specifically but can send our love to this entity as well, and this we do.

Is there another query, my sister?

Carla: Yes. Thank you on behalf of P. As for myself, I thought you would answer the first question by suggesting ways of increasing one's polarity to gain harvest but you concentrated on one's being and on serving when one is asked. I wondered if you could comment on that? Is it necessary to try to serve more or want to serve more?

I am Q'uo, and am aware of your query, my sister. Each seeker previous to the incarnation has laid a plan or created a pattern, shall we say, that will encompass all such steps that are necessary to be traversed for the harvest. The desire to seek and to follow this path is thus a gift of the self to the self. Each portion of the one Creator seeks to become one again with the one Creator. Thus, this basic desire is embellished in a fashion that is in accordance with the desires of the entity that has become individualized to the extent that it is able to choose its own path. Thus, during the incarnation it is well if one attempts to be oneself, to be that pattern, to be that choice, to be true to the self, for the self to which you are true is the greater self, the higher self that has laid the path before you in a fashion which allows for the free will interpretation of many, many details and yet which assures each entity that the path has been laid and laid clearly.

Is there a further query, my sister?

Carla: No, thank you.

I am Q'uo, and again we thank you. Is there another query at this time?

B: Yes. I have a question concerning the Law of Responsibility. I am confused by the concept of forgiveness. My experience teaches me that forgiveness has many strings attached to it. Could you give me a higher perspective on forgiveness?

I am Q'uo, and am aware of your query, my brother. To forgive is, shall we say, to give love for whatever has been given to you. Thus, there is no condition other than a relationship and an interaction between entities. The desire to forgive is enough with which to begin. If one places conditions upon the forgiveness then one is beginning in a fashion which will yet require refinement, for to truly forgive another one must erase all conditions. There is the giving of freedom by removing conditions, the allowing and accepting of free will by removing conditions. The gift freely given is the one with the greatest value, shall we say.

Thus, if you are able to wipe the slate clean within your own heart and mind then you have truly forgiven. There is much of one's own experience at being forgiven that conditions one as to what it is to forgive and to be forgiven. If you feel that you have accepted another's definition that no longer fits that which you wish in your own life pattern then you are free to construct your own definition and to put it into exercise by applying wherever appropriate. And we are aware that within your illusion there is much opportunity for practice.

Is there another query, my brother?

B: No. Thank you, Q'uo.

I am Q'uo, and we thank you, my brother. Is there another query?

Questioner: *(Inaudible).*

I am Q'uo, and we would be glad to entertain one or two more queries before closing this session of working, if there are any further queries.

T: How may I best be of service to my son in raising him so that I do not interfere in his spiritual path and yet teach him what I know in the spirit of love and guidance for whatever is best for him?

I am Q'uo, and am aware of your query, my brother. We have found that it is well in teaching another who seeks your assistance to first set the pattern of your own behavior in a fashion which exemplifies the basic principles which you wish to share. In this instance we feel that you desire to share in large part the seeking of the one Creator and the serving of that one Creator in all that you see. This shall be the greatest teaching to the young entity: that which he observes in the daily round of activities shall teach him far more than words and patterned instructions, though words and instruction are indeed important.

It is well to realize that even a small entity is an honored seeker of truth, one who has traveled as many trails as has any, and who seeks within this incarnation to move with you in your seeking and to learn from you. Thus, to observe, support and appreciate the free will choices that such an entity makes is most important while balancing this appreciation of free will with your own guidance given in a fashion that respects the entity rather than confining without explanation.

This is a great honor and privilege: that of teaching the young child and one which cannot receive too much appreciation from any, for the responsibility is large but, as we have said before, the rewards are as large, at least.

Is there a further query, my brother?

T: No. Thank you for what you have shared.

I am Q'uo, and we thank you, my brother.

(Pause)

I am Q'uo, and as it appears as though we have exhausted the queries for this session of working, we would once again thank each present for inviting our presence this day. We are most gratified to have been able to blend our vibrations with yours and to speak our thoughts and opinions in response to your queries which we have found helpful in our own patterns of seeking.

We would at this time take our leave of this instrument and this group, leaving each, as always, in the love and in the light of the one infinite Creator. We are known to you as those of Q'uo. Adonai, my friends. Adonai.

L/L Research

L/L Research is a subsidiary of Rock Creek Research & Development Laboratories, Inc.

P.O. Box 5195
Louisville, KY 40255-0195

www.llresearch.org

Rock Creek is a non-profit corporation dedicated to discovering and sharing information which may aid in the spiritual evolution of humankind.

ABOUT THE CONTENTS OF THIS TRANSCRIPT: This telepathic channeling has been taken from transcriptions of the weekly study and meditation meetings of the Rock Creek Research & Development Laboratories and L/L Research. It is offered in the hope that it may be useful to you. As the Confederation entities always make a point of saying, please use your discrimination and judgment in assessing this material. If something rings true to you, fine. If something does not resonate, please leave it behind, for neither we nor those of the Confederation would wish to be a stumbling block for any.

CAVEAT: This transcript is being published by L/L Research in a not yet final form. It has, however, been edited and any obvious errors have been corrected. When it is in a final form, this caveat will be removed.

© 2009 L/L Research

Sunday Meditation
April 21, 1996

Group question: Traveling the spiritual path, it seems that many get burned out after a while, and we would like to know what it is that burns out—our inspiration, our desire, our will, what is it, and what is the best thing to do to get our inspiration again? What is the wisdom of resting along the path?

(Carla channeling)

We are those of the principle known to you as Q'uo. We greet you in the love and in the infinite light of the one infinite Creator. We thank you for calling us to your group this beautiful day. Your springtime has cycled around again, that time of expanding light, and even in the purely physical illusion your colors bloom and blossom rejoicing in the increase of light. There is the palpable lifting of vibrations among your peoples as the light increases in its daily amount each of your days. The self-aware life of your planet actually increases in its fidelity to the original Thought. As light increases so does remembrance of love increase.

This is as a blossoming on the metaphysical plane, so springtime redounds very much to the finer densities and is not at all simply a surface phenomenon. Indeed, each individual, each kind of thing, has its seasons and its cycles of being and for the spiritual seeker such cycles are to be expected.

We do not wish to forget to remind each, as always, not to take our words as those of authority but as those of fellow seekers, fellow wanderers upon the spiritual path. We are not infallible. Indeed, no source is infallible, for to speak is to err. It is only possible to approximate understanding or truth at the level at which words and symbols have meaning. Truth lies behind all appearance. This includes the finer densities as well.

As we ponder how to discuss this interesting topic we find ourselves moving to the consideration of that which is the essence of each individual seeker. That essence is, in all cases, the perfect vibration of love which is the great original Thought distorted in a way chosen by the individual into patterns which are unique to that one individual so that each entity is congruent with each other entity and at the same time, and antithetically, each individual is entirely separate and different from any other, for truly, as with the snowflakes, there are no two entities just alike.

Just as each entity has the fingerprint that is unique to it, so the individual spark of consciousness that has coalesced into that sub-sub-Logos that is each seeker, that coalesced entity has its unique soul-print or signature of self. This means that each entity has, in addition to the commonly held cycles of time, of season and so forth, additional cycles unique to that one individual. There are tendencies that are common to seekers, but in the deepest sense each individual seeker must chart its own cycles and come to penetrate the mystery of those cycles for himself, for that which is perfect for another is not likely to be the optimum way of dealing with these spiritual cycles for the self. One can pick up many, many good tips, good tools and resources to use in searching out the deeper truths of one's nature, but one must always depend upon that discriminatory faculty that lies within the self.

This power of discrimination is not a passive power entirely. That which fuels the power of discrimination lies within the precinct of the deep mind and can be seen as potential memory. In other words, implicit within the essence of self, truth articulated within what you would call your past lies stored; not only the universal spiritual truths but also and more importantly the way in which these spiritual truths have come to have meaning for the infinite entity which is your consciousness.

Much, much work has been done by the being that you are. Much has been stored. Within the subconscious these potential memories lie as hidden treasure. The key to that treasure is the process of affirming the self that begins with silence, with meditation, with the opening within of the door to that inner sanctum, that holy of holies where beyond time and beyond space you, the consciousness, dwell with the Creator in an eternal tabernacle of adoration, praise and thanksgiving. Within the archetypical self lies this deep identity, and it is into this portion of this identity that you wish to move. From this sacred place comes the faculty of recognition of that which is your own. When we or another speaks to you in ways that resonate with that deep faculty of discrimination it is as though that potential memory has been given permission to move into the conscious planetary self which is your waking personality.

The use of meditation, silence and the practices of contemplation that are various is to open the avenue from the deep mind into the conscious, temporal, incarnational mind that is in cooperation with infinite consciousness, living and giving structure to the living within your illusion. Each entity will have fairly regular cycles of enthusiasm and a lack of enthusiasm. Now, each has been calling this lack of enthusiasm "burnout," and this is one name for the point in the cycle in which the seeker feels unexcited. The truth of the essence of the self is not much connected to these seasons of enthusiasm and seasons of burnout. That which each is learning can be processed by the self which puts itself into the silence regardless of the emotional weather taking place at the surface of the mind, for even in the stormiest ocean the movement beneath the surface is far profounder and far less obvious, and this is also true of the deeper processes of consciousness.

You are learning in season and out of season and what you do in terms of emotional response to surface condition is actually relatively unimportant if in season and out of season you simply remember, in a non-dramatic way, who you are and what you seek. You do not have to wax poetic to be a seeker. You do not have to sustain enthusiasm to do your work as a seeker. It is not necessary for each day to be a carbon copy of each other day in terms of a rule of life. Each seeker will need to adjust its rule of life according to its surface weather, its felt needs at the level of the surface, at the level of time and space and connections within the illusion. It is not only satisfactory but recommended that each alter the rule of life as needs, hungers and desires are felt.

Let us attempt to clarify this. Just because one has ceased to feel enthusiasm for a given practice that does not suffice as a reason to alter the practice. As long as one is not hungering for another specific practice it is well to be persistent in enthusiastic weather and in the reverse weather alike. However, as long as the seeker moves into that listening, that silent listening regularly, the seeker can feel fairly confident that it will have the inspiration and the desire to alter its practice when that alteration is appropriate.

If an alternate practice, then, moves the seeker, by all means let that seeker alter its practice in accordance with this new enthusiasm. But when the nature is simply dry and the spirit feels isolated, arid and generally in the desert spiritually, this is the time to persist. This is the time to ask of the self that in memory of those deeply held desires that still seem fair, though the yearning is missing, it is extremely well done to rely upon those memories. And in the absence of another practice continue with the practice that has seemed fair up until this point.

This instrument would suggest that it has said in the past it is easier to find a good job if you already have a job. In seeking also, it is well to persist and to be loyal to a practice that affects daily life and causes the self to come into remembrance of the Creator, regularly, inevitably, daily. So if there is the practice that no longer feels new this is still an acceptable practice. Those periods of regular silence and asking are all-important, for the Creator and you together have crafted an elegant plan for your incarnation. All those things that are needed for learning and for service have been prepared. Thusly, it is to the entity that has learned to abide that the fruits of a deeper contentment and a deeper commitment may come.

There is an art to seeking the will of the one infinite Creator. That art is grounded in the faith that you do have a proper path. And we do say to each that each does have a very appropriate path. Now, each path is open to the free will of the individual, but as that path unfolds each will be unable to avoid following the path, for it is not a straight path. It is often a roundabout and complex path, but all variations of your path lead you to the infinite love of the one infinite Creator. No matter what general permutations of your path you choose you still are upon your path, for the path is more a journey of self than a journey within time and space.

These concepts are almost impossible to share using your language. We apologize if we seem to be vague. But it is deeply so, we believe, that you cannot ruin your path. You cannot fail to continue to have constant feedback from all experience that offers a constant and self-renewing source of catalyst to the self.

In the terms of movement there are times it feels well to race upon one's path and then we urge your feet to have wings. The cycle will contain those times when the body of emotions has been beaten and it needs to rest and recover, and in those times there will be the pausing upon the path. But all of the various moods that consist in the emotional weather of self are acceptable.

We would at this time transfer this contact to the one known as Jim. We leave this instrument in love and in light. We are those of Q'uo.

(Jim channeling)

We are those of Q'uo, and we greet each of you again in love and in light through this instrument. At this time we would ask if there are further queries to which we may attempt to speak?

R: Could you give me a suggestion as to how I can maintain the silence when I sit down to meditate?

When we are asked to join any entity such as yourself in the meditative state it is our ability and our honor to attempt to blend our vibrations with yours in a fashion which tends to reduce the peaks and valleys of alertness, the beta waves of your brain's working. This allows the perceived environment to move by your notice in a much more peaceful fashion. It is as though we were taken upon the back of your brain activity and given the opportunity to ride the waves, bringing each more nearly to the point of harmony or that which would be seen as more of a ripple than a wave in the physical sense.

When we do this blending of vibrations we tend to work from the violet ray or crown chakra down to the heart chakra and work with the reservoir of accumulated love that is the essence of your being by blending our love vibrations with yours and aiding the opening of the meditative state or the reduction of the conscious state. We then hope to offer a more calm and peaceful environment in which you may practice of the one infinite Creator. The responsibility that you and we share in this blending of vibrations is the responsibility to use this blending in service to others. Whatever essence or kernel of love you may feel and connections you may make in your own understanding is a fruit, shall we say, that may be of service to others as you put it to work in your own life pattern. The same is true for us.

Is there a further query?

B: I want to know how to deal with a person at work that I often seem to battle with. How do I keep from battling?

I am Q'uo, and we may comment. We are aware that this other wishes to be confrontive and gain the upper hand in each encounter so that there is a system of dominance established, and when you are required to be in this entity's presence it is difficult to refrain from engaging in the conflict which this entity appears to enjoy with not only yourself but others as well. There are many, many kinds of personalities which have formed around free will and individual expression of this will. It is inevitable that there will be conflict and confusion, for the free will expression of personal identity is an activity that third-density entities are liable to use with or without discrimination and yet the expression of this free will is central to all choices made and most importantly central to the choice of polarity that is the gift of this density. Thus, each entity is in its own way attempting to carve out that vehicle of personality that shall carry it to those places it wishes to go.

There is, however, as you are well aware with acute sensitivities intact, much of friction or wasted energy it would seem that occurs when entities inhabit an area of work that is the place where the personality shall find its fullest play, and the play of more than one personality conflicts with others. This is the very stuff of your density, my brother, for whether the interactions are long or short, intense or not, there is always the opportunity to give love for whatever is received from another, each instance offering a certain degree of difficulty, yours being more challenging than most for you at this time. Yet we can assure each entity that each personality and opportunity to interact with them is given in a way that is possible to achieve, to give love rather than conflict. We can only suggest to each entity that the meditative state be used as often as possible in order to return one's own desires and intentions to the proper tuning.

(Tape change. During this time, Q'uo finished the previous answer and B asked another question.)

(Jim channeling)

As you have observed previously this day it is difficult to be vulnerable. When one is wishing to give love and acceptance in place of any conflict offered to the self, one is placing oneself in a vulnerable position, for there is not the attempt made to protect. To protect is the more common or natural response from entities who are working their way towards understanding. It is not easy, as you are well aware, yet it is always possible and it is for the possibility of such a breakthrough that such efforts are made.

Is there a further query?

B: Sometimes I wish to serve and find no one to serve. It is very frustrating. Do you ever find yourself in such a position?

We have felt great desire, as have you, to be of service to others. However, we are somewhat more accomplished at feeling the opportunities and answering in a manner which is appropriate, for it is always possible for us to simply send the vibrations of love, light and healing to those who are in pain and who call for such healing with their anguish. It is not so easy for you to do this, yet it is also possible if this is a ministry that one would wish to take upon one's shoulders.

There are many entities that one meets in the daily round of activities and even the smallest smile or offer of assistance can mean much to any entity. To give even the smallest amount of time and energy to another is to assist. To wish to assist is to lighten the vibrations of this planet by the simple desire to serve another in love rather than to bring difficulty and grief to another through machinations of the mind and the random thoughts that accompany such random desire. Thus, the tuning of one's own mind/body/spirit complex in the desire to be of service to others is in itself and in its essence a service. Where there is desire to serve, there is always the opportunity to serve.

Is there another query at this time?

(Pause)

I am Q'uo, and we are most grateful, as always, to have been with each entity this day in this circle of seeking. We feel that when the queries are from the heart the depth and power with which the desire to know is [enhanced]. And we are grateful to each for allowing us to be a part of this most personal sharing of concerns, ideas, inspirations and confusions, for all of these are a part of the one Creator in each entity. [Each] entity has a portion of a great puzzle and when we come together in sessions such as this we see and feel and are much more than any individualized portion that we were before. For this opportunity to grow and to serve we thank you with all of our hearts. At this time we shall take our leave of this instrument in the love and the light of the one infinite Creator. Adonai, my friends. Adonai.

L/L Research

L/L Research is a subsidiary of Rock Creek Research & Development Laboratories, Inc.

P.O. Box 5195
Louisville, KY 40255-0195

www.llresearch.org

Rock Creek is a non-profit corporation dedicated to discovering and sharing information which may aid in the spiritual evolution of humankind.

ABOUT THE CONTENTS OF THIS TRANSCRIPT: This telepathic channeling has been taken from transcriptions of the weekly study and meditation meetings of the Rock Creek Research & Development Laboratories and L/L Research. It is offered in the hope that it may be useful to you. As the Confederation entities always make a point of saying, please use your discrimination and judgment in assessing this material. If something rings true to you, fine. If something does not resonate, please leave it behind, for neither we nor those of the Confederation would wish to be a stumbling block for any.

CAVEAT: This transcript is being published by L/L Research in a not yet final form. It has, however, been edited and any obvious errors have been corrected. When it is in a final form, this caveat will be removed.

© 2009 L/L Research

Sunday Meditation
April 28, 1996

Group question: The question this afternoon deals with wanderers and the problems that they face. Ra mentioned at one point that wanderers were more likely to have psychological problems fitting in with the vibrations of this planet. We are wondering if Q'uo could speak about the kinds of difficulties that wanderers face that might be specific to them as opposed to the kinds of difficulties that natives of this planet might face, and special recommendations that Q'uo might have as to what wanderers might do to harmonize their situations.

(Carla channeling)

We are those of the principle known to you as Q'uo. Greetings in the love and in the light of the one infinite Creator. Thank you and bless you for calling us to your circle of seeking this day. We are most grateful to have this opportunity to blend our vibrations with yours and to offer our humble opinion. We ask only one thing, and that is that you take with you that which you feel is useful of what we say and leave the rest behind without a backward glance. Trust your discriminatory ability, not another's authority, for you have your wisdom deep within you and we only help you remember parts of it. That is what we hope is our service to you, and we thank you for your great service to us, for without those who seek and hunger and desire to know the truth we would have no right to share our views.

You have asked us this day about a subject that is very dear to our hearts, as this instrument would say, for we have been wanderers and have dealt with the experiences of being one who is not native to the vibration of birth. We know the call to serve as a wanderer and we know of the tremendous effect the veil of forgetting has on the young wanderer that [is] so, so far away from any vibration that feels native, and yet we have not regretted in any way our service as wanderers, and we hope that each of you can come to feel that the service that you wish to provide is worth the sacrifice of comfort and the many feelings of difficulty and isolation that a wanderer is almost bound to experience.

This is a large subject and [at] this particular meeting we would like to speak using the organization of energy centers to allow us to share our thoughts in a somewhat more logical way than simply taking the various challenges of the wanderer one by one.

We are aware that each has a good understanding of the various energies that lie on the path or pole line from the entering energy at the root or red-ray energy center and that move upward through the body's [energy centers] to exit finally at the violet-ray center, moving, as does each of you move, from the basic to the more advanced lessons of love which you have come to learn anew as if you had never known them before. Remember to turn in thanks and look once more to find what depth you have not yet plumbed in each energy. In each, shall we say, division of incarnational lessons there is an unending subtlety and refinement of what we may loosely call understanding or balance. There is no end to awareness and there is no end to the path each of you shares, but only an ever more profound allowing of the natural balance to come into manifestation from that great well of potential that is the human heart.

We would begin with the red ray, that great and powerful …

(Carla deals with Mo the cat wanting to climb into her lap.)

As each wanderer comes into being in an incarnational body the very cells of that physical vehicle, having been inundated and marinated in that consciousness that it now carries for a lifetime, shrinks and quivers with the mismatch of vibrations between the physical body of that consciousness and the energies which can be called public opinions, those cultural entities which mold and control, for the most part, the surface beliefs and habits of a culture. Your peoples, by their very basic ways of moving through their days, their seasons, and their years create a tremendous and powerful ethos driven by fear, driven by hunger, driven by need and desire that many of your peoples truly believe can be satisfied through the attainment of money and power.

These beliefs, so native, so normal and so very widespread, simply fail to ring true to the wanderer on the most basic of levels. And so that red-ray energy center is challenged first by the very instinct for survival, for it feels to the consciousness of that body as though it will not be able to survive.

Perhaps the most basic corrective of this feeling is the observation that each has in fact survived, and we may not create joy by telling you that each will continue to survive until all that you have wished to do is done, all that you have desired to learn has been learned. Being a wanderer does not condemn the body to an early grave. Rather, it promises a chronic situation of mismatching vibrations. This is often expressed, manifested, or shown in allergies, illnesses and mental and emotional difficulties.

Now, what can each do to open and strengthen this all-important first ray? We ask each to spend the time when the self is grooming and bathing and clothing that physical vehicle to care for it, nurture it and do those things that you feel will help it. In all ways find the way to give the most respect and love to this fragile, hard put, physical vehicle. Rock it in your mental arms. Hold it and tell it, "I love you. I love you. Rest easy, for I love you." You are that body's only human connection. You are that entry way where consciousness of self meets self, and you have been given this precious physical, chemically driven body. It has offered itself freely, given its instinctual life over to that consciousness that has never been born and will never die. This is a complete sacrifice of the body which, until recently, lived the instinctual life of the great ape. Know that you can nurture this body and that it needs your love.

The other way that you can open this energy center is by coming to grips with the sexuality with which this physical vehicle was supplied. Gaze at experience and come into ever closer awareness of the sacramental nature of this energy. That which is called sexuality is only the surface expression of that driving force which has created the densities. It is as though each of you had within the self a port upon the ocean of eternity, for through the physical vehicle of woman flows the ocean of life and to its shores come each male energy to enter and know infinite love, infinite energy and the miracle of birth from the forever into the now. And to the male has been given that driving enthusiasm that is manifested in that seed which is fertile and which takes hold and offers life within the ocean.

And male and female, energy and energy, come together and flow into each other and create all the polarities, all the densities, all that you can think of. All polarity has its first expression in red ray, so whether you express this energy or are celibate, it does not matter, for if you know and respect the goodness of that basic energy it will well up within as the never-failing spring, always life giving, always life enhancing.

That second energy which is often associated with the belly is the orange-ray or second chakra, and within this energy come the difficulties and the dynamics of the self's journey with the self and the self's interactions with other selves, one at a time. For the wanderer whose experiences of other selves are often difficult, the orange ray presents the challenge of remaining open in a hostile environment of, as this instrument would say, taking the slings and arrows of challenging fortune and still remaining eager for further contact with people.

It is often true that the wanderer will not be completely aware of its difficulties of accepting itself. Therefore, the wanderer will project that difficulty outward and it will then feel that it cannot deal with other people. Yet other people are the mirrors which reflect the self to the self. It would be possible to work through the lessons of love without other entities but it would not be probable. It is the mirrors that touch your life that give you the information you need to turn within, and, little by little, find ways to deepen the love that you have for yourself.

Now, each would say, "Of course I love myself." And yet there is the self that criticizes self, that asks the self for more, that is never satisfied with what has been done. This instrument would call it being hard on yourself. Yet this is not an adequately deep expression of the kind of damage most wanderers do within themselves because they do not have mercy upon themselves. Somewhere, dimly remembered, each wanderer feels there is the possibility of giving, serving, doing, being more.

We do not deny that there is always more, but we ask each to see that this is not at all the point. To aid the orange-ray center we ask each to work at becoming more able to accept, forgive and support that self that is living by faith alone in a difficult environment, that is hungry for food that they cannot find and that becomes weary with every passing revolution of the sun. As each becomes older the weariness increases and yet this is not necessary for the one who has learned to accept the self as it is, with its dark side intact, not regenerate, not born again, but the self in all its dirt, with every mole and wart and running nose showing proudly.

Beloved ones, know that your physical vehicles will always be challenged. Your reactions to other selves will always contain the inevitable biases which handicap you in physical and emotional ways but enlarge your area of action in other ways. So, perhaps the one word that expresses our advice on dealings between self and self would be mercy. Compassion and forgiveness heal. They heal the self and they offer others a place wherein they too can chose to heal themselves. Let your witness with this strong energy be that of the loving and the merciful.

This instrument would say shepherd, but that is not the concept. We simply cannot give this instrument a more accurate word.

Moving up into the solar plexus we find the yellow ray that is the primary ray of this density, that is the ray within which the greatest work of learning and service can be offered. This is that ray within which wanderers must learn to work within various groups and institutions of your peoples. The yellow-ray difficulties mirror and extend those difficulties of orange ray. However, dealing with group dynamics is in one sense simpler, but in the normal sense far more complex than the dealing of one person with another.

Within this energy nations are built and destroyed. Religions are started and abandoned. Peoples move across continents and cultures evolve, mature and fall away. And within each group there is the more balanced and loving and compassionate path. Within this large assortment of groups that each entity will encounter within a lifetime lie the matings, the marriages, the belongings, the revolutions that shape the present and the future. In this energy each comes into deeper contact with the group mind, the national mind, the racial mind and the archetypical mind. This is the seat of power within the entity. This is where the instincts of control and influence dwell. This is the place where the spider builds its web or decides to become another entity. This is the crucible of your lessons in love.

Perhaps the most common and challenging of these groups is the family. Within this small group entities have the most steady, deep and lasting opportunities both for weal and for woe. Each is capable of becoming a portion of the so-called good of another's experience or becoming the nemesis and the avenger that can destroy another. This family is so deeply a part of the experience of third density and so fully fertile with opportunities for service to self and to other self that we cannot overstate the opportunities for polarization that lie within the challenges and circumstances of the self dealing with groups.

Community is something wanderers understand instinctively. That much almost always comes through the veil of forgetting that marks the beginning of an incarnation upon your planet in your density. The remembrance of a loving, supportive and steady family. The remembrance of men and women and children that are not only connected by names and by association but also by commonly held beliefs in service make the wanderer's plight very, very lonely within what this instrument would call the nuclear families of your Earth, for within these families there does not seem to be a constant and steady atmosphere of love, for when faced with challenges of yellow-ray energies many entities, wanderers and natives alike, move back into orange-ray energies and remove themselves from groups insofar as possible, or, alternatively, entities can choose to immolate themselves within a certain group or "ism" that there is no longer the necessity for making personal choices.

We encourage each to catch those feelings of retreat and even panic and to express to the self the word "remembrance," for if the wanderer can but remember that there is a good reason for having come, there is a good reason for dealing with these entities, these groups, then there is still the weariness, still the pain, but also courage and strength that comes from the knowledge of who you are, why you are here and where you are headed.

Now, this triad of energies is difficult, is hard work for any, native or from elsewhere. In fact, we may go as far as to say that it is well for the wanderer to realize that in choosing to come to offer this service at this time the wanderer has put itself into the situation identical with that of the native of your Earth. That is, to graduate from this plane of existence it is necessary for wanderer and native alike to walk the steps of light that offer with each step more fullness, more density of light, and if the wanderer becomes caught in the pain of living and creates a lasting imbalance in energy, the wanderer will then as surely as any Earth-born native need to remain within third density until that wanderer has again become balanced and polarized sufficiently to bear to endure that fuller light that is the experience of fourth density.

Now, in fourth density there is the dropping of the veil of forgetting. There is the greater awareness of each as the self. There is the lifting of limitations and boundaries so that each is unique, yet each shares the thoughts and experiences of each other in harmony. This sounds paradisical to the Earth entity yearning for manifestation of unity. Yet we ask each to remember that each density has its own challenges and lessons, so that there is never an end to the learning. There is never an end to challenge. Within manifestation there is always the awareness of self and the awareness of other, and as the densities refine that awareness the consciousness asks with more profundity the nature of oneness, the nature of unity.

Moving into the heart, the green-ray chakra, that heart energy center, we stop and ask each to think upon the way in which energy works. Now, if there is a tightness, a stringency or a blockage within red, or orange, or yellow, to the extent that that energy is baffled, energy into the heart will not be as much, for there will be the energy bleed-off before the energy of the one Creator reaches the heart center. The energy that reaches this center is, in practice, that energy that the self has available to begin to work upon consciousness. The disciplines of the personality—learning to communicate, learning to find the sacredness of all things—these lessons of love are not well undertaken by those who have not come to some degree of balance within the lower energy centers, and this situation is perhaps the most typically devastating to the wanderer of all situations we could explore, for wanderers yearn so for the vibrations, the feelings and associations of home that they do not have the spirit and the energy to clear those blockages to allow confusion to reign as it will without becoming enmeshed in that sea of confusion.

We are being told by this instrument that we are taking too long to speak with you this evening and that the energies are somewhat flagging. And so we would simply halt at this point, realizing that perhaps at another session the circle may wish to explore this interesting subject further. We ask each to know that each is perfect and whole and in total unity with all that there is. This is reality. The rest is illusion. For each his star. Know hope and faith as you know your fingers and toes, and dwell in love. As the one known as Jesus has said, "Love the Creator. Love each other." Dear ones, if you can but remember these simple things each day will [be] doable, each night a cause for thanks and praise.

Because there is some energy for questions we would wish at this time to continue this contact through the one known as Jim. We would leave this instrument in love and in light. We are those of Q'uo.

(Jim channeling)

I am Q'uo, and greet each again in love and in light through this instrument. At this time we would ask if there might be further queries that we might address. Is there a query at this time?

R1: I would like to ask how we as wanderers can better serve the Creator and the creation?

I am Q'uo, and am aware of your query, my brother. Whether one is a wanderer on a distant sphere or an entity of third-density illusion which has grown from roots on its home sphere, to love is to serve. To seek ways of serving more completely fuels this desire and the opportunities then present themselves to one who wishes to serve more fully. Thus, my friend, we say to you to desire to do so is to begin the process.

Is there a further query, my brother?

Carla: I have a follow-up. I know R1 is talking about helping people to network via computer and so forth and to make a place where wanderers can get together to combat the loneliness. Are these kinds of things useful or is our service mainly just living?

I am Q'uo, and am aware of your query, my sister. These many choices are but mechanics and detail. The desire to serve is the foundation upon which all shall be built according to desire. Fuel, then, this desire. Seek to serve in whatever way is yours and those ways which are yours shall come to you and through you.

Is there a further query?

E: I would like to know if there are entities that actively work against the progress of wanderers, and if so how does one recognize them?

I am Q'uo, and am aware of your query, my brother. There are indeed those which you may call the dark angels which serve in their own way by providing the catalyst of which you speak. Any crystal shall fracture along its most flawed line. Thus, look into your own pattern of beingness to see those opportunities presented that tempt you away from love and service to each entity that you meet. When these opportunities present themselves it is your free will choice as to how you shall proceed. Perhaps the choice is made in action rather than in thought, thoughtlessly rather than in contemplation, seemingly by accident [rather than] a choice, and upon the foundation of this choice the dark angels, or loyal opposition as they have also been called, may offer the intensification of that choice which has been freely made. Then the wanderer who is like unto a light is tempted to dim that light of love and service. If possible, the dark angel would seek to put out or control such a light. Thus is their service offered and thusly do they evolve in the negative sense of the service to self, the putting into order, and the gaining of power over others. They are a part of the illusion as surely as is the light, for the one Creator blinks neither at the light nor at the dark that makes up the nature of the creation itself and its expression in this third-density illusion.

Is there a further query, my brother?

E: As one becomes more aware, does karma become more instantaneous?

I am Q'uo, and am aware of your query, my brother, and feel that you are most perceptive in your recognition of this principle, for as one becomes aware of what it is that one wishes to accomplish and clears the way for such activity and is successful in achieving it, so then are the challenges more intensive and the feedback more immediate. This is efficient learning, though its disguise is often pain and suffering and confusion. Yet [by] persistence, utilizing the faith and will that are the rod and staff of the seeker of truth, one may move through this pain, suffering and confusion.

Is there a further query?

R1: Can we erase karma while we are in the third-density illusion?

I am Q'uo, and am aware of your query, my brother. We would suggest the [word], perhaps, balance because to erase karma is to erase those lessons which have been programmed previously to the incarnation and this would be like erasing a portion of one's existence, whereas to balance those lessons programmed is to remove the effect of the karma which ties one to the incarnation until the balance is achieved or until the will is depleted.

Is there a further query?

K: Do wanderers have to remain within the third density until they have achieved a balance in their own light at the fourth-density level?

I am Q'uo, and am aware of your query, my sister. The wanderer, as with any other third-density entity, must meet the same standards of giving love, of offering compassion, of opening the heart to the unconditional kind of love and compassion that are the fourth-density hallmark. Thus, the wanderer must meet these same standards.

Is there a further query?

K: Do wanderers get to go back to their home density after completing the harvest here?

I am Q'uo, and am aware of your query, my sister. The wanderer may do so if this has been the agreement and may do otherwise if the agreement has been, for example, to remain for a certain portion of the experience of the planet that it has chosen to serve.

Is there a further query?

R2: I am curious if you, after the meditation is over, stay sort of in the background and eat food with us?

I am Q'uo, and am aware of your query, my brother. We are always delighted and filled with the love and light of this group as it meets in workings such as this one. And as you disperse from this circle and share your light and love with each other in meal and conversation we are able to partake by experiencing this light and this love in its movement between you.

At this time we would again thank each for inviting us to this circle of seeking, hoping that you will forgive us for speaking overly long but we are not aware of the passing of time as we speak with you, and we are always glad to be with you. At this time we shall take our leave of this instrument and this group. We are known to you as those of Q'uo. Adonai, my friends. Adonai.

Sunday Meditation
May 12, 1996

Group question: We would like to continue the session from two weeks ago where we were discussing problems that wanderers have in this density. We were working on the energy centers and we had gotten up to the green, and now we would like to complete this information.

(Carla channeling)

We are those of the principle known to you as Q'uo. Greetings in the love and in the light of the one infinite Creator. We are most privileged to be asked to offer our opinions and to join your meditation for this session on this lovely springtime day. The energies of your growing things are most active and excited at this time and their light is beautiful to behold. As we share our opinions we ask each to take that which is of help and discard the rest of what we have to say. We trust your discrimination and ask that you be careful to trust it yourselves, for there are many who would like to replace personal discrimination with group discrimination. Yet all who seek spiritually seek uniquely and the world views of your culture do not always ring true. We simply ask that you pay attention to that ringing of truth. Trust it when it comes. Trust yourself when it does not come.

In working with the challenges that wanderers might especially have a tendency to face upon your planet of third density we have been making generalizations and will continue to do so. Each entity seeks differently and so we encourage each to question and work with this material actively, asking for further information on points which seem unclear so that we may be more able to be of service to each who is present.

We had begun to discuss the green-ray energy center and its special challenges as the, shall we say, dissertative part of the previous gathering ended, and so there we shall pick up the subject, noting that with the heart energy comes, in one sense, a fruition, a place of rest and repose where one can gain an overview of the nature of being, the nature of being in an incarnative body, and the nature of that great road which the heart walks.

The heart is that seat of wisdom that is bathed in compassion. That is its eventual destiny, and often the wanderer is able to feel that deeper centrality which is the property of the tuned heart. Yet the heart energy is also very vulnerable to mismatches of energy which block, over-activate or in other ways distort the red, orange and yellow ray energy centers. Furthermore, even when the seeker has become balanced to a high degree in the lower three chakras, still the heart, in offering information to the senses, does in most instances generate a good deal of noise along with those deep and true signals that are the essence of the open heart information.

We pointed out previously how vulnerable the green-ray energy center is to low energy coming through the lower three chakras. This is a cardinal point, for each wishes so deeply to experience that blessed open heart energy and to move into the higher energy centers that the wanderer has the natural tendency to wish to move on from the work of the lower energies into the heart, then into those energies of communication and work in consciousness which offer so much blessing and are the balm to so many wounds experienced by the wanderer.

And so there are two reasons why it is well for the seeker to go slowly and to monitor the self so that the self does not spin its wheels, shall we say, attempting the work of higher energy centers while experiencing low energy into the green-ray center. The lessons of love seem to be more uplifting in the higher energy centers. To the intellect especially this is true. However, it is our opinion that the advent of true openhearted energy takes place only when the seeker has begun to value each energy center equally and begins any conscious work with a brief examination of each center so that imbalances can be seen by the self and attended to before the self takes the consciousness into those higher centers and asks it to function.

This group has spoken often of the feelings that the self has the dark side and each has worked with this dark side, seeing how it can unhappily distort red, orange and yellow-ray energies. We encourage each, then, to find more and more appreciation of and tolerance of those lessons that seem so basic, for in truth each energy center has the same degree of preciousness. Each ray of self is beautiful to the infinite One. So the task becomes that of attempting to clarify and refine the sense impressions that arise from catalyst as the present moments seem to pass. If there is work to do with self or with other self in clearing these lower energies, we encourage an attitude of enthusiasm for doing the work it takes to get to the heart of whatever distortion or blockage has taken place.

Judging not but only nurturing the self, finding out what you truly think and feel and then, without judgment, turning once again to the open heart. Each within incarnation shall make many errors. The illusion was set up to force errors, to bring about helpful challenges. The catalyst that seems so heavy is an expensive gift of the higher self to the self. When one can take this, shall we say, on faith, one has overcome a great stumbling block that stands in the way of the open heart.

Now, once one has made peace with the first three energy centers, once one can feel that full energy is moving into the heart, there is another consideration to deal with before further work is done. This is a subtle, careful, work. It is the sifting and winnowing of the feelings and thoughts within the heart. Each entity has within the heart center all the expressions of love from the most refined to the most inchoate, unorganized and distorted. All feelings of the heart are true at some level, but the upper levels, the surface emotions of the heart, can be as the red herring in a mystery story, clues that lead in the wrong direction. If each can see itself as a kind of distillery and can see emotions as the raw products which go into the creation of the wine, there might be a good analogy of what it is to explore, refine and purify emotion, for the grape, with its skin, its fungus and its stems, the sugar with its impurities, the water with its impurities, [these together] are wine. However, they do not yet manifest as wine but rather as a collection of ingredients, mishmashed together, not yet finished. These are the emotions that the heart receives to begin with when new catalyst comes. Seldom is the entity receiving catalyst able to listen, see, touch or feel clearly. Usually, there is some degree of confusion in the response.

Therefore, it is not well simply to advise the seeker to follow the heart and no more than that be said, for truly one needs to follow the heart, but first one needs to allow each experience to be refined and be purified by that distillery that is carried within that heart by each. It seems that each is a prisoner of time, and yet in the sense that we are using this analogy it is only in the freedom of the illusion of time and space that this first purification of self-aware emotion can be accomplished. These raw feelings that the heart senses instantaneously may be already pure. But it is well to ask the self to refrain from impulse and to honor all feeling by moving back to it when one can contemplate it, and in that centered and balanced mode allow the deeper truths of what has been felt to move through that refining fire which distills pure emotion from the dross of ingredients that are no longer needed.

In other words, the heart puts out a lot of garbage which needs to be placed where it can be removed. Let us say that you have within your heart a curb.

Place the can at the curb, and when you feel you have found the dross of some feeling, that which was not fundamentally clear, the wanderer can visualize the action of physically placing those stems and skins of raw emotion into the trash to be removed by time, while the precious and pure emotion is filtered into the deep heart that contains purity, compassion and its own wisdom. Discrimination is such a valuable activity. Each has it. We encourage each in its frequent use.

Now we stand within the open heart, gazing backwards at those powerful energies that make us strong, and gazing forwards at those energies which more and more merge with the metaphysical. This green-ray center has but one true polarity, and indeed those who seek in the path of service to self must needs bypass the green-ray energy center. So, for each who wishes to serve the Creator by serving others, we say spend as much time as you can within the open heart, for it is central and the light that it sheds moves backwards to the root and forward to the crown of all possible energies. The word passion, like the word love, has far too many connotations to be a pure word, and yet we say to you that the passion-pure heart is the greatest power within the universe. It is that seat where manifestation moves from within your incarnational experience. Its keeping clean and clear is a task that cannot be overdone.

Now, with the movement into the throat chakra, or the blue-ray energy center, we move into that area wherein gifts of the Creator have often been given generously, for wanderers are communicators. It is ironic that the usual experience of the wanderer is one of frustration at being unable to communicate. This is, however, not because the wanderer cannot communicate, but because the wanderer is not speaking on the level at which others may be listening. The skill of communication is certainly in a large part simply the thinking and expressing of thoughts, knowing what is thought and finding the way to say it. However, the penalty for communicating in ways in which the other is not presently thinking is a failure to communicate.

Therefore, a signal skill of a communicator is the listening ear that is able to distinguish just where the other entity is dwelling within its own mind and heart. It is obvious that one cannot communicate to most six-year-olds as one can communicate to a sixty-year-old. Yet the differences between the consciousnesses of various entities within your density is such that a six-year-old wanderer may be able to understand what you say better than a sixty-year-old entity who sleeps still in third-density unawakened bliss.

Therefore, we encourage each to practice the skill of listening and of attempting to tailor that which is communicated to the needs of that particular entity. This is careful, subtle work, yet we feel that it is a good discipline and one which is badly needed by the wanderer, for it is a wonderful gift to share one's essence with another. Yet if that speaking does not hit the mark because the entity has been careless in giving to that individual to whom it is speaking, then those powerful energies have to some extent been misspent. Therefore, we do not say simply hold the tongue, but seek to assess the needs of that entity to whom you speak and then attempt to communicate directly into the heart of that energy. That gives the other full respect, and it shall aid in effective communication.

As we move into indigo ray we find that perhaps the greatest problem wanderers have is an obsession with and hunger for spirit to an extent which cannot be held in a balanced manner within the full range of energies. Work in consciousness seems like the hardest work possible to those who have not awakened. To the wanderer, work in consciousness is likely being done piecemeal, whether or not that wanderer has awakened, simply because of the various mismatchings of vibration between the spirit and the culture into which it has come. The great attractiveness of indigo-ray work is seductive. We encourage each to the great work of disciplining the personality and of doing that work in consciousness that better refines the self and its awareness of self, but we encourage each to do this work slowly, carefully and reverently, taking small steps and setting small goals, for work in consciousness is something that shall be more and more refined in higher densities.

Third-density work is largely within those first three energies, so that while we encourage each to work in consciousness as the opportunities are given, at the same time we also encourage each before starting into work in consciousness to turn and gaze at the self and its alignments, energies and energy transfers, and if there is work of a refining nature that needs to be done to tune to that work not with the feeling of having been punished but with the feeling of gratitude that here within this illusion of space and time you have the opportunity to move back into that open heart that you have just attained, and from there see the balance between that which is considered basic and that which is considered exalted, for it is truly said within your holy works that the first shall be last and the last first. All that you see as base is in fact that which is powerful. The right use of power is truly basic work in consciousness but it expresses through improvements through the lower rays.

What we are attempting to communicate is that third density is not the place from which to take off into the ethers. Rather, it is the place to refine your basic choice of paths: service to self, or service to others. This seems a simple and basic choice, one easily taken and out of the way, clearing the way for important work. Yet, this is the chief work of your incarnation, the purification of that choice for the light. Into that light you will take your entire universal, as this instrument likes to say, three hundred and sixty degree self. You shall not be judged on the contents of your heart, for all have light and dark within. You shall be judged by the self on your capacity to accept an increase of light. Those who truly think of others first are automatically increasing their ability to withstand the more dense light of the next density.

Therefore, wanderers, just like those native to this third density, need to see the chief importance of making, and remaking, and remaking this choice. It is not made once for all. It is made again and again and again. Temptation to shut down that open heart, to go away from the light, comes every day you dwell within your illusion, so that you can go through this process of refinement which has many temptations and tests.

Perhaps to say that there is a shortcut would not be incorrect, and that shortcut to which we refer can be summed up in two words: praise and thanksgiving. No matter what is occurring within your life experience, within the experience of your groups or of your planet, it is a gift. Many of these gifts are brutal: death, pain and suffering seem like dark presents indeed, and yet each situation is a chance to choose praise and thanksgiving.

If one can take that imagery of the distillery, we can say that often the darkest of grapes and the mustiest of fungi and growth and stems, when given time and allowed to sweeten, can offer the most profound blessings. Thus, we encourage each in all emotional weathers to find the faith and the will to offer praise and thanksgiving for the time and space in which to be conscious, aware and making that great fundamental choice: the darkness or the light.

(Transcript ends.) ❧

Sunday Meditation
May 26, 1996

Group question: Today we would like some information on addictions, whether the addictions be of food, drugs, friends, rituals or whatever. Is there any value to addictions? Almost everybody has some addiction. How do we work on addictions? What is the proper attitude to take with an addiction? Do you try to solve it, correct it, or accept it? How do you know that you are getting anything done when you work with an addiction? Is there any value in working with addictions or in addictions themselves?

(Carla channeling)

Greetings in the love and in the light of the one infinite Creator. We are those of the principle of Q'uo, and we greet you in the unstopped love and the limitless light of the one infinite Creator. We wish to thank each of you and to bless each of you for calling us to your circle this day. You have given us a precious gift in asking us to blend our vibrations with your own and asking to hear our opinion concerning addiction. As we speak through this instrument we will offer you some thoughts, and we ask that as you listen to them you take those which please you and which have the subjective ring of truth to them and to leave the rest behind, for each is upon an unique journey. Each has an unique path and each has his own personal truth. Your discrimination is all-important. It is well always to trust that instinct within that knows and recognizes its own truth, for others may feel strongly that their opinion is correct and yet you are the only one who actually knows what is correct for you. Some truths last a month, some a year, some a lifetime, yet all will one day be overshadowed by a higher and broader truth. So the relationship betwixt the seeker and all of those opinions that come from the outside is that of the connoisseur who chooses just those fruits and vegetables that are ripe. You know which truths you are ripe to receive. So shrug off any thought whatsoever that does not satisfy you.

In speaking to you about addiction we would like to begin by working with the word "addiction," for this word is to your people what the word "vice" was in a previous age. Both describe the condition wherein an entity feels driven to do or use or be some thing, or some way. This calling of vice addiction makes it sound more vulnerable to, shall we say, the quick fix, and, indeed, for specific addictions there are quick fixes. However, the nature of addiction or vice can be seen to be that which takes a good thing and simply overdoes it. What drives entities to addiction very simply is the instinct that the body, the mind and the spirit has to seek comfort, enjoyment and peace.

As each spirit enters incarnation it is without preference because it has had no experience. Immediately a soul is born into flesh and breathes the air it begins to weep because it is cold, uncomfortable and hungry. All of those needs were met within the womb, but now here is life given to a baby in full complement with all of the ins and outs of the character that it will learn how to express as it grows older. But in the short run this entity is helpless. It knows only when it lacks comfort, and when it lacks that comfort it learns to express displeasure and need. And when the parents hear that innocent cry they quickly learn to feed, or bathe, or change the infant that is squalling and thus upsetting the peace. The only tool that this young entity has to work with in the manifested body state is its inarticulate voice, and so the trials of incarnation begin with the sobs of the newborn.

(Transcript ends.)

Sunday Meditation
August 25, 1996

Group question: Most people feel totally overworked and pressed and we are wondering how we can refill our batteries to do all the work that lies before us. How can we keep our spiritual balance in the world that requires so much worldly things of us?

(Carla channeling)

We are of the principle known to you as Q'uo, and we greet you in the love and in the light of the one infinite Creator. We thank each for calling us to this circle of seeking at this time. It is always a delight and privilege to be asked for our humble opinions and especially since it has been some time since we contacted this group. We bless each who comes looking for truth, looking for the path that is that path which is destiny for each. We too pursue our destinies, and as the road ahead is a mystery to you, so it is to us. Just as each of you must live by faith and not by words, so must we. We are your brothers and sisters, not infallible authorities, and as we share our thoughts with you we ask that each take those concepts which have that ring of personal truth from that which we offer and leave the rest behind. Always use that discrimination that reflects your own faith in yourself, for each knows all that there is to know already. It is simply that the veil of flesh has dropped for each of you. You have, shall we say, signed up for a few moments, a few years, within incarnation. You chose to move into this flesh, this abode, this animal of second density that carries your consciousness about and allows you to have hands that serve and legs that walk upon the dusty road of your illusion.

This instrument once heard a visiting preacher talk about his experience as a missionary in Africa. The story went that this person and his wife, both doctors, had gone to a country in Africa that was very poor, a place in which there was much suffering. A few years after they came to this post the country experienced both drought and an outbreak of disease, and these people worked so long and so hard they did not know how they could go on. Because these doctors were also priests they decided to get up early and pray, and this they did, taking two more hours from their small allotment of sleep so that they could pray to strengthen their faith, and for them this worked. They became energized and found more than enough power within to move through their days in grace.

Now, this is an extreme example of how the way one lives and gazes upon reality as it appears before the eyes can affect changes in consciousness that bear fruit within manifestation. Several of you were saying earlier that the culture in which you live encourages the doing rather than the being, and this is a true and substantial point. Take a moment and gaze at the expectations which each has of the self. There is the expectation of enough supply to be able to amass a dwelling, vehicles within which to drive to various far-flung locations, numerous responsibilities having to do with duty to family, to loved ones, to friends. There is the requirement of collecting the various gadgets of your people, the what this instrument would call electronics that make the life both simpler and infinitely more complicated by their use—the telephone to be more in contact, the various parts of the computer that this instrument is so fond of that offer new efficiencies in storing data and require more and more hours of work in offering this machine its daily bread. Yes, you live within an environment of consuming, collecting and doing. And, yes, you have absorbed these values.

Now, let us back up from gazing at the outer world, that world of flesh and bone and deeds. Let us call upon the deeper reality, that structure within the self that is infinite and eternal. It is this consciousness that is not a part of space and time that chose to move into just this perverse environment, just this materialistic society, just exactly this one and no other. Why? Why feel that it is a prize to achieve an incarnation of such suffering, such distraction and confusion? Sit with this "why" and know that only one answer will suffice, and that answer is love, for love is the beginning and the end and all things in between. Love it was, that one great original Thought of Love, infinite love, creative, powerful love that bore light. Each photon, each particle, if you will, of light is a pure manifestation of love and of this light are builded all the vibrations and nexuses of energy that form the universe and all that is within it.

And into this infinitude of worlds beings of light come, sparks of the heart of the infinite Creator—you and all of the family of humankind. Each of you unique as a snowflake. Each of you infinitely beautiful and valuable. Each of you powerful and able to serve, for you are love. Yes, within this veil of flesh each has distorted these structures and ideas and thoughts of love so that they do not shine like the diamond but are rough. And so within the flesh each feels the frustration of knowing her own imperfection. And this is a treasure, this awareness of the self in its illusory form as imperfect. This treasure is so precious because within this illusion, this seeming imperfection, entities have the greatest chance of choosing to live in love by faith alone, for there will never be any proof that there is a spiritual reality beyond that which can be seen, felt, heard and tasted.

It is just this difficulty, this confusion that you have sought so that you may play your part in the shadow world of Earth. Each of you comes as a messenger of light, a vessel full of love. It does not come from you. It only comes through you. You are not responsible for loving the world but only for allowing space within yourself so that a channel of life through you may be made from the infinite Creator. Through your smile, through your eyes, through your outstretched hand to the world flows the infinite love of the one Creator.

Yes, each of you has, shall we say, bogged down in the mire of too much to do. Yes, each of you is weary and this is exactly what you hoped would happen. This very suffering, this crown of thorns that the too short days are, is the destiny you have hoped to achieve, for it is in this very place, this very time that you can both learn the most about service and love and offer the most powerful service and love.

When all seems confusion and energy seems gone we encourage each to take a moment to say to the self perhaps just one word: love. This instrument, being a follower of the mythical system of Christianity, says one word: Jesus. Others might say Christ-consciousness. Whatever this love, this principle that has created all that there is is named. It is an infinite source of energy and calling upon love you shall be strengthened.

Beyond the attitude of love and service and faith that all is well the tool most likely to be useful when energy is low is the sense of proportion that enables each to see that they are tiny creatures standing upon a ball in the far reaches of an unimpressive galaxy in the midst of an infinite creation in which ten thousand years is an eye blink. Truth is eternal. The knower of truth is eternal. Each of you is an infinite spirit. The more you can remember who you are the more easily shall you be able to find that center, that place of knowing that is the holy of holies within. That place where the Creator waits for you patiently, hoping that you may stop. Open that door and tabernacle with the Most High. Feel that heart within you open as you think of love and know that the most important thing you will ever do is find that place and live there. It matters not whether you follow your head or your heart; there are no mistakes. But if you wish to cooperate with destiny you will consult your heart first.

We would at this time transfer this contact to the one known as Jim, thanking this instrument. We leave it in love and in light. We are those of Q'uo.

(Jim channeling)

I am Q'uo, and I greet you in the love and the light once again through this instrument. At this time it is our privilege to offer ourselves in the attempt to speak to those queries which those present may have for us. Is there a query to which we may speak briefly?

J: Would you speak a little about the dynamic of love and faith. I think of love as active and of faith as being passive. Could you talk about them?

I am Q'uo, and am aware of your query, my sister. Love is in our way of thinking and being an activity which when experienced in its fullest is shone about much as your sun shines the light throughout the system of planets which is in its provenance. When one loves one is engaged in an activity that is the heart of being itself. Yet, one loves with the faith that to love is that which is most appropriate, most helpful, and is at the center of one's being, that this is the reason for which incarnation was taken; that throughout all of the experiences that one may accumulate within an incarnation that there is the distillation of how well one has loved that is the measure of the success of the incarnation. Yet, as we have said, there is the faith that also permeates this experience of love. Faith in the self to love, faith in those about one that are loved, faith in love itself to be able to transform one's own being and often the life pattern of those about one.

Thus, we see love and faith much as the tresses of a maiden, plaited up together and inseparable, if one is to be fully aware of the ramifications of love. There is the faith to continue when it seems that any response but love would be appropriate. The faith that to make oneself seem foolish and love when other, less harmonious, responses would seem to be called for is the situation in which the seeker of truth will find itself frequently as one loves in the face of all that comes one's way.

Thus, we can recommend to the seeker of truth no qualities higher or more difficult to achieve than having the faith to love and loving in spite of all obstacles that would seem to hinder or obliterate the possibility of love.

Is there any other way in which we may speak to you, my sister?

J: No. Thank you very much.

I am Q'uo, and we thank you very much, my sister. Is there another query at this time?

(Pause)

We feel a great joy at the opportunity to blend our vibrations with those of this circle, for it is in such serving that we are able to share that of our love with you and to feel with you the journeys that you travel, the steps that you take, the missteps that seem far too frequent and the lessons hard-won from all steps that are taken. We would wish each here to know that there is no step taken in any incarnation that is taken alone, for not only do we walk with those who call us to walk with them but each entity within your illusion is surrounded by friends that may not be seen or felt in any physical or mental way, yet there are those teachers, guides and friends who have been called to you by your own seeking and the nature of your experiences who watch you walk and who walk with you, and who hold the hand in the metaphysical sense when those moments of stress and trauma appear.

Call, then, upon these unseen friends whenever you feel that you are alone and need the support of another. Know that all such calls are answered, perhaps not in the exact way that one would imagine but in a way that has substance and lends support to the journey that is taken, for each of you here has made agreements with many who are also here and also with those who walk with unseen treads and who find great joy and meaning in assisting you on your journey, for this is a journey which all take together and none arrives home without aiding and assisting the journey of another. This is the way that the journey is accomplished.

At this time we would again thank each for inviting our presence and would take our leave of this group, leaving each as always in the love and in the ineffable light of the one infinite Creator. We are known to you as those of Q'uo. Adonai, my friends. Adonai. ☙

L/L Research

L/L Research is a subsidiary of Rock Creek Research & Development Laboratories, Inc.

P.O. Box 5195
Louisville, KY 40255-0195

www.llresearch.org

Rock Creek is a non-profit corporation dedicated to discovering and sharing information which may aid in the spiritual evolution of humankind.

ABOUT THE CONTENTS OF THIS TRANSCRIPT: This telepathic channeling has been taken from transcriptions of the weekly study and meditation meetings of the Rock Creek Research & Development Laboratories and L/L Research. It is offered in the hope that it may be useful to you. As the Confederation entities always make a point of saying, please use your discrimination and judgment in assessing this material. If something rings true to you, fine. If something does not resonate, please leave it behind, for neither we nor those of the Confederation would wish to be a stumbling block for any.

CAVEAT: This transcript is being published by L/L Research in a not yet final form. It has, however, been edited and any obvious errors have been corrected. When it is in a final form, this caveat will be removed.

© 2009 L/L RESEARCH

Sunday Meditation
September 8, 1996

Group question: The question this afternoon has to do with how to contact that still, small voice within when we are dealing with our catalyst and are confused about what to do. What might we do to reestablish contact with that voice within?

(Carla channeling)

Greetings in the love and in the light of the one infinite Creator. We are those known to you as the principle Q'uo. As always, we are most grateful to you for calling us to your circle of seeking this day. To allow us to share our opinions is a great service to us and we most heartily thank each of you for the opportunity to share in your meditation and the process of seeking the truth. We too seek that which is truth and we too continue to seek, for that which is truth ever recedes before us as we approach it, so there seems no end to the seeking or to knowing in love, for we find that this mystery and all metaphysical mysteries come at last to that by which we know no other better name than love itself.

As always, we ask each of you to take what thoughts may aid you in your own seeking and please leave the rest behind, for we are not infallible but those simply upon the same path as you, filled with the same hope. It is a pleasure to be here through this instrument and we just thank you for this opportunity.

Your query concerns how to know what your greater Self knows, and so we would begin to answer this question by commenting upon the true size of the individual soul or spirit. When entities upon your world gaze upon each other they see a curtain of flesh which covers that which cannot be limited by time or space. It is the normal reaction to gazing in the mirror to see the self looking back. And, indeed, for the duration of your present incarnative experience that image, for all outward intents and purposes, is you. However, that which dwells within that habitation of bone and flesh is an entity of such power and strength that one of the ways of expressing the self in densities to come will be to participate in being a star. The strength and power which is you is an infinite quality. We do not limit you to even the most extravagant measure of power, for each of you recapitulates that great original Thought of Love which created all that there is.

Your roots lie in eternity. Your hopes for this incarnation lie in focusing that power and strength by disciplines of the personality learned under the conditions which you now enjoy. Now, let us gaze at these conditions. Why would an infinite quality known to itself as a soul leave the full awareness of Self to adopt a personality shell and a physical body and a process of forgetting all that it knows? Why would any of us seek to draw the veil over all of the information that gives us a full awareness of the self?

Gaze in mind about you, about your environment, the home, the workplace, the meeting place, the stores, all of the environments into which you walk, with which you interact. All of these environments place you cheek and jowl beside a great many different, equally powerful entities, likewise dwelling in human form, likewise unaware of their true power, and likewise seeking in each his own way to find the just right place in time and in space, each for himself.

This process of unknowing, of forgetting, is something that those experiencing the full Self gaze at as thought it were a summer camp full of the most enjoyable and interesting activities, for when you are your greater Self and not within one or another incarnation you become aware of all of those little strings and tatters, little imperfections, little places of weakness that you perceive in the fabric of your very vibration, and you look at those things upon which you yearn to make progress. And you are aware that the fastest, most efficient place for sharpening and honing those skills of discipline of the personality are found in the deep illusion of third-density incarnation. This is in addition to the desire to serve that has brought each of you to this planet at this time. You also wished to aid your own progress upon your spiritual path, and this your Earth world is by far the most skilled teacher. And if each student can find the way towards her own center this experience shall indeed yield for you all that you hope.

For the most part, this illusion works upon you not in spite of the veiling process but because of it. It works because it throws you continually into confusion. It works because it causes you continual frustration. It works because it knocks you from your center and sends you spinning. You, as a higher self, wanted this spinning, wanted the frustrations, wanted this aggravation of not knowing. Why? Because only in the ignorance of unknowing can a person choose to operate solely by faith. All the wisdom that the mind seeks pales before the wisdom of simple faith. All the ways of gaining what you have called control, good as they might be, pale before the efficiency and efficacy of the employment of faith.

Once one is aware that one is being apparently limited but with great resources which lie beyond space and time, that seeker can choose much more consciously and much more on a daily basis to make use of the various catalysts that cause confusion and to see these experiences as positive opportunities to exercise faith. The exercise of faith is simply that willingness to believe and to act upon the belief that there is a plan that is in effect and that cannot fail, and that that plan will constitute a destiny that is a safe passage regardless of the many twists and turns that always occur.

It is not that one must have faith in a destiny that is absolute, for that is not the way the world of spirit works. The lessons that each came here to work on are not lessons to be learned literally. They do not constitute specific wisdoms. Rather, they are lessons of the nature of, perhaps we might say, a seminar upon one issue or another. The issues are always about love. Some must work more on how to love. Others must work more on how to accept love. Some must learn how to love without possessing. Others must work on how to love with commitment and possession. But always these lessons are a theme. If you do not choose to go one way and get the lesson there that lesson will simply follow you along the path that you have chosen. One path might give you a more easily understood or more rewarding example of a way to learn this lesson than another. But always we ask you to keep in mind that you cannot make a serious mistake. The reasons that you are here will follow you faithfully, and you shall have ample opportunity to work upon that personality that you experience as yourself.

The goal here is not to be full of the self. Rather, the goal is to be familiar enough with the self that you exhibit at this point of space and time that you become transparent to that infinite love which flows through you which brings you the energy to live and which flows through you to the world as undiluted, infinite love. You are seeking not to consolidate as much as to know the self. It is not that you wish to push this self around. Rather, you simply must learn that essence of self that is most truly you. Once you have come into a relationship with that self that is most deeply you you are in the position to open to infinite energy and to allow yourself to be a channel for that energy. And thus each can become that light upon the hill that the one known as Jesus spoke of. The bushel that you are hiding your light under to some extent is that consolidated sense of self that is opaque to love and to the changes that spirit always brings. For spirit grows constantly. Love moves without end. Its very nature is a flowing and a vibration. There is nothing static about that great original Logos that is Love.

When that solid self is most confused and when you seek to find the way that is for you we might suggest that your first activity might be to affirm that you live in utter faith that there is a way for you that is prepared. You do not know what it is, but you can ask in meditation and in prayer for that awareness to come to you. Now, where is this awareness coming from if all are one? You may conceive yourself to have within the subconscious mind all that there is. The top of the subconscious mind is full of distortion, but as the roots of mind move downward into the cultural mind, the national mind, the racial mind, the mind that is Earth, as you move down through these levels of awareness to the very roots of the archetypical mind you come upon purer and clearer and more lucid conceptions and awarenesses of that unspeakable truth that expresses itself as emotion.

And so in meditation what you are doing is moving down to that subconscious mind, opening up that conscious mind by not using it, allowing the self to sink down, down to those roots where the information is clearer because it has no words. That still, small voice is truly silent. It is a rare entity which hears a voice which says, "Do this. Do that." What you shall hear is nothing. But for the one who waits in faith in the tabernacle shared with love itself there shall come a feeling of peace. It shall be either the peace which knows, "This is what I shall do," and can point the finger just there and knows its place and is content. Or it may come with that peace which says, "I shall cooperate with whatever happens because I know that what is mine will come to me." Both of these awarenesses are emotional feelings and both of these awarenesses contain great personal truth. We encourage each of you who seeks to know the next step, the next way, to move into meditation seeking that next step, asking humbly to become aware of that which is destiny for you.

We encourage each to allow time to pass. Sometimes there is an immediate apprehension, an immediate peace and it only takes a few seconds to become aware of the next step. At other times one must invoke faith and patience again and again. These times of waiting, though difficult, are as the times of fertilizing the ground. And if you are waiting, wait happily, we encourage each, for in this waiting much is taking place. The ground is being prepared. Faith is not something that you may buy or something that you may work towards. Faith is something that comes to you after you take the leap into empty space. Once you are falling you feel that [emotional] parachute and you know what faith truly is, but you must jump first.

This instrument is encouraging us to move ahead, as we have a tendency to use too many words, and so at this time we shall transfer this contact to the one known as Jim. We thank this instrument and leave it in love and in light. We are those of Q'uo.

(Jim channeling)

I am Q'uo, and I greet each of you again in the love and in the light of the one infinite Creator. At this time it is our privilege to offer ourselves to attempt to speak to those queries which those present may have for us. Is there another query at this time?

P: Is there any other way to know faith besides jumping?

I am Q'uo, and am aware of your query, my sister. We are aware of entities who are able to express the quality of faith as a gift of the incarnation and for those who are blessed with the gift of faith both the expression of the faith without jumping and the expression of the desire to jump and to know faith more closely is more easily accomplished. We know of no way to gain faith other than to become vulnerable to your incarnation and to your destiny within your incarnation, for as you face the uncertainty of this or that catalyst at various times during your life pattern, it will come to you that the only road to travel with any confidence is that road that has faith as its milestone and marker along the way.

Is there a further query?

P: When do we know it is a temptation to jump as Jesus was tempted to jump by Satan and when it is an act of faith?

I am Q'uo, and am aware of your query, my sister. This is the central question of this meeting, for it has been asked of us when and how to know that still, small voice, and it is this voice that we could suggest that one listen to in order to know those times when it is appropriate to jump and those times when it is appropriate to wait. Thus, in all situations in which there is doubt it is our recommendation that one practice meditation. Meditate upon the action or inaction, for as long as it is necessary for you to hear that voice and to feel that impulse in one direction or the other. As we stated previously, it may happen in a moment. It may take a great deal of time, and while this process is going on again we counsel faith that the process itself and the action itself and the entire incarnation will unfold as each should, for this is not a universe in which chance plays a significant part. It may seem so for many, but in the overall scheme if one could look with far-seeing eyes outside the incarnation one would see that there is the hand of the Creator in each event. That, indeed, not even a small sparrow falls to the ground without the knowledge of the Creator. Thus meditate, my sister. Meditate and have faith and go forth confidently.

Is there another query?

B: How can we find the balance between being vulnerable and protecting the self?

I am Q'uo, and am aware of your query, my brother. We can only counsel that you surrender to your destiny. This instrument has heard it said frequently. And by this we mean that you must, as all warriors of consciousness, go forth into your daily round of activities and experience that which is yours to experience. In some instances you will feel that you can become more of what you call vulnerable. In other instances you will feel the need to withdraw to some degree behind a certain safe construct or wall, shall we say. As you move through your daily round of activities experiencing and experimenting with each possibility you will find that some feel more fulfilling than others and you will find this balance yourself. You must learn to trust yourself, your inner impulses, this small voice of which you have been speaking, until it speaks to you as often and as clearly as your best friend, for indeed it is such. And as you seek to hear this voice, and await the words, await the feeling, await the intuition, it will become more easily accomplished and you will indeed be apprised of the situation by this best friend, this small voice that is still within where peace resides at the heart of your being.

Is there a further query?

(Pause)

I am Q'uo, and as it appears that we have squeezed the last query from the tube of queries, utilizing this instrument's imagery, we shall again thank each for allowing us to join your circle of seeking and to express our thoughts and opinions that have been helpful to us in our own journey of seeking. At this time we shall take our leave of this instrument, leaving each in the love and in the ineffable light of the one infinite Creator. Adonai, my friends. Adonai. ✣

L/L Research

L/L Research is a subsidiary of Rock Creek Research & Development Laboratories, Inc.

P.O. Box 5195
Louisville, KY 40255-0195

www.llresearch.org

Rock Creek is a non-profit corporation dedicated to discovering and sharing information which may aid in the spiritual evolution of humankind.

ABOUT THE CONTENTS OF THIS TRANSCRIPT: This telepathic channeling has been taken from transcriptions of the weekly study and meditation meetings of the Rock Creek Research & Development Laboratories and L/L Research. It is offered in the hope that it may be useful to you. As the Confederation entities always make a point of saying, please use your discrimination and judgment in assessing this material. If something rings true to you, fine. If something does not resonate, please leave it behind, for neither we nor those of the Confederation would wish to be a stumbling block for any.

CAVEAT: This transcript is being published by L/L Research in a not yet final form. It has, however, been edited and any obvious errors have been corrected. When it is in a final form, this caveat will be removed.

© 2009 L/L Research

Sunday Meditation
September 15, 1996

Group question: The question this week has to do with the feeling that we won't have enough time to do the work that we came to do. When is this work really done in relation to time? What is occurring when we worry? Talk to us about time, worry and spiritual work.

(Carla channeling)

We are those known to you as the principle of Q'uo, and we greet each of you in the love and in the light of the infinite Creator. May we thank each for coming to this circle of seeking. We are so grateful to have been called to your meeting and to speak to you on the subject of time and some of the implications that lie in that concept of time. As we speak we ask each to use his own discrimination, for each of you has the power and the wisdom to recognize the truth that is yours. It is as though your truths lie waiting for you to rediscover them and to remember that which is already known. If some of our thoughts have that ring of remembered truth then by all means we offer them to you with a full and happy heart. If we do not hit that mark, then we ask you to simply drop those thoughts and go on.

Talking about time is talking about one of the prime distortions that makes up your illusion. Let us then start with our concept of time and space. Although we cannot be sure of this, it is our opinion that time is a building block that exists in order for the illusion of sequence to offer the Creator's children a seeming sequence of events, small and large. It is half the basic building block of your perceived consensus reality, the universe as your culture and science know it. It is as though the Creator took the Logos, which is Love, and paired that great original creative Force with the means to make it into a perceived illusion. The means of this impregnation of love to create a kinetic universe is light, the basic unit of light. The photon, we feel, is combined with one unit of love to create space and time. It also creates time and space.

Now, the perceived physical creation about you we have labeled space/time, that is space-slash-time, indicating the apparent ascendancy of space over time. That is the illusion in which you dwell during an incarnative experience. There is a universe which this instrument prefers to call the universe of spirit or the world of spirit. This metaphysical universe is created of time/space, or time-slash-space, or time over space. Within this creation it is the illusion of time that has the ascendancy and in this illusion conditions are much different. However, both the physical universe of space/time and the metaphysical universe of time/space are equally illusory and are created for a combining and overarching purpose, and that is, as we said, to create an illusion of sequence. As far as we know the least illusory state is that state in which there is no space or time. This is the truth in which all are rooted and all are members of that which lies beyond space and time entirely.

However, without the illusion the creation rests in unity. It does not dream or talk to Itself. Indeed, one might somewhat whimsically call space/time and time/space as the dream of the one infinite Creator, and in this dream the Creator hopes to know Itself. The Creator hopes that each unit of Itself, each being that is love, which each of you are, will experience those things which add to the knowledge the Creator has of Its nature, for it has generously given Its complete nature to each co-Creator of the universe. To us, to you, to the highest, and to the seemingly lowest of creatures that has an awareness of the self is given one nature and that nature is love. Through the machinations of time/space and space/time choices are made. Each unit of love finds itself progressing, finds itself offered any number of actions and thoughts and avenues and directions. And there is no attempt to control the thoughts and reactions of any, for each is treasured as it is. The Creator loves so completely, so utterly, so purely that It loves each and every tiny thought or kind or state of being whatever, including all of those facets of the self which this instrument often calls the dark side of the personality.

Loved as you are there is nowhere to go, nothing to accomplish that can create between you and the Creator any greater approval or any more vehement or intense love. Before any thought of you was visible to the most metaphysical eye, you were already created and loved, for the units that have been sent out to experience and to come back into unity have gone out and come back many, many times and as far as we are aware this is an infinite universe.

Now, what is the nature of this grand illusion, space/time? How can you use it? What is the nature of time/space, and how can you use that? Firstly, we ask each to consider the possibility that the right use of time is first of all the right use of consciousness or attention. Within your culture the weight of importance is generally given to actions undertaken and completed. There is much spiritual encouragement along the lines of "by their fruits you shall know them," which entities almost always take to mean the fruits of time and attention which are money or projects completed or services offered in love, and surely all of these achievements are excellent and show that stewardship of talents and gifts that is, as far as we know, the right use of those gifts.

However, what this point of view misses is the far deeper importance of the way your consciousness is aligned with respect to the vibration of the one original Thought which is Love. Indeed, you may grade yourself, firstly, on that tuning with which you meet consensus reality moment by moment. To our mind, we cannot conceive of running out of time to do one's main job because one's main job is to experience in as clear and undistorted way all of those catalysts which come before you with that vibration which is most essentially yours which is closest to the tuning of love. This tuning, which one may think of as a constant such as the speed of light—let us say, the speed of love—is the same for all entities. However, each entity is unique, and so each entity's path is unique. And each entity's way of tuning the self moment by moment must be his own and not something taught to a group by rote, each person doing precisely the same as each other. The path to the clearest self-awareness is unique for each seeker.

However, we encourage each when thinking about the right use of time to remember to consider before all else whether the self is tuned to match the vibration of love. Each feels this constant within and we would pause for a moment at this time to allow each person to move into the heart, move the attention into that place within that is the metaphysical equivalent of the heart, the green-ray energy center. Here is the seat of love coming into the created body. Here is that holy of holies where love dwells fully, undistorted and pure. Moving into this sacred place within, open the heart and feel the love of the one infinite Creator.

Like the sun lights up the sky, the Creator rests in full strength within you, lighting your way. The key to this door, the key that opens the door into your own sacred heart, is silence, a turning within to listen to the silence. And this habit of turning within, of centering first upon the Creator which is love, shall stand each in very good stead as each attempts to seek the truth of its own being and its own journey.

Thus, one can finish an incarnation and only then realize that one has run out of time [for that] which one has come to do. Yet that [for] which one took flesh is available to be done in every living moment.

We would greet the one known as O, as he squeaks happily and high, and assure this smallest of our circle that we rejoice with him.

Moving from that place within which contains truth, which contains love, one may begin to feel an energy—which has nothing to do with how much sleep one has gotten, or how healthy the physical body seems—beginning to enhance and energize not the body but the spirit which moves the body about. Each may find this a very present helper as she goes upon her way. This aid will enable each to know, recognize and acknowledge those gifts which have been given to each, for each has come with at least three things, at least, to do: to experience, to learn personally, and to use one's gifts in service to each other, for in serving each other you serve the one infinite Creator.

We ask each to see each other as the hands, the voice and the face of the Creator. The Creator cannot smile upon any nor reach a hand to any, nor feed nor clothe any. The Creator's voice, hands and actions are yours. You represent and give meaning to love by your service to the Creator within those with whom you share your fragile island in space. It does not matter whether these services are small or great or considered important or unimportant by any society or way of thinking whatever. What matters is that you are attempting to open the heart, are attempting to use your gifts, and are attempting to make what sense you can of your experience. These are your basic commitments in incarnation. These you may do minute by minute and day by day, and to the world you may be doing nothing useful. But each who has come within the glow of your smile or the friendliness and cheer of an open handshake or hug knows that more is going on than just passing the time.

When entities attempt to think of time as a value inevitably they become completely frustrated. The reason for this is that time is illusory. It is tied into space as space is tied into time to create the illusion that something is happening, that there is a past and a future. In actuality, it is our understanding that we are all without space and time, without separation. All is occurring within this one instant that ever has or ever will occur. It is one whole. It is love. Through the illusion of time love is articulated and mirrored back to its source, and this is deeply, deeply satisfying to the infinite Creator.

So when you think of how you spend your time release yourself from the judgments of those who have strictures of what constitutes service and love, for by the way your being meets the world that it perceives through its senses each of you is giving the greatest gift of all to the Creator, to each other, and to the planetary vibration, and we feel this is worthy of being emphasized. For as your planet and as the entire solar system of which your planet is a part rotates into a never before entered part of time and space, it is nearing, closer and closer, true fourth-density space/time.

The nature of space/time is beginning to alter. The nature of the way each perceives time and space is slowly altering. Even values that your physicists attempt to understand, subatomic particles and new—we cannot find the word for this instrument, but those things which are newly discovered by your scientists—are various new particles which are part of space/time in fourth density. Your planet is being prepared to enter this environment as are all of the global inhabitants, and at this time we are very pleased to say that much progress has already been made in lightening the planetary consciousness.

Wanderers who come to this planet from other densities have served as beacons of light through song and art and government and through all of the little-known and seldom understood ways in which simple vibrations aid the planet. And each of you is as a beacon of light. That light will grow dim or grow bright as you allow the infinite love that comes from the Creator to all to move freely through the ever-opening heart and out into the world. You cannot love, for your human love will be very limited. There comes a time when the effort must cease and no matter how firm the intention, love cannot any longer be expressed in a human sense. It is only when one quits trying to be love and allows love to come through the self from infinity that one becomes able to withstand that great force and to be able to offer it on a continuing basis.

So, each is encouraged to think of the self as a kind of light house or radio station with the light being brighter or the tuning being higher the more one's heart is stayed in love, and is open to love, and is open for loving. All of these things are yours to give before you rise from your bed to begin the busy day. And no matter what gift you give the world during those daylight hours of commerce and satisfying accomplishment, that which is the deepest service shall always be your vibration, your signature that we would recognize from any other entity in the creation, no matter in what density or under what circumstances we met you. You are yourself, full of glory and full of a life that is unending.

There were concerns about the use of time and the use of energy and what effect worrying would have upon the service that one offers in time, and we can say to each that there is no need to worry about using time poorly. If one worries, if one frets and takes up the time in the mind, then one is vibrating at a certain rate. Perhaps it may be true that worry affects the open heart to some extent, contracting it, holding some of the light within because of over-concern. But this is acceptable. It does not alter the basic vibration.

What alters the basic vibration of any entity are those thoughts that one has and that one moves back into time and time again. Thoughts of "not enough." Thoughts of "unworthiness." Thoughts of "fear." These keep that heart closed. However, when one gazes at whether one who does great things in the world is superior to one who does nothing greater than re-diaper the baby or take care of a pussy cat or simply get through a difficult day without complaint, [one finds they] are doing completely congruent acts because what is important with any act is the love with which it is done.

The one known to you as Khalil Gibran, in one of this instrument's favorite quotations said that work is love made visible. Whether your love is invisible, except when you smile, or whether your love is incredibly visible with a thousand accomplishments, that love is that love and it is that vibration, not the acts which accompany it, that are your true gift to the infinite One.

So, if you worry, by all means get it all out of the closet. Number your worries. Revel in them. Roll in them as Scrooge McDuff in his money piles. Do that which concerns you to do whether it seems foolish or wise, whether it seems useful or useless. Your intuition may sometimes suggest to you odd things. To the extent that they do not interfere with your health or another's freedom, by all meaning do those things which you have a hunch which are the right things for you. And worry not about whether you are centered if you are worrying, for truly we say to you that if you are a loving person worrying, then your vibration is very little affected by worrying or by anything else that does not close the heart. Each of you remembers a better way, and we would call that way the way of the open heart. Compassion opens the night and makes it daytime. Seek always, then, to center in love to revel and enjoy being loved by the infinite One. And that which your love is to do, those places where your love is to shine, will come too and you will know them.

We would end this instrument's part of this first larger question with a look at faith which is simply that quality that enables those who cannot see into the metaphysical world to act as though they could. In the metaphysical world which your spirit rests in at this precise moment and at all moments, you are a larger being by far. You have chosen many, many things about your present experience that have deep reasons for being as they are. Faith is a matter of trusting that this experience is on the track that you intended it to be before you came. But you will never receive an objective proof of any of [the] thoughts that we are sharing because it is essential that each entity within these illusions make the choices that they make without the advantage of knowing that they are right. It is always your free choice to love and serve the infinite Creator and to do it in this way or that.

So, know that you are underpinned, bolstered by a Self that is as sturdy as you are frail and as wise as each of you feels foolish. When one feels secure in one's moments, when one feels that one is on the track, is in the right place and so forth, then a great weight is lifted off the attention, and one is not nervous or concerned that one has missed the boat. Allow little seeds of faith to grow in your garden of thought. Invoke faith without knowing that it is reasonable to do so. Live as though you had perfect faith, that your destiny will come to you and all that is for you will simply be attracted to you as it is time for it to appear. Live as though it were true and notice those subjectively interesting hints and suspicions and suggestions and synchronicities that say to you, "Yes, you are on the right track." Each of you will have various experiences that, for you, grow to be the signal for, "Yes, you have got it right. Yes, this is what you should be doing." And you will find greater and greater satisfaction in these subjectively interesting coincidences.

We thank this instrument for the services which it has provided and would leave this instrument in love and in light and would transfer to the one known as Jim. We are those of Q'uo.

(Jim channeling)

I am Q'uo, and greet each again in love and in light through this instrument. We would ask at this time if there are any other questions from this group that we may speak to?

P: Concerning the change to fourth density on our planet. How is it affecting the lives of the children?

I am Q'uo, and am aware of your query, my sister. The young entities upon this planetary sphere are those who have by seniority of vibration chosen to enter incarnation at this time of harvest. Thus, these are entities who are old upon this planetary sphere for the most part although there is a great influx of those you have called wanderers. So that those who are taking incarnation at this time are those who are full of the essence of life, shall we say. These entities have come with a full agenda, with much history, with great expectations, with talents both active and latent that will add to the richness and the variety and the intensity of experience upon your plane for many of your years to come. These are entities who will seem to many to be of another breed, a different race, as it were, for the energy awareness at their disposal is great and is like the sack of seeds that is ready to be sown by the great Sower. The harvest, indeed, draws nigh and many are those who shall partake in it.

Is there another query, my sister?

P: What can we do to ease and aid their work? There seems to be a discrepancy between the old mindset of the world and the work that they are to do.

I am Q'uo, and am aware of your query, my sister. We would recommend that interaction with these entities is most important, that the relationships of the family be emphasized and be supported in all their many expressions of excitement, interest and dedication. These entities, as each generation notes, seem to be of another order so that the ways of the culture, though providing many foundation stones for the new building, yet do not fit in every instance, so that there is the need for the individuality of each entity to be recognized, nourished and directed with a means of giving praise and thanksgiving to the one Creator in a regular fashion and in a way which gives the young entity a sense of wonder for the immensity and the infinity of all creation. The young entity needs to find his or her place within this infinite creation, and as the family and friends of each young entity provides support, the young entities are able to test their new legs in a safe and supportive environment. Give each entity those values which are most important to you, those means of discipline that show it that there is a way to approach any situation that takes into account the individuality of the entity and the rights of others as well. Make your discipline that which is both loving and firm that the young entity be made aware that it is indeed surrounded by those who care.

Is there a further query, my sister?

P: From my classes I was shown a picture of a race in Egypt with larger craniums and I wondered about their history. Could you comment on them?

I am Q'uo, and we would need more information as to the time and the place of any entities that we would attempt to identify for you.

P: I'm not certain of the time. The place of Egypt and time of the pharaohs at least 6000 years ago. They seem to have a skull about three times larger than ours.

I am Q'uo, and am aware of your query, my sister. There are among the Egyptian peoples the interbreeding and intervention of other sources and places of origin that are other than this planetary sphere. Many have referred to these entities as being those who were representing the sun and have made drawings and statues of these entities and passed these records as lore to succeeding generations so that there is a mixture of places of origin for these particular entities of whom you speak. Thus, the folk traditions and historical records are mere remnants of the appearance of these entities amongst the Egyptian peoples a great portion of your time in your past. These entities have been known by various names, the name most similar to this group being that of Ra. However, we again caution that there has been much cultural overshadowing and infusion of sources, shall we say.

Is there another query, my sister?

P: Not at this time. Thank you.

I am Q'uo, and again we thank you, my sister. Is there another question?

Carla: Yes, O'B's friend, R, who has just had had a kidney transplant. Could you give her a special message?

I am Q'uo, and am aware of your query and the request. We would say to the one known as R that the surgery and transplantation which has been effected is that which is designed to lengthen the span of life in this incarnation, for this entity is yet full of that which is the desire to serve, to know the Creator, and to learn that known as love. We would assure this entity that there is no power upon this planet that can remove it before its time and when its time has come, with rejoicing it shall go. It is also appropriate to inform this entity of that about which it is already aware, and that is that there are many upon the inner planes that move in rhythm with this entity, lending assistance where necessary, inspiration where asked and guidance at all times.

Is there a further query, my sister?

Carla: No. Thank you, Q'uo.

I am Q'uo, and we thank you. Is there another query at this time?

(Pause)

I am Q'uo, and we shall take our leave of this instrument and this group at this time, leaving each, as always, in the love and in the ineffable light of the one infinite Creator. Adonai, my friends. Adonai.

Sunday Meditation
October 6, 1996

Group question: The question today has to do with our darker side because each of us have thoughts of injuring another who has wronged us, and that makes us uncomfortable. We would like to know how to deal with this darker side because it is part of us that needs some kind of recognition. Could you talk to us about how we could relate to that darker, shadow side of our selves?

(Carla channeling)

We are those of Q'uo. Greetings in the love and in the light of the one infinite Creator. We are most happy to be called to this circle of seeking, and we thank and bless each whose search for truth has led you to this place at this time. As always, we ask that it be known that we are not infallible. We make mistakes. We have opinions. We are those who walk with you. We are not those over you, but pilgrims such as yourself. And we share a royal road together, for there is a kingdom whose head is Love itself, and on that highway to Love we are comrades. We thank you for the company and for your great desire to progress and become more of who you truly are. This is the great journey to the heart of the self.

At this session you wish to have some thoughts from us concerning the darker emotions, more especially anger. We are aware at even this remove from your density at the power and attraction of that magnetic emotion that you call anger. If we needed to put a more accurate term to it we would call it a kind of fear. However, upon the surface that emotion is anger. It is … as we say, we do remember that it is very uncomfortable. It is extremely difficult to ignore, for regardless of whence the anger has come, its base is in the survival chakra, the red-ray energy center. One who is enraged is fighting for survival. That is, the body and the second-density brain of the creature that carries your consciousness about is honestly, genuinely concerned for its survival.

The second density is not a density in which reason has a great part. And those instinctual angers that come from a feeling of being invaded or threatened have as the natural response deeply held emotional consequences to the individual moving through incarnation. Anger and the darker side in general are not things which we would encourage you simply to ignore or to brush aside, for you cannot tell your physical and emotional second-density body not to be angry because it is not spiritual. This does not make sense. It is only in that consciousness which is abstracted from the incarnation that one has either the ability or the right to work deeply with this dark side.

So, the first thing that we would say about the darker emotions is that they deserve a place, that they deserve respect. They deserve attention. If such inner pain is not addressed and honored it can shrivel the most robust nature.

Now, let us look at what we said earlier, that anger is a kind of fear. In your language you use words that are approximate and we cannot find words in your language that satisfy us in speaking through this instrument to distinguish between various aspects of anger and fear. However, generally we would say that love, that original Thought that created all that there is, is of a nature that is purely expansive, moving outward and radiating in all directions from every point. It is the great celebration that lasts to infinity. When that love pours through the vehicle—physical, emotional and mental of the entity within incarnation—that love moves into the field of the body at the base or red-ray chakra, that survival chakra, and if it is blocked there by contraction, by fear, not much energy can come through to move into higher energy centers. The same is true for each energy center.

Therefore, the first work upon the self having to do with anger is to see its place and to forgive the self for having this nature, this nature that contracts against threats, that defends against the enemy. That which is not love is illusion, yet that which is love is also illusion within your density. So when you as a seeker find yourself radiating within in hostility, aggression, anger, rage or resentment your first duty is to yourself and it is to validate and support that dark side, for that dark side is very concerned with your health and welfare and it needs to be reassured, comforted and held as gently and lovingly as the baby at the breast.

The response of the seeker to its own dark side needs to be, in the beginning, an acceptance of what seems to be a less attractive portion of the self. The objects of anger and resentment, spiritually speaking, only seem to be other selves. Actually, you may look at each other self with whom you interact as a mirror which reflects to you those things you like about yourself and those things you do not wish were a part of yourself, and the angrier that you are at that other entity, the more a part of yourself you are recognizing and responding to.

It is as though the anger were a vampire type of spirit threatening to take you over, to suck from you your life and strength. And yet how does one cause vampiric activity to cease? There is only one way, and that way is to accept into the heart that vampiric energy, to cradle it and to know it as the self, and to say in compassion, "This, too, is me." Yes, you shall have fear. Yes, you are worthwhile. Your illusion was created so that you could not but help but respond blindly to incoming catalyst. It was not intended that an incarnation in third density be without conflict and suffering. Indeed, that portion of you which is your higher self rejoices when you feel that catalyst of rage, resentment or anger, for now you are doing the work that you came to do.

The source of a great deal of anger is the dynamic betwixt two entities, yourself and another, and so although all fear has a red-ray blockage, many feelings of anger also are generating orange-ray blockage, as that is the ray in which you an working with yourself and one other self. That is the relationship chakra, the belly chakra, the chakra where many entities will try to control from. The person that has a lower belly tension is often reacting to another being who is attempting to control or is reacting because the self is attempting to control another. In either case, not only the red-ray but also the orange energy center is experiencing some blockage and when the anger has to do with anger at society or at the culture or at groups, this anger is also generating yellow-ray blockage.

What this means is that you as an energy user are put suddenly on short, short rations so that although the energy coming to you is infinite, the energy that is making it up to the heart chakra where it can open the heart is much diminished, so once you have accepted yourself for having this dark side you have the basis for a long program of work doing what we might call coming out of a hidden place. We gave this instrument the vision of a closet. It is as though your fear, your blockage, as you experience the catalyst that creates anger, contracts you into a crowded, small space and you feel that you would explode if you could to make that place larger, yet the skillful way to work with this anger once it has been identified, accepted and forgiven in the self is to see that there is a real concern which can only be addressed by love itself.

In this work of addressing fear it is well, as this instrument would say, to maintain the baby step and not to attempt to walk out of the closet into brightest noon saying, "Well, I am out of that closet and I'll never go back." Because no matter what your station, circumstances or vibratory nature you will again be in that space as long as the veil is drawn between you, your conscious mind and that great store of information which lies below the consciousness mind.

It takes faith to gaze at a situation in which you have gotten angry again and again and still be able to say, "I will open the door just a little more. I will not try to become a person without anger, but I will try to become a little more light, a little more lifted from fear, a little freer than I was a year ago, a month ago, a week ago, or an hour ago." Do not try for the dramatic breakthrough. These things do occur, but they cannot be forced. Try, instead, to pour your compassion into that closed place and allow the compassion itself gently to move the being back into the light. Baby step by baby step. See the darker emotions as a darker color and the peace of compassion of service as the light, and see your being moving gently and slowly two steps forward, one step back, throughout the lifetime, and feel good about that, for work in consciousness is a maintenance program. It is not a college one graduates from.

All the created universe exists because of opposites. It exists because there is light and dark. The dark side within each of you is as it must be in order that you may manifest at this time, at this place. You cannot get over your humanity. You cannot become an entity without polarity. You must be that which your nature is. You are top to bottom and side to side entities of three hundred and sixty degrees, the full circle of personality from lightest and brightest to the deepest and darkest. The skill lies in seeing your emotions as information bearing energies, offering to you the fruits of your own past and the seeds of your transformation into an ever emptier, ever lighter, ever hollower self. The earthy part of the self, that soil in which the dark nature hides, is a heavy thing, and it is that soil in which truth and beauty and those mysteries which call you forward grow out of this very soil.

So, we encourage each to gaze unafraid at those dark emotions within, to love and accept them, and gently and persistently and with humor to work with them, putting them in perspective, seeing them for the vampires that they are and allowing compassion to flow as you enfold your dark side in your heart. The goal here for each is to open the heart.

We would at this time transfer the contact to the one known as Jim. We thank this instrument and would leave it in love and in light. We are those of Q'uo.

(Jim channeling)

I am Q'uo, and greet each again through this instrument in love and light. At this time it is our privilege to open ourselves to any further queries which may be upon the minds of those gathered. Is there another query at this time to which we may speak?

P: How can we help another person who is enraged with anger?

I am Q'uo, and am aware of your query, my sister. It is a situation in which one's intuitive capacities are often called into play, for it is a most fluid situation to experience the anger of another, especially if one is the focus of such anger. We can recommend that one attempt to accept the other entity for having such anger and through this acceptance to seek communication that might clarify not only the present situation in which the anger is being expressed but which might also move more deeply into the origin of the anger within the other entity. This kind of communication is that which is most easily accomplished with those who are close friends and those who are willing to explore with you a portion of the self that is not pleasant to expose. If the entity does not wish to speak of the anger at the moment it is being expressed then it is well to wait until there is a time in which the entity is willing to speak upon this matter, the emotions having been drained away concerning the situation. We recommend, first and foremost, however, that acceptance is the foundation upon which all further communication and interaction may be undertaken.

Is there a further query, my sister?

Carla: I would like to follow up on that. I've watched a couple of relationships which were like this. One person refused to communicate and was simply abusive. This can't help but hurt. Is there any way to defend oneself against being personally hurt by such abuse? Even words really do hurt.

I am Q'uo, and am aware of your query, my sister. The most effective means by which we have found that one may deal with such a situation is to work internally upon the self for the building of the confidence that one has not truly generated such feeling but that the entity experiencing the anger has the responsibility of generating that anger, for as those known to this group as Ra have mentioned, there is truly no emotionally charged situation.

There are only emotionally charged responses, and each entity will respond to each situation in the way that the entity has biased itself in consciousness previously to this incarnation.

Thus, the one experiencing the anger and expressing the anger has the responsibility of dealing with that anger and its causes. The one feeling the anger has the responsibility of dealing with the emotions that come up as a result of experiencing the anger. Thus, if it can be kept in mind and in perspective as to who is responsible for what, it is most helpful, for if the entity that is around another expressing anger takes that anger into the self and feels one way or another, the feelings are this entity's with which to deal.

Is there another query, my sister?

Carla: I just wish I knew some technique which wouldn't shut out the other person but would make the person getting the abuse safe.

I am Q'uo, and we would ask if there is a specific query to which we may speak?

Carla: I'm just concerned for P, who is a strong person and who is reduced to rubble when exposed to the anger of her spouse.

I am Q'uo, and am aware of your concern and your query, my sister. This is the stuff of the third density illusion, the interacting of entities whose motivations, intentions and talents are varied, whose paths cross and re-cross bringing into play all of the pre-incarnative catalyst that was intended to be looked at in each incarnation. There is confusion, there is anger, there is doubt. There are many emotions that come into play as each relates to another and to others. There is in one sense no safety, for one is vulnerable at all times when one opens the heart in love to another. And in another sense there is only safety, and no damage can be done, for each is an eternal entity and all seeming damage is only that which exists in the moment to be worked upon as catalyst for future growth and the strengthening of the concept of the self.

Is there another query, my sister?

Carla: No, thank you.

(Tape ends.)

Sunday Meditation
October 20, 1996

Group question: We would like information on the concepts of being in a rut or accomplishing ritualized behavior for a specific purpose and expanding our horizons and learning new things. Our own subconscious, the High Priestess, seems to be the means by which we are led into new directions. Male and female relationships seem to be characterized by the female being more willing to learn new things, whereas the male is happy to be in a rut. So what we would like to know is the strengths and weaknesses of ritualized activity and expanding our horizons.

(Carla channeling)

We are those of Q'uo. Greetings in the love and in the light of the one infinite Creator. We thank you so very much for calling us to your session this day. It is such a blessing to us to be able to share our thoughts with you and we thank and bless each of you for allowing us to share our opinions with you. As always, we ask that it be remembered that we are often in error and are not authorities but rather pilgrims along a limitless, timeless path, as you are also. And so we are companions along the way that is always the same and yet is unique for each and every seeking spirit.

This day you ask us concerning the achieving of balance, that balance of yin and yang, of reaching and waiting, of being bold and being quiet, of being fond of the usual as opposed to being fond of the novel. May we say that there is no one correct balance that persons should aim towards achieving, for each spirit has its own stored harvest of previous distortions which means that each energy center, each line of, shall we say, electrical-body impulse is wired or arranged in a pattern unlike any other, so truly that which is balance is balance for one entity at a time. Each entity shall have its own strengths and its own weaknesses. However, there are some general principles which a seeker may attempt to follow in seeking that point of balance that signifies a level of physical, mental, emotional and spiritual comfort, that feeling of being comfortable within one's own skin, and pleased with one's own company.

If you are an entity which enjoys itself you have achieved an enviable state of balance. It is the work of much compassion and hard-won wisdom to fall in love with the self, to be a support to that self in all of its uniqueness, with all of the quirks that signal and trumpet the imperfection of self. Each entity is uniquely distorted and each should celebrate and enjoy those distortions while keeping the weather eye out to find those quirks whose laughter is not kind and to work with those portions of energy until the same stimulus triggers, not a different response in terms of emotion, but rather a sense of compassion which embraces and accepts that which is seen as distortion.

The entity in balance is one which has achieved a state wherein judgment of others or of self has accuracy tempered with gentle kindness.

One of the ways in which entities within third and fourth densities tend to gauge balance is by placing one set of—this entity does not have the appropriate word. She would say "symptoms," but we speak of ways of thinking and ways of reacting—that should be given to the female and the opposite given to the male principle. In fact, although it is so that the second-density physical vehicle that carries men's and women's consciousness about in those densities have distinctive sex related patterns of behavior, it is emphatically not so that the infinite and eternal spirit that is the true self is bounded by or even very conscious of these instinctual behaviors.

Gazing upon the young of your species, it is fairly easy to see that the male and the female children tend to play differently regardless of the toys which they are given. Each within this circle is aware of lifelong patterns of behavior which have been taught by those of good character and strong morality throughout their childhoods, so that the adult seeker not only has the built in biases of the biological body which it has for the space of this incarnation, but it also has a very thorough and often crippling grounding of what it means to be a biological male or female.

Even taking these two sets of distortions into consideration we may note that it is certainly not true that all entities respond in the same way to the various conditioning experiences of their lives. There is, then, no fixed limitation as to how a spiritual seeker must express its own being. However, the choice of sex as well as other major choices concerning the incarnative period were made by each seeker before incarnation with an eye towards setting up an appropriate and fertile learning situation for the incarnation. This is especially true as the great cycle of evolution rolls around to a whole new and beckoning density, a time of harvest, transformation and what this instrument would call resurrection. As this scenario unfolds sensitive entities such as yourselves are more and more eager to find and to be the best that they can be, the most balanced, the most alert, the most aware that they [are] personally able to be. There is a great hunger for that feeling of poise, that comfort of self that is able to view, to respond and to be without the agony of self-recrimination and self-doubt.

For those who are of the biological female in body it may be said in general that the lessons which have been chosen are likely to deal with increasing the ability of the self to accept, to nurture, to forgive and to understand the self and other selves. For those who are born in the body of a male, the lessons in love frequently revolve about being one who can fulfill responsibilities and duties without recrimination or ill feeling.

The simple differences are deep and we hope that each can see that one cannot take the differing lessons of males and females too far without losing sight of those things which are deeper, wider and broader than the entire spectrum of sexual differences. However, if you are female, often the quiet of meditation shall bring to you new ways to accept nurturing of a passive kind, and for men, the same offers the burden of accepting in an active way. In other words, the female principle flames brilliantly with dreams of many colors, and it is the work of a lifetime to find roots for all the wings of imagination. For a man it is the work of a lifetime to allow imagination to become powerful.

Certainly the most efficient way for spiritual seekers to work upon themselves is to be in relationship, especially the primary mated relationship. This is a great advantage for those who are aware of the process of spiritual evolution to accept in a conscious way the burden of communication so that differing viewpoints about commonly witnessed catalyst can be shared without judgment and with mutual respect. It is also valuable to have any relationship, regardless of sex, in which there is open and clear communication, for each entity has within the self an unique balance of yin and yang, the male and female, if you will, within the self regardless of the biological sex of the entity.

We look upon the attempts of each of you to make sense of the lessons of the incarnation and we see within each a persistent lack of charity in dealing with the self. Often this lack of charity is projected outward and it is felt by the self that there is judgment upon others. However, the other selves are as mirrors to the self, and whether an irritable point has caught the aggravated eye of self from one's own behavior or another's, the message given to the deep mind is a judgment against the self.

It is so easy, my friends, to have judgment and so very difficult to refrain from that judgment which does not stop at being accurate in describing but rather moves on to evaluating the morality, ethics or beauty of a situation. It is well for all beings to attempt to gaze upon the world with sense wide open, attempting ever more an efficient prioritizing of incoming catalyst.

This is a key way of working upon the balance of the self. Each hour offers much to see and sense, and it can be arranged within the mind in many, many ways, several of [them] perhaps equally valid. In working upon one's balance one is seeking to find the point within the self where there is poise, comfort and calm within so that the seeker may be ready to take in more rather than being swamped with what has already been taken in.

Now, let us look at the question of the male and female within the self. Again, we do not feel that there is any one way which is the correct balance for all entities. Indeed, there is a complete 360 degrees of possible balance for any seeker, male or female, in terms of the kind of energies and combinations of energies that run the electricity of the personality, shall we say, that work those emotional bodies that express self in the more finely tuned inner densities of light, for each entity's existence is at the same time that it is upon the Earth world also existing, learning, working and evaluating on other unconscious inner levels. So much of what you actually do within an incarnative experience is completely unknown to the entity within incarnation. You in your conscious state sense dimly the movements of forces that are within you, and yet we say that deep within you lie the energies that created all that there is.

So, perhaps to sum up, we encourage each to discover the self new each day, to find those areas which seem to be blocked or over-eager or in some way out of balance and to attempt to find time for silence and listening and reflection, time in which to open the self to that possibility of a better configuration of energies. It is a small thing to the conscious mind to pray as this instrument does, "Lord teach me Thy ways." This sentiment can be said in many other phrases. However, that simple desire to know the better way has much more efficacy than the attempt to know precisely what to do next upon improving the self. The true work of spiritual evolution is done below the surface of consciousness, so you as a conscious being are working with your personality, working with your balance, working to aid your own evolution. When you choose to disengage the machinery of mind from the ephemeral business of the passing hour to the point where you become aware of the nature of the creation and of the self, when you can know that all is love at the same time you are expressing distorted views, you have indeed become wise.

(Tape ends.)

Sunday Meditation
October 27, 1996

Group question: How can we really know what is happening in our relationships with others in this illusion? How do we know how to conduct a relationship, by planning or by intuition? Should we be true to ourselves even if it seems to hurt another? If we are always changing, so do relationships. Could you give us some clarity on relationships?

(Carla channeling)

We are those of Q'uo. We greet you in the love and in the light of the one infinite Creator. We of Q'uo wish to bless and thank each within this circle for allowing us to have the opportunity to share our thoughts upon the broad subject of relationships at this time, and we are most happy to do so and simply request, as always, that our words and all words be evaluated by you, for you have the ability to recognize your truth. And if our words have not your truth, then we ask you to pass them by, for we would not wish to make you stumble but only to offer our thoughts.

When speaking of relationships, it is well to begin with the self as it comes to relationship. The one known as B was speaking earlier of knowing who you are and what your situation is as being a foundation for spiritual work and spiritual evolution. This is indeed so. Each who comes to relationship comes first to relationship with the self. Indeed, it can, we feel, be said that each and every relationship which you experience upon the Earth plane is in an important and basic way a projection of a relationship you are having with yourself.

The question mentioned that there was a good deal of mystery left to the detective wishing to know the self more completely. This is inevitable, for the self which your culture and your Earth world sees is actually a shell of flesh together with a metaphysical shell of personality. The incarnate human upon Earth is experiencing in a conscious way only the shadow of what is actually transpiring as each self walks through the moments of space and time that contain those precious moments of incarnation betwixt the date of birth and the date of death.

We notice that among your peoples that these dates are placed after the name of one who has gone on, and find it interesting to note that the whole of the human experience is expressed by the dash between the two dates. It is a little precious gem of a life and within this gem-like construction in which you experience incarnation your personal goal, that with which you arrived into life in the physical body, is to experience more and more truly that which is occurring. Thusly, the one who wishes to know the self becomes an entity who pays attention to the movement of energy within the body, the thoughts and the emotions.

These tides of expression within mental, emotional and spiritual bring with them gifts which cannot be gazed at over a long period of your time, but rather your moments pass with blinding speed. And suddenly, all too soon, your time of learning and growing within the Earth plane and its school of learning lessons of love is all done. And yes, it is a summer vacation when the death arrives, yet it also closes that precious door within which there was confusion and movement and passion and life such as you cannot know outside of the chemical distillery which moves you about and which you call your body.

So, in the beginning of attempting to perceive more accurately relationships one must attempt to move ever more deeply into the business of choosing what you will pay attention to and how fearless you can be in maintaining responsibility for that which you perceive. Now, as you go through these few moments of life an enormous amount of information comes at the self through all the senses of the physical body and the finer bodies as well. Consequently, the choice of what to heed and what to pass over is on a continual basis crucial and the chances and changes of your mortal life occur with great speed. It is more than any entity can do to know the self. However, the attempt needs to be made.

Now, we would say a few words concerning knowledge itself, for it feels to you within incarnation as though you wish to know, to be sure, to pin it down. And we must say that in our opinion that which is called knowledge is, itself, an illusion. We ask you to consider, for instance, those within your culture who are absolutely sure that they know the spiritual facts of life. They then cling to that knowledge and often in such a way that it precludes loving all of those with whom you might be in relationship, for some might not agree that the way that you know is right is for them also right.

The entity who wishes knowledge will penetrate illusion after illusion, and yet each penetration shall uncover another illusion. Knowledge—may we say that which will help you in your quest for the balanced, the loving, the simple, the pure in relationship, and we know that is what you crave, the truth which lies behind that which binds any two entities together—knowledge will fail you. However, we ask you to step back to the beginning, to that impulse which brought each of you to this point, that great overwhelming of being awake for the first time, and feeling for the first time the craving for truth, the hunger and the thirst for love, for that which is true and that which is love are congruent and identical. And the truth which cannot be got at by knowledge can be attained through love, for each of you is love. Each of you is created as love, in love, for love.

That which is you, that which is most deeply yourself, is that portion of self that is love. That ground of being for each of you is the same. There is only one life. There is only one being. There is only unity which expresses and manifests in distortion within your density, within each succeeding density, though each succeeding density is more densely filled with light and the lessons become finer tuned, yet still we move from illusion to illusion, growing and learning. And as we grow, giving and evolving until finally the last realization occurs, not to just one, but to all, and there then becomes that time of resting between creations in an infinite progression of awareness and experience and harvest and coming to breathe inward again the wonderful sweet water of duality and illusion and motion and life and experience.

These times, then, are very precious and [are] art. And you hoped when you came to this illusion to become more able to stand firmly upon the ground of your person, upon that being that is at the bottom of it all and be able to love and be loved with the least possible distortion.

Now, let us ask you this: What do you have in common with everyone whom you meet? We are aware that we have given you the answer. What you have in common is love. Yet, you cannot relate to another by saying to yourself "I am love. She is love. We are love." You simply have conjugated the sentence. You have not got to love yet. But when you realize that the ground of your being is love, you can turn to love itself and know not the being but the love. The love is that which holds you and another together. You can depend upon the love. You can know that that love is true, that this is the truth of any relationship. It comes to you through love, or it comes not to stay.

We feel that entities who face each other without the awareness that what is between them is love find it of varying efficacy to relate, and because of the nature of illusion even the most earnest attempts to connect with another shall often fail in any human sense. However, if you can remain aware that the connection is not between one and one but between one and one with another one so that there is the go-between, there is the middle man, and that middle man is love. That entity between is the truth, distortions move into that, shall we say, globe of metaphysical light and love that speaks as the entity that is the two is relationship.

When you can envision that which is between you and the other as standing not between you and you but between each and that us which is in love, which is in the Creator, then you give yourself and the other the space, the time, the patience, the permission to relate imperfectly, to misunderstand and work things through very slowly. It is inevitable that the illusion will fool all of its children again and again. This does not change the truth of love. And love will express through distortion. It is not fazed by imperfection. It is simply a matter of your being able to keep a constant awareness of love, for there lies truth.

In all else it is as though life were sometimes effervescent with trouble, as a bubbling glass of your liquid that storms and rages and blows bubbles into its being until they burst forth from the charged water and reach into the atmosphere and explode and then are gone. That is the experiencing, that is the catalyst, that is the movement. That is the life. And when the bubbles are gone, still the drink is what it was. It has simply bled out all of its charged water. The bubbles have popped. There was that experience and that experience. There were trouble bubbles. There were joy bubbles, and they are gone and then there are no more bubbles. There is simply the essence that is you.

We are aware that casting life as a soft drink may not be the most exhaustive analogy. However, we wish you to grasp that each of you is the soft drink. Each of you is a delicious, delectable mixture of all that you have experienced and all the distortions that you have chosen and all of those attempts that you have made and think that have failed and those [you] have made and you think have succeeded. One is almost never accurate within the illusion, but as we have said, the illusion is not about being accurate. It is not about knowing. It is about loving.

When those entities to which we have referred to before within your religions have judged all others because of whether they believe as you do or not, have they loved all entities? When you choose to separate yourself from someone behaving poorly, are you still acting in love? You see it may be that to love most clearly and most purely it is the time to sustain a painful relationship, giving yourself the opportunity to remember love as the true bond betwixt, or it may be exactly the opposite and it is not in knowledge, it is not in thinking, it is not in planning that one can come into a sense of whether it is time to stay or time to go. Rather, it is in that moment when you can let yourself be bubble-free, when you can stop the effervescing, get into your essence, become aware of that silent voice that speaks with thunder to those who can listen with the heart open, that the truth will come out and you will feel it, not think it. It will be that feeling within that feels just right, that feels loving, that feels peaceful. And you may come to that feeling about relationship in a moment, or a month, or a year. And so much of wisdom lies in waiting, in not attempting to make decisions but rather attempting to flow in cooperation with the energies that you sense from moment to moment.

You see, getting at the true nature of relationships through the mind is not efficacious. Moving from heart, moving from the open heart, is far more efficient.

There is more to say upon this interesting subject. However, we feel that there is sufficient material here for this particular time of working, and so we would transfer the contact to the one known as Jim. We hope that you may by your queries fine-tune our responses and that if you wish to move into more information upon this topic that you consider these things before you query again upon the same subject.

We thank this instrument and would leave it in love and in light. We are those of Q'uo.

(Tape ends.)

Sunday Meditation
November 3, 1996

Group question: How can we work with relationships and feel safe in doing so?

(Carla channeling)

We are those of Q'uo and are again with this instrument. We find ourselves much amused by your difficulties with the crying baby and the crying tape recorder. We send best wishes to both sensitive media and hope that all is well.

We were speaking of those text books that you are to each other, learning those lessons of love that you have come here to learn, for, indeed, each of you has come here not only to serve others. The call to the Brothers and Sisters of Sorrow who have become wanderers upon your plane of existence have truly hoped to be of service but also each who incarnates within your Earth sphere as a wanderer comes with a hope of doing work in third density that may lend clarity and crystallization to that entity that you have evolved into through the vibratory levels to that of your home density. You see, each goes through this school of love in third density without learning everything, without achieving perfection, but merely tending toward the direction of service to others and unconditional love to the point where you may enjoy and bask in that fuller light that characterizes each succeeding density. So each of you has been through the school of love before, some upon this planet, others upon other planets. But wherever in the infinite creation you have matriculated into third density, you have graduated from it without attaining perfect understanding. And as the densities succeed and as you progress upon your path you find yourself feeling the lack of one or another of those inner strengths, those cores of steel that constitute a real experience of realization of one or another aspect of those lessons of love. So each of you has asked of the self in incarnation at this time that it go back and attack with appetite and enthusiasm those remaining little tangles of feeling and emotion and sensitivity and self-awareness that have knotted and been snarled throughout succeeding densities, lessening in confusion through time, and yet the self is aware that it has work to do, and in the higher densities there is not the opportunity to work through faith alone that there is in third density. In higher densities the veil is lifted and you are able to remember all that you have done, all incarnations that you have enjoyed and experienced, and so you do seek to refine that choice of service and love that you made in third density.

And yet you have not been able to unsnarl that lack of understanding. And so each of you has a real hope at the unconscious level that you will undergo the ordeals which set up the situation for learning about loving and about being loved, about possessing and about being possessed, about caring and not caring. There are many seeming drawbacks to third density, specifically, the veil that traps the conscious mind within the context of a life bound in flesh, able to move only one step at a time, able to think only to the self and not in communion with others. It is as though in third density you are dumb and blind and numb and all the sensations that are so clear in the mind have a confusion in the experiencing of them. And, we hear you say that, "This is a good thing?" And we say to you, yes, the confusion, even the terror of living without proof, without knowledge, and by faith alone is a good thing, it is in fact a thing so prized that there are, shall we say, lines waiting to get into your third density at this time for the opportunity of service and personal growth is excellent among your peoples in your culture at this time.

Now let us explore what it is to live by faith. The floor under the entity that is yourself is hidden from you. We have heard the one known as R speaking of the difficulties of getting to know your own self well. There is tremendous confusion that would hit any entity when he cannot see his feet before him, when he cannot see the terrain through which he is traveling. An entity within your density cannot see the lines that link person to person to person, cannot see that flowing oneness that takes the illusion of flesh and moves through it as through the medium of your air. The fact that you cannot see the connections betwixt yourself and other selves is certain. The fact that, nevertheless, each entity is one with all that he meets is also true. The only way that the seeker then can walk is without looking at what the appearances of things are, for the appearances are that each entity is a monad. Each entity walks alone, and this feeling of isolation is a tremendous source of suffering among your peoples and yet when an entity stops looking for his feet and simply moves ahead, step by step, an unusual and unpredicted thing occurs, and that is that the steps of one who has stopped trying to see connections are more assured and livelier than those who are pressing with urgency against that envelope of blindness that surrounds the metaphysical self. So the suggestion of the one known as R to relax, to allow, to let things be, is an excellent suggestion. It is, in fact, the only procedure which gives the element of faith its proper centrality.

To live at all is to live by faith. Now consider this, what if one day your system decided that it did not wish to function. Does your heart simply stop beating? Do you simply forget to breathe? Never. For that second-density body which has offered itself up to carry your infinite consciousness, untroubled by self-awareness continues. It does not forget to make the heart beat or to make the lungs breathe, or to make the blood collect all that it must collect and take it to all of those places within the body that calls for each element. Nay, you can have faith that you shall breathe, that your heart shall beat, that your sense of balance and so forth will allow you to move about your illusion anywhere your free will chooses for you to go. And this total trust, this complete unerring dedication to that nature of self, has the potential of working within seekers such as yourselves in much the same way except then that you are working with your mental, emotional and spiritual bodies, and with the emotions, with the mentality, with the spirituality the entity who wishes to know the self must first make connection, make contact with the sense of rightness and trust and faith in those finer bodies that are part of the complex of vibrations that is you.

It is not to those who speak many things and write many words, necessarily, that self-knowledge comes, but rather it is to the one who has learned to trust in the energies and sweeps or ranges of energetic cycles that self-awareness shall come. Perhaps we could use this instrument's example of the watched pot that never boils. Living in faith is turning on the fire under the water and trusting the water to bubble when it is ready to bubble. There is the human desire, perfectly natural to an entity imprisoned in flesh, to wish to control the processes that have to do with survival and comfort, and certainly there is tremendous discomfort in the processes of learning those lessons of love which you have come to learn. The natural reaction, when there is pain, is to draw back, to contract against it and to guard against further contact with it. And yet the process of learning is one which does cost the entity learning that energy which it takes to apprehend and work with and grasp that changes are taking place. There is, as far as we know, no way to avoid some degree of suffering. Indeed, it is one of the beauties of your density that you are in confusion and pain much of the time, at one level or another. And, therefore, are more open to rapid learning than one who is not in pain, is not suffering, and knows the score, shall we say.

We speak from experience, for we had in our third-density an unusually easy time of it because the ethos of our people was more loving. Therefore, there were depths which we did not learn in fourth density because we had not enough difficulties and confusion to take our human pride, shall we say, and break it. For you see each of you has an inner idol which needs to be cast down and broken. You can name it one thing or another. This instrument would call it pride, and this instrument works upon its pride very consciously. However, it has to this moment found no answer to its difficulties, for pride seems to grow upon itself.

Each of you has this sterling opportunity to break through the defenses, the shells, the masks that each has gathered about itself to defend itself from those pains which it fears. And the answer to these pains and difficulties is simply to accept them, to embrace them, to walk through them by faith, working in each case to see the love that is in the moment and to be a part of that which is good for all those whom you meet. You see, the confusions, the difficulties, the suffering are symptoms, shall we say, of the process of change or transformation when you have incomplete information. Each of you has woefully incomplete information in the conscious mind.

There comes a time when an entity has disciplined the personality to the point where it sees its own suffering. It sees the pain and the confusion and at the same time rests in peace and in faith in the knowledge, that knowledge that comes to the open heart without proof that beyond all of the appearances the one thing to focus upon is love. This is at its most important when the entity faces itself, for only when an entity has learned to love and forgive its own self can the entity turn open-heartedly to embrace another in intimacy of spirit, of mind, and of body. Until the self is seen for that creature that it is, with dark and light mixed together, can the self move from self-absorption into radiating as does the lighthouse, as does the fire upon the hill. Your lighthouse self, that self that you came to share with Earth, awaits that moment when you turn from all the confusion and simply embrace the moment, looking at that moment with the realization that all is well and that all shall be well, whether it be life or death, good times or difficult times. Still and always you are loved. You are held in infinite care in the tender arms of the Creator whose nature is unbounded love.

We ask each to see the self as a fortress, that fortress of flesh that defends and guards and has fears. And to see the hope of the incarnation being that process of dismantling the armament, of taking off one mask and then another, one layer and then another until the self is transparent and empty, and is a vessel through which love may flow.

The deeper that you are able to take this process of becoming naked the more intimacy you shall be able to endure, the more of love that you shall be able to channel through yourself. The controlling, fearful seeker wishes to give love and receive love. The entity whose pride is dust simply is and in that bare being lies infinite unbounded love. So when the striving is over and the heart has room and time to open, there is love itself and in that love there is all the awareness and understanding that is needed. So, indeed, the next time the seeker feels itself reaching and grasping or pushing away and defending we ask that seeker to remember that nothing is as it seems but all things are full of love, even those which seem the darkest. There are many distortions, but beneath and above and around and penetrating all distortion is perfect love and there is within that holy of holies, within that open heart that each of you has in potentiation, that perfect instinct for love.

You may think of your life in faith as a process of mining where you bring up the ore and sort out the dirt from the gems. Each of you is a marvelous, beautiful gem. You are simply in the process of tapping away the dirt that surrounds it. And that tap, tap, tapping will continue as your years increase. That tap, tap, tapping of life working upon you to refine you. This is what you came for. This is what you thought was a glorious chance, though there is pain associated with this learning. We encourage each to allow the pain to be, for it, like any other sensation, is your sister and your brother. And as you are able to open, to be fearless, to be simply yourself, with no masks, so shall you come closer and closer to that center of self which is infinite and eternal.

We would at this time open the meeting to questions. Is there a query at this time?

R: You seem to be with us before the session begins. Do you also stay with us after the session is over?

We are those of Q'uo, and we certainly can share comment on the process of speaking with each other for we find that each is of great aid to each other within the circle, and we encourage the sharing that you do within your group. We are pleased that each wishes to invest time in seating these thoughts that we share and we wish all of you much fortune in enjoying each other's thoughts and company. You are correct, my brother, in thinking that we are with you as you gather and speak before we channel. We, indeed, are often with those within this circle of seeking, for all that we need is the mental thought and we are there. That is one of the pleasures of being within other densities of creation. The ability to be intimately aware of each other is very much enhanced and we do make use of that ability to be with each as we are called. Because it is an infringement upon free will we are not with entities until they request or think of our presence, but if it is requested we will be with each at any time. We do not attempt to share concepts with our presence but rather function as a kind of carrier wave undergirding and strengthening the basic vibration that is the essential entity.

May we answer you further, my brother?

R: I see you as different from my guides but all still of one source. Could you correct my thinking there?

We are those of Q'uo, and believe that we grasp your question. The character of a personal guide is much like the character of a Confederation entity, so it is easy to think that they all are the same. However, shall we say, inner guides and ourselves have a different address. The guide that is a personal, shall we say, angel or advisor to you lives within your planet's inner densities and comes to you as one who has experienced the Earth plane and is in relationship to you and has been in relationship to you at other times. These inner guides have the perfect right to infringe upon your free will to the extent of giving information specific [to] subjects such as other incarnations, the problems with diet, and other kinds of specific information that would be to us an infringement upon free will. We are one of many entities and groups of entities that comes to your Earth plane from elsewhere and do not and cannot claim Earth as the home of our particular spirits. Because we are not of the Earth we have clear guidelines as to that which we can offer without detuning the contact which we have with this or other instruments.

May we answer you more fully, my brother?

R: I still have some confusion. I'll think about it and ask more later.

We are those of Q'uo. We also wish to thank you and encourage you in these approaches of thoughtful inquiry, for these are fruitful areas to ponder.

Is there a final query at this time?

B: In the upcoming Aaron/Q'uo workshop how can I help Carla maintain her energy levels?

We are those of Q'uo. We would say to you that by your concern there is automatically a conduit opened which this instrument may draw on without any conscious thought upon your or her part. Beyond this basic aid which is the greatest part of being the battery there is simply that loving attention which suggests rest when it seems appropriate.

May we answer you further, my brother?

B: Do you mean rest for myself or rest for Carla?

We were referring to the one known as Carla. However, it is a good point that to care for another is not so helpful if one is not caring for the self also.

May we answer you further, my brother?

B: No. Thank you.

We thank each as well. We would encourage each to go forth rejoicing, for love is all about you, and you can walk by faith with a merry heart. We leave you in the light and the love of the one infinite Creator. We are of the principle known to you as Q'uo. Adonai. Adonai. ❧

L/L Research

L/L Research is a subsidiary of Rock Creek Research & Development Laboratories, Inc.

P.O. Box 5195
Louisville, KY 40255-0195

www.llresearch.org

Rock Creek is a non-profit corporation dedicated to discovering and sharing information which may aid in the spiritual evolution of humankind.

ABOUT THE CONTENTS OF THIS TRANSCRIPT: This telepathic channeling has been taken from transcriptions of the weekly study and meditation meetings of the Rock Creek Research & Development Laboratories and L/L Research. It is offered in the hope that it may be useful to you. As the Confederation entities always make a point of saying, please use your discrimination and judgment in assessing this material. If something rings true to you, fine. If something does not resonate, please leave it behind, for neither we nor those of the Confederation would wish to be a stumbling block for any.

CAVEAT: This transcript is being published by L/L Research in a not yet final form. It has, however, been edited and any obvious errors have been corrected. When it is in a final form, this caveat will be removed.

© 2009 L/L Research

Sunday Meditation
November 10, 1996

Group question: We would like you to speak to us about how we might develop the proper relationship or perspective on our darker sides.

(Carla channeling)

We are those of the principle known to you as Q'uo. Greetings in the love and in the light of the one infinite Creator. We thank and bless you for calling us to your meditation this evening. It is our distinct pleasure to have the opportunity to share our humble thoughts with you, and we do so as always with the clear understanding that each of you shall take only those things that appeal to you from the thoughts that we offer and leave all the rest behind. We would not wish to be a stumbling block to any of you and encourage each of you to use your own excellent power of discrimination.

This day you wish to consider the proper relationship of the self to its own dark side and any thoughts that we might have on how to appropriately relate to this portion of the incarnate personality shell. Perhaps the first thing that we would wish to observe is that the duality of light and dark is not, in our own opinion, the ultimate reality but is, rather, an artifact of incarnation, for in the world of manifestation in order for there to be observed manifestation there must be duality.

Unity, when it is absolute, is without awareness. Each of you is a portion of that unborn and undying awareness, that heart of all creation that is the one original Thought. Within that thought of infinite love there lies no shadow. However, we as well as you walk the path of duality and exist within a series of physical vehicles, enjoying the experience of living within various densities and conditions of body, mind, emotion and spirit. In all of these densities of unimaginable variety lies duality.

Thusly, it is well to remember that the light side and the dark side of your self alike are portions of that shell of manifestation which represents the totality of your self. The learning, the experiencing, the growing that is done within incarnations throughout the densities is a growth hemmed in on every side by limitation. Within this world of finity the light and dark create a tremendous dynamic. Within this dynamic rest all of those who sleep; that is, all of those who are within incarnation yet who are not yet aware of themselves [as] consciousness experiencing itself. Those who are spiritually unawakened rest in the center of that dynamic betwixt light and dark.

Some of the things such sleepers think and say and do carry some positive charge. Others carry some negative charge. However, to the sleeper this is not interesting information. The question of how to be simply does not arise until that moment [when] the self perceives the self as larger than life, as that which is beyond the limitation of flesh and human thought.

To the sleeper who has awakened this dynamic is useful and very fruitful, for in striving to accentuate and increase the rate of learning or evolution in a spiritual sense the polarity of intended action can carry a very strong message to the deeper mind and the more difficult it is to find a positive polarity, that is, the more the dark side of the self is engaged in working through catalyst, the greater the opportunity to polarize positively the seeker has.

Thusly, when things seem the darkest, when the self sees the self as that darker side, this situation in itself is a gift and the way to open that gift is simply to accept and absorb that awareness of the self's darker side while allowing the heart to remain open. When that open heart approaches the darker side of self its gift is to be able to know the light while gazing into darkness. Thusly, in the spiritual or metaphysical sense there is no such thing as a disaster or a catastrophe. An old hymn this instrument knows is, "The Body They May Kill, His Love Endureth Still."

When the darker side roars within and the self feels the power of that darkness there is the opportunity to exercise that muscle that you call faith, for in faith there is the sure and certain awareness of the light. The light, metaphysically speaking, can shine in any darkness. It only takes the bringing to conscious awareness of that truth to place the dark side safely within the bounds of self that it may not cause the self to infringe upon the free will of another.

This instrument is aware of that which the one known as Don called the "180 degree rule." We find this phrase pleasant to use, for it is succinct and accurate. One's relation to one's dark side should be one of gratitude and love, for the dark side is that which strengthens and enables the light side. Each experience of the darker side of self is that which burns away pride and what this instrument would call egotism. It is well when one sees that side of self which has those vices and sins, if you will, in abundance not to turn away but rather to embrace, to love, to accept, and to forgive that part of the self for being.

In grasping the necessity for having a 360 degree range of personality lies a peace that will serve you well. When the myth of Christianity that this instrument is familiar with addressed the beginning of creation, it stated that the first act of the Creator in the manifested world was to separate the light from the darkness. This says it well. There is, in the manifested world, that duality which enables each of us to wend our way back to the Creator, for we did not come from the light or darkness if we speak of true origin. Rather we are, with no past and no future. Before all created things that which is each of us at our base is. Each of you, each of us, is consciousness itself. And within the purview of those interior rooms lies all that there ever was and all that ever shall be.

How else could each of us be one with all but that we are all holographs of each other? We speak here of mysteries that we do not know the answer to. But we have, indeed, found a tremendous strength in coming to know, to love, and to discipline all portions of self, be they considered light or dark.

There is infinite energy which moves into the system of mind, body and spirit, physically speaking, from the base of the spine upwards. Within each energy center, where the dark side of self has created unresolved catalyst, there the instreaming light of the one infinite Creator must stop and dwell with that darkness. Therefore, the hope of each seeker is to balance and allow a clarity to move over these tangles of self-judgment and self-criticism and to smooth them away with love and tenderness. Sometimes it takes many of your years fully to address a tangle in one of the centers, a place where repeatedly the self has come up against its darker side and has found self-judgment to be unavoidable. And we say to you to be patient with self. Take each day as a new, unique and one-of-a-kind experience. Do not accept those thoughts of, "I can do nothing with this energy." For each of you is Creator and co-Creator of the experience of your incarnation. Each of you can remember the light and allow that memory to shine as the lighthouse in the stormy sea of difficult days.

You will find the great allies of this work in consciousness to be the sense of humor and the ability to appreciate other selves as they too struggle to become that which they hope and cherish they might be. Each of you can be the light for another when that other's light is lost. And each of you in turn shall find a time to accept with humility the light of others when you are lost and forlorn.

We would, at this time, transfer this contact to the one known as Jim. We thank this instrument and leave it in love and in light. We are those of Q'uo.

(Jim channeling)

I am Q'uo, and greet each again in love and light through this instrument. It is our privilege at this time to ask if there may be further queries to which we may respond.

Carla: We have a workshop coming up in a couple of weeks and we would appreciate any thoughts that you might have about that service.

I am Q'uo, and am aware of your query, my sister. In attempting to serve others it is well to give that which is wholly from your heart and from the desire to be of service. We are aware that there is much of administrative detail in being certain that attendees are well taken of. We would recommend that each simply move with the desire to serve and to make those preparations which you know to make. Then with a light heart allow that energy of desire and love to work its way through you at the appropriate moments, giving little care or worry about outcomes, for there there is that entirety that is the group that shall gather of which you are a part. Each will play a role. Allow the full expression of each energy.

Is there any further query, my sister?

Carla: No. Thanks for that, Q'uo.

Is there another query at this time?

(No further queries.)

I am Q'uo, and as it appears that we have for the nonce exhausted the queries that are upon your hearts and mind we would again thank each for the great privilege we feel at being asked to join your circle of seeking this day. It is an honor that we cannot fully describe but can feel within our hearts. We would at this time take our leave of this instrument and this group, leaving each as always in the love and in the light of the one infinite Creator. We are known to you as those of Q'uo. Adonai. Adonai. ♣

L/L Research

L/L Research is a subsidiary of Rock Creek Research & Development Laboratories, Inc.

P.O. Box 5195
Louisville, KY 40255-0195

www.llresearch.org

Rock Creek is a non-profit corporation dedicated to discovering and sharing information which may aid in the spiritual evolution of humankind.

ABOUT THE CONTENTS OF THIS TRANSCRIPT: This telepathic channeling has been taken from transcriptions of the weekly study and meditation meetings of the Rock Creek Research & Development Laboratories and L/L Research. It is offered in the hope that it may be useful to you. As the Confederation entities always make a point of saying, please use your discrimination and judgment in assessing this material. If something rings true to you, fine. If something does not resonate, please leave it behind, for neither we nor those of the Confederation would wish to be a stumbling block for any.

CAVEAT: This transcript is being published by L/L Research in a not yet final form. It has, however, been edited and any obvious errors have been corrected. When it is in a final form, this caveat will be removed.

© 2009 L/L Research

The Aaron/Q'uo Dialogues, Session 31
November 22, 1996

(This session was preceded by a period of tuning and meditation.)

Group question: Since we are all channels, how can we bring our energy through more purely? What would be the appropriate techniques to aid in becoming more clear?

Aaron: I am Aaron. My greetings and love to you all. I cannot overly state the joy it gives to us on the spirit plane to gather together here, incarnate and disincarnate, to share our energy, our thoughts and our deepest seeking together. I thank you.

I smile at the way Jim has written this question because it reflects a primary distortion. Your deep concern as humans is always, "How do I do it with more purity, with more clarity?" The question might be better phrased, "How do I do it with more love?" More love will probably bring that greater clarity and purity, but not necessarily. If there is fear which is creating distortion and you bring love to that fear, in the long run it will help to resolve the distortion. In the beginning it may not.

What bringing love in will do is not to guarantee absolute purity but to enhance your compassion. My dear ones, if you plan to allow the universe to channel through you with absolute purity, then why are you in incarnation? It is very easy on my plane. Here is the greatest gift: to allow the expression of the Universe filtered through the human! You are not here to learn perfection. You are here to learn faith and love. You are here to learn compassion also, although that is mostly the lesson of fourth density; but each of you is moving into that density.

The human is never going to be perfect. These fears that arise in you which create some sort of blockage to your work are not problems; they are gifts. They are reminders to have compassion for this human vehicle with all its complex mechanisms. This does not mean you are not responsible for what comes through you. If it becomes increasingly distorted, you are responsible for recognizing that distortion and doing the inner work to clarify the distortion to the point that it is again adequately clear. I stress *adequately*. I can channel the universe with absolute purity, but it lacks the gifts of human interpretation.

Can you see that it is only fear that drives the desire for perfection and not love? So may we phrase the question: "How do I learn to become a channel which offers what most is needed in the deepest spirit of love which is possible for me; and secondly, when I experience distortion, how do I greet that distortion with love?"

It does not matter what form your channeling takes; there is going to be distortion. And that very catalyst which creates distortion is the greatest gift, because only through that distortion can you really practice compassion and kindness.

It was our idea that my dear brother/sister/friend of Q'uo would open this session. So with joy I hand the microphone to Q'uo. I pause.

Q'uo: We are those of Q'uo, and we greet you in the love and the light of the one infinite Creator. May we add our thanks and our gratitude to the one known as Aaron, for each within this circle of seeking has sacrificed much to come to this circle; and we are aware in our memory of the seeming lack of time when in incarnation in your density.

The choice of where to place the attention is a choice full of weight within the incarnative scheme or nexus or arrangement of priorities; and scheduling of time simply to have come to this circle creates that opening, that opportunity, that cannot be purchased at any price. You have given yourself this chance and have given us an enormous gift, for you enable us to be of service. Sharing our thoughts with those who might find them interesting is our chosen form of service, and you enable us to progress in our own destiny. You could not give us a more precious present; and we cherish this occasion, asking only, as always, that each seeker use her own powers of discrimination and retain only those truths which resound within as if she had already known those truths but had forgotten them. Those are the truths that are yours personally. Allow us to share all our thoughts, but allow those thoughts which do not echo of recognition within to be left gently behind.

Let us then begin by gazing upon what this instrument would call the human condition. Each dwells in two distinct worlds, if we may oversimplify for the sake of discussion. There is the physical portion of existence within which each has a physically difficult time of second density, of what this instrument would call the great ape variety and what one of your philosophers has called the featherless chicken.[11] This earthly, mortal, limited vehicle contains brainpower designed specifically to solve problems, to make choices. This is practical and useful within the Earth world. We do not scorn the human brain. We simply note that it is either a servant or a master. Those who would advance spiritually are well advised, in our opinion, to reduce the dependency of the consciousness on the choices and intellectual structures which the human brain is so good at creating.

Within this earthly plane you are still completely a citizen of the universe. You are infinite, eternal, omnipotent, omnipresent. You are what has been and what will be. You are a child of the Creator; and indeed, we all seek together for that place in space and time when we shall cease to be citizens of duality and move back into the heart of the one original Thought, which has created all that there is. That Thought is love, and each of you is love. Consider yourself within the earth plane as one who is upon a journey, sent forth from the beginning of time and space to gather experience—and always, always returning, circling back to the source, to love. And at the same time that you are upon this plane, you are perfect, pure, unblemished, without error; and this identity remains absolute no matter what your perception of yourself or your progression might be.

When you as a seeker, then, begin to desire to clear the channel for more clear channeling of the love and the light of the infinite One, there is the tendency to think in terms of working from the viewpoint of the one who wishes to take from work in consciousness that which does not belong. However, the concept that may in actual practice do the most to clear the channel is to go against logic and instead move back into those energies that, were the human structure as a house, would be in the basement. The clearing of channels continues in the progress made in joining the self with the lower energies in a loving and non-judgmental way, through gazing with care upon the arrangement of what this instrument would call the dark side of personality—that side wherein reside those instincts for survival, sexuality, human relationships with self and other selves.

The feeling is to get away from the body and its millions of complaints and needs, yet in actuality you worked hard to deserve the opportunity to come into your physical body and into physical incarnation. The nuts and bolts, the nitty-gritty of bodily awareness, is continuingly important to attend to and embrace. The confusion that swamps the entity because of the sensory input of the physical vehicle is a problem, for in confusion nothing can be known. The physical body is a blanket of confusion; and by dwelling within it you are removed from knowledge of the truth as to what your energies are actually doing. In the body you have no choice if you are spiritually oriented but to find faith and use that faith in order to make your

---

[11] *Lives of the Philosophers, Book 6*, Diogenes Laertius, third century A.D.

choices, beginning with how you relate to your self: to your intransigent need to continue to survive, to continue the species, to attend to all of these things.

Do not brush these things aside, for the greatest of choices begins with these choices; and as you embrace and involve yourself, so do you open the way to that center within called the heart chakra or the green-ray energy center. The opening of the heart is possible only when the seeker gives up on the intellect and moves in unknowingness. The seeker lives in faith. What does this mean? As this instrument would say, we'll talk.

We turn over the microphone to our friend, our beloved brother Aaron, with great delight. We leave this instrument for the nonce. We are those known to you as the principle of Q'uo.

Aaron: I am Aaron. As I begin to speak, I wish to echo Q'uo's thought. Please take what is useful of my words—that which rings true to your own deepest truth—and allow it into your heart. As for the rest, discard it without a second thought.

Q'uo has spoken of the two aspects of your being, what I call the angel and the earthsuit. You are angels in earthsuits. If you wanted just to be angels and manifest perfect clarity, you would not have chosen to incarnate. Any can manifest its energy with great love and clarity as an angel. Can you do it in the earthsuit? Even more important, what happens when you bring the balance of these two together? For you are not only the earthsuit; no, no, no! You are the angel *in* the earthsuit.

It is through this balance—taking the constant catalysts of the earth plane and drawing them into the heart of love—that you not only learn for yourselves, but that you manifest your energy into the world with increasing purity and love and thus offer that energy to all beings. Very often you become lost enough in the earthsuit catalyst that you lose view of what you are really doing. You are simply forging ahead blindly, and yet sometimes one has to do that.

Speaking of her drive to perfection, once, with this instrument, I asked her a simple but difficult question. I said to her, "Imagine that you are with a group of people on top of a mountain. You are walking, when suddenly the weather turns, clouds roll in, it begins to snow. Where you had been hiking was very steep, with many precipices. You feel that you cannot walk because of the density of the weather, and yet you recognize that you must get off the mountain. What you really want is someone to come along from the group and say, 'I know this mountain so well. Follow me and I will lead you down.' But no one comes. Everyone sits down and shakes from fear and from cold. You are fully aware that in less than an hour of this treacherous wind and cold, people are going to enter into hypothermia, people are going to die. You do not know the path. You only had a glimpse at it as it lay ahead, just as the clouds rolled in. What are you going to do? Are you going to wait there for somebody else to say, 'I know the mountain. I will lead us,' or are you going to do it yourself? What if you are not perfectly prepared?"

When is it ego to say, "I will lead"? When is it love? More correctly phrased, when is it the voice of the small self who acts in service to that self, perhaps to enhance or self-inflate? When is it the voice of the large self that acts in service to all beings?

First, you must allow that both voices are going to be present. You are this angel in an earthsuit. While the angel's voice may come through loud and clear, the human voice also must be present or else you are not having a human experience. Perhaps the angel's voice says, "I think I can do this. If I move very carefully, I think I can do this." Then you hear ego's voice saying, "Oh, won't everybody make a fuss over me when we get safely to the bottom." Hearing that second thought, you may surmise, "This is not my deepest truth that says it can lead the descent. This is only ego." If you strike out in anger against that ego's voice, then you cannot hear love's voice. You become so much at war with the small-self aspect of you that you shut out the existence of anything else.

On the other hand, you can hear that small self's voice and just say, "Aha, here is self that wants recognition. Here is self that feels pain, and it wants to be a hero. *Shhhh*, I hear you. I hear how afraid you are, and I hear the ego self grasping at this opportunity for some notice." When you treat the small self with kindness, its voice quiets. Then you have the opportunity to reopen once again to the greater self, that voice that is still whispering insistently, "We must get these people off the mountain or people are going to die. It will take courage from all of us, but it can be done."

When you ask, "How can I become a purer channel?" that absolute purity is always accessible within you. Confusion and distortion are also always there. If my friends who have heard this example before will pardon me, a very simple illustration of your being is to take a very smooth white sheet of paper with absolutely no wrinkles, wad it up into a ball and squeeze it tight so it becomes wrinkled. Then open it out again; the sheet appears filled with wrinkles. Look at that sheet of paper. Can you see that the perfect sheet of paper still exists? It has not gone anywhere. The wrinkles also exist. We are not denying either truth. Which do you choose to practice? Do you choose to practice the wrinkles or the perfect sheet of paper? To practice that perfect sheet does not mean to deny the existence of the wrinkles, only not to need to enact them—and even further, not to fixate on them in any way. This is of tremendous importance.

This shadow aspect of the self will exist. Do not fixate on it in any way and do not deny it. You do not need to be ruled by it and you do not need to fight against it. Your work is to draw it into the heart of love. When the conditions have ceased which gave rise to that particular wrinkle, it will go if you are not relating to it in a way which gives it further conditions from which to perpetuate itself! It will go. You do not need to push it away. To fret over it is a way of practicing it—can you see that? When you are busy attacking the wrinkle, you are giving solidity to it. In karmic terms, your energy contracts around that particular wrinkle and it plants the seeds for the next moment.

I think it is very important to understand how that works. Let us use as a hypothetical example, the thinking of the self as unworthy. This concept is the wrinkle. To strive to become a worthy person sets up a pattern of contractions every time there is an opportunity to be generous or kind. The generosity and kindness are gifts to another, of course; and yet if there is a strong *somebody* being generous and kind, it sets up reverberations which solidify the self. That somebody who is struggling not to be unworthy is struggling to be worthy. In either case, it solidifies this self who must push away unworthiness and grasp at worthiness. It does not acknowledge the deeper truth that there is no such thing as unworthy or worthy. How could any human—any being on any plane—be unworthy or worthy? Generous maybe, wise/unwise, skillful/unskillful; but worthy/unworthy?

Even such a movement as generous or greedy can set in motion this pattern of solidified self. You may see yourself as clinging, greedy, and make the decision, "I'm going to defeat this wrinkle. I'm going to become generous each time fear arises"—and with it a clinging pattern. You castigate yourself and say, "Look how bad I am to have this fear energy. I'm going to be generous," and you push yourself to give.

So long as you are fixated on being the generous one, you are going to continue karmically to enact situations in your life in which clinging or giving are primary. The mastering of this lesson does not involve only giving freely even when there is fear. That giving will come naturally when there is no obstruction to it. The idea of the generous self here serves as obstruction. The entire notion of the self as giver or clinger, of self which must be "fixed," must be released. Freedom from perpetuating this pattern comes when you can release fixation on the whole movement of clinging and giving.

Note the fear from which these patterns arise. Note that certain conditions give rise to that fear. Observe the self which is fearful with a great deal of kindness and compassion. Then this solid self is no longer the one who is giving or clinging; then the heart knows what to do. There is no more giver; there is no more clinger; giving happens. There is no subject and object, no one who gives, nothing which is given.

The fear does not disappear automatically any more than our would-be guide on the top of the mountain loses its fear when it says, "Follow me," and takes the first step. The fear may be immense. That is just it! If you were just spirit, Pure Spirit, giving or leading people down the mountain, there would be no fear and there would be no challenge. The challenge is not to be fearless. The challenge is to bring love where there is fear.

The work is to cease to fixate on getting rid of anything—fear, jealousy, greed, anger—but instead to draw all of these emotions and the causes for them into the loving heart. Then you can watch these patterns come and go in yourself; and a loving heart knows what to do. As Q'uo said, the brain stops directing the show and the heart becomes the ruler.

At this point I would like to pass the microphone back to my brother/sister/friend Q'uo. I pause.

Q'uo: We are those of Q'uo, and are again with this instrument.

We can sense all of you experiencing these thoughts, feeding them back into your consciousness and sorting through them as through items at a rummage sale, and appreciate the bewildering effect of so many old and new ideas countermingled. But have faith; there is a part of yourself that overarches and interpenetrates all of your self and experience, which you can rely upon. You already know that which is needful for you at this particular juncture, so relax the desire to comprehend and practice that trust in your own deeper intuition that constitutes one way of expressing things.

We would like to describe for you an entry into that portion of self that has its selfness in faith. It lies within the heart center, is literally and figuratively at the heart and of the heart. As the energy moves into the physical body through the feet up into the root chakra or energy center at the joining of the legs, it encounters a beautiful, crystalline … we give this instrument a picture of a geodesic dome, a structure in time/space that enabled that energy of red ray to express the energy from the red through that co-Creator's ready energy center. And as the energy gathers, that energy becomes more crystalline and transparent to that love/light that is expressing into manifestation from unmoved love. Moving upwards it encounters another beautiful crystalline structure that resides in the belly itself, that contracts against dangers of association with the self and with the complexity of dual and triple, completely unusual and conflicting needs of the self and one other self. As the seeker gathers experience, the choices made can more and more energize this nexus of energy; and the energy allowed through moves up to that place where belly meets chest, that omphalos of power. This is the plane of your Earth. This is the social energy center where the self deals with society and its associations, whether experiencing as a member of a family, as a citizen of a country, in any group in which you are working with distortions of the yellow-ray energy center; and again, the choices that you make can, through the incarnative experience, help to crystallize and make transparent this center.

As one works with all of these energies to balance them, one is literally making more room for energy from the Creator to pour in its original strength into the heart center. The problem with attempting to work in consciousness with ascended masters or entities such as we is that one is working from the top down, whereas the stable basis of energy shall always first depend upon the amount of energy that comes into the heart from the root chakra upward. No matter how much energy is called into the system from the heart, it must move downward to the place where the energy from the Creator has originated its entrance into the mind and body complex. Thusly, you see seekers who find themselves in desperate straits because they are attempting to open the heart by inspiration, and yet they have no home in which to place this inspiration; and so, like a bird, all that is felt from contact from that source flies away like lost hope and is gone when the eyes open and the entity is once again within the busyness of everyday life.

But come with us into the heart, just for a moment, where we feel that there is the need to experience love; and we wish to tell you that you can do this at any time. But come with us now. Feel that energy coming through those distortions in each center, yet moving upwards to the heart. See that energy coming from above, as it were, that calls for inspiration and flows like liquid into the heart; and these two meet where lions guard the door. And you bow to the lions and you do not say, "I deserve to be here"; you say, "Have mercy on me, for I seek love." And the lions bow to you and the door opens and you walk into this room, this holy of holies. This is the open heart. Sit down. Take your shoes off. You are upon holy ground. Now you are with the Creator, who can give you rest. You are loved with a passion that creates and destroys worlds. Oh, how you are loved. We turn the microphone back to our beloved friend Aaron.

Aaron: I am Aaron. Where is that place of most brilliant light and love? Is it somewhere out there? Is it something you must attain through self-purification or other types of pursuit? No, it is within. It is that perfect sheet of paper that still exists, even though the wrinkles are also there. That Pure Heart-Mind is always available to you, my friends. It is not the existence of the wrinkles, of the shadow, that keeps you from that brilliant inner light. It is your relationship to those wrinkles, to that shadow.

I am back to the same point. The wrinkles will come and go. You are human. If you step on a tack, there is going to be pain and contraction of the physical and emotional bodies. If somebody screams at you insultingly, rudely, there is going to be a contraction of the emotional body. If you are very hungry and somebody takes away your meal, there is going to be fear. These movements do not prevent you from resting in that light nor manifesting from that brilliant and loving heart. They are simply fear, desire, anger, confusion. They need no reaction from you.

You cannot get rid of these by forcing them out. By strong will power you can rid your outer experience of them; but they still lie hidden in the ground, simply waiting for a break in your fierce suppression so that they can sneak through. But if you learn to allow these kinds of emotions and confusion, which are the human experience, to move through you—and never lose that place of center—then you need fear them no more. You know will never lose the awareness that you sit in the light. The Pure Heart is always accessible!

I would offer an example of what I have just said, and even more, of what Q'uo said preceding me. Returning to our guide on the mountain … you are this guide, and you have said, "Stand up and walk with me. I will lead us to safety." For a while you follow the path. The snow has not yet obscured it. Then the snow drives harder and the wind is stronger. You become aware that you have lost the path. What are you going to do? You stop and acknowledge, "I've lost the path and don't know where I am."

Fear may come up very strongly for those of you who aspire to live your lives with love. It might be a very fierce self-critical fear which said, "You knew you couldn't do it. It was all ego that said, 'I'm going to lead.'" So what are you going to do, just tell everybody to sit down in the snow and die because you made a mistake?

What if it was fear that said, "I will lead"? Are you denying that there was also a deep wisdom which said, "We must make an attempt to get off the mountain"? It is certain death versus a possibility of survival. As soon as you open your heart to yourself, as soon as you hear your pain and fear, you reopen into the wisdom and clear heart. And the clear heart says, "Okay, I made a mistake; I got lost." That does not mean that negativity was leading, even if negativity was there. The loving heart was also there. Coming back to the loving heart, you simply pick yourself up—trail or no trail—and begin moving slowly down the mountain. On the trail it is easier; off the trail it will be a little harder. The task is the same: You have got to get down from the mountain.

There is a teaching in both Buddhism and Christianity which I find useful here. This instrument has been reading a very clear book, written jointly by a Zen master, Robert Aitken Roshi, and a Jesuit priest, Brother David Stendl-Rast. It is called *The Ground We Share*[12]. The focus of the book is to explore the commonalities. Aitken Roshi speaks of a Buddhist teaching given the very technical name, *Three Kayas*. The word *kaya* means "body." It talks of the "truth body" or *dharmakaya*, the everperfect; and at the other end, the "form body" or *nirmanakaya*. This is not just the material body; by form I mean any kind of a form. A thought is also a form, as is an emotion. This is the outer-expression body. There is a bridge that joins them, called the "wealth body" or *sambhogakaya*. I call this the "transition body." Think of the everperfect; think also of the final expression. The wealth or transition body is a bridge of intention, of karmic force and other elements, which serves as vehicle for the everperfect to express itself into the world.

A very simple example would offer the sun as a metaphor for the everperfect. The expression of the sun on the earth plane might be the heat that you feel on your back when you sit in the sun, or a patch of sunlight on the grass. The atmosphere, the clouds, and so on carry the particular qualities of the sun and permit them to be expressed onto the physical plane. It is not a perfect metaphor, but you can see the two ends and center of it clearly.

In Christian terms, within the Trinity we can substitute Father for everperfect, Son for the form body, Holy Spirit for the wealth or transition body (the intention energy level). This is not a perfect match but quite adequate. You may think it uneven because the Son contains God, is direct expression of God. Yes! And the nirmanakaya contains the dharmakaya, too, and is direct expression of it! I find this a very valuable teaching for this reason. No

---

[12] Shambhala Publications, 1996.

matter where one looks on your physical plane, you see the self-display of the divine.

In the teachings in the languages of both Buddhism and Christianity, the inner core and outer expression are not separate: the Son is voice of the Father; the Son is the expression of God in the world. In Buddhist teaching, everything on the form level or in outer manifestation is expression of the everperfect. You cannot separate them. This is vital.

In the transition body, we pick up the many energy streams which may offer distortion of the absolutely pure core. *Please remember that within this core are the possibilities of distortion, or distortion could not occur or would be dual with the core itself.* The negativity in you is not in dualistic opposition to the divine, it is simply a distortion of the divine. Love is also a distortion of the divine.

Some distortions, when you play them out in the world, may do harm. Then clearly you are responsible for that harm. You must clean up your spills. Some distortions may be of great service to others; nevertheless, they are distortions, carry adhering karma and must be attended. They are all a display of the divine. My dear ones, you do not have to be afraid of what moves through you. There is nothing there but God. When you ask, then, "How can I manifest my energy more purely in the world?" remember that there is nothing there but God, sometimes being expressed with distortion, or even great distortion. "How can I come to a reduction of distortion?"—by offering forgiveness and kindness. Hatred will never dissolve hatred and negativity. Only love will dissolve negativity. Only love will dissolve confusion and distortion. Whatever distortion expresses itself, you must bring it into the heart of love.

Ah yes, the question is, "How do we do this?" Perhaps that is best left for tomorrow's discussion. I would leave you tonight only with this thought: *There is nothing which is not God.* Therefore, when you see in dualist terms, that is an invitation to remind yourself that what you are seeing is itself a distortion and is the voice of fear. Instead of trying to chase it away with a big stick, do as this instrument would do: Hold out a goody in your hand and invite it to come and take a taste of it. Offer it loving-kindness. Embrace your fear in that way; do not hate it and order it away.

The distortion-free place is always accessible to you. When you are reacting from a place of fear, which is creating increasing distortion in the outpouring of the energy that flows through you, that is not a statement that absolute clarity and love are not available. It is only a statement that you are increasingly practicing the wrinkles. Then you must come back to the everperfect. As I said, I would prefer to leave the *how* of how we do that to tomorrow so as not to overtax here with too many different thoughts.

At this point, and with great thanks for your willingness to hear me and open your hearts to these thoughts, I turn the microphone back to Q'uo. I pause.

Q'uo: We are those of Q'uo, and would give you farewell fairly briefly.

We would make a request of you. We are aware of the questions within the group, and we and Aaron naturally planned to open the dialogue to questions on the morrow. It would be helpful, we feel, if the circle spoke together before the next session to work out what the group feels it wishes to offer as the next input to this dialogue. That we would appreciate, for the more total the group's comfort with each other and with the activity comes our own greater ability to communicate with a corresponding focus.

We would leave you this evening with a brief return to the one known as Aaron's topic. We would take you into the office and place the paper with the wrinkle on the machine and make the copy. On the copy you may see every wrinkle. Turn the paper over. It is clean. This is actually more like what your situation is than the simple paper, for you yourself are as a shell of personality. As the mark of that toner upon that paper describing those shadows of wrinkles, that shell of personality that is living your incarnation and interacting with your human function is only as thick as a sheet of paper. All that you are resides in fullness. Each wrinkle, each shadow, is sacramental. Each energy center is holy. The trick is to know each energy as a sacrament within.

Dear ones, we wish you deep sleep, joyous dreams, and a fresh day beginning oh, so soon. For now, we leave this instrument in the love and the light of the one infinite Creator. We are known to you as those of Q'uo. Adonai. Adonai. ☙

L/L Research

L/L Research is a subsidiary of Rock Creek Research & Development Laboratories, Inc.

P.O. Box 5195
Louisville, KY 40255-0195

www.llresearch.org

Rock Creek is a non-profit corporation dedicated to discovering and sharing information which may aid in the spiritual evolution of humankind.

ABOUT THE CONTENTS OF THIS TRANSCRIPT: This telepathic channeling has been taken from transcriptions of the weekly study and meditation meetings of the Rock Creek Research & Development Laboratories and L/L Research. It is offered in the hope that it may be useful to you. As the Confederation entities always make a point of saying, please use your discrimination and judgment in assessing this material. If something rings true to you, fine. If something does not resonate, please leave it behind, for neither we nor those of the Confederation would wish to be a stumbling block for any.

CAVEAT: This transcript is being published by L/L Research in a not yet final form. It has, however, been edited and any obvious errors have been corrected. When it is in a final form, this caveat will be removed.

© 2009 L/L RESEARCH

THE AARON/Q'UO DIALOGUES, SESSION 32
NOVEMBER 23, 1996

(This session was preceded by a period of tuning and meditation.)

(On this occasion, Aaron and Barbara presented practices.)

Barbara: I use this practice to remind myself that I have the ability to become a purer vessel and to remind myself to tend to all three areas of my extension into the world—body, speech, mind.

The positive precepts—traditional Buddhist.

With deeds of loving-kindness, I purify my body.

With openhanded generosity, I purify my body.

With stillness, simplicity and contentment, I purify my body.

With truthful communication, I purify my speech.

With words kind and gracious, I purify my speech.

With utterances helpful and harmonious, I purify my speech.

Abandoning covetousness for tranquility, I purify my mind.

Changing hatred into compassion, I purify my mind.

Transforming ignorance into wisdom, I purify my mind.

If it were not possible, I would not ask you to do it. Abandon what is unskillful. One can abandon the unskillful. If it were not possible, I would not ask you to do it. If this abandoning of the unskillful would bring harm and suffering, I would not ask you to abandon it. But as it brings benefit and happiness, therefore, I say abandon what is unskillful.

Cultivate the good. One can cultivate the good. If it were not possible, I would not ask you to do it. If this cultivation were to bring harm and suffering, I would not ask you to do it. But as this cultivation brings joy and happiness, I say cultivate the good." (The Buddha[13])

Barbara: Aaron will lead us in guided meditation and prayer.

Aaron: To begin, draw in and exhale several deep breaths.

(Pauses are indicated with ellipses.)

…

Relax the body, tension leaving with the exhalation, mind letting go, coming into *this* breath, *this* moment.

…

---

[13] *The Anguttara Nikaya: Book of the Twos*, #10.

Make yourself at home in the universe, resting in that space which truly is yours.

…

Be present for this one eternal now.

…

Open totally.

…

If something hangs on or if there is aversion, it is okay; it will go on its own. Nothing to do but touch all arising lightly with choiceless awareness.

…

Opening into this precious moment, allow to arise in yourself the awareness of your connection with all that is—no longer your joy or your pain but *our* joy, *our* pain.

…

Seeing the joy and pain of all beings, allow to arise in you the aspiration to serve all beings, to move beyond your own small fears and troubles; and instead, to use energy, courage and awareness to alleviate suffering throughout the world.

…

This statement of intention is important, bringing awareness from *my* suffering to *ours* and offering the self as instrument for the alleviation of suffering.

…

Rest in that intention for several minutes, allowing awareness to spread, moving beyond the small self.

…

As you expand outward and come to rest in the divine self, the eternal and pure awareness, feel the presence of the divine in all its aspects.

…

Rest in the nature of pure awareness, pure mind.

…

Allow yourself to rest in that space, feeling the energy which surrounds you.

…

Now the second step: to ask for help from all that surrounds you. Open to the spirit plane and to the divine in your own nature.

…

In your own words, ask for the ability to hear that wisdom and to share it for the alleviation of suffering of all beings.

…

Offer yourself as a receptive instrument, not for your own benefit only, but for all beings.

…

And rest in that space, open and attentive, heart unbounded, ready to listen with that loving heart.

…

Finally, offer thanks for whatever you will be given. Then sit for several minutes in silence.

…

Aaron: I am Aaron. My love to you all. Bring yourselves into your body. I request that you allow yourselves the experience of the inhale and the exhale—to come deeply into your body for this particular meditation. I would like you to feel that inhalation and exhalation in the belly. Breathe in … belly breath … feel the breath coming into the abdomen and then breathe out. Let the body be soft and open. Now, let attention move upwards from the body to the heart. This living heart is the core of your being. The brain is the servant. It is in the heart where the true Christ or Buddha self dwells.

The body may experience pain and react by distorting itself or contracting. The brain may experience fear or discomfort and turn to what it is good at, which is directing the show so as to protect the organism from that which it fears or finds discomforting. The heart can watch all of that movement and know that it is merely the superficial movement of waves on the surface and does not affect the true being.

It is in this heart that I invite you to rest. Whatever physical sensations may arise, you can attend to them skillfully, without fixation. Whatever thoughts or emotions may arise, you can attend to them skillfully, without fixation. From a loving heart, we offer the deepest affirmation of our being. Please join me silently in offering that affirmation if it feels appropriate to you:

Today may I offer my energy in a loving-kindness to all beings, including myself. If judgment, fear, greed, anger, or any such contracted emotion arises within me today, may I greet it with love and invite it into the heart where kindness may soften and transform it. I offer myself fully as a servant of the light. To be a servant is not to be somebody but to be nobody. I simply offer my energy that the divine may make use of it in ways that the divine itself determines, not the ways which I determine. As much as possible, I offer my energy in that spirit and my whole being in service of God, of love, of light. I ask for whatever help may be offered to me by all loving beings on every plane to help me express and nurture this resolve. Through allowing myself to be an instrument of light, may I help to bring more light into the universe so that increasingly all beings everywhere may be free of suffering, may be happy, may find perfect peace.

Barbara: The last writing on the page is also from a traditional Buddhist prayer. Please read it with me if you would like:

"By the power and truth of this practice, may all beings have happiness and the cause of happiness, which is loving-kindness. May all be free from sorrow and the causes of sorrow, which are fear, hatred and delusion. May all never be separated from the sacred happiness, which is sorrowless. And may all live in equanimity, without too much attachment and too much aversion; and live, believing in the equality of all that lives."[14]

It is traditional in these teachings to offer outwards whatever merit comes from this work, not to take it for oneself, but to offer it back out to all beings. The offering reminds me of Jesus' words from the Bible, "not my will, but thine."[15]

May whatever merit comes from this practice go to the enlightenment of all beings. May it become a drop in the ocean of activity of all of the Great Ones and their tireless work for the liberation of all beings.

Group discussion: *(A question was formulated to address the concern that, while there may be no intention to harm, harm does sometimes occur: How do we work with this harm and with our own distortions so as more clearly to offer our energy with non-harm?)*

Aaron: I am Aaron. My love to you all. We are talking of how we serve others and of purification of the self to be offered in that service. I would toss a question into your stew pot here. Some years ago C. and Barbara met with a man from their church. He was very negative and expressed tremendous fear. He was violating the spirit of the meeting by bringing his fear in and publicizing it out to the meeting, condemning and judging specific people vocally within the meeting.

The three of them spent a number of hours talking together about what he calls his righteous anger and need to denounce these others who had done him harm. The women were able to hear his pain. He was not really able to hear them and their suggestions that he bring love rather than hatred to these places of perceived harm.

One would have to say that this man was bringing in a very distorted channeling of his own negative bias. He was being a channel for fear and dissension. It caused much pain for many members of the church. C. and Barbara experienced his fear and negativity, not with pain or fear, but with a sense that they really could not speak to it. Yet this man opened so many doors for so many people through the catalyst he offered. Was he being a good channel or a bad channel? Was what he offered of harm or of benefit, or some of each? What does "good" mean? What does "bad" mean?

Clearly you do not intend to offer your energy with the intention of harm. And yet, even when there is no intention of harm, sometimes harm is what comes out. This man had no conscious intention of harm. He felt it a moral necessity to let people know that he felt they had harmed him, not to let them continue what he perceived as *their* distortion. That does not release him from responsibility for the great pain that he caused. But the negative bearing of his attack on others ultimately served as catalyst which brought much insight for many. So it needs to be understood that there are many factors which determine the labeling of "good" or "bad." That is all.

Q'uo: We are the principle known to you as Q'uo; and we greet each of you in love and in light, those lasting and active principles of the one Creator.

We come to you as brothers and sisters of sorrow, for we hear the call of your Earth. We hear and are pierced by your sorrow and distress; and we thank you always for this call, this willingness to work with the catalyst which comes to you, not cynically, but

---

[14] *The Tibetan Book of Living and Dying*, Sogyal Rimpoche; Harper San Francisco, 1992.

[15] *Holy Bible*, Luke 22:42.

hopefully. The deepest sorrow and the greatest pain are as fallow fields within which is sown the kingdom of love. There is the parable within the holy work known as the Bible, of the kingdom of love being one precious pearl buried in a field. The one who seeks the pearl sells all that he has and buys the field.[16]

We hope to help each of you relate to your humanity. But there are subtleties involved when the self-aware seeker turns within. The mind sees the self. It sees the self watching the self. It sees the self who is watching the self who is watching the self. When the self perceives negative emotion, it sees the self seeing negative emotion and the self seeing the self seeing negative emotion. This creates the crowded universe and does not enlarge mercy. And so, we would suggest that as you watch yourself, as you perceive dealing with seemingly negative catalyst, that you remain within that first self-awareness which observes—the observer in a court room typing out what is said and who is responsible only for getting the words set down aright. There is no judgment involved in reporting what occurs. Last evening the one known as Aaron and we worked with that crumpled piece of paper; and it is always helpful to remember that no matter what you are perceiving, it is still no more than a temporary chimera, a shadow flashing upon a sheet of paper whose other side remains completely clean and untouched.

In working to become better, may we suggest that what each is actually responsible for is becoming more oneself. The urge to be better is answered within your earth world by a list of preferred adjectives: worthy, generous, loving … You could think of desirable qualities for a good long time and create wonderful, inspiring lists of good qualities. However, you are an unique being. You are like the snowflake, that crystal that is quite obviously snow, yet whose kaleidoscopic patterns are unique. Only you in all of the created and uncreated universes is you. Therefore, we ask that you encourage within yourself the perceptive ear that notes those moments when you can feel yourself being who you feel you are.

Each of you within this circle has by seniority of vibration earned the opportunity to incarnate at this time. Each of you has two main goals: You wished to move through the intense incarnative experience, repeating for yourself your lesson of loving, which you felt could use more polarity; and you wished—for you, too, are brothers and sisters of sorrow—to lighten the planetary consciousness of this sphere you call Earth.

Your instrument is your self. Learning to play this instrument involves doing those practices, those scales if you will, which enable you to develop a sweet melody as you live your life. If you can see the flute or recorder or any reed instrument, perhaps you can see your energy centers as those buttons which you press to make your melody. Thusly, you wish in each case to clarify the energy that is there, to make it more itself, to make each energy true—not another's truth, not a teacher's truth, but your unique note of sound. For example, let us take the note of any ray, say the yellow ray. Your hope is not to make brighter or larger that energy, but rather to find the truth, the balance that does exist. Once all the energies are played upon consciously, they begin to adjust and balance themselves.

We would at this time transfer the microphone to our beloved brother Aaron. We are those of Q'uo.

Aaron: I am Aaron. Q'uo's example of the melody of the flute brings to mind another image, which is that of a pure spring giving rise to a series of streams running in different directions, eventually drawing together again as they enter the sea itself. The water that enters each stream from the pool around the spring is absolutely pure.

Think of yourself as this streambed; this pure water flows through you. Some streambeds have accumulated a good deal of debris. The purity of the original water never changes. If you add something into that pure water and then lift it out, the water is unchanged. If silt falls to the bottom of the clean, rocky streambed, it will affect the water until the streambed is cleaned again. Then the water will once again be pure. Even if you add chemical pollutant into that water and then filter it out, you have the same pure water again. But for some periods of time it will be affected by the quality of the streambed or the additives.

As you experience that pure water moving through you, you bring different ingredients into it. Figuratively speaking, you bring chemical pollutants into the stream of Pure Awareness through fear, greed and anger. If you do not attend to the

---

[16] *Holy Bible*, Matthew 13:44 - 46.

pollutants, do not then filter them out, the person downstream who wishes a drink will receive water that is chemically impure. The pure water is there, but somebody has got to filter out the pollutants.

You have two areas of work, as I see it. One is consciously to deepen your intention to offer your energy with love. This means to pollute the water as little as possible or not at all. And second is to understand that because the human is what it is, it is going to pollute the water at times. Then you must be responsible for what you have created.

The problem is not that you occasionally pollute the water, but that when you do so, you then turn on yourself with shame and judgment instead of turning your energy to clarifying that which you have polluted. You let the pollution go past because you are so busy condemning yourself that the water became clouded in the first place.

My dear ones, if you were already perfect, if you did not occasionally offer your energy in distorted ways that give rise to cloudiness, you would not be here in incarnation. The more you can stay in each moment, noting the various contractions of mind and body which give rise to the distortion of fear—which distortion tends to pour pollutants into the water—the less you actually have to pour those pollutants out into the stream of life.

By way of simple example, your intention is to offer your energy with kindness. Somebody who is feeling much fear and pain approaches you and belligerently attacks you with his words. When you notice your own arising defensiveness—arising of discomfort and desire to attack that which is the source of your discomfort—the more present you are with that arising in yourself, the less you have to act it out. Noting how much discomfort there is in the self, you might also note the discomfort in your assailant. Allow your heart to open in compassion to that assailant. Then you respond from the heart, responding to his pain instead of reacting only to his words.

This response may be the statement, "No, you cannot attack me like that." The *no* is offered from a place of love, not from a place of need to defend, not from a place of fear. There is no ego involved in that *no*. It is the kindest thing you can say at the moment for yourself and for the assailant, who is creating a great deal of negative karma for himself: "No, you may not speak like that to me; and I will not stay here and hear it."

To be loving does not mean to be a doormat to negativity. It means to speak the truth from the heart. Step one, then, is to practice being present as much as is possible. Within that presence, you watch the conditioned arising of the body and mind and understand how you move into negative mind states which wish to cling or defend, and which thereby poison the situation.

A very useful practice is what I call "clear comprehension of purpose." This practice has several parts. I would speak here only of the beginnings of the practice. First is to understand your primary purpose. To defend yourself against that assailant is a purpose. It is not bad to wish to defend yourself. But there is a higher purpose, which is to create increasing harmony and understanding. Will you look at these two purposes and your choices of words or action that lie before you? Which choices are most suitable to the attainment of the highest purpose?

In this practice of clear comprehension in a given situation, we note our highest purpose and we ask, "Is this proposed speech or action suitable to that highest purpose?" If it is not suitable, and yet the intensity of the catalyst is such that you enact that unsuitable movement and offer outward whatever reactivity may have been called forth by the catalyst, then you will have a new catalyst and may again examine the highest purpose: Is it to save face and lay blame elsewhere or to accept responsibility for what you have wrought?

Let us return to our metaphor: The water is polluted; do you have the courage to be responsible for it? Your self-judgment, even your sense of shame, are not ways of being responsible. They are deterrents to responsibility. What are you going to do, sit there and condemn yourself while others drink your poisoned water? Or are you going to go and clean it up?

You clean it up in very simple ways. You observe the source of the pollutant and close it off. If the source is great anger, you close off the anger by opening your heart to it, making a bigger container for it within you so it does not need to pour out of you into the world.

Anger is not bad; anger is just energy. When there is a lot of it, it needs a big space. If the source of the pollutant is seen as pride or jealousy or greed, you attend to each of those in the same way. There are many specific practices that are available to help you create this bigger container. One of my favorite comes from the teacher Thich Nhat Hanh.[17] It is very simple: "Breathing in, I am aware of my anger; breathing out, I smile to my anger …" and again and again until you feel that space enlarging.

You must both acknowledge the heavy emotion and also offer a willingness to embrace it instead of attacking it, thereby to invite it into the ever-spacious heart. That is one way to become responsible for the pollutant that is already pouring out of you. The other is simply ask for forgiveness. You cannot ask for forgiveness while distortion is still pouring out. You have got to attend to it first, and then you mop up. Mop up by asking for forgiveness. If you are clinging to your shame and self-judgment, then those mind states are what need the bigger container. That is where the poison is coming from.

Remember that the pure spring is always there. Remember that in human form, you are never going to be a perfect channel for that pure spring. There is always going to be some distortion. Deep mindfulness will reduce that distortion; and a sense of loving responsibility will mop up and readjust the flow, will clean up whatever distortion has been created.

Do you think you teach more when what flows through you is absolutely pure? Would it just be possible that you teach more when what flows through you does become distorted, and then you very lovingly attend to that distortion, thus helping others also to learn that they do not need to be perfect—they need to be conscious, loving and responsible? Your distortion also offers a catalyst to others through which they are given opportunity to practice with their own fears and distortions. This learning is, after all, the primary motivation for incarnative experience. This is not justification for poisoning the waters; but when the entire movement is deeply considered, it may be better understood that as long as you are human, there will be spills, and they are all part of the learning process of the incarnative experience.

I would ask the same question also in a different way: In which way do you learn more? What would self-perfection teach you? This is the old story. One does not need pain to learn; but pain says, "Pay attention," and that attention allows learning. The pain of your mistakes does not teach you, but it does catch your attention.

My friends, you do know all the levels on which you are working. You can never excuse great intentional harm to another by saying, "Well, it's their karma," or, "I'm working on a different level." When you are working to the best of your intention, noting the arising of fear within you and attending to that fear with skill, cleaning up after yourself for the bits of fear that have sent themselves out into the world, then you have got to have faith that, while some of this fear did escape and created a pollution, out of that situation can come some good because of the heart's great desire to offer its energy with love.

This highest intention to offer your energy for the good of all beings is of utmost importance. It is not up to you to determine how that good is going to come about, only to constantly ask yourself, "What is my highest purpose here?" and to work with clear comprehension of this purpose.

You know that the highest purpose is to offer the energy with love. Remember, you are in third density largely to learn faith and love. If you did not have this veil surrounding you so that you clearly understood exactly how different movements of energy through you became distorted, why they became distorted, and in what ways that distortion might actually be of service, you would be denied the opportunity to learn faith around these distortions. This is not to be taken as instruction to consciously perpetuate the distortions; but if they occur, both trust them and ask how you may purify them.

You wished for a clear-cut question and answer. There is no clear-cut answer, except for one: Pay attention and act with love. Be willing to be responsible and to learn. Do not be afraid; but if you are afraid, do not be afraid of your fear. Give that also a bigger container so it does not need to pollute the water. Where it has polluted the water, clean it up.

Whatever flows through you when your primary intention is to offer your whole being in loving service to all beings, the divine will take and use for

---

[17] Reference is pending.

holy purpose. It is that in which you need to have faith. Let the loving heart offer its intention for service. Act, speak and think based on this intention and with awareness, and offer that which is prompted by fear and the notion of separate self to the divine. Trust the divine plan for even your fear.

I would turn the microphone over to my brother/sister/friend of Q'uo. I pause.

Q'uo: We are with this instrument. We are those of Q'uo.

The loving energy that is you is impossible to dissect. It has an integrity unique to your system. Often seekers target one or another aspect or energy center for renovation, and feel that this energy needs to be improved, cleansed, or altered. This is a less skillful model than that approach to improving the instrument which sees as its first goal the balance of the instrument as an whole. Some entities have little strengths compared to others, yet because they have somehow found the balance within and have harmonized that scale of being, that melody arrests the listening ear with delight. To have a more powerful indigo ray, for instance, has less virtue than to have an indigo ray which is euphonious and promotes travel between it and the other energy nexi.

In working with the self in this regard, we find it helpful to ask that which the one known as Ra first offered to this instrument: "Where is the love in this moment?" By turning to this universal question, by asking, by desiring that quality, that question, you open doors within your deeper Self—that self which abides in the awareness you do not have access to in your conscious mind. This deeper Self knows where the love is. Therefore, by asking that question and then by abiding in faith with patience and an inner knowing, that which is sought shall come to you. The thousand and one specific details of everyday occurrences are taken from that world of manifestation and handed up as a noble and holy offering to the Creator: "Here is my confusion; here is my pain; here are all my emotions; here is my confusion; here is my mental anguish." And that great Being which lies within embraces the self, the concern, the anguish of unknowing, and responds in silence with love.

Within the moment of asking lies the perfect and balanced response. The skill of the seeker is to trust that process and to keep the mind upon the question, "Where is the love?" and to keep the mind upon the moment wherein the question is asked. If you can come to the present moment and know it, you have entered eternity. If, when you come to that present moment, your question is, "Where is the love?"—in that moment you have entered love. The concern about articulating and beautifying or crystallizing the energies can then be set aside, for in the moment-by-moment-by-moment succession that the illusion of time offers, your instrument shall be aided; and rehearsal always helps. Each moment is another rehearsal. The whole of your life removed from the illusion of space and time is a song. You can no more know the song than know your life. You are in the middle of creating a life which is a gift to the one infinite Creator.

The way the question is asked is far more important than what is asked, for the attitude that asks the question is that point of view which will limit the answer. Thusly, abide in love and look in all things for love—even with rage, with fury, with the strongest and heaviest of emotions. There is at the heart of that emotion a purity and an essence, a color; and there is the same beauty in those dark colors as there is in those dark colors that create variety and depth in a tapestry. All things you experience are as these threads going into the tapestry of your life. To identify this or that thread, then, is to lose sight of the picture, the whole of your tapestry.

At this time, we give our farewell to you for now, unless there be queries after the one known as Aaron has completed the material that he wishes to share at this session. As always, we ask that you hear us with discrimination. Thank you beyond our ability to express through this instrument for this wonderful chance to share love with love. We leave you in that love which is all that there is and that light which manifests in all this world of duality. We are those of Q'uo.

Aaron: I am Aaron. I would like to share one thought with you and then ask for your specific questions. Last night we spoke of the wrinkled sheet of paper, of the relative reality that the wrinkles existed and the ultimate reality of the ever-perfect sheet. We suggested that both realities are true and that it is useful to stay balanced between the two. When you are working with the wrinkles, with the so-called negative distortion of your being, are you any less perfect? Are you any less whole?

Most of you relate to yourselves as broken. When you ask, as Q'uo suggested, "Where is love to be found?" can you see that the love is to be found in both the idea of brokenness and in wholeness? The love is always there in the wholeness—that is easy to see. The sense of brokenness is catalyst which sets you looking for the love. Therefore, the love must also be in that sense of brokenness. The love is in the inspiration which inspires you to seek the love, and that inspiration is often the negative and painful distortion. Nothing is dual here. Within the shadow is found the sunshine!

When you begin to experience with more clarity that love is in everything—not just in the ultimate perfection of you but in every expression of that perfection—then you do not need to worry so much over distortions nor to enhance judgment and shame about them, but simply to attend to them. Recognize, "This distortion does not separate me from wholeness, nor from the divine. It is simply a distorted expression of that wholeness."

When you work conscientiously in this way, instead of each distorted expression becoming something that grabs at your energy so you must frantically go and fix it, each distorted expression just becomes a reminder to ask, as Q'uo suggested, "Where is the love? Where is God in this fear, in this anger, in this judgment? Can I find God right here?" If you look, you will find you can.

When the expression is distorted and causes discomfort to self or to another self, it must be attended; but regardless of its effect, it is still expression of the divine. I would ask you to visualize a crystal. If you hold it up to the sun, the sun plays through the crystal and creates a rainbow of light. That rainbow is direct expression of the sun. When you look at that rainbow of light, can you see that the sun is there? If the light is shining in somebody's eyes so that they are uncomfortable, then you must attend to the crystal; but there is no good or bad to it, just sun and its various expressions.

Using a different metaphor, when you sit in the sun and feel its heat on your back, that is a direct experience of the sun. It is of a different intensity than if you could fly up into the heart of that sun, but still it is the sun. Sometimes the heat on the back feels warm and gentle. Sometimes it may burn. We do not say that only the pleasant experience of the sun is the sun. Every experience of the sun is the sun.

When you ask, "Where is love to be found?" especially when involved in a painful experience, it is a way of reminding yourself, "Even right here is God." With that reminder, your energy field opens. When you are closed and defended it is very difficult to learn. When you remind yourself, "This is okay; it's workable. And the divine is present even in this," you allow that opening of the self which is willing to be present with the experience with all its discomforts. Then love announces itself.

Here is where you become increasingly willing to offer that which has arisen, to let it be and allow the divine to use it as it will. To offer it does not mean to get rid of it. It does not mean to say, "This one is bad, God, please take it"; rather, it is a statement, "I haven't the faintest idea what's going on here, but my deepest intention is to use all of this turmoil and confusion and everything that is coming through me as a way of offering service to all beings, for the good of all beings." You can say to yourself, "I don't know how to transform this mess. I don't know what to do with it. All I can do is offer love." It is this way that you offer it.

There is a discarnate energy which is a guru to this instrument. He comes into her experience on occasion. During this summer she was on an extended meditation retreat and experienced the presence of this one. In offering her instruction, he offered the suggestion, "Let go of everything; give everything away." At first she misunderstood: "Am I to give away my house, my car? What does he ask of me?"

Through the following months she moved to a deeper understanding of what "give it all away" means. Are you identified with your fear, with your unworthiness, with your shame, with your judgments? Give away the identity with it. You may say you *want* to be rid of it, that it is very painful and unpleasant—fine; but nevertheless, you are invested in being that person who is fearful or is self-judgmental and who is going to be the one who improves. There is so much "somebody" in these notions. Be nobody; give it all away.

Within this rising intention to allow whatever comes into your experience and offer to God—not to hold on to any of it—lies the ultimate path to service, because with that offering "somebody" disappears and "nobody" remains. In more precise terms, that which is contracted can stay contracted or can open itself. This process means not making anything special happen, just allowing an open heart which watches it all moving through and continually offers whatever moves through with a trust that the divine will make good use of it.

I would ask of you during your afternoon and evening to watch closely something which arises in your experience. In very simple physical terms, if there is a loud noise, such as a shout, *"Hey!"* do you feel your body energy contract around that noise? Fear and the energy of fear contract. There is nothing bad or good about the contraction; it is simply a knee-jerk kind of reaction of the body. You may feel the reverberations of that contraction for a bit, and then eventually it will dissolve again. If, instead of a physical noise like a shout, what you experience is an energy catalyst such as somebody else's sorrow or anger, there will also be response. You have emotional nerve endings as well as physical nerve endings. Your energy field will contract.

What if, instead of one shout, there was an ongoing unpleasant noise and growing discomfort with that noise? The contraction changes from contraction as reaction to pure hearing, to a contraction around the feeling of strong aversion to what is being heard. That pure sense awareness, hearing, is not the aversion to hearing. The relationship to the hearing is not the hearing itself. In hearing there is just hearing.

Each mind or body experience will have its own energy movements. Can you feel the difference as I demonstrate it here, how in that one shout, *"Hey!"* there is that momentary contraction, which then may continue with some reverberations and then release? It may have been unpleasant, but it is passed; there is nothing holding it. When it continues, then fear may arise: "How am I going to get rid of this?" Then there is a contraction around the contraction, a secondary contraction. Or perhaps there is contraction and then judgment around the contraction, a different sort of secondary contraction.

What I would ask you to do is to deeply observe the movements. Note the physical or mental catalyst, the physical object contacting the physical sense or the thought touching the mind. Note that there is a contraction carried in the body when this occurs.

The contraction in itself is just a contraction. There is no adhering karma in it. There is nothing that needs to be done with it other than to relax and observe it, just to know that it is present. Smile to it! If it is a difficult experience, do as Q'uo suggested: Ask, "Where is the love?" with a truly open heart and mind.

If there is some relationship with the contact and the resultant contraction, note that as a new contact. For example: Judgment or aversion, each, is a thought; they have touched the sense base of the mind. With that thought there will again be a first contraction, just the wind rippling the water, so to speak. Again, note it as contraction. Is there anything which follows?

It is not the experience of hearing, seeing, touching, knowing and so forth that pulls you out of center and into a place of self where adhering karma is created, nor is it the contraction around that touch. It is your relationship to that contraction. It is this truth that I would ask you to observe for yourselves this afternoon and evening.

My deepest thanks to you for allowing me to share these thoughts with you, and for your willingness to attend to your experience and do this deep work. That is all.

Questioner: Q'uo spoke about energy entering the being from below, through the feet, and from above, and that there was a meeting place for these energies that is somewhat dependent on the allowing of energy through the lower centers. Could Q'uo speak about what this meeting place is; and is this a place where energy entering into the illusion enters in a different way than the light issuing from the other energy centers?

Q'uo: We are those of Q'uo, and believe we grasp your query.

The meeting place of the upward spiraling light and the instreaming inspiration has been known within your cultures as the kundalini; and the ability of the self to become transparent to whatever distortions exist within the energy centers leads to an increased ability to experience a freely flowing upward motion so that the kundalini, in your culture's terms, rises. This involves being friends with the various energies of the mind, body and spirit; not the perfecting of those energies, but the balance of them in the acceptance of self as self without explanation or apology—that relaxed self-confidence that this instrument would say makes one comfortable within one's own skin.

Does this answer your query, my brother, or may we speak further upon it?

Questioner: So it is that the distortions in the centers do not limit the rising of the upward spiraling light, but rather the relationship, as you said earlier this morning—the relative harmony of the entity's acceptance of the aspects of self.

Q'uo: This is so, my brother.

Questioner: So this is … this sounds to me like what Aaron mentioned earlier when he asked us to consider the possibility that the distortions provide us with opportunities to learn and to enhance our abilities to offer learning experiences that help others, through our loving attendance to those distortions.

Q'uo: The entity who loves self, who loves self as it is in all its dirt, is an entity with mercy to offer to others in all their dirt.

To allow a knot to be a knot, a tangle to be a tangle, is the beginning of the end of that tangle or knot. To ignore is not to allow; but to see, to love, to accept, to forgive and to move on, knowing the whole—that is helpful.

Questioner: So, it is the distortions that allow one to increase polarity?

Q'uo: This is perceptive, my brother. Polarity is exquisitely central to your task here upon the third planet from your sun. You have one great choice to make: Shall you radiate or shall you contract and hold, giving it all away or grasping all for self? That polarity of radiance is the service-to-others path. It is what we came to share, and we say to you that it is your radiance within all the suffering of every day that expresses this polarity of love.

May we answer you further, my brother?

Questioner: No. Thank you.

Questioner: I don't understand the seeking polarity. Selfish or unselfish what?

Q'uo: To serve others is to serve the self. To serve the self is to serve all that there is. There is no answer to your question. The attempt to separate selfishness from unselfishness works upon a false premise. The self is an whole, so polarity is expressed moment by moment as you choose to forgive, accept, allow and look for the ability to do this in difficult situations; and is that which will move you into a finer degree of awareness. Thus, the very time of difficulty where you see that the love energy is sacrificial and painful—that is time to rejoice; for in loving the unlovable, you are truly choosing to polarize in service to others.

We are those of Q'uo; and as the energy is moving away as we speak, we would close this meeting with the promise to ask for further queries at a future session. We leave you and yet leave you not. We leave you in all that there is. In the company of each other, see the face of the Creator. Adonai. Adonai, each light. We are those of Q'uo. ✤

The Aaron/Q'uo Dialogues, Session 33
November 24, 1996

(This session was preceded by a period of tuning and meditation.)

Aaron: My greetings and love to you all. My joyous welcome to this circle of seekers, and in gratitude for the invitation to join you in your circle.

I want to return to this aspect of your experiences as a balance between human with its physical body, which has aches and pains; its emotional body with its joys and sorrows; its mental body with its mix of clarity and confusion; and its spirit body. The balance is between this human expression and the ultimate essence of love that you are.

You speak of taking incarnation and experiencing a veil of forgetting of who you are—a veil which pushes you deeper into the seeming confines of the human. This is just as it needs to be, because through this human come the greatest expressions of compassion, generosity and love.

I give you a very simple example. If I had a vast apple orchard, literally thousands of healthy, vibrant apple trees, what if a being knocked on my door and said, "Please sir, would you give me an apple?"—and I gave him one? One might say that was an act of generosity. If I gave him a whole bag of apples, one might say that was an act of even greater generosity. Certainly it is; I have freely given something of mine to another. But there is a clarity within me of the infinite abundance which lies behind me. There is no fear which prevents my giving or in some way influences my giving and makes me pause. Yes, it is still generosity if we define that word to mean a free giving from oneself, but what a difference if I have but one apple in my pocket and no access to more. I know this is my supper. I have walked for ten miles and just sat down under a tree in the shade, pulled out that apple and polished it on my shirt; and I'm looking forward to its sweet juiciness to quench my thirst as well as my hunger. Then you approach me and say, "Please, would you give me your apple?" Fear now may arise: "If I give, what will I eat? Will I be safe? Will my needs be met?" Through that fear, the voice of love must speak with resounding clarity in order for the apple to be offered. It is the force of this voice of love that I define as true generosity.

You can offer that apple for many reasons. You may practice self-discipline: Push the fear and annoyance away and give the apple. Or the fear may remain—silent, unspoken, beneath the surface. Then the apple is given but not with joy. To give the apple with real joy, you must have acknowledged and transformed your fear. Within fear is generosity. Fear, transformed, is generosity.

Here we have a different experience of giving. It is not just that joyful giving which comes out of the strength of knowing infinite abundance, out of ten thousand apples. There is a deep joyfulness because you have moved through the fear with love. You have not allowed fear to control you, but been able to give despite the fear and to transform the fear. It evokes faith that your needs will be met, although you still may not understand how, because that was the only apple.

There is a different possible scenario. If the other is grasping, punishing, in order to shame you into giving the apple, there may be anger but also a fear that says, "I *must* give this apple in order to feel good, feel generous." Here the primary fear is not whether one's needs will be met but is the desire to be "good," to please another. One need not be slave to that fear. "I *must* give" is a harsh judgment which considers the self to be less worthy to receive than is another. That is also a fear which love can transform. Here the outcome is to say no to fear and to the asker, to keep and eat the apple, or perhaps to share it. One does not act to punish the other but to affirm that the self's needs are also to be honored. There is nothing wrong with this response. It is a different practice of generosity, responding lovingly to the fear by kindness to the self. The point is that when fear is not the master, the innate generous heart will know how to respond. Fear is the catalyst offered to the human, which prompts it to learn how to transform that fear into loving-kindness or generosity.

This is the love which the earth plane offers you the opportunity to manifest and express out into the world. I do not want to talk about degrees of love here, but love which is manifest in the face of fear is a far more transformative love, transformative because it touches that fear with kindness and teaches you the ultimate lesson that there is nothing to fear. Only through practice with fear do you learn that you do not have to be reactive to your fear but may relate from the ever-opening heart.

Your earth-plane experience constantly offers you such lessons because you live with this veil of forgetting. Of course, as you reach a point of deeper spiritual awareness, the veil has holes poked in it. It becomes translucent in parts so that the light shines through. It is even quite transparent on occasion, but as long as you are in human form it will never be continually transparent.

Your fear is not an obstacle. Your fear is wisdom itself when you abide with it, smile to it and are not ruled by it. It is then that the heart develops, then that you truly begin to live in the heart and express from that heart out into the universe.

You are in incarnation for a purpose. That purpose is not to have discarnate experience—not even continuous discarnate clarity—but to be incarnate and to work with the catalyst of your incarnation with love.

Here I would like to turn the microphone over to my beloved brother/sister/friend Q'uo. I pause.

Q'uo: We are those of the principle known to you as Q'uo, and we greet you in the love and light of the one infinite Creator. Let us give thanks to you one more time, each of you in the circle, for this opportunity to be a voice to you upon the path. We find your companionship heartening. We marvel at your courage, for you must express within this veil of unknowing.

There are two distinct ways to proceed upon a heartfelt path of learning and serving; and as we were saying to the one known as J. last evening, either technique or method of seeking is fruitful. However, the seeking with mind and opinion is that seeking that takes place in the shadow world of night with just the dim moon to offer its mysterious light to the darkness. In this dimness it is very easy to misrepresent to the self that which is seen. Discernment is difficult. Upon the other path, the path of the open heart, the light of noontide is offered to those who can surrender their small will and their hopes and expectations set upon defining that which is developed and manifest in the future.

Let us give a concrete example of the mix of these two ways. We describe now the way the one known as Jim came to the conclusion that he should join this instrument and the one known as Don. The one known as Jim had lived a simple and monastic life for some years before he encountered the ones known as Don and Carla. He also was a good friend of another teacher who lived some 2,000 miles from his home in rural Kentucky. He had decided that it was time to embark upon a path of service to others instead of remaining alone. His mind said to him, "I shall go 2,000 miles and offer my service." Thusly, this entity packed his worldly resources in the back of his truck and drove the 2,000 miles. When he arrived he found good work to do, but his heart kept knocking at the door of his awareness, saying, "Is this your place?" Finally, this entity honored that knocking on the door and determined to sit in silent meditation for the period of the weekend. He completed all his chores having to do with the service to the teacher and retreated for a long weekend alone. After all this preparation, he went into meditation and immediately he knew he was to drive 2,000 more miles back to Kentucky and join this instrument and the one known as Don.

Could the one known as Jim have come directly 70 miles down the road to L/L Research? We say to you, no; he could not. He was too sure that he knew his way. He had plans in hand, and therefore he had to work through these concepts and opinions. The miles were not at all wasted. There were no errors in this roundabout journey.

Now each of you seeks the most efficient way to serve. And whenever the grace comes upon you to stand in the noonday of that sun within, then we say, "Wonderful, exquisite," yet it is not often the case that sufficient surrender to the spiritual forces molding your destiny is enough completed that the apparent short cut through can be taken. Most often there is the mixture of the self attempting to predict and control the flow of energy with that openhearted surrender.

What we wish to impress upon you is our honest belief that the longer and seemingly roundabout route is not merely acceptable as a substitute for the blazing purity of surrender, but offers valuable catalyst which enables that sun within to begin to manifest within the inner consciousness. It is for this seemingly roundabout journey, this peering into the folds of velveteen night, that you donned what the one known as Aaron has called the earthsuit. We hope you may find it in your heart to embrace this walk in the shadows of mortality. We hope you may come to value and enjoy your swim through the seas of confusion, and may find play and sport in the swim and flow of inner tides. You shall be tossed about in these currents of unknowing; and as you suffer, you may often doubt the efficacy of your own seeking. This is the very situation you came to Earth to experience. Within, at noontide, you claim your wholeness easily. But you hoped to come into the shadow world and act as if you saw the noonday sun. Faith is that throwing of the self into the midair of complete surrender.

Against all logic, there comes in cycles the time of blind choice. At those cusps there is the desire to do right; and the instincts of mortality are to hold, to control, to reach and pull. The muscular take of those who choose to develop these cusps is that brave decision to release and surrender, and to claim the surety that all is well, that all will be well, and that for the moment it shall be given you what to do.

We would at this time offer the floor to the one known as Aaron. We are those of Q'uo.

Aaron: I am Aaron. Can you see that efficiency is often the voice of fear? There is within the human that which wishes to stay in control, not only for its own safety but also for the safety of those around it. It wishes to pattern the universe and make it predictable.

On the astral plane there is never a sense of being unsafe in the way that the human experiences such danger. It is clear on the astral plane that there is nothing that needs to be ordered or controlled, but that disorder has its own delicate and lovely order, and you can just let it flow.

Who wants to be in control? Often your reasons may be the highest: wanting to offer one's energy in service to all beings, wanting to alleviate suffering. But my dear ones, life is chaos; life is messy. Thoughts and emotions do not arise only when invited, and like good little children reporting themselves and then stepping back into a line. Thoughts and emotions are a class of rowdy children raising their voices out of turn. This is human incarnation.

It is easy to keep your equanimity in heaven. You are here incarnate to learn this equanimity regardless of the catalyst and even regardless of your response to the catalyst. Then, while you are shrieking, *"Eeek!"* and running from the mouse, there will be that within which is centered, still and knows its safety.

In very practical terms, in fourth density you are going to move into telepathic energy groups. Every thought or emotion that arises in you will be telepathically received by your peers in the group. Every thought and emotion that arises in them will be heard by you. This is the nature of fourth-density experience. Thoughts and emotions are not going to cease to arise just because you are fourth density. If this circle was fully telepathic now, would that be okay with you? Is there something that has been said or thought which you would not wish to share with the whole group? Did you glance at someone across the room and think, "Her hair or clothing looks frazzled today," or, "Why did he frown at me?" Certainly each of you has had what we would call negative thoughts or emotions in the past three days. Would it be okay if everybody heard this, or would there be a sense of shame? What if you heard this from your neighbor? Would there be discomfort with that hearing?

You are not incarnate to stop thoughts and emotions from arising but to find equanimity with them so that when you enter fourth-density experience, everything within you can be shared, everything from without can come freely to you. And judgment does not arise, shame and embarrassment do not arise; rather, there is complete equanimity with those thoughts and emotions so you can fully hear each other.

Now you are limited to learning from your own direct experience. What if you could totally empathize with another? Can you see that, then, others' experiences also become very viable tools for your learning? This is why compassion is learned so deeply in a higher density, and wisdom also, because so much more experience is directly accessible to you.

So, here you are in this third-density form, experiencing this wide array of thoughts and emotions, of confusion, joy and sorrow. Your first instinct is to wish to order this madness, to force it to stand in line and salute; and report, one at a time, and only that material which is pretty. But you cannot do it. That is not the nature of human experience. The nature of human experience, while it is often beautiful, is also dirty, smelly, chaotic. You are here to learn equanimity, to learn to open your heart to that chaos. The chaos is not your enemy; the chaos is your teacher.

When you ask, "How can I be a clearer channel in the way I wish to channel?"… The fear of which Q'uo just spoke wants to order experience. It wants efficiency: "Cut out that four thousands miles; go straight to Kentucky." It does not leave room for the great journey in which you are immersed and which purifies you, which teaches you.

To desire order and efficiency is not bad. Of course some of that desire is from a place of love, which wishes to release disorder to alleviate suffering. Only some is fear-based. Can you distinguish? If it is fear-based, can you observe that movement with kindness and without fixation on it? This instrument has a magnet in her office which says, "Bless this mess." It is precisely that attitude that you need to bring to your lives.

I would share a brief story about efficiency. Some years ago this instrument worked one day a week as a volunteer for a service organization known as Seva. She worked in the office, where her job was to receive the order forms for donations offered as gift in another's name, such as to commemorate a birthday. She would send a thank you to the one who had paid for that particular donation and send an announcement of the donation to the one in whose name it was made. These were all very loving donations in support of many beings. They were financial donations; merchandise ordered for self or other; and service donations, such as a cataract operation offered to a blind person in Nepal or a goat offered to a woman in Guatemala, which goat would provide her some means for a livelihood.

Barbara sat down one day with a great stack of these forms to be sent out. She saw how many thoughts she had, which slowed the process. She said, "This isn't efficient. What I'm going to do," she thought to herself, "is to go through the whole list and write all the donor address envelopes, then choose the appropriate card that says, 'Thank you for your donation', and slip it into the envelope. Then I'm going to go through the whole pile again and write recipient envelopes. I'll simply pull out the individual card: 'A cataract operation in your name'; 'Happy Birthday'; 'Merry Christmas'; 'A hundred dollars in your name'; 'With blessings to you'…" So she started separating these gifts, creating an efficient order of replying. She spent a day on it. By the end of the afternoon she was weary, and she had not really covered more ground. She took a walk and asked, "Where did I go wrong? Why didn't it go faster?"

Suddenly she realized the heart had not been present. Her previous process was slow because she would read the words and feel happy about how Mary Smith in Seattle offered this cataract operation with great joy to help another, and how much love Mary had for her mother to honor her and offer this gift in her name. When she wrote the cards, then her own joy at such generosity was a part of the writing. She was involved in the whole process and honoring the process. The cards were done more slowly but with love.

My dear ones, it is so easy to fall into the trap of cutting out your heart, finding a mechanical path that does not have to feel the pain of the Earth. Mechanism insulates you against chaos, pain and disorder. You are never going to create perfect order; you are not here to do that. You are here to find equanimity and love.

I am asked sometimes, "Aaron, if this disorder does in fact add to suffering, then why is it bad to attempt to order it?" To attempt to order it is not bad, but attachment to ordering it creates the suffering, not the disorder itself. When there is attachment, the motivation is largely fear-based; "I've got to fix this" is the stimulus. When there is no attachment, there is a willingness to go into things the way they are, to feel the wind blowing and pushing on you and the trees, to sway back and forth, to feel the currents of the river ebbing and flowing, to feel the whole movement of life.

When you feel in this way, in connection with all that is, then the loving heart can respond with an intuitive awareness: "If I offer love here, it will shift that current so beings are not drowning in it. If I offer kindness there, it will gentle the push of that wind so beings are not blown off their feet." Then that movement comes from a place of deep love, which trusts the ways of the universe, which does not need to fight a war with the universe but offers its deepest love as co-Creator of the universe. Offering that loving force, which the universe may draw into itself and use in the best ways, you are no longer saying, "This has got to be fixed." You are saying, "Here is love, which can apply itself as it is needed."

This is the greatest skill you can master. You master it first by observation, by seeing how fear serves as a giant pusher, how your energy field armors itself and wants to push back. As these pushes keep coming fiercely within this realm of chaos, you learn to dance with the energy. It pushes and you yield a bit and observe it; as the pushing stops, you let the energy flow back. There is no longer anyone who yields or pushes, only the play of the unconditioned, the play of God. It is a dance of love, not fear. It is a very masterable skill. In order to learn it, you must first of all be present. You must observe the way that the physical world of material objects and thoughts pushes at you. You must observe the discomfort with that push and the small ego self that wants to be safe, wants the others it holds dear to be safe. You observe the one who wants to fix the push or fight it.

As you observe the flow of these movements in yourself, increasingly you will see how much choice you have. The heart of love opens! You will cease to need to attack the voice of fear in yourself, but instead will offer compassion to it. This is the second phase after presence—a nurturing of the deepest truth and resolve to live that truth until each moment of the mind and body cannot help but reflect truth. Thus, the lessons offered you by that arising fear will be mastered, because fear will become increasingly a catalyst for compassion. And you will become a force in the world which is centered and offers love. Not less important, you will ready yourself for fourth-density experience.

Each of you has some kind of mindfulness or meditation practice. It is very useful to use this time of practice, at least in part, as a way of observing your relationship to the aspects of life which push at you and at fear's reaction to fight back. To all of this you offer love, both to that which wants to fight back and to the catalyst itself. The more you practice this, the easier it becomes, and the more freedom you have to live with great joy and peace within this chaos that we call third-density experience.

I would like to offer the microphone to Q'uo. Whenever Q'uo has made whatever statement it wishes to make, I will open the floor to your questions. I am Aaron. I pause.

Q'uo: We are those of Q'uo; and before we speak, we would suggest the time is right for the seventh-inning stretch. We shall be with you when you have stretched. We are those of Q'uo.

(Pause)

We are those of Q'uo, and would offer to you last thoughts before the question period. To know yourself as human, as the featherless biped, may seem a great restriction, a great inconvenience. But no, know and trust that the moonlight is glamorous and deceiving, and that your wandering steps are all perfectly as they need to be. Take yourself lightly. Take love with profoundest dedication. Know that your greatest treasure, your central purpose and your patience are all wrapped up in the everyday life lived devotionally. In the world of the Father, all things are featured. Persist in your attention to the daily; for each task, each tale, each silly piece of paper in the paper mountain of your culture is full of learning for the one with ears to hear and heart to understand. Know that as you touch others, you meet yourself. The one known to you as Jesus offered two rules of life: to love the infinite Creator and to love the other self as the self. These suggestions encompass all you need for your journey.

This instrument sang this morning, "To give and give and give again, as God hath given thee; to spend thyself nor count the cost; to give right gloriously to the Lord of all the worlds that are and are to be."[18] May your worries be blessed with quietness, your concerns touched with grace. May your heart open.

We would at this time open the meeting to queries of Aaron or ourselves, or both. Please proceed with the question.

Questioner: Q'uo, I am interested that the path to equanimity seems to be anything *but*. It is not a process. How much of the instructions that we garner are just keeping us busy or stopping us in our tracks, and how much a ladder to our goal?

Q'uo: We are those of Q'uo.

My brother, all of the seeming missed steps and mistakes are necessary. This instrument has a memory: the story from a friend whose cat, upon finding her mistress at the front door, would race around and around the living room, run between her legs, dash into the kitchen, jump up upon the counter top, run around the counter, dash around the floor, jump at the refrigerator and then walk to her bowl. The cat knew that only after she did these things would her mistress provide food. The human mind says, "But it simply took that long for the woman to reach the storage place for the food. All the running was for nothing." We say to you, did not the cat enjoy the exercise, enjoy the time between the coming of the mistress and the food?

You must do something between this moment and when you die from this planet. You can choose when you rest and sit and await without motion. How this defeats the desire for which you entered this veil of illusion! The times of your life are instructional. They give you exercise; they give your emotions opportunity to refine. That process creates the beauteous and clear emotion, the mellow and harsh tones of the various positive and negative emotions. And so, it is the work of incarnation to begin to listen to and appreciate the dance of the emotions and mind and habit and encountered parts, confusingly and seemingly wrong-headed as these things must be; for it is in the fires of these steps of learning that realization of wholeness is found. So embrace the seeming trading of goals for mistakes, for seeming roads wrongly taken, and see that, truly, you cannot waste time as long as attention persists. Simply keep paying attention. Pay that treasure of time and talent. Pay it without concern for whether it seems worthwhile. Simply give of yourself as you see aright to do. And the moment of *samadhi* shall take you in the midst of that sea and never leave it for a moment, that confusion.

May we answer further?

Questioner: No, thank you.

Aaron: I am Aaron. I would like to add an illustration to the thought that Q'uo has just provided, taken out of the experience of this instrument.

At one time she took a walk in the woods, in a lovely wooded park. Since her last visit, the trails had been changed. She knew from prior walks that there was a shortcut that led to the beach. She walked down a path that seemed to go in the right direction, but it became narrower and narrower. Then ahead she saw what seemed to be a dirt-covered clearing—a patch of dirt, not quite as big as this room.

On the far side she saw the continuation of a trail. She stepped out into it and sunk literally up to her armpits in mud. She had the presence of mind to fling her arms out as far as she could. She was quite alone. Her feet were not touching the bottom, so there was nothing solid to push from. Slowly she grabbed the sticks and leaves that were within reach and built some kind of cushion for her body. Slowly she inched her way out of that mud, certainly not without fear. She crawled out to the other side, literally covered with black mud from head to toe.

She decided she needed to go back to the main trail, to stop looking for shortcuts, so she sought a way around this patch of mud. She tested with a stick and saw that the patch of mud was not an isolated one but was a strip of marsh which cut off the land nearer the beach from the land where she had at first been walking.

---

[18] Words by Geoffrey A. Studdert-Kennedy (1883 – 1929); melody, "Morning Song," attributed to Elkanah Kelsay Dare (1782 – 1826).

The undergrowth was very dense beside the trail which she followed. Thinking that eventually it would take her to a passage across this strip of marsh, she walked and walked for perhaps two hours. She found herself walking in circles, came back and said, "But I was just here. Was I, or was it just a look-alike?" She began to leave a small mark and proved that she was going in circles.

At first there was anger when she observed the circles. "I am wasting my time," she thought. She was not concerned about getting into serious trouble. She knew she could push through the dense thorns to the beach and simply come out with some scratched skin. She knew if she did not return by nightfall, people would set out to look for her. By morning she would be found; but the night would be very cold, and all she wore was a bathing suit.

All of these dark and dreary thoughts went through her head as she came to the same tree for the third time by a different route and said, "I'm still going in circles." It was only after she had been around four times that she finally had the wisdom to simply sit down. She walked a bit until she came to a patch of sunshine where there was a clearing in the trees. She sat in the sun, which warmed her a bit, and began to meditate.

When she opened her eyes, finally now at ground level, she saw before her a deer trail. She had only been walking on old human trails. Clearly, if anybody knew how to get through this, it was the deer. So she proceeded again but this time crawling, following the deer trail, which took her across that strip of marsh by a very thin ridge of solid land and back to the main trail. She recognized the trail itself. The way back was but fifteen or twenty minutes.

Were those first few hours wasted? She could not have come to the readiness to crawl and thereby find her way out via deer trails until she had explored the human paths. I find this a perfect metaphor. Perhaps as you become more wise and experienced, you cease so strongly to be reactive to the voice of fear and begin to hear the voice of love earlier. Maybe then you only have to walk the unnecessary but once before wisdom steps in and says, "Settle down and listen." Part of being human is not only learning how to listen, but how to listen *through* the voice of fear when it is going to set you walking in "meaningless" circles for awhile.

As Q'uo was talking just now, this instrument said to me, "The question is that I waste so much time walking these meaningless circles. I seem to learn so slowly." But, my dear ones, you learn as you learn. However many times it takes before you finally learn, it will take. Once you have learned it, that is it. Then the next division in the trail appears.

Again, you practice the same thing: It is very easy to hear love when fear is not shouting. When fear is shouting, you must quiet yourself enough to hear the whisper of love beyond the shout of fear. As Q'uo just said, no time has been wasted. You are learning to hear better.

May we speak to your further questions? I pause.

Questioner: Aaron just said that we come to the same lesson again and again. This is the lesson of love? And the teacher is always fear? A question: Is the teacher always fear?

Aaron: I am Aaron. Fear is nothing but a distortion of love. Please do not think of the teacher as fear. Think of it as love in one of its many guises. I pause.

Questioner: Aaron has often said that whatever we choose to do is our own free will, but we will learn to make more skillful decisions. Q'uo said that there is no way to waste time. We learn from our mistakes. I have a belief that we may ask for guidance from God or spirit as to which path is the clearest or most skillful path at any moment. Could either Aaron or Q'uo speak to that? Is that correct?

Aaron: I am Aaron. Both Q'uo and myself may wish to address this. I will speak first.

In accordance and full agreement with Q'uo, it is *impossible* to waste time. It is not wasted time. You are learning; and yet when you do not pay attention because of the force of your fear, your learning takes longer. This is not to be viewed as wasted time. It is what you needed. Yes, your learning can be less painful and more in accord with the paths of love. With that aspiration in mind, yes, you certainly may ask for help.

Your asking is a statement of your free will, a statement of your readiness to receive. In the story I just told, Barbara dashed in mad circles before she was finally ready to sit down and say, "I need help." Fear was directing her, and it took her an hour and a half to settle her fear enough to simply realize that there had got to be a better way, to sit down and meditate and ask spirit, "How can I get out of this? Where is the path?" The time was not wasted precisely because the next time she came into a figuratively similar situation, she remembered the lessons of this situation and asked sooner.

What was driving her in the beginning? First there had been real terror in that pit. She screamed for help. There was nobody around. She realized that she literally could die in that mud hole, which was over her head, and that she had to get herself out. When she finally got herself out, then she allowed herself to give way to the terror she had felt and which she had pushed aside in order to find her way out.

If one were to find oneself in a similar situation, literally or figuratively, and remember how one had learned to bring kindness in, how to ask for help, then increasingly one will walk an harmonious, clearer path. Your primary question here is, "How can I become a clearer channel?" Everything you need for clarity is within you. Everything that prevents clarity is within you.

Clarity is only one goal. Learning, growth and the expansion of the path of love are equal goals integrated into the whole tapestry. To grasp at clarity is to negate the other goals. I hesitate to use the word goals. I think a better word would be fruits—clarity is just one fruit. To grasp at clarity is to turn your back on the other fruits. At what cost, then, is that clarity attained?

You have stated your belief that we may ask God or spirit for clarity as to the most skillful path. Yes, of course you may, but the most skillful path to what end? In the desire to avoid pain and confusion, do you wish clarity for comfort? Do you wish to cut out some of the loops because you are exhausted? Do you wish to cut them out to impress others or to feel like a "good" person? Do you wish to cut them out even because they seem unskillful in their impact on others? But perhaps those extra loops are precisely what is needed, as in the case of Jim's trip west before he knew where he must really go or this instrument's circles in the woods. The path is a treasure hunt. Clues are everywhere.

To ask is to acknowledge your confusion. It is to state your highest purpose, which is to enhance love and harmony. But what is the primary motivation for asking? Is there still desire to control and fix? Asking cannot be fruitful if it comes from a place which merely seeks avoidance of pain. To ask is not to request clarity about the path itself but to seek equanimity with the discomfort of the confusion. You open your heart to that discomfort. When the heart stays present, then as you just suggested, you open the heart and pray for guidance. It is not that the time would have been wasted otherwise. It is simply that you are now ready and expressing that readiness through your prayer. So the answer you requested becomes more available to you. Do you see how it works? I pause.

Questioner: There is an aspect of fear … Specifically, J. and I may work in Detroit in a hospice community. We have had one conversation with staff there. The opportunity came through a friend of mine. After one conversation we set a time for another. I know there is no necessity to do this work. It has come to us in a way. Part of what was discussed was teaching a class of staff members about how to meditate, how to work with their burnout. We are still looking at what will be taught, what is needed. Nothing is set. I see the fear rising in me saying, "I can't teach that kind of class," yet there are many things I know that can help those people. My question is that I am aware of many places where our service would be appreciated and needed. I have been praying for guidance about this. When I hear Q'uo saying there is no way to waste time …

I am not motivated by fear. My motivation is, "What is the wisest path? Is this the path to follow at this time?" Comments from Q'uo about making this choice wisely and not primarily out of fear?

Aaron: I am Aaron. C's fear suggests that there is a certain goal, which is to offer the self in service and for others to benefit from that service. Fear suggests that anything that sidetracks from that is a waste of time and energy. To offer the self in service and for others to learn and have some of their suffering alleviated by that route is a fruit. For you to learn about the fear in your self is another fruit. If the first time service is attempted, it falls short of what you would desire in terms of the final offering, if you thereby learn what you still need to practice, if you thereby learn to relax and allow your great wisdom to flow out of you, nothing has been lost. Such learning is a great fruit.

Can you see how you are clinging to what you believe must happen, looking for a specific result? You are not being a co-Creator with the universe, you are trying to direct the entirety. Instead, you may offer your intention that you and all beings may benefit by this situation as much as is possible. You must acknowledge that there is also motivation to be the "good servant" and fear that you will fall short— even motivation, if such exists, to be helper to others or win approval. Noting all the motivations and that love is primary, you may enter into the situation with an attitude of surrender of control, without expectation that something special is going to happen for you or anybody. You take these multiple motivations and with loving and earnest heart offer the entire confusion to God while reaffirming the primary motivation. Then, whatever happens can be taken as learning. I pause.

Questioner: I have the same question. Is there guidance? I see that it is okay to go ahead with it. What I am asking for is, are there wisdom and guidance around in making such choices? No fear, just love. Is that available?

Q'uo: We are those of Q'uo. We are with this instrument, and, my sister, we believe we grasp your query.

Of a certain, guidance is about you and about all at all times. The world of spirit greatly desires to support and strengthen each beloved spark of the infinite One. It is indeed a skillful and loving thing to ask for guidance. This instrument has a short phrase which it uses constantly within itself: "Lord, show me thy ways." It prays daily, "Lord, in all we do today, help us to serve you."[19] This passionate embracing of guidance does not in any way fail. However, sometimes the answer from guidance is a silence and a lack of further information. Sometimes the answer is even, "No."

One who passionately embraces equanimity is upheld from moment to moment, and of this you have been the witness many times. However, when the guidance is negative or simply silence, then it is that the human must move forward without that feeling of being supported. The support is there; but at that crux, the guidance and support is opening by its silence the opportunity for moving in confusion. One may move for months or years, sensing into and cooperating with the outpouring of one's destiny. But inevitably for some entities there comes the desert experience where the air may be full of night, the heart is blind and the fear is joined by doubting. At that time when the seeker feels most alone, when guidance seems gone, the act of love is simply to persist in faith in that memory of how it is to live with guidance. In those times when spirit seems silent, we suggest persistent attention to the subject coincidences and synchronicities of the moment-by-moment experience; for all of the creation is alive and is connected with you, and your hopes and desires.

There is much time and skill behind your query. And we feel that you are aware of the guidance to a point that denies the possibility that there is none or that it is unwise to rely upon the support network of spirit. Certainly, always open to the help available. But when that revolution of cycles comes and suddenly you find yourself riven, then it is for you the opportunity to walk by faith alone, untroubled by seeming flaws and disasters, large and small.

The human experience seems to be about doing things well. But you are not here to do things. Primarily you are here to develop an attitude, a core vibration of being, shall we say, that is as close as possible to the original vibration of love. As you live through confusion, the way to maximize the proximity of your vibration to that of love itself is to surrender any holding on to the web of support and in allowing it to seem to fail without becoming upset. You then have the chance to express a shining faith that says, "*Whoops*. I know nothing. I haven't a clue. But all is well and all will be well. And embracing that health that demands that I am whole, I have no clue at the moment, but I still know that I am precisely where I am, and it is good." To view the mess that sometimes occurs and to dance in the tatters and in the cleaning up, and to joy in all of it—that is faith.

May we answer further, my sister?

Questioner: Thank you. No.

Q'uo: Is there a final query for Aaron or us?

Questioner: My observation is that as we experience this equanimity, we can have joy despite turmoil. Guides that work with us provide a short cut, and part of their gift is quiet—letting us learn patience and love at a deep level. I really have no question, just my observation of what has been shared these past few days.

Q'uo: My brother, we could not say it better.

---

[19] Reference is pending.

Questioner: Thank you for your gifts.

Q'uo: We truly thank you. We bless each. Enjoy your dance, my sisters and brothers, and know that no sorrow is wasted, no joy unheard. We are those of the principle known to you as Quo, and we leave this instrument and you in the love and in the light of the one infinite Creator. Adonai.

Aaron: I am Aaron. I would also thank you for the great gifts that your seeking brings to all beings, and the gifts of your sincerity and loving hearts.

When there is confusion in your lives, can you remember to greet that confusion with love? The one known as C. said about this upcoming work, "I don't have a clue." That is a highly accurate statement for most of you at most times in your life. You often have no idea of what you are really doing while you are busy doing what you think you are doing. What can you do but smile and trust and take the next step? And when you do, you will find love there, I assure you. My blessings and love to each of you. I am Aaron. That is all. ♣

L/L Research

L/L Research is a subsidiary of Rock Creek Research & Development Laboratories, Inc.

P.O. Box 5195
Louisville, KY 40255-0195

www.llresearch.org

Rock Creek is a non-profit corporation dedicated to discovering and sharing information which may aid in the spiritual evolution of humankind.

ABOUT THE CONTENTS OF THIS TRANSCRIPT: This telepathic channeling has been taken from transcriptions of the weekly study and meditation meetings of the Rock Creek Research & Development Laboratories and L/L Research. It is offered in the hope that it may be useful to you. As the Confederation entities always make a point of saying, please use your discrimination and judgment in assessing this material. If something rings true to you, fine. If something does not resonate, please leave it behind, for neither we nor those of the Confederation would wish to be a stumbling block for any.

CAVEAT: This transcript is being published by L/L Research in a not yet final form. It has, however, been edited and any obvious errors have been corrected. When it is in a final form, this caveat will be removed.

© 2009 L/L Research

Sunday Meditation
December 15, 1996

Group question: From the Law of One information we have the statement from Ra that "It is the way of distortion that in order to balance distortion one must first accentuate the distortion." We are wondering if this is done consciously or subconsciously. How does this work in the daily round of activities? How does this work with emotions? Can or should we attempt to control our emotions when we are attempting to balance catalyst?

(Carla channeling)

We are those of the principle known to you as Q'uo, and greet you in the love and in the light of the one infinite Creator. We thank each of you for calling us to your circle on this occasion, for thereby you enable us to serve, for communications such as this one through this instrument constitute a large portion of our present way of serving others. We have this in common with many positive entities who surround your peoples at this time, ready to offer the love that lies within them to those upon your planet who in their heart are crying out. We hear the sorrow of your planet and it moves us greatly, so we feel privileged to be able to share our opinions.

We are aware that you wish us to speak of balance and of emotions. Perhaps we should begin with gazing at emotions and the role, shall we say, that they play in the shadow dance of life within the veil of flesh which each of you enjoy as those in third-density incarnations. The emotion that is pure is as a note upon a scale upon your musical instrument. The entire range of notes or tones of emotion create what has often been called the music of the spheres, for the purified emotion has the deep level of truth that moves from unknowing to unknowing. Within the illusion of your daily lives emotions are almost never present in a purified manner. The incarnation begins with the seeker already possessed of many basic biases in thought. These biases create ways of perceiving incoming information in a distorted manner. Some distortions are slight, some are substantial, and some are so exaggerated that it is difficult to recognize where the truth within that emotion lies.

However, no matter how biased the emotional attitude or presenting of self to the moment with regard to the material seen in the moment, all emotional feeling bear truth. It is just that because of the distortions present within each these truths are clouded or impure. You may think of emotions as being of a crystalline nature and of impure emotions as being of a nearly crystalline structure but with the impurities which create the cracks and faults within crystals. So each of you has your unique instrument. The notes of all emotions from the most positive to the most seemingly negative. Each of these feeling states is a truth of your being, but insofar as you dwell within the body of flesh the veil has dropped so that you do not have a good example of pure emotions to emulate. For all within the illusion partake in that illusion and many distortions are built into the being that presents itself to incoming information.

So you may look upon the disciplines involved in purifying emotions within yourself as that job that the piano tuner does when it takes its vibrating instrument which, when struck, vibrates the A below middle C, and then attempts to tune the corresponding note upon the instrument to that precise vibratory rate. Each of your emotions has a perfect crystalline nature. It is buried within the distortions that keep you from seeing and hearing the beauty of that note of feeling, that emotion. So when you experience emotions, know that you are receiving information from a deep source, that is, from that large portion of your consciousness that resides at a level below the threshold of conscious awareness. Where words cannot go, emotions become vocabulary.

So as you gaze at yourself reacting emotionally we ask that you realize that it is not at all your job to remove emotion. Nor is it desirable, in our opinion, that the emotions be altered because you feel they should be altered. Rather, we would suggest that [with] these emotions that strike you as being less than pure, to sit with that emotion, to re-experience that emotion, to move about in that feeling state, and to gaze without fear and without haste at that experience that you have collected. As you spend the time to contemplate that situation in which the emotion became embedded, perhaps you can begin to see some of where the distortions are within your own vibratory complex. This is valuable information, but not to the conscious mind. Rather, it is the subconscious mind which reaps the benefits of your contemplating those things which have moved you.

We have often said that your third-density incarnation may be seen as a school in which the illusion's purpose is to drive the third-density seeker from the head to the heart, whereas intellectual thoughts have light energy, shall we say. It may be said that emotions have heart energy, and because of this the emotions contain more profound information than any wisdom which the brain can encompass and speak concerning. For emotions move in waters too deep to contain words, and it is at this depth that the changes that you desired to make prior to this incarnation may be affected. Thusly, even though it seems as though reflecting upon one's emotions is the work of analysis and intellect, indeed it is actually exercising that muscle of faith and allowing that opening between conscious and subconscious mind to be kept open while you do what you can to open the self to a wider and deeper grasp of the situation in which the emotions were concerned.

The way to work upon that balancing then, that balancing of the emotions, the balancing of energies, is to allow that door between subconscious and conscious awareness to be allowed to keep open while the play that you have just finished can play again within the being. And in that review of the soap opera of the day, let us say, there is the opportunity to allow through the threshold of conscious thought the whole range of that particular emotion. For you may see that each note, for instance, upon the piano has its octaves. It also has its harmonics, and it is of these notes, tones and harmonics that the emotional tone poem of your particular vibratory nexus is built. So you may see the balancing exercise as a beautification project, working with what may seem like slums of feeling with that faith that does not judge the self for having distorted emotions. [The more] the self softens and allows the space for that dynamic between the polarized emotion and its opposite, the more the individual becomes as a clear tone and is able to have a more and more tuneful instrument.

Because of the tendency of entities within this heavy illusion you experience to avoid the work upon difficult emotions and because it is well to allow time to pass in your illusion before dealing with this difficult material we do not suggest, in general, that the time to work upon balancing emotions, thoughts or actions be as soon as these have occurred. But rather we would suggest that the sun be allowed to go down and come up again and then perhaps go down again, before you personally and subjectively feel that you are ready to work upon this particular experience. When you feel that you are ready in a good and stable place and able to do work in consciousness, then is the time to reexperience that situation which caused your conceptual feeling of a knot or tangle of emotion to occur. Move back into that caught or knotted place. Envelop it. Be it. Not only remember but allow the feeling to come again and allow it to be strengthened. When the bicycle approaches the corner[20], those who ride their bicycle will tend to lean the other way when turning that corner. To turn right, there is the lean to the left. This is because if one did not lean to the left when making the right turn one would lean inevitably and perhaps catastrophically to the right. Sometimes balancing means not just gazing at it to grasp it in its splendor but rather to see that corner turning, see that dynamic of movement where you lean into the way you wish not to go in order to give balance and stability as the turn is made into the right way or the way that you feel is the opposite of that knot or tangled emotion.

We have spoken of your beings as having the characteristics of instruments and we wish to emphasize that this is true to the best of our limited knowledge. Each of you has an unique signature made up of all of the tones of emotion, truth and beauty that make you up as a metaphysical personality. The vibration of perfect love, the vibration of the great original Thought is that perfection of which each of you are possessors. That is, the great thought of Love lies perfected within you, not outside in a book, in a teacher, or in any experience, but, rather within awaiting the patient and persistent seeker who is able to wade through distortion supported only by faith. You may see yourselves as being a grand chord of being with notes that create just your signature, and you may see your work in consciousness that balancing requires as the working out within illusion of your personal polarity. The one who is not attempting to polarize may work upon his emotions, may work upon her experience, or she may not. It is simply whether she feels as if she might do this work. As long as the efforts are now and then, sometimes yes, sometimes no, the person will find continuing difficulty in maintaining polarity.

Now, polarity is extremely important to your third-density experience. The unpolarized entity is as a pendulum which has no emotion. In a busy emotional individual the pendulum gets moved about, back and forth, back and forth, but there is no net gain in positive or negative. The challenge of one who wishes to become a metaphysical being, an awakened consciousness within this illusion, that entity must begin to move that weight which is as a pendulum in such a manner that it does not return to the zero point. This take patience, persistence and faith. As you work with your emotions there will be many, many temptations to stop the work. The faculty of judgment has been talked about during your conversation previous to this session, and each of you judges the self for playing bad notes upon your instrument. The piano tuner does not become upset because B-flat is not at pitch. He simply adjusts the string until it vibrates an accurate B-flat. You have these pure, truthful, truth-filled emotions within and simply need to see them, all of them, as valuable precious, priceless objects which hold clear and crystalline truth. Even the deepest notes of terror, pain and all of those ways of suffering that flesh is err to, as this instrument would say, these notes too contain enormous beauty, earth-shattering intensity, and in the melody of your existence you may see yourself attempting to purify those notes. This is indeed an effort worth maintaining, for to the one who persists shall come that tremendous inner peace that spreads over the consciousness of one who has stopped judging on appearances and is willing to listen to the most distorted feeling complex with the steady and sure faith of one who knows that beneath the distortions that hide the crystal there does lie the virtue of perfect emotion.

We believe that this is sufficient for this particular session and would at this time transfer the contact to the one known as Jim. We leave this instrument with thanks, in love and in light. Take those thoughts helpful to you and leave the rest behind. We are those of Q'uo.

(Jim channeling)

I am Q'uo, and greet each again in love and in light through this instrument. It is our privilege at this time to ask if there might be further queries that we may speak to. Is there another query at this time?

R: I have a question to clarify the previous channeling. You used the example of leaning into a turn when riding a bicycle when balancing an emotion. You used the example of leaning opposite to the turn, but that will cause a crash. Was that a miscommunication. Is that right?

I am Q'uo, and am aware of your query, my brother. Indeed, it was our intention to suggest that one must lean into the turn, to lean in the direction of the

---

[20] See the first question by R for further clarification regarding this section.

turn in order to accentuate the distortion upon which one works. We did not mean to cause a crash, my brother.

C: I have a question in relation to spirit guides and ones like yourselves. I wonder if you could speak more upon the different types of guides available.

I am Q'uo, and am aware of your query, my sister. There are guides, as they have been called, teachers and friends available for each seeker, and a great variety at that. There are for each entity at least three of those in whose care each seeker may rest. There is the guide of the masculine nature, the guide of the feminine nature, and the guide of the balanced or androgynous nature. These are primary to each entity and will work with each entity according to the needs or level of work upon which the entity has focused its attention within the incarnation. In addition to these, there may be those such as ourselves that move in service to those who are what you would all wanderers within your illusion. Thus, we serve as a guide, or what you may call a Comforter, to many of those who are in harmony with our vibration and from a level of service which seeks to aid those upon this planetary sphere.

In addition, there are those friends or teachers who are called to a seeker's service at specific or intensive times within the incarnation of the seeker. These entities may have a more narrow or specific purpose to fulfill in guiding the third-density entity. Many times those who are creative within the fields of artistic expression will feel a guidance from such an entity at particular periods of production or creative inspiration.

There are also those friends who may serve as guides who are of the third-density entity's family, shall we say, and when we speak not only of the Earthly family and one who may have gone through the doors of death and rebirth before the entity to be guided but also of the family of the entity which works from incarnation to incarnation, perhaps one serving as guide or teacher while in the discarnate state and the other in the incarnate state, these trading positions from time to time or incarnation to incarnation.

There are other types of guides as well that are far less usual, shall we say, and of these we can say little except that they do exist and may give a kind of guidance or inspiration upon request, such as that of the prayer, the contemplation, the heartfelt emotion that cries out to all creation and elicits the response of such entities such as these.

Is there a further query, my sister?

C: No. Thank you. That was very helpful.

Is there a further query at this time?

Carla: I felt there was a time when something got away from me where you were talking about the one original Thought. I would be glad to hear through Jim anything I forgot to say.

I am Q'uo, and am aware of your query, my sister. At various times during the channeling process for an instrument such as yourself which is most sensitive there are those crossroads which will augment the understanding of the information we are giving. If one is able to travel each road successively, oftentimes the concentration is so well focused on one road, there is the beginning of this road, the traveling of this road, and then the continuation upon that portion of that explanation rather than the returning to the crossroads to give another aspect or viewpoint of the information. There are, in fact, many, many roads or aspects of any point being discussed which could aid in the elucidation of the point, but the ability of an instrument to perceive all of that which is available must be focused and one-pointed in order for any information to be transmitted. Thus, an instrument must not feel too discouraged if some aspect is omitted. That one has become aware of such omission or deficit merely is an indication of the increased ability of the instrument to function as an instrument.

(Side one of tape ends.)

(Jim channeling)

I am Q'uo, and am again with this instrument. Is there a further way in which we may speak, my sister?

Carla: No. Thank you.

I am Q'uo, and again we thank you, my sister. Is there another query at this time?

R: I have a question about guides. I listen to your words, but when I try to open a channel to my personal guides, I wonder if it is appropriate to try to consciously open a channel or whether a thought is enough?

I am Q'uo, and am aware of your query, my brother. The desire upon your part to be guided in the seeking of love and the service to others and the growth of the self is all that is required for such guidance to be received. To become aware, consciously aware, of the guidance is yet another task. For one may move throughout the entire incarnation with the faith that guidance will be received and indeed shall be correct and shall be guided without perhaps ever becoming aware of exactly how the guidance worked. For those who wish to be more closely aware of such guidance it is well to pick a manner of receiving. Some are able to perceive thought concepts such as those which we transmit through these instruments. Some are able to perceive concepts through writing within their own journal where they are able to give over the control of the manuscript. Others are able to utilize implements such as the pendulum and work in this way to become aware of guidance. Others may utilize the tarot deck of cards containing images and meanings, energies and directions. Others may find more personally tailored manners in which they can become aware of guidance, each technique dependent upon each seeker's personal preferences and talents, whether they be through some endeavor which will allow a certain kind of feeling to be transmitted, perhaps through music, movement or some game of chance, shall we say, the falling of cards, the ball through the basket, the technique dependent upon the individual's selection firstly, and secondly and most importantly upon the individual's continued utilization of this technique on a regular basis so that a channel is set up that may be utilized again and again

Is there any further query, my brother?

R: One more point. I assume that as you ask for guidance the guidance will be given appropriate to your stage of development. You walk your own path and when you receive guidance, this does not mean that someone else walks your path for you. Is this correct?

You are correct that another cannot walk your path. As one receives guidance you are always free to accept or reject all or any part of the guidance. The feeling of recognition, of rightness, of being in the flow of energy, shall we say, is often the signal to the seeker that the guidance received is good and perhaps shall be adhered to. However, one is always able to choose one's own path, for at every turn there is always guidance whether it comes from another or from the self.

Is there a further query, my brother?

R: As one asks for guidance, there is a responsibility to use the guidance well. Is that all the responsibility?

To that responsibility we would add one further and that is that one seeks with a whole heart in each endeavor in which one asks for guidance. It is not always possible for the seeker to listen clearly, to hear clearly, or to act well, but a seeker can act with a whole heart and seek with the intention of knowing in order to serve and to grow.

Is there another query?

R: No. Thank you.

We thank you, my brother. Is there another query at this time?

(No further queries.)

I am Q'uo, and as it appears that we have exhausted the queries for this session of working, we would at this time wish to express our great gratitude at the opportunity of joining this circle of seeking. At this time we would take our leave of this instrument and this circle of seeking. We leave you in the love and in the light of the one infinite Creator. Adonai, my friends. Adonai. ☙

L/L Research

L/L Research is a subsidiary of Rock Creek Research & Development Laboratories, Inc.

P.O. Box 5195
Louisville, KY 40255-0195

www.llresearch.org

Rock Creek is a non-profit corporation dedicated to discovering and sharing information which may aid in the spiritual evolution of humankind.

ABOUT THE CONTENTS OF THIS TRANSCRIPT: This telepathic channeling has been taken from transcriptions of the weekly study and meditation meetings of the Rock Creek Research & Development Laboratories and L/L Research. It is offered in the hope that it may be useful to you. As the Confederation entities always make a point of saying, please use your discrimination and judgment in assessing this material. If something rings true to you, fine. If something does not resonate, please leave it behind, for neither we nor those of the Confederation would wish to be a stumbling block for any.

CAVEAT: This transcript is being published by L/L Research in a not yet final form. It has, however, been edited and any obvious errors have been corrected. When it is in a final form, this caveat will be removed.

© 2009 L/L RESEARCH

Sunday Meditation
December 22, 1996

Group question: We would like to ask about discernment. We are aware that we know whatever we know through the intellect, through the experiences that teach us, and we know through intuition, through the subconscious mind, through any entity that might communicate through the subconscious to give us an indication of the rightness of a thought, direction or action. We are wondering how to find or discriminate the highest knowing, the best knowing, the way that we can act according to what we know that we are doing the best we can, both to know and to act? How much of this is dependent upon faith?

(Carla channeling)

We are those of the principle known to you as Q'uo, and we greet each of you in the love and the light of the one infinite Creator. What a blessing and privilege it is to be called to your circle of seeking on this day of chill and grayness, when the days are so short and the longing for the light is at its greatest. We greatly appreciate this opportunity to share our thoughts, to share with you those things that we feel that we have learned. We ask, as always, one thing of you and that is, if we may use the word, discernment. We do ask that each of you trust her powers of discrimination, for there is within you a very powerful knower. And that keeper of your own personal truth awakens when you hear that which is true for you, that which is of use to you. It is a feeling of remembering or recognition of that which was already dimly known. Then that is yours. If you have no such recognition of those things which we say then leave them behind, for we are not speaking as authorities but as those who walk the same path as you and those who have perhaps in the illusions of time and space walked a few more paces than you have.

The wish to obtain and purify the faculty of spiritual discernment is surely a common one because of the nature of the spiritual journey. It is not given to any to have proof of rightness. In other avenues of your daily existence where the world of the physical holds sway there are ways that seem to approach exactitude, of knowing and measuring quantities and qualities of those things which are manifest within your illusion. One of these things which is manifested in your illusion is the physical, mental and emotional bodies that you have taken upon yourselves as one would don a suit of clothing in order that you might have a beingness within your world of illusion during your incarnation here. That body is at once a wonderful gift and a gift to be grasped and understood as a part of but not all of that which is yourself. In particular, that mental and emotional mindset that comes with the body that you have, that follows the instincts of the body that you have, is also that which makes it very difficult to see into that darkness in which spiritual things are always hidden.

The hallmark of the spiritual inquiry of the seeking and searching after truth, of the thirsting for righteousness, is the darkness, the perversity, the inability to see clearly that is typical of a world that is in darkness in which the only light is the light of stars and of the moon. The one this instrument knew as Don used to say that the moon was more important that the sun because it gave light in the night, when you need it. This is very true. It is into the spiritual night that the light, so dim yet so precious, of discernment must come. It is not in the noonday of consensus reality when choices seem clear, but rather at the midnight, the dark night of the soul, which in some levels goes on all the time beneath the tempo of your everyday life.

It is as though the greatest of treasures was hidden in a darkened theater, or a darkened field. If within a theatre, then, it is not simply the audience but those upon the stage that gaze about and look for that hidden gem that is truth. If within the field of night, then, we might bring that parable that this instrument has from its Christian education of the merchant who sold all that he had to buy a pearl of great price. That pearl lies buried with the field, and it is the decidedly unglamorous job of the seeker of truth to dig in the dirt. Now, each of you has a different way of approaching the dichotomy which is sometimes not clear and is sometimes excruciatingly obvious betwixt the second-density great ape physical vehicle with its attendant mind and emotions and that consciousness which was before all began and which shall continue after all has ended in the stream of time and space.

To most entities it is very difficult to move from the choice-making, comfort-seeking mindset into that consciousness which has no characteristic of time or space or momentum but rather which exists in the eternal, in the infinite, in the unknowable. All that is unknown in spiritual discernment does indeed lie safely, most deeply within the heart, within that great center within which you may visualize as a tent of meeting, the tabernacle, the holy of holies in which resides the Creator, that great original Thought, unconditional Love. That power that is the Logos is absolute.

When there is that golden moment and the self somehow moves into that space where one is tabernacling with the infinite One, one is in the light, and one becomes the love. When those moments occur we suggest that you write them down in your memory and know that you have gleaned a precious gem from that field which you are digging in. Or know that one of the characters upon that stage has come to life because somewhere in that theater that little bit of truth was found. Those moments are absolute. They cannot be transferred to another, but for the self they are tremendously important, for very often, while in the physical illusion, the seeker must run on faith and hope alone. And when this is the case, it is memory that feeds faith and sparks hope. Memory of the self is a blessed gift of the moment, and another and another, and as the years of your incarnation roll by there is a growing collection of precious, precious gems of moments in the light, moments when love and the self were not bounded or separate.

This instrument has often attempted to write of these moments of ecstasy in a way that would spark others to find the fullness of joy in the Creator, and yet there is no communication that can transfer this kind of moment of pure awareness. So the seeker, as always, is upon an unique path. There are no two sparks of love, no two souls, shall we say, that have the same path, though many may say, "Oh, I have a Christian path," or, "I have a Buddhist path," or whatever path is named. Yet one path is not equal to another. Each is unique. The difficulties of sharing and helping each other when discernment is being searched [for] is monumental because one path is not just like another, regardless of how two people use words to describe that path.

Your nature as an entity is at the same time unified and extraordinarily complex. If the soul that you are works better moving from feelings it is perhaps desirable to cue to the unitary nature of experience that all is one and that in experiencing any one is experiencing one experiences, in the end, the All. For the one who is more aware of the internal workings of the mind, that one who is aware of the layers of meaning and of consciousness, the image of a subtle and complex network of mind works better. The mind has great depth, moving ultimately into that Self which is All. There is a kind of geometry to the mind. There are pathways within it. And there are entities within your culture, within each culture upon your planet, who have moved deeply into subtleties in discriminating betwixt one level and another, betwixt one tone poem of a mood and another, between one awareness and another.

Either of these kinds of path will work. It is simply that one must find the path or the combination of thoughts that will yield to the self that which is sought, which is an increased trust that all shall be made clear in good time.

The simple use of time is recommended to those who wish to work with the processes of perception. When an entity takes time with the self it is a great help to the inner workings of that self. Some find that the greatest gift that they can give to themselves is silence, and we do recommend, always, the daily silence, the listening within to that still, small voice that speaks in that silence with thoughts beyond words, with food that feeds the deeper person. Some find conversations with the Creator very helpful. These are often cast as prayers, but any conversation with that mysterious higher power qualifies as prayer, as this instrument has often done, getting very angry with the Creator, complaining and otherwise getting negative emotions expressed. Sometimes yelling at God is suitable and appropriate for what someone has been through and what someone is attempting to integrate into that combination self of awareness and mortality that each is within your illusion. Certainly allowing time to pass, allowing sequences to build up, is extremely helpful when one is attempting to discern and there are subtleties that cannot be voiced. The simple allowing of time to pass can bring into your awareness those subjective signals that work only for you, those little nudges that you begin to get when you turn your life over in complete surrender to that truth that you seek and that you wish to be.

There is a freedom that comes with the surrender to that higher power, to that attitude that says, "Not my will, but Thine. Teach me Thy ways. I want to know how to fulfill my service to you. Give me a hint. Give me a sign." Then allowing the time to pass, asking the question, and waiting. There are times when the waiting period is very, very short. There are times when one waits for years. However, always these questions continue to work within you until you have found your way. Fortunately, it is in how you meet the conditions of life that the quality of life inheres, not in the events or circumstances themselves. It is easy to forget that consensus reality is illusory because everything looks very real and seems very solid. Scientifically speaking, you are aware that within each piece of furniture and within your own body there is far more space than anything else, with electrons dashing about as tiny little galaxies. Almost all space. No real matter. All an illusion. How hard it is to wipe out, sometimes. And to find that patience that seeks more deeply, that is not impressed with seeming success or put off by seeming lack, that sees beyond the appearances and the chances of a mortal existence.

But discernment is all about moving into that uncomfortable darkness, where things are almost impossible to see aright. The colors are hidden, even the shapes. Oh, the light could not be dimmer without going out entirely. This is your spiritual situation, and that is why the faith with which you meet the good and bad fortunes of your existence is such a signal and powerful portion of a walk that can be termed spiritual or devotional in nature. Since nothing can be known, one must choose either to stop trying to understand or to invest in faith.

If the seeker is able it is very helpful in pursuing truth to work with those entities with which you come into contact, for as long as you are thinking internally and turning the gaze inward, the mirrors which others offer to you are not used. It is very difficult for one within the tangle of life that each entity creates in his incarnation to see that tangle in a balanced and helpful way. However, those others with whom you share your environment have the happy faculty of being mirrors without effort, for you shall catch off of their mirroring only those images that provoke reaction within you, and as you react to those entities seemingly outside of yourself you may know that you are now working in an area where there is something to work on. Your interest has been awakened, perhaps rudely. Perhaps you do not like what you see. Perhaps you love what you see. Either way, you as a seeker have been served by the mere being of the other, who without any effort whatsoever is able to show you the truth that is hidden within you. When you have the untoward or the negative reaction, take that gift and look it over, for it has much to tell you. Perhaps in the end, when speaking of spiritual awareness, we must admit that in terms of final things we as yet do not know anything. The mystery continues to recede before our eyes in an infinite and spacious way.

And this seems to us to be satisfactory. We are content at this point in our own evolution to serve according to that which we value and that is why we thank you for allowing us to speak to you. For to us, the cries of those upon your Earth for understanding, illumination and peace are gripping and make us feel much sympathy. We feel the sorrow and the desire for the higher way, for the loving way, for the truthful way, for that quality of life which turns the everyday into an object of beauty and truth. We feel these desires within you and praise them. As you move in response to them you are accelerating the rate of your spiritual evolution and beginning to live a life larger than yourself in that as you attempt to live from moment to moment, fastening upon those things of greater importance, the vibration of your being lightens, and as it lightens the planetary consciousness lightens also. It is as though with your being, with that essential you that breathes in and breathes out and yet remains beyond all breathing, you have the power to change the world. And indeed, quite literally, each of you is changing the world to the full extent of your choices in respect to how to serve.

The great choice, as you know, is between the radiant, the giving [of service to others], and the attracting and holding and controlling of service to self. Each of you has chosen the path of radiance and each of you is making a difference.

There is perhaps nothing greater that we could say than to love one another as you have come to love yourself, and if you have not learned to love yourself, that task is your first one. For it is difficult to do work in consciousness until one has become at peace with one's being, in its full nature, with all its shadows and its dark side. So we ask you to love, to find ways to love the self, and to nurture that self and appreciate and respect the sacrifice of that second-density great ape being which has given you the opportunity to walk upon the earth and to make a dent in it and to live and to choose. This is a very precious thing, this incarnation. Each is aware of how quickly it is going. We wish you every blessing and shall be with you at any time that you request our presence, not to speak but simply to sit in meditation with you.

We are aware that there are questions that remain and so we would transfer to the one known as Jim so that we may probe further in this interesting area. We thank this instrument and leave it in love and in light. We are those of Q'uo.

(Transcript ends.)

Year 1997

January 5, 1997 to December 29, 1997

Sunday Meditation
January 5, 1997

Group question: The question for this afternoon has to do with discipline in the sense of the disciplines of the personality that Ra spoke of in the Law of One information. We would like Q'uo to give us a little better idea as to what this discipline of the personality amounts to and how it is arrived at and the attitude one has when one exercises it as opposed to, say, our normal idea of discipline which is an idea of doing something rather out of the sense of duty or being ordered to do so or because you think it's right, then it doesn't have a very pleasant connotation about it, and we would like to have Q'uo talk to us about disciplines of the personality.

(Carla channeling)

We are those known to you as the principle of Q'uo, and we greet you in the love and in the light of the one infinite Creator. It is, as always, a privilege and pleasure to be asked to share our humble thoughts with you, and we are honored to do that, asking only that discrimination be used by each to pick up those things which appeal to you and to leave undesired thoughts behind.

You ask this day concerning the disciplines of the personality. May we say that this is a large subject. The question entails gazing at the stuff of which humanhood is made, for it is within the human situation that the discipline of the personalities becomes challenging. When one is between incarnations, or when one is within densities where the truth is not veiled, the disciplines of personality are a much more straightforward challenge because there is that simple measuring stick of the vibration of the one infinite Creator against which to view the considerable material of that personality which is your unique gift to the Creator and to the creation.

It may be more difficult to achieve meaningful progress when the truth is not veiled, but it is more difficult within the third-density strictures to perceive the directions in which one is well-advised to proceed, and it is just for the sharpening of this challenge that the veiling of third density was chosen by the sub-logos responsible for the structure of your particular physical universe.

Each of you is, shall we say, a new and improved product, since much has occurred in creations before yours which has suggested to the newer sub-logoi that this veiling take place. What is the personality? This question, this concern has generated millions of words among your peoples. Always it seems that your culture is fond of the list-making, that the personality is Number One this, and Number Two that, and so on. The shape of the truth, however, is athwart [of] the list-making tendency of your peoples.

It is easier, shall we say, at least for this instrument to conceive of the personality and the structure of the mind that fuels this personality as an instrument of musical kind. An instrument is that which is to be played upon; an instrument can produce many tones within the limits of that instrument's nature. This instrument is familiar with musical instruments such as the piano and the recorder, which is a kind of flute, and, in each of these instruments, the way the instrument has approached [it], the nature of the particular touch of the fingers is quite substantially important, for it is the production of lucid, pure tone that the player of the instrument is attempting to achieve.

You may look upon the structure of your mind, emotions, mentality and spirituality as an instrument, that each is a different kind of instrument. Some personalities are those which must be struck, such as the piano or the drums. Others are entities who have various strings of character and nature that individually can be tuned and then plucked or vibrated in such a way as to produce tone by friction. Other instruments require energy, the pressure of breath forced into a shape and then air opened and denied in order to produce various notes. Each spark of the one infinite Creator that is each of you is an unique instrument with the ability within its potential to produce pure, clear, beautiful tones.

Thus, one may perhaps see that the first concern of one approaching the self and wishing to do work in consciousness is to investigate the nature of one's own instrument. Because of the veil, this is excruciatingly difficult without help, for it is hard for a person to see its own character. One may most accurately see into one's own personality by reflection. It is no mistake or coincidence that your third-density experience is determinedly social, for it is in the interactions of personalities with each other that the truth is projected to each from the other.

When you relate to a sub-logos such as yourself, those things that you like in the other are likely to be those things which you like within yourself, and vice versa, those things which offend you in someone else reveals to you those considerations and issues which are far from settled within your own self. Moving deeper into this heart of consideration of personality, one may attempt most successfully with other entities' help to penetrate the outer forms of personality and to move into that subterranean spring of personality from which you are as a fountain bubbling up into manifestation.

The personality that you are, may we say, is an artifact of distortions that have been created by the choices that you have made in pulling from the archetypical and racial mind those elements which you have decided to work upon within your incarnation. Although each entity is unique, then, each is standing from material that is very deep within the unconscious mind that links all sub-logoi with the identity of the Logos. The Logos in potentiation cannot be said to have personality. By the action of free will, the potentiated Logos becomes that intelligent energy in which the seeds of personality are sewn. Each of you springs from one soil. More than this, each of you springs from one kind of seed.

Through the circles and cycles of life after life and density upon density, through the processes of seemingly slow moving time, you have created the distortions that identify you as unique. So, part of the goal of one who wishes to play that instrument of personality is to move through each distortion to find the parent stem that all share; then, when one has more of a feeling of those things which are congruent from person to person, one may then move back up the trunk of consciousness into those branches of conscious thought that ramify into the personality that you express at a present moment such as this one.

Were each personality not to have come from one source, it would be an entirely different thing to learn the disciplines of this particular instrument that you possess, that you have created up to this point in your cycles of manifestation. But you can stand upon firm ground in receiving information from any other human source, because each is most assuredly and truly a distortion conglomerate whose roots are identical to your own. This is why so much can be learned in the interaction of person to person. Moving deep enough, one treads common ground with all entities. It is equally important to grasp the common ground and to grasp the peculiarities and specialties of your particular instrument.

Now, when you have more or less begun to identify the tones that your instrument can produce—and this is the work of many lifetimes—you can move forward. These tones are emotions, so-called by your culture. The music that personality plays is a music made of pure emotions when the discipline of the personality is somewhat advanced. However, as in any entity attempting to learn to play an instrument, the sounds produced by one who has not practiced can be discordant and unpleasant to the ear, and, in most cases among your peoples, those who have not yet learned discipline produce many unpleasant tones.

There is the feeling of one sitting down at, say, a piano but knowing not where the keys are or how to make harmony, and, unless certain keys, certain key information, that is, is made available, the piano continues to be a large physical object which produces nothing that is pretty. When one sets oneself to learning to play the piano, one practices each piece to find the harmonics of that particular key. Then, and only then, can one begin to make music.

So, as you have emotions, as you experience emotions, what you are first attempting to do is find that purity that lies within the distorted feeling that you have concerning this emotion. For the most part, emotions come upon one in a way that is blind, and one spontaneously discovers oneself vibrating on a certain note or a certain kind of emotion. The usual non-practicing person assumes that, however this emotion has hit, however this emotion has felt, [it] is instantaneously the true tone. It is the concern of those who wish to work in consciousness to hear that tone in all of its distortions and to treat it with that reverence which finds the center, shall we say, the good of that emotion, the true heart of that emotion. Once one has begun to grasp the notes, one can begin to allow the discordant distortions to fade from that particular tone or emotion.

This is the work, as we have said, of lifetimes. It is slow work. However, we think that each of you as seekers will find this work enjoyable. It is not an intellectual process but rather a sensing or feeling or intuitive process to find the heart of emotion, and we would simply suggest that each of you, as it feels right to do so, begin to sense into the emotions that spontaneously arise, loving, supporting and respecting them as they come to you and, at the same time, allowing the heart within to search for the heart within that particular emotion, for the purification of emotion is very central to the process of working with your consciousness to achieve the discipline of the personality.

Your personality, your character or nature, your essence—we correct this instrument. Remove "essence"—is a group of manifestations stemming from the vibratory complex that is you. What you are attempting to do, then, is express your true nature, become more yourself. You're searching for the truth of your being. You're not attempting to end distortion within yourself, you are attempting to see and play with the beauty of each of your feelings or senses.

So, we have given you two steps. First, beginning to name your own personality, trait-by-trait and nature-by-nature. This done, you are attempting then to practice the self, practice the being of the self, play with the self as it experiences incoming sensory data, begin to play the scales of the instrument. One thing there is that the musician must have, and that third thing is music, and each of you is seeking that music, is certain that there is music written for your instrument. Each of you hungers and thirsts for this music to be laid before you, and this music is the path that you choose to take and the choices that you make in hewing to the chosen path.

The musical pieces that you play with the instrument of self have a significance and a depth that comes from that free will that blows the spirit hither and yon. There is no end to the music of the spheres, and there is no end to the music that you can play once you have learned your instrument.

We would at this time transfer the contact to the instrument known as Jim. We leave this instrument in love and in light. We are those of Q'uo.

(Jim channeling)

I am Q'uo, and greet each again in love and in light through this instrument. At this time, we would ask if there might be a query with which we may begin this portion of the working?

Questioner: Yes, Q'uo, if I understood correctly, I'll use an example *(inaudible)* describing what I think I heard you say with respect to disciplines of the personality, discipline with disrespect … I find it very difficult to *(inaudible)*. The discipline aspect really doesn't have anything to do with saying to self either, well, I'm going to do this anyway, because I know it's good for me but rather indulgent, if I might use that word, the emotion to determine … well, indulge the emotion feeling in all of its aspects and then find the heart of it. Is this correct? Is this the essence of discipline? *(Inaudible)*.

I am Q'uo, and am aware of your query, my brother. We are, in large part, in agreement with that statement which you have made. We would add to it by suggesting that the discipline of the personality would have an effect upon your decision to meditate or not, an effect upon the attitude with which you viewed your decision in that it would be that heart of yourself which would entertain all these thoughts. It would be that primary stance that you assume as you encounter or meet any situation in the life pattern. It would be the expression of that heart of self, that personality, if you will, that would undergird all potential responses to this thought. It would be the flavor, shall we say, the distinctive mark, the impression that would be the guiding factor in your choice of actions or responses to this thought within the self that one should meditate.

Is there a further way in which we may speak, my brother?

Questioner: No, thanks, Q'uo.

I am Q'uo, and we thank you, my brother. Is there another query at this time?

Carla: I was kind of surprised that I didn't receive anything concerning love or faith or meditation. It occurred to me thinking about that after I finished channeling that, perhaps, when you talk about the ingredients in a personality, you're talking about something that's already there and that it's just like an ingredient *(inaudible)*, but I guess one conclusion that I might draw is the discipline of the personality is equally important for negative and positive polarities, but where does this learning to play the instrument intersect with love and faith? Is that in the lifestyle chosen or the path of life chosen?

I am Q'uo, and am aware of your query, my sister. The entity which seeks to discipline the personality, to become a metaphysical being, to exercise the way of the magician in attempting to arrive at changes in consciousness, these things are done primarily through those qualities which you have spoken of when you spoke of faith and love.

The entity which seeks to become a metaphysical being and to exercise the expression of its personality finds in the positive polarity that the ability to love comes forth from the primary faith that the entity has been able to nourish and to cause to grow within the self. All of these elements of the personality and the ingredients that make up the multifaceted being that each is find the necessity to give and receive love the primary building block and energy of all creation with each portion of the life experience.

Thus, the entity who wishes to be a metaphysical personality stokes its internal furnace with faith, and the energy which is output is likened unto love, the means by which it is done, the many facets of the personality that has been disciplined and is available as a resource, that one may [write the tone poem] of life with an unique and distinctive flourish, that gives a glorification to the one Creator in that it is a means by which a metaphysical entity begins to express its nature as the Creator.

Is there a further query, my sister?

Carla: No, thank you, Q'uo.

I am Q'uo, and again we thank you, my sister. Is there another query at this time?

Questioner: *(Inaudible)*. This falls within the context of today's subject, and *(inaudible)*. I've really been experiencing a great deal of feelings [of] very, very deep sorrow and sadness *(inaudible)* particularly with respect to this group and with you, and I'm absolutely certain *(inaudible)* felt this way before. In dealing, can you speak *(inaudible)*, please towards working with this *(inaudible)*?

I am Q'uo, and am aware of your query, my brother. Most positively-oriented entities who wish to develop that quality known as compassion in a larger degree will program for the incarnation the seeming lack of this quality of compassion. For the positively-oriented entity, this programming of lack of compassion will be for the self rather than for others, for it would not be appropriate for a positively-oriented entity to enter an incarnation with the programming of lack of compassion for others.

Thus, internally the entity works upon the palate that [is personal]. These feelings of lack of worth, of lack of compassion, a feeling of a loathing for the self, are a kind of angst that is meant to cause the entity to dig even more deeply into the self than the sense of selfless or less worth would indicate.

To state this in another way, the entity with the lack of compassion for the self would do well to look upon that self as a child within one's care and attempt to give it that love and support that any child would need when learning new lessons, realizing failures will occur and are most valuable, for they teach much about what is workable and what is not, what is helpful and what is not. Thus, if one would take under one's wing that semblance of self that has such small value, such lack of worth and love from self, there could begin to be …

(Tape ends.) ✣

Sunday Meditation
January 12, 1997

Group question: We are taking pot luck today. No particular question.

(Carla channeling)

We are of the principle known to you as Q'uo. Greetings, dear ones, in the love and in the light of the one infinite Creator. We thank you, as always, for inviting us to share our thoughts with you at this time. And we must say that the topic this time is interesting.

As we chat we ask, as always, that you please take only that which sounds good to you and leave the rest behind. Use your discrimination. We thank you for doing this, for we offer our thoughts to you freely, knowing and trusting that you will not allow them to be a burden or stumbling block but only to use them as possible tools and resources in your path of seeking.

The term "pot luck" is interesting, the connotation being that of the meal, the choice of food, for truly we are those who deliver a kind of grocery. There is the food for thought that definitely fills an appetite, and perhaps today we would talk a bit about that appetite for more, that thirst and hunger for the truth. How hard it is even to find the truth of the self. Each of you sits within a framework of flesh and bone, apparently limited and mortal, fenced about by circumstance, with only a marginal degree of control over much of the experience of the incarnation. And as the seeker awakens, as the spirit within stirs and rouses and rubs fists into sleepy eyes and looks about the manifested world, at first glance it would seem to know the self is a simple thing, and yet as the being within incarnation grows in stature, in age, in years, there is that moment when the unthinking child becomes a seeker. There is that moment of awakening, that movement of awareness as if someone had suddenly opened a door and the fresh air from the outside came in and beckoned. And suddenly you do not want to be indoors anymore. You want to be out in the world seeking the truth, looking for it as if one were a traveler searching for a lost homeland.

And who is that person who has awakened, who has walked out of the comfortable, sheltered life of those who sleep? One of the penalties of awakening is the realization that you do not know yourself. And so the seeker seeks to know the self, and each journey that the seeker makes reaching outside for learning, going to the classes, the seminars, the workshops, each of those experiences offers a tantalizing glimpse of a variety of those who also seek, perhaps one or more who teaches, who has a point of view that seems to beckon and have truth, rubbing shoulders with other seekers that have points of view that seem enticing, provocative. Soon the new seeker can be swamped in the projected thoughts of self from teachers, from fellow seekers, and from various portions of the being within that is awakening.

And so awakening often brings not a simpler or more peaceful mind, but an awakened, searching, uncomfortable mind that is looking for deeper and more lasting truth. What is that self that is seeking the truth? Let us go in search for that self at this moment. Scan that which sits and listens, the skin, the hair, the clothing, the weight of the body. It is this outer shell of manifested being with which each of you meets the world. And for those who sleep it is that simple. That is that person. "I recognize that person's face, that person's clothes." That is that person.

Going a little deeper, we find the roles that each has played: student, teacher, brother or sister, mate, friend, lover of this or that hobby or interest, the froth upon the waves of being. That also is you. Now let us move further into that interior of being. Let thoughts of body go. Let thoughts of roles go. What remains? Allow the mind to ask this question. What remains? And as naturally as waves beat upon the shore the truth comes—love, love. That is your truth, your deepest truth of being is that you are a creature of love called into being by love, chosen by love to manifest that the Creator Itself may experience the illusion of a dream. If you have thought recently that life sometimes has a dreamlike quality, we say that you are very much in tune with the way we feel that things are. For even that which lies at the heart of the manifested universe is still an illusion, and the only thing that is not illusion is unknowable, for in the dualism of known and knower the truth has already been abandoned in its pure state.

Yet, if the hand that cast each of you forth has meaning at all, and we feel that it does, then that illusion that holds the most light serves as the truth. And that, I think, is what each person does seek, that truth that is deepest for that person at that particular time and that particular place. When the seeker has at last relaxed into a sure and certain awareness that the truth will come bit by bit, little by little, realization by realization, then the heart is at last free. What frees the self from its agonizing search for identity is a surrender to the realization that knowledge of the self and knowledge of truth shall always be partial, with the mystery forever receding before one's grasp. This realization sets the soul free

to play, to reside in peace, and to rest in the natural joy of being aware.

When it is winter it is not particularly obvious that nature is a world or a creation which dwells in a state of pure joy, for the trees seem barren and bitten, the blossoms of winter are sticks and dried berries, and it is not clear how joyful the creation is. The winter chill brings that movement of contracting, pulling in the radiant arms of summer and nestling in that period in which rhythms are slow and the resting is paramount. And yet we say to you that in all weathers the natural creation dwells in a state of joy. This level of joy is available to the seeker in third density. However, as was spoken earlier today in your conversation, in order to experience this one must let go.

We give this instrument a vision of the starry sky, of that depth of space in which no planet or sun is near, and we say to you, "This creation is inside you." This experience of creation that seems outer is actually taking place within your awareness and is an experience which not only comes to you but with which you interact. When first the seeker sets off on this journey of seeking the truth there is that concept of some place to get to, and yet the seeking pulls you out and out and out further, only to disappear into the self. Whether one studies the outer or the inner world, one is studying the same thing.

But it is valuable to be aware of the space and of vast distances with the self. Literally, on a microscopic level, you are a creation with billions of star systems. Even the physical illusion that builds the chair upon which you sit and the body which sits in that chair is largely, if not altogether, empty. What is there is light, and that is what manifests all things. And that which calls light into being is the love that you are.

We have walked you about the universe with these foolish thoughts of ours, and yet always we bring you back to the heart that rests within, within which the Creator resides in glory and holiness and in utter truth. All of the reaching outward ends within the realization that you already have and already are the truth. That truth is always and ever the same. All that there is is love. You are love. And because you are a spark of manifested love you have the opportunity to become one who deals lovingly. It is as though to those who seek and simply go about their day there is a woodenness, a deadness. It is that quiet of one who sleeps. And to each who sleeps there is an alarm clock set, and when it is time that entity, each entity, shall awaken, so it is not a concern of any to bring another to wakefulness. But only to know the self as having awakened to a life that does not begin with birth and end with death but is eternal, infinite, unitary.

As you breathe in this depth of union, this oneness, it is a life-giving intake. Each of you hungers and thirsts for the truth of your being, and yet the end of all your journeys of seeking shall be your own heart, and you will learn to warm yourself at the fire of creative love which dwells within you. A tremendous hearth, a blazing fire of being rests in that holy place within where love resides. There is no cold within the illusion that the warmth of that fire cannot thaw, for the worst that the world can do is render lifeless the body that limits you to time and place. This is a realization that enables the weary seeker to laugh and relax and take the self lightly.

We would at this time transfer this contact to the one known as Jim. We thank this instrument for its service and leave it in love and in light. We are those of Q'uo.

(Jim channeling)

I am Q'uo, and greet each of you again in love and in light through this instrument.

The taking of the self and the experiences of the self lightly is the work of a lifetime, and each entity who engages in such work will find that there is much of effort and much of that which you might call a lack of effort, that is required to take oneself lightly. There are those times in which one finds it easy to be down upon the self, shall we say, to berate the self and to list in detail those difficulties one has faced and the shortcomings one has felt in dealing with them. And yet in this illusion of limits each entity finds that there is a limit beyond which he or she seems unable to go. And when there is this limit then it is often easy to expend the energy one would wish to expend exceeding limits in berating the self for being unable to do so.

This is the kind of situation in which the forbearance [to refrain from] berating the self is laudable yet difficult to achieve. The ability to hold back self-criticism, the ability to see the self as whole and perfect in a situation in which the self seems to have been revealed as quite disjointed, imperfect, unable and wholly lacking in the effort necessary to achieve success by one's own terms. There are those times where it would be well for the acceptance of the entity if the entity would speak for the self, engage in an effort to offer the self as that source of inspiration and motivation which not only the self but perhaps another would benefit by experiencing, to put the self forward, to engage another entity in simple sharing of being, the give and take of the ordinary daily routine. And yet one holds oneself back because one does not wish to make such an effort. It seems perhaps to be either doomed to failure, to be too much of an effort to make, or there is something easier that one can do instead. It is a form of self-acceptance to put one's self forward in instances such as these. And yet, as each knows, there is often a lack of the attempt to do so.

Yes, to take the self lightly and to take one's daily round of activities lightly does seem in many cases to be just beyond the grasp. And yet the effort to do so, we suggest, is worthwhile however many times it needs repeating or reminding. To pick one's image of oneself up from the floor, to dust it off, to try it on again, and to move forward, the effort is often too much to make and we understand this, my friends, for the illusion in which you live is indeed one which is constructed carefully by all who enter and who partake within it to offer you just these opportunities, for as many times as you have been unable to put the self forward, to take the self lightly, to feel whole, full, and perfect, as many times more shall this opportunity be offered, for though this is an illusion and has its limits, there are no limits to the opportunities each of you have offered to yourself within this incarnation to take that moment of inspiration and run with it, to take that moment when one feels whole and full and to allow the self to express this exuberance and this unity, yes, these are the moments which each remembers, for they are unique. And your incarnation has been engaged in order that these moments might present you with the opportunities that you have wished for,

to face the challenge as is necessary in order to find a smile where once there was a frown, in order to find one small measure more of acceptance where before there has been none. These steps forward may seem small when one looks at the long run of things and the picture that seems to get larger and larger with opportunity. Yet we assure you, my friends, that each of these opportunities, however small that they may seem, can become the turning point, the axis, shall we say, upon which a new world turns for you. For as one is able to develop the light touch, the sense of humor, the tolerance of the self, then can become a new beginning for each of you. By just such small measures can the fulcrum point be turned and the momentum of the life path shifted.

So, as always, we recommend to each seeker that perseverance can become one's greatest ally when seeking tolerance and acceptance of the self. Continue, my friends, for one never knows when that moment will come that will offer the turning point of the incarnation, the opening of new vistas, the filling of a heart that felt empty, and the movement of a point of view to a wider perspective that sees and experiences more and more compassion, love and acceptance from and for others, from and for the self, especially the self, my friends. Do not neglect to have compassion for yourself. May we assure you that each of you does indeed deserve it, and when you, yourself, are able to give it then you will find a new and risen being within your midst.

At this time we would offer ourselves for any further queries which those present may have for us. Is there another query at this time?

(A cat is heard mewing in the background.)

Carla: It's too bad that you can't answer Abbey's question.

I am Q'uo, and we would take this opportunity to suggest that each of you is like the small creature that calls for love and protection. This second-density creature does not know not to call and not to ask for that which it needs, for its perceptions are quite clear and simple. Each of you can become as clear and simple in the perceptions.

Is there another query at this time?

Carla: No. Thank you.

I am Q'uo, and at this time would thank each of you for offering us the inspiration of the incarnation that each of you lives, for to live within the seeming darkness of your illusion is a valiant undertaking, and we are aware of the difficulties within this illusion. Do try, with all your might, to take the self more lightly every now and then, if only as an exercise. Perhaps, as with meditation, you will find that there is a value in so doing and will wish to engage in this activity upon a daily basis. We do not mean to suggest that there is not much that can be learned and that there is not much of value in the learning. However, we do suggest that the earnest seeker needs a rest and deserves compassion from itself, and will find the learning is much easier to accomplish with the light touch, with the sense of humor that sees a sense of proportion in the life pattern of the self and in the greater pattern of events and entities about it. For all are individualized portion of the one infinite Creator. You do not deal with anyone else, ever, within the incarnation. It is only the Creator and you. Speak kindly and lovingly to each Creator that you see, including the one in the mirror.

At this time we shall take our leave of this instrument and this group, leaving each, as always, in the love and in the light of the one infinite Creator. We are known to you as those of Q'uo. Adonai, my friends. Adonai. ☙

L/L Research

L/L Research is a subsidiary of Rock Creek Research & Development Laboratories, Inc.

P.O. Box 5195
Louisville, KY 40255-0195

www.llresearch.org

Rock Creek is a non-profit corporation dedicated to discovering and sharing information which may aid in the spiritual evolution of humankind.

ABOUT THE CONTENTS OF THIS TRANSCRIPT: This telepathic channeling has been taken from transcriptions of the weekly study and meditation meetings of the Rock Creek Research & Development Laboratories and L/L Research. It is offered in the hope that it may be useful to you. As the Confederation entities always make a point of saying, please use your discrimination and judgment in assessing this material. If something rings true to you, fine. If something does not resonate, please leave it behind, for neither we nor those of the Confederation would wish to be a stumbling block for any.

CAVEAT: This transcript is being published by L/L Research in a not yet final form. It has, however, been edited and any obvious errors have been corrected. When it is in a final form, this caveat will be removed.

© 2009 L/L Research

Sunday Meditation
January 19, 1997

Group question: How can we live from the open heart?

(Carla channeling)

We are known to you as those of the principle of Q'uo. We greet you in the love and in the light of the one infinite Creator. We thank each of you most profoundly for gathering and calling us to share our thoughts with you at the gathering. It is our blessing and our privilege to share these thoughts with you. As always, we ask that you remain careful in what you take in from that which we or any source might say, for you are the guardian of your temple. You will recognize the truth that is your own. The rest you may leave behind without a second thought.

You ask us this day concerning how to live with the heart opened and vulnerable, and we say to you that this question is central in attempting to make the choice of service to others or the choice of service to self that this incarnation that you are now experiencing is so much concerned with. There is always an abundance of ways in which we may speak of the ways of service and the ways of polarization, and yet nothing is more direct a way of addressing the issue of polarity than to speak of the open heart. Those who wish to serve the Creator by serving others are those who truly wish to open the heart. Those who wish to follow the path of service to self find a closed heart necessary in order to polarize negatively. Now, as we speak of polarization in consciousness it might be helpful to think about polarization in more familiar terms.

If there is a weight hung in space it is, first of all, going to respond to gravity and will hang directly downward. If the pendulum that this represents is very heavy it might take a great deal to get it to sway from side to side. And the first time that the effort is made to swing towards one or the other extreme will most likely be barely sufficient to break the lack of momentum of the downward hanging pendulum, and there will be just a slight movement. What happens with most entities, and this includes those who seek most earnestly after truth, is that [with] the effort made to polarize towards a radiance of being, a generosity and an openness of being, there is an equal and opposite reaction that contracts against fears and makes separations betwixt one thing and another in order to feel more safe. This brings the pendulum back so that there is a slight movement towards service to self. And the pendulum never gets very far in either direction.

What you hoped to do as you attempt to work with you own consciousness in order to accelerate the rate of evolution of your own spirit is to be enough consistent in opening and radiating love that the pendulum begins to move more and more towards the extreme. The more polarized the reactions, the more obvious it will be to you when you make an error. And this means that it can be very poor judgment to become involved in gauging one's polarity or assessing one's progress. You have heard that a watched pot is slow to boil, and the over-concern with how one is doing in polarizing will actually be a brake upon the very activity that you had hoped to emphasize.

So the first thing that we would suggest to those who wish to open the heart and to live in the open heart is to refrain from attempting to give the self a spiritual grade. Avoid thoughts of how you are doing. They will come regardless of whether you encourage them or not, but it is your choice if you are wise to allow those thoughts to come and go, for within the illusion that you have worked so hard to enter it is almost impossible to be aware of how one is actually serving. One must simply serve in faith and allow that faith to be sufficient.

There is within your earthly condition a great array of choices which face you every day, every hour even. And it is easy to begin to look at the things that occur and to think these things have no spiritual nature. "These things are of the world and do not need my attention but only my activity." And yet we say to you that all things are full of the Creator and by this we mean every stone, every bit of earth, every iota of the wind that blows, and the rains that fall, every diaper changed, every dish washed, every chore, every onerous task, all of these things are instinct with the magical, utter life and that life is love. And the life within you is love also.

When one is attempting to live with the open heart every missed step seems to be a difficulty, and this is because the attempt to live with an open heart is neatly and fully circumscribed about by the perils and tests and round robins of a very active spirit that watches over each with the firm intent of offering the maximum amount of helpful catalyst. When this catalyst hits the sensory input of your being the earthly, normal thing that one does is to contract around that thing, assess it, and decide what to do concerning it. These actions tend to close the heart. This is not to say that the way of the open heart has no input from intelligence or thought but, rather, to emphasize that much of one's care in assessing incoming data has much to do with the lower energies of the body, and as one gives these concerns priority the self tends to continue acting from a place within what this instrument would call the head. And, using that terminology, we can say that the spiritual life of third density is a journey from head to heart.

And we have noted before that the energy that comes into your being is infinite, but that there are ways in which each of you, by the choices that you make, contract and narrow and limit the amount of energy that can come into the body and move up the spine. The first center—we will simply summarize—has to do with issues of life and death, breathing, eating, the sexual polarity. These are the concerns of red ray. The concerns of the next ray, the orange ray, are those that the person has with himself or herself, and the person in relationship with one other person, the dynamics betwixt self and self, and self and other self, without reference to groups, but just one person and another. These are the concerns of orange ray. The concerns of yellow ray, this being a yellow-ray density, take on a good deal of centrality of importance. This is the heart, shall we say, of third density—the relating of self to groups, the opening of self that will in fourth density become the social memory complex when thoughts are shared, private thoughts simply skirted about, seen, appreciated, respected and left alone. There will be other lessons to learn in fourth density, but this lesson that you now work upon, of opening the self without fear, this one you will work upon until you are able to feel that contact with other selves as an identity of one to one, heart to heart, and love to love.

Now, those issues of red ray, orange ray, and yellow ray are neatly designed and most tidily packaged to maximize your confusion and to limit the power that you may bring and allow up to the heart center, the next one after red, orange and yellow. Each time that you put yourself down, each time that you are harsh, each time that you feel so isolated and alienated that you deny your brotherhood with all that is, you close down a little bit of that channel which is bringing in infinite creative energy to your body, and each time that occurs there is less energy into the heart. So, basically, those who have not worked through the issues that confront them at these three levels—self, self with another, and self with its groups—each time that you allow these issues to come and to be feared you have shut off some of the power that you need in your heart in order to live the life that you wish to live.

May we say that the conversation preceding this message was, we felt, most enlightened, for each was speaking of the being as opposed to the doing. You see, it is the love with which you do things that radiates; it is not the things that you do. Among your peoples this has been much misunderstood, for people look to see if there is some service that can be their spiritual gift to the world. They are looking for a dramatic role to play, to teach or to heal or to prophesy. And yet these things are forever secondary to the primary mission of each of you upon this particular planet in this particular density at this time. The mission before each of you is simply to address all of that which comes to you with an open heart, just that. And yet just that is the work of lifetime upon lifetime, for how can a person in a heavy illusion such as you now enjoy be fearless? It is not within the physical body to be fearless. It is not within the earthly brain, that choice-maker, to be fearless. Indeed, only the foolish are fearless, and yet the teacher known to you as Jesus the Christ has said that it is only to the foolish that the wisdom comes. It is only to those who live as little children that the kingdom is inherited.

How can a sensible, sane person, gazing upon a rather dangerous world, feel no fear? This is the crux. Here is the center. Just here, where fear shuts the door of the heart, here lies the opportunity to learn. This instrument has moved past the death experience and returned. Consequently, this instrument's life since that experience has been relatively fearless. We bring this up to emphasize that what each fears in an archetypical sense is the cessation of being. When one feels threatened those emotions which do not have intelligence but are simply instinctual rise up to defend and protect. And it takes a great deal of care and discipline and perseverance to teach the self to lay down its arms and to be peaceful with the self.

Each of you has the issues of all the world within you. This instrument is concerned for the peace of the world and prays for it often, and yet if this instrument prayed for peace within itself, it would be the same prayer. Indeed, it is our humble opinion that the most efficient way to bring the world to peace is to learn peace within the self, for as you think, as you are, so your universe *in toto* is also, for your consciousness is as a field and each bit of fear that you are able to let drop, each time that you find your heart expanding, the consciousness of your planet is being lightened. There is no lag time between the open heart of self and service to the planet, that lightening of the consciousness of planet Earth. You came among these entities of flesh and bone. You took that flesh upon yourself and buried yourself in a world of shadows because you wished to make a difference. You heard the sorrow of those who dwell with you now. And you wished to stand among them as a witness and as one who was a channel for love. This is your great chance. These are the days you hoped and prepared for, and now the time is upon you, and how quickly, my friends, it is going. Is it not?

You have sped through childhood and adolescence and adulthood, and each is thinking to the self that, "Well, it's all downhill from here." And yet we say to you that as the physical vehicle hews less and less to the electrical body's blueprint, so the heart, so much more experienced [than] when new to the planet, has its time to open and flower and blossom. You see about you so many entities who have maturity but without joy. Who have wisdom but without love. Who have become bitter rather than sweet, and tart rather than mellow. Learn from these people how not to be, for these are the entities who are forever attempting to move out of the gravity well of neither service to self nor service to others but just back and forth, good days and bad days. You are hoping through your life to bear witness to a love that loved you first. You are hoping to be as the keepers of lighthouses, that your love, that love that flows through you, not from you, may shine upon that sea of confusion in which all are swimming and might warn entities of those rocks of despair, and anguish, and hopelessness.

There is suffering involved in each door you open in life, wherever you look, in whatever land, in whatever subject you find that those who would be true servants have made tremendous sacrifices, even unto giving up the life for others. You find people in each situation whose heart has remained open regardless of the circumstances. And you feel the strength of inspiration from those entities, those people who make the news for a day or two because they have leapt into the water and saved five people before they drowned or went into a prison and released the prisoners, paying with their lives. And these stories touch deeply within your being and let you know of the depth and profundity of love that you have within you and [that] resonates and exalts and expresses the light and joy for knowing the beauty of those spirits and their great gifts.

But we say to you that there are many, many millions more whose sacrifices and suffering you never see, for they suffer emotionally, and mentally, and spiritually, bearing witness to love, being givers of light regardless of the circumstances that would fell a lesser being. And each of you has opportunity after opportunity to meet situations without fear, to open to any catalyst whether it seems positive or painful. The faith to remain steady is to be prized for there is in steadiness a vision, clear sight, and in persistence of openness, healing and forgiveness. And these do not come from you, for from you can come very little until you run completely out.

These things must come through your channel. You simply have to allow that channel within not to get clogged up with the lower energy concerns. If we could leave one thought with you this day it would be not to despise your lower self but to love, support, respect and make allowances for the instinctual behavior, the needful behavior of that being that you are, part animal, part angel, and rather a hash between the two, holding you together. Love, care for, and nurse this physical vehicle of yours. Know that this is the building wherein the Creator now lives, and the ground on which you stand, or upon which you sit, is holy ground; not somewhere else, not when you were better, but now, exactly as you are. This is your moment of holiness, and all moments are potentially sanctified, and what sanctifies but the recognition of love in all things.

We do not want you to think that we consider this easy. We do not. We remember most keenly being in third density, living without the memory of things as they really are, and having only that yearning of desire and that movement of faith to rely upon. In this you are wise to encourage relationships with those who have the same concerns, for the gift of one entity to another, both being spiritually concerned, is the gift of the clear mirror that lets the other self see what it is doing, how it is coming across. You cannot see yourself. You must depend upon others to help you, and this is profoundly the work of third density.

We would like, before we open to questions, to address a concern which was given in the conversation preceding this session. And that is the concern that perhaps we of the Confederation of Planets in the Service of the Infinite Creator get bored or tired of saying the same thing over and over. We assure you that we do not. Each group that calls to us is in an unique position, even if you are the same group time after time. The point at which you are within moves and the combination changes each time so that while there is a stability of recognizable dynamic in the interplay of each of your vibrations which makes up this circle, there is also something new each time that the circle meets, for you are other and more than you were before. That is what the illusion of time is for: to enable entities such as you and we to have that illusion of sequence and to see, if only illusorily, that progress is being made.

So each time that the question is asked to us that may have been asked before, we speak to entities who are in a new place, who are looking at the same subject but from a different level. And there are as many levels of being to you as there are to an onion, and you are a big onion with many, many layers, and as you peel each away it looks so smooth and whole and clear. And yet it too falls away, and there is a deeper truth, and so forth. And this goes on, as far as we know, infinitely.

Each opportunity that we have to speak is unique. And we ask you never to fear that we are weary of your concerns. This is why we have come among your people in the inner planes of this planet. This is why we have placed ourselves here, simply to talk with those who would find what we have to say possibly useful. This we do with an open and loving heart, and we assure you that we shall not tire of speaking about love.

Before we would leave this instrument we would ask if there are any questions that you might have at this time?

B: Does it interfere with your service to us if we hold back on expressing our concerns?

We are those of Q'uo, and, my brother, service to others is a very ticklish business, and the key, we feel, is that service may be characterized as a response to a request for service. That is, we identify our service as that of answering those concerns which you bring to us. If the concern is not ripe within you and is not ready to be plucked but still has growing to do in order for that concern to develop its final nature, then that is not a question that is ripe for the asking, and we do not feel inhibited or limited because we cannot answer that which has not been asked. We feel that this opportunity to share thoughts [with] you is that which you …

(Side one of tape ends.)

(Carla channeling)

… We feel that by your coming together you ask us to share thoughts with you, and that defines our service. We would not be able to preserve the free will of those to whom we speak were we to take up concerns whose help you have not asked for.

May we answer this concern further?

B: I'm looking for whatever way I can find to help you accomplish your service. Is there anything that any of us can do to assist you in your service?

My brother, we would simply ask you to hone your appetite for the truth. This is your service to us.

May we answer you further?

B: Hone the appetite for the truth? I don't understand.

[I am Q'uo.] That which is love within your density may be described also as desire. The desire that brings each to this circle of seeking is the desire to know and to share love. That hunger, that thirst for righteousness, as this instrument would say, that desire to be a positive in the balance of life, that hope that there is a greater meaning behind the suffering that seems inevitable. These are the desires and hungers that call us to you. And as the desire is sharpened and the appetite is whetted for more, then that contact with us becomes stronger. And the keener the desire, the better the contact.

Does this make sense to you, my brother?

B: Yes, it does. My image has always been that I come here in need of help myself. But now I see that I can work with you to help serve others. Does that make sense?

We are those of Q'uo, and yes, my brother, this makes sense. Remember always, that in the spiritual sense all is already perfect. All is as it should be. It just looks weird. So in order to get at the heart that lies beneath the often uneven surface of ordinary happenings one simply looks with eyes of love. And each time that you find yourself looking upon a world with eyes of love you will know it, for a world seen with love is a place of surpassing beauty.

Is there another query at this time?

R: *(Inaudible).*

We are those of Q'uo, and yes, my brother, that is the usual way. The excitement of that which is new, over time, fades and the work that is not obvious at first blush begins to take the center of the stage. Actually, my brother, in this instrument's way of measuring time we can say that your fidelity to seeking is unusual, for many who have come to these sessions through the years there was a place perhaps five or six months into the experience of these meetings [where] there was no longer the will to attempt to live the message that was heard, and when the attempt to continue fails, then it is that we must repeat and repeat. And then those entities who did not wish to hear of work the first time wish even less the second and the third, and so there is that natural parting of the ways, and that entity has gained all that it can. Therefore, we commend you for your faithfulness and note that it is the big flashy beginning that looks so wonderful, but in truth it is the quiet, persevering heart that continues quietly but persistently to love that is the true star, the true flash, the true victory.

May we answer you further, my brother?

R: *(Inaudible).*

We are those of Q'uo, and we thank you, my brother. Can we scare up any more queries by our speaking, or shall we call for a motion to adjourn? This instrument has been at a church meeting today, and she is full of it. Our apologies to this instrument. Yes, my friends, how good it is to laugh, to take the self lightly. We leave you in the wonderful sense of rightness that laughter is, in the love and in the light of the one infinite Creator, now and always. We are those known to you as Q'uo. Adonai. Adonai. ✻

Sunday Meditation
February 2, 1997

Group question: How should we deal with negativity in our daily round of activities, from situations that we perceive as negative, to people who would like to control us? What is the best way to deal with negativity, a situation, a person or even a thought in our own being?

(Carla channeling)

We are those of the principle known to you as Q'uo, and we greet you each in the love and in the light of the one infinite Creator. We thank you for this privilege of being called to your circle of seeking. We thank each of you for the seeking, the desire, and the persistence that has brought you to this place at this time. We thank you because you have blessed us with the ability to serve in the way in which we have hoped to serve by being within your Earth's spheres at this time. To be able to share our opinions and our thoughts is all that we could ever hope to do. We have been limited, and will continue to be limited, by those who offer us their service as channels. And so when there is a group and a channel and we are able to be among you to enter into your sense experiences, to feel and sense anew the courage and the stamina that it takes to seek by faith alone, we are overcome by appreciation, and we thank each one of you for all that you have endured in order to be able to seek and to hope and to wish to live in faith, for that is what we come to suggest to people: that there is a center to that life which does not end.

There is heart to the truth. And that center and that heart is love. Love is a pale and useless word, almost, because your peoples have used it in so many, many ways. We use it in the sense of unconditional and freely given love, the loving that persists when there is no return, when there is no obvious reason to continue to love. This is the love in whose vibration we come and in whose vibration you each have also come into incarnation because all that there is, is love. The raw material of your universe is love interacting with light in order to produce energy fields. Each of you is an energy nexus, a complex of vibrations and fields of energy. And this complex of vibrations is as your name or your signature. We do not need to know the names that you are called by in order to recognize each soul, for as you come to us, as you sit in meditation, you are as the song that is sung, or the painting that is before the eye, every detail, every nuance so beautifully collected. We are aware of how rattled and how chaotic you find your own selves. The heavy illusion in which you now enjoy living is specifically designed to promote confusion and being lost and at sea and unable to order the universe by means of your intellect. This is what your illusion is supposed to do, to pull you off that intellectually safe balance point from which you may carefully judge and logically grade all incoming sense date, thereby insuring that your universe shall continue to be as you have set it up to be.

The Creator, wishing to aid in developing each spark of love in each unique way, is delighted to offer each entity those confusions and difficulties and losses and limitations which shall involve the seeker in learning those lessons to do with love and loving for which you took incarnation, for each of you here has personal work to do. Each of you came to incarnation carefully choosing your relationships, your gifts of personality and character, and aiming that self within incarnation at the kind of life and the kind of learning which you and your higher self felt would be the most helpful use of your incarnation, for this time within physical incarnation is rare and valuable. The opportunity to live by faith alone is given only to the density in which you are now enjoying the experience of living.

So as you ask the question about dealing with those entities which come into the experience with seeming negative service to offer, our first comment, shall we say, is to move back to that beginning [of] all things which is love, the one original Thought, that Logos that is Love Itself, that Love that is the All-Self, the Creator. It is well to move back always to one's basis for being, to be sure the feet are standing upon solid metaphysical ground. Starting with unconditional love is always correct and accurate as a mental or logical beginning. Now, as sparks of that original love, each of you has, through many incarnations, distorted in various ways this original vibration. And each of you basically yearns to more and more closely approach the original vibration which is unconditional love. So in that sense each of you is seeking to become the Creator, seeking to be lost completely in unconditional love. This thirst and hunger that you have to be closer to the source and the ending of all things is that thirst and hunger that the awakened spirit feels.

Once you have awakened to your spiritual identity, you cannot go back to sleep. You have to see your life and your priorities from that point on in a way which deals with the fact that you are now on a journey whose end you do not know, whose next steps you may not know. And you are on this journey with nothing more than your hopes and dreams and some companions along the way.

So as you interact with the people about you it is well again and again to move back into the awareness of the self as a vibration of metaphysical self, as that self which overshadows the illusion and the problems and concerns of that illusion. Whatever the day-to-day actions, behaviors and thoughts concerning dealing with negatively oriented entities, it is well always to come back to the remembrance of who and what you truly are, for in realizing more and more fully your own nature you are becoming more and more aware of the nature of those about you. Many are the entities in your world that prefer to gaze upon the self with different priorities. Those priorities may seem very negative. In actuality, most entities upon your planet are neither [very positive] nor very negative but, rather, are in a gravity well, in between those two polarities, neither working hard enough to serve others to polarize towards that path, or working hard enough to gather power and control over others to progress along the polarization towards the negative path.

The great temptation for one who is seeking to serve is to forget that all other entities in your creation are identical to you, in that both of you are of the one great original Thought. No matter how deep the imperfections of that entity may seem, the basic nature of that entity is congruent with your own, for each is perfect. The distortions are apparent in the illusion. All those who go through incarnation in third density distort the vibration of infinite love. The one you know as Jesus distorted this love. It is impossible to live and experience a lifetime in third density without distorting appreciably that original vibration. It is for developing these distortions that you came to this experience.

From the level of soul to soul, then, whether you are gazing at someone whom you feel is acting in a petty way, or you find someone being critical in a small way, or you find someone being righteously indignant, or you find someone willing to massacre thousands, no matter how widely distributed along apparent diversity the souls you meet are, each of them is an image of you. Each of them tells you something about who you are, including that dark side entities may not wish to explore. And so, from that soul level, the question of what to do with this entity becomes less than difficult in that from that level each entity is to be loved as you love yourself. To love the Creator, to love the self, and to love others as the self; these are very simple suggestions, and from that soul level they are fairly comprehensive instructions.

Now, it is often not on the soul level from which entities wish to move. And when one leaves that safe ground, shall we say, metaphysically speaking, of loving from the soul level unconditionally, the ground becomes rapidly much less simple. The terrain can be very puzzling, and so if one does not wish simply to express love or to feel love for another, or to move lovingly without disturbing another, one then has to take some responsibility to look at the self, to look at the gifts of the self, to look at the lessons that you feel that you are working on as a seeking entity, to see, as this instrument would say, to see where you are coming from. Are you objecting to this entity from a red-ray point of view? Do you find the negative actions of this entity to threaten yourself, or someone else, or people in general? Are you coming to the question, "How do I deal with this entity?" from an orange-ray energy where you do not know how to relate to this one entity that you feel that you have to make a connection with as an individual? Or are you coming to dealing with this entity from the standpoint of a person being in a group; that is, using the yellow-ray energy? Or are you coming to this person from the open heart? Or from that level of communication or even from that indigo-ray energy of work in consciousness?

All of these levels of connection with other entities have their own best ways of expressing, and I think that it aids the entity to grasp exactly where the energy [is] moving from and where you would hope that it would go to.

Once that you have fairly well become satisfied with your own self-knowledge of why you have singled this entity out to practice on, shall we say, then you can look at the gifts that you have. Do they include more nonverbal or more verbal skills? Is your gift more in the line of praying for an entity or speaking with an entity? The gifts that one has are important. It is well to think [of this] when you are seeking the highest and best way that you can be with someone else and very helpful to know what you have that might be of service. So often the gifts that one has, if used well, create a life experience that is utterly different than that entity who, gazing at its gifts, chooses instead to move in a way in living and working in relationships that is logically or mentally thought out and makes good sense but may not be a comfortable habitation for that eternal creature that you are.

Let us think now in terms of what that entity that is acting negatively would wish of you, for in giving service to others entities find themselves in very confusing waters. Perhaps the most common mistake that positively-oriented seekers make is the mistake of feeling that they know what another entity needs. Indeed, it is the work of some patience to come to that place where you are willing to wait until you are asked in order to attempt to be of service. This sounds very simple but is very difficult when you feel that you have something to say that will help another. When this feeling hits there is the urge to share, and we do not say that this is wrong. We simply say that it may not be service to others, for what entities desire they shall ask for, and it is when that other entity asks that that precious gift of service may then be shared.

In truth, we do not feel that there is one way for all people to treat all people, for if each entity were perfectly in harmony with each other entity this would not be third density. Before the matter is investigated it would seem obvious that the better that each entity treats each other entity the more harmonious and beautiful the experience of living. And yet the collisions that occur when intimacy is sought either with the self or with others are not harmonious and from the standpoint of each individual within the illusion of mortality and space and time it simply seems impossible that one will ever know enough. And one comes to the conclusion that one does not know much at all. And when one comes to this realization it is a great gift because the great mistakes are made by those who think they know exactly what to do. And there is great healing in the awareness that not only do you not know but that you are not supposed to know, and you are not here to know the right thing. But rather you are here to experience and to learn and to share the essence of yourself with the planet that you came to love and serve. And this is not that which is spoken. This is not that which begins with working with another entity. This is that which begins with breathing in and breathing out. Here is your vocation, in the living, in being, in the breathing, in being where you are with your senses alert and your heart open, paying attention to that moment that is the only such moment that you ever shall have.

So, again and again, one comes back to the fact that in the illusion you must follow your gifts, know yourself as well as possible, and then share the self as honestly, as lovingly, and as much in accordance with those gifts that you have as possible. In this you shall again and again fail. You shall find that you have said what you would not say. You shall find that you shall allow moments to go by when you wished you had said something but could not find the courage. See all of this, if you can and when you can, as nothing more than the grist for the mill, as the one known as Ram Dass has said. And when you perceive negativity, see yourself and say to yourself, "I am that also." For each has that dark side that is so shiningly mirrored for you. And if you see this again and again then that gives one pause for thought. "Why have I invited this? Why did I feel that [I] needed this rasp roughing up the surface of my life? What does this image of myself tell me that I need to know?" For you are that self and the appropriate emotion is always love.

When inappropriate emotions are felt, however, we cannot say that it is wrong to express those feelings which may sound negative, for it may be your gift to that person to take away the mask and give that entity another way to think about the negativity that that person is doing. There is no one way to relate. You must simply toss upon the waters those actions and those words that you would most want to be shared. And know that each word that you say and each action that you do is not what it seems, and that the ripples of each action and each word will become confused and will tangle in to other actions and other energies that you have set in motion.

There is an art to becoming clear enough within the self that the self becomes almost transparent. The art in this is that when the self becomes enough transparent then the self does not any longer relate so much to the mirror images that come within one's view. If that dark side of self is seen clearly enough already, then the emotions arising in response to that negative person coming into your purview is perhaps a small disturbance, an awareness of disharmony, perhaps not even that. The more work that you do in knowing, forgiving and accepting yourself, the less work that you shall have to do *vis à vis* other selves. And the more powerfully you defend, understand and respect that dark side of yourself, the less you shall have to defend against the dark side of others.

Each within the group has had experiences with negative energy, had run-ins and painful times with disharmonious entities, and each has that sense of wishing to make it all better. And you may do precisely that at any moment that you choose by stepping back into the remembrance of the one great original Thought. You are doing nothing more and nothing less than vibrating in the original vibration that is your true nature. The rest is details. May you enjoy the details of your life. Knowing them to be temporary does not make one less fond and appreciative of the opportunity to live and love and seek in a world in which by faith alone can one find one's way. May you love as you are loved. May you love each other, care for each other, pray for each other, carry each other's burdens, tell the truth to each other, and bring each other home.

We would at this time transfer this contact to the one known as Jim. We thank this instrument and leave it in the love and the light. We are those of Q'uo.

(Jim channeling)

I am Q'uo, and greet each again in love and in light through this instrument. It is our privilege at this time to offer ourselves to speak to any other queries that those present may have for us. Is there another query at this time?

Carla: We were talking before the meeting about how positive channels go awry, and I was wondering if there was anything that you wanted to add to that discussion?

I am Q'uo, and am aware of your query, my sister. We find that you have covered those external appearances and experiences which groups such as this group have suffered in the loss of their original contact and its replacement by sources of information that are perhaps other than desired. The only further comment that we would make would be that those who have the honor and responsibility of serving as instruments for contacts such as ourselves would do well to examine carefully the qualities and responsibilities of such an instrument. The exploration of this service is that which is often not undertaken by those who seek to serve as instrument. It is too often the case that entities are so overwhelmed by the experience that they seek only to continue as they have previously in their efforts at being instruments and channels for information, whereas it is most helpful for each entity serving as an instrument [to] become aware of the necessity for preparing the self for this work, not only in the daily round of activities and in the type of standards that one wishes to keep for the self, but in the actual performance of the service, that is to say in the tuning of one's own internal mechanism, the setting of the desires of the personal nature aside for this time of service and the exercising of the tuning, as we find it has been described by this group, the setting of the internal radio dial, if we may use this radio analogy, to the highest source that one can stably maintain.

The ability to discriminate between spirits is also an exercise which is well undertaken by all who would serve as instruments, for it is indeed a crowded universe and many are those spirits who would seek access to those instruments that they might speak and do as they will with or without regard to the welfare of the instrument or the group to which they speak. Thus, one wishing to serve as instrument finds that quality within the self that is the foundation stone upon which they stand in the discrimination between contacts. It is well for the one serving as instrument to find that quality for which it lives and for which it would die if necessary, and in the name of that quality, or entity, or concept, challenge those contacts which wish to speak through it; that they ask if they come in the name of—for this instrument in particular—the Christ consciousness, for others, perhaps, Jesus the Christ, for others, perhaps, the quality of love, of service to others, and so forth. When those who wish to serve as instruments have mastered the ability to tune the self and to challenge those entities who wish to speak through their instrument, then we feel that the one who wishes to serve as instrument has prepared itself well and is then able to enter into this service in a fashion which can be sustained and in a fashion which may truly be of service to others.

Is there a further query, my sister?

Carla: No. Thank you.

I am Q'uo, and we thank you once again. Is there another query at this time?

B: I would like to serve as an instrument one day. How can I practice discriminating between contacts?

I am Q'uo, and am aware of your query, my brother. The practice of the discrimination between contacts is undertaken best when done with the assistance of an experienced instrument that will work with you on a periodic basis so that it is able to assist you in this discrimination in its initial stages.

Is there a further query?

B: Yes. Perhaps later, since I forgot what it was.

Is there any other query at this time?

V: Are you speaking of working with someone in the physical or in time/space when practicing this skill?

I am Q'uo, and am aware of your query, my sister. For the vast majority of entities within your third-density illusion we would suggest that entities work with teachers within the third density who are themselves instruments and who are willing to work with those who wish to learn this service.

Is there a further query, my sister?

V: No. Thank you.

I am Q'uo, and thank you, my sister. Is there another query at this time?

Carla: I would bet that P would love to have a message from you. I am pretty sure that she is scraping the ground in low spirits right now.

I am Q'uo, and am aware of your request, my sister, though it is somewhat difficult to speak to an entity who is not present within this circle of seeking and who, herself, has not requested a speaking for her.

We are aware that this entity and others as well suffers its own form of anguish in its current experience. To all those who feel the suffering and the difficult circumstances we would ask that each take a time during the daily round of activities each day and sit in meditation, releasing all the fears, the doubts, the worries of the day, letting these fall aside for this moment, and within this moment seek the presence of the one infinite Creator. Rest therein for as long as one is able and feel the unity once again with all that is. Feel the center once again to the self. Feel the feet upon firm metaphysical ground. Feel again the hand of the one Creator moving within the life pattern. Feel the love and light of this one Creator coursing through one's being. Feel those special touches of heart to heart that are available in these times of seeking the One. Rest in this nourishing flow of experience, and when it feels appropriate move once again into your third-density illusion. Feel the quiet and peace of the meditative state moving with you and ever available as a resource within as one moves in this daily round of activities that brings the challenges, the catalyst, the opportunity to use that which one knows in the heart, the opportunities to love where it does not seem that love would go, to bring light to those who move in darkness, to become as a beacon, one who gives the love and light of the one Creator to all those about one. In such situations, many are the doubts, shadows and fears that will fall by the wayside as one continues to seek the inspiration of the one Creator in daily meditation.

We would remind each that all that lies before you you have placed there for a purpose that is of a service-to-others orientation. There is light in each doubtful situation. There is love in each fear-filled heart that can erase the fear and remove the doubt. It is not an easy journey, nor would you wish it so, for there is much to be gained by bringing love and light where there is darkness and doubt. We wish each seeker a good journey through this illusion, for there are many sideroads that can distract, confuse and fill [one] with fear. But there is always love and light from the one Creator available to each within one's own heart. Never could it be closer. There seek to find the nourishment that will carry each of you that await on your journey of seeking the one Creator.

Is there a further query?

V: I am aware that dreams give us needed messages from the subconscious, but if one is not able to remember these messages in dreams, is there a way to work in the conscious state to aid their remembering?

I am Q'uo, and am aware of your query, my sister. The subconscious portions of each entity's mind are filled with the patterns of the incarnative experience and send various portions of these lessons and experiences to the conscious mind in the form of the dream, that there might be a dialogue with the conscious entity seeking to uncover the treasures of the subconscious mind. In order to be able to work with these dream images it is well that the seeker send a message to the subconscious mind that it is ready to work upon those messages in dreams. This may be done by reminding the self before bedtime to attempt to remember one dream this night, to further reinforce this desire by placing the appropriate instruments to record the dream whenever one is able to remember the dream, whether it is shortly after the dream or upon waking in the morning. It is through the constant repetition to the self, the subconscious mind, that one wishes to work with these dreams that the subconscious mind will become convinced that the conscious self is serious and serious in this desire, and will then begin to release to the conscious mind dreams which will be able to be remembered.

Thus, it is a matter of setting up a dialogue with the subconscious mind and to express one's sincerity to continue this dialogue by the continued repetition of remembering the recording devices, whether they be the tape recorder, the pencil, the pad, the flashlight or whatever. In this repetition, then, lies the building of a bridge betwixt the conscious and subconscious portion of one's own mind.

Is there a final query at this time?

B: Is the setting aside of the personal worries as one is about to serve as instrument the same as activating the magical personality?

I am Q'uo, and we would answer in the affirmative, for when one wishes to work upon the experiences and services of an instrument, one is indeed working in the time/space portion of the magical or metaphysical self. Thus, when one is able to see the concerns of the day, label them as they are, see them put in their box, see the box set aside, then one is entering into that portion of the unmanifested self that is called by some the magical personality or by others the higher self. Thus, one is also with this work establishing the bridge betwixt the space/time illusion in which you find yourself now working and the time/space portion of this illusion in which one works as a metaphysical personality.

Is there a further query?

B: Should one work on that during regular meditations?

We feel we grasp your query. If one works in the meditative state to set aside the waking consciousness and its concerns in order to establish the magical personality to serve as an instrument it is well that this be done only in a circle of seeking such as this one so that the new instrument has the experience and protection of the experienced instrument and the circle of seeking as well. An individual doing this work alone would be unable to make the initial discriminations to serve in a stable fashion for positive contacts.

Is there any further query?

B: No. Thank you.

I am Q'uo, and thank you once again, my brother. And at this time we would thank each once again for inviting our presence to your circle of seeking this day. As always, it is a great honor and privilege for us to be invited to join you for during this time we are able to partake for the moment in the intensity, the variety, and the vividness of your illusion and are able to serve in our own humble way by offering the opinions and experiences that we have found helpful in our own journey of seeking. We would, however, advise each to use personal discrimination to decide which words we have spoken that are useful to you in your own journey. Please leave behind any word or concept that does not ring true to you. If any word does not ring true to you it is not useful at this time no matter how much it may shine.

We are those of Q'uo, and we leave each in the love and light of the one infinite Creator. We are those of Q'uo. Adonai, my friends. Adonai.

L/L Research

L/L Research is a subsidiary of Rock Creek Research & Development Laboratories, Inc.

P.O. Box 5195
Louisville, KY 40255-0195

www.llresearch.org

Rock Creek is a non-profit corporation dedicated to discovering and sharing information which may aid in the spiritual evolution of humankind.

ABOUT THE CONTENTS OF THIS TRANSCRIPT: This telepathic channeling has been taken from transcriptions of the weekly study and meditation meetings of the Rock Creek Research & Development Laboratories and L/L Research. It is offered in the hope that it may be useful to you. As the Confederation entities always make a point of saying, please use your discrimination and judgment in assessing this material. If something rings true to you, fine. If something does not resonate, please leave it behind, for neither we nor those of the Confederation would wish to be a stumbling block for any.

CAVEAT: This transcript is being published by L/L Research in a not yet final form. It has, however, been edited and any obvious errors have been corrected. When it is in a final form, this caveat will be removed.

© 2009 L/L Research

Sunday Meditation
February 9, 1997

Group question: Today we are taking pot luck for our general question.

(Carla channeling)

We are those of the principle known to you as Q'uo. Greetings and blessings in the love and in the light of the one infinite Creator. We thank you for the privilege of sharing in your meditation, more especially we thank each for calling us to speak with you and to share our poor thoughts with you. You allow us to be of service and that is that which means so much to us, for without those who seek we do not have any possibility of such sharing. So we thank the instrument and each within the circle and ask of you all just one thing, and that is not to relate to those things which we say as if we were an authority but, rather, offer our opinions as any to your powers of discrimination, for deep within each entity lies that sure and certain indicator that will, if listened to, let the seeker know when she has come upon a thought that has personal value. When that reaction does not occur, then we ask you to let our opinions slide away and be lost, for we would not wish to cause anyone to stumble. We hope to offer thoughts which might prove to be resources, assets or tools for the use of the seeker who wishes to accelerate the rate of spiritual evolution within his own being. This is our goal and we know that it is your goal as spiritual goals go.

The common goal is to seek and to know truth, and yet, ironically, in the way of all spiritual truth, that which is held on to is as rust and ashes, for truth within illusion is that which flows and has its own rhythm and motion. Indeed, we would ask each of you to consider that you are like the radio with a beacon that sends out a signal, that sends out desires into the universe that is listening to prayers, hopes and desires. And in the natural way of rhythmic living, that which is desired is drawn to you in the fullness of time so that that which you see before you as the present has its beingness deeply within those patterns that you have completed in the past. The faculty of free will so often seems somehow abridged by the circumstances of destiny, and yet it is your sending out your desire that has called your being into manifestation in this present lifetime. And on that preincarnative level it is the desires that are deepest within you that have organized and carefully arranged in series that you can survive each and every lesson you hoped before birth to learn.

So you are as the magnet and that which is yours comes to you at the proper time. Woe to the heart that is not listening to the silence, for it is within the silence, within the quieted heart, that that illusive truth abides. That which is outer in experience is a projection and manifestation of that which is occurring completely within your heart, within that center that is opening little by little as it learns not to fear, as it learns not to panic, finally as it learns simply to listen in faith that the silence holds that illusive truth. And that clinging to that unfindable truth in that silence is the key that activates the patterns that you wish to call forth into your experience for your further development. We encourage each of you to become ever better at listening, for as you listen the quality of your listening reveals to you that level of truth that you are ready and willing to bear.

We are aware that there are several concerns within your minds at this particular time, and we are very glad to work with what this instrument calls potluck, just as we are equally glad to take the group question or to go from question to question. To us, the format is not important, because to us that which we truly are offering lies beneath the words that are channeled through this instrument, because what it is that carries these words is the energy that in sharing becomes our service. We offer thoughts but our value lies in our being with you and allowing our energy to mingle and merge with your own. The wonderful dance of harmonization is beautiful to us, and as we move through the group energies and the individual fields of consciousness the love that is offered to us and the love that is very deep in our hearts for you becomes that truth that is greater than any words, and, indeed, we suspect that in the end we shall find that one cannot know the truth ever, but one can become the truth. That for us lies ahead. We have not found the key that unlocks that last door, but we are patient and we find joy in contemplating the mystery that lies always before us, always riveting and always unknowable.

Before we open to specific questions we would perhaps say a few words concerning the concept of—we give this instrument the concept and it does not find the words. Let us say that the illusion that you now enjoy is as the landscape. The natural tendency of entities within the illusion is to assign value to what this instrument would call mountaintop experiences, and perhaps to define spirituality in terms of that feeling of being overcome by the special beauty of a mountaintop experience. It is not that the Creator is not there within those moments of personal witness to glory, to ecstasy. Indeed, the Creator is gloriously there in every fiber of those moments to remember, and yet if each of you as a seeker thinks of spirituality as the occasion that must be risen to, he cheats himself out of the spirituality that lies within, all of that which this group has recently called the drudgery of the chores of living.

Earlier, the one known as R was speaking of the way that the truth seems so often right there, and this is so. Not just in that which you put quotes around as spiritual. "Love," "truth," "beauty," these words reflect an awareness of the divine. And we would turn your eyes to the divinity of the ordinary, to the majestic and marvelous beauty of the everyday, of each and every mote and iota of manifestation within the illusion. For as the one known as R said, "Is not everything made of this perfect love?" Therefore, is not the Creator literally in everything? These are words of great wisdom. If we could but share with you our perceptions of our environment and its amazing beauty we would love to set you awash in awe and wonder.

And yet we grasp the fact that there is a limit to the amount of spiritual awareness that can be carried within the soul while it is functioning. It is just that it is our experience that the way of accelerating the path of spiritual evolution includes an ever growing tendency towards the awareness of holiness in each moment. It is the self that is brought to each moment that creates the perception of that moment. It may seem at times as though it is impossible really to get into those attitudes that govern perception. However, since there are several entities within this group much familiar with computers we may say that just as any software within a computer can be altered by one who grasps the principles by which those programs were written, so too the seeker who knows the self and has begun to be conscious of that self's thoughts can begin to go into the programming and alter according to preference those deeper processes which produce perception.

It is not impossible to begin the transformation within the self. There is the opportunity for transformation at any time. So we encourage each to become a little more conscious of how that biocomputer, the mind, is working because these ways of thinking can be played with. And the—this instrument wants to say "manipulated," but there are difficult connotations to deal with in that word—but let us say that the building blocks of the mind can be taken down and restructured by one who has the patience and the tenacity to be persistent about self-observation. We would not encourage overemphasis on this kind of work, for truly the essence of spiritual seeking is in becoming more and more oneself, and that self rather fades before the eyes while one is doing work on one's deeper programs. The true spiritual earth of self lies far below that level of program and that is the ground of being that you hope to affect in some small way by the cumulative experience gained in your present incarnation.

So you are going to a school. This metaphor for the spiritual life is useful, for there is the classroom, your planet, the lessons you chose to work on for your courses, and, of course, the graduation to larger life at the end. That is a graduation no one fails.

Now, we have had our fun with that concept of truth that eludes us all. Let us open this meeting to the questions that you may have at this time, the concerns that are upon you. Is there a question at this time?

B: It seems that the mind is like an inverse pyramid in that the surface of the mind has more blocks that can be played with which all come from the original Thought. At what level are you rearranging these blocks? Are you just substituting one illusion for another illusion? Does it not accomplish the same thing to remain focused on the original Thought? Do you have any thoughts on this subject?

We are those of Q'uo, and, my brother, we have thoughts on almost anything … which we are glad to share. To the best of our limited knowledge there is nothing but illusion. The only thing that is without illusion is unpotentiated Love, which has no awareness of Itself. By the play of free will the Creator is able to seek to know Itself, but the act of manifesting love is in itself an illusion, a distortion, certainly a primal distortion, but distortion nevertheless, so that no matter what density of experience or length of study that describes one's situation, one is experiencing an illusion and one is distorting the truth. There is nothing but a steady progression of more and more light-filled densities which offer a more and more pleasant light-filled way of distorting the one original Thought.

The concept of distortion is sometimes not an easy one to get the mind around because there is that feeling in the mind that says that there must be something that is unchangeable, that is without distortion. However, we do not know anything that does not contain some distortion. Our only perception of undistorted truth is that state of being where one is lost in awareness of the Creator that speaks within the silence of the heart. So perhaps we could say that the most light-filled distortion available to one in third density is that state of mind where the attention is focused upon that which is known to be holy ground. That inner sanctum lies within your green-ray energy center, the heart chakra. This is why when entities are moving from the open heart that they seem to have a healing influence regardless of what they are saying and the relative wisdom of it, for that energy of the open heart contains the sanctification that is available to that opened heart.

May we answer you further, my brother?

B: No, thank you.

R: *(Inaudible).*

We are those of Q'uo and, my brother, we would be very happy to take you upon a walk with us. Let us begin by becoming aware of the physical vehicle as it rests upon the chairs and couches. Feel its heaviness. Feel the substance of that which you sit upon. Sense into the energies that hold the chair in position, that hold the body in position. Feel the liveness of the dwelling place, the energies of furnace and refrigerator and electricity as it moves through this place where these physical vehicles abide and enjoy the many cycles and energies of incarnation.

Sense now into the everlasting strength of your earth, that powerful terrestrial awe that is right beneath your feet. Sense down into that earth energy, for each of you has the roots within the earth. Each draws power from the earth. Sense the quiet joy of the daffodils pushing through that earth seeking the uncertain warmth of early spring. Sense those bare and dignified trees that lift their articulate branches through a bitter sky. Sense those few birds that yet dwell in the winter.

And now lift up from the body and the location, and rise up until you can see that island in space that is your home. All the cities have disappeared. There are no boundaries, no line that says United States and Canada. No pink Wyoming. No blue Kentucky. Just one tiny globe whirling through the never-ending night of your space/time. From this lofty altitude one can become philosophical about millennia, about great eons of time and great reaches of space. There is no body to that awareness that sees this planet.

Open now to the subtler levels of life. Become aware of the millions of entities that dwell within the Earth in spirit without their physical vehicle, those whom you have called angels, fairies, devas. Sense into that liveness that fills the air with the sound of wings, and rest back upon that band of angels that is with you and let it carry you back down into the Earth's sphere and come to rest in a more equable clime. You stand at the base of a mountainous area, on the shore of an ocean. The sun is golden and seems closer than it is possible to be. So warm, so toasty, so comfortable. The physical vehicle loves that feeling of sun, responds as does a flower to the warmth of life. Here in this private beach the Creator may walk with unshod feet. Breathe in that warmth and that presence that the sun is. Breathe in that love which fills the air. Feel how cherished you are as you rest there upon the sand with the ocean beating its susurration at your feet, wave upon wave of clear aquamarine water. Get up, lazy bones. Go for a walk. Sink your feet into the sand. Look out over the expanse of water. See the curve of Earth. That is the end of the eyeshot. How can the eyes see all the way to the curve of the Earth? What hundreds and thousands of miles of water does the eye take in in order to see to the curvature of the Earth? Standing here looking out, one must face the fact that there is a mystery that cannot be resolved. It lies just beneath every event of circumstance.

Let us walk far away from the beach and up into the warm shady foothills, walking the worn dirt path, finding the way from one valley to another until you have come to that waterfall and lagoon that lies at the heart of this mountainous island. Come now over the ridge of that hill into a place where that lagoon lies, that spring of fresh water that feeds it, and gaze around you. The trees so love the water. Willow, cottonwood, grand creatures that dip their toes in the deep springs and overhang the quiet water. Here in the shade it is warm, not hot, and you may lie down and close the eyes and rest, and as you rest you fall asleep and you dream that you are actually living in Louisville, Kentucky, sitting in a living room, and working on the spiritual journey.

Are you, then, those who are dreaming of a beautiful trip to a magic island, or are you living on a magic island dreaming?

(Side one of tape ends.)

(Carla channeling)

… finally to penetrate your winter heart and know that that which you can imagine is real. Come back now, if you have not already, into your body, into your circumstances, into the patterns with which you now work and feel the sun within. Know that that sun is love, both as it shines upon you within the illusion and as it flows and warms you within your heart.

This instrument is expressing to us that forty-five minutes is long enough for this session, so we would ask if there is a final question at this time?

B: Is clearing blockages more like cleaning the dirt off of a window or like popping the cork off of a bottle?

We are those of Q'uo, and we believe that we grasp your query. Let us say, rather—we give this instrument the image of an entity that is within a cave. The door to a cave is naturally open and when the energy within an energy nexus is without blockage there is the perfect ability to come in and go out as one wishes. When an energy is blocked it is the action of fear that causes the heart to contract away from that which is feared, that causes what you might see as a strand of knotty material that comes down over that opening, and when there is enough crystallized fear it seems that there is so much material at the head of the cave that there is no way to get out or come in. Entities often try to use large blunt instruments to remove such blockages from the mental, emotional or spiritual body. However, it is not the way that we would suggest. We would suggest that as entities work day by day it is a matter of taking a little of the material away so that a little more space is made for energy to move around, enter and leave. It is far more effective to work a little bit again and again and again than to attempt to, as you said, pop the cork and cause the energy to become unblocked in an explosive manner which can do damage to the structure of the mouth of the cave. The skill lies in knowing how much material can be laid aside. There is no time limit on this practice, so that if too much material is laid aside and the entity is seeing itself contract away again and move more into blockage that entity can stop and allow that blockage because that blockage for that entity at that time is necessary. What one is working with really is fear. Fear is the antithesis of love. As love radiates, fear contracts. To use explosion as a way of clearing a blockage is in itself a kind of use of the energy of fear, whereas the energy that radiates is that which is respectful and careful not to harm the knotted material that is taken away, the cave itself or the entity who wishes to have a more free energy center.

We fear that we have mixed a few metaphors, my brother, and apologize for that, but perhaps you see the direction of our thoughts.

May we speak further?

B: No. The images were helpful.

We thank you, my brother, and we thank each again and again. You have greatly enriched our lives, and we treasure each of you and thank you for this opportunity. As we leave you, we do not leave you, for are we not all one? Yet we shall cease speaking through this instrument and leave you in the love and in the ineffable light of the one infinite Creator, glorying in that mystery that ever draws us onward to our source and our ending. We are those of Q'uo. Adonai. Adonai.

(Pause)

I Yadda. I Yadda. We got the call from R, so we are here. We greet each in the love and the light of the one infinite Creator. We have only to say "hello and goodbye," but the one known as R asked for our voice, so we came. We Yadda. We leave you in love and light. Adonai. ✦

L/L Research

Sunday Meditation
February 23, 1997

Group question: We would like to know what the function and effect of ritual is upon the seeker of truth.

(Carla channeling)

Greetings in the love and in the light of the one infinite Creator. We are those of the principle known to you as Q'uo. We bless each of you and thank you for calling us to your circle of seeking. We thank each individual and each individual's desire for a fuller truth. We see each desire as a kind of tone or color and it is as though we were gazing at a circle of jewels. We are most, most happy to share our humble opinions with you, always with the understanding that we are not incapable of error. We are not an ultimate authority. We are seekers of the One, pilgrims of the mystery that is love. And we follow that love, which we find to be our very essence, in the hope of rejoining all that there is. This journey is far from over for us, and each of you has a few more steps than we to go, but we journey together and truly feel blessed in the company.

The question for the beginning of this session concerns the nature and function of ritual. This is indeed a substantially large subject. There are two types of rituals, the one being more an adaptation from the second-density roots of the vehicle that carries your consciousness about, the other being the creation of humankind in its search for deeper states of clarity in emotion and consciousness. The second density heritage that your bodies carry includes a generous helping of instinctual ritualistic behavior. An example of this kind of imprinting ritual is a favorite of this instrument's, that example being the cat which, upon hearing its owner at the door, begins to run about the living room, to jump up upon the door, to race from the door to the kitchen and back several times, to jump up on the cabinets, bounce off the refrigerator, go over to the dish, and then the cat is fed. Having once done this [the cat] associates all of the movements preceding the food in the dish as necessary to bring the food to the dish. It does not occur to the mind of a cat that the owner must go get the food and put it in the bowl. To this little mind, this little ritual of movements is quite essential.

The experience of each entity's life includes a full list of imprinting situations. The instinctual imprinting first shows itself as the mother suckles the newborn infant. There is a deep emotional content to this simple act which has life-long consequences for the mother and for the child. Again, that first experience of intimacy with the opposite sex creates an imprinting so that that first experience is instinctively retained as being the perfect sexual experience, and the rest of the incarnation is affected by those circumstances which were local to that imprinting first experience. As each goes through life experiences …

(R leaves the circle, coughing.)

We are those of Q'uo, and we request this instrument to say, "It's OK, R." We shall continue.

There are various times within the incarnation other than the imprinting of parents and the imprinting of sexuality. They largely include those individuals who have been effective in bringing to the surface some hidden desire. This is normally the function of the teacher/pupil relationship and is not uncommon between mates when each may be the teacher of the other. These imprintings are fields of energy which affect one entity for one particular period of incarnation.

The deeper and more typically human kind of ritual has its roots in instinct also, for there is an instinct for repetition of the familiar as a means of feeling no longer isolated, no longer alone, no longer as confused. There are rituals chosen by entities to solemnize changes such as the marriage and certainly each service of what this instrument calls the holy Eucharist or the holy communion is a good example of an effective and powerful ritual. In the use of ritual for the acceleration of changes in consciousness the term magic has often been used as a descriptive term suggesting ritual behavior which has a hidden spiritual significance.

We feel that it is this kind of ritual that the question was sparked by, for there is within this group a sincere and deep appreciation of the power of ritual. Each has experienced that purifying and clarifying effect that is gained through some ritual that is entered into by the self and by others with a common and, shall we say, non-terrestrial desire. The rituals of spirit, those rituals that this instrument would call religious, the many ritual orders of brotherhood within your various cultures, are all examples of collections and arrangements of words, tones and progressively more deeply touched emotions that have been repeated many times.

The reason that the ritual continues becoming more effective through generations and centuries is that within your inner planes, as this group was discussing earlier, there are many entities that are discarnate, that is, [that] do not have the physical vehicle that you enjoy in third-density incarnation. Yet they have, when incarnate, moved through these great rituals of religion, spirituality and religiously oriented brotherhood. When those who are in incarnation move through those same rituals, depending upon the ritual a relatively large group of discarnate entities may be awakened to the energy of this ritual and join in the ritual, creating an unseen—and what this instrument would call angelic—element so that to the individual moving consciously through this ritual comes the combined energy of a great heavenly host as well as those within the group that are participating within the ritual. These so-called magical rituals are very useful to the type of person that will seek a group worship or the cache of hidden things. To some, it is enough to be with the group to experience the movement of emotion that is possible when one participates deeply in the form of the ritual.

There are certainly many, many souls who do not feel the desire to participate in group ritual in order to clarify and purify the magical personality. To this entity comes the opportunity to create rituals for the self, and in many cases this attempt is well thought and well done. Many are the pilgrims whose rituals have to do with very humble ordinary things: the placement of cup and spoon and bread at a simple meal; the cleanliness and order of personal effects; the thoughts that one moves through before meeting another and honoring that entity. These are all examples of personal rituals. And these rituals also are not the terrestrial imprinting ritual. These are the rituals designed to effect changes in consciousness. To effect these changes in consciousness it is not necessary to be in a group. That group experience is available to those to whom it appeals, but to those weary souls who cannot enter into group ritual or group worship those emotions and changes in consciousness yet remain available. They simply do not call forth the degree of angelic assistance that is alerted by group worship.

When an entity has decided to choose the lonelier path of seeking then that entity is as the artist with the canvas washed and ready for the image. Both of these strains of ritual behavior, the solitary and the group, have but one goal, and that brings us to the consideration of what this instrument calls magic, or to be more specific, the white ritual magical tradition of the western or occidental world.

This instrument's definition for magic which she has read from the author, Butler, is that magic is the creating of changes in consciousness at will. Anyone who has attempted to see things in a spiritual way, to penetrate the outer skin of experience and know the gist and the core and the heart within experience will find ritual quite helpful, for the emotional body and the spiritual body are affected deeply by thought. There is for each entity one particular way, one particular possession of learnings and realizations unique to that one speaker. And yet in common to all seekers who wish to work with ritual is the innate tendency of the consciousness within to flow more easily through the consciousness, the physical, emotional, mental and spiritual bodies, when habit has been chosen carefully and followed persistently over a period of time. This instrument has been told that it takes three weeks to learn a new habit or to break an old one. This is the direction that we are suggesting is useful in ritual.

Take a look at the self and you can see that as the roots of self move through the threshold of consciousness down into the roots of mind there are passageways that are crystalline and regular in shape and function. Each ritual aid that opens those passageways, especially within the emotional body, is helpful in regularizing and enlarging that ability to channel light and love through the deep mind into the roots of mind, securing the self, rooting the self again and again in the deepest truth possible, the deepest truth that is seen, or felt, or sensed by that individual. The deeper mind has a desire to be used, a desire to open, a desire to yield its contents. One could, in terms of computers which have many qualities in common with the mind, one could see these deeper structures of mind as programs that are hidden and are only accessed from within other programs and are never directly accessed. Ritual is a tool which does eventually connect the self more and more with one's deeper and more accurate programs. The knowledge, shall we say, or inarticulate wisdom of the deep mind which lies beyond word and even beyond concept can be triggered by ritual. Therefore, ritual can be a great aid in becoming more the person that one truly is, for each is well aware of the number and the subtlety of the masks that each has worn within the lifetime. The heart yearns for that which lies behind that mask. And certainly ritual is a resource that aids in revealing the self to the self.

Why do seekers always wish to be able to effect changes in their consciousness? Certainly primary among the reasons for this … we must pause. We are those of Q'uo. This instrument, unfortunately, moved into a trance state which resembled sleep. Consequently, we found ourselves unable to continue channeling. We will attempt to alert this instrument.

We are those of Q'uo, and are glad that we have a good contact with this instrument so that we can continue. As this instrument is somewhat low, we feel it would be advisable to open the meeting to queries. We perhaps have not given you all that we had intended, but perhaps we have given enough so that you can follow up with queries. Are there any queries at this time?

B: Is there anything that any of us can do to prevent this type of losing contact?

We are those of Q'uo, and we feel that it is not frequently that the channel will fall asleep. There is within this instrument significant distortion towards weariness and discomfort, and it is the energy of this circle that gives this instrument relief from this discomfort. Therefore, we do not see the outcome of losing contact as a bad thing but merely an inconvenience in the context of the group energy waiting for the finish of our thoughts. We cannot think of any particular thing that would guarantee that this instrument would be able to erase weariness. However, my brother, we can assure you that the laying on of hands, the discussion, the social converse, these are things which affect this instrument in a positive way. The sharing between all of love and the gifts that each brings to this circle are what feed this instrument and, indeed, what feed all within the circle. Perhaps it is well to think of that energy as the unity of the group and realize that our communication is coming through the group first and this instrument second, so that the special gift that the one known as B has of having the healing touch, this can be helpful before or after the session. But, in general, the greatest gift is the comfortable and natural flow of love through the group.

May we answer you further, my brother?

B: No. Thank you.

And we thank you, my brother. This instrument was not in trance. This instrument was merely asleep. Is there another query at this time?

V: *(Inaudible).*

We are Q'uo, and are aware of your question. The suppositions of entities within incarnation do indeed have some effect upon their experiences immediately following the passage of the spirit from the physical vehicle and into that form-making or light vehicle that is their body immediately after the process of death and separation from the physical plane. In general, the effects of expectation last a fairly short time after cessation of the life experience, for the majority of entities have little enough certainty concerning the hereafter that they are open to being received by someone familiar to them. This guide, whether it seems to be husband or savior or some other entity, serves as the guide who leads by the hand as the entity is taken to a place of healing and restoration, for most entities tend to leave the incarnation in some metaphysical disarray to the extent that they have been injured spiritually, emotionally or mentally within incarnation. They will have the space and time necessary for full restoration of the true self. Once the entity has come to the realization of that fuller self that one is when one moves beyond that veil of flesh the period of review of incarnation then can begin and in this the entity and its higher self simply move through the incarnation, gazing at what has occurred, what has been learned, what has not been learned, and gradually they develop a plan for what the next step will be.

If that entity finds it has become able to graduate from the density now experienced then the guide takes it to what may be seen as a stairway of light, each stair being fuller of that one great original Thought of Love than the one before. The entity moves up the stairway until the intensity of light becomes uncomfortable. If that stair step is in fourth-density light, the entity goes on to lessons within that density. If the entity stops short of that demarcation and is remaining within third density then the self and its guidance develop a plan for the next incarnation. There is then that time taken to chose the parents, the friends, the mated relationships, and other important and central figures for the life to come. The lessons then are set up, depending most often upon the relationships and where those interactions lead the self.

If an entity has a strong and fixed vision of the afterlife, that afterlife scenario may play for some of your space/time. This entity then remains caught in space and time and hovers in the inner planes living out the expectation. However, this is always a time bound phenomenon, and eventually all entities awaken and move on. Certainly when an entity has been bound to the previous experience for some length of time, once the entity awakens to its true nature it will spend a significant amount of time in the healing mode before moving on.

May we answer you further, my sister?

V: *(Inaudible).*

We are those of Q'uo, and, my sister, it is often the case that one cannot infringe upon the free will of another. The key to await is the asking. If an entity asks you for your views or in some other mode of questioning indicates a desire [of] an alternate view, then certainly you may jump in and do your best to share your own vision. However, when an entity has a determined and anchored view, the only level of help available to one who wishes to observe the Law of Free Will is prayer. One may pray that the loved entity may be set free from limiting confusion. One may visualize the entity awakening to a higher way. And in this way one may place about that entity the angelic aid that such prayer alerts. And again, prayer is a kind of ritual, and when prayer is given from the heart it does alert what this instrument would call the angelic host so that when this entity moves through the veil of death there is more angelic light or love around the entity and more opportunity to sense a fuller truth during this transition. We would say, my sister, that it is not a great difficulty in terms of the experience after incarnation for the expectation to be deliberate, codified and incorrect, for the entity has an infinite amount of time to travel back to its source, so time considerations which seem drastic within incarnation become considerably less impressive when seen from the viewpoint of eternity.

May we answer you further, my sister?

V: No. Thank you.

Is there a final query at this time?

C: I have a friend who has a very serious illness and seems to be dying. Would prayer be the best thing for her since her illness seems to be a mystery to all of the medical profession?

We are those of Q'uo. My sister, when dealing with those approaching the entrance to larger life one does well to open the self to intuition, for each entity approaching this metamorphosis is wounded and the pain of incarnation begins to crystallize as the entity approaches the end of the experience. It is always new to each entity and unique to that entity what may give it more peace. To one entity it might be the talking, the sharing, the ability to listen to difficult emotional content, to another it might be that the gift of silence is the greatest gift, that support that does not ask for attention, and does not seek any effect, but rather is present. To one entity it would be the sharing of your gift, whether it would be the cooking, the singing, all the gifts that entities have to share with each other.

So there is always the delicacy of listening [with] that purity of attention that is willing to flow into that pattern that is sensed that will be the greatest gift. In general, we would say that the gift of prayer is always helpful because of the alerting of consciousness so that the entity is less and less able to feel alone or abandoned. When entities become ill it is common to those about it that the illness is ignored and there is a lot of pretending that everything is the same. The bare ability to abide in closeness with one who is in distress is a very helpful and healing influence. So we would say prayer and attention and the lack of drawing away would be the most likely avenues of aid.

May we answer you further, my sister?

C: No. Thank you.

We are those of Q'uo, and we thank you also, my sister. Each has such a power of love within. Each has such beauty to share. Each is so powerful to give assistance or to withhold it. We urge each to love each other, to care for each other, and to take the hand and give it the squeeze that says, "I am with you."

We would at this time leave this delightful group, rejoicing in the love and in the light of the one infinite Creator. We are known to you as the principle of Q'uo. Adonai. Adonai. ✧

L/L Research

L/L Research is a subsidiary of Rock Creek Research & Development Laboratories, Inc.

P.O. Box 5195
Louisville, KY 40255-0195

www.llresearch.org

Rock Creek is a non-profit corporation dedicated to discovering and sharing information which may aid in the spiritual evolution of humankind.

ABOUT THE CONTENTS OF THIS TRANSCRIPT: This telepathic channeling has been taken from transcriptions of the weekly study and meditation meetings of the Rock Creek Research & Development Laboratories and L/L Research. It is offered in the hope that it may be useful to you. As the Confederation entities always make a point of saying, please use your discrimination and judgment in assessing this material. If something rings true to you, fine. If something does not resonate, please leave it behind, for neither we nor those of the Confederation would wish to be a stumbling block for any.

CAVEAT: This transcript is being published by L/L Research in a not yet final form. It has, however, been edited and any obvious errors have been corrected. When it is in a final form, this caveat will be removed.

© 2009 L/L Research

Sunday Meditation
March 16, 1997

Group question: We are asking about service today. First, we seem to need a sense of self in order to know what it is we have as resource to serve with, and secondly, we would ask if it is even appropriate to concentrate on serving others in our daily round of activities, or is it more a part of our beingness to serve in a less directed effort? What is the true nature of teaching when it comes to serving others?

(Carla channeling)

We are those of the principle known to you as Q'uo. We greet you in the love and in the light of the one infinite Creator. It is a joy and a privilege to join in your meditation and share in your vibrations. We cannot express the blessing that each of you brings to each of us, for we remember well third density, that time in the crucible. It takes courage to allow the conditions for the choices that you make to be felt, expressed, named and accepted. And we are inspired by the genuine and authentic desire of each to seek and know the truth. We also thank you for your calling us because our service and the way we ourselves are progressing at this particular juncture is by sharing our experiences and opinions with those companions along the path that dwell on your Earth plane at this time. There is a tremendous calling that redounds throughout creation when a people such as yours approaches a cusp and is not ready and yet senses, however dimly, that call to march, that feeling of purpose and mission. So we thank you and bless each and ask one thing of you in return, and that is that you use your personal discriminatory power in keeping those things we might say that seem to you to be worthwhile and allowing the rest to fall away, for we would not put a stumbling block in front of any.

We were the proverbial fly on the wall listening to your discussion, and we agree with this instrument that truly this particular group does not need a formal channel, but, rather, there is a conjoining of kindred spirits so that each is teacher to each. You shall find this occurring more and more frequently as many among your peoples in all your nations do awaken, do find themselves in the sense that, for the first time, they relate to themselves as a spiritual identity. When each entity does awake, there is that feeling of almost a panic, a desperation of desire to become oriented in the metaphysical world in which thoughts are things and things are only thoughts. What a different and uniquely alien landscape appears before the newly awakened spirit who, for the first time, realizes that she is not a body with a mind, not doomed to death and limited in time, but, rather, a citizen of an infinite and eternal unity.

As each progresses, many are the questions and issues that arise. Many are the dogfights and wrestling matches with angels in the dead of night. Many are the ties that seem broken and the pieces that seem never to fit. And great is the suffering of each spirit as that metamorphosis occurs and the wet and still unborn butterfly fears to leave the cocoon. And in this experience, were each of you not to want to help others [it] would be remarkable. It is natural and appropriate for each of you to hope and, indeed, to know that you can serve. If we could leave you with one thought it would be that one: you will serve. Fear not. Do not be distraught because you are confused or because you have not that mountaintop experience on this particular day at this particular time. You shall perform your mission. Each of you shall serve effectively that light and that love that you so adore. You cannot fail at this, for as you breath in and as you breath out you are an essence. You are a personality shell in a second-density body that hides your consciousness from yourself and, to a lesser extent, from the world around you. You are the one great original Thought. You are Love.

And those who are joined with us on this particular day all have native homes in densities that are sweeter and more open and closer to the original vibration of unconditional love. Beneath the masks and roles that are appropriate for each to play in your dance on the sea of confusion you are who you are and it is that essence that is your gift and your main service. As you breathe in and as you breathe out, you breathe the world, you breathe illusion, and you are love. As you have breath so shall you be mortal, and this mortality clothes one in a flesh that creates a lack of memory, a lack of contact with those things that pertain to your infinite self. This does not disturb your essence. You can lessen the ease with which your native vibrations can ripple out. You can be blessed, expressive of essence. You can be more true to that underlying and encircling essence, but you shall, without fail, perform your service and complete your mission because your basic mission is to live a life amongst those people with whom you find yourself, having a heart that is consciously open as is possible on a stable basis.

When one worries and strives and struggles it may seem that the night falls and nothing can be seen, yet always the self lies waiting for you to allow its depths to rise up into conscious awareness. There is a spring inside each in that sanctum of the heart, and it bubbles forever with the clear water of light and love. The Creator has placed His tent within this inner sanctum and patiently, lovingly and personally waits for your touch upon the door, for your step upon the stairs, hoping that you shall come in and sit with It. And there is no greater joy that the Creator has than that joy of being joined in communion within the heart. The Creator has enormous infinite love for you. There is a personality, a personhood to that quality of love. It is not impersonal. It is not general or vague. The Creator finds each vibratory complex beautiful and loves each just as it is.

For those in third density and within incarnation such unconditional love is not particularly easy to find access to. And we are aware that you hope to find more resources to help you become a better servant. Certainly our first suggestion to each would be to enter into a deepening and more comprehensive awareness of the self, especially those parts of the self this instrument would call the dark side, for this complete and total self encompasses all that there is. Each of you has made repeated choices in this incarnation, and those choices have been to emphasize, for the most part, the positive qualities. However, your culture does not teach you to deal with the other path of the self with the appropriate kindness. And so each has faced that self that murders and steals and blasphemes and envies and lusts. And each has turned a hard heart to the self and said, "I judge this part unworthy."

It is not that we disagree with how wretched each of us is, for truly when one is all things one does encompass the pain and suffering of all time and all space as well as the brightness and glory of the light. But it is our humble opinion that these parts of self are actually other than they seem. Within third density, however, the knowledge that nothing is what it seems is a cold and unpersuasive thing. We are not sure how to suggest to each of you that you find the courage and nerve to forgive yourself for being human. In the world of illusion you, too, must be of the same stuff made. You cannot bring into this illusion an undeniable reality, for the whole purpose of illusion is to so confuse you that you finally give up using the tools of intellect and logic in order to make sense out of life, for life does not make logical sense in the normal use of that term. Certainly each has been in that state of mind wherein all things were seen to be perfect. And these are moments of rare beauty and joy. And yet they feed only the self. You cannot give them as presents to others or persuade any because you have been persuaded, for this is the density of choice, and each entity must face that choice of whom to serve, how to serve, for himself.

However, we can assure you that there are ways to be of service to others besides simply being. It is just that it all begins with loving yourself. We cannot overemphasize this step, nor can we say that it is an easy or simple thing, for the self must first be plumbed and seen, not in great detail, perhaps, but in the sense of facing that ravening wild beast that dwells within each and that has the power of the vampire, pulling on the energy of self when it is not loved. Each of you has forgiven others tremendous things, but have you forgiven yourself for the small things, much less for the things that you consider large? How difficult it is to turn and see self. Many never achieve knowledge and must project all that occurs with them in their life upon other entities, and this is one of the things that other entities are here to offer. Indeed, each of you has played that part for others, being the mirror that reflects and offers catalyst. Each of you has experienced that great feeling of seeing self for the first time because someone else was a good mirror. But the first mirror we suggest you hold up to yourself.

The one known to you as Jesus was reared in a climate of what this instrument calls the Old Testament, the Ten Commandments, the Law of Orthodoxy. This teaching was tempered by much mysticism, but when this entity began to teach others it suggested that all of the law and all that the prophets had said could be replaced by loving the Creator and loving others as one loved oneself. One cannot become able to love others unconditionally until one has forgiven the self. We encourage each to press on towards self-acceptance, self-forgiveness and that feeling that each day is a new one, each moment is a clean and untouched thing.

When one seeks to serve others one has chosen the most subtle of activities. Certainly there is never any harm in perceiving an entity in need, of offering aid in a general sense, of suggesting that you are there for that person. Certainly when one is asked to be of service in this and that way one may respond to one's fullest for this is the green light that says, "Please impose your values. Express your feelings to me. I will listen because I am seeking." Seldom is service that simple. Often it is a matter of dropping seeds. A smile is a seed. An open book that says on the front, prayer, or meditation, that is a seed. Those who come into your environment see what you are reading and something in them is refreshed, for are we all not one? An open hand. A kind word. The commonplaces of ordinary life. These are riches indeed and within them lie all the service imaginable, for as you speak to one and to another in the normal run of things you speak to all. Release the concept of numbers. It does not matter how many perceive that which you offer. One is enough. One is a bounty. For that one is the Creator. Each entity is a holograph of all that there is. There is no loss. There is no way to be lost. You are in the creation.

To a deeper level let us move and look at this being, this essence of self. We always greet each of you in the love and in the light of the infinite Creator because it is our opinion that that is all that there is. The great original Thought is a vibration known as love, that insipid word for which we cannot find a substitute for. All that is created is created of light which is the product of free will acting upon love. At this level is the identity and beingness of each. At the level of pure vibratory complex you cannot help but be yourself. Within third density there is tremendous opportunity to accelerate the rate of spiritual evolution. And so as you go forth each day, realize that this process will take you and shake you and things will come rattling loose from time to time. Change, as this instrument says, is often uncomfortable. And change you will if you are listening and acting upon the desires of your heart. It is sometimes a tough, brutal journey. The landscape is sometimes very barren. As each goes through those initiations and that dark night of the soul that this Lenten season is so appropriate for is experienced, you do not know when you approach another what state that person is in. You do not know to whom you are an oasis. You are the water that quenches the thirst by your being.

Before we go to questions and answers we would ask you to rest in that beingness and experience yourself as we experience you. How precious you are. How beautiful. Touch into this beauty, this grace. Feel that light as you move into the place of love within self. Feel the radiance beginning. And know that it is not from you that that radiance comes. All you can do is prepare the channel for the infinite love and light of the one Creator to flow through you into the world of manifestation. The suffering, the questioning, the doubting, the pain, and the suffering and agony of all that you experience is for one thing: to hollow you and to focus that emptiness so that it is ready to receive. For those upon the service-to-others path, those to whom we wish to speak, what is being received is infinite love and as it flows through you into a channel that you have cleared it radiates into all of your Earth world. It is for this that you came: to live a life filled with many sacrifices as things fall away and you begin to know what is valuable, what is beautiful, what is true. You are a witness, and yet you are what you witness in that wonderful paradox that is the signal of the metaphysical world. It will always baffle the mind and it hopes to so baffle it that you will make the trip from head to heart.

As you wash dishes, as you attend your daily toilet, as you diaper a child, as you pull a weed, as you sit in a blue funk and wish everyone were dead, you are serving the Creator. It does not matter how many you serve. But only that you be yourself and experience as fully as possible what the Creator has placed before you, for those things that are for you will come to you. You have prepared for yourself a line of growth. When one resists this line one may go in other directions, but there is only one place you are attempting to get. You can make your journey longer by resisting, but it shall be that same journey. Consequently, it profits one to contemplate how to cooperate with this rhythm and vector you experience in the flow of your own living. Know each thing in terms of praise and thanksgiving. Many things are easy to offer praise and thanksgiving for, and yet as each of you has said in the discussion prior to this channeling, as this instrument calls it, each has made that point.

So we simply urge you to love. Love the Creator. Love yourself. Love each other any way you know how to. Any which way. You cannot err. You can seem to fail again and again. Yet you truly make no mistakes. For you are, at all times, secure, safe and centered. You will learn to experience more and more how to allow yourself to feel that center that is already there.

We would at this time open the meeting to questions. Are there any at this time?

R: D has discovered he was someone close to Tesla and now he seems to be getting psychic attacks, being paralyzed from the waist down, his gear is breaking down, and a dowser has found alien energy in his house. Could you comment in any way you feel is appropriate?

We are Q'uo, and we grasp the query. When one is attacked it is natural to defend, and yet in the sense of psychic greeting the defense creates the prolongation of attack. The one known as Jesus has said, "Resist not evil," and we would say know this greeting as coming from the self, as the child has been spurned by the parent. This child does damage, hits people with the toy truck, bangs on the piano. This is not lovable behavior, and yet this too is part of self. We would suggest that when an entity is faced with a new part of self the solution is, as always, love. These footsteps, this paralysis, find the courage to give praise and thanksgiving for this and any condition. Find the serenity to seek the heart of this greeting, and see that heart as that which, when loved, shall be transformed. There are reasons that a veil of forgetting drops when an entity enters into incarnation. When this veil is penetrated within incarnation an entity feels she is seeing self and yet this self is but a shell and that self is but a shell, and the essence lies beneath, between and around both and yet is neither. When the feared is finally seen with love then shall phenomena make little difference.

We would be glad to continue further if the entity who asked this question would wish to requery. Is there another question at this time?

B: No question. Just wanted to say that you said some things in today's session that really moved me. As I prepare to move off into my next step of growth I just want to say that I am really going to miss these Sunday sessions. And I just want to thank you for everything.

My brother, we thank you as well and could not put it better. Is there another query at this time?

Questioner: *(Inaudible).*

We are Q'uo and are aware of your query. My sister, the runaway technology, as this instrument would put it, of your peoples is that of the child with toys. The child is not large enough to grasp how to care for and treat his objects of interest and amusement. This shall be very confusing which is as things should be. We cannot comment upon specifically what effect or direction your culture shall move but only encourage each to see the innumerable and ephemeral ripplings of the ascent of intellectual knowledge with equanimity. Whatever seems good or evil, whatever seems hopeful or disastrous, is illusion. And so we encourage each to turn always to that place within which connects the self in incarnation to the self in eternity.

May we answer a final question at this time?

Questioner: *(Inaudible).*

My brother, we are so glad that you brought that up. We love milkshakes. We consider each of you a delicious milkshake. We could eat you for breakfast. We leave each of you in the ineffable love and light of the one Creator. Love each other. Love each other. We are know to you as those of Q'uo. Adonai. Adonai. ✸

L/L Research is a subsidiary of Rock Creek Research & Development Laboratories, Inc.

P.O. Box 5195
Louisville, KY 40255-0195

L/L Research

www.llresearch.org

Rock Creek is a non-profit corporation dedicated to discovering and sharing information which may aid in the spiritual evolution of humankind.

ABOUT THE CONTENTS OF THIS TRANSCRIPT: This telepathic channeling has been taken from transcriptions of the weekly study and meditation meetings of the Rock Creek Research & Development Laboratories and L/L Research. It is offered in the hope that it may be useful to you. As the Confederation entities always make a point of saying, please use your discrimination and judgment in assessing this material. If something rings true to you, fine. If something does not resonate, please leave it behind, for neither we nor those of the Confederation would wish to be a stumbling block for any.

CAVEAT: This transcript is being published by L/L Research in a not yet final form. It has, however, been edited and any obvious errors have been corrected. When it is in a final form, this caveat will be removed.

© 2009 L/L Research

Sunday Meditation
March 23, 1997

Group question: Concerning seeking and searching. We often have things happening inside of us that are quite intense and we don't know how to work with them. How can we work with these situations? Grab hold of them and try to understand them or let them go and develop on their own?

(Carla channeling)

We are those of the principle known to you as Q'uo. Greetings and blessings to each in the love and in the light of the one infinite Creator. We thank you for calling us to your meeting this day. The experience of blending our vibrations with yours in meditation is a lovely gift, and we thank you as well for being willing to let us share our opinions and thoughts with you, asking you, as always, to discriminate as you are listening to that which we say so that you may take those thoughts that seem good to you and leave the rest behind.

This day your query is the—we give this instrument the concept of a national anthem or a favorite song of the wanderer—that is, how to learn from the catalyst that occurs to one who is walking the spiritual path; how to use that catalyst that is yours with the most efficiency, the most respect, and the most success. The spiritual path is often described in terms of difficulty, as though the losses and limitations that affect all within the heavy illusion of your third density were puzzles that could be deciphered, riddles that could be solved, equations that could be completed. And in a very real sense this is so. Yet in a very important way this is not so, and this paradox is, as always, the hallmark of the spiritual concern, befuddling the intellect, defeating logic, confusing the seeker. And to what end is this the desired spiritual occurrence? From the commonality of the difficult experiences for each seeker, the answer would seem to be in the affirmative. But what is there to enable the spiritual seeker to be more skillful in looking at those things that are points of confusion and occasions for the many emotions surrounding fear and frustration?

First, let us address the happenings themselves, those things that come, seemingly at random, upon the unwary seeker: the auto accident that is visited upon one out of nowhere, the sudden loss that is unacceptable, the limitation that seems to be directly athwart every hope of progress. The heart of this question moves into the reason for your density of experience at this juncture of time and space, that is, third density itself. For, indeed, your illusion is specifically designed to place each seeker repeatedly in situations of limitation and loss, situations that trigger every fear, every confusion that the human heart possesses. Although it may seem that the Creator that helped mold the nature of your illusion is either mischievous or mean or possessed of a poor sense of humor, the truth seems to be that the

Creator wished that each spirit, each spark of Self, once radiated out from the Creator, would have the experience of falling into the chasm of the unknown with no parachute except faith.

This is the point the spirit of Love wishes each of Its sparks to attain, that point where it is realized that faith is a way that lives upon itself without any scientific support. The Creator hungers for each entity to turn towards It, to be drawn so to the great original Thought of Love that in spite of every limitation and loss and difficulty each heart remain faithful and of each entity's own free will to cleave unto creative love itself and to stand firm in a serene knowing that despite all appearances, things are as they should be.

When one is experiencing privation or difficulty certainly the last thing that seems a good idea is to fold the hands and say, "This is perfect." And yet this statement, that is, "This is perfect," is the deepest truth in any situation. The more it looks like an untruth, then, the greater the part that faith must play within the mind and emotions and heart of the seeker. We believe that in older creations than your own, free will was not so valued and, therefore, third density was offered without the veil, without the forgetting that occurs during the birth process so that each entity who awakens upon the Earth plane is kept from knowing its spiritual identity and the spiritual nature of the surrounding creation. Although the second density continues to speak volumes to one who has the ears to hear concerning the endless generosity of the Creator and the infinite way in which each part of creation serves each other part, the veil being drawn over all existence except that which you are experiencing at this moment creates a situation that is ripe for confusion, and we are not surprised to see that each seeker within this circle has been confused again and again.

And in this confusion each has set the stage for the choice between reasoning based upon fear and reasoning, if you would call it that, based upon love. For faith is the active application of love to situations that astound, confuse or befuddle you. This instrument once at a time near death placed a motto above the bed in which she lay. That motto was, "Faith, the final frontier." And for each of you this faith is as the Grail that is desired, that is sought after, that is hoped for, but how actually to attain this spiritual attitude?

There are many ways to help awaken that faculty of faith, but we feel that in the mix of things needed to pursue faith paramount is a willingness to jump off into the unknown, and to believe that all is well for no reason except faith alone, for no reason except that deep feeling that there is order, that there is purpose, and that there is a rhythmic way to progress. The more jangled events and voices and tempers become, the more the intellect is locked—this instrument would say grid-locked—with the nonsensical nature of such occurrences. The spirit of Love hopes that such times of crisis will trigger within the seeker the realization that this is another crux at which faith may be invoked.

Faith can begin with very small things. Faith that you shall wake up when you go to sleep. Faith that you are who you think you are. Faith that the sun will rise, that the birds will sing, that the seasons will progress to a time of blooming, when things look grim and dark. It is like a muscle that must be used and not when it is convenient alone, but when it is inconvenient especially. Many are the signs and wonders offered to the illusion by energies and essences within spirit. Many are the visions of those who seek visions. Many are the miracles of healing, prayer and love. Many are the occasions to note and marvel at the faith of others. Many are the stories whose burden is that faith and faith alone has pulled the seeker through.

This instrument recalls an instance when a missionary couple were fighting not only the ignorance and poor conditions of an aboriginal tribe but also a terrible outbreak of illness. No matter how hard they worked they could not keep up, and they were becoming more and more weary. Being people of rare faith they chose to meet the situation by arising even an hour earlier and praying in silence and in peace, knowing that all was well, knowing that there was enough. And as these affirmations spiraled heavenward this couple found peace. And they were able to meet the impossible demand of the situation with humor and dignity. They did not hold their burdens, you see, but made a point of giving them to the Creator, of taking every burden, worry and care and placing all as if giving a present in the capable hands of love. For truly the Creator broods over each of you, so in love with each of you. We cannot express the intensity of that love that we have perceived coming to us and to all from the infinite One. We are His heart's darlings. We are the children of creation, and this describes our nature beyond all illusion.

When this has begun to become a part of who the seeker is, when this feeling of being so loved and so precious has sunk in and taken root in a subtle and ever-changing way, the life begins to be transformed because the self finally accepts the Creator's opinion of self and can begin to see by faith alone that whatever is upon the surface, the self is the Creator's own from its very origins upwards. This is the native land. This is the home. This is the safety of each, not the power, security or any manifested part of how the world thinks about itself, but, rather, the safety and security lie in remembering whose child you truly are, whose service you truly wish to join, whose love you truly wish to channel through yourself and into the world.

Now, some of what you asked this day concerns how the seeker can tell that something is occurring that is of a pattern that is especially meaningful to look at, and we would say to each that when there is a time of testing, trial or temptation the key aspect of the situation is pattern. When you can spot within your thinking a repeated theme, a repeated motif, then you can tell yourself in good authority, "This is something I want to look at more closely, more deeply. What is there in this pattern that has caught me? Where am I stuck?" Since the heavy illusions guarantees that nothing is what it seems, the powers of mentation are not particularly useful at deciphering the pattern. However, if the seeker will move into the feelings and emotions that have arisen in connection with this pattern then the seeker may be able more easily to use this material, because it is in the responses that are chosen to catalyst that occurs that the self expresses self.

So we would say in meditation allow the silence to do its work. But in contemplation simply allow the self to move into those states of emotion that arise in this pattern. Feel that state. Enter into every nook and cranny of this emotion or of this nexus of emotions. Allow association to move your feelings and see if there is a constellation of events or memories that seem to trigger this same type of emotional response. In this way you are working on your consciousness without departing from the situation at hand, for there is a self that is beneath all of these experiences that come within the incarnation. As one goes through the illusion day by day one can more and more find composure where formerly there was conflict simply because the attitude of faith has begun to take root and the need is not felt so quickly to move into patterns that take one away [from] faith and into the doubtful waters of opinions and words and points of view.

What we have to offer to you is a very simple thing. We are here to speak of love because love is truly all that there is. The energy of love, when touched by free will, has created the manifested world, but all things that are in this world still vibrate with the one great original Thought, and you are those on their first voyage as self-aware entities that are citizens not just of time and space but of eternity, and within incarnation you are attempting to sail the ship of flesh and at the same time realize that there is a deeper ocean of spirit, and that the deeper identity is the one launched upon a shakedown cruise upon a metaphysical sea which cannot be seen or felt or heard or touched but which is dearer in the heart than any manifested things to the seeker. So you are dual citizens, and to combine the spiritual and the earthly is sometimes an interesting challenge.

We encourage each in two ways: firstly, we encourage [you] to, as this instrument would say, validate the self, to stand up for the self, to feel good about the self, to take care mentally, spiritually, physically to love the self. And we encourage you to release fear as it feels safe to you to do so and to replace that quite understandable emotion with faith. Simply to live by faith is to bring an end to paradox and confusion, for to faith all things are acceptable. All experiences are those of love and the distortions of love. Faith is, shall we say, a code word suggesting a vibration that is more like the vibration of love itself. So wherever you are when you suddenly feel challenged, turn inward for the remembrance of your real and overriding nature. You are not simply a person caught between birth and death in a dance of no meaning. You are also a citizen of eternity, a child of the Creator and a dweller in light.

We would at this time ask if you have further questions.

V: There seems to be something missing as far as I can see. I am not sure where I am supposed to be and what I am supposed to be doing. Could you help me with that?

We are those of Q'uo, and believe that we grasp your query. My sister, we would say that those who seek spiritually do indeed have an urgent and telling purpose. And yet that purpose is not one which naturally occurs to those within the illusion, for within the illusion there is always that feeling of doing something in order to be useful. And as spiritual entities, that translates into the feeling that one has to be doing something, some career, some vocation or calling whose activity serves the spiritual purposes of humankind.

However, it is our opinion that the mission and the purpose for which each of you took incarnation was simply to live, to offer your vibrations to the planetary consciousness. It may seem that this offering of self to lighten the planetary web of consciousness is a small thing, perhaps a useless thing, for seekers generally do not feel that they are operating at a high vibration. Yet with all the confusion and all the distortion surrounding reactions to the confusion not withstanding, living moment by moment with the heart open to love is enough purpose and mission to cram a lifetime so full that it radiates life.

Certainly some entities are offered careers or callings which are obviously helpful, and for those people there is the siren call of, "Look at what I am doing. I can be proud." You see, this is a secondary or indirect way of serving. It only seems direct because of the way the manifestation seems. The actual direct and common career of each seeker first of all is to live and be an entity of loving and being loved, an entity of the open heart.

May we answer you further, my sister?

V: No. Thank you very much.

We thank you as well, my sister, and wish you well on your journey. Is there another query at this time?

B: Concerning red-ray energy. I am in a position where I have chosen celibacy and I am wondering if I can offer this red-ray energy towards the planetary healing. Is there a way someone like myself can do this?

We are those of Q'uo, and we do grasp your query. We believe that we can certainly confirm that which you say, that simply the offering of all of self to the Creator is the central or key act, metaphysically speaking, for when seen from [that] standpoint, whether that energy of sexuality is offered in exchange with a partner in the act of intimacy or whether that energy is offered whole and pristine back to the Creator, it is that turning of self to Creator with the desire to offer all of self that is the important thing.

There are many ways in which seekers have found good use for sexual energy, in the giving of it and in the holding of it. We cannot say that one way is better than another, although certainly those who have to be celibate—and here we refer to those among your peoples called monks and nuns—feel that theirs is the higher path. And yet the simple gift of the complete self to another is as the offering of the virginal self to the Creator when each is done with the same purity of dedication to the Creator.

There are many possible ways to vent and express the red-ray energy which have not much virtue, metaphysically speaking. The key is simply to gather the self and offer that self completely. Once this is done the knowledge that what is yours will come to you rhythmically and naturally may perhaps keep the mind at peace with this decision; that is, to express the sexual nature only as a gift to the Creator. Once this decision is made, whether that gift is a gift of celibacy or an energy exchange with another who also wishes to serve the infinite One, the result is precisely the same.

May we answer you further, my brother?

B: No. Not on that subject. Concerning the archetypical mind, why do seekers touch the archetypical mind? How is the way made possible for them to do so?

We are those of Q'uo, and we do not mind being confused, my brother. We rather enjoy it.

The archetypical mind is a part of the deep mind of each entity. The roots of mind begin with that region closest to the conscious mind's threshold and as one follows these roots one finds various levels of group mind within the mind. The ethnic group mind, the geographical group mind, the political group mind, and so forth. Deeper than these are the planetary mind, the archetypical mind, and the all-mind or the Knower that is the Known. The archetypical mind is a set of structures that create a way to think about the self as a metaphysical being. Within a mythical system there are characters with which one may find identity. Each who has used that identity to further deepen one's own spiritual nature will be familiar with this.

For instance, this instrument shall, during the coming week which it calls Holy Week, be following the footsteps of the one known as Jesus, deeply identifying with this entity's sacrifice, deeply rejoicing in this entity's [triumph] over death. The archetype that is being explored is the archetype of transformation. As spiritual beings there is far more to the self than can be imagined or [en]compassed, and so as the mind struggles to process information which has no words, that which transcends words becomes increasingly useful. The drama, the comedy, the painting, the opera, the art that pulls an entity beyond words into emotional states, these are valuable things because they trigger truth from the standpoint of emotion or the heart rather than the concept of the mind. And the seeker is attempting to get to the heart of the self, to live from the heart of self, and so these archetypes which carry great rivers of purified emotion within them are extremely helpful.

As the seeker meditates it is offered material which is beyond words. It is that still, small voice that moves upon the sea of feelings and emotions. The seeker will come again and again to realizations which cannot be summed up in words and in this process, which is so subtle, the use of the archetypical mind is constant, seldom breaking forth into the conscious mind in most cases but always going on beneath the surface. This is the way that consciousness works. In an easy and comfortable partnership with the consciousness that is yours within the personality shell, the mind, and the body that are given for this incarnation alone. There is constant communication between consciousness and the personality shell itself. And as the seeker becomes more comfortable with truths which have no words the self can more and more reside in that way of being which does not need words. And from this point of view there can be an ever increasing ease of motion in switching from that state of being which is deeply peaceful to the self that meets and greets and acts with the illusion, wresting ever more abundant harvests of experience from the catalyst offered.

May we answer you further, my brother?

B: What particular archetype does Judas represent? I appreciate what you have offered.

My brother, this is your meat to chew. May we have a final query at this time?

B: One more about the archetypes. The particular myth that the seeker would be attracted to in touching the archetypical mind, is that unique to the seeker or to the commonalties between seekers?

We are those of Q'uo. My brother, for the most part, entities find themselves most comfortable with the myth that is shared by the culture. When the culture does not identify greatly with any mythical system then it is that the seeker is challenged to explore possibilities for itself. We find your culture at this time in such a state of flux. The lip service given to the mythical system of Christianity and Judaism remain current and widespread, yet the emotional involvement of the culture as a whole in this mythical system is at a low level. In this atmosphere each seeker will find ways to create from a synthesis of various systems or from within the self a unique path. And this is more and more the way that those within your culture are moving.

May we speak further upon this subject?

B: No. Thank you.

We find that this instrument's energy runs low and the circle's energy to listen perhaps even lower. We would have no problem talking with you right through the supper hour, but we are sure that you would not wish it so. And so we will leave you glorying in the fellowship that we enjoy with you, thanking you for the dedication and courage that brings each out of his and her way to this meeting of souls. We leave you in ineffable love and light. Now and always. We are those known to you as Q'uo. Adonai. Adonai.

L/L Research

L/L Research is a subsidiary of Rock Creek Research & Development Laboratories, Inc.

P.O. Box 5195
Louisville, KY 40255-0195

www.llresearch.org

Rock Creek is a non-profit corporation dedicated to discovering and sharing information which may aid in the spiritual evolution of humankind.

ABOUT THE CONTENTS OF THIS TRANSCRIPT: This telepathic channeling has been taken from transcriptions of the weekly study and meditation meetings of the Rock Creek Research & Development Laboratories and L/L Research. It is offered in the hope that it may be useful to you. As the Confederation entities always make a point of saying, please use your discrimination and judgment in assessing this material. If something rings true to you, fine. If something does not resonate, please leave it behind, for neither we nor those of the Confederation would wish to be a stumbling block for any.

CAVEAT: This transcript is being published by L/L Research in a not yet final form. It has, however, been edited and any obvious errors have been corrected. When it is in a final form, this caveat will be removed.

© 2009 L/L Research

Sunday Meditation
March 30, 1997

Group question: Today we are taking pot luck.

(Carla channeling)

We are those of the principle known to you as Q'uo. Greetings in the love and in the light of the one infinite Creator. We thank this group for calling us to share with you our vibrations and our thoughts. As always, we find it a great honor to offer our opinions and we do so hopefully knowing that each of you will use your discrimination in deciding which of our thoughts to take further and which to leave behind. There is a particular flavor or feeling that comes when a truth that is an important resource for you is first heard. That feeling is like remembering something that one knew once but had forgotten. Trust this intuition, and when that intuition does not speak, then please allow our words to pass away like water.

We find in this instrument's mind choruses and violins and tunes and harmonies of a feast day that is much beloved and blessed to this instrument, that day whereon that love that came into the world and was slain by the world was freed from the grasp of death. When it is Christmas time we speak of the seeker resembling the infant Jesus, born brand new into a spiritual identity previously unknown, the child within that is the spiritual infant that has the language of spirit to learn and the ways of spirit to become comfortable with and used to. When it is this time that you call Easter we tend to suggest to the seeker that she see herself both in the sacrifice of love for the world and in that resurrection from the death of the body that is the birthright of every seeker who has become aware of his spiritual identity. We encourage each of you to contemplate the sacrifices that each of you has made to come to this particular moment, not simply to this particular house or to this particular group but certainly involving that momentary situation that is shared by all of you at this time.

It is a measure, a clumsy one, but a yardstick of sorts, when looking at the self and its travail and difficulty in walking the spiritual path to reflect upon the amount of love, the amount of, shall we say, even surrender that is brought by the self to the chances and changes of mortal existence. For, truly, it is not so much a question of what one does to be of service as it is a question of how much love was brought to offering the service. A common misperception of those that walk the spiritual path is that there is something specific, some vocational career, that someone is supposed to be doing. There is this urgency of feeling that it is time to serve. "It is time to move on with the mission for which I came to this place," and as we have said before through this instrument, it is our feeling that that idea of a career is a chimera unless that career is seen to be a vocation of being. There is that within each of you that is perfect. Each of you is a hologram of the one great original Thought, and this is carried in an undistorted form in every cell of your physical body and all of the subtler bodies which make up your mind and body and spirit in its complexity.

You cannot take a breath that is closer to you than the Creator in all of Its perfection. Therefore, as each seeks to be of service and to know what is next, what is the pattern, what is the rhythm, no matter how many tools and resources the seeker finds in other people in the way they live, in what they teach, in what they have written, and so forth, yet within the self, in those caverns and labyrinths of self within the mind the help that is hungered for lies waiting to be touched by the spirit willing to plunge ever deeper into that system of roots of mind that bring one from the present moment through all of time and space and all the ways of humankind, shall we say, to that ocean of oneness within which each of the sparks of love that you are is swimming in, as the dolphins swim in the waters of your planet. Within you is the creature that knows and loves the ocean of consciousness within. And yet within the illusion, you walk upon the dry land and can only carry that ocean within. And upon the dry land there is dust and time and sorrow, and the heart grows weary and the spirit lags. And yet within each cell of your body there is rejoicing and gladness in fullness. Oh, to be able to touch the realization that lies waiting.

As each of you knows well, we always recommend the daily time of meditation. If it be only for five minutes, that is a time that you have carved out that is held for no one but the Creator. This is a gift of self to self, and no matter how poorly you listen to the silence, no matter how many voices rise and fall away within the mind, yet still that intention has been made. And as this is repeated and repeated through your time there comes to be that feeling of habit that helps the seeker to continue the journey of discovery that she has begun. For like anything else that uses up time, it is something that can be made habitual and the choice to do that, to get into that habit, is truly a choice that will deepen the feeling of working with the spiritual path and having some input as to how that path is walked.

We have also suggested many times the light touch, for as the seeker grows more persistent there is the need for balance so that each time that there is a rededication of self then so there should be a reacquisition of the awareness of the self as the Fool. For it is that which inspires and draws on which is to be greatly loved and greatly taken seriously, whereas the self with its many distortions and illusions indeed often plays the Fool. So the seeker is in the position either of attempting to rationalize foolishness or simply recognize, accept and love that Fool that truly desires the highest and best of truth and beauty.

There is an art to aiding the self and we are aware that the one known as B especially is seeking at this time for ways to nourish the self, to take spiritual vitamins, shall we say, so that when the spirit gets a cold there is some aid that can be turned to as a resource. The ways of the world with their specificity and their perfectly natural desire to control and shape events in order to achieve a perceived goal do not serve the seeker particularly well. The self may be seen to be an absolute that is moving through a series of illusions and is experiencing relative truth, relative realizations, and relative—we find no word for this concept in your vocabulary, but shall we say—ways of balancing nonjudgmentally that which has occurred.

Perhaps it might aid to visualize or conceptualize the spiritual path of any one entity as a thing that rides that razor edge between predestined destiny and destiny only as a reflection of free will. There is neither predestination nor free will in an ultimate sense, but rather each entity has delimited the way the spiritual journey shall occur along the lines of the lessons which the entity and its guidance or higher self have decided would be most efficacious before the process of incarnation begins. It is not that there is a route that must be taken from point A to point B. Point A is set. Point B is set in terms of being hoped for. The route from point A to point B does not stop at one way, but rather as the scroll of time and space unrolls, the wings of [destiny] turn and events roll into consciousness and back out of it as time itself rolls along within the incarnation.

No matter what choice is made at a certain crisis or cusp, wherever that has landed the seeker between the roads A and B, the seeker can be assured that there is still a way to point B. In that sense you cannot make a mistake. But in the sense of accelerating the process of learning it is well to work within the self to realize that there is a drift or tendency that can loosely be called destiny, and it is safe, we feel, to say that this destiny is a benign and helpful one, worthy of faith and trust and, to some extent, able to be made visible by the seeker who is willing to listen and feel and intuit and, truly, in each way that you can simply pay attention. For the way of the Creator is overwhelming. There are signs on every side, synchronicities and coincidences that mount up rapidly when one is paying attention.

And so perhaps this is what we would say would be the most helpful of skills to work at, the skill of cooperating with those rhythms of self as movements of spirit that seem to lift one and take one upon the way. When this kind of energy is perceived allow the self to lean into it, to practice that habit of faith and trust. We are not suggesting that it is always the best way, to be passive. This is not so. There are times when the seeker will feel [the need] to act and if that is felt, that is right. It is not passivity we are suggesting but an intelligent consideration of the catalyst which comes your way. Above all, that which nurtures and nourishes the self in its seeking and in all of its striving is remembrance of who and what one is and where one is headed, to come back into that tabernacle shared with the Creator, if only for a second, yet still, that is a powerful thing and it is always available, to turn and turn and turn again, and in all conditions know and see the Creator. This is the work of many lifetimes.

We have talked of the open heart and we are aware that many times when the heart is open it will be hurt. We encourage each to remain vulnerable to hurt, to allow the self to be made uncomfortable when it seems the appropriate situation or space to be dwelling in at that time. Many times a fear of being destroyed or being brought completely low may keep one in a protected or defensive stance. When this is necessary we encourage it, but whenever possible we do encourage that continuing willingness to offer the sacrifice of time and attention and feeling to that Creator that has created all things in love and given each iota in creation one request and that is to love.

We would at this time ask if there are any questions from the group?

B: *(Inaudible).*

We are those of Q'uo, and would not mind commenting on that, my brother. When one works with this material one has entered an arena where the ways of confusion must be carefully kept. Therefore, we can perhaps best say to you that there has been a good beginning by you in attempting to see into the architecture of the deep mind and we feel that you have some good beginning concepts. We would suggest that it would be fruitful to continue contemplating this very substantial and helpful part of the mind. The mind, the body, and the spirit are indeed greatly connected. However, we would suggest more thought upon the perception that when one of these three are activated that all are activated. There is certainly intimate relationships betwixt those three systems which feed into that unity that is the self. However, each to some extent, especially the spirit, works in its own rhythms. We would further suggest that the correspondences betwixt each matrix, potentiator and so forth be considered, for one may see the archetypical mind as a way of creating music, for instance. The various themes harmonize and in that harmonization structure [is] the ability to think about mystery, that mystery that draws each of you to this spiritual community at this time.

May we answer you further, my brother?

B: Not on that topic at this time. *(Inaudible).*

We are those of Q'uo, and, my brother, we did not take the bite. Is there a further query at this time?

(Abigail the cat meows.)

We find that the one known as Abigail has a question, and that is, "Shall this entity stop talking soon?" And to that we find we are going to give an affirmative, for the energy within this group is dancing away, even as we speak. It has been a great privilege and a blessing to be with each of you as you go about your living and your days. We are always there as a silence that you can lean into to help you with your meditation. We express great love for each of you and leave you in that love and that light that is the one infinite Creator. We are known to you as those of Q'uo. Adonai. Adonai. ✣

Sunday Meditation
April 6, 1997

Group question: We are taking pot luck today.

(Carla channeling)

Greetings in the love and in the light of the one infinite Creator. We are known to you as those of the principle of Q'uo, and we thank you for calling us to your circle. As always, we consider this a signal blessing, an opportunity to share with companions on the way whom we have come to care deeply for. It is a blessing to be here and we in turn offer blessing to each. As we share our humble opinions we ask, as always, that each seeker use her own powers of discrimination, selecting carefully those tools and resources which shall give good service and leave the rest behind.

We find within this circle this day no set query. That being the case, we shall simply share through this instrument those thoughts and musings which we bring to this time and place, this moment of shared joy.

We find that each of you has come to this day, this hour, and this meeting, hungering and thirsting for the truth, for that ineffable verity which each of you senses and feels must exist providing the solid foundation on which the cycles and wheels of the universe turn upon. And we can add to your thoughts our own hopes that this mystery that so defies the unraveling yet does have in it a ground of being that is unified and that moves from the finite to the infinite and from the time bound to the eternal. Truly, we do find an ever unfolding, ever more detailed concept of the intricate harmonies of consciousness. The illusion which you now enjoy within incarnation at once seduces and teases, and we are aware that each has pondered where truth lies, where this ground of being is.

We encourage each in this questioning. We encourage each to work upon the relationship with deity as you would any other relationship, for to engage the Creator in deep conversation is a practice most beneficial and productive of clarity. The Creator does not flinch at those who express anger. Indeed, the Creator welcomes the strong emotions, both positive and negative, that each self develops while wrestling with the angels of life and death, good and evil, the road taken and the road not taken. The more visceral and muscular that wrestling with deity, the more deeply the subconscious mind becomes alerted to the needs of the personality shell which float above the threshold of consciousness, for each is, in addition to that self that the world sees, a substantial and complex personality that bears the fruit of many, many incarnations.

In this instrument's mind we find a continuing concern for those of her spiritual family not present, and we find to some extent that same concern from each within your circle of seeking. We would address this concern by asking each to take a journey with us in the mind. Imagine the self dwelling within your ocean. The characteristics of the water create the necessity for constant motion. When one embarks upon the life of one seriously seeking the Creator, it is as though one were to climb aboard a vessel of uncertain strength and efficiency. There is no way to alight once more upon that shore which was left the day the spirit awakened to its identity, nor is there a compass to tell the sailor what direction he may be headed. Nor are there maps of this trackless deep. Each seeker is a voyager upon eternal waters. Within the life pattern there is that feeling of setting out with all of the excitement and optimism of one who has enjoyed the champagne of the bon voyage party.

Gradually, the ship sails until there is no land to be seen. The seeker finds herself completely lost. This is the precise position from which the life of faith is lived. Faith is not that which is connected to reason. The apostle known as Thomas was one who did not believe the disciples who had seen the one known as Jesus returning in resurrection glory. Thusly, Thomas the Doubter has become a character with which many may find a common identity: that desire for proof, that craving to put the finger in the wounds of wrist and foot and the great wound upon the side of the Creator's Son, so-called, into which he would wish to place a hand simply to be sure that he was not wrong in placing his faith. And the one known as Jesus blessed and welcomed Thomas the Doubter, and yet he also said, "Blessed are those who have not seen and yet believe."

There is a persistent lack of seeing, a continual lack of proof, in the worldview of the seeker, for those who move by reason, deduction and proof there are many things to control, to plan and to order. For the one who has set off upon that sea that is the path of the spiritual seeker these conveniences are forbidden. To offer proof would be to take away from the seeker the opportunity to live by faith alone.

We would suggest to each that there is a constant and marvelous opportunity within incarnation to express to the self the complete lack of knowledge and the complete lack of need for knowledge. If one has no compass, no way to navigate, and no port or any dry land of any kind to look forward to, then ultimately one becomes a citizen of the infinite and the eternal, even while in incarnation. Indeed, for some the experience of first realizing that not only is there no compass, there is no need for a compass—the reaction can be giddy and much laughter can fill the air when the seeker first sees the self in its true state; that is, in the middle of everything, directly upon all that there is. Time and space telescope and disappear for the one who has at last grasped the situation.

So much of the machinery of self stemming from the biological intellect is concerned with control—controlling the environment for survival, food, reproduction, shelter, breath and the necessities of life. There comes a continuing urge to take control, to understand to the end, to look at all the variables and to make arrangements and patterns so that the philosophy of living might be reduced to a finite code. And certainly these terrestrial patterns of organization are what create the possibility of living in an orderly and comfortable social setting. But, you see, the Earthly intellect is only a small portion of the self which thinks and expresses through your being. For every iota that dwells within incarnation expressive of self there are hundreds and thousands of iotas of self which did not and do not fit within the container of self and the limits of intellect, and yet all of these portions of self lie within the deep mind. It is simply that they are not available in words. This instrument has often mused upon the seemingly higher truth of emotion compared to the truth of intellect and logic. Each has experienced those hauntingly beautiful songs and melodies, symphonies, motets and all of the creations of sound, and each of you is as one in a great orchestral chorus. The self on dry land finds great difficulty in harmonizing the self minute by minute and day by day, whereas that portion of self which is created, that consciousness that knows no boundaries, has as its nature the ability to swim in and enjoy the infinite waters of consciousness.

We are not suggesting that each entity forbid the self to think, or to reason, or to order the chores and duties of the day. Rather, we encourage each to allow the self to become more and more open to the experience of living in two worlds at once. That life upon dry land is the life that retrieves the salary in order to feed the self, that keeps the self covered and fed and housed. Yet this self does [not] deny but rather is completed by that unmanifest and always mysterious self that is too large for words or concepts, for each of you is an immense and many-storied citizen of eternity.

As each entity opens to that dual existence and finds it easier and easier to slip between the two back and forth, each will find the experience of living more rhythmic and more able to flow. There are many, many ways to see the spiritual path. Almost always it is envisioned as a circular journey and we might even suggest that it is the journey of no movement whatsoever, for if all things are one where is there to go, for one is always within the creation, and the creation is kept like a precious gem within the heart of each which seeks the ways of love. So we encourage each to be able to flow through the water, to dive deep, to enjoy the ocean and to find ways new every day, for this is very true: that each moment is unique and each is born new through each sleeping and awakening again.

Rest, for though the boat is frail, yet it shall endure. Rest, and watch the stars.

We would transfer this contact to the one known as Jim. We thank this instrument as we leave it in love and in light. We are those of Q'uo.

(Jim channeling)

I am Q'uo, and I greet each once again in love and in light through this instrument. At this time it is our privilege to offer ourselves in the attempt to speak to any queries which those present may have for us. Is there another query at this time?

Carla: I would like to ask for a few words of inspiration for P. You were probably listening to us talk before the meeting and know that she is depressed and under stress. She would appreciate whatever you could tell her.

I am Q'uo, and am aware of your request, my sister. When we observe those of your peoples in difficulty, feeling lost and depressed and without immediate hope for the rescue, we observe those within the depths of darkness living within this illusion and without the guiding star, shall we say. Each entity who enters this illusion does so in the hope that there will be, as a fruit of this effort, a movement along the line of serving others and of realizing the Creator in all that there is. As this is an infinite journey, it is not surprising that there are for many, indeed, at some point for each, a portion of the journey which moves into those kind of difficulties that can sap the spiritual strength of even the strongest seeker of truth. In such times it is well that friends such as are gathered here today remember the entity in need and hold this entity each in his and her heart as each here has done for the one known as P.

The sending of love, whether by phone or by heart, is felt and does its work, for there is nothing in your illusion but love. The one known as P could at this time testify that this love has many disguises and there are a multitude of the forms of love that offer the challenge to the spiritual seeker. When one is challenged as is the one known as P and can find no easy or obvious remedy or way out of the difficulty, then it is that the inner strength is tested. Then it is that the earth within one's being is being plowed, shall we say, being made ready for a seeding that will, in its time, produce the flowers, the weeds, and the grasses that are being produced now by your springtime weather and the turning of this planet on its axis.

So, too, must each seeker who finds itself in travail begin to turn the inner self so that this inner self is able to see some light once again, is able to see hope on its path that the journey might proceed with more ease and with more harmony. The inner strength and the seeking for the light within are the rod and the staff which comfort the seeker as the seeker walks in that valley wherein lies many shadows and much darkness—danger it would seem, and confusion it is certain.

The one known as P is a seeker who has a strong inner compass and a great desire to know the Creator's will for it that it might do what it can to serve the Creator. When all seems to be crumbling in and the ground even gives way under the feet we encourage each seeker in this situation to remain, to continue seeking, not just for the momentary remedy, but for the part or piece of the puzzle that represents the overall plan for this entity. In each struggle and difficulty there is a pointer, a reminder, a milestone that will illumine a portion of the darkness for the eye that is ever aware, and watching and waiting. There is much to be said of the difficult times within your illusion, for these are those times in which great strides are made inwardly, metaphysically, though there is little that will show to the outer eye. The seed there planted, nourished by hope, given strength by faith, will crack the hard shell that protects the treasures inside and the seedling will send out roots, will send out leaves. There will be a growth that comes from this difficulty that will be able to provide for the seeker the sense of purpose and certainty that each feels the need for. There will be a progress where the feet will continue moving upon the path though the mind seems confused. At such times it is well to continue those routines that give one strength: the readings of inspirational material, the singing, the dancing, the poetry, all those means by which an entity can reinvent itself, nourish itself, inspire itself, and keep the faith that all is one and all is well.

We encourage the one known as P to remain strong in heart, and dedicated to service, dedicated to learning, and to remember that even in the difficult times such as it now experiences there is much to learn, and much service to be offered. It is also well that each seeker in this position remember that it does indeed have friends which are both seen and unseen who walk with it on its journey. No seeker travels alone. All tears, all bruises, all difficulties are seen and shared and treasured, in fact, by those who walk with unseen feet. The time upon this planet may seem interminably long when difficulties are encountered. We can assure each that your time is but the blinking of an eye. Be sure to notice that situation in which you find yourself and to remember that you placed yourself there for a reason. Persevere. The reason is there. It remains. The joy can be found. The purpose is at the center of one's heart and, all around, friends cheer you on. You are not alone. You shall walk again in sunshine.

Is there another query at this time?

B: I have a tendency to take your words and the words of other authorities and run with them. Everything is so subtle and related and I get blindsided often by something from another front. Would you have any suggestions for me in my confusion?

I am Q'uo, and am aware of your query, my brother. We are aware that you utilize the tools of persistence and faith to a great degree. It cannot be overemphasized to any seeker how persistent and yet how, shall we say, relaxed in that persistence it is necessary to be over the long run of the life experience, for as you have mentioned in your query, to run wholeheartedly with each idea can be wearing upon the vehicle—physical, mental and emotional—of the spiritual seeker. Thus, there is a kind of balance, as in all things, between the kind of persistence that needs to be exercised upon a continual basis and the attitude of mind that exercises this persistence without, shall we say, a wholeheartedly dedication to the outcome, an effort which is much like the one known as Jesus mentioned in the casting of the bread upon the water. That the effort is made to the best of one's ability, and then one gives oneself permission to rest, to relax, to allow the fruits of this effort to manifest that they, in their own time, may be noticed.

We know that the illusion in which each entity moves upon this planet is difficult and confusing, full of what seem to be mistakes or misturns. And yet we would suggest to each that there are, indeed, no mistakes, even being over-dedicated to an outcome, being hard on oneself, failing to forgive oneself, all of these actions and efforts designed by oneself to move one forward do, in their own way, that very thing. However, each entity, being fully apprised of free will at each moment, is free to choose how to place the feet upon the path.

When we are asked for advice as we are this day, we give advice in a way which allows each seeker the freedom to accept or refuse that which we give, for we are well aware that the only true authority for any seeker resides within that seeker. What may be appropriate at one moment may not be so at another. This is the fluid nature of the experience that you have as conscious beings in a heavy chemical illusion. When we give advice, when you seek advice from a book, from a friend, from whatever source, we are aware that that *élan vital*, that energy of life within you, will take that advice and move with it in whatever manner is appropriate. If you in the moving decide that there is something that is yet to be realized in your choice of moving then we applaud you in your second choice, in your third, and your fourth, and so forth.

We do recommend that you move with those feelings that grow from within and that you move with them until you feel another feeling; that you continue in this fashion for as long as you feel the motivation to do so. Continue to gather information. Continue to seek from every source that which it has to offer. In this way you constantly reevaluate, reposition and take yet another step in the dance. When it is said that there are no mistakes it is truly said, for the dance you do is just for you, and you do it well, no matter what you think.

We hope that we have not confused you. Is there another query?

B: No, thank you.

Is there another query at this time?

(Pause)

I am Q'uo, and as it appears that we have exhausted the queries from those present we would take this opportunity to thank each again for inviting us to join your circle this day. We are aware that the season of spring indeed fills every portion of air. We hear through this instrument the wind that moves pollen through the air, the sound of the cutting of your new spring grass, the movement of entities to and fro in your world, and we are also aware that the seasons of your world greatly affect each entity upon your planet, and we hope that with this new season of growth that each will find within its heart a new spring bursting forth with love and joy in full bloom, for in your springtime there is much of joy that can be rekindled in every heart that feels any opening at all—just a crack will do.

There is inside of each of you a seed that will send forth its roots, and stem, and leaves, and flowers. Nourish that seed, my friends. It is the seed of love, the seed of hope and faith, the seed of unity, the seed of whatever quality you feel is highest and best in your experience at this time. We feel through each here a feeling of renewal, a feeling of rededication, of purpose and place, a centering within all that is. We encourage each to be the gardener: to pull the weeds, to water the seeds, to give praise and thanksgiving to the One who provides all that is necessary for this growth and movement through this illusion.

Remember, each, that you do have friends. They are here with you. They are always with you. They are legion. At this time we shall take our leave of this group. We leave each, as always, in the love and in the light of the one infinite Creator. Adonai, my friends. Adonai.

L/L Research

L/L Research is a subsidiary of Rock Creek Research & Development Laboratories, Inc.

P.O. Box 5195
Louisville, KY 40255-0195

www.llresearch.org

Rock Creek is a non-profit corporation dedicated to discovering and sharing information which may aid in the spiritual evolution of humankind.

ABOUT THE CONTENTS OF THIS TRANSCRIPT: This telepathic channeling has been taken from transcriptions of the weekly study and meditation meetings of the Rock Creek Research & Development Laboratories and L/L Research. It is offered in the hope that it may be useful to you. As the Confederation entities always make a point of saying, please use your discrimination and judgment in assessing this material. If something rings true to you, fine. If something does not resonate, please leave it behind, for neither we nor those of the Confederation would wish to be a stumbling block for any.

CAVEAT: This transcript is being published by L/L Research in a not yet final form. It has, however, been edited and any obvious errors have been corrected. When it is in a final form, this caveat will be removed.

© 2009 L/L Research

Sunday Meditation
April 13, 1997

Group question: We would like to know what you can tell us about spiritual community, how one can be formed and how we can partake in a spiritual community.

(Carla channeling)

Greetings in the love and in the light of the one infinite Creator. We are known to you as the principle Q'uo, and we thank you and bless you for inviting us to blend our vibrations with your own in this circle of seeking. As always, we ask each of you to [realize] that we are not authorities, but, rather, travelers upon the road which you travel who treasure the opportunity to share with those who might have the interest in knowing our opinions and thoughts on those various subjects which seekers revolve about in their minds and ruminate upon in cycles throughout their incarnate and discarnate times of being.

Each of you dwells in a very heavy illusion, but each has penetrated that illusion to the extent that each has seen the illusion as illusion and love itself as a truth that is higher than the seeming truth of fact, figure and measurement. We, too, have our illusion. We, too, move towards a mystery which we cannot plumb. Our illusion is sheerer, yet the work of evolving is far slower. So, we do not feel that we are in any way your superiors, but, rather, companions, very, very honored and privileged to have the chance to speak with you, especially upon a subject which is dear to our own hearts in that we find spiritual community the infinitely appropriate way of looking at all that occurs between that spark of Creator that is one and that spark that is another.

For what is it to commune? The very first syllable of that word means "with." Further, we have the prejudice or bias that the spiritual community is the preferable form of dwelling within vehicles of light, whatever they may be, for entities come together for many, many reasons and yet in that all groups consist of the one infinite Creator and in that all entities are made of the very stuff of love, all community is, if healthy, possessed of a spiritual aspect.

Let us look together, then, at third density, the density of dramatic and pivotal choice. An entity by itself must make many choices, but that entity makes them, if completely alone, without friction; that is, with only the resistance of self against self. Although the work of self with self is often subtle and sometimes very difficult, it is not the same experience at all as that of working with other entities and choosing how to manifest to those other entities the heart of self.

So community is as the natural state of third density. The reason for the nature of the illusion as each sees it is that this configuration of awareness and perception offers the richest potential for entities to learn about love and about polarity.

Now, love itself is infinite and without polarity. It is the unlimited infinite and eternal light that is the manifestation of the love of the one infinite Creator. Each who incarnates into third density does so with the expressed purpose of interacting with the society, the community, the neighborhood into which she has been placed by birth, by circumstance, and by that personality shell which has been chosen for the most efficient use of the hoped for processing of catalyst, especially at this time as the sphere upon which you enjoy your incarnation enters into a new area of space and time, and the vibrations are moving through that birthing process. Each entity that achieves incarnation has won her place because of seniority of vibration. That is, those who have most hope of achieving harvest, that illusive fifty-one per cent service to others, have been allowed to come at this particular time.

Some of those who seek to graduate are, shall we say, natives or those who have not come from higher densities. Some of those who seek to graduate have indeed come from other densities, yet each, regardless of the history of self, is in precisely the same situation at harvest. That is, there is one and only one way to graduate into the next density or back to the home density, and that is to be of the essence that can welcome the intensity of light, the fullness of illumination which is the characteristic of higher densities.

The very word, density, is misleading, for it would somehow suggest that each succeeding density is more pallid or frail. The opposite, however, is true in that [in] each density further than the last there is a higher density of light. There is no emotion involved in moving from density to density by graduation. There is simply the ability to enjoy light. As entities reach the light at which they feel most comfortable they simply stop. If it happens to be in the fourth density then that is the future for that entity. If that entity stops on the third-density side of this division of quanta we call density, then that entity shall enjoy more of the third-density light, and work for another period upon those lessons of love and polarity which he came to ponder.

There is no particular reward for moving onward, any more than there is a reward for moving from the grade in school to the next highest grade. And yet there is tremendous emotion in the process of becoming that essence that does welcome light and that has chosen how to use, how to spend, how to offer or allow the increase of that light through radiation through the self.

So community is that necessary and natural linking of energies, often by geography alone, sometimes by family, usually by environment. Each entity deals with the family community, with the work community, with environments of those who are involved in one particular hobby or interest. It is part of the nature and character of each entity to link with other entities. It is as though those sparks of the Creator, which infinitely fly from the heart of creation out into that manifestation of experience that starts that great spiral of being moving back to its source, each have the energy and urge to link up with those of like mind, for each craves the mirror that shows the self to self.

Now let us look at spiritual community. When this instrument says the words, "spiritual community," she immediately thinks of her church, that Christian edifice of stone into which she pours, and has poured for many years, great devotion and love. And those feelings which this instrument has about that spiritual community are characteristics that each tends to seek. This instrument is not different from those who cannot find community within the traditional church in what she craves but rather in finding a way to deal with the many irregularities which have crept into that institutionalized church over many centuries of history. She moves into that environment in order to worship, in order to be taken out of the self, in order to spend time and attention upon the divine, upon the blessed, upon the sanctified and holy things which she hungers for.

These are the things that a spiritual community does offer. Looking further at the experiences of this entity, the particular church to which she goes worships together by taking a stylized and ritualized meal, by the taking of food and drink. And that magical ritual which this instrument calls Holy Eucharist or holy communion is a way of placing into the very cells of the flesh and blood of physical vehicles the essence and energy of the Creator It is said that the one known as Jesus asked his students to eat and drink together in remembrance of him. It is written that he took bread and when he had given thanks he brake it and gave it to them saying, "Take. Eat. This is my body which I give for you. Do this in remembrance of me." Then he took the cup and drank when he had given thanks and gave it to the disciples saying, "Drink all of you of this, for this is my blood, a new covenant. Do this in remembrance of me."

The center of that church is manifest only by symbol, and yet there is deity in that wafer and that sip of blessed and holy food. That service brings Christ consciousness not simply to that place but to each member of that place, and then it sends each into the world to love and serve. This is the essence of spiritual community. A spiritual community is a place that has moved through the sacrifices necessary to allow it to offer spiritual food to those who would wish to share such food. The center of a spiritual community is not the people. It is that ideal that is worshipped and loved and believed in by those who gather to remember the one infinite Creator, to spend time and attention in community with and in worship of the divine that is so hungered and thirsted for.

Upon the surface the question of what is a spiritual community, what makes a spiritual community, almost answers itself and yet as one probes more deeply one can see that the heart of community is very open-ended. Certainly, it is the nature of a functional community to find ever more ways to foster and nourish, nurture and support each other. And as one finds such a community and enters into communion with those in that community there is a strengthening and a stability which becomes possible only as entities group together and offer themselves for that which is greater than they are.

When two join together there is already a community. It is a strong and powerful community, and yet the addition of one more entity doubles the strength of that group and the next entity doubles the strength of that group until soon you have a few people and yet the strength of thousands. Or a thousand people and the strength of millions.

Now, at this particular time many who may call themselves wanderers are awakening to their spiritual identity. As the awakening occurs there arises within the seeker a great hunger to know more, to find ways to serve, to become comfortable with this state of consciousness that is so completely different from that round of work and play that is not reflected upon. The routines may be precisely the same but the viewpoint has changed. And once awakened the seeker cannot return to sleep but must live awake within the incarnation.

Each intended to remember his own nature. Each felt fully confident that she would be able to break through that veil of forgetting. And each of you has indeed become more aware. The community, as this instrument said before this contact began, has that function of being the focus point which acts as a spiritual or metaphorical anchor or point of stability or leverage. The desire to serve is greatly enhanced by those who have banded together in order to support each other in service. So the community feeds entities and at the same time entities feed into community by their participation in the activities seen and unseen, by their sharing with others that which they have thought and talked about in community. It is as though there were a net being made of golden thread, and each time one awakened wanderer links up with another and establishes a spiritual community another piece of the net is woven, and eventually that net will cover your orb like a golden seine and the Earth shall be completely surrounded in unified love. We see this occurring at this time. It is moving towards fuller manifestation rather quickly as more and more entities awaken and establish connections and share with others their own focal points or spiritual communities so that more and more entities may feel secure and stable and part of something that is higher and bigger than the everyday concerns of living, for truly these concerns are constant throughout third-density experience. It is completely up to each seeker as to how she wishes to express the self and the love of the infinite One in each person of the daily round.

At this time we feel that we have spoken enough to prompt thought, and if there is further interest we would be happy to speak further upon aspects of this interesting subject. For now we shall simply say to each that each truly serves within the community that is meeting within this dwelling place. Each embodies that communion that flows between those present. Each carries within the self the seeds of divinity that have been planted, aided by the energy of the group as it turns its heart and attention to the one infinite Creator. Each shall hope to serve greatly, and each shall be disappointed in the self, and yet each shall have done so much that is not and cannot be known, for light radiates in ways each seeker cannot know, and service is done in many cases that are not known to those offering their services.

Thusly, we encourage each to enjoy that peace that dwells in the hearts of those who do have a spiritual community, a source of support and encouragement, safety and dwelling. But there is that hunger to evolve that can only be realized in community. Each of you is a blessing to each.

We would at this time transfer the contact to the one known as Jim. We leave this instrument in love and in light. We are those of Q'uo.

(Jim channeling)

I am Q'uo, and greet each in the love and in the light through this instrument. At this time it is our privilege to offer ourselves in the attempt to speak to any queries which yet remain upon the minds of those present. Is there another query at this time?

(Tape ends.)

L/L Research

L/L Research is a subsidiary of Rock Creek Research & Development Laboratories, Inc.

P.O. Box 5195
Louisville, KY 40255-0195

www.llresearch.org

Rock Creek is a non-profit corporation dedicated to discovering and sharing information which may aid in the spiritual evolution of humankind.

ABOUT THE CONTENTS OF THIS TRANSCRIPT: This telepathic channeling has been taken from transcriptions of the weekly study and meditation meetings of the Rock Creek Research & Development Laboratories and L/L Research. It is offered in the hope that it may be useful to you. As the Confederation entities always make a point of saying, please use your discrimination and judgment in assessing this material. If something rings true to you, fine. If something does not resonate, please leave it behind, for neither we nor those of the Confederation would wish to be a stumbling block for any.

CAVEAT: This transcript is being published by L/L Research in a not yet final form. It has, however, been edited and any obvious errors have been corrected. When it is in a final form, this caveat will be removed.

© 2009 L/L Research

Sunday Meditation
April 20, 1997

Group question: Today we would like some information on the personality shell, the identity we form in this illusion. What is its purpose, and how does it work in our evolution?

(Carla channeling)

Greetings in the love and in the light of the one infinite Creator. We are those of the principle known to you as Q'uo. This day you wish to explore the thinking behind that joining betwixt the second-density body and the consciousness of self-awareness which you have called the personality shell. As always, we are delighted to share with you those thoughts that we may have upon this interesting subject, with the one request that each seeker judge our thoughts by the standards of her own personal discrimination, for this power was given unto each to know that truth that has come at the right time and at the right level, for those truths ring clearly and distinctly. If our thoughts do not ring true for you, we ask you to leave them aside and move on. If our thoughts provide a resource for you, we are most pleased. In any case, we thank each of you for calling us to you at this time, for truly it is a blessing for us to be able to serve in this manner.

As each of you relaxes upon this beautiful spring evening the surroundings of your domicile vibrate in an unending song of joy. Each tulip and daffodil, each dogwood and red bud, opens its blossom to the air and rejoices and dances and skips like a lamb. There is that bliss of full knowledge, for each flower knows the Creator and nothing but the Creator. Each animal has that same instinctual awareness, that feeling of being completely, totally at home. For these plants and animals there is no self-doubt. There is not the concern for the opinions of self or others, for there is no self-awareness. That which comes, be it the wind that blasts the flower, or the injury that ends the life of a small animal, all is accepted as perfect. If there is pain, it is endured.

Into this perfection of animal awareness something is given and something taken away in order that third density may offer its opportunities for learning, growth and the evolution of the spirit. Into the instinctual awareness and brain of that hairless great ape that is *homo sapiens* comes that startling and stunning awareness of self. No longer does the animal look into the mirror and see nothing or perhaps see another animal like itself with whom it might wish to play. Now the image that looks back from the mirror is that self of which each human is aware.

Blocked from this human being in third density is that knowledge that is beyond telling, of the perfection of one's place in the flowing dance of life and rejoicing. It is not for the human to know beyond doubt, beyond awareness, that all is perfection and that there is nothing but love and the rhythmic echoes of love answering to love. The great gift of self-awareness walks hand in hand with the startling reality of free will and places the third-density seeker into a dilemma to which there is no final answer, at least not within the incarnation.

Thusly, there is the meeting of the instinctual biological entity that is the vehicle of awareness that meets the one great original Thought that is pure and creative consciousness. This consciousness has no personality, has no limits or characteristics that can be directly described. Efforts to characterize love inevitably fail, for no matter how fulsome the praise of love or how painstakingly accurate of the observation of its passing, love itself remains that creator and destroyer that is beyond all telling and cloaked forever in mystery.

The animal within is dumb. It does not speak. Consciousness is also silent and has no words. And so consciousness has no way to express itself to that biological entity that carries you about. And so before you, as a spirit, undertook to enter into that great ordeal known as incarnation you and that self that is the heart of your self, your higher self, thought long in choosing from the full Self that exists beyond space and time those characteristics of the self so far explored that you felt would be useful in bringing you as a self-aware entity into certain configurations of mind and ability and energy that seems to you promising in that these gifts and blockages and characteristics of all kinds would color and characterize and particularize that limitless light of love so that manifestation and learning might take place.

The self that chose the personality shell was not a self that hoped for a popularly lived or easily enjoyed incarnation. Rather, it was designed to make the incarnative self uncomfortable in this or that situation so that the self was caught on the hook of this or that characteristic of personality. You did not hope for an harmonious and pleasant existence. Rather, you hoped for the self to be able to confront, examine and process those learnings about love and loving and being loved that you felt still needed more work. And in this regard and to this end you artistically and creatively crafted the combination of strong points and weak points that would bring you again and again into face-to-face meetings with the self that hopes to choose ever more purely and deeply the love of the one infinite Creator.

Further, each chose the endowments, talents and gifts that you thought would be most appropriate for sharing as blessings with others. If there is within the personality shell a marked gift for the art, for the scholarship, for the science, for working with people, and nurturing families, or for any marked talent whatsoever, this was given to you on purpose. However, not all talents are intended for the using in the way in which one automatically thinks of the use. For example: with this instrument there is the talent for the dancing, the scholarship, and other gifts that have not been used to any great extent in a direct fashion. And yet these endowments create for this entity a cluster of gifts that can be used in the movement of energy between those entities which are about the instrument and which may turn to this entity for counsel or advice. When one looks at the personality of the self, then, there is almost never a direct one-to-one relationship between one's gifts and the most obvious use of these gifts.

We find within this instrument's mind, and indeed within the culture in which you live in general, that feeling that the self is the personality shell. And yet within each seeker there is that call to live beyond the personality and beyond the personal. There is that call to live the impersonally lived life. And so the personality shell is often undervalued and underappreciated by the spiritual seeker who sees the personality simply as part of an illusion that needs to be seen beyond. We feel that this is not an opinion which gives the appropriate amount of respect to the personality shell. It is indeed full of error in that the characteristics of personality inevitably color and bias and prejudice the instreaming sense data and cause the seeker to think and to express the self in biased and imperfect ways. Especially aggravating to the seeker are those blockages brought into the incarnation that catch the seeker and take the seeker from the catbird seat of full awareness of who he is and where he is going.

But we would commend to your attention the virtue of confusion, the virtue and helpfulness of being caught, of being puzzled, of being taken out of oneself so that self is revealing self to self in a spontaneous manner. These characteristics of self provide the structure for learning within third density. They present to the seeker carefully orchestrated choices that are subjectively oriented to offer the best opportunity for polarization of consciousness. Without personality but simply with self-awareness and the choice before one the seeker will move without error into full awareness. Yet this awareness teaches nothing. It does not connect with that biological entity in a way which furthers spiritual evolution. It is the foolish personality, the ego, the self that thinks a million thoughts and does a million deeds in its heart, and that foolish entity alone that interacts with free will and finds ever deeper and truer choices that create and recreate and recreate the self ever anew.

It is these perceived imperfections, then, that make that nebulous and necessary connection between consciousness and manifestation. Therefore, we encourage you to glory in and enjoy your personality. We encourage each to appreciate the real value of confusion. As each finds herself becoming too intense, or too this, or too that, take the time to speak to self tenderly and to say, "I know that you are feeling foolish, but this is the folly that teaches." Therefore, abide in peace and allow the confusion to do its work, for from these concatenations of circumstances hitting that personality shell shall come the catalyst that gives to you the seeker all that you desire: the opportunity to intensify and accelerate the processes of spiritual evolution within the spark of the Creator that is your eternal and infinite self.

We would at this time transfer this contact to the one known as Jim. We thank this instrument and leave it in love and in light. We are those of Q'uo.

(Jim channeling)

I am Q'uo, and greet each again in love and light through this instrument. At this time we would ask if there might be further queries to which we might speak?

B: Could you clarify the phrase, *(inaudible)*?

I am Q'uo, and am aware of your query, my brother. We were speaking with that phrase and the thought about it that the entities that exist within the third-density illusion, the human beings that live upon your planetary sphere, are not those who are able to appreciate the fullness, in some cases even the existence, that has created all, the love that is the energizing force within each entity's incarnation, for within this heavy chemical illusion there is the covering and hiding of almost all of the jewels, shall we say, that the Creator has bestowed upon each of the entities that inhabit this sphere. The reason for this is, of course, the choice-making ability and responsibility that each entity within this illusion partakes of. The love that is so magnificently formed into each portion of this illusion is, though ever present, ever hidden from the entities that move in their daily round of activities and pursue the myriad of goals, some having to do with this love, others not. Yet always is this love available for inspiration, support and the connection of all things one to another.

May we answer you further, my brother?

B: No, not on that topic. I have another query about the archetype of the mind, the Fool. We never really have all the information that we need to make correct choices. Is this why it is called the Fool?

I am Q'uo, and we believe that we grasp your query. We ask that you query again if we have not satisfied you with our response. The archetype of the Fool, the choice-making entity, is the archetype which can represent [or] which places each choice within the illusion as a portion of its form or creative personality, or it can represent the entity which has been able to master the energies of mind, of body, and of spirit and which, with that mastery in hand, is now able to choose the further path of its evolution from this density. Thus, you see in some instances the Fool being numbered zero, which would indicate the continued choosing ability of the neophyte seeker. In other instances the Fool is numbered twenty-two, which would indicate the entity which has mastered the illusion and which now proceeds from this illusion to a finer illusion.

Is there a further query, my brother?

B: No. Thank you very much.

And we thank you, my brother. Is there another query at this time?

Carla: Let me follow up a little bit. So when we as people feel that we know the Creator, it is not a perfect knowing because we are still aware of our personality shell?

I am Q'uo, and am aware of your query, my sister. The feeling of knowing the Creator has in some of your cultures been refined to a greater degree so that the knowing of the Creator yet contains the existence of the personality shell which knows, so that the entity knowing the Creator knows also it remains an entity. There is the knowing of the

Creator in which the entity who experiences the Creator does not any longer, during the knowing, experience itself as apart from the Creator in any way whatsoever. Thus, this is considered by many as a higher knowing of the Creator.

Is there a further query, my sister?

Carla: During my channeling I got the impression of faith swimming around in the muddy waters of the personality and the personality somehow making faith possible. I couldn't make anything out of it to channel. Could you explain it a little more for me?

I am Q'uo, and am aware of your query, my sister. The quality of faith is much like …

(Tape ends.)

L/L Research

L/L Research is a subsidiary of Rock Creek Research & Development Laboratories, Inc.

P.O. Box 5195
Louisville, KY 40255-0195

www.llresearch.org

Rock Creek is a non-profit corporation dedicated to discovering and sharing information which may aid in the spiritual evolution of humankind.

ABOUT THE CONTENTS OF THIS TRANSCRIPT: This telepathic channeling has been taken from transcriptions of the weekly study and meditation meetings of the Rock Creek Research & Development Laboratories and L/L Research. It is offered in the hope that it may be useful to you. As the Confederation entities always make a point of saying, please use your discrimination and judgment in assessing this material. If something rings true to you, fine. If something does not resonate, please leave it behind, for neither we nor those of the Confederation would wish to be a stumbling block for any.

CAVEAT: This transcript is being published by L/L Research in a not yet final form. It has, however, been edited and any obvious errors have been corrected. When it is in a final form, this caveat will be removed.

© 2009 L/L Research

Special Meditation
April 26, 1997

Group question: The question this evening has to do with a phrase from the Ra contact which said that the price of each action of a positively oriented nature was in direct proportion to the purity of the action; and we would like some information upon this price that we seem to pay with each desire we have to be of service. And the situation that it puts us within presents us with challenges, difficulties, confusions and so forth, and these seem to be part of this price. We would like to have any information that you could give us as to the price that we pay, how we pay the price and what it is that we've bought with this price.

(Carla channeling)

We are those of the principle known to you as Q'uo. We greet you with the light, in the love and in the light of the one infinite Creator in Whose name we come to serve. It is such a pleasure and a privilege to spend this time with you, to enjoy the blending of your vibrations and the beauty that lies about your domicile, and we thank you from the bottom of our collective hearts for this privilege. It is a true service to us, for it allows us to be of service as we hope to, and this is a precious thing to us. So, we thank this instrument and, indeed, all of those who comprise this circle of seeking, for as we have said before, each of you has made sacrifices in order to be sitting in this circle at this time. And as this is your requested topic of the evening, we shall share some of our thoughts, always with the understanding that each of you shall exercise your full discriminatory dominion over your own truth and your own way, for within your heart lies that awareness that is absolute of that which is yours, and when those gems of truth come to you, you shall hear them or see them and recognize them as if remembering them. If truth does not fall upon your mind in a grateful[21] way, allow it to pass and do not be concerned that there might be a point that you have missed, because each seeker has those triggers for transformation that are subjective and unique to that one seeker. And so, each will react in a way unlike any other. We may say the same thing any number of times, and each time there is a novelty in the approach that cannot be gotten at in any of the preceding ways of stating that simple truth which, in fact, we do come to offer; and that is that all that there is is love. And all that is manifest is love, quantized and rotated and turned into light.

Each of you is as a starry messenger that has become tangled in flesh. There is that portion of yourself that is eternal and infinite. That eternal and infinite

---

[21] Carla: This is a musical usage of the word, "grateful." A particular piece of music is grateful to the voice if it is easy to sing. A lot of composers cannot write for voice well, and their music, especially Beethoven's, is considered ungrateful to the voice. A synonym is "hard to come by," for grateful does not mean "easy," but "complementary to/possible for."

being is steeped in unknowing—truly a mystery of mysteries. Each entity is as deep a mystery as the mystery of the Creator, for each, truly, is one face of the Creator. And in each manifested illusion, each entity is the face of the Creator and each face shall be unique. But to all these sparks of love sent forth upon the winds of free will there is given the knowledge of home and the desire to be moving in the direction that home lies.

In the portion of the spirit's journey through the present octave that is third density, the crux or focus of the learning that is offered in third density is The Choice. This archetype of The Choice was referred to by the one known as *(name)*. This archetypical image is of a young man stepping off into thin air—no suggestion of a bridge, no suggestion of another shore, but simply the walking off of a cliff in perfect faith. As each entity awakens to her spiritual identity, that which has awakened is in part that fool, and that which lies before that entity is a step into midair. And once that step has been made and the air has seemed to solidify about the new vantage point, a cliff will appear once more and the fool must needs step over that one as well, and the next and the next. And each time that this occurs, that seeker, that fool, has recomprised the choice.

To define this choice is a deceptively simple thing, for the choice is that either/or of morality and ethics that seems straightforward. We have called it service to self as opposed to service to others, negative as opposed to positive, following the way of attraction and control over others as opposed to following the way of radiation and the releasing to all others of that which flows through. The creation of third density gives evidence, again and again and again as one observes the natural world about one, that this is a world of duality—of light and dark, heat and cold, and so forth. Mentally, emotionally, spiritually … repeatedly the nature of this experience of incarnation causes entities to see their dilemmas in terms of clear-cut choices. When things do not seem so clear and the choice likewise is unclear, the person tuned to hear the ethical either/or is in a quandary, and often in the midst of change, a seeker shall have to simply wait with patience that is difficult to come by, simply wait until all the ripples have quieted and the horizon can once again be seen. And in those times there is no choice except the choice to trust. To trust in what—this is a subjective thing. But to trust, certainly this is the recommended action. For indeed, to deal with concern by moving the mind in ceaseless circles is a wearying thing. Trusting, upon the other hand, is a release that can be seen to be helpful.

You have asked about the price of choices made by those who wish to serve others, and have said that the one known as Ra suggested that the more purity with which the choice is made, the steeper the price will be. If you can enter into the deeper portions of your own mind, perhaps you may see the heart as a dark room, full of shadows and yet containing the Most High, the infinite One. In that darkness nothing can be discerned, and yet, this is where the learning comes. And that which is taught one in those deep, private moments has a tendency to spring forth once the seeker has gone out into the daylight world again and joins that dance of manifestation that you experience as you live within incarnation. Within that deep and dark heart, within that holy of holies, that portion of you which is beyond space and time dwells, perfect, complete, ineffably whole. It is as the buried treasure.

If one attempts to take the self that has not realized the nature of its heart, the holiness of its center, and asks it to make a choice, the entity may make a positive choice, but this entity is making a choice that has no depth of root. A little wind can blow it over, a newer idea can take its place. And so the entity that has not gone down deep, diving into the heart, may skate happily across the pond of life, skittering along the meniscus, happy as a dragonfly in the summer sun, and like the ephemerid, it shall pass, and it shall not pay a price, for it has not bought very much. To the one who has begun to discover the utter and intense purity at the heart of self, a choice that is made is made not simply upon the surface, but in profound depth, and to the extent that the purity of the heart has been penetrated in the making of a choice, this action in the metaphysical world is as that which turns on the bright light.

When entities consciously choose the service-to-others option in a difficult situation because of pure awareness of the purity of self within the heart, this takes the clay of flesh and shaves it aside until the light begins to shine through. The more deeply the entity knows his own heart, the more pure that choice can be made; and in the world of time/space, this movement of light is an energy flow that automatically triggers the attention of what this instrument has often called the loyal opposition, for there are those forces within the dualism of third, fourth, and fifth densities that appeal to entities who wish to take the path of service to self. And they hunger for the light that they may use that light for their own purposes. Attracted by this light, entities move, looking interestedly to see what they might see: Where is this light coming from? What is this entity's weak points? How can we put this light out?

There is a very wide range within which entities can experience imbalance. Indeed, we encourage seekers not so much to work upon the energy centers one at a time as to become the entity that knows its instrument, and in a state of balance allows the energy to flow freely through that instrument, making those intonations and notes that naturally flow from the rhythmic intersection of the self and the moment. To an entity of negative polarity, such activity is irresistible; and once attention is drawn, the natural course shall be that each weak point or imbalance within that energy web of self shall be offered. And this is, in a very real sense, a service, for at each point of testing, the seeker being tested has the opportunity to see the test, to see through the test, and to see that attack and defense is not necessary, but rather, that these times are the times to trust and have faith in the self and in the perceived light.

Indeed, the greater the purity of desire, the more numerous and the more telling shall be the challenges to that positive choice in a state of balance. What the natural resistance of negative thought in essence wishes to do is move entities who are radiating light off balance so that they become less than transparent, so that they become fearful and defensive and ruled by the impurity of considerations that are based upon fear. And yet, we say to you, once you are able to touch the purity within that deep, dark heart, once that light within has been perceived for but a split second, never again can that seeker truly say that she does not have faith, for she has touched the heart of the Creator; and this is a knowledge that none can remove from the seeker who once claims it.

We encourage each of you to seek within the self for that heart, to look for and to bless the purity within that has values and ideals that are completely impractical and unearthly. We encourage each to dream the highest dreams, love the deepest beauty, and know the deepest truth, and embrace, as this instrument said earlier, the deepest and most authentic passion. And if that purity calls forth the testing and the trial, we hope that each shall be able to know that the fire that burns does not burn away the heart of self but only the dross of flesh. Fear not that fire, and if that which is called the ego by your peoples loses a bit of a chip here and there, is that any great loss? For that which replaces that small self, though far more impersonal, is that which marries peace and ecstasy, quietude and joy.

May you each go forth rejoicing. This instrument kindly informs us that we are asked to shut up now, which we shall do, sparing each the traditional question and answer session in the interest of this instrument's failing energy. We thank this instrument and this circle for bringing us to you this evening, and you to us as well. And we leave you in all that there is—the love and the light of the one infinite Creator. We are those of Q'uo. Adonai. Adonai.

L/L Research

L/L Research is a subsidiary of Rock Creek Research & Development Laboratories, Inc.

P.O. Box 5195
Louisville, KY 40255-0195

www.llresearch.org

Rock Creek is a non-profit corporation dedicated to discovering and sharing information which may aid in the spiritual evolution of humankind.

ABOUT THE CONTENTS OF THIS TRANSCRIPT: This telepathic channeling has been taken from transcriptions of the weekly study and meditation meetings of the Rock Creek Research & Development Laboratories and L/L Research. It is offered in the hope that it may be useful to you. As the Confederation entities always make a point of saying, please use your discrimination and judgment in assessing this material. If something rings true to you, fine. If something does not resonate, please leave it behind, for neither we nor those of the Confederation would wish to be a stumbling block for any.

CAVEAT: This transcript is being published by L/L Research in a not yet final form. It has, however, been edited and any obvious errors have been corrected. When it is in a final form, this caveat will be removed.

© 2009 L/L Research

Sunday Meditation
May 18, 1997

Group question: Could you tell us about The Choice, how much we make consciously and how much subconsciously, what we discover as we go through our lives as we consider being of service to others. What about giving over one's identity in serving another in what are called co-dependent relationships? How does that differ from true service? What really are we doing when we make any choice?

(Carla channeling)

We are those of the principle known to you as Q'uo, and we greet each of you in the love and in the light of the one infinite Creator whom we serve. We bless and thank each for making the choice to be a part of this circle of seeking and for inviting us to share with you our humble opinions. We are most happy to share with you. It is for this reason that we are within your inner planes at this time. It is of great service to us to be allowed to speak through this and other instruments, for this is our means of being of service at this time, and you make this service possible. Thus you teach us much more than we you. As always, we ask one thing of you and that is that you discriminate carefully in listening to us and any who would seek to offer their views and thoughts, for each entity is the guardian and keeper of its own heart and soul, and each has within that ability to discriminate that ability to recognize personal truth. If we are fortunate enough to offer a thought which is a resource or a tool we are happy, but if we do not we are just as happy if you will put our thoughts down and move on, for truly we wish for each to find his and her own way, as each is as unique as a snowflake and as crystalline and as delicate.

This day you wish to consider that choice that is the hallmark of the third-density world which you now enjoy. And certainly the density is one of endless choice, but let us look first at the first choice and that was the choice of the Creator to know Itself. In choosing to know Itself the Creator flung from Itself innumerable and infinite sparks of love which coalesced into each awareness that dwells within the infinite awareness. Each of those sparks of awareness is the Creator, and yet, because the Creator chose free will in the manifesting of sparks of self, each spark is unique and has been unique since before time began. Each of you is eternal and in many ways immutable, a citizen of infinite nature, worth and value. Each one a holograph of the Creator and yet each one different.

Thus, the choice that birthed each of you was a choice to know the truth, to know the self, and as the Creator is love, so is each entity love. This is the central truth. This is that which does not change. Yet this is that which is ever wrapped in mystery. Each within this circle has come through many planes of existence, has learned a great deal, and each within this circle chose not only this incarnation now being experienced but also that cast of characters with whom each entity interacts in the family, in the close associations of friends, and all those who have significant connections with the self. There were agreements made before incarnation, most notably with the parents and those within the bonds of kinship of blood and of commonality of interest. Each difficulty, each crux that leaves one in a position of being forced to discover the self has been placed not with a hand that desires to punish but with a hand of loving self that wishes to serve ever more deeply, ever more purely.

Before incarnation it appeared to each of you that remembering who you were and why you came would be possible, indeed, might be easy. Such is the attitude of those who gaze upon a thing from the outside. With the first breath taken as an infant newborn into a strange world the veil of forgetting who you are, where you are going, dropped. And the illusion, an excellent illusion, became that which was real. And yet within each of you there was that awareness that this was not quite as it should be, that this culture, this way of being and relating and living was significantly different and substantially less harmonious than each somehow remembered deep within the self. And so was born a divine discontent within each breast, a restlessness with the surface illusion, a desire to penetrate that veil of forgetting and come to an honest and authentic realization of who each entity is. And where each is going. And why.

There is a hunger that overtakes the spirit when it has recovered a sufficient amount of that memory that cannot quite be veiled. And so each that hears these words has already made difficult choices, sacrificial choices that enable the seeking process to gain momentum and to become more valued within the life pattern.

We are aware that each is quite familiar with the choice of service to self or service to others that is the foundation choice of this particular density. In addition to this choice of service there is a component which has to do with the purity or extremity of service. We have often called this aspect of the choice polarity, for something can be chosen with a wide range of urgency, a wide spectrum of intensity of desire. There has been the puzzlement expressed in the conversation preceding our remarks concerning how one can truly be of service. The paradox is that when one is of service to others one is automatically serving the self, for that which is offered is returned a hundredfold. It seems clear that each other person is also the self, is also the Creator, and so serving others is serving self. Further, before one can be free to serve another, one must come into relationship with the self, and the process of arriving at a love and acceptance of the self may seem very selfish and egotistical.

The hallmark of spiritual issues is paradox. The answers trail off into mystery without exception. Thusly, we cannot define for you or make absolutely clear to you with any words, no matter how lucid, the whole and complete nature of choice. However, we would speak to you of the will, for this aspect of self is heavily involved in work upon the self, especially that work upon self which would best be described as indigo ray, for there is work upon the self at each level or each energy center of the being. It is appropriate and important to work at each energy level, to work with issues of survival, of relationship, of groups, to work at opening the heart, to work at open communication, and to do this work one must use the will. Yet it remains the greatest challenge of this particular illusion to find the right use of will.

In what is willed and what is desired lies the teaching, the learning, the confusion, the difficulties, all of that which comes forth from that desire or from that use of will. For the polarity which is service to self, the use of the will is never in question, for the will is that which takes charge. Whatever is decided to be desired is simply willed and the negatively-oriented entity has full sway in determining that which will come to him. To such an entity the will is sent to grasp and take. In many ways, although this sounds like plunder, service-to-self's [use of] will can be uncannily hidden, and it is not at all obvious to the service-to-others polarity when something is appropriate to desire and when it is not. All things that come into the sensing apparatus seem natural and it is only by extensive repetition that the entity begins to form a structure of priorities which listen to the incoming data and chose what to pay attention to.

This instrument, for instance, is notorious for not knowing where she is, but this is not because this instrument is not paying attention. It is simply that this instrument has chosen to prioritize some of the deeper levels of incoming data so that that which is occurring upon the surface is often left far behind by this instrument as it desires to penetrate to the heart of catalyst. This has been a progression spanning this instrument's incarnation which is well over half the century that the one known as Jim is now rejoicing at achieving. Each of you has done to some extent—some greater, some lesser—conscious work in disciplining the awareness so that the incoming data will make not only some sense but more and more a particular kind of sense.

In the parables of the one known as Jesus this entity frequently said at the end of a story, "Let him who has ears to hear, hear." And this is the quest of each seeker, to develop ears that hear ever more accurately the song of love that rushes through each moment of experience. Third density, your Earth plane, is a world of great solitude and sorrow, with each entity shut up from each other entity in ways that do not occur before this density or after it. This is a density of metaphysical darkness lit only by that pale moon of hope and faith. And yet in this dim light there lies a depth of truth that shall never be touched again, for only in this density has the Creator given Itself the luxury of not knowing. Thusly, as each experiences himself, the Creator experiences Itself in an unspoiled and untouched way, totally spontaneous and totally free, and if that entity that is you finds that heart of love that is the deepest truth, that finding is completely real for it is not at the surface of things that this truth is obvious. It is not obvious that all is one. It is not clear at all that each entity is a creature and a child of love. Indeed, it is only by blind faith that we can begin to apprehend that which we do not know and yet that which we do know, love itself.

So when the seeker comes to those moments of startling lucidity, when that knowing which is beyond unknowing lights the sky of consciousness with that fullness of light which is true self-knowledge, there is a degree of joy that cannot be attained by those who already know the score. Around this habitation we are able to see each flower and plant and tree moving rhythmically in the joy of perfect knowledge. The second-density world embraces itself without self-knowledge but with full knowledge of love. There is no doubt. There is no argument. There is no confusion in the growing of seed into bud and bud into flower, in the dying down of that which is born and in the rising again from seed. All is felt in that cyclic rhythm that is perfect, and all harmonizes, each serving each in infinite detail.

Beyond this density, the choice having been made how to serve, the veil is again lifted and each is again aware—in the way that each of you is aware of the shape of this house and the color of the paint upon the walls—that all are one. Each knows the thoughts of the other and sees the complete commonality between that and the thoughts of the self. Yes, there is a great deal more to do beyond third density, but it is finicky work, careful, time-consuming, tedious even compared to the adventure that you now are embarked upon, who live and breathe the air of the Earth world. This is then, in a real sense, your moment of glory.

And so what is the choice, precisely? Although we cannot speak precisely, although the choice is always veiled in mystery, we would point in the direction of the will which is as the verb in a sentence in which the nouns are made of faith, hope, love and charity. What is the right use of will? The one known as Jesus spoke very clearly when it said, "Not my will but Thine." For you see, the choice truly is to surrender. The choice of the Fool is to leap into mid-air, knowing absolutely nothing about what lies at the bottom of the chasm of unknowing. One chooses either to have complete faith and thus to remain calm in the midst of this sea of confusion which is the Earth world. This is not an obviously good choice. The choice to believe blindly seems quite foolish and may we say that it is foolish. Upon the surface of events such a choice as pure faith shall only rarely be obviously validated by experience and yet the energy that is released when a seeker chooses to live by faith is tremendous. It certainly flies in the face of logic. Logic dictates that one maintain control in order to better serve.

And yet the way of logic is the way of death, for service is a living and vital thing. It blows as does the wind, and to be of service to another is an art. The beginning of this art is the refraining from using the will in eagerness to serve. As you attempt to serve others, always ask the self, as this instrument said earlier to the one known as B, "What is being asked of you?" For it is in response to what is asked that one may serve another. And upon a deeper level, as events impinge upon you, a good question to ask as a touchstone is, "What does the Creator ask of you?" The answer to this can be known only from the heart, only from the intuition, for what the Creator asks is often illogical, often puzzling, even though one feels to do or not to do something. One cannot precisely explain why. But when there is a strong intuition, we recommend and encourage the will to follow that intuition.

Now, we do not suggest that you give up desiring. Indeed, we would encourage you to hone your will, to sharpen your desire, but let that will and that desire be to know the infinite One. For the basic choice of one who is, shall we say, trapped in time is how to meet each moment of that time. Do you meet this moment with your heart open and with your spirit at peace? If you cannot say that you do, then there is introspection, thinking, ruminating, meditating that might aid in achieving your clarity. There is a great art to nurturing that self which has so much within it but which needs the kindness, the acceptance, the awareness of a supportive self.

We leave you, as far as this first question is concerned, in mid-air. This is not the density of firm ground. Truly, when at last you do not mind free-falling you shall have arrived at a reasonably comfortable metaphysical stance from which to gain a somewhat more accurate view of the rhythmic beating of destiny. Blown by the winds of free will, that destiny has a surety, a sure-footedness that cannot be moved by decisions that turn you from one direction to another. You cannot go away from the right path, for those lessons that you came to explore, those lessons of how to love and how to allow being loved, are fluid and living and they can move with you wherever you go. So, in the sense of making tragic errors, we ask you to be fearless. You cannot make a mistake, metaphysically speaking, for your lesson and your destiny shall follow you wherever you are moved to go. Yet to cooperate with that defined destiny is often to allow the little world to die away that the greater self and the greater will might be presented more clearly.

We would at this time transfer this contact to the one known as Jim, thanking this instrument for its service and leaving it in love and in light. We are those of Q'uo.

(Jim channeling)

I am Q'uo, and greet each again in love and in light through this instrument. At this time it is our privilege to ask if we might speak to any further queries which remain upon the minds of those present. Is there another query at this time?

B: I just want to express my gratitude for your speaking to us at these meetings.

I am Q'uo, and, my brother, we share your sentiments, for it is in these joining together of vibrations in these circles of workings that we are able to not only be of service to you but are able to experience much of what you experience as you query us concerning your life patterns. We are most grateful to each for these opportunities.

Is there another query?

Carla: When Abigail hollers like that is she talking to you and responding to your vibrations?

I am Q'uo, and am aware of your query, my sister. We are aware of the entity known as Abigail and that this entity is, indeed, able to perceive our vibrations. In many cases this small entity finds our vibrations somewhat jarring, and, indeed, as the contact was transferred to this instrument the one known as Abigail vacated the lap [of] this entity in this working. The one known as Abigail was also responding vocally to the other second-density creatures feeding outside the window.

Is there a further query, my sister?

Carla: No.

We thank you. Is there another query at this time?

B: Is it in the application of the will towards the deeper desires that brings the lessons to an entity so that they might hone the application of the will and desire?

I am Q'uo, and am aware of your query, my brother. We would substitute for the word, "application," the word, "surrender" of the will. As the entity moves further along its path of seeking, the ability to fall freely through the experience is an ability which opens the entity's inner resources and channel, shall we say, to such an extent that the preincarnative choices are more easily accepted and danced with. The attempt to apply will and through discernment plot a practical and wise course is in itself useful more for the direction of intention and the cultivation of one's motivation than for the actual plotting of the course.

Is there another query, my brother?

B: *(In general, the query concerns just surrendering the will and going along for the ride.)* Is this correct?

I am Q'uo, and am aware of your query. In general we would agree with your summation, but would also emphasize the importance of the means of surrender—that the entity seek within the meditative, prayerful and contemplative state to open the self to such a degree that the one Creator moves through the being; that the entity surrender to the Creator, rather than to circumstances or to other entities.

Is there a further query, my brother?

B: I am still confused by "application of will" and "surrender of will." Could you elucidate?

I am Q'uo, and am aware of your query, my brother. One applies the will well when one is able to look at the experience about one, to ascertain the choices available, the opportunities presenting themselves, and much as one feeds this information into a computer and lets the work of the mind take place, then it is the balancing operation to seek in meditation the voice of the greater will. There one surrenders preconceived ideas about how the experience should be and the entity should partake. There this surrender opens the self to greater possibilities, to the greater will, to the higher self, to the one Creator, and when this has been felt at the heart of one's being, whether the choice be yes or no, to follow that choice though it may present difficulties to the mind and preconceived notions.

Is there a further query?

B: When a seeker chooses to seek the Creator are the difficulties that arise from that choice like initiatory experiences, the letting go of preconceived ideas?

I am Q'uo. Again, in general, this is correct, for the perceived difficulties [of] the nature of the experience in its entirety is the meeting of the incarnational self with destiny, and various notes in this musical score that we are calling destiny may seem discordant, disharmonious and out of place, yet when examined carefully and taken within the being as a portion of the self there can be harmony achieved and the great score of the preincarnative composer may then be completed.

Is there a further query, my brother?

S: Sometimes one has traveled a goodly distance down a certain path before one realizes that it is not the path one wishes to travel, but one has invested a certain amount of emotional energy in that path. Can you describe the need one feels to continue down the path because of this emotional investment?

I am Q'uo, and am aware of your query, my brother. The path is the path for each whether every portion is recognized or appreciated. Many times the need to change a course is more the need to clarify the present moment. Each entity will move itself upon its path in a manner which is most comfortable to that entity in the metaphysical sense, for much in the physical illusion will seem to be greatly discordant and very uncomfortable.

It is well for each to remember that no seeker travels alone, though each may feel great loneliness. It is well to remember that unseen hands—teachers, friends and companions from before time—move with each entity and offer guidance and counsel whenever sought by the seeker. It is well again for each seeker to remember that the course being traveled was chosen, that this is not the density of understanding, it is the density where little is understood, yet within this environment and these circumstances it is possible to so strengthen the will and the faith that the experience gathered is vivid and unique, pure and of great variety that would not be possible were there great understanding here. Thus, this is the treasure of this illusion. The constant need to understand what cannot be understood builds great strength of faith and will.

Is there a further query, my brother?

S: No, thank you.

I am Q'uo, and we thank you, my brother. Is there another query at this time?

R: It is very comforting to know that you are our friends.

I am Q'uo, and we indeed are your friends. We walk with you upon your journey. We consider it a great honor to do so at your invitation.

Is there a further query at this time?

(Pause)

I am Q'uo, and as it appears for the nonce [we have] exhausted the queries once again, we would once again thank each present for inviting us to join you this day. It has been a great honor to do so. We would remind each that our words are but guides and possibilities. Take those that ring true to you and leave behind those that do not. We are known to you as those of Q'uo, and we shall take our leave of this instrument and this group at this time. We leave each in the love and the light of the one infinite Creator. Adonai. Adonai. ✣

Sunday Meditation
May 25, 1997

Group question: No group question. Potluck today.

(Carla channeling)

We are those of the principle known to you as those of Q'uo. Greetings in the love and in the light of the one infinite Creator. We are most happy to have been called to your circle this day, and have enjoyed your conversation. It is beautiful to us to see those of you who have sacrificed much to be within the circle of seeking move in ways small and larger to attempt to be of service to each other as each deals with the daily diet of catalyst that is the grist for the mill of seeking experience.

We have an almost giddy sense of "What shall we talk about first?" because of your broad range of topics and the possibilities of relationships between various portions of those things which are upon your minds at this time. And yet perhaps it is best to move back to a place within the mind, within the heart, within those halls of eternity where your citizenship truly exists, to sound once again the glad bell of union and love, for beneath all of the illusions that tease and delight and frustrate mind, all—with no exceptions—are deceiving, and beyond all of the illusion and chimera there lies the One, that Thought which is love in its creative and fiery sense. Not the love of mates or friends or family, not the affection, or the *agape*, or any of the myriad of words which exist in your language, but a love that is beyond any word, a love with the power to create and to destroy. It is this stuff that you are made of, this and none other. It is the mating of this thought of love with light that has builded the entire universe. It has made all of the interpenetrating illusions of inner planes and outer planes throughout the infinite creation. It is that love of which each of you is made.

And if love can be said to have the body then that body is that spark that is without weight, without form, but most specifically is within the heart of each, in its perfection, undistorted, undilute, a perfect spark of that love which created and sent each forth to gather experience, to ripen, to become heavy with the fruit of learning and loving and being loved. How loved each of you is by this love that made you and that awaits your return. Yet at the same time you are already home, for there is that spark of perfect love within, for there is a secret tabernacle within each, that soul's shrine wherein one may lay down the sorry candles, burned to guttering, of the day's efforts, the day's emptiness, and all the concerns within the sea of confusion within which your illusion dwells.

That shrine can be forgotten. That shrine can be closed and become dusty. One waits there whose love is beyond all telling. This instrument would call this consciousness Jesus. However, the one known as Jesus would be happy for us to call this energy perfect love. But this perfect love is for you, unique to you, awaiting no one but you. Patiently. Silently. This energy, this essence of love, waits for you to put your hand upon the door, to turn the knob, and walk through, from that outer heart that sees the light of day to the inner place that only you can go. There is nothing in this holy of holies except you and the Creator and the perfection of that shared vibration that is love itself. Whatever trouble, whatever the illness of mind, emotion, body or spirit, this love wants to share, wants to embrace, desires nothing more than to tabernacle with you. There is no judgment there. There is no test to pass. There is only absolute love.

When your center of self dwells within that shrine the sea of confusion continues all about you and you swim and do may things and go many places and see many people, and yet as long as there is that awareness of perfect love you do not drown in the sea. You do not become lost of heart when relationships do not seem to be availing either with learning or with peace. We are aware that it would not be desirable in terms of incarnational learning for an entity to spend all of her time in that secret tabernacle, and we do not suggest that the life pattern be changed so that the indwelling spirit may be beheld and enjoyed full time. We are aware that none of you wishes to come into incarnation and then dwell in the shadows of that incarnation. Rather, each has an urgent and profound feeling or sense of purpose. Each of you wishes to accomplish that true vocation that each feels within has been made or prepared for each. And we feel that this is a true and authentic sense or feeling, the feeling of having a purpose that is spiritual in nature.

When the soul awakens to its spiritual identity concomitant with the gladness of knowing who one is comes the honor and responsibility involved in the feeling that there is work to do, and for each entity that work has been prepared in the sense that each seeker has gifts and talents for which there is a use. We encourage each to flow with those talents, to support the self in using those gifts that have been brought into incarnation, that have been carefully chosen by each for the outer service, for the actions and accomplishment that each may choose to offer.

However, far more important than these outer ministries or ways of being of service there is, as each is aware, the true and central service of each which is to be the self, to be that self that rings the truest and the deepest. Simple to say; difficult to do, to truly be one's self. For how can one connect with the self? Is it not more often gotten through the echo gotten back from others that each sees the self most accurately? How can one be and know that that is the best being? The values of your peoples' culture make it very odd to be thinking of how to be, for your people value fruits. The one known as Jim was saying, "I like to get things done." And all could identify completely with this sentiment.

You are in an illusion full of things and you want to see things accomplished. You want to see where you have been, yet in terms of being you cannot see where you are, or where you have been, or where you are going, for the value of being is in its unforced spontaneity. What evolves for the seeker, then, is the challenge of learning how to take away from the self extraneous material and enlarge that freedom of movement of the spirit vibrating without thought, for there is a native vibration that is as the signature of each entity. We know each spirit within this circle not by the name but by the music that each heart is singing, that complex of tones and harmonies that is each person, each spark, and each is uniquely lovely. There is no repetition. There is no possibility of boredom, listening and joining in with the songs of each person and each two people in relationship, and then each within the group creating that song of the group.

Beyond the illusion, beyond the extraneous material there lies the music that is within each that must sing and will sing and does sing. The one known as B was saying that the word "allow" was very helpful to him and we offer this word again, for each is already singing a perfect song, but this is a silent and hidden part of self and it must be allowed the room, the space and the attention of silence. It is for this reason that we often remind each of the benefits of a regular, daily period of silence. Certainly, as we hear through this instrument's ears, between the snores of her pussycat and the calls of the ravens, the silence within may not be literally silent. However, the point is to attempt at any rate the disengaging of the mind from the gears that work continually and churn out so much to consider.

It is not even important that that babble of self be stopped. What is important is that the effort be made to disregard it and to tabernacle with the infinite One and to listen, to simply listen to that silence within and then to hear the door open, and at once to feel the bliss of that presence that awaits.

We have come to a place where we feel it would be helpful for questions to be asked. And at this time would transfer this contact to the one known as Jim, thanking this instrument and leaving it in love and in light. We are those of Q'uo.

(Jim channeling)

I am Q'uo, and greet each again in love and in light through this instrument. At this time it is our privilege to offer ourselves in the attempt to speak to any further queries which may yet be upon the minds of those present. Is there another query at this time?

B: Could you explain more about what healing really is?

I am Q'uo, and am aware of your query, my brother. Indeed, the area of healing is that area which encompasses the entire incarnation, for healing of any distortion is the balancing of that distortion in such a fashion that the particles of experience are made whole, that that which has been torn is brought together, and that which has caused injury is found to be a portion of the experience which has taught a lesson that has been planned by the entity itself, either before the incarnation or as a portion of the incarnation.

The apprehension of any experience, the perception of stimuli, are all means whereby the seeker interacts with its environment, with its larger self. Thus, as one perceives in such and such a fashion one prepares the self for experience, for the perception, the apprehension, the experience of an entity is a reflection of the lenses through which the entity sees. By being biased in one fashion or another, the entity in effect throws off a portion of the balanced self so that it spins or pulls the entity into a certain mode of receptivity. There is the phrase, "preconceived ideas," that is applicable here. As one conceives a thing to be, so it becomes for that entity, and so that entity experiences that which it has conceived previously in a fashion which allows a kind of dance to occur. The entity focuses upon that which it perceives and moves with it in its experience until there is an harmonious blending of entity and experience which you would call healing.

Many times the dance between entity and experience—or to be more precise, between entity and catalyst—is what is often called a disease or a disharmonious experience, for the entity, or some portion of the entity, is thrown off its normal balance and forced by the imbalance to pay attention to the dance it is now engaged in. When this perception and this dance is accomplished mentally and emotionally then there is a reestablishing of the balance, of the harmony, of the seeker. When the perception is distorted enough—or perhaps we should say ignored enough—then it may be that catalyst is given by the mind to the body and physical ailments of one form or another ensue to further guarantee the capturing of the attention of the seeker. This kind of discomfort then focuses the attention of the seeker upon that catalyst [that] has not been well used. As catalyst is used and the dance is completed then also is that which is called healing achieved.

Healing, then, is that balancing of distortions so that that which is perceived more closely approaches love, compassion, understanding, tolerance and so forth rather than the distorted perceptions that come when love is not seen.

Is there a further query, my brother?

B: I am assuming that balance is achieved in relation to the self as well as the other self?

I am Q'uo, and am aware of your query, my brother. This is most emphatically true, for all balance must begin with the self, with other selves simply playing a role for the portion of the self that needs balance.

Is there a further query, my brother?

B: What does the one who serves as healer actually do in the healing process?

I am Q'uo, and am aware of your query, my brother. The one serving as healer provides the opportunity for the one who has sought healing to open its centers of red and violet ray that hold in place the current level of awareness in its expression in the entity's incarnation, so that that which has been held in place may for this moment be released, and if it be appropriate for the one to be healed then this entity at that time will release the old manner of being and will accept a new manner or attitude of being, this then being the healing process.

Is there a further query, my brother?

B: At the deeper levels is healing simply the realization of the perfection of the entity?

I am Q'uo, and am aware of your query, my brother. This is indeed so, for each entity is a portion of the one Creator, whole and perfect, with the free will to choose the path of its seeking. The third-density portion of this experience, and, indeed, the higher densities as well to a lesser extent, is a process whereby an entity has forgotten a portion of its perfection, has forgotten its unity with all creation, has forgotten these foundation stones of being in order that it might provide the Creator with experience that will enable It to know Itself. Such experience cannot be gained when each portion of the Creator knows itself to be the Creator, whole and perfect. Thus, it is what you may call a great service and sacrifice for an entity to engage in the forgetting in order to voyage forth into the creation with the desire to serve the Creator.

Is there another query, my brother?

B: As you answer these questions I feel a tightening in my lower energy centers. Does this affect the contact in any way?

I am Q'uo, and am aware of your query, my brother. The impact is to intensify seeking, and thus aids in the overall experience of each in the circle of seeking. The manner and reasons for this action and occurrence within the energy centers described we must leave to your own discrimination.

Is there another query, my brother?

B: No. Thank you very much.

Is there another query at this time?

Carla: What is the best way of thinking about people's emotional pain? I have trigger points in my body that are very painful but it feels good to release it by pushing on it. Do people have such trigger points to release emotional pain? How to handle it?

I am Q'uo, and am aware of your query, my sister. The points of pain that trigger the emotional response are those areas that may be seen both physically and metaphysically as a knotting or tying into knots of portions of the physical and metaphysical vehicles so that when one is able to find such a point one may focus the attention upon the untying or releasing of pain.

In this experience lies an entire field of discovery, for each entity has woven into the life pattern a number of these points which may then lead to a greater and greater understanding of the nature of the entity, leading eventually to the fully experienced presence of the one infinite Creator, many steps along this path.

Is there a further query, my sister?

Carla: Do you have any suggestions how a listener like myself can support this process?

I am Q'uo, and am aware of your query, my sister. To listen with the compassionate ear, accepting that which is heard without judgment, is the most nurturing attitude that one may assume in such a relationship of entities. The answers to the puzzle, the untangling of the pain, is a process which can only be accomplished by an entity for itself in the ultimate sense. Other entities such as yourself may provide the listening ear, the compassionate heart, and occasionally the insight or wisdom to direct the entity where one's intuition discerns that motion and movement may take place profitably, shall we say. It is the seeker itself that must engage the listener, that must engage the self, that must search relentlessly for the clues in this untangling process. It is this experience of untangling that which has been tied and fused together that provides the means whereby the entity will eventually find the Creator within, and the Creator within will come to know Itself more fully because of the experience of the seeker.

Is there a further query, my sister?

Carla: Just one more. You have talked about untangling, but you have not talked about cutting the knot out like a mother will often do with a child's hair that is tangled beyond untangling. You can't just cut it out, can you?

I am Q'uo, and am aware of your query, my sister, and would agree wholeheartedly, for each portion of the knot is a portion of the self and of the one Creator. If the surgery is attempted, another knot will grow.

Is there a further query, my sister?

Carla: No. Thank you.

I am Q'uo, and we thank you again, my sister.

(Tape ends.)

L/L Research

L/L Research is a subsidiary of Rock Creek Research & Development Laboratories, Inc.

P.O. Box 5195
Louisville, KY 40255-0195

www.llresearch.org

Rock Creek is a non-profit corporation dedicated to discovering and sharing information which may aid in the spiritual evolution of humankind.

ABOUT THE CONTENTS OF THIS TRANSCRIPT: This telepathic channeling has been taken from transcriptions of the weekly study and meditation meetings of the Rock Creek Research & Development Laboratories and L/L Research. It is offered in the hope that it may be useful to you. As the Confederation entities always make a point of saying, please use your discrimination and judgment in assessing this material. If something rings true to you, fine. If something does not resonate, please leave it behind, for neither we nor those of the Confederation would wish to be a stumbling block for any.

CAVEAT: This transcript is being published by L/L Research in a not yet final form. It has, however, been edited and any obvious errors have been corrected. When it is in a final form, this caveat will be removed.

© 2009 L/L Research

Special Meditation
August 3, 1997

(Carla channeling)

We are those of the principle known to you as Q'uo, and we greet each of you in the love and the light of the one infinite Creator. May we thank each who sits within this circle of seeking at this time. We are aware of the choices and the sacrifices each has made in order to be a part of this circle, and we offer our thanks and our blessings to each for all that they bring to the honest search for the deeper truth.

We are honored and privileged to share our thoughts and ask only that each of you listens with the ear that hears that which is truth for you. Those thoughts which do not ring true to you we ask that you leave behind without any thought, for when your truth comes to you, there is a special resonance which your discriminatory powers will offer to you. Use that discrimination not only with regard to that which we might share from our humble experiences but also *(inaudible)*, for that power of discrimination which each has is [knowledge], and its impulses are worthy that *(inaudible)*.

We find the group energy most pleasant and thank each again for allowing us to be a part of this session of working. We ask ourselves what we would wish to offer before moving to questions, and we find we have very little to say that has not been said by the one known as Carla and others within this circle. Our basic message is always the same. It is a simple message, too simple for most to believe or to use. However, it is what we have to offer, and that is that all that there is is love, not *(inaudible)*, words describing romance, not a [pale] word describing friendship, nor any of the ways that the word love has been used, for the love in which we come is the Logos, that one original Thought from which all else has *(inaudible)*.

Using free will, the Logos chose to create the manifested illusions which you now are in the midst of enjoying. As you dance through these illusions, we simply ask you to remember that each is love, each is a creature of that love which creates and destroys. The love within each entity's energy nexus is as are all things within your illusion, quite *(inaudible)*. If a seeker attempts to offer love from the self, that seeker shall soon run dry of love and be left in the emotional [precincts] of exhaustion and irritation. However, each has the ability to so clear away the daily clutter that the interior can become calm and silent, and, within this hollowed out space within, there can flow through the seeker an infinite love.

We suggest to each the effort to remember who you are, to remember why you came to this difficult illusion. What was important enough to pull you into the great illusion of the Earth plane? As far as we ourselves know, that reason in each case has been the wish, the genuine wish to serve the infinite One.

Each has worked hard to gain the right to incarnate at this especially critical time within your present cycle of learning. Each was able to come here because of the seniority of vibration of each, that is there being fewer physical vehicles than souls who wish to use them. The vehicles have been given to those whose vibrations more nearly accommodate the fourth-density love and light of the one infinite Creator.

Each of you, then, is either here as a wanderer from a higher density or here because you have the ability to graduate within this present incarnative experience. We find there are both wanderers and what we might conveniently, if inaccurately, call Earth natives within this particular circle. Know that each of you, whether wanderer or Earth native, is completely and equally beholden to that light [that] awaits at the end of your present incarnation, for the steps of light that each shall walk are one in the same for all.

Even if an entity has *(inaudible)* into the third-density experience from fourth density or fifth density, yet still, through incarnation, those entities have become Earth natives in the respect that they must enter those steps of life carrying each and every experience, balanced and unbalanced, which have occurred within the present Earth density incarnation. In other words, wanderers can get caught in what this instrument often calls a karmic situation.

So we suggest and encourage each to take the time daily to center the self within the heart, to spend that moment of knowing that you are loved and that you can channel infinite love to a world that is starving for that vibration that is unconditional love; for this you came into this incarnation. Whatever your manifested excellences and achievements, they shall always fall far short of the service that you are doing by being who you are and by meeting the moment with the maximum amount of love which you may find yourself able to open to within your heart.

We would at this time ask for the first question.

Questioner: What is the meaning and purpose of reincarnation?

We are those of Q'uo, and, my brother, we are aware of your query. The concept of reincarnation has at its core the assumption that entities continue before and after and during each incarnative experience not as those bounded by time and space but as those bounded by eternity and infinity. These arrangements of densities and the repetitive lifetimes within those densities have been developed from creation to creation as each sub-logos, that being one of your suns, has taken the basic offering of the previous creation, those densities that have been developed so far, and offer in each case a slightly different way of approaching the matter of learning.

The reason for reincarnation is that previous octaves of creation gradually discover the need for periods of learning followed by periods of rest, recuperation, healing and planning. The goal of the entity throughout all incarnations remains singular, that being the effort to more and more approximate the vibratory complex of love itself, for each of you has within you that perfect and unconditional love that created all that there is.

It is a matter of the untaught self being as the rock from which the elephant is carved. In each incarnation, the seeker chips away at that which is not an elephant. Imagine how many strokes of the tools of sculpting it takes to create—we correct this instrument—or, shall we say, recover the articulated statue. So each of you gazes at the self before incarnation, ripples the pages of previous incarnative experiences and comes to conclusions concerning what facet of love, loving and being loved needs the most study, for each entity is unique, each entity has its own path.

Thusly, each of you in the present incarnation has a plan, has made sure that there are ways for you to be presented with the circumstances in which you may choose to enlarge your ability to give and to receive unconditional love. There are many angles to coming to this realization of love itself and so each of you will find at times that there are few to talk to about your particular task. Nevertheless, trust your inner guidance and the perseverance in following that guidance, for this is the precious opportunity. This is, as this instrument has said previously, the opportunity to offer love by faith alone, knowing nothing, sensing everything.

The more that you may find yourself able to release attachment to any *(inaudible)* and well in love, the more you are able to cooperate with that destiny which you have set [up] for yourself. Mind you, we do not suggest that you can learn more by giving up more. We do not wish to suggest that you must go begging with a bowl in order to gain understanding. Rather, we simply suggest that each will have impulses and intuitions and feelings of rightness that are trustable, and so we encourage each to have faith in the destiny and in the self that can fulfill that destiny that has been set up. In every case, there shall be the confusion and suffering that comes because there is a forgetting of the scheme of oneness and *(inaudible)*, a forgetting of true nature. As one takes on the curtain of flesh, one shuts out the knowledge of unconditional love and [unity]. Nevertheless, that unity lies within you, so we encourage each to visit that heart within that is the sanctum within which your work may be done.

May we answer you further, my brother?

Questioner: Thank you for your response.

We thank you, my brother. Is there another question at this time?

Questioner: I am curious as to why this group of people is assembled at this place at this time.

We are those of Q'uo, and grasp your query. Ah, my brother, what a delightful question! Why, indeed, is each of you here? What have you sacrificed, what have you done, what have you failed to do in order to be able to arrive at this remote and unlikely destination? Within each, there is the knowledge, there is that recognition, within each, there is the ability to sense those meetings with entities with whom one has work to do in service to the light. Within each is the heart that responds to the benefits and the blessings of companions along the way. Upon each head rests a crown, and it has thorns. Upon each shoulder, there is a burden and a harness to pull that burden [that is his], but, if each pulls together, the load is shared, and though the crowns may prick a bit, there is so much blessing in companionship that the duties and the labors of the light are glad and merry.

May we answer you further, my brother?

Questioner: [If you wish.] It was a very beautifully put answer. I do understand.

[Very well, my brother]. At this time, we would transfer this contact to the one known as Jim. We are those of Q'uo.

(Jim channeling)

I am Q'uo, and greet each again in love and in light through this instrument. We would ask if there would be another query at this time?

Questioner: Yes. Once we attain and realize our inner unconditional love, what then should we seek?

I am Q'uo, and am aware of your query, my brother. The great quest for this "pearl of great price" is that quest which, for most, encompasses the entire life, for to open the heart in unconditional love to those about one is a task difficult enough that it eludes and confuses most. For it is far, far too easy and tempting to take offense, to give offense, to be confused, and to move through the incarnation on unsteady metaphysical feet. However, when one has been privileged to taste that unconditional love moving to and from one's own heart, then the blessings of this experience tend to open for one the next step and the next and the next so that the opportunity to share this love is ever present.

This love has a power unto itself that is like no other. It draws to one who expresses it those experiences and those entities which are in need of the service of unconditional love. Worry not, my brother, about what you shall do, for it is set before you, and it shall be yours.

Is there another query, my brother?

Questioner: That's fine, thank you.

I am Q'uo. Again, we thank you, my brother. Is there another query at this time?

Questioner: Yeah, I'd like to know if there's a relationship between what we call spirit and what we call consciousness.

I am Q'uo. Indeed, my brother, there is a most close relationship between these concepts. Each entity here and all entities, indeed, are those portions of the one Creator that have been sent forth much like explorers, adventurers into the great unknown of creation to discover the relationship between the self and the creation and the Creator, to discover that these are all one. Each portion, then, has a need for the various vehicles and accoutrements of each density or level of the creation.

Within this third-density illusion, there is the necessity of the physical vehicle so that the spirit that is whole and perfect within each may have a means by which to experience that which this illusion offers concomitant with this physical vehicle and preceding and *(inaudible)* is the consciousness, the identity of each entity. The spirit, then, through the use of the mind, the consciousness, utilizes the physical vehicle and most particularly the energy centers or chakras of this physical vehicle which move upwards from the base to the crown located within the physical brain in order to form the incarnational patterns that each will travel in order to discover the Creator within and in order to give that Creator the experience of the self as a means for the Creator to know Itself.

Thus, the consciousness that each possesses is the dynamic rules by which each may co-create the illusion in which you move, that each may co-create the experience of giving and receiving love. These experiences are many, through many incarnations and many densities, for this creation is rich and varied and offers to each seeker the full reach of the one infinite Creator.

Is there a further query, my brother?

Questioner: So, is it that spirit and consciousness are one and the same thing, or are they closely related, or does one create the other, or what?

I am Q'uo, and am aware of your query, my brother. The spirit of each entity, the soul identity, if you will, is the core concept with which all begin. From this core concept, then, comes the creation of the consciousness that shall inhabit various physical vehicles, both the vehicles and the consciousness being the tools of the spirit or soul's identity.

Is there a further query, my brother?

Questioner: No, you clarified it for me, thank you.

I am Q'uo, and we thank you, my brother. Is there another query at this time?

Questioner: Who is Q'uo?

I am Q'uo, and am aware of your query, and we congratulate you on being far quicker than either this instrument or the one known as Carla in asking this query, for those entities took a great deal of time before remembering that there is a meaning to this title, this name that we have chosen for their benefit. We are a principle that has been created to maintain a stepped-down contact between those of Ra and this group. The ones known as Latwii are also a portion of this principle and are also students of the ones known as Ra and offer to this group a means by which there is the possibility of communication upon the many concerns of the incarnational experience.

Is there a further query, my brother?

Questioner: The word, principle, is unclear. Could you attempt another description?

I am Q'uo, and am aware of your query, my brother. Those of Latwii, being also students of those of Ra, serve as an intermediary, shall we say, a kind of relay so that the entities known as Ra may blend their vibrations in some degree with those of Latwii and continue the communication through this group.

Is there a further query, my brother?

Questioner: Then, who is Ra?

I am Q'uo, and am aware of your query. Those of Ra are the social memory complex or planetary consciousness of a group of entities formerly residing upon the planet known in your terminology as Venus who have for a great portion of the history of this planet attempted to teach the Law of One, of singularity, of unity to those upon this planet who have sought this information. There has been success in some cases and some lack of ability to communicate in others, yet they persist to serve the One in each.

Is there a further query, my brother?

Questioner: Not at this time.

I am Q'uo, and we thank you.

Questioner: Thank you.

Is there another query at this time?

Questioner: Yes, is our species from different planets? Is there an indigenous Earth species, and are there other species that in ancient times may have interbred with our species on Earth, and is mankind from diverse locations in the solar system or even farther?

I am Q'uo, and am aware of your query, my brother. The population of this planetary sphere is, indeed, from many places located throughout this galaxy. The planet itself has generated its own population as well from its own first and second-density vibratory *(inaudible)*. The number of other sources is sixteen, as other third-density planets have reached the culmination of their seventy-five thousand year third-density cycles and found a portion of the population unpolarized and therefore unable to proceed to fourth density. Thus, these planets have contributed to the population needing further polarization to this planetary sphere, some entering sooner than others and, as you have mentioned, some experiencing the mating or interbreeding with what you would call extraterrestrial sources in order to work with the genetic make-up hoping to aid in the ability to polarize in either the positive or in the negative sense so that the evolutionary process for each may continue beyond this third-density illusion.

Is there a further query, my brother?

Questioner: Well, just historically, are there any important points in history when these beings from other locations have intervened that we should perhaps investigate or be aware of?

I am Q'uo, and am aware of your query. We find this information is relatively harmless and unimportant, thus, we give it without recommendation that study is necessary. At the beginning of this seventy-five thousand year cycle there was the transfer by Confederation entities of the population of the planetary sphere known to you as Mars to this planetary sphere as it was beginning its third-density illusion. The entities upon the planet known to you as Mars had engaged in bellicose activities to the extent of rendering their planetary sphere inhospitable to third-density life-forms. In addition, there has been and continues to be a transfer of entities form the planet known by some within this solar system as Maldek to this third-density illusion in order that these entities, having destroyed their planetary sphere through warfare, might also begin a series of *(inaudible)* restitutions and continue their evolutionary journey through the third density within this planetary sphere.

Is there a further query, my brother?

Questioner: That is wonderful. I thank you.

I am Q'uo, and we thank you, my brother. Is there another query?

Questioner: I have a question about the bellicose activities. Is there a purpose and a need for bellicose activities? Do the higher powers need a group of people to try to destroy the planet in order to enhance spiritual growth on the part of certain people, or is it a test of the human species to try to protect the planet against these bellicose-wanting people?

I am Q'uo, and am aware of your query. It is not so much that the bellicose activity is needed for spiritual advancement as it is the case that entities of higher densities need to be of service to those who follow them upon the great evolutionary journey in order to continue their own evolution, for the process of service to others for the positive polarity posits the need to be of such service in order to continue the process of polarization in consciousness and the evolution of the entity. The activity of the bellicose nature is that which proceeded within this solar system …

(Side one of tape ends.)

(Jim channeling)

Is there another query, my brother?

Questioner: If someone is a victim of bellicose activity, does that retard their spiritual growth?

I am Q'uo, and am aware of your query, my brother. We would look first at the term, "victim," and suggest that each entity in every situation has chosen at some level of his being to participate in the experience whatever its nature, for all experience is of the one Creator, and all experience teaches some portion of love, light or power that is in relation to the one Creator.

The second point which we would investigate is the term, "retard." We would suggest that some learn [more] than others, as in all studies and in all students. However, all shall learn the lessons of love, for there is as much time as is needed for each entity to proceed through this illusion at whatever pace is comfortable to that entity, for indeed each entity partakes within an infinite creation and will find those lessons most pertinent to it at its own pace.

Is there a further query, my brother?

Questioner: Not at this time. I thank you very much for answering those questions.

I am Q'uo. We thank you, my brother. Is there another query at this time?

Questioner: Is the Earth soon to [birth] into fourth density and the people upon it to ascend to fourth-density vibration state?

I am Q'uo, and am aware of your query, my sister. This planetary sphere has entered the fourth-density vibration approximately fifty of your years ago and continues to move into this green-ray vibration at a steady rate. This planetary sphere is indeed to become the home planet to fourth-density positive entities within the near future with some aid from elsewhere.

Is there a further query, my sister?

Questioner: Are we soon to go into the photon belt *(inaudible)* to transition us to fifth density by 2012?

I am Q'uo, and am aware of your query, my sister. Though some students do indeed learn quickly, we find that it shall take a great span of time longer than the figure which you have named in order for this planet to enter into the fifth density of wisdom. Indeed, there is within this planet the fifth, the sixth, and the seventh densities in potentiation. However, the fourth density is one which spans a great portion of your time, and those lessons await the fourth-density population.

Is there a further query, my sister?

Questioner: Thank you, no.

I am Q'uo, and we thank you. Is there another query at this time?

Questioner: I have one. Is Ra in any way associated with ancestry of the people we know as Maya?

I am Q'uo, and am aware of your query, my brother. We find that those of Ra have had an influence upon these entities. It is one which is telepathic and information giving in nature, inspirational, shall we say.

Is there a further query, my brother?

Questioner: Who is on the outer planets?

I am Q'uo, and am aware of your query, my brother. We are assuming that you are referring to the outer planets of this *(inaudible)* solar system.

Questioner: Correct.

And it is our view that there is a population of entities from elsewhere who are utilizing these planetary spheres as kind of bases, for at the present time there is no second or third-density population which inhabits these particular planets.

Is there a further query, my brother?

Questioner: No, thank you.

I am Q'uo, and we thank you, my brother. Is there another query at this time?

Questioner: I want to ask one question. Are there any techniques, physical or spiritual techniques, that we can use to help stimulate our awareness of reality and the truth and help us to grow in our quest toward the goal that we should be directed in and assurance of which way we should, what our ultimate goal of becoming loving beings is, things that we can use, tools that we can use to help ourselves?

I am Q'uo, and am aware of your query, my brother. We always recommend one great tool for each seeker of truth, for it has shown its value to us throughout our experience in the processing of experience and the learning of the ways of love and wisdom, and this tool is that of meditation. Retire within, my friends, to that quiet room in which you go to be in communion with the one Creator. Shut there the door and on a diurnal period each day retire there to listen with the heart, with the being to the voice of the One.

When you have found this peaceful place within your heart, look then to the daily round of activities which has preceded your meditative time. Look there to any injury, difficulty, joy, learning, inspiration and so forth that has left its mark upon your mind. Look to those difficult times, re-experience in there, see as much as you can how they came about, the part you played, how you could re-script that situation, how you might heal that which was injured, how you may unify that which was broken, how you may clarify that which was confused.

Resolve in this place and at that time to take whatever steps you can to do these things that will restore love to your heart and to the heart of any others about you. Make this a portion of your daily round of activities, for, during most of your days, you are active: you think, you do, you speak. There needs be a balance, a time during which all of this activity and the possibility of learning that depends therefrom needs be seated within your being that it might be used for further learning or growth into love and into the unity with those about you.

To meditate each day for a short period is a simple thing to do, yet it is a means by which you may reconnect yourself, your consciousness to the infinite Creator, to receive the eternal, life-giving waters that nourish one's very soul. Look there, my brother, for love and share this love then with those about you.

Is there a further query, my brother?

Questioner: I do have one more question. I thank you for that wonderful answer. The other question I have is, are there beings out there that will try to take the place of the one true infinite Creator God and try to misrepresent the true God during these meditations, that we have to be aware of and watch out for?

I am Q'uo, and am aware of your query, my brother. Indeed, those entities who have chosen the service-to-self path as the means by which they shall move beyond the third-density illusion are entities which, by the nature of the path chosen, attain further progress upon this path by controlling the power of others.

This third-density sphere has a population that nears its graduation and which seeks in many, many ways to grasp the nature of this process. For those who have engaged themselves in the process of spiritual seeking in general and in the channeling or receiving of channeled information in particular, there must needs be taken those steps of engaging one's discrimination in order to determine those who serve others and those who serve themselves, for those who are upon the negative path, the path which tends to absorb the light rather than radiate it to others, are most desirous of replacing the positive efforts of their brothers and sisters who serve the light.

Thus, we recommend to each the engaging of the discriminatory powers so that within your own being you search for that feeling of lightness or its lack when appraising any catalyst which comes your way. For those who serve as instruments or channels, it is most necessary to find a means whereby any entity wishing to channel information through it might be challenged in whatever concept the instrument would live and die for so that those who come to it and wish to speak through it might be filtered, and only those who serve others and radiate the light of the one Creator to all may be allowed voice through any instrument.

Is there a further query, my brother?

Questioner: You're saying that when we meditate within ourselves in these quiet times that you spoke of before, that, if we can discern that the spirit is right, we know that we're talking to the correct person? Is that correct?

I am Q'uo, and am aware of your query, my brother. There are two aspects of seeking with which you deal. The first is the seeking, within your meditative time, of the one Creator. These times are your sacred, spiritual journey and are far, far less likely to be encroached upon by those of negative polarity than those times during which an entity would seek to be an instrument and to channel from other entities information, inspiration and so forth.

When one seeks to be an instrument of that nature, it is most necessary to have a means of challenging spirits. For one who does not wish to serve in this capacity and merely wishes to seek within the meditative state, there is not the necessity for the challenge and for the protection as there is for an entity who does wish to serve as an instrument. For one who does not wish to be such an instrument, it is well, however, to engage the powers of discrimination so that when one hears information, reads information, speaks with other entities, that always the discrimination is used to determine that which is of value and that which is not to the entity's own spiritual *(inaudible)*.

Is there a further query, my brother?

Questioner: I think that answers my question. Thank you very much.

I am Q'uo, and we thank you, my brother. Is there another query at this time.

Questioner: I have a question I'd like to pose on behalf of a sister of mine who's shy. Does there exist a spiritual form of virus which influences human behavior?

I am Q'uo, and am aware of your query, my brother. We would need more definition of that which you have described as a spiritual virus, for there are many interactions between the population of this planetary sphere and those from elsewhere of the negative polarity that could be described as a virus or means of infection.

Questioner: A virus in terms like a biological virus causes damage to our physical structure. This would be a virus that would cause damage to the spiritual structure.

I am Q'uo, and we feel that we more fully grasp your query and would respond by suggesting that, to our knowledge, there is not such a virus, for the spirit of each entity is whole and perfect and resides in complete unity with the one Creator at all times.

May we answer any further questions, my brother?

Questioner: Can you clarify your definition of the [word] "spirit"?

I am Q'uo, and am aware of your query, my brother. We call spirit that individuated portion of the one Creator that has chosen to take form within the physical universe in order to proceed upon the great evolutionary journey of seeking and knowing the one Creator.

May we speak further, my brother?

Questioner: Yes.

I am Q'uo. We do not mean to confuse. We meant to ask if you have a further query.

Questioner: No, not at this time. Thank you.

I am Q'uo. We thank you, my brother. Is there another query at this time?

Questioner: I have a question. What are the essential foods that are ideal for our bodies and then, in turn, our minds and spirits, and what effect does having artificial pesticides and other things in our foods have on our spiritual growth and our spiritual being, and is meat intended by the infinite Creator to be eaten by people?

I am Q'uo, and am aware of your query, my brother. It is intended by the infinite Creator that each entity have—we correct this instrument—has an exercised free will. Thus, each entity is free to do as it will. As far as the foodstuffs which may be ingested to the benefit of the physical vehicle, we are aware that many within this circle of seeking are aware of those food stuffs. To be brief, we would suggest the virtue of the grains, the vegetables, the fruits, the, what we shall call, secondary animal products such as your milk, your cheese, and so forth, the preserved animal muscle itself, to be utilized upon one's own discretion in the minimal quantities and of the highest level of quality, shall we say. The use of your chemical additives is that which is not recommended, for the intensity of their chemical nature often produces detrimental results upon various portions of your physical vehicle.

Is there a further query, my brother?

Questioner: Yeah, and does that detrimental effect on our physical vehicle, in turn, affect our spiritual consciousness and awareness and our spiritual vehicle?

I am Q'uo, and am aware of your query, my brother. We find, rather, the cause and effect relationship to be reversed. That is, that the entity's ability to express the nature of his spirit is that which determines the kind of foodstuffs that are utilized in this incarnation.

Is there a final query at this time?

Questioner: I understand, and I appreciate your answer, thank you.

I am Q'uo, and again we thank you. Is there a final query?

Questioner: Third density has a seventy-five thousand-year cycle, approximately. What is the cycle in fourth density?

I am Q'uo, and am aware of your query, my sister. The third-density experience is by far the briefest experience in the evolution through the seven densities of this particular octave of experience. We speak of octaves with the understanding that the total unification of all portions of the one creation at the end of seventh density completes the octave. The fourth density experience is the second-shortest experience, being thirty million of your years.

At this time, we would once again wish to thank each entity present for allowing us to speak with you and to join you in your circle of seeking this *(inaudible)*. It is a great privilege for us to be able to do so, and we look forward, as you would say, to each opportunity.

We are those of Q'uo and hope that we have been able to be of some small service to each present. Again, we recommend that each take only those words and thoughts which ring of truth to you, leaving behind all others that we have spoken that do not ring of this truth. We are those of Q'uo and would at this time take our leave of this group and this instrument. We leave each, as always, in the love and in the light of the one infinite Creator. Adonai, my friends. Adonai. ☙

L/L Research

L/L Research is a subsidiary of Rock Creek Research & Development Laboratories, Inc.

P.O. Box 5195
Louisville, KY 40255-0195

www.llresearch.org

Rock Creek is a non-profit corporation dedicated to discovering and sharing information which may aid in the spiritual evolution of humankind.

ABOUT THE CONTENTS OF THIS TRANSCRIPT: This telepathic channeling has been taken from transcriptions of the weekly study and meditation meetings of the Rock Creek Research & Development Laboratories and L/L Research. It is offered in the hope that it may be useful to you. As the Confederation entities always make a point of saying, please use your discrimination and judgment in assessing this material. If something rings true to you, fine. If something does not resonate, please leave it behind, for neither we nor those of the Confederation would wish to be a stumbling block for any.

CAVEAT: This transcript is being published by L/L Research in a not yet final form. It has, however, been edited and any obvious errors have been corrected. When it is in a final form, this caveat will be removed.

© 2009 L/L Research

Wednesday Meditation
November 19, 1997

Group question: The question this evening has to do with individual or group efforts to make energy or technological advances available for humanity. The Confederation of Planets had this problem in pre-World War Two when they were giving information to the Manhattan Project scientists who then developed the bomb. Is humanity ready for further technological such as free energy, or if we wish to be of service to … *(inaudible)*.

(Carla channeling)

We are those of Q'uo, and we apologize for our premature beginning. We were saying how much of a privilege we consider it to be asked to speak with you and share our thoughts. As always, we would ask that you pick and choose among these thoughts, taking those which are helpful to you and leaving the rest behind. For we have no illusion that our own concepts of the truth are any final word; rather we are happy to share our opinions with those who have discrimination. And each does indeed have that discrimination that recognizes that which is one's own personal truth.

The question this evening concerns the application of gifts and we would, as we often do, wish to begin by placing the concept of gifts in some kind of context.

When each incarnate being gazed upon the incarnation to come, each selected from the infinite self those gifts and quirks of being, thought and attitude which would provide the resources and tools to prosecute various purposes for which the incarnation was chosen. Often, these eccentricities and biases do not seem in the life experience to have any direct application. However, the indirect use of gifts is frequently an enlarged group of service. Secondly, we would encourage the concept of the personality shell that makes use of these gifts and a kind of focus for the deeper reasons for incarnation. As the self gazes at the self, the self is actually gazing at the personality shell. This is the first fruit of self-knowledge, that knowledge of the personality shell. Now, this personality shell is created of the blending between the second-density life-form which is your physical vehicle, and whose mind and instincts are unimpaired, and the consciousness that is that infinite self within its vehicle.

Far beyond the apparent nature of the self, with its temptations and duties and positive and negative thoughts about many things, there is a deeper self, a self that may ultimately be identified as the great original Thought, which is love. This Logos is complete and utterly within and it, love itself, is the nature which you may come to know in the most trustworthy way. For love is love. Love created all that there is. There is no sham, no falsity to divine Logoic love. And this is the vibration, this is the essence which each is beneath the personality shell.

When one considers what one is to do with one's gifts, we would encourage each seeker to contemplate first the greatest gift, that gift of consciousness. There are duties and responsibilities that go hand in hand with the awakening of awareness of one's spiritual identity. One responsibility is to remember who you are, and what you are. For it is that essence that you came primarily to offer as your service. As each comprehends these words, each is fulfilling her major, primary service. For the primary service is to share sacrificially the essential vibrations of self with the planet that you call Earth in order that the planetary consciousness may be lightened at this critical time, metaphysically speaking, in Earth's history. So no matter what occurs within the outer world, as the one known as C observed, no matter whether one devolops a new physics or works and retires, the primary service is performed as you breathe in and out, and as you are most deeply and truly yourself.

It is this vocation for which you took flesh. Primarily, this is why you came. You came here to be yourself, to offer yourself sacrificially to a world greatly in need, a relatively unbiased vibration of love. The sacrifice is life itself. Not that which is within the life. It costs something for each to come here. You have paid that price. We encourage each then, to relax, to trust, and to surrender to that destiny which is a gift carefully chosen by yourself before incarnation. You have prepared ways to serve in the outer world. It is not terribly important whether or not this or that which was prepared is taken up and manifested. However, it is from this standpoint, and from this context that we would prefer to deal with the question of the use of gifts.

As each contemplates the future, each is immediately aware of a sense of tumultuous change as your solar system rotates into a new area of space. The vibrations are changing, the density is changing. Time itself is altering. And the old paradigms grow increasingly awkward. There is in such a time a need for those who are able to move with the rhythm and the information surrounding that change, that energy, or dynamic of transformation. In such a situation as your Earth is at this time, it is to the scientists who look carefully at the actual knowledge of humankind a time when there is seen by all to be a crying need for a new paradigm. Much goes into shift or transformation in consciousness. The entire panoply of arts and sciences, disciplines of every kind, factor into a new creation, a new way of being, that model known as life experience. And so it seems simple and true that if one's gifts include a vision of a transformed physics, cosmology, economics, social model … this would be a good time to explore areas which seem to draw you forward. This instrument, for instance, knows she must write a book. This instrument will continue to question her ability, her knowledge, her rights, her worth; however, this entity is persistent and will produce that fruit of her particular gift of which she is capable. And we encourage each to move with those gifts that draw your interest forward.

We are aware that the one known as C has serious concerns, for indeed many are the newly discovered items that have quickly been co-opted for their military use, or otherwise been used for the detriment of humankind rather than its welfare. And indeed we agree that the only safe area for an entity to work is within the self. Working with the self, it is difficult to infringe upon anyone's free will. It is difficult to find oneself suddenly aghast over the misuse of the fruits of your labor. For that which you do within yourself is yours to do, there is no possibility of infringement. And this work is at the center of the life, this being rather than doing. We realize that we are more or less simply describing the situation which the question attempted to address. We wish to eliminate the landscape rather than to choose one road or another as this instrument and the one known as Jim both said earlier. We are not those who feel that any should do this or that; this is not a concern of ours whatsoever. Our concern is simply to share anything that we know or think that might constitute a resource to those seekers who we came to communicate with and to serve.

There is a delicate, yet surprisingly robust, middle or golden mean, or as this instrument would say, there is a groove coming from the jazz groups that she has. And when one is in that groove, one is simply responding to a rhythmic unfolding of destiny. It is this feeling of rightness and rhythm that will come to the one who is making right use of her gifts. And we commend to your processes of thinking the inclusion of that feeling sense that lets you know when you are on the beam and when you are not. For each has the intuition and the inner knowing that one can draw on and depend on.

It is after all, your creation, for each entity, whether it be one of us, one of you, or any within the creation of the infinite Father.

(Pause)

We are those of Q'uo, and we must apologize … we are those of Q'uo. *(Laughs)* This instrument almost went to sleep on us and we are sorry, and the instrument is sorry, and we must regroup. We were saying that each within the creation of the Father has an infinite rightness for each is a citizen of the time, each is a spark of the infinite Creator and from creation to creation, the sparks shall fly out, become homesick, and return. And you are flying and wishing for home—and you shall return—only to be sent out again by an ever inquisitive Creator to see just what love can be, what it can do.

We would at this time transfer this contact to the one known as Jim. We are those of Q'uo, and we leave this instrument with thanks and love and light. We are those of Q'uo.

(Jim channeling)

I am Q'uo, and greet each of you in love and the light through this instrument. We have attempted in this session of working to speak to the query which has been most important upon the minds of those present, especially the one known as C. And we would ask at this time if there is any further query that any present might ask.

Questioner: Well, I don't have a question, but my mind sure was wandering all over the place and yet I wanted to thank you for your words because there seems to be some general truth in it because I usually find inspiration in dealing with my concerns that are on my mind.

I am Q'uo, and we are grateful that we have been able to provide the information that has set your mind in motion. We are always hopeful that we are able to speak in some way to the heart of the concerns which are offered to us in the form of queries. We are aware that much within your illusion is confusing and difficult. There is the need for the ray of light, shall we say, within each daily experience of each seeker to shine the way for the seeker and to inspire the dedication to service. And to give the seeker the knowledge that to be is the greatest service that any can offer. For to be is to reproduce the nature of the Creator in the individual incarnation. For the Creator exists in a fashion in which the creation is much like your computer program, running in such and such a fashion with infinite participation and possibilities. There is great harmony within this intricate and infinite moving energy individually expressing as each personality. If you can be and allow the harmony and the love and the light of the one Creator to shine through your being in your words, in your thoughts, in your actions, then you have offered that is which most helpful to offer. An incarnation, an illusion, and all those about you, as you move through your incarnation within this illusion it is your free will choice what you shall do with your being, but first be, my friends. Then that which is appropriate for you to do will present itself as clearly as the sun shines on a clear summer day.

At this time we shall take our leave of this instrument and this group, thanking each again for inviting our presence, and cautioning each to take only these words we have offered that ring of truth to you, leaving all others that we have spoken behind without a second thought, for we would not be stumbling blocks upon your path. We leave you in the love and in the light of the one infinite Creator. We are known to you as those of Q'uo.

Adonai, my friends. Adonai. ✣

L/L Research

L/L Research is a subsidiary of Rock Creek Research & Development Laboratories, Inc.

P.O. Box 5195
Louisville, KY 40255-0195

www.llresearch.org

Rock Creek is a non-profit corporation dedicated to discovering and sharing information which may aid in the spiritual evolution of humankind.

ABOUT THE CONTENTS OF THIS TRANSCRIPT: This telepathic channeling has been taken from transcriptions of the weekly study and meditation meetings of the Rock Creek Research & Development Laboratories and L/L Research. It is offered in the hope that it may be useful to you. As the Confederation entities always make a point of saying, please use your discrimination and judgment in assessing this material. If something rings true to you, fine. If something does not resonate, please leave it behind, for neither we nor those of the Confederation would wish to be a stumbling block for any.

CAVEAT: This transcript is being published by L/L Research in a not yet final form. It has, however, been edited and any obvious errors have been corrected. When it is in a final form, this caveat will be removed.

© 2009 L/L Research

Sunday Meditation
December 29, 1997

Group question: We would like to have a look at the information, if possible, today about the earth changes that may be occurring in the next few years, what form they might take, and what impact they might have upon our lives as spiritual seekers.

(Unknown channeling)

Greetings in the love and in the light of the one infinite Creator. It is a privilege and a pleasure to be called to your circle of seeking at this time. We are most grateful for your desire to seek the truth and for your calling us, for sharing our opinions and views is our chosen form of service at this time and each time we are able to use instruments such as this one to share these views, we feel that we have offered our service and this is very precious to us. We ask only that you use your discrimination for we have many opinions and we are known to be wrong and would not put ourselves forward as any authority. We ask each entity to know that there is a good and adequate power of discrimination given to each seeking soul. There is a genuine and authentic feeling that accompanies the hearing of what we may call a personal truth. Many are the views discussed that may appeal to one and not to another, for many are the paths of seekers.

So we ask you to listen and take what you will, leaving the rest behind. We do not come as those in authority, but rather as those who also seek the truth. We share the mystery to which we are called, for which we hunger, and upon whose end we all gaze with awe and worship, for each entity is as a spark of love that is precisely like love itself, that great original Thought for which there is no better word than love.

Many are the distortions. Very general is the confusion of many people with distorted views attempting to see clearly that which cannot be seen clearly. That is to say, you now inhabit a very deep delusion. Within you is the truth and you are the truth that you seek. And yet, in order to have the opportunity to accelerate the rate of your spiritual evolution, each of you has chosen to come into precisely this confusion, precisely this space and time, for here you have found a chance to work upon your own polarity, a chance to work upon that faith which is no accomplishment without the confusion of the illusion-ment.

So you are here specifically to be confused. And to undertake to follow the desires of your heart. It is easy to gaze upon the world about you as a thing, a geographical location, an island in space. The heard music of language and culture, of buildings and ways of relating, all those things that make up the environment and habit have prepared you to attempt to make sense of this illusion. In many ways you have succeeded in carving out each for yourself that identity that you are pleased to wear as the mask of self, that face that you wear to meet those whom you meet. Yet each mask that you see is the Creator and you yourself are also that love divine, which is the Creator.

We describe this essence that is you, to be able to stand at this viewpoint and then gaze at that which is occurring upon the physical planet whose surface you now inhabit. This planet of yours is indeed under much stress. The details of the havoc that has been reached by third-density humankind is all too well known to those here. And we do feel that there is the potential for difficulties such as your floods, your earthquakes, those ways the planet has of being comfortable within its own skin, for it, too, is a living being.

This level of concern is appropriate. It is well to be aware that the ground under you is alive, and that that life is compromised by the actions of humankind. We also are aware, however, that each difficulty has a solution and as the wheels of destiny turn, there will come balance and renewal and new life where there is to the eye now only death and barrenness.

Upon a level deeper than this, we would speak of the roots of mind, for as you move over the threshold into the unconscious, and move deeper within the memory, you pass through a level at which the earth changes, as they are often called, strike a chord with humankind's fear of not continuing. For those who are fascinated with Judgment Day, Armageddon, or conversely the New Age, the Second Coming, and so forth, we would suggest that, archetypically-speaking, one is gazing at the self, gazing at death, the death of the personal self, for each knows that it is physically a creature of dust. It is made of earth, and that bone and sinew that moves this vehicle about shall one day again be dust. All of the civilization and training that the culture gives upon this death of self has a tendency to be very fear-driven. Thusly, it may be seen that those who follow intensely a scenario of planetary disaster may well be more concerned with issues to do with the self than those to do with the planet. It is our opinion that at this time there has been a radical upswing, shall we say, in awakening souls. It is for this reason that some within this group chose incarnation upon this sphere at this time. This is indeed a harvest season for those entities who now dance the dance of third density.

This is the time when each of those who has been allowed to incarnate has the possibility of graduating into the next density at the end of the incarnation. The line to get into the physical third-density planet Earth atmosphere is a long one, for the need here is great at this time.

Focusing upon the difficulties having to do with magnetic shift may reward one with some meager harvest of information. However, we would suggest that a more appropriate response to that feeling that the fields are ripe with harvest is to dedicate the self more and more to being a spiritual entity first, and an actor who functions and does things second. If indeed there were a planetary disaster, a chance at survival would not in any case avail. Indeed, when one sees difficulty and disaster, there is a choice to be made as to what you will think about. Many things enter the senses of your vehicle, far too many things for you to be able to acknowledge and think about them all. The way one prioritizes the incoming data, therefore, is quite important. And we would encourage each when faced with thoughts of difficulty or disaster to consciously and eagerly to move into that tabernacle within, for the Creator Itself sits in light and in perfect love.

That sun within that warms the soul waits for each to come to its own heart and knock and enter. The joy of opening the heart cannot be described. The experience of flying free of judgment, borne on the arms of compassion, is a heavy one. And this is the response that best addresses the difficulties of your planet. To the outer person, this sounds patently absurd. How can meditation or prayer or the centering within the self upon love affect a deadening ocean, a deadening land, a deadening atmosphere, and all the numerous other difficulties your culture is aware of? And yet, it is at being at peace within, and thusly being free to open the heart and allow the love and light of the infinite One to move through the self and out into the world, this is, by far, the most effective answer that you can give to the world of concerns everyday. For each of you is as a star. Each eternal, each unique, and each *(inaudible)* truly perfect. Incarnation and learning are peculiar things. It does seem peculiar to want to come into a darkened world, and spiritually speaking, there is some darkness upon your planet at this time, which you were speaking of earlier.

Know this and all darkness to be but the reflection of the darkness within. Know all confusion, all difficulty, and all disaster, as reflections of those parts of the dark side of self within. That which you see is as a visual aid explaining you to yourself. And as you enter this season of harvest, you know there is service to perform and you wish to be about it. We say to you that the way to serve the Creator at this time is to open the heart to the present moment and practice that precious oneness with the Creator. When there is confusion, when there is awkwardness in the rhythm of the day, move back into the heart where the Creator waits patiently.

Again and again, center the self upon its deepest truth. And you will gaze at a world made different because of the way you think. And as more and more people find peace within themselves, the harvest will begin to be plucked. So, we ask you not to fear. It is written within one of your holy works, by the one know as John of *(inaudible)*, that in the beginning was the Word and that Word or Logos made all that there is. And this entity also described the earth scene as a spiritual darkness, and concluded by observing that, as the light came into the world, the darkness has never overcome it. Each of you is a being of pure light. Each of you has complete freedom to choose the way in which you will manifest that life. All these so-called evils of the world are but love distorted. We encourage you to find ways to choose love over fear, light over darkness, surrender over control, for the attempt to control is a hard service to self.

Know as deeply as you can, and as often as you can, who you are, where you are going, and for the rest, trust destiny. For as the one known as M and the one known as L have both said, one is led to the work that has been prepared for you to do. But the greatest work of all, and the work that will harvest this planet in safety, is being who you most deeply are, a child of the Creator, a miniature of the love that is so powerful that It has created all that there is.

We would at this time transfer this contact to the one known as Jim. We thank this instrument and leave it in love and in light, for we are those of Q'uo.

(Jim channeling)

I am Q'uo, and greet each again, in love and in light, through this instrument. It is our privilege at this time to ask if there might be further queries which those present would find value in the asking. Is there another query at this time?

Questioner: Well, I have a question. You mentioned the change in the magnetic field. I was wondering if the difficulty has something to do with our rotating into the new area of space that our planet hasn't been in before.

I am Q'uo, and am aware of your query, my sister. To this query there are many components that comprise the answer. There are indeed new and more available, shall we say, energies in the portion of time and space through which this planet now moves. There is also the effect of the planetary entity realigning itself because of previous distortions offered by the third-density population in the way of the deleterious effects upon the planet. There are those entities in your circles of government who have sought to influence the patterns of weather. All these together may be seen as potential influences that have caused the patterns of weather to become somewhat more erratic. However, each of these potential sources may, as we have said, be affected by the love that emanates from the open heart of each seeker within your illusion. Thus, each may offer healing to this planetary entity and to all other entities, as well, each time the heart is open in compassion, forgiveness, understanding, mercy and tolerance.

Is there a further query, my sister?

Questioner: Not on that subject, thanks, Q'uo.

I am Q'uo, and we thank you again, my sister. Is there another query at this time?

Questioner: Our experience here on Earth is described as an illusion. Is the illusion basically just that so many of us have in a sense separated from God or from the Creator, and from each other? Is that what is meant by the illusion?

I am Q'uo, and am aware of your query, my brother. You are correct in your assumption that the illusion is that which is more than it appears to be, for each does appear to be separate from each other entity and from your environment itself. The unity of all things is the underlying truth in this matter. The illusion of separation exists so that each portion of the one Creator, the personalities who each of you are, may have the opportunity to explore within the one Creator's boundless field, the opportunities for discovering love and service for each other, though these may not seem to be the primary reasons for which each was incarnated. The illusion offers many other alternate answers for why each is here: to gather wealth, to be powerful, to do this or that great thing. All of these are but means by which each entity may find the heart of love and unity within itself. Each uses the artifacts of the illusion to travel the spiritual journey, though all around one the material world is given ascendancy.

This is the illusion so finely created by each portion of the one Creator for the purpose of finding the one Creator's love and light in each heart and also providing that one Creator within the opportunity to know Itself in ways that would not be possible were this illusion and your choices within it not creative.

Is there a further query, my brother?

Questioner: No, thank you.

I am Q'uo, and we thank you, my brother. Is there another query at this time?

Questioner: Just a follow-up to his. When you say illusion, I sort of think of the fact that no one has seen an electron even as far as mass goes. They see the path of energy that is left behind but they can't find any mass, so that's really where I was thinking the illusion came in is just that level where there really isn't anything but energy. Does that have validity?

I am Q'uo, and am aware of your query, my sister. This is indeed true, and is a most salient observation. The nature of the illusion may be described in many, many ways. And in your pursuit of the explanation of particles of creation that you call physics, there is the discovery by more and more of those who pursue this field that indeed, what each sees is most mysterious. There are a variety of ways that explanation is offered, and yet, none satisfy completely unless one sees the entire creation of many-ness as a unified concept of the one Creator's expression of love and light.

Is there a further query, my sister?

Questioner: No, thank you.

I am Q'uo, and we thank you, my sister. Is there another query at this time?

Carla: I had a guy write in from Turkey and he was very upset over people being born retarded, and otherwise handicapped or born starving, and what was that all about. I just wrote him back and said that it was part of the mystery, that we all did suffer, those that obviously suffered and those that don't look like they suffer at all. Everybody suffers. I wondered, do you have any comment on that? I'd love to be able to answer better.

I am Q'uo and am are of your query, my sister. To love and to find love is an easy thing when there is no barrier to perceiving love. Within your illusion, there is a great deal of darkness, shall we say, spiritually speaking. So that it carries far more weight [int the] mind/body/spirit totality that you call the spirit or soul to find love and light in an incarnation in which there is great difficulty, great darkness, great challenge. Each entity which incarnates within this illusion enters into the undertaking of this challenge and will gain in the spiritual awareness and power, shall we say, by being able to accomplish the discovery of love where it is most difficult to find.

Is there a further query, my sister?

Carla: No, thank you.

I am Q'uo, again we thank you, my sister. Is there another query at this time?

Questioner: I have a question. In my search throughout my life to find out more about myself and what my path is in life, I've had many thoughts, so to say, that have followed me throughout my life and I'm wondering if these thoughts are symbolic of what I am to do. But they have troubled me in their authenticity of what they actually mean. I was wondering if you had any comment, so to speak, on that?

I am Q'uo, and am aware of your query, my brother. Each entity which incarnates within this illusion offers to itself those guideposts or milestones, these thoughts which you have described, that pose to the incarnated entity the questions that [you] are indeed asking yourself. These thoughts, these images, these impulses within, then seek to guide, to lead, if you will, the entity within a certain line of inquiry that will eventually prove fruitful to the entity as it faithfully follows that which it feels within to be leading it. You will within your incarnation discover certain synchronicities, coincidences, the bringing together of information of entities, of experiences, of shared thoughts and dream. These will serve as those kinds of directions that will lead, that will nurture, that will inspire and support when the way seems difficult and dark. Look then, especially in your prayerful times, and in mediation and in those times where you seek within the answers that are of importance to you. Look there upon a regular basis that you might inquire into the wisdom that you have provided yourself, and which the Creator and those angels and spirits about you have provided you, so that you may become inspired at those times when it is open to you to seek and to ask, to serve, to give. That you are aware of these images, these thoughts, is important. Important not only at this time, but throughout your incarnation.

Is there a further query, my brother?

(No further queries.)

I am Q'uo, and as we perceive that there are no further queries from this circle of seeking, we would at this time offer our gratitude to each entity for inviting our presence and for sharing with us your thoughts and your concerns. We are honored to have been a part of your seeking this day. And would remind each again that the personal discrimination is most important at all times, including listening to our words when information is being sought that has meaning in your own journey of seeking the truth. You indeed have the answers that you seek within and when there is information given to you that rings of truth, then you may welcome into your …

(Tape ends.)

Year 1998

January 11, 1998 to December 20, 1998

Sunday Meditation
January 11, 1998

Group question: We would like to ask about the two ways that we experience ourselves: being caught up in the illusion, wandering about from thing to thing without being in the flow, of being there, and of enjoying the love and the light of the harmony of the moment. The other is being in the flow, which is the goal which most of us have. We are wondering if Q'uo could give us a description of how work in the metaphysical sense is being done both when we are not in the flow and when we are.

(Carla channeling)

We are those of the principle known to you as Q'uo. Greetings in the love and in the light of the one infinite Creator. We regard it as a great privilege and blessing that you have called us to your circle of seeking this day. We are very glad to share our feelings with you, asking only that you use your discrimination and not simply accept our thoughts because they are our thoughts. Let your own sense of recognition be the standard by which you accept information. You will find that your power of discrimination is great for you can indeed recognize and have a certain feeling towards that which is your own personal truth, that which for you is a resource and a tool. Let the rest go.

You ask today about the relative merits of attempting to live life consciously, aware of the self as a spiritual being, observing and, conversely, being caught up completely in the illusion. Were we to recommend one mode of expression over the other for third density we would be forced to choose the confusion and the babble of the unthinking everyday carnival, with all its amusements and rides, that greets you each morning as you gaze out of your physical senses at the physical world. It is not that living consciously is a lesser thing. Indeed, whole densities are spent in such work. It is, rather, that third density is valuable because of and not in spite of that heavy pall of confusion and illusion that animates this Earth world.

Were each present to be able to satisfy herself that all was being done appropriately in the moment to moment relationships there would indeed be a kind of bone-deep pleasantness to the incarnation. However, although weary, battered and tired as you are you may now wish for the contentment and peace of the lifting of the veil, as spirits you hunger to come into this illusion because it is only within the illusion that an entity can work upon that pivotal first choice: service to self or service to others. When one has all the rules in hand, knows all the players, knows all the values, one may play well at that game but feel or learn nothing. It is when the spiritual entity is thoroughly mixed up with the clay and mire of life in the physical illusion that the challenge may be raised to live by faith and not by what you see.

It is felt by the spirit who is descending into matter that incarnation within the material world is a pearl of great price, something eagerly hoped for by far more entities than can be accommodated at this time. Your sphere experiences [numerous] forces inevitably moving through that which can be considered a dying and rebirth or a time of initiation and a time of peace, and since this is a harvest time, each of you hoped to come into this confusion to paddle about in it and to meet each choice in a way that discovers the self to the self. One thing that one cannot do as an observer is surprise the self, and it is when you surprise yourself with who you are that you feel and sense into your spiritual identity, which is quite a bit larger than your physical identity. You are a personality shell; that is, you are consciousness which has adapted itself to incarnation within a second-density physical vehicle.

This consciousness cannot be brought completely into the illusion, for this consciousness that you are is all that there is. To bring all of self into the illusion would be to erase the illusion, and this illusion creates for each of you other selves to relate to in order that you work upon yourself by reflection. Lost in the running of the everyday chores you make choice after choice after choice, in little ways and in larger ways, and when those choices are easy and obvious the polarization value of them is measured. Those moments when you discover yourself being or acting in an unpredicted or unpredictable way are little nuggets, little treasures. For this personality shell that you are was carefully chosen to contain those gifts and limitations of character and personality that will best serve you at this time. The material before you, the relationships in your life, all of these things you gave yourself as gifts. Some of them gifts to wallow in with pleasure, some of them gifts to challenge yourself. And the entity unknowing is the entity at the cusp of choice.

We would balance speaking of the unknowing, incarnational self by talking also concerning work in consciousness, the other alternative, shall we say, that life observed that each thirsts for. This instrument, by nature, by the gifts of personality, character and will, which she and the Creator cobbled together for this particular incarnation, spends a good deal of time, perhaps a higher percentage of time within incarnation than most within this circle, being completely within the moment, having that experience of the present self observed. To this instrument this is not a gift or an accomplishment. It is a simple fact of her nature. This instrument, therefore, is more aware of the negative aspect of such a frame of mind than the positive aspects. To this entity it is simply irritating to discover time and again that one has not been on the right page or even opened the right book as far as knowing what is occurring. So this entity has the inner experience of scrambling upon the surface of life in order to take a look around at the illusion. Therefore, this entity, more than most, grasps the value of the unobserved self, the self completely within the illusion. For this entity finds itself involved in causing inconvenience to the self and to others because of her lack of awareness of space and time.

There is, of course, much to be said for the entity who has been able to so live the life so that a rhythm has been caught and that marvelous beating heart of all that there is informs, enables and blesses all experience. It is a joy indeed to find the self in that holiday delight, that thrill of knowing that all is as it should be. These moments, however discovered or achieved, are wonderful, true and lovely. We encourage each, when those moments of delight occur, to mark them down in the heart, to look at the significant self, for these are moments of truth when the illusion falls away and all is real. It is not the reason that you are in the Earth world. Nevertheless, such moments are most blessed.

This instrument has a favorite phrase, "the prayer without ceasing," and this is her version of being in the flow or being the observer, and there is such feeling in those measured moods of awareness when the self feels awake and alert to the world about. There is such pleasure in staying within that upper triad of energy centers, the heart, the throat, the brow, of green, of blue, of indigo. And this is the crux of the situation. Each spiritual student hungers and thirsts for these feelings of certainty, of orientation within the larger universe. It desires to cast off the shackles of culture, to spend all of the time, if possible, rejoicing and delighting in the beauty, the truth, and the unity of all that there is, for the joy to be aware permanently that you are part of that harmony.

Yet this Earth world remains that extremely vast stage upon which you and those about you dance and sing and speak with each other, discovering self, other self, and offering the reflection of self to self.

This instrument has often said to those working upon the path of spiritual evolution, "Try not to work in the upper energy centers more than you work in the lower energy centers." And we feel that this is a key to your own use of both modes of awareness. Mental, emotional and physical health as well as spiritual health are a matter of balance. Each entity is unique and has an ever moving, ever developing, always spiraling path of energy flow. When one has not yet awakened to one's spiritual identity yet still one is aware of the flow when one is in it. There is not anyone who does not do good work while asleep. There is a drawback to those who are not awake and are not consciously aware of wishing to accelerate their rate of spiritual evolution, nevertheless this does not keep them from progressing. And in the fullness of time the entity most completely immured in the illusion shall one day, without conscious effort achieve realization. Evolution is absolutely inevitable. The rate of evolution is that which is questionable.

And with this instrument we would encourage each not to be laggardly or to feel better than the entity who is not aware of spiritual evolution. Insofar as you have become aware of the process of evolution, of the kind of thing spiritual evolution is, yet still you are equipped with the full array of challenges, physically, mentally, emotionally and spiritually, and all of these threads of being have their own best luster and strength. So much of the tapestry of life is created from difficulties, the dark side of things that we cannot overemphasize the value of these lower energies and working upon them as though they were as exciting to work with as the higher centers.

You see, work in consciousness proceeds from the heart. However, the heart's energy is entirely a creature of the power, shall we say, that is brought to the heart. Those who wish to skip working on the self in relationships, with regards to issues such as sexuality, survival and so forth, may wish that they could spend all of their time working on communication and consciousness itself, yet unless the energy centers of red, orange and yellow, of survival, self-identification and association with others, are addressed, and that with respect, there will be a lessening of the flow of energy into the heart. And one can only work from the heart upward with that energy that has come through to the heart. Those who have experienced the rising of kundalini, that flow of energy up the spine, know that its origin is the root chakra, those organs of generation, reproduction and elimination that together form the great taboo, the great unspoken subject in your culture. Yet there is great need here for much balancing with regard to the issue of life itself. This is strictly red-ray. And so much depends upon that way in which you meet this opportunity for life.

The self in orange ray seems a bit drab to work upon. "How do I comfort myself?" These questions of self to self can burn the midnight oil within one's mind and create endless and often agonizing tangles. Often work in this energy center is not fun. And with yellow ray there comes an even greater burden of the learning curve which must be achieved in each and every relationship, in each and every joining of all groups, working with all desires. The heart may wish that it could break out of these cages of lower energies and burst the illusion of maya. And yet you came here specifically to be tied down, specifically to be confused, and to work within this great unknowing.

We cannot make the lower energy work more fun by sugar-coating the process involved. It is hard work to work from the self in relationship, the self with issues, and yet it is that for which you have come. You have come here to be confused, to be challenged, to enter a learning situation such as this one. We encourage each to see the whole panoply of the self from the lowest to the highest reaches as one seamless wheel, each part of which is as important as the other. There is not a favorite place in which the personality shell shall choose to work. Indeed, the most reliable method of becoming one with the flow of things is simply to wait until they come to you, as the ones known as R and J have both expressed. And how difficult is that waiting, yet once one has been able to surrender in one wise, on one front, once one has been able once to say, "OK, I give it up. I don't care. Whatever your will is, that is what I want," that surrender makes the next one easier. The life of faith, if it has a beginning, begins in the dirt, the dust, and the mire.

That clay self must be tossed into mid-air and this is the way it must be for you again and again. And each of you has found far more than once that moment of resolve, that moment of choice, and you have said, "I surrender. Not my will, but Thine." We encourage each to continue to have the courage to take that leap into mid-air. When you are not one with your environment, when you are at odds and are very much a human being, know that you are still learning. Indeed, you are probably learning more than you are in those moments when you feel supported, for the learning is in the strife and friction of life. Consider yourselves as little distilleries. Now, a distillery is something that takes a raw material and refines it until its nature changes. And each of you is a spiritual distillery taking in the odor and muck of daily living.

And so it is that in yielding to it and cooperating with it in trust, hope and faith, that you maximize the transparency of your self and your personality. When you are suffering, when you are confused, when you are lost in the illusion, know that you are working, that you are on the journey from head to heart. Of course you are not within the heart all of the time, not within this illusion! It is far better that you stay within the illusion. When you come out of that illusion and have those moments, this is wonderful. This delicious. This is dessert. But the meat of living is in the ordinary and the often ignored daily affairs. Your mind is infinite. If you could only see into the self, the roots of mind come through the life of one self into the life of many, into the greater and greater groups, and finally into the All. And each of the steps and ramifications is a universe unto itself, and this infinite repository and resource indwells each of you. You have all the material that you will ever consciously pursue and adore resting comfortably and in fullness within your being. A portion of that infinite Self that begins with your personality shell knows this fire. But for you within this density at this time, embrace the confusion. Do your best to live consciously, aware of the issues of free will, love and service. But do not be upset or discouraged with the self or with getting lost within the illusion. You are supposed to be lost most of the time. This is how you learn. And this pattern of the discovery of your self, it will show you to yourself, and that self that it shows you, ah, what an infinite thing you will find!

The self unaware, the self aware. The self undone and the self composed. These are one. It may seem like a vast difference to each of you, but we assure you that the basic vibration inside of incarnation and outside of incarnation is the same. You may muddy your vibration by being unhappy with the self or unhappy with others or in some way moving athwart of living, but you are still yourself and you are still at work on your path no matter how deeply confused or suffering you feel.

This instrument hears the unpleasant cry of two of this instrument's cats in the upper floor of this dwelling. These two entities are deeply enmired in their illusion and yet they too learn and they sound unpleasant to other ears. But each thing that they do is appropriate for them. Begin to have this kind of feeling about yourself. Know the satisfaction of putting up that first floor before ascending to the higher second floor of inspiration.

We would at this time transfer to the one known as Jim. We leave this instrument in love and in light. We are known to you as those of Q'uo.

(Jim channeling)

I am Q'uo, and greet each of you again in love and in light through this instrument. At this time we would offer ourselves to any further queries that those present might find the value in asking.

R: I am confused. You are not saying that there is no value in mediation and opening yourself to the energies that work with you?

I am Q'uo, and am aware of your query, my brother. We spoke at the beginning of our response to the primary query for the day by saying that if we had the necessity to choose between these two ways of being we would choose the confusion of your third-density illusion over the feeling of atonement and peace that each seeks within this heavy, physical illusion. Our choice would be thus for it is within this confusion that one can learn a great deal more than is possible to learn in a more harmonious environment. Indeed, this is the reason that this third-density illusion is such an intense place for growth and such a valued experience for each spirit which seeks incarnation here. The learning that is possible when there is mystery and darkness all about carries far more weight in the total beingness of an entity than does the learning which is inevitable and obvious in the harmonious realms of existence. We also recommended, my brother, that when these opportunities [are present] for feeling atonement and the presence of the one Creator in all His or Her perfection, that one enjoy and luxuriate in them, for they are the frosting on the cake. However, as we spoke earlier, the meat of this incarnation is to find love and light in the confusion of the daily round of existence. To find those gems of inspiration embedded in the muck and mire of everyday experience is far more valuable.

Is there another query at this time?

R: No. Because I am much lost. I will think about it some more.

I am Q'uo, and we would make an addition to our response. When one finds oneself at the cusp of choice and is confused as to how to respond, perhaps with another entity, an argument, a disagreement, a miscommunication, one has at one's disposal the entire previous store of experience from the incarnation to [use in creating] a response to the situation. One has a range of emotions that the choice may be embedded within. One has a range of reactions from the one with whom one speaks and interacts. All of these are bits of information, opportunities to learn, to learn the power of the love of the one Creator to transform, for instance, when one is able to tap into this resource. To learn regret that one has caused injury, to learn the determination that one shall not do so again, to learn a vast array of possible responses. Indeed, the experience offers an example of the infinity of the moment. In this moment one may learn how to give love in a way that is much quicker, intense and efficient than this learning could be accomplished where harmony, oneness and the power of love and light are obvious and the proper response is given without thought, without effort, and the entire mind/body/spirit of the entity is affected but little. Whereas in the intense moment of third-density confusion the love and light that you find there carries a great deal more value and weight in your total beingness and moves your mind/body/spirit further along the line of evolution than is possible in the same amount of experience within the higher realms of harmony and oneness.

Is there a further query at this time?

J: What is the value of meditation in the daily experiences?

I am Q'uo, and am aware of your query, my sister. As one has gathered about one all the various confusions, experiences, communications and so forth one draws certain tentative conclusions about how best to respond within the incarnation in order to determine how to find and share those qualities of love, of light, of harmony, of service, and so forth. Within the meditative state these tentative conclusions and experiences may seat themselves in a manner which allows their influence to have its sway within the total being. One is able to more clearly make sense of one's experiences by allowing a certain kind of settling out to occur, and for the allowing of inspiration to make its natural response as one considers the events of the day, allows them to have their weight and go their way, and then finds the sitting and the listening to the one Creator to produce an inspiration, a motivation, or simply a recognition. It is in meditation that the confusion and distraction begin to fall away and the foundation of one's being begins to be revealed and becomes more accessible to the entity in the daily round of activities when found in meditation.

Is there a further query, my sister?

J: No. Thank you.

I am Q'uo, and we thank you. Is there a further query at this time?

(Pause)

I am Q'uo. As we have apparently exhausted the queries for this session of working we would again take this opportunity to express our gratitude to each entity here for inviting our presence and again remind each that those words that we have spoken that ring of truth, take them and do with them as you will, letting all others fall away. We are those of Q'uo, and at this time would take our leave of this instrument and this circle of seeking. Adonai. Adonai. ♣

L/L Research

L/L Research is a subsidiary of Rock Creek Research & Development Laboratories, Inc.

P.O. Box 5195
Louisville, KY 40255-0195

www.llresearch.org

Rock Creek is a non-profit corporation dedicated to discovering and sharing information which may aid in the spiritual evolution of humankind.

ABOUT THE CONTENTS OF THIS TRANSCRIPT: This telepathic channeling has been taken from transcriptions of the weekly study and meditation meetings of the Rock Creek Research & Development Laboratories and L/L Research. It is offered in the hope that it may be useful to you. As the Confederation entities always make a point of saying, please use your discrimination and judgment in assessing this material. If something rings true to you, fine. If something does not resonate, please leave it behind, for neither we nor those of the Confederation would wish to be a stumbling block for any.

CAVEAT: This transcript is being published by L/L Research in a not yet final form. It has, however, been edited and any obvious errors have been corrected. When it is in a final form, this caveat will be removed.

© 2009 L/L RESEARCH

Sunday Meditation
January 18, 1998

Group question: The question today has to do with the concept of, "Not my will, but Thy will," and when we are able to realize that this is the way we wish to behave and to live, what else can we do intellectually to assist bringing forth "Thy will" into our lives? How can we know "Thy will" and get out of the state of confusion in which we most often find ourselves, having given up our will and yet no particular direction shows itself to us? Is there anything that Q'uo could recommend to us that might strengthen our faith and our will?

(Carla channeling)

We are those of the principle known to you as Q'uo. Greetings in the love and in the light of the one infinite Creator. We are always pleased to be called to your group, and this session is no exception. We thank and bless each of you for turning once again to that interest that we have very much in common, that consciousness that lies between us, linking us and all that there is into one vast being, one consciousness, one basic core vibration. This is the mystery that drives us ever onward, seeking always that which lies beneath illusion.

We have found many illusions, and we are aware that you also have your experiences within the illusion of your Earth life. We are glad to speak to you of that issue of confusion and decision, for, indeed, there is an art and an appropriateness that one can only sense, one can only record finding. It cannot be created by will. It cannot be created to a time frame or a schedule. Indeed, in issues of will, this is subtle work. When one perceives working upon one's own consciousness it is easy and tempting to stay within the confines of that particular issue, that particular concern. When you as a human being in your illusion decide to make the purchase of the choice of everyday things, there is usually a very superficial level of will involved. Many, many things simply need to be done. However, what you ask about this day is that way of knowing when the will of the infinite Creator has been expressed to one. There is, indeed, the rub, as Shakespeare would say. There is the difficulty, for one can make decisions using logic, using the will, using each and every aspect at the command of mind. And that decision has no promise of being the will of the Creator in any way of knowing that can leave one at peace.

Intellectual questioning into the issue of, "Is this Thy will or mine?" almost always involves one in a tautological circle, like the dragon eating its tail. It is forever eating and forever unfinished. However, now that we have taken away the habitual and normal use of mind, what have we left for you to work with in this particular kind of larger decision? We have left your consciousness. Let us look at that which remains when logic and mind and intellect are, if not removed entirely, certainly placed in a less conspicuous and influential position in respect to decision-making. We have an entity whose resources are infinite, whose citizenry is of the universe, who does not belong in space and time. We have a stranger in a strange land. Indeed, were we to pull back to see where the self is in self, we would find each of you and all of your affections in the illusion that you now enjoy to be but the merest shell, your personality shell, that expresses perhaps one or two percent of the total beingness and experience which you possess within the deeper reaches of the roots of mind.

Having taken the conscious mind out of the consideration we now chose to use the unconscious portion of mind, for within it lie the resources needed to sort out issues of will and faith. Whatever your energy level within the illusion, resting back in the divine, letting the self be, evokes a contentment that does not reach nor does it shun those things which are about one. This is the self that is often accessed by meditation. One of the benefits of meditation, indeed, is that the door betwixt the conscious intellectual mind and the subconscious in the roots of mind is, if not wide open, at least ajar. Time spent in the silence is time spent listening to the voice with no sound that indeed does carry the messages of faith and choice, but not to a schedule. And this is where the entity within your illusion, feeling confused, loses that quality that so well supports the spiritual seeker. That quality is patience.

Patience is a powerful spiritual quality. The one known as Jim spoke earlier of persevering no matter what. This is another way of stating the same sentiment. If one can become patient and willing to wait whatever time it seems to take, one then is prepared for messages that do come from the unconscious self. This instrument has seen a popular cliché on refrigerator magnets that reads something like, "Lord give me patience and give it to me right now." And that is where the third-density illusion comes in and kidnaps the spirit who is not completely staid upon patience. To be content to wait is an attitude that will always prove the best resource possible for the spiritual seeker. For the person who does not mind waiting no matter how long it takes, results can often come quickly. When the entity moves at all from the attitude of "waiting is" and "waiting is good" then comes in the desire. It

is not [that] the desire is wicked or wrong. The universe moves upon desire. It is that beyond a certain point the seeker cannot know himself. There is just so much inner work an entity may do, and that work is more deleting confusion from the way the mind works than it is adding information to the mind. You are in the situation of having a wealth of knowledge that purports to be about the spiritual but having almost no assets concerning and dealing with that which lies beyond the words.

It is a frightening and seeming illogical choice to move beyond logic and trains of thought. There is no victory promised the seeker who chooses to wait. Entities persistent enough to wait a long time have spent incarnations waiting when there was a need to express this quality in order to balance the personality shell. And yet there is no glamour or reward to the practice of waiting, to the practice of patience. Yet that willingness, that abandoning self can and will communicate at the appropriate and rhythmically right time. You see, you experience life within the illusion as if you were walking down a road or moving down a river. There is motion involved from yesterday to tomorrow, from Louisville to Chicago. There is space and time and someone occupying both. In reality this is an illusion within an illusion within an illusion. That which seems so full of self is only the paltriest shell of personality from that powerful Self that you are in totality. Time and space actually do not exist, and there is no possibility of making a wrong choice, for all has already occurred, and all is perfect.

For those who are not able to have hearts to understand, this entire concept makes no sense, and we accept that. We do not attempt to make sense but rather to share our observations of how things work. What you are attempting to do is in reality not to make the choice but to be the person who puts the self to the choice with the most desire, the most polarity of desire. Both of these are important. The most desire. To hone the desire is so important. To move within those well-worn words, "Not my will, but Thine," not once, not twice, not a hundred times, but with every breath. This is the goal: to consume the self in the divine. To so empty the self that the divine makes its own colors moving through you so that you have only to say, "Oh see, I should do this now. Here this is." There is a level upon which this is possible for each entity within the illusion, yet this soft spot is surrounded by hard rocks on every side. For truly it is difficult to let go.

Perhaps one suggestion that we could make to one who feels decisions must be made to a schedule is simply to say that if something does not strike before someone's schedule comes to an end, perhaps this also is information being communicated. Know that when the right time comes you will know the choice that the Creator has for you, and you will feel it to your bones, to the end of your heart, to your depths. And you will be able to jump on it and work with it with all of your self.

Let us look again at this question of mind, for we feel that it is always the razor's edge to work with the mind within incarnation. Upon the one hand, if you use no mind you cannot communicate with others or share your observations with others. You may be a wonderful light, but you cannot teach except by your being. On the other hand, any use of the intellect tends to pull one away from that seat of joy and delight that is present in the one infinite Creator. The heart that dwells in this opened love, or the heart that is open to this love and willing to allow it to run through that heart and into the world of manifestation, has done healing work for the planetary energy, the local energy, and the energy of self. In a normal decision-making the programs that are used are those run by logic. As the one known as R says, "The pros the cons, for and against," and one can indeed line up all of the pros and cons. They do not add up to a tidy sum, for nothing is simply that surface appearance. Things have the necessity of being more real than that, more subject to free will, more uncatchable than that.

As one becomes more able to use that surface mind without becoming emotionally swayed by one's rhetoric, one can open more to what this instrument would describe as deeper programs, programs below the level of consciousness that do not work on logic or linear thought but, rather, contain the essences of self that have been purified and worked upon through many, many incarnations and many experiences. These are the assets of the deeper self and it is here that the soul must go who wishes to learn patience, for patience lies within you, a powerful, slumbering elegant beast. Truly your brother and your sister, if you are seeking spiritually, there is no friend that is more faithful than patience. There is no challenge that cannot be won with patience. Letting go of the surface of things, being willing to rest in the mid-air of not knowing, this is an art, and it is this that we encourage you to practice. You have, not simply "the answer." You have all that there is.

To the surface of things, you attempt to make a certain choice. To the reality of things, you are working upon your vibration. Whatever situation you are in or will be in is a fine and splendid opportunity to develop the self, to work on that vibration. And so we encourage the slowing down, the resting, the quietness of mind that is willing to pass up an opportunity if the time is not right, and is willing to grasp an opportunity when that inner knowing occurs, and it will. In a moment you shall know. Yes or no. And for you that will be the correct decision.

We would at this time transfer this contact to the one known as Jim. We are the ones of Q'uo, and we thank this instrument and leave it in love and in light.

(Jim channeling)

I am Q'uo, and we greet each again in love and in light through this instrument. At this time we would offer ourselves to the potential answering of any further questions that those present may have upon their minds. Is there another query at this time?

Carla: I have a question. I wonder if you could comment on my frame of mind. Sort of feeling listless and lethargic and at the same time not being discontent or upset.

I am Q'uo, and am aware of your query, my sister. We may speak in somewhat of an abbreviated fashion, for, indeed, it is well for the student to have a fairly good grasp upon her query before we may respond without the problem of infringing upon free will. We can note that which has been noted concerning this attitude of mind, that being that the one known as Carla has in her past served as an instrument for a contact which has as a residue a certain amount of weariness that is inevitable. For when one has been able to contact those more harmonious realms of being, as the instrument known as Carla did during the Ra contact, and has been faced with the necessity of returning to a more dense, in illusion that is, realm of being there is the relative experience of wearying the physical vehicle. This has a cumulative effect, and the one known as Carla has experienced this in some intensity, shall we say. There is within the mind complex of this entity dual needs to achieve and to rest. This is not unusual for many of your entities, for there is the need to accomplish activities and projects that are concomitant with your third-density illusion. All within the illusion experience the drive to move, to gain, to master, to achieve. This is the nature of the illusion. This is the grist for the mill, as we find has been described accurately.

However, there is also within many entities, and this entity in particular, the feeling that to be is sufficient. And this is indeed correct, especially when seen through those eyes that are metaphysically oriented. The being that one expresses is the heart, the essence, of one's self. And in truth each entity is whole and perfect, having entered this illusion with such wholeness and perfection in abeyance that there may be further exploration into the individuation of consciousness that each entity has undertaken as a portion of the one Creator. The fueling of the beingness being sufficient is a feeling which we can encourage in entities, for it is not only accurate, but within the illusion that you inhabit, a proper balance for the unending activity and seeming restlessness that so signifies those of your peoples that partake in the daily round of activity and experience.

That this entity feels somewhat ashamed of being uninspired, as she says, may be examined for the particularly biased view of the self that this entails. This entity is not unfamiliar with its own criticism of itself. Thus we feel that we have reached the limit of that which is helpful and we ask if there might be any other query that this entity might ask of us?

Carla: No, Q'uo. That was very clear and helpful. Thanks.

I am Q'uo, and we again thank you, my sister. Is there another query at this time?

R: I have noticed a little fear or anxiety when I participate in these sessions. I sometimes just want to ask a question as if there was an opportunity lost if I do not ask it. I do not know where that fear is coming from. I feel like a little boy standing with a group of grown-ups and am saying, "Me too. Me too." Could you talk about that please?

I am Q'uo, and am aware of your query, my brother. We feel that this query concerns an area which is natural for the human experience; that is, when faced with what seems to be the wiser or more informed point of view, one wishes to partake of that point of view in order to enhance the evolutionary process, feeling that if the opportunity is not taken it shall be lost, and there will be the failure to move forward as quickly as would be possible as if the opportunity were taken. We appreciate this experience of our blending of our vibrations with your own, and we appreciate the opinion that you hold us in, but we would again remind each entity that we and others who serve as teachers and guides for each third-density entity are available at all times so that in your own contemplative or meditative times you may ask whatever query is upon your mind or upon your heart and therein find a response that will point the direction in the same way that we would frame a response to your query within one of these sessions of working. This again moves back to the primary query for the day and to the remark that we made concerning how an entity may perceive the Creator's will when it stands before one and remains unrecognized. Oftentimes it is simply a matter of realizing the perfection of the moment, for each entity has spent the entirety of its previous life experience to reach the moment of the present. All that has gone before has brought one to this point, thus there must be something important in the present moment. And we would again affirm [not only] the perfection of each entity but of the moment in which each entity finds itself. This is not to say that there will not be changes in what you call your future, for, indeed, there shall be many of these. But each of them, as well as that moment which you now experience, shall be perfect. And when you are able to accept the perfection of the moment, the perfection of your own self, then perhaps you shall not feel quite the fear or anxiety of missing an opportunity to find a more perfect moment.

We hope that we have not further confused you, my brother. Is there another query?

R: No, you have not confused me. I do believe what you have said. Another thought is that I feel a lot of gratitude for these sessions. I feel some love flowing that generates the response and oftentimes I have no questions but just feel like I want to say, "Thank you for speaking to us."

I am Q'uo, and we are aware of the experience of which you speak, my brother. Indeed, the gratitude for the blessings for the one Creator that come in various forms is a blessing in itself, for it creates within the mind/body/spirit complex of each entity feeling it a certain ambiance that enhances the experience of unity and of harmony that is available to each. When one has been able to feel true gratitude for that which one experiences then this is a kind of opening of a door through which the entity wishes to pass, in that it moves into a finer appreciation of that which it is and that which it experiences. The gratitude of the spiritual seeker is a kind [of] lubricant that enhances the friction of daily experience and relieves much of that which is rough and unrefined.

Is there a final query at this time?

(No further queries.)

We are those of Q'uo, and we would take this opportunity to express our heartfelt gratitude to those present for once again inviting our presence within your circle of seeking. It is a privilege and an honor for которыйwe cannot express enough gratitude, my friends. At this time we shall take our leave of this instrument and this group. We are known to you as those of Q'uo. Adonai, my friends. Adonai.

Sunday Meditation
February 15, 1998

Group question: The question today has to do with guides. What guides are available to us? How are they available? How might we gain access to them and feel that we are being guided?

(Carla channeling)

We are those known to you as the principle of Q'uo. We greet you in the love and in the light of the one infinite Creator whose servants we are. May we thank you from the bottom of our hearts for calling us to your session of working this afternoon. We thank each in this circle for hungering for truth and for being willing to allow us to speak through this instrument and share our humble thoughts with you. As always, we ask that each of you listens with discrimination, for you shall recognize those thoughts which are able to be resources and tools for you in your path, a path unique and not like everyone else's, so that no two entities can take all of the thoughts that may have merit in a general sense but, rather, each will find those that are companions and fit into that puzzle that each is putting together in the search for what is loosely called the truth.

You ask this day concerning guides, angels, guardian spirits and guidance in general, and this is a subject peculiarly unsuitable to words. Indeed, the very nature of the metaphysical universe is such that the guidance which is always and constantly with you is not that which translates into materialistic or fleshly body-oriented thinking. The common concept of a guide or a guardian angel is of a specific being. However, not all of those who are part of your guidance system are beings in the same sense that you consider yourself an individual self.

In order to clarify we must retreat first to express some more general concepts. Firstly, let us look at the concept of personhood or personality, for each of you is a person and has personhood. This is, within the illusion, something that you can trust. The flesh that rests upon your bones is flesh, and it shall continue until the spirit that enlivens that vehicle needs it no more. A skeleton remains a skeleton. The organs remain the organs. These things are physical, and they are obvious. Consequently, entities, even spiritually oriented entities, tend, by and large, to think of the self as the flesh, the bones, the organs, the body, as though the self had no other connections before, or will have no other connections after, the incarnation that you now experience. Certainly it does not occur to many that you have within the physical vehicle connections with and contact with non-physical and non-bodily energies and essences which are as much a part of who you are as those things that can be named, counted and measured concerning your physical beingness.

However, we feel it is true in our observation that the personality shell that animates the incarnational body is a very shallow, very limited selection of portions of your self, in the greater or metaphysical sense, that you have chosen because these are the attributes and the limitations that you put together in order to be challenged and in order to meet the challenges you would find within the body and within incarnational experience. As beautiful, sacramental and worthy as this bodily personality shell and all that you see of yourself in the mirror is, it remains as insubstantial as a shadow next to the profound and infinite nature of your whole self. Indeed, it is difficult to explain or express, but within this very limited mind which you sense within yourself and are aware of within yourself, you have direct connection to all energy whatsoever. The entire universe is within your self and with care, regardless of the circumstance of incarnation and limitation within a body, there are ways in which the seeker may improve its connections with these deeper energies of self. It is in these deeper strata of self that the many kinds of guidance available to the seeker dwell.

One of the advantages, therefore, of meditation that is silent is that when the inner silence is entered the door betwixt the conscious and unconscious levels of mind opens, for some very slowly, for others with a great bang, for most at a steady but relatively slow pace, interrupted occasionally by real leaps forward in awareness. This is the general pattern for people who have become conscious of their spiritual identity and now wish to accelerate the pace of spiritual evolution by making more efficient and thoughtful use of the resources available.

Secondly, let us look at the concept of vibration. It may be helpful to you to begin to see into things as vibrations. This instrument produces a sound vibration by moving air through a voice box while distorting the face in various ways in order to produce what you call language. Language has to be made up of words because it is finite. It has to be made up of units of thought that are smaller than a concept. This, in itself, is very troubling to those in the metaphysical system of illusions that are attempting to speak with you because the common communication used in the metaphysical universe is concept sharing or telepathy, as this instrument would call it. Communication by concept is a direct envisioning of a whole system of thought that is in a certain pattern and that can be offered as a whole. To unravel a concept and exhaust its possibilities can be a lengthy process, the translation into words being awkward and elephantine compared to the cleanliness and lucidity of concept communication. This is but one kind of vibration.

Most within your culture are aware that heat is a vibration, light is a vibration. Most entities are not aware that all things are vibrations, and certainly it is not a common thought within your Earth plane that qualities, consciousness, essences and energies are vibrations. Indeed, if one could choose one term to describe the manifested world it would be vibration. The first vibration is that infinite Love of the one Creator, and each of you is a system of distortions of that vibration. Very simply put, the goal of the seeker is to become more and more congruent with the undistorted vibration of Love, infinite, universal Love. The Love that creates. The Love that destroys. The Love that is the "I" of you. This Love is not a manifested vibration. The first manifestation of vibration within the outer world which you now experience is light, which this instrument has learned to call the photon. And it is from this building block of light that all collections of vibrations and systems of rotation spring , [as well as] all your elements that you have learned go into the making of the various things that you can touch and see. All of these things are systems of vibration.

When you seek guidance, you are not simply asking a friend to talk to you, not unless you wish to access a certain person who is within the inner or teaching planes of your illusion. Now, this instrument does not crave, shall we say, the personal guide and, therefore, has not had experience with that specific contact that comes from finding an inner planes teacher. For those who desire a named person, a person to count on as you would a being with that personhood of personality shell, we recommend studying within the Oriental systems and Asian systems of philosophy and theology, for it is within these cultures that the concept of the Creator as teacher creates a place or a space for inner plane guides. To become more familiar with that entire way of devotion is to bring the self more into the kind of setting, shall we say, of the inner expectations that would be more likely to produce the experience of contact with a specific entity.

Within your Western philosophy, although many spiritual teachers are greatly revered, esteemed, and loved, they are not worshipped as incarnations of the Creator. Consequently, their beingness within the inner planes is quite different and, generally speaking, will move more into the vibratory levels wherein one is contacting a consciousness field of a certain vibration. For those who simply wish by whatever means to surrender to the will of the infinite One there is the feeling of the way, the tentative moving towards an orientation with one's own energies, with one's own essences, with one's connections into the deeper and deeper portions of the self. It is not necessary in order to be guided that you have any particular vision of your guide. However, as this instrument has often said, it is helpful to choose a mythical system such as Christianity, Buddhism or any other spiritual or religious system of thinking and realizing the cosmos that you feel, personally, the most kinship to. This is a matter not necessarily of the mind but, rather, of the emotions and of the spirit.

The universe is far from blank. It is filled with the vibration of all that there is. Consequently, guidance is always very, very near. Using one spiritual system to realize guidance for yourself is wise. It organizes the effort made. It gives you some starting points from which to move forward. This instrument, for instance, desires to be led by what she calls the Holy Spirit. In choosing the Holy Spirit this entity has done two things. Firstly, she has chosen, within the mythical system she has felt most kinship to, to trust and cast her loyalty upon a certain kind of entity. Secondly, she has called upon herself, for guidance comes from the deeper or higher self. Each mythical system gives one a way to realize these connections.

Without choosing a mythical system to work with the seeker must create a way of proceeding. Shall it be to name the name and to call upon that name? Shall it be to call upon a certain vibrational level that is desired? This is creative work in consciousness for the individual seeker. The one thing that is sure is that guidance is all about you. The one known as Jesus often said, "He who has ears to hear, let him hear." And certainly in this instrument's experience we find a constant conversation with the forces of nature, with beings of bird and bush and flower and sky, an overheard comment, and chance happening. Anything and everything is material for this instrument because this instrument has come to the belief that all things are sacramental. Each person, each seeker, must first realize her own way of perceiving, her own belief system, her own need in terms of guidance. Some need a named person; some need a level of vibration. But behind all of the mental and conscious ways of gaining access to this guidance there lies the identity of self with self. All guidance is from your self in a less distorted configuration of vibration to the self within incarnation, that incarnation in third density being deliberately and carefully cast into confusion and disarray.

It may seem that there are emergencies where guidance must be had, but, indeed, the greatest friend to one who seeks guidance is Sister Patience, for there is the abiding, the waiting for the rhythm of things to come into the configuration which is harmonious and right. There is that moment when the one who has the heart to understand can almost feel the situation clicking into rhythm. And when that moment of the feeling of rightness comes, there is no doubt. There is only the awareness of and the great gratitude for guidance.

Each kind of myth creates ways of thinking about this guidance. No one way of thinking is wrong. Each is an attempt, by finite intellect, to describe processes that are infinite and that take place outside of the bounds of time and space. Consequently, there are as many ways to think about guides and guidance as there are systems of thought. To this instrument the mind goes to angels because this instrument has been steeped in the Christian faith. To other entities familiar with and finding comfort in other systems' doctrine there are other kinds of beings configured a bit differently, moving perhaps from a different inner plane, and these are all genuine. For what is happening is beyond all of the systems of thought. It is energy relating to energy, love reflected in love. That is what guidance truly is, love reflected in love.

To attempt to tell one about guidance one must use finite words and thus great confusion is born. "Well, is it this way, or is it that?" It is all the ways that you can think of and none of them at all. With this paradox we know again that we are in spiritual territory. Yet that which is sought is ever at hand, closer than your own body, closer than your own thoughts, for the silence within those thoughts and within that body is beyond all time and space. And however you realize your guidance in this little life of the Earth plane, you remain a citizen of eternity, and your guidance is sure.

In third density a great veil drops and one cannot see into the metaphysical universe, or to put it in terms of the mind, into the subconscious mind. One is not supposed to see into this mind for the reason that it is this density's lesson to learn to live by faith, by those qualities of love, faith, patience and trust that defy the limitations of personality and confusion. Within each of you there is a stubborn and sure conviction that this little life is not all that there is, and when you have thought this for the first time it is as if you have become awake in the land of the slumbering. We can only say to you who wish to become more aware of the guidance sought that it is all about you, that there are ways of thinking about guidance and methods of guidance that you may consider and choose between, but know this: beyond all of your choices the information that you need comes to you again and again and again. If you miss it this time, there will be another time. Your work, indeed, can be very simple if you choose to make it so. If you choose to be a simple and unintellectual seeker you may simply sit in the inner silence expecting nothing, desiring nothing but communion with love, and that desire you may encourage and feed with the fodder of your thoughts, the branches and the trunks of your emotions.

There is a yearning within each seeker for home. And when the angel, or the guardian, or the guide, or guidance itself, is sought there is that hope of a letter from home, of a pat on the back, or a hint of what the situation is from an older and wiser relative. Whatever the way you choose, you are seeking that home when you seek guidance. You are sensing that you are on a journey, and you are asking for some information closer to the source and ending of that journey. Be aware that you may be someone else's guide. Be aware when questions are asked of you, for that which is love may speak through you if you are empty enough and clear enough. Be aware that others may be your guide for a moment without any conscious intention, or with conscious intention. It makes no difference. For what is happening is that vibration is harmonizing with vibration, or not. And connections are being made, or not. Thusly, if with patience you attend to the present moment and desire as purely as possible to know the love of the one Creator, that which is yours to do and that which is yours to be shall rhythmically come to you and express to you. And when you feel resistance, stop. Wait. Be aware. There is something that you need to know. Make space for that knowledge. Go into the silence and ask. Then be prepared to wait for that moment when the heart knows, and there is no more doubt.

May Love always be reflected in love for each of you, and may all of those difficulties that are such good teachers find their ways into your heart as blessings indeed. May we thank each again for inviting our presence within your circle of seeking this day. We shall now take our leave of this instrument and this group, leaving each in the love and in the light of the one infinite Creator. Adonai, my friends. Adonai. ✲

Sunday Meditation
March 1, 1998

Group question: Our question today concerns the principle of spiritual pride. We are wondering how it fits into the sequence of catalyst that each of us works with in our lives. We all work with pride at some time or another. Some have said that it comes up last in our pattern, that it is sort of the culmination of all of our work. We would like for Q'uo to give us an idea of what spiritual pride is and how we work with it and if there is any particular time that is more appropriate to work with it than any other?

(Carla channeling)

We are those of the principle known to you as the vibration, Q'uo. And we greet you in the love and in the light of the one infinite Creator, in whose service we are. We feel very privileged to be called to your circle at this session of working, and we bless and thank each within the circle who has come to seek the truth. We share that seeking and are glad to share our poor thoughts, as long as each of you will feel completely comfortable, listening without needing to agree or to disagree, for if you disagree we would ask that you would leave behind those thoughts. And if you agree, then we would ask that you would simply make those thoughts part of your own resources and tools, always subject to the moving rhythms of learning and experience, for personal truth is both clear and moving. There are journeys to take in this seeking of truth, ways of going that develop and lead to other levels, other facets of that infinite mystery that is Love.

This instrument finds it amusing that one of the cats that is a denizen of this house has chosen this moment to begin to snore. We hope that that is not in reaction to our words, but we cannot be sure. At any rate, we find it humorous, for we are not proud, and we take pride in that. We seek to be humble, and we know that we may be speaking complete nonsense to any of your ears, and if that is the way that it comes out, that is fine with us, that is what we wish to say. For you are the arbiter that is important to you. It is your judgment that counts and no one else's. No authority. No book. No person. For within you is all that there is, and within you is a finely honed system of sense, the physical senses being but the beginning of those senses into which you may pour your attention and from which you derive the biases that distort your life in just the way that you live it. These biases and distortions are yours. No one else's. You are unique.

We are aware that you wish to talk about spiritual pride, and we find that, as is often the case, when we are asked concerning a specific subject we need to move back into the generalities upon which we may base those opinions that we would share with you.

Let us look at this concern of pride. What is the general concept of pride? When someone is proud it is generally of some thing. A person may take pride in many things: his physical strength, her physical delicacy, the abundance of supply, or the lack of dependence upon supply, the work that one does, or the work that one will not do, the relationships that one has, or the barrier to relationships. In all these things one may take a certain pride, may say, "I feel that this is a strong point of my being. I feel I can be proud of this accomplishment, this relationship, this situation." And there is nothing more distorted about pride than there is about the illusion in general. However, in general the illusion is very dense, and this illusion creates the distortion that it is what one does that is the avenue for pride, for feeling worthwhile. The conversation of strangers tends to begin in your culture with an examination of the work that each is accomplishing in order to make money or in order to express self. Whether the work is routine or creative, it is a starting point that people recognize in each other, the place of comfort where one can divulge something about the self and be receptive to hearing something trustably understandable from others. It is very awkward to go up to a stranger and say, "What sort of vibration do you have? What kind of being are you?" Entities tend not to take pride in who they are, in the being that they express moment to moment. So you may see all of spiritual pride as a thing basically one with mental and emotional pride and physical pride.

Now let us look at pride as [in] your religions, especially the Christianity, the Muslim, and the yogic systems. In those systems spiritual pride is considered a negative value. Why is that? It is assumed that if one is proud, then there is something that must be overcome in order for him to continue with his spiritual unfoldment and evolution. Perhaps the principle, the spine, shall we say, of reason for the mistrust of pride by spiritual systems is best illustrated in the little story within your Holy Bible wherein two men are described, one of whom has made it very obvious by the way that he is dressed, by the spiritual accouterment of his costume and the books that he holds, and beside him a beggar man with tattered clothing and dirty skin, an empty stomach, and a full awareness of his iniquity. While the rich and well-satisfied man is praying, "Oh Lord, I give more to the temple than anyone else. I fast three days a week. I pray without ceasing," the beggar is saying over and over, "Lord, have mercy on me, a sinner." Can you see the walls that have come up about this rich man, the wall of wealth, of dress, of possessions, and of actions? All of them offered in a sincere effort to be holy but offered as an accomplishment. These walls make it possible for this man not to realize that in addition to all of these things that he has done right, there remains a basic and intrinsic identity within the illusion which the rich man and the beggar share with total equality. And that is the human state. The human state itself is the basis of pride, for it seems to each human, without recourse to any physical evidence, that she is alone, that the walls of skin surround the self and cut it off from oneness with all else that there is.

To those who are not seeking spiritually, this may seem fairly obvious and not worth mentioning. Of course each entity is separate. Of course each entity is alone. Each has common concerns with others of like mind, but with physical eyes, physical senses, there is no question but that each entity is alone, apart from and over against other selves, outer situations in general, and the entire environment in which the entity dwells. It is instinct, the instinct of the physical body, that carries you about, that begins this discriminatory process. The infant slowly realizes that some of its needs will not be met. It begins to realize that some things can be hurtful and does not want to repeat experiences of pain. And so the walls begin to go up about the young heart. "Don't touch the stove. Don't pat the cat too hard. Don't pick up the dog. Don't. Don't. Don't." As the child grows it learns how to defend the self. It experiments with ways of relating to other selves. And except in very unusual situations, by the time this entity is considered a mature adult by the surrounding society, this entity has become one to some extent controlled by fear.

We changed from pride to fear because the one known as J was asking which was the ultimate catalyst to be dealt with within third density. And we would respond in general that the only catalyst dealt with in third density is fear and love. The entity begins its babyhood wrapped in love, love known throughout its system, and it learns to close itself, to become apart, and to become defended because it seems fairly obvious that there are things to fear. There are entities and objects out there that can harm and hurt. So the spiritual life within third density may be described as either a learning how to love or a learning how to release fear, for fear is that distortion of love that posits a separation betwixt beings and things, thus occasioning the necessity of having some sort of response to these persons or things that will tend to increase safety and comfort.

We are not saying that these contents are incorrect, for the entity's fears are real. There is that which is feared. It is an illusion. However, the illusion cannot be brutally penetrated and torn away, for that would also do harm to the developing self. Indeed, when one is working with one's fears, attempting to see the love behind the apparent separation, the most nearly correct attitude is simply the slowing down of self, quieting the mind, stilling the emotion, until you are able to sit with whatever fear that is, not removing it harshly, but perhaps moving away strands from that tapestry in front of you, gradually making an opening through which you can see the light beyond.

We could picture the fear in one as [being] within a cave of safety with a good stout blanket over the hole of the cave to hold back those things of which they are afraid. If one rips away the blanket, then one must deal with all of the distortion at once. However, if one is satisfied to sit with and accept and be conscious of that particular fear that you are experiencing, then one may gently, gradually, with persistent effort, see a lightening of the burden, see a nearer and nearer distance to where that blanket has a place in it where one can go in and out and venture a step or two into that world beyond the cave.

Each of you has come to feel comfortable with imaging and ideating of the self as a spiritual being. Each of you is awake in a land where many slumber. And so to each of you there are special opportunities, both for service and for pain, and spiritual pride is a distortion which each seeker becomes aware of in a subtle way, over time. It is that which remains when the fears have been shaken up and the cave has been left. It is the distortion or fault peculiar to those who have worked the hardest to realize who they are, and where they are going, and whose they are. So let us look at the possible way to work with this dynamic of spiritual pride.

Within this instrument's spiritual system, pride, like envy, greed, lust, sloth, is considered more of a vice than an actual sin, a kind of excess of a good thing. It is good to be humble, and yet one can justly be proud of one's good works, one's good habits, one's ethics, one's conduct. When one is attempting to do everything that one can to live a good and holy life,

one is peculiarly apt to feel some pride in oneself. Now can you see how that feeling is a separator between the self and the world about the self? It is based upon the assumption, which is an illusion, that one is responsible for the self and at the base of the self, one is oneself. This is a sticky, sticky point and we would ask you to look closely at this matter of identity, for as long as there is self there will be pride in self or a feeling about self that does separate one from other. If one is still thinking that one is still living one's own life, one is not yet beyond spiritual pride. This instrument is aware that she is not beyond spiritual pride and has often said that this is the one vice that she cannot find a way to remove from her personality, for even though she attempts to work on her humility she has a pride of self that thinks self is right. There is a righteousness there. There is an inherent lack of eagerness to taste other souls' flavors. There is a desire to retain some boundaries, some uniqueness of self, which is completely understandable in an illusion where there is no way to discover in any way that can be proven that one is not separate, that one is not, at base, oneself. And yet we say to you that as far as we know, at base there is only the one great Self, that Love which is reflected in each of the Creator's children, which each of you is.

As long as you think that you have a self that you need to defend you shall be working with spiritual pride, and so entities for the most part are working with this no matter how persistently and purely and devotionally they have sought year after year, yet still there is the sense of "I" am searching. "I" am looking. "I" am seeking to become the best that "I" can. Conversely, we have found that coming into a fuller awareness of self is actually a process of subtraction, simplification and elimination of things from the defended self until finally the self is empty and the barriers are down. Is this safe to do within your density? No. Not at all, not in the sense of the preservation of the physical body, the emotional body, or the spiritual body within incarnation.

What we are trying to say is that it is not a terrible thing to be working with pride or in general to be working with one's fear. This is part of what one is doing in this illusion. This is what you are supposed to be doing. This is your subject matter: fear and love. Boundaries and unity. Each time this instrument tunes she repeats a prayer that we would like to repeat at this time. "Lord, make me an instrument of Thy peace. Where there is hatred, let me sow love. Where there is injury, pardon. Where there is discord, union. Where there is doubt, faith. Where there is despair, hope. Where there is darkness, light. Where there is sadness, joy. Oh, divine Master, teach us to seek not so much to be loved, as to love. Not so much to be consoled, as to console." And this instrument often says, "Not so much to be controlling, but to allow control. For it is in pardoning that we are pardoned. It is in giving that we receive. It is in dying that we rise to eternal life." Do you see the imagery of this prayer? The darkness that separates. The light that joins. The hatred that separates. The love that unites. This Prayer of St. Francis is the outcry of the soul who wishes to be free of self and subsumed into the service of the infinite mystery that it worships and adores.

And this is the door that opens into a larger and less fear-filled view of living within the illusion, this realization that there are different ways to look at each situation, that it is not terrible to have faults or to have sins or to have pride about the good things and fear about the bad things. That one is intended to be very confused by this illusion. That there is positive value in this confusion in that it, and it alone, tear most people away from those things that they cling to in fear.

You are attempting to set yourself free of an illusion, and yet within you there lies the self that is completely free, and often this instrument will recommend to people that instead of working intellectually upon some perceived problem that the person simply visualize a perfect state that is the actual truth of the situation. In truth, all is love. In truth, all is perfect now, this instant, just as it is. For there is no time or space. This is an illusion. This is the stuff of the illusion. And each of us upon our journey are illusions also. And yet unique and wonderful beings, beloved of the Creator and persisting through octaves and octaves of creation to infinity, as those very sparks that learn again and again more and more as the creation's heartbeat pulses and universes live and die and other universes are born.

It is easy to think of the spiritual life as a kind of school out of which one shall one day graduate, and certainly within the illusion of time life is graduated by larger life. There is a periodicity to things. Then for that universe in the fullness of that system of illusions, all the sparks of the Creator will have completed their journey and lost themselves within the Creator again. And all comes together in that universe at that time in an unimaginable ending of illusion into nothingness. For when there is no one to perceive, what is there but the Creator? And then the Creator dreams again and a universe is born, and the sparks are sent out again to learn more. And so you are all on a journey that the Creator is fascinated with. You cannot do anything that will turn the Creator against you, for the Creator loves all that It has made with an unimaginable fervor and absolute tenacity and embraces each spark with a love so profound and so great that it cannot be expressed.

We recommend to each the Prayer of St. Francis. When working with fear and working with pride and working with any perceived distortion that keeps one from that tuning that is the truest and the highest of the self the remembrance that there are always ways of perceiving things that change your choices and options is a tremendous tool. Simply remembering that you can explore any situation for alternate ways of perceiving it, for alternate patterns into which to put it is a great resource. We encourage each to go ahead and be proud and to know that that is a distortion that is not particularly service-to-others oriented. And so you shall work with it as you shall work with all you perceive false, and yet you shall remain human and error-prone, as we are error-prone. But beneath the time and space, the incarnation and the concerns of the incarnation, there abides a well of being that is infinite within you, an identity which creates unity with all that there is. And those moments when one is lost in communion with the source and ending of all things are moments of blessing and healing where there is no distortion, for time and space have flown away and you are tabernacling with the Most High.

The next time that you experience the catalyst of feeling that you are yet an incomplete spiritual being, remember the truth of subtracting, of dropping away that which is not. And as you experience those realizations that enable you to drop a part of the ego away, rejoice. You cannot make it happen. You cannot rush it. But there come moments and you perceive that you no longer have that pride or that particular fear. And of that you may be proud and happy, and if that is a distortion also, then so be it. For you are not here to go beyond distortion but to live within distortion by faith, to express within this confusion a trust in the plan that placed you here, a trust in the destiny that is absolutely yours. A feeling that cannot come from proof or words that all that is yours will come to you and that you do not need to reach but only ask "Thy will for me today. What is it? And I will try my best." That is all that you must do. So do not give up upon the self because it continues to have distortions and confusions. That is all right. You are not supposed to be without illusion. Ah, precious incarnation. If we could but share with you the opportunity that is now yours. If we could share that perception with you fully you would jump for joy. You would rejoice most fully and heartily, for here is the place where you choose by faith alone, and this choice, this expression of faith, however imperfect, creates within that permanent self which is beyond space and time tremendous changes in consciousness which you cannot achieve outside of this third density of yours. For in other densities the veil of knowing is lifted and what virtue is it then to realize that you are your brother and that all those things your brother has are you? There is no virtue in perceiving the color red if your eyes are open. But, ah, with the eyes closed, here you are in a world of color with your eyes closed. For you are in the equivalent of a black and white movie. You are up there on the screen watching yourself. The pigment of the movie screen is grainy, and some of the voices are distorted, and it's kind of a corny story, and it's over too soon. But, ah, when you come out of the theater into the light and you look back on that black and white movie and you see the hope and the faith and the caring and the love and the compassion that you truly have had, with no reason for it but just that constant desire for love, to know love, to know the truth, to express that love. Each of you is a gallant, gallant soul and we both envy you and honor you, for you do much that you do not know; even as you suffer, you heal worlds.

So be content. That is what we would say to you. Be content, and simply look carefully, and more carefully, and with opener and opener eyes at all that there is about you. And see into things as you can, as you are able, as you are given grace, remembering who you are, remembering in whose service you are and letting yourself be yourself, for that is a wonderful and special thing. Each of you are very beautiful.

We would apologize for our wordiness upon this subject but we feel that this concern is a very deep one and wish to probe into it somewhat. We thank each once again and would leave this instrument in love and light, transferring to the instrument known as Jim. We are those of Q'uo.

(No questions asked.)

(Tape ends.)

Sunday Meditation
March 15, 1998

Group question: We would like to know if there is a best way to deal with a balance between the need to do something and waiting to let things happen naturally when we are going through big changes that may be an initiation or transition of a major nature in our lives? What is the balance between the work of the heart and the work of the mind in dealing with these changes?

(Carla channeling)

We are those known to you as the principle of Q'uo, and we greet each of you in the love and in the light of the one infinite Creator. May we say how privileged and how humble that we feel to be asked to share our opinions and our thoughts with you at this time. We are aware that this week the concern upon your minds is that of change. There are many ways of looking at this necessary and inevitable process. Perhaps for us we would take a step back from the soul in transition and attempt to describe what we see as the situation against which this drama of change and transformation plays itself out. The one known as S has expressed a love of the concept of the holographic universe, and, indeed, we also feel that each of you is as the hologram of the creation and of the Creator. This, of course, is not obvious or manifest within your third-density illusion, and yet there is a spot within each awakened soul that lies far below the level of sense and rational thought where the spirit knows self, and that basis or fundament is a kind of knowing of self that does not change with time or space or occasion, but rather is the essence of self, the infinitely subtle and unique patterns of vibration which create that complex perfume of light and color that is the spark which each of you is. It is difficult to express this concept in a language which measures by size, for you as a citizen of eternity are both infinitely large and infinitely small. However, in both views of this basis of self, the spark of self is a reality in the midst of confusion, a feeling deep within that endures beyond all experience. When it rises to consciousness for even a moment the conscious life is transformed for that moment.

And when these moments of clarity occur to each who is upon a shadowed path and feeling the stress of change, we encourage the careful etching into memory of that moment, for the bare memory of the realness of self is a balm and a comfort against the sometimes very difficult emotional and mental experiences of one who is in the process of change. Beyond all other resources, for the one who perceives herself as changing this basic resource of knowing that holographic self within and remembering the way that feels is a powerful and saving memory.

Let us look now at change using the word, suffering. When the life of flesh is born it immediately begins to change. Within the physical world all things that grow bodies and appear in the illusion as part of the Earth plane change continuously through their time of bloom, ripening and decay. The source and ending of all these changes for physical flesh is dust and ashes. We do not for a minute suggest that the source and ending of the change within the spiritual seeker is dust and ashes. However, it is well to realize the absolute inevitability of constant and unremitting cycles of alteration and transformation, and within each transformation there is the decay, there is the loss of what is left behind. And there is that time when loss has occurred but new life has not become apparent. Those times, which this instrument has often called the Dark Night of the Soul, are times of gravest pain and bewilderment for many. Certainly the mind grasps the concept of change. And as this instrument was saying earlier, the mind views change as a problem to solve. This is the natural tendency of a brain, and we make this distinction clearly between intellect and consciousness, that the form was created simply to solve problems, to make choices that tend towards the safety and comfort of a physical vehicle.

However, when the spirit awakens from Earth's pleasant slumber, it beholds not simply the natural processes of a life, not simply the earning of money, the acquisition of needed items and so forth, but far more acutely there is the sense of the mind's being unable to grapple with or solve the process of spiritual change. So often those in the midst of spiritual change do attempt to use the intellect. It is a natural and a common resource. After all, the mind is consulted continuously, is working continuously, and when it is faced with the subtle nuances of that which is deeper than words, it finds itself uncharacteristically boggled. There are things upon which the intellect cannot work. There are situations which the intellect cannot make into a problem to solve. There is that feeling of being out of control, and intellectually speaking, this feeling is accurate. For there is little that the brain can do to promote peacefulness of heart or that wonderful feeling of grace.

This inability to bring the resources of the mind into play and fire away at the situation is not easily understood by those who have not awakened. They do not see beyond whatever material concerns are at the surface of the change or are happening concurrently with the change that is sensed within, and consequently the spiritual seeker is cut off not only from his own abilities of intellect but also the intellectual resources of those about him.

Conversely, those who grasp and fully sympathize with the subtleties of spiritual regeneration cannot bring words to bear upon a process which is far deeper and less personal than words and language in general might offer. The issues involved in spiritual transformation are profoundly impersonal as well as uniquely personal to each seeker. That is, at the same time that the seeker is experiencing unique perceptions because of the unique pattern of distortions for that particular entity, that spark is also melding with and creating dynamics with a greater Self, which process is very difficult to express in language, for this Self is at the same time that spark that is you and all that there is. The layers of self as one moves down the tree of mind are infinite, and as the experiencer moves through and takes part in this process of spiritual change it may at one moment be at one level of mind; at another moment at a bewilderingly different level of mind, skimming and diving deep, coming up and leveling out, and at the same time not knowing that one is in motion. The spiritual sea is three-dimensional, and you can breathe the water.

So there are experiences of being taken to the bottom of self, of becoming the planet, the star, the sun, the creation; at the same time, those infinitely small awarenesses of the self as a thought, as an ether, as an object such as a beautiful butterfly, or a perfectly blooming flower, or given the sardonic nature of certainly this instrument's mind, a pile of garbage. All of these levels and feelings that the senses cannot process within incarnation are in play and in play with a good deal of freedom while the entity is attempting somehow not simply to survive this process but to embrace it, to make a welcome for it, and to cooperate with it and perhaps accelerate the process. Yet the essence of spiritual change is suffering. There is a shallow suffering to being without a home, keen but not bone deep. There is a deeper degree of suffering in becoming aware of either the depth of suffering of the self or the suffering of the world. And this can crash in upon one with mind-numbing power and intensity and cast one into a great pit of despair.

This is part of the creation. This, too, is to be embraced, this death, this pain, this limitation, this very pain is to be embraced somehow. The self does not see any possibility of becoming able naturally to embrace suffering. Here is where the heart may become an ever more helpful and useful resource, for while the mind is an excellent tool for the outer world of decisions within the outer world, it is within the heart and the deeper emotions that spiritual change shall take place. And, therefore, it is to the heart that the seeker may reliably and trustfully come; sometimes for comfort, sometimes for encouragement, and sometimes simply for a place to be held and comforted and loved. Whereas the mind must think itself sacred, the innermost heart is already holy ground, and awaiting there is the Creator, that intelligent infinity that so curiously loves every spark from which It is learning about Itself. As you sit within this temple and remember the Creator and feel that holiness within, the self may find surcease from pain just for that moment. And, oh, what a relief that moment is!

We would at this time pause and ask for a redirection of the question, for we realize that there were several strands to the information requested this day, and we would like to have further direction. Is there a question at this point that someone would wish to throw in so that we could, shall we say, get our bearings? We are Q'uo.

V: How does the releasing of past traumatic experiences or past programming relate to the progress that can be made and the changes that will be necessary at this time to go further in the ascension process?

We are those of Q'uo, and we thank you for your question, my sister. The past often seems to be a kind of permanent burden, at least the less pleasant portion of that past. There are crystallized nuggets of pain, emotional and spiritual pain, that are locked deeply within the personality and character of each seeker. Any attempt to analyze or therapize them into a new configuration is limited in its success because it is not seen by most therapeutic entities that the issue is forgiveness. The deeply buried programming and crystals of pain are seen as that which need to be taken out, to be pulled up by the roots, seen, in other words, as weeds in a garden. And yet this approach only tends to build walls thick enough to protect one from those crystallized areas of pain without coming into a balanced awareness of that pain. One cannot give it away. One can only give away what one has forgiven oneself for feeling, and the triggers for this forgiveness are different for each seeker. The key, however, is forgiveness of self, forgiveness of others, forgiveness of humanity. For truly it is the very nature of the physical world as you know it, this heavy chemical density in which you abide, that almost nothing can be known.

However, when the senses are awakened by that final iota of forgiveness it is as though someone has lifted the burden from the shoulders. As to how to approach that moment of release we can only encourage persistence of desire. It is written in your holy works, "Ask and you shall receive. Knock and it shall be opened unto you." And this is true. We always say through this instrument, "Be careful for what you wish for." For truly, all desires will be granted to you. And yet what does a spiritual being wish for? Does it wish for surcease of pain, or does it wish to serve the Creator in whatever way it may serve the Creator? Are not the paths of those spiritual entities which are inspirations to you within your world those lives which have experienced much pain and suffering? And yet you see in those lives a joy, a delight, a passion that somehow transforms the experience of suffering. This instrument's path to the Creator is the teacher known to you as Jesus the Christ. This entity deliberately sought its suffering and simply dedicated it to the suffering of all beings, opened its arms to the world and said, "I take all of the pain, all of the suffering, because I want there to be less suffering, and this is what I can do."

In many ways you also may take upon yourself the sorrow of the world, and this is a spiritual practice that many have pursued. We ask you to gaze with a cold eye upon the suffering involved in transformation, for this attitude is a balanced one in our humble opinion. It is to the person who is able to gaze upon the Dark Night of the Soul, which this instrument spoke of, with an indifferent eye but a full and willing heart, that this process may begin to come easier. By releasing and yielding to your suffering, by welcoming that which must be suffered as a brother and as a sister, by offering the hospitality of your life, your body, your mind, your strength, and your will to this process, the heart is opened as if by magic, and you find that no matter how intensely you hurt, it does not kill but, rather, cleanses, empties, renews and readies that instrument to be an ever clearer, purer and brighter channel for the light that must come through into the world or the love that must come through into the world, not from you but through you.

As you embrace this process those emotions of release and humility, humbleness and nothingness, become an offering to be lifted up unto the Creator as "all that I have." "This is all that I have and this I give to you. Do with me what you will. I am a boat. Life is the ocean. Toss me somewhere. I shall attempt to sail." This kind of abandon, this action of the Fool is powerful. And as you become ridiculous, as you embrace this darkness, you embrace also the light that follows. For truly in the Dark Night of the Soul there is a moon setting and a sun rising. And that sun is a glory beyond all space and time signifying a Love that created all that there is. We would encourage that moment of abandon within each of you where you not only say but feel, "Not my will, but Thine." For, you see, there is a cyclic nature to manifestation of any kind. As the Creator's heart beats, creations are born and die. The one thing that remains, whether it is perceived or not, is that intelligent infinity that we can only call Love in your language, this vibration which is the one great original Thought or Logos is what you are, with no past or future but simply a moment of being that is infinite.

Move back into this awareness when you have done your work with the mind, with the emotions, always you are the branches reaching down to the roots of the vine, for your roots are those of perfect Love. And as you spiral ever upward, you shall be light and dark and light again and again and again. And that which has become a burden will be sloughed off again and again and again, for you shall mature, not by adding things unto your self, but by allowing them to fall away from the self. In fear, you see, you collect and armor and harden. As love is able to touch those difficulties that have crystallized within, they are subtracted from the already whole, already perfect being that is your reality.

We realize that what we have offered may be slim comfort to those to whom this present moment is a vale of tears, and we would remind each of you that the Creator's love can only be expressed, that support can only be given, by the hands that are of flesh. You are the Creator to those about you. Your support is the only way the Creator can support within the incarnation, within the illusion. Your hands. Your voice. Your smile. Your eyes. These things are your gifts to your brothers and sisters. Sorrow is essential to this experience that you call third-density life. But your attitude towards this sorrowing, grieving and changing process can create for you a peace that surpasses all understanding. We encourage each of you to see that heaven, even if it is from afar, to know that the angels and ministers that have always loved you, love you now and are here to help you, though unseen they hover, waiting to comfort, looking for ways to confirm any glimmer of hope within. You are never alone in this process. This is a guarded and protected process, and the haven does abide. May each of you help each other to find your way home.

(Transcript ends.) ❧

L/L Research

L/L Research is a subsidiary of Rock Creek Research & Development Laboratories, Inc.

P.O. Box 5195
Louisville, KY 40255-0195

www.llresearch.org

Rock Creek is a non-profit corporation dedicated to discovering and sharing information which may aid in the spiritual evolution of humankind.

ABOUT THE CONTENTS OF THIS TRANSCRIPT: This telepathic channeling has been taken from transcriptions of the weekly study and meditation meetings of the Rock Creek Research & Development Laboratories and L/L Research. It is offered in the hope that it may be useful to you. As the Confederation entities always make a point of saying, please use your discrimination and judgment in assessing this material. If something rings true to you, fine. If something does not resonate, please leave it behind, for neither we nor those of the Confederation would wish to be a stumbling block for any.

CAVEAT: This transcript is being published by L/L Research in a not yet final form. It has, however, been edited and any obvious errors have been corrected. When it is in a final form, this caveat will be removed.

© 2009 L/L Research

Special Meditation
April 4, 1998

Group question: Our question has to do with a quote which Ra made, "The source of all distortion is the limitation of the viewpoint." We are wondering how, since each of us seems to bring various distortions with us into the illusion, these distortions affect that which we produce, whether we raise a family, create laws, beauty, dance, channel, whatever we do? How do our distortions in our personalities affect that which we hope to produce in our learning and our service in this incarnation?

(Carla channeling)

We are those of the principle known to you as Q'uo, and we greet you in the love and in the light of the one infinite Creator in whose service we come to your peoples. We want to thank each of you for calling us to your group, for enabling us to learn from our own way of offering service. For truly without your call we could not be useful in our present occupation, for we hear the cries of the sorrowed of the Earth, and we seek to lighten that sorrow by sharing our thoughts and our opinions. We ask that each of you exercise discrimination in listening to our words or any words. For we are not authorities, nor is anyone else when it comes to the spiritual journey, for each person is unique. Each spirit has its own journey, and though there are many, many points of similarity each path is unique. Each spark of the Creator is unique, and each will recognize and treasure those truths that are meant to be heard. Those thoughts that we offer that do not meet that demanding criteria, we ask that you leave behind. For truly you shall recognize those concepts that can be to you a tool or a resource in your evolution.

Your query this evening concerns distortion, the distortion seen in personality. And in order to discuss this we must move back to examine that concept of distortion. This is the way that we use the word distortion. To our way of thinking, all that there is in the manifested world is distortion. The lack of distortion, when absolute, describes intelligent infinity, the Creator Itself, in Its unpotentiated state. The first distortion which approaches the unmanifest intelligent infinity is free will. This produces that manifestation of the Logos which is known to this instrument as intelligent energy and known to your scientists as the photon, or light. When we come to you in the love and in the light of the infinite Creator we are coming to you in those distortions, for were we to come to you as undistorted Creator we would have no being in a manifested universe. We would be unable to act in any way, for all would be one in an absolute sense.

So when we gaze at the distortion of a particular personality shell, at the systems of energy blockage and bafflement which causes what seem to others as an unbalanced or distorted personality, we gaze upon distortions of distortions of distortions. We gaze upon systems of energy, all of which are distortions of the one great original Thought which is Love. To us, then, that a person is distorted in such and such a way, in the context of an incarnation, is not a bad, a wrong, or an incorrect thing. For we are aware that each entity before incarnation selects the personality shell which contains those gifts and those physical, mental, emotional and spiritual limitations which will create biases or distortions, which will then set up both the personal learning for that entity for that incarnation and the path of service or paths of service that become available to the entity during incarnation, given that various systems of distortion do indeed prove to stand the test of incarnational time.

It is not that an entity incarnates with one mission and can either fulfill it or fail to fulfill it. Rather, there is the setting up of circumstance which may provide the catalyst which was considered desirable by that spirit before incarnation. The system of distortions or biased opinions can show themselves very simply in the growing entity as preferences. Each young spirit in incarnation discovers things that it likes, things that it wishes to avoid. As the incarnation progresses there are repetitions and cycles of experience that lead the entity repeatedly to the crossroads of incarnational choice, not simply once in an incarnation but reliably and dependably again and again. Each spirit will face one or more basic incarnational questions. For instance, this instrument is already aware that its incarnational desire for personal learning was to find situations in which it was able to give without expectation of return. This is, in fact, a fairly common incarnational goal. And to this end, certain biases were chosen by this particular entity. In just this fashion each evolving spirit will in the processes of incarnational living meet situation after situation in which the metaphysical question is repeated, and the choice may again be made for service to others, for service to self.

So the biases given to oneself certainly create avenues of learning and avenues of service. However, the metaphysical twist, shall we say, of fate deposits in each spirit's experience a universe in which gifts are not necessarily used for what that entity thinks they should be used for. The ability to dance, the ability to sing, the ability to do mathematical equations, the ability to do any particular thing which is considered unusually skillful or to constitute a talent or a gift may logically be assumed to lead one to a specific career or line of work or avenue of expression. In many cases, this is simply not the goal in a metaphysical sense. Because one can, for instance, play the piano it is not necessarily one's fate to become a pianist. The delicacy with which the music is heard and felt, the dexterity of mind and muscle that is involved in producing a heartfelt and intelligent piece of music has many metaphysical uses which are not necessarily apparent and do not have much to do with music.

Consequently, biases in the form of talents and gifts, in a metaphysical sense, do not equate from talent to expression. There is always the mystery of that rhythm of destiny which, if looked for and listened for and heeded when heard, can greatly facilitate and ease the accomplishment of that destiny which was, in fact, metaphysically hoped for, illogical as it may seem in Earth terms.

In the sense in which the question was asked, the distortions had to do with producing a pure channeling, the three entities involved in producing this channeling being obviously distorted and biased and in many ways unbalanced. The question put to this instrument by the original questioner in this regard was, "How can such an unbalanced group produce a pure and clear contact?" And we say to this entity, the one known as J, and to this group, as we have said before and as others have said through this instrument, that, metaphysically speaking, it is the intention, the desire, and the hunger of the entity in visualizing service that creates the service, not the system of distortions which have set up a particular dynamic. However, it is to be noted that in line with what we have said about distortions, although it is in no way obvious that various distortions would create these dynamics, nevertheless, the distortions chosen by each of those three entities were exquisitely utile in creating an atmosphere in which three confused and highly distorted entities could support each other's desire to serve and could support such with a purity of intention that, for each, had been honed over a period of time.

Again, we note that distortion, seen in a metaphysical sense, is a matter of mechanics, of setting up a situation which may produce a system of energies that harmonizes for a specific kind of service. When any group unites for service there is a great explosion of potential energy, and it is to those entities who have spent the time or the effort or have the gifts to be of a sincerity that is profound that service in a group shall be most successful. The way distortion feeds into group effort, then, is both obvious and mysterious. Obvious in the sense of seen attributes, talents and gifts. Forever mysterious in that seen by human eyes each entity is less than perfect. Seen as systems of energy that may harmonize, distortions may be seen as most fortunate and most powerful in combination.

We are those of Q'uo, and we would welcome further queries upon this point before moving on to another question.

H: I want to know if you can enlighten me on my father who died last August and the fact that I have a real sense of him being with me, and I am not sure what I mean by that. Perhaps you can help me understand a real sense of his presence with me at this time?

We are those of Q'uo, and we grasp your query, my sister. When entities leave the Earth plane there is, in many cases, much healing that needs to take place, and adequate time and space for this healing is supported, nurtured and provided. There is no time limit upon this period of balancing and review of incarnation, and often a portion of this healing is the continued ability to, as this instrument would say, keep track of those entities [which one has] a particular kind of connection, affinity or dynamic with. In many cases there is the opportunity during this period for comfort in the company of those still living who have this particular connection, affinity or dynamic. This is not necessarily evident from closeness within incarnation and, indeed, when there has been some lack of communication within incarnation it is extremely healing for the entity moving through that review of incarnation to sit on the shoulder, indeed, to lie within the heart as comforter and supporter. And most of all to breathe the odor of a beloved personality, for even though the personality shell is chosen out of a vast self that is the true self for incarnation, that personality shell is turned into art, turned into beauty by the creative spirit. And when an entity gazes back over an incarnation and sees that bright light of a particular shell that for this entity has shone, or as the song said, "Helped the universe to shine," for this entity, there is great comfort in the company of that entity. It is not that there is a great message to be shared or that there is a concern, but, rather, simply an enjoyment and appreciation that could not be felt within incarnation but that is seen from the wider standpoint of larger life beyond that veil of illusion which is the Earth plane.

May we answer you further, my sister?

H: What I think I hear you saying is that the entity that manifested on Earth as my father is now sitting on my shoulder in appreciation of having a broader view now that he is no longer manifested physically. He is more of a total spirit. It is more like that entity is looking at me, and that is an interesting perspective for me to see because I wondered if I was in some way invoking him. Or wanting to or this was a hope. I didn't know where it was coming from. Thank you for your explanation.

We are those of Q'uo, and we thank you, my sister. We believe that you have the gist of it as we offered it. This instrument is having difficulty expressing this concept. The puzzle of personality is that puzzle where pieces keep trying to fit together and after incarnation after incarnation is experienced each entity in relationship finds the fit a bit better and a bit better. And as entities move in and out of illusion they can, when out of the illusion, have far greater appreciation of the healing and healthful aspects of a given relationship and find transformative healing within appreciation of the living entity that is within incarnation seen from that broader context. Indeed, for a person to heal from incarnation there is the self to be forgiven. And each relationship is gazed upon. The surprises involved in this gaze from larger life are many. And we would simply say that in most cases where there is that intuition of presence the source of that intuition is not the self in [the] personality shell of incarnation but the other self that is in relationship and that is relating from larger life as a part of its healing. So in a way that entity that is you is a healing presence to this entity as it is in larger life reviewing the incarnation that has been and gazing at the self to see what perhaps shall be the next choices of incarnation, of personality shell, of mission, of purpose.

Is there a further question, my sister?

H: Thank you very much. That was very clear.

We would at this time transfer this contact to the one known as Jim. We thank this instrument and leave it in the love and in the light of the one infinite Creator. We are known to you as those of Q'uo.

(Jim channeling)

I am Q'uo, and greet each again in love and in light through this instrument. We would continue to entertain further queries that those present might have for us at this time.

E: I am wondering if it is possible to meet yourself in the form of another person in this life?

I am Q'uo, and am aware of your query, my brother. In the largest possible sense this is always true with each entity that you meet, for each entity is an other self, an other aspect of your self and of the one Creator from which all aspects move into experience through the illusion. In the sense which we feel you are asking at this time we would also suggest that is also quite possible for entities to have the opportunity to interact with other portions of the self which have incarnated from other periods of the, as you would see it, the river of time moving from one point to another. However, we would suggest that this experience is one which has the purpose of allowing each aspect of the larger self to integrate with another in order that there might be a more complete experience for that portion of the self which might be termed the oversoul or the higher self. This portion of each entity's self exists at a level of experience which can be seen as existing in your future. However, it also is that which exists in what you see as your past. The experience of each of its portions is undertaken in order that an overall balance might be achieved.

Is there a further question, my brother?

E: How would you recognize such a meeting?

I am Q'uo, and am aware of your query, my brother. We would suggest that the recognition is most difficult, for the great majority of the third-density population is unaware of the possibility of such an experience and would not be able to identify the feelings of familiarity and the intuition that alerts the conscious mind to the recognition that is subtle, profound and powerful.

Is there a further query?

E: No. Thank you. I think that that was a very accurate answer.

I am Q'uo, and we thank you, my brother. Is there another query at this time?

Carla: H and I were talking about how I could help myself with diet. I feel that I am living on faith and nerve pretty much after a lot of experience with diet. Why would I give myself such a bankrupt system? Why would I not react to food which I so love to see growing and that I so love to cook for other people? I have no logical anything to illuminate that feeling. It's just an intuition.

I am Q'uo, and am aware of your query, my sister. As you are so well aware, the experience which you have had with the ingestion of foodstuffs has been one which has seen a full circle of variety and preparation, tailored so that the gastrointestinal tract which your physical vehicle is saddled with may be able to pass the foodstuffs in a regular fashion. There has been the preincarnative choices to limit the physical vehicle in many ways in order that the efforts of the incarnation might be focused inwardly and might look toward those areas towards which it has looked. The side effects of the physical vehicle's limitations are many, including those concerning the ingestion of foodstuffs, as you are aware. The fact that the physical vehicle is still incarnate is a fact that should bring great rejoicing, for this physical vehicle has gone through much stress and difficulty throughout its incarnation in order that the focus be maintained. It is part of your present understanding that the low-residue diet is of central importance, and this suggestion is one which we continue to recommend. This in itself has its limiting factors according to the variety of foodstuffs that are within the range of the low-residue diet. If there is the desire to further improve the diet we are aware of some small measures that can be taken but in the overall sense would continue to recommend the course which has been traveled of late.

We would at this time once again thank those present for inviting our presence in your circle of seeking this day. We are known to you as those of Q'uo, and we leave you in the love and in the light of the one infinite Creator. Adonai. ❧

L/L Research is a subsidiary of Rock Creek Research & Development Laboratories, Inc.

P.O. Box 5195
Louisville, KY 40255-0195

www.llresearch.org

Rock Creek is a non-profit corporation dedicated to discovering and sharing information which may aid in the spiritual evolution of humankind.

ABOUT THE CONTENTS OF THIS TRANSCRIPT: This telepathic channeling has been taken from transcriptions of the weekly study and meditation meetings of the Rock Creek Research & Development Laboratories and L/L Research. It is offered in the hope that it may be useful to you. As the Confederation entities always make a point of saying, please use your discrimination and judgment in assessing this material. If something rings true to you, fine. If something does not resonate, please leave it behind, for neither we nor those of the Confederation would wish to be a stumbling block for any.

CAVEAT: This transcript is being published by L/L Research in a not yet final form. It has, however, been edited and any obvious errors have been corrected. When it is in a final form, this caveat will be removed.

© 2009 L/L Research

Sunday Meditation
April 19, 1998

Group question: Our question this week concerns the concept of gratitude. How does gratitude work in the spiritual or metaphysical sense? It is said that it is a powerful force to have in the heart, just to be alive, to be breathing, and to serve the Creator. How does gratitude affect our spiritual growth, even in the worst of situations?

(Carla channeling)

We are those of the principle known to you as Q'uo. We greet you in the love and in the light of the one infinite Creator. We bless and thank each of you for all that you have done to come to this circle of seeking at this time, for all that you have sacrificed and the choices that you have made that have brought you, as seekers of truth, to sit together and open your hearts to each other, to the universe whose citizens that you are, and to those thoughts of ours that might have use for you. You have truly given us a great blessing and a great gift. We hope that those thoughts that we share with you shall be helpful to you. If any thought does not please you, we simply ask that you release it and forget it, for we do not have authority but, rather, are as you: pilgrims sharing that which we have come to feel is our truth, hoping that it might be a resource for you as well. As always, we encourage your careful discrimination in listening to any and all opinion, for there is no authority as great as that which rests within you and which knows what is yours.

You ask this day about gratitude, thankfulness. We realize that this is peculiarly difficult to come to in any situation, for within the illusion that you experience as your incarnation the atmosphere is not full of clarity and illumination but rather often full of confusion and negative seeming emotion. The heart within desires to experience only a greater and greater amount of solitude, peacefulness and beauty, but that which the world seems to offer is crowded with many different people with many different opinions and certainly seems far from peaceful as the timbers and rafters of your own personal mental interior shake and stagger under the many confusions that reign and that shall always hold sway over the incarnation, over the experience throughout the incarnation, for truly, as we often say, no one who takes incarnation upon a third-density planet is hoping for a clear and peaceful existence, but, rather, is hoping to be utterly confused and yet to remember, somehow, those truths which can only be known by faith, which can only be remembered by faith, and which can only yield hope, praise and gratitude within the transformed heart.

It is that transformation of experience that each hopes for again and again within the incarnational experience. And as each of you looks back over patterns that have been completed in the past, each may see the working out of seemingly insurmountable confusion in ways that were unexpected and yet elegant, difficult and beautiful. Such is the bittersweet quality of realization amidst the sea of confusion that is consensus reality within your Earth world.

What is the spirit that it should be mindful of such things as praise and thanksgiving? It is at this very basic level that so many among your peoples cannot grapple with the issue of life itself. What is the spirit within that it must take flesh and be thrust into a world of sensation that overstimulates with glorious disarray and confusion? The spirit, from the instant that it awakens into the Earth plane until that moment when the last breath leaves the body, what is this entity that it should feel anything, positive or negative? It is in facing this question of identity that the search for true thankfulness must begin. For just here, just upon that spot where the slide is under the microscope, there at that first glimpse of light of that which changes, we get the first scent of the dangers and the glories of this ephemeral and all-to-short process of incarnation. Each of you begins with that spark of light that is your essence and your core. It is in no way different from or lesser than the Creator Itself, for it, as all things, is infinite and divine love.

The clay from which you have been formed expresses that love but is not that love. There is no thing about each of you that one can pick up and say, "This is the essence of this person." No, the essence of you is much closer to you than your body, is much more a part of you than your breathing or your heartbeat or the rush of blood through your veins. You are love. It is this identity that is the only explanation for praise and thanksgiving, for positive or negative expression of any kind. When one can realize, even momentarily, that deep identity within, that congruency with the Logos Itself, the seeker then has his feet on solid ground and may say to the self, and in response to the world however it comes to him, "I am love. I am in a state of utter confusion. But I am love. This is my nature. I take this on faith." When one can begin with this much confidence then one is able to move into that attitude which this instrument would call the positive path or the path of service to others. If one thinks to oneself, "I am responsible. I did these things," or "These and these things have been done unto me," then one has become willing to begin, not from that place of love, but, rather, from a place where masks have been put on and a stage play is being acted. Once one has moved into that level of interaction and the various responses to each other's catalyst that characterize relationships one no longer has a quick or short route to that positive place of rest within which knows, "I am love, and the I am that is me is the I am that is you."

Without this feeling of self as love, one simply begins to see oneself as positioned in such and such a way and aiming to get positioned in such and such a way. Then the self has a story that is not being created in rhythm and according to destiny's often slow pace, but rather the self is creating the self with masks at a level which does not fill the heart. The conversation before this meditation several times touched upon the many ways in which that feeling of humble thankfulness comes to one as a blessing and a special visitation much like the spring rain feeding the young plants. We encourage each of you to be willing, when thinking upon this subject of identity, to see the self as a deeply impersonal, a deeply true, entity. For truly each of you is that which is beyond personality, and if the spirit can rest in that most basic and profound identity there stems from time and attention spent here a strength and flexibility of emotional responses that is part of the rhythm of faith.

We are often aware of the degree of suffering among your peoples. The sorrow of your peoples is great, the yearning for that which is remembered is great. There is a hunger for heavenly things, as this instrument would call it, a thirst for that meat and drink that feeds the soul, and yet in so many ways the restless heart cannot find quiet enough to connect with that great heart of Love Itself, which is the source and ending of each and every spark of light within the infinite creation.

When entities attempt to feel gratitude they may well fail, for gratitude is not that which may be approached head-on with the most effectiveness but, rather, a sense of thankfulness or gratitude comes as a natural efflux or emanation from the soul which is willing to be still and allow the world to find its balance within the self. This is not something that is easily done by those within incarnation, for the living without faith is that which is taught and practiced by your culture, not here and there, but as a general rule. Young ones within your culture are taught to work, to give a good effort, to follow certain paths in order to further ambition. The soul is taught that worth is in what one does, and so each growing spirit faces the self, attempts to find that which will earn the money, attempts to prepare the self for doing this, and then spends the life following a certain career, profession or job, and as one is wending one's way through the various obstacles that seem to pop up from day to day in the execution of these various professions and jobs and so forth, any entity that is able to help or facilitate one or another of these ambitions is seen as someone to whom to be grateful while those who are stumbling blocks seeming to be in the way between the self and the ambition are seen to be irritations and of negative help.

When we, or any, attempt to speak upon spiritual things we are often tempted simply to tell stories, for there is within stories that which words alone cannot express. And when dealing with gratitude perhaps the story that this instrument is most familiar with is the story of the Prodigal Son. There are several different ways to look at this little story that was told by the teacher known to you as Jesus. In this story the sons of a wealthy man have two different natures. The older son is the good son, and this son never thinks of anything but simply staying at home and working on the family estate. However, the younger son is impatient and ready to have fun, have a good time in his life. And so this younger son asks his father for his inheritance. He has decided that he wishes to go to the city and have a good time. The father is willing to give his young son his fair portion of his accumulated fortune that he has to offer. And so the Prodigal Son trots off to the big city and engages in various excesses of various kinds until he becomes penniless, homeless and forlorn. Finally, the young man is reduced to living with the pigs, eating what is given to the pigs in order to stay alive. And it occurs to this Prodigal Son, "You know, I could go back to the country, back to my father's house. Of course he wouldn't take me back, but I could be a slave and eat much better than this because my father treats his slaves much better than this." And so off he goes, but when the father sees him coming he rejoices greatly and orders a great feast to be prepared. Now the older son is very jealous of this, and says, "Gosh, dad, I've been with you all the time. I've always been a good boy. I've done everything you wanted me to do. You never killed a fatted calf for me, and here you are having a huge party for my idiot brother who never did anything." The father says, "But don't you see? I thought I had no son and now I do."

Look at the gratitude in all of these people. The father grateful because he has regained the son whom he loves. The Prodigal Son who is grateful simply to be accepted back as a slave, much less as a younger son. And look at the hard heart, the pain of the older brother who does not feel his father's love since he has never done anything wrong for which his father has had to forgive him.

Each of you is a prodigal. Each of you has squandered precious things. Each of you greatly and humbly seeks to return to the house of the Father, to that place of love that is undefiled and pure. For in that state gratitude is natural and flows effortlessly and this is a great truth [for] each of you, that you are loved deeply, that you are welcomed in spite of any and all failures, and that the Creator does give great thanks for you. Truly, it takes the movement of thought from the little self experienced in every day to that self that each knows is a truer and deeper self. Gazing at life from the standpoint of the everyday self there is hardly ever a completely trouble-free or worry-free experience. There is hardly ever a reason to feel completely or profoundly grateful. And yet if one can move back into that prodigal self that is coming home, you may see that all of experience is such that the only response is thankfulness and praise.

Why is this gratitude so powerful? Simply because it is the truth. In truth everything that occurs to you is a gift. Each situation delivers to you the sisters and brothers of experience, Sister Sorrow, Brother Pain. The list is different for each entity. Brother Anger. Sister Depression. Each spirit will have its own guests that seem to be difficult indeed to be hospitable towards, and yet each of these guests comes with great gifts to give you. There is a natural rebellion against having to see things from such a deep perspective. The mind does not want to move to this level where it can be seen that all things are gifts. The mind wants to distinguish between things. The mind wants to make choices and stack everything in neat and orderly piles. "This is that. This is the other. This is something else entirely." But that spark of true self within you is ever ready to spread and illuminate the spirit within, the heart within.

Each entity, each spirit that has taken flesh comes to the experience of incarnation with an agenda, with the hope of learning and the hope of service. It seems very simple before incarnation, this whole remembering of things through the veil. And it is not so simple, for the veil is surely there and surely appropriately thick and impenetrable. But for those who can live within the open heart, who can face the difficulties of the day from that place of the open heart, there is the opportunity to see each day as part of a dance that is all too short, a dance of rhythm and grace, a dance of living and feeling and expressing the truth within. We hope for each of you the grace to see into that rhythmic and muscular pattern that is prepared for you to walk upon. May each of you have the courage to wait when it feels right, to wait even though to the world this may make no sense. For if each of you can stay within the heart and can sense for the rhythmic delightfulness of things, that attitude of gratitude shall come easier and easier until finally you may experience whole days at a time for what they really are: one moment, one now that is ever fresh, ever beautiful, and ever perfect.

May you learn to express this faith by an increasing stubbornness in holding to that attitude that has its source in the spark of love itself. For the attitude which you bring to your experience shall make a great deal of difference in that experience, and every moment that you spend attempting to center the self and balance the self, turning always again to that center of love within, each moment is an experience of truth. We realize that this is a concept difficult to work with words, for the emotional content of thankfulness is far greater than words can express. The power of a thankful heart is truly infinite. May your heart have that great benefit of your protection of it, of your nurturing of that spiritual self within that more and more yearns to dance the dance of incarnation with rhythm, grace and beauty.

We would at this time transfer this contact to the one known as Jim. We leave this instrument in love and light. We are those of Q'uo.

(Jim channeling)

I am Q'uo, and I greet you once again in love and in light through this instrument. At this time it is our privilege to offer ourselves in the attempt to speak to any further queries which those present might have use in the requesting. Is there a further query at this time to which we might speak?

T: Could you comment on my meditational experience from last Sunday?

I am Q'uo, and am aware of your query, my brother. We may speak to a certain extent. The boundary which we do not wish to cross is that which infringes upon your own free will. However, we find that we may suggest that the catalyst which faces you now in the world of illusion is that which has significance to a deeper portion of your being. And as it does have a potency it therefore affects the perceptions that you experienced when you attempted to enter the meditative state and reach down into a deeper portion of your conscious mind in order harmonize your vibrations as a part of the group meditation. The difficult nature of the catalyst which you now face had its effect upon the images which were being fed to you from your subconscious mind and were attempting to give an indication of the effect of this catalyst upon a basic portion of your personality structure. Therefore, the distortions in your perception occurred as a means whereby the effect of the deeper levels of your being was presenting itself in symbolic form to the conscious mind.

May we speak to any other query, my brother?

T: No. Thank you.

I am Q'uo, and we thank you, my brother. Is there another query at this time?

Carla: I would like to ask about this sense that was suggested to me that my reluctance to work on this book was related to it being my swan song, the last thing that I would do before leaving this incarnation. Could you comment on this possibility?

I am Q'uo, and am aware of your query, my sister. Again, we may speak only in a limited sense in this instance. To look upon a project or an activity as that which shall be the final statement of an incarnation is an attitude and an experience which could be utilized at any time by any entity within the incarnation, for, indeed, no entity knows the length of days which await in the future, as you call it. Whether this particular project is indeed the final curtain of your incarnation has little value in whether or not an entity such as yourself might decide to undertake it. For to think in this manner is to put a limitation upon one's own perceptions and experience whether the perception may eventually be true or false. Thus we would counsel you, my sister, to worry not in this regard for it is well said in one of the cultural sayings of your people that "what will be, will be." Your attitude in partaking in this experience is that which will make it as it will be for you.

Is there a further query, my sister?

Carla: No. Thank you.

I am Q'uo, and we thank you again, my sister. Is there another query at this time?

(No more questions.)

I am Q'uo, and we would once again thank each entity present for inviting our presence in your circle of seeking this day. It is always a great privilege for us to be invited to your meditation gathering, for we, in these experiences, are able to have our being within your illusion and are able to see the Creator in each and every entity and activity, observing the effect of illusion upon love. We would remind each that there is no entity which walks this path alone. For each here and, indeed, each person of your planetary population, has a guide, a teacher, a counselor, a friend, and many of them that accompany each upon this journey. Within those moments of meditation, of prayer, and of contemplation retire you there to speak with those who walk with you and who offer you unseen hands in times of need. We are known to you as those of Q'uo, and we leave each of you in the love and light of the infinite Creator. Adonai, my friends. Adonai. ♣

L/L Research

L/L Research is a subsidiary of Rock Creek Research & Development Laboratories, Inc.

P.O. Box 5195
Louisville, KY 40255-0195

www.llresearch.org

Rock Creek is a non-profit corporation dedicated to discovering and sharing information which may aid in the spiritual evolution of humankind.

ABOUT THE CONTENTS OF THIS TRANSCRIPT: This telepathic channeling has been taken from transcriptions of the weekly study and meditation meetings of the Rock Creek Research & Development Laboratories and L/L Research. It is offered in the hope that it may be useful to you. As the Confederation entities always make a point of saying, please use your discrimination and judgment in assessing this material. If something rings true to you, fine. If something does not resonate, please leave it behind, for neither we nor those of the Confederation would wish to be a stumbling block for any.

CAVEAT: This transcript is being published by L/L Research in a not yet final form. It has, however, been edited and any obvious errors have been corrected. When it is in a final form, this caveat will be removed.

© 2009 L/L Research

Sunday Meditation
May 3, 1998

Group question: Our question today has to do with how we travel from head to heart in any spiritual belief that we may have and in the spiritual journey overall. It is easier to intellectually understand, for example, that all things happen in their time, than to actually wait for that time to come and accept it. Is it grace that brings this about? Just the right time?

(Carla channeling)

Greetings in the love and in the light of the one infinite Creator, in whose name, in whose peace, and in whose power we come as witnesses and as fellow pilgrims on a common path with you and with all who seek to know the infinite Creator. We are extremely grateful for [you] calling us to your session this beautiful spring day. We thank each of you for the time and attention that each gives to the spiritual life, for each brings that to the circle, and each becomes part of a circle whose strength is in all of its members. This spiritual community we find so precious, and we are most grateful for this opportunity to share our thoughts with you. Please take those which please you or seem useful to you and leave the rest behind, for we are not authorities but only your brothers and sisters.

We are aware that each of you has a vision, a basic concept of how a spiritually oriented being behaves. It is indeed true that orientation as a spiritual being is a primary importance in allowing the spirit to transform Earthly life into that Garden of Eden, that heaven that does lie closer than breathing, nearer than your hands or your feet. What each of you seeks is fairly clear within the mind. And your question is simply how to move from the situation where the mind grasps the concept to the point where the being lives the concept. And this is indeed a challenge. It is the challenge for which you took flesh and came into a world of shadow. For each of you seeks in this incarnation both to learn and to serve. Each of you to whom we speak, we can say with authority insofar as we are able, is one who has earned her place upon the stage of your Earth world at this time, for many more spirits than there are bodies for have wished to incarnate at this particular time. In your Earth plane's development as a planetary spiritual being those who have made it are those who are very close to having learned those primary lessons of love which involve making that choice to follow only the good, only the true, only the beautiful and to attempt to allow the love and the light of the Creator a place to flow through into the Earth plane. For this is, among other things, what you are. You are, as it says in your holy works, a lamp upon a hill. It is not your light that lights the lamp. It is the Creator's. What you are able to do as you work with your mind and your heart is, little by little, to clean the panes of your lamp so that they are transparent and so that the infinite light may shine through, each of you, though you deem yourself unworthy. For you cannot give love to the world. You shall shortly run out in your persona as a human being, as a time-bound entity. Everything is finite, and it is as though you are in a cage of flesh and illusion. There is that within you which remembers paradise, which knows a better way, which is at peace and at rest. But that part of the self is very difficult to find access to. Until the day comes when, as the one known as R said, the journey from head to heart is made.

The culture which has birthed each of you and cherished you and supported you to this point in your incarnation has many qualities to offer, many values to express, and some of these values tend towards working athwart spiritual principles. When we speak of such things we cannot over-generalize, but there is that tendency in your culture to value accomplishment of whatever kind as a positive asset and to value motionless being as either a zero or a negative quality in that to those who have their life flowing from their being the list of things to do for the day, or for the week, or for the year, may never seem as important as the yellow wheat in the field or the blue of the sky on a sunny day, or the tips of the trees as they first embrace the air with their new, furled leaves. There is slim value for being within your culture, and we feel that this is a key disadvantage when it comes to that journey from head to heart. For the head is the place where things get done. The heart is the place where things get cherished and cared for. For the head there are choices of a right and a wrong, a movement to the right or a movement to the left. For the heart there is, rather, the flowing of things. Into the heart time and space themselves flow, for each of you is a citizen of eternity, and you are taking part in time during your incarnation in order to learn and to serve.

Now, how can you work to neutralize the result of a lifetime of learning? For this is what occurs as the culture nurtures the young mind and helps it to grow into a mature ability to cope with that which is within the illusion. It cannot be done with the head. To attempt with the mind to move the center of being from mind to heart is to hire a rustler to protect the cattle. There is no way for the mind itself to break one habit and begin another. We would introduce the concept of the will. There are those here such as this instrument whose will has been given to a specific lord or Christ symbol. This instrument has given her life and her spirit to the one known as Jesus the Christ. It is well to choose a principle that speaks to you most deeply of infinity, eternity and holiness and to deposit in that basic core of belief every bit of will and faith and hope that you possess. For this is an appropriate and an honest gift to the Creator, the surrender of the light, the willingness to follow with heart and soul and mind and strength a life lived in faith.

The tools to help you with this work are several. The very first and always the central one, in our opinion, is time spent with the Creator, time being with the Creator. The eyes that see the world see a human being sitting. The heart within knows a different reality. In that world within the self is a pilgrim seeking entrance to an inner sanctum in which the Creator already dwells in full glory and strength; from before time began until there is no more time, this is so. Before you were, before the world was, before all things, the Creator rested in Its universe. And as you are part of this universe of love so that love incarnate dwells within you. See yourself as a pilgrim walking up to the door of that inner sanctum, inserting the key of silence, walking in and sitting, not with other human beings, however worthy they may be, but with the infinite Creator. This communion awaits you constantly. It is not that the Creator is not with you, for the Creator is your companion from the instant of your beginning until the last fell knoll of life's bells. It is the self within incarnation that does not remember where to go to tabernacle with the infinite One. We would encourage each who wishes to move into the heart to attempt daily to sit in silence and allow the Creator within to make Itself known to you with no words, with no dramatic fanfare but that still, small voice whose message is far beyond concept but whose surety is absolute.

The eventual goal of those who wish to be and to move from that flowing beingness is to gradually replace expectation with curiosity. The ways of the mind and of expectations and so forth involve energies which seem to grasp and hold and stop the flow of rhythm and attempt to control that rhythm. Frequently, it seems that such manipulation works. And usually entities can convince themselves that they are in control. However, in the spiritual sense the only control is in how to surrender the small will and the small self to an infinite One whose wish for all is to give and to receive love. Each time, then, that you find yourself having imaginary conversations, moving into circles of concern and worry, and, in general, finding oneself knocking up against the corners of life, find ways to stop the momentum of that relationship with what is. Stop and remember that you are a child of the Creator, a child of eternity, and a child of love itself. You need do nothing but welcome the rhythmic and rightful destiny that awaits. And we are not saying that there is one fate for each entity, for it is our understanding that each has free will and that each must, of her own free will, choose service to others or service to self. Rather, it is a question of whether you wish to go a straight route or a roundabout route. If there is control attempted in a working pattern, that will change the pattern. The more faith that one is able to express in the moment to moment rhythm, the more gently one may meet the unfolding of your particular story. And the shorter will be that moment of centering the self within that identity of being.

Issues of this magnitude are not done with during an incarnation. They will revolve again and again into your experience, into your stream of living. What you learn at this time you shall see again. It may be at another level. It may be somewhat different, but the issues shall be the same: to offer the self with no expectation of return. Each of you came into this incarnation wishing to sacrifice the self for love, wishing to brave the forgetting of all the spiritual principles that were known and held so dear, daring to come into a world most illusory and seemingly far from the Garden of Eden, as this instrument would call it. Yet in faith and in hope you took on this lifetime, for you wished to love the Earth and its people. You wished to serve, and this is your opportunity. In truth, it matters not what is occurring upon the surface of your life as long as you are attempting to be an instrument of love, a harbinger of peace. Practice being. Practice at odd moments, allowing the self simply to be aware, and resting in that deep peace that is awareness of the Creator. You shall certainly get lost in the sea of confusion again and again. But that too is illusion. Trust that heart within, and as you are given the grace to do so, work with those concepts of being and doing until you begin to have a lucid idea of what it is to be yourself. This is an art of profound moment and we encourage each of you to take it up. In your hopes and in your prayers, surrender all to the Creator and know, in confidence and in quiet, that that which is needed for you to learn and for you to serve will come to you. May you see all things with the eyes of love.

We would at this time transfer this contact to the one known as Jim. We are those of Q'uo, and we leave this instrument in love and in light.

(Jim channeling)

I am Q'uo, and I greet each of you again in love and in light through this instrument. At this time it is our privilege to attempt to speak to any further questions which those present may have for us. Is there another query at this time?

T: I have a question about the sudden appearance of a little bird that I had never seen before just after my meditation. Was there a significance to this bird, or was it just a little bird that was lost?

I am Q'uo, and am aware of your query, my brother. As we find there is already certain knowledge within the subconscious level of your own mind moving into the conscious levels we may speak concerning this small bird which you have observed. The decision to take your journey or not to take your journey was that concept to which this appearance of the small bird spoke, the meaning of the appearance having to do with the bird being as much out of place in your sighting of it as you would have been upon your journey.

Is there a further query, my brother?

T: No. Thank you.

I am Q'uo, and we thank you, my brother. Is there another query at this time?

R: Thanks for the food for thought on the concept that I spoke about earlier.

I am Q'uo, and we are always honored to be able to look upon those concerns which come from each heart and to give them the attention of our experience and our desire to be of service.

We would ask if there is any further query at this time?

Carla: I get so much out of worshipping with a spiritual family, and I want to share it with others, but that seems so impossible. Could you speak to that dilemma?

I am Q'uo, and am aware of your query, my sister. Each seeker that moves along the path of seeking the truth, of seeking the love and the light and the unity of the one Creator has a unique way of moving upon this journey. Many there are who feel similarly to others and who gather together with them to worship as you say, in a community of seekers, and in this community they take comfort, joy, inspiration and find a great meaning. This is well for each seeker, to find a path which speaks to its heart, whether there be a great company with it or a small company of one. To look upon the journey with the heart that desires to travel and the mind that seeks answers, the passion of the desire is that which is most important for each seeker. For though one seeker may find fruits upon the journey and wish to share the nourishment of them with others it is difficult to do unless those others with whom one wishes to share have the similar desire, for each has the lessons of love to learn. And the greatest sharing that each seeker can make with others is to travel his or her own journey with a full heart, with alive compassion, and with the sincere desire to know that which you call the truth. The radiance that comes from within for each seeker so traveling is as a beacon, a light to others that, when they wish to inquire as to the nature of the journey, it is most appropriate to share with them that which you have found.

Is there a further query at this time.?

Carla: No. Thank you for your thoughts, Q'uo.

I am Q'uo, and we thank you again. Is there a further query at this time?

R: Many times you say that you are grateful for the sacrifice that each makes to come to the circle of seeking, but I want to come, and it isn't a sacrifice, so what is the sacrifice that you are referring to?

I am Q'uo, and am aware of your query, my brother. Each entity which finds itself in such a circle of seeking as this circle has for an entire incarnation moved upon a path in such a way which has brought it to that point in that circle. Each entity has sacrificed much in each incarnation to gain that of understanding that it has gained, to have gained that of tolerance, to have gained that of continuing in the desire to seek with others. One may find oneself in such a circle and ask the question that you have asked, feeling that the sacrifices have not been that obvious. But if each searches in its own memory and experience, each will find that there were steps that were, at one time, difficult to take, rituals and routines and responsibilities that were difficult to initiate, to continue, and to accept. Each seeker has accomplished much of work in this manner before being able to join in such a circle. These are the sacrifices to which we have spoken often, and we continue to offer our gratitude to each seeker that sacrifices much in order to join in these circles of seeking, for there are a great numbers of things that could occupy one's time, activities that could take one's efforts, and other concerns that would satisfy one's desire to spend an afternoon. Thus, we are grateful for each sacrifice, great and small, that each entity has made in order to join in this circle of seeking.

Is there a further query, my brother?

R: Isn't it like a fruit that, once tasted, you do not wish to give up because there is truth in there?

I am Q'uo, and am aware of your query, my brother. It is true that as one continues upon a journey, a ritual, a philosophy, or a practice, that the effort is easier and easier as the memory of the body, mind and spirit begins to exercise itself within the new parameters. Indeed, this is the nature of the seeking. As one is able to continue upon a path, a program, or a path of seeking, one will find that there is a kind of rhythm or momentum that gathers behind the effort to aid the effort and to enhance one's experience of it.

Is there a further query, my brother?

R: Thanks for talking about it.

I am Q'uo, and we thank you, my brother. Is there a final query at this time?

(No further queries.)

I am Q'uo, and as we have exhausted the queries for this session of working we would again thank each for asking our presence in your circle of seeking. We are most privileged to be able to share our opinions with you. Remember, my friends, that we do not wish to provide a stumbling block for any seeker. Take only those words that we have spoken that speak to your heart, and leave all others behind. We are known to you as those of Q'uo, and we leave each in the love and the light of the infinite Creator. Adonai. Adonai, my friends. ☙

Sunday Meditation
May 24, 1998

Group question: We would like information on the difficulties in relationships. We have times of doubt, fear, lack of trust and faith, and we want to know how to resolve these difficulties skillfully. How can we use contemplation, prayer and meditation to find harmony in our relationships?

(Carla channeling)

We are those of the principle known to you as Q'uo. Greetings in the love and in the light of the one infinite Creator. We bless and greet each in the name of Love, that one great original Thought. It is as servants of Love that we hope to offer our service to those such as yourselves who are seeking the truth. And so it is a blessing to us that each of you has come with your desires and your seeking, for we hope to serve the Creator whom we love. Without the inquiry and the interest, we could not do so in this way. So we thank each one of you for each step that you have taken against whatever resistance to bringing you to this moment you have experienced. It is a precious one to us, and we are glad to share our thoughts, always reminding you that we are not authorities but only friends along the path. We will share our opinions and our experiences in the hopes that they might provide food for thought. Please, however, take anything that we might say that does not meet with your personal feelings of "this is helpful" and simply leave it behind. We do not profess to be without error. We are as you: pilgrims.

And the road is long. Endless, perhaps. And so we may delight in that sometimes dusty walk together and encourage each other, for though we each seek through illusion, there is that which is not illusory. And though it recedes before us, yet it calls us onward. And that call seems to be our deepest spiritual instinct.

Your question this day focuses on that which is at the heart of your third-density experience for which you took incarnation at this time, for relationships are the basis for much learning within your illusion. Your entire makeup as a physical, mental, emotional and spiritual being in this environment calls you to be with each other. It is obvious that, physically speaking, the male and female call to each other to perpetuate the species. And this, indeed, is the beginning of many, many relationships. Yet there are others that have just as much use with companions, friends, teachers. Perhaps even those who have not met face-to-face but have meant a good deal, those with whom you feel the intimate relationship that comes from the reading of deep truths shared. This hunger for society, society that fits with your own nature, is a powerful force, an instinct within you. Naturally, it propels the seeker into confusion and chaos quite often, for that is one of the intentions of relationship. It is in learning how to love a mate, a companion or friend, family member, or lover, that we learn by reflection how to love ourselves and how to love the creation of the Father.

Each density has its basic learning. That of first density is the simple beginning of awareness, the beginning of being in a manifested environment. The elements earth, air, wind and fire are of first density. Rock and ocean is of first density and they are learning, not self-consciousness but manifestation. And, as in your holy works, it describes the light separating from the day and the earth from the water, the fire from the air. Such is the learning of first density. The becoming of one element or another. The beginning of the long road from the Source to the Source. In second density the learning turns towards that of movement, of being drawn towards the light and the love of the one infinite Creator. The flower turns to the sun. The greenery breathes that oxygen which animals need, and animals breathe that carbon dioxide which plants need. There is the instinctual sharing of environment, the instinctual harmonizing of each thing finding its place as all things reach towards light and love. And yet there is not a self-awareness. That is the gift of third density. It is the first density in which the spirit within may begin to find conscious expression. For although plants and animals experience harmony and love and a feeling of rightness, they are not conscious of so doing.

When that step into third density comes, there is a veil drawn across that deep knowledge that all is well, for it is within this third density that the newly awakened soul within begins to work through the body, the mind, and the emotions to render them instinctual again through decisions that you make in each and every day. The spiritual work of third density has sometimes been seen as a single decision following one particular religious system, and for some, this is the experience that occurs. However, for many the awakening of the spirit within comes slowly, step by step. And yet small decisions create evolution of spirit, and there is no matter that is too small to become filled with the love which you as a person of faith put into the response that you offer to that which is in the moment before you.

In looking at relationships perhaps it may help to take a step back and to look at the process itself and what we wish to be focusing towards in this process of living in incarnation, behind the veil of forgetting, in the sea of confusion that you call life. To put it in one way that this instrument is fond of saying, third density is intended to be a journey from head to heart. To put it another way, third density is a kind of spiritual boot camp in which one overriding question is put before the spiritual seeker. This question is, "How do you wish to serve?"

The choice in service is of service to self or service to others. Those who choose service to self basically feel that the Creator is them and they are the Creator. The environment about them is that which may be controlled or manipulated in order to best make the self happy, comfortable and so forth. This is not a consciously negative attitude in many cases but simply the day-to-day working pattern of self expressing. The other choice is service to others, and the one who chooses this way of expressing love is intending to, at the expense of the self, put others first. The service-to-self polarity and the service-to-others polarity is like the north and south poles of a magnet. In third density each begins somewhere in the middle in a kind of well of inertia. There is no positive charge or negative charge when experience begins to be accumulated by the awakened soul within incarnation. It is little choices, like whether to share your peanut butter sandwich with the other kids in fifth grade, whether to go sit with the kid with a broken leg in second grade, whether to help the parent who seems to need it. These seemingly small and everyday decisions are those in which one either decides to attract to the self that which is needed or to give away the love that is within one for the benefit of others.

We are those who seek to be of service to others for we feel that others and ourselves are one, even though it is not something that we can see and certainly not something that you can see. You cannot see that your hands do not stop at the ends of your fingers and that the other person's hands next to you similarly do not end there but that each is touching each. Each energy field is moving to find comfort and [harmonization] with each other entity within this dwelling place and, in general, this has a tendency to occur, people finding ways to make each other more comfortable and to smooth and oil the social machinery that helps each person to feel better about whatever situation is occurring. These are not small choices when viewed in the context of the basic purpose of third density, for in a nutshell, the way you graduate from this third density to the density of love and understanding is by making decision after decision after decision based, not upon evidence, but upon faith. Faith that the love and the hope and the charity and the good feelings that you experience within your heart are real and are not foolish or naive. Faith that things are well and that things will be well and that you do have comfort to give to yourself and to others.

Faith is only of importance when there is no real knowledge, and so it is in your environment in third density that the truth is hidden from you. There will not ever be any specific proof of your belief that will stand up, shall we say, in a court of law or in your discussions with someone who simply does not get it, who is still slumbering to the spiritual self and the spiritual identity that lies within, whatever your orientation. For instance, this instrument is Christian, and that literature and community of the Christian church feeds this instrument and gives this instrument ways to work upon faith. Whatever the orientation of each, it does include resources and tools that are available to all and can be used in the acceleration of spiritual evolution.

So when we say that this sea of confusion is given on purpose and not in a cruel or unthinking way we are simply referring to our feeling that it is only when there is no way to prove belief, hope and love that the choosing of those values and the manifesting of those values in a life experience has metaphysical weight. And, indeed, each choice that you make polarizes you a little bit more to the service-to-others polarity. We are assuming that each within this dwelling is a service-to-others oriented entity, as are we. We do not wish to say anything negative about those who seek in service to self, for we are aware that this too is a valid path as far as it goes. It does not take one as far as the path of service to others, and it must be abandoned, not in the next density, or the next after that even, but in the sixth density. For the fourth density, the one to which you hope to graduate at the end of this incarnation, is the density of love. The density after that is the density of wisdom, and the sixth density is the density in which love and wisdom are balanced. It is at this point that negatively oriented entities must switch polarity, for they discover at this point that they are unbalanced and that they can go no further because the deepest [choice] of all is towards evolution. Eventually each negatively oriented seeker chooses to become positive and to move onward towards the Source.

So the situation for each is a walk in semi-darkness, metaphysically speaking. The light is that of the moon, and there are many shadows, and the comfort of companions along the way cannot be overestimated. Naturally, each entity is drawn to the birds of a feather, as this instrument would say, those of like mind, those of like nature with whom they feel more comfortable, and the mating of men and women is a constant force towards the activation of catalyst that will teach the seeking soul to love. And the best of catalyst is gained with those with whom one is in contact with continuously. Those whom we see from time to time are those with whom we can plan to be our Sunday selves. We may wish to show all of our dazzling good points at once, or we may give them out one by one. But as long as it is the occasional friend that we are seeing we can offer the best of ourselves to that entity in each and every occasion upon which we meet. But for mates this is virtually impossible, and thank heavens for that impossibility, for it is necessary to work, it is necessary that we have catalyst to work with. And since we all came here to work on whatever density we are experiencing life, this seeming catalyst of pain and suffering and not understanding and wondering—this is the friction that we need to move us towards learning. And as we learn, we begin to realize that in each case we are looking not just at a situation but at an opportunity to find the love in that situation and to express that love. Consequently, often the catalyst itself becomes less painful to us because we are able to work upon our response to that catalyst; rather than simply being overwhelmed by the catalyst itself.

You asked what do entities fear when they are working on relationships, and perhaps we would say that the greatest fear is the loss of love or trust and the betrayal of security in whatever distorted way that security is felt by the self and by the other self. Many issues have their heart in this emotional security. The surface of an issue may be money, or health, or where to live. It may be almost anything in which two people have a different view, but whatever the seeming issue there is a deeper issue, a singular issue involved and that is not necessarily a doing issue but a being issue. It is the way of being or an attitude that we would like to encourage each to explore. The one known as Ra has offered the question, "Where is the love in this moment?" and it is this instrument's favorite way of centering the self in times of confusion. For each of you is love. Each of you is a projection into manifestation of the infinite love of an infinite and divine intelligence that has created all that there is and is all that there is. Of course, each entity in manifestation is distorted from the original vibration of the Logos. Without this distortion, without this mismatch, shall we say, in space and time, there would be no universe filled with light. There would be no way that the Creator could know Itself. And yet, simply being in manifestation posits that there be illusion. As long as each of us is a being, an entity, apart from Love Itself, each is dwelling in some degree of illusion. However, in this illusion each is the Creator to each, and in relationship, especially the mated relationship, this awareness is a healing balm that may help and prove a resource to those who are in pain because they feel abandoned or rejected or misunderstood.

What people fear is being betrayed: offering trust and having it betrayed. There is within each the dancer that would fly and soar and leap in joy. And yet when we let that self out we are as foolish as little lambs playing in the pasture, and we can be easily squashed. And so it is a scary thing to surrender to those feelings of love and joy and enthusiams that are in our very heart, for are we all not love?

One of the big illusions is time itself. And as this instrument was thinking earlier, considering the various things that had been said around the circle, many times it is just that waiting that is so difficult. And what is it that mates or anyone in relationship would wait for when there is confusion between two people? We would say that it is as though there were a dance that all of nature and all of humankind is engaged in in third density. It is a dance with meter, rhythm, harmonization of movement, and the plants and animals are aware of that. And the moon and the sun and the stars dance also, and within each of us there is that completely aware dancer also. And to that completely aware part of ourselves which we may touch from time to time, there is no such thing as waiting but merely pausing and resting until it is time to move into the next step of the dance. But to the human heart lost in confusion, anxious to put things right, there does not seem to be much rhythm or harmony. There does not seem to be a clear cue as to when to enter the stage or when to change one's step or even in what line to say. And as entities repeat lifetimes working upon one dynamic or another of loving and being loved it is as though you were in a situation comedy, or, shall we say, a karmic book, and the jokes sometimes go right past you because there is too much sorrow, too much suffering, and too much angst. And you feel like a living "Dear Abby" letter in search of the impossible solution to a complex knot of problems.

We encourage each to love that part of you that does not get it. You cannot wake up out of this illusion. That is not why you came here. You came here to be buffeted and pummeled by suffering and pain and limitation until finally, finally you surrender your intellect. You give up your logic and you move from head to heart. My friends, it is in the heart that the Creator is waiting for you, whole, complete and loving you with an intensity and utter compassion that is so real and so vital that there is no response but to love the Creator in return. This is not something for which you must reach. This is not something for which you can reach. You may sit in meditation for days and weeks and months and you will feel spiritual, but you will not necessarily be spiritual. For spirituality is in the being. It is in the self as you bring your self to the moment. It is in the attitude of self that, by faith alone, waits for that still, small voice, that intuition, that guidance that will tell you when to come in and what to say, that will enable you to look at a hopeless situation as far as harmonizing with another and say, "I reject the hopelessness of this situation. I will rest and wait for the rhythm to catch up.

In this endeavor you are crucial to each other, not simply mates, but everyone whom you pass on the street even, for you may in passing smile at someone who is hopeless and that realness may jolt that entity out of hopelessness into hope that bears much fruit. You do not know what you do. You cannot know the impact that you have as a being. [You may] not necessarily [seem to be] as those who are fruitful in the world. Some are. Some do not seem to be. And within the world this means much. Within the metaphysical world it means very little unless each thing that is a fruit is also one that was done with love, with a desire to help, with that stubborn naiveté that says that "I want to give the best that is in me, and I want to see the best that is in those around me." This encouragement of simple being cannot be overstated. May you have encouragement and support for each other, for you are acting upon yourself when you so do. And may you nurture and cuddle and hug that small self within that is so often hurt by a very bruising world. There is much unseen support for work in consciousness, for prayers, and for a life lived in faith. We ask you to lean into that support. This instrument would call it angelic support and say that there are angels everywhere. Other entities would describe this far differently, but the concept remains the same. There is guidance. There is help, for the Creator is constantly communicating to you using everything: nature, the environment, other people, coincidences. Be alert. Begin to see the spiritually interesting coincidences and you shall be much encouraged thereby.

We would at this time transfer this contact to the one known as Jim. We leave this instrument in love and in light, thanking it as we leave it. We are those of Q'uo.

(Jim channeling)

I am Q'uo, and I greet each of you in love and light once again through this instrument. At this time it is our privilege to ask if there are any other queries to which we may speak. Is there another query at this time?

Carla: To follow up on the first question, are there times when it would be the spiritually rhythmic thing to do to separate from the mate?

I am Q'uo, and am aware of your query, my sister. In the run of things, as we observe the great majority of relationships, it is well to stay with the relationship in which one finds oneself in order that the learning might proceed most efficiently, for there is much work in the, shall we say, building of the foundation of trust and of faith that takes a noticeable amount of time and effort in your terms. This time and effort must needs be repeated if there is the leaving of a relationship that has the purpose of the teaching the basic lessons of the incarnation, for in whatever relationship that one finds oneself, there will be the repetition of the pattern, the lessons to be learned, the difficulties to be experienced, the confusions endured. However, in some cases we find that the confusions and the difficulties are in what may be seen as an out-of-control mode where confusion builds upon confusion. Opportunities are lost and lost again, and momentum fails. And perhaps there is the injury of the mental, the physical, the emotional, and perhaps even the spiritual nature that can occur. In such instances we would suggest that each entity within the relationship retire to the silent room within and, in the meditative state, appraise the situation, as one may do in any situation. And surrender the small will, which places its desires foremost in the field of the vision, and ask what the greater will of the Creator or the higher self might be in this situation. We always encourage the reliance upon the small, still voice which resides in each entity, so that this source of information may be found in each instance.

Is there any further query, my sister?

Carla: No. Thank you.

[I am Q'uo.] Is there a further query at this time?

(Tape ends.) ❧

Sunday Meditation
September 11, 1998

(Carla channeling)

… which is known to this instrument as the chambered nautilus. As this sea creature grows it becomes too large for his previous shell and creates for himself a larger one and when in the course of time he then grows, he then creates a larger shell and so on in a beautiful and unending spiral until such time as he has no need for it whatsoever, for any physical vehicle, the consciousness having left this form. Then, my friends, all the shells are empty, having served their purpose.

There are two distinct stages to the development of your mental vehicle. In the first stage, it is primarily important that you constantly be aware that in each situation there is freedom, and you are not iron-bound by any restrictions from the outside. In order to fashion this awareness, it is in this stage necessary that you construct for yourself a larger mental shell, a larger home in which to dwell. Each time that you find that a situation is impressing you as limiting or difficult, it is time for inner work, my friends, in which you explore and discover the larger and more spacious mental atmosphere that is necessary for your balance.

There is a certain point in your development when you will find that you do not need a shell at all, but instead, in the vulnerable body of consciousness, you may swim out into the waters of the universe and merge with all that there is. In that moment, my friends, you will have discovered that there is no need for any vehicle whatsoever, for all things are one. And as your home is the universe, and as all things are one, no protection is necessary.

We are aware that this second stage is, for the most part, a very distant goal and yet we wish you to know that it does exist and that within it is a larger reality which in good time will supersede the limitations and the difficulties of your present state of consciousness. Meanwhile, enlarge your shell, my friends, through meditation and contemplation. Open yourself within, for the world without only seems to press in upon you. In reality, it is pressing upon itself and you are free.

We are enjoying this contact and find that transfer of information is very smooth at this time. We would like to leave this instrument at this time and use the instrument known as N. I am Hatonn.

(N channeling)

I am Hatonn. I will continue. Our intention, my friends, can be compared to food … to the food of the sea creature, the food the creature must eat in order to grow. To outgrow the old shell and to *(inaudible)*. Your intention is food from the Creator, so to speak.

At this time I would like to transfer to another instrument. I am Hatonn.

(Carla channeling)

We are with this instrument and again I greet you in love and light. At this time, if you have a question I will request that you ask it.

Questioner: Hatonn, hi, it's been awhile. I've been reading a book in which it states that a man named Timothy Leary has said that the discovery of DNA was a very, very important scientific and spiritual discovery. I wonder if you could comment on its importance and non-importance?

I am with the instrument, and I greet you, my brother, and affirm that we are never away from you as you think of us and question our existence, yet always send us your love. We always send you ours and never question your existence.

Questioner: I don't really question your existence but I question your form.

I am with the instrument. That, my brother, is a simple question. We will attempt to answer the question on DNA for it is an interesting one and, indeed, central to an understanding of the essential nature of evolution. For evolution is of a unitary nature and is not physical as opposed to metaphysical, for all things function in a certain way which is a way of, shall we say, the broken circle, or the spiral.

When the Creator sent all things into darkness to begin the great trip back to Him He defined the infinite circle and, yet, as we climb from cycle to cycle, we seem to be moving. And, indeed, we are moving within the parameters of what we may call the spiritual journey. But at the end of the journey we will find what we have been describing: not a spiral, but a circle.

To understand the building block of your physical vehicle is to begin to get a model also for the building blocks of [the] journey towards the light. You begin to see that which is physical as an extremely complex but completely understandable and programmable series of bits of information which are capable of reduplication and progression in space and time.

That which is programmable is reprogrammable. And so evolution—on a physical level—has its existence. It is a simple truth to realize that the nature of your spiritual journey, of the journey of your star system, of the journey of your galaxy, and of the journey of the universe as you know it, progresses along a similar series of programmable and reprogrammable cycles. What your scientist have not yet discovered is that there is a purpose behind the existence of consciousness, whether it be the consciousness of the self, the consciousness of a being of a race, of a star system, of a galaxy, or of the universe.

Without the understanding of this purpose, those of your scientific community who deal with genetic and that which is called [recombinant] research may act irresponsibly and, yet, this has been done before and its consequences and planetary karma have been reaped and, yet, my friends, the cycle goes on.

Does this answer your question?

Questioner: Actually, no, not fully. I do understand what you're saying, I appreciate it. But what I was thinking was that DNA is sort of like the cosmic telegraph office between the message of the Creator and the cells of our body. I was also thinking one night in a somewhat questionable visual state that the DNA, the matrix plan for the DNA is also that of rejuvenation and a lot of the basic drives for reproduction. Rather than just the creation itself, it also has sort of that [duty.] The telegraph office of the *(inaudible)* would deliver the message to create the unique mind and personality and drives. Am I correct?

I am with the instrument. That which is DNA is as a blueprint for the construction of a vehicle. Those drives which are part of the vehicle—that is, those of hunger, reproduction, desire for oxygen, and other necessary functions of the vehicle—are blueprinted by DNA. However, that which makes a being a being, is not DNA oriented but rather is within the, shall we say, eternal nature of the spirit or soul which inhabits and animates the actions of that vehicle for the time in which that vehicle will remain viably conscious on the physical level.

Now, there are, shall we say, blueprints which are the counterpart of DNA on the eternal or spiritual level …

Questioner: What about mental level?

That which is mental is a matter of programming as you know that are aware from what you have said and can be reprogrammed and this is what we were attempting to say about DNA itself. As the vehicle slowly follows evolution of a species so your mind can be reprogrammed by your conscious direction of will in appropriate circumstances. However, that which is eternal within you and which is related not to a day-to-day activity but to the personality which expresses itself in a timeless and instant vibration at all times, is not being fully reprogrammed by a mental reprogramming but is influenced over many lifetimes and many experiences.

However, a serious and concentrated effort can gradually make a distinction into the vibration of the being. In fact, at any moment your will and desire were strong enough you could instantly change your eternal being. It is simply that instant of will and perfect desire is not easily come by.

Questioner: Doesn't the will and desire already influence the genetic message? See, what I'm trying to get at is that it appears to me that people who have genetic malfunctions, like in their biases, they get karmically imposed, genetically, from the genetic message delivered by the soul so that *(inaudible)*.

Let us separate theories of karma from the genetic structure of a physical vehicle. May we say first that each *(inaudible)* of incarnation is individual and not all genetic malfunctions are due to that which is known among your peoples as karma. However, if a soul is removing karma by a certain situation which it chooses, he does not form a physical vehicle with that genetic imbalance but rather chooses a physical vehicle which already has that imbalance. The imbalance itself is guided by the rules of DNA in its random combination. The parents of a particular physical vehicle might, by mediation, cause the randomness of DNA selection to be less random. However, this is due to the action at a distance effect of the mind upon physical particles—such as spermatozoa and ova.

The soul and its philosophical nature must not be considered to be interacting with the physical DNA genetic code prior to incarnation. The soul chooses the vehicle which best suits.

Questioner: Does that *(inaudible)* of longevity and perhaps even immortality or this *(inaudible)*. Is that a conscious spiritual union of, through meditation, of the spiritual mind of the DNA genetic code?

That which is long life is desired by some among your peoples but in your present vibration it is not truly desirable. There will come a time when longevity is natural. Efforts to precede this natural moment by means of scientific and technological advances may perhaps be fascinating and inspiring to your peoples. However, when longevity is a desirable tool which you may use to good effect—learning and growing throughout a longer incarnation—the exterior vibrations will of necessity, have, shall we say, ameliorated and wars and violence and other negative aspects will have lessened in their impact on the planetary vibration.

The efforts of single individuals to have lives on the planet which do not take into account the outer negativity of the planetary vibration are lives which, shall we say, are those of a *(inaudible)* and may not be as rewarding to the progress of the soul. However, we realize that we are not addressing ourselves to your question but it is not a question that we can answer simply.

Questioner: Are you saying that it would do just as much *(inaudible)* to spend a great a deal of time *(inaudible)* trying to communicate *(inaudible)* with our genetic code *(inaudible)* that would pretty much be a waste of time at this point?

Our basic feeling is that those who work in this area are great pioneers and as their work is perfected it is greatly hoped that that golden age so richly deserved may come to pass and all things will come in good time. However, while those who are working in this area continue, we have noticed that the planetary vibration itself becomes, perhaps a little darker, perhaps a little brighter, but basically the same. And our basic suggestion is that to help the planet grow is at least as desirable an activity as to help in an esoteric understanding which cannot be fully used until it can be used by all.

Questioner: Well, thank you very much. As usual, I have more questions now then when I started. I really appreciate that.

We thank you for allowing us to share our thoughts with you. Is there another question?

Questioner: *(Inaudible)*.

I am aware of your question, my sister. First let us elucidate the question of the one known as Ra for his description of longevity as we understood it included not merely a long life as we now know it but that which you would term an impossibly long life such as one which spans two centuries or more.

And, indeed, we enjoy a longer life than you by many centuries for our whole sense of time and space have changed as we have entered new vibratory patterns.

Now, secondly, let us address ourselves to your question of a normally long life being perhaps not desirable. May we say to you that lives as you know them, whether long or short by any standards, are in a certain pattern which you have chosen before you enter into the pattern. As a result of going from the beginning to the end of this pattern your spirit hopes that it will have learned certain lessons and thus have improved and refined the vibration which is its essence in the sphere of eternity in which all of you truly dwell.

When one contemplates and then does that which is known as suicide, one cuts short before the natural end the time of learning. And more often than not, the lessons which that soul had hoped to learn have not been learned. Consequently, it is often so that rather than alleviating karma, the action of taking one's life adds more karma to the burden which is already carried and you are trying to discharge by the expression which is the lifetime which you are now living.

Thus, when you reenter incarnation, you have not only the original lesson to be learned but an additional severity to that lesson which is brought on by that pain that you have caused to those whom you have previously loved. Many times this type of karma is alleviated by the total forgiveness of those whom you have hurt. However, it is simply desirable to live until it is time for the lesson to be through, for your burdens to be laid down. It is a truism, we are aware, but we must repeat that you are not given those things which you cannot bear; thus, working through what is difficult.

When you finish with a lifetime, at its natural end, whether it be short or long, you can then go on and learn other, perhaps, more agreeable lessons in other, perhaps, more agreeable spheres of vibration. If you may think of your existence as having a natural rhythm and an ongoing purpose, perhaps it will be easier for you to understand that suicide, as you call it, is a stoppage of that rhythm in an arbitrary manner. Instead, it is desirable to proceed with the rhythm of your existence, always seeing the many blessings that are about you and letting the realization of love flow into you from the Father. If you can keep these realizations before you, your life, in this realm and all others, will be enjoyable and fruitful.

Does this answer your question?

Questioner: *(Inaudible).*

We thank you, my sister. Is there another question?

(No further queries.)

I am with you. Please, my friends, know that the love of the Father flows throughout the cosmos on the wings of all of the universe—to you, through you, from you. I am Hatonn. I leave you in that love. Adonai vasu borragus.

L/L Research

Sunday Meditation
September 20, 1998

Group question: The question today has to do with acceptance. There are a number of people in the group today facing the possibility of a change in their life, of moving to a new location in the country or a new location in working or a new situation at home and we would like some information about how we can accept what the universe or the Creator gives us even though it might not look like what we wanted or what we had in mind. If Q'uo could talk to us about the quality of acceptance, the peace of mind and the harmony that we can achieve by acceptance, we would appreciate anything Q'uo could say.

(Carla channeling)

We are those of the principle known to you as Q'uo, and we greet you in the love and in the light of the one infinite Creator. As always, it is a privilege and a blessing for us to be here with you, to share in your meditation, and to rest in the harmony of your vibrations. We apparently will be sharing this communication with the one known as M and we welcome this entity. This entity speaks the truth.

You have requested that we speak upon acceptance, and that we are most pleased to do as long as it becomes and remains clear to each of you that we are not the voice of authority but your brothers and sisters, imperfect, as are you in any sense that can be rationally understood. We make mistakes. We have opinions. We share the opinions and hope not to share the mistakes but undoubtedly we shall make mistakes. Not all of our opinions shall be those that will aid you and so we ask, as always, that you use your discrimination and trust your guidance within to the exclusion of other voices when necessary. For we have utter faith that you shall know the truth that is for you. As long as that is understood we are delighted to talk about acceptance.

As we search through this instrument's store of experiences, we find that this word of acceptance has overtones of toleration and even a grudging or somewhat difficult transaction within. The acceptance is not an easy thing sometimes, that sometimes it is difficult to accept, and we would like to remove that overtone that is implied in that bare word, for acceptance is a word that does not ring of joy. It does not have the freedom of feeling that we would like to talk about. Our choice of words would perhaps be faith. When this instrument was very close to death some years ago, she put a motto above the hospital bed where she lay. It read "Faith, the final frontier." As each of you does, she wished to find the joy of acceptance. It is well to have that kind of reminder when one is working upon a situation in which one is not yet comfortable and does not yet feel positively or affirmatively concerning the situation.

The one known as Jim has talked this weekend somewhat about becoming the fool, and we are the first to confirm that in any rational sense that faith is a foolish thing, that archetypical image of the fool walking off the cliff into dead air. This instrument immediately thinks of the coyote in the Road Runner cartoon, who is running at top speed to the edge of the cliff and beyond and continues running in the air until he realizes that there is no more cliff. That realization plummets him to the depths. The teacher known to you as Jesus called to the one known as Peter who was in a boat. Jesus was walking across the waves towards him. At Jesus' call, Peter left the boat and was walking on the water also, until he realized that he was on water. And as his faith fell prey to rational observation, he sank like a stone. So each of you is vulnerable when being full of faith to accusations of foolishness, of not getting it, of not being aware of the true situation, and like any fool there is almost no answer that will satisfy one who critiques the actions of faith.

(Long pause.)

We allowed this instrument to remain without any information for some few seconds in order that we might demonstrate immediately, and within the context of the moment, the type of energy that is involved in the faithful. This instrument did not attempt to fill the silence that it perceived from us with its own opinion or any words that might put off the need for the next meaningful thought. The instrument was content to be silent if we were silent. It is a lesson that took this particular instrument some years to learn. And, indeed, each of you has spent lifetimes already working on this precise discipline of the personality and of the mind.

When each of you is not within the veil of forgetting, each of you is full of faith and power and purity. Each of you has been eons in development. Each of you brings to this moment a tremendous array of gifts. And each has created for itself each and every opportunity that you and your higher self, as forces of soul or spirit, felt that you would wish to have. As the character this instrument calls Clouseau[22] would say, "Every move you make is carefully planned." We say this as we watch you falling over the furniture of your life, tumbling through doorways, bumping up against walls you didn't see, and walking through the walls that others

---

[22] Inspector Clouseau, from the movie *The Pink Panther*.

see. And yet within the confines of the incarnational self, how difficult, indeed how impossible it is to remain aware of who you are.

It is difficult to gather the self together to meet such a challenge as prompted this question. For that which you deal with upon the surface is extremely seamless. It is an excellent illusion. It is a thorough going in rich illusion, a tapestry of detail that is incredibly intricate and absorbent. And yet all of this is as the thinnest shell, and has as much life in comparison to the self that you are within that shell of personality as does the shell of an egg compared to that life within, that the shell protects, that the forces within the shell feed.

Many of you have spoken this weekend concerning the desire to move out of that shell, to become a citizen of eternity and not a person with a body and a lifetime, a beginning and an ending. And yet this is your time within the shell. This world of shadow is your time of being unborn and developing that being which shall hatch upon the entrance to larger life which you call death. Within this shell is marshaled infinite power, wisdom and love. Within this shell lies the food that you shall need, those drinks of water that are guidance, inspiration and hope. And so we ask you to abide within that state of being in the learning situation of the unhatched egg. Unlike the little shell of the egg, your shell is large. You may move about. You may express yourself within the illusion in many, many ways. However, you are constantly and infinitely protected. That physical vehicle that sustains life within this density, within this illusion, shall fail. Just as it had a beginning so shall it have an end. So each moment that you have within the time and space of this illusion is precious, for it can be given only the one time. There is no recapturing a second of experience, opportunity, challenge. And of course we urge you therefore to be alert, to be vigilant, to pay attention, for the winds of your thoughts are rich with useful concept. There is constantly coming to you from many sources guidance by sign, by metaphor, by physical experience. And as you use your intuition to notice coincidence and synchronicity and pattern, you may begin to find your environment more and more full of information and this is helpful to one who is attempting to live a life in faith.

For one who is looking for a job, looking for a way to make money, there is that feeling of panic. "Yes, I have faith, I have faith that the Creator loves me, I have faith that I am something more than my body and my mind, but I need a job." We encourage each who has concerns to voice them not to the self, but to the Creator. This instrument often argues with the Creator. The Creator doesn't mind. We would encourage each of you to have conversations with deity however you may envision that, at any length, at any time, with any emotional import whatsoever. With this conversation is more than any emotional colloquy. When talking with the Creator you are opening lines of energy within the deep mind that marshal and enable forces that are helpful to you. Let your faith be in something you can talk to. Let the deity have whatever face it has for you. Let the Creator be real to you. For, truly, as you move from this veil of forgetting, much will be restored to your knowledge, and you will marvel that you could ever doubt the eminence and reality of infinite intelligence, that great Logos that is love.

We do not know how to make real to you the Creator. We can suggest conversation, we can encourage silent listening, but in general we can simply say that any way that you can engage yourself in converse with intelligent infinity will be helpful to you. Indeed, you are speaking with yourself. However, it is helpful to speak to the greater Self and not simply to run the small circle of thought that goes nowhere. When the issue is acceptance or faith, the last thing that you need is rational thought. Here is a situation in which the intellect and its logic will not be useful in most cases. Now let us look at that for a moment. The logical mind that you have working for you is extremely helpful in making choices. That is the nature of intellect. It discriminates, it compares, it sees options, and chooses one. Much of the incarnational routine, shall we say, of daily life needs this kind of attention, organization, good choices made that will move you through the day and through the week and so forth.

There are entities that spend their entire incarnation without need for the recourse [of] faith. These people have the bliss of ignorance and having not yet come to the crossroads when logic fails. And one must move into the realm of unknown and mysterious things. For those who have come to be awake within the sleeping world, for those who have chosen to dive a bit deeper into quality of life, times when faith alone will serve come ever more rapidly and frequently. And indeed for many there are times when intuition and faith alone will steer the ship that can read no direction from the stars, yet how to inspire within you that quality of attitude that we call faith? Certainly one suggestion we may give you, and we do that again and again, is to learn to appreciate the still, small voice that speaks in silence. The Zen Buddhists have a saying that this instrument is fond of which is, "I held stones in my mouth for twenty years until I learned to be silent." Where does that urge to fill up the silence come from? There is that fear of silence, that reluctance to move into the unknown, the ineffable, the trackless, and yet this is the very stuff, the very material that you so value as a soul, as a spirit looking for the opportunity to work upon the consciousness, the polarity of that infinite and eternal self. Indeed, you wished to come here to be of service, but you also wished to learn. You wished to place yourself at risk. You make yourself vulnerable in order that you would have this opportunity to work on faith.

Move into now your body, feel that physical vehicle, feel the gravity that makes it rest upon your seat. Feel that contact, feel the shape of your bones and your flesh as you sit in meditation. Pull back the view and see yourself sitting with your feet pointing towards the center of the Earth and your head pointing outward from the side of the planet as it revolves in infinite space at the edge of the small galaxy, nowhere near the center of the universe. How tiny, how infinitesimal each of us is and yet each contains the creation. It is this sense of the infinite riches within that we would like to share with you as we encourage you to cooperate with your destiny, to recognize that it is well to move from the safety of intellectual and rational thought to the illogical and foolish ways of faith, and knowing that all is well, and all shall be well. There are so many mottos about taking it one day at a time that we can hardly speak about that concept without trivializing our conversation. And yet one great key in living in faith is taking it as it comes. This instrument has a friend that likes to imagine the worst: "What would I do if the worst possible scenario occurred?" This friend causes itself many worries. We would encourage you that when you have that craving for surety, to think upon the fool in mid-air who does not look down, who chooses, illogical though it may be, to trust.

Each of you will move through your days and meet your eventual physical demise with a mixture of easy and difficult times. We encourage you to watch for the pattern, watch for those things within you that cause you to stop and contract and move into that worried state where the thoughts move in small circles. Watch for those, being aware that your earthly pilgrimage is a journey from the head to the heart, a journey from past and future to the present, a journey from dark and light to oneness, a journey from right and wrong to love. Focus upon your love that you can give, that you can receive. Honor and respect that, follow that, and for the rest having done all those logical things which one can do in a situation, then crawl into the hands of infinite intelligence and rest easy. We encourage you to strive. We encourage you to help your situation in any logical, rational way that you can. But when those things have been done and there is still concern we encourage you to walk upon the water, to jump into mid-air, to toss yourself into the sea of confusion in faith that the Creator will toss you where you are to go and will bring to you the fish you need to eat and the water you need to drink and the understanding you need to grow.

You have but a little while upon this Earth. May you use the time lovingly, sweetly, insofar as you are able. There is for the fool a peace, a peace that the world cannot know. It is the peace of absolute trust, that the one who watches the sparrow also watches you. That no matter what occurs, be it starvation or death, this too is acceptable, this too is part of pattern, a beginning, middle and ending. When once again this body that you now enjoy is dust, what you shall value about this incarnation is the suffering you have successfully undergone, the challenges that you have been able to take advantage of as opportunities to express faith.

There is no way to prove spiritual truth. This is not an elementary mistake that the Creator made but rather a careful example of the refusal to infringe upon the free will of each spirit, That each may learn and each may be guided by faith alone, to rest in confidence and quiet surety. We encourage each to work upon these difficulties with a light heart and with a peace within that simply says, "I'm looking, I'm watching"…

(Side one of tape ends.)

(Carla channeling)

… in your faith, in your serenity, and as you go about this work to remain aware of those about you. For they too are moving through crises of faith, initiations that cause them to be up at night, to be concerned and disturbed. For each of you can be to others that bright light that remains faithful and steady, and remember the unknown stranger as well. Turn your mind to the crisis of faith of those many, many of your tribe of human that you know not, that you shall never know within incarnation and who are yet a part of you, and you them. And lend them your faith, let it wing where it will, where it is needed, for just in such a manner can you love and serve without leaving your chair, without moving a muscle, and serve right well, and in a very important way. You are not the only entity adrift on this sea of confusion. The archipelago is crowded, my dear brothers and sisters, with many frail barques, with many wandering souls, and each of you is to the other an anchor, a mast for sail, a rudder for direction. You know not when you shall be able to be used to aid another.

This instrument is informing us that we have talked long enough on this subject and with our customary humility we shall, therefore, fold our tents on this subject and steal away in order that you may ask other questions that you may have at this time. We would at this time transfer this contact to the one known as Jim, thanking and leaving this instrument in love and light. We are Q'uo.

(Jim channeling)

I am Q'uo, and am with this instrument, and we greet you again in love and in light. At this time it is our privilege to offer ourselves in the attempt to speak to any further queries which those present may have for us. Is there another query at this time?

Questioner: As entities, did we always exist, as we shall continue to forever exist?

I am Q'uo, and am aware of your query, my brother. To the best of our knowledge, which as we spoke before is limited, each here and each that is now in creation in any portion of the creation has existed before any creation began yet not as you exist now, for you are rich with experience gathered through many, many lifetimes in different locations within this creation. However, as [a] point of consciousness, as an awareness of being, yes, indeed, each has existed, and shall exist, in the future as you see it.

Is there a further query, my brother?

Questioner: No, thanks.

I am Q'uo, and we thank you, my brother. Is there another query?

C: We had a question yesterday that I thought was very interesting and it was "how do you see us?" and we thought, well, you see us as vibration because you have mentioned that and I believe you've mentioned color. I wondered if you wanted to add to that. How do you see us?

I am Q'uo, and am aware of your query, my sister. We see in a manner which is much like your sensing, that there is within your presence another presence. If we choose we may see you as emanations of vibrations that itself can and does produce light, that which you call your aura. We see you often as accumulations of experience and as potentials for further experience. We see you when we look to the heart of your being as ourselves, as the one Creator. We see you in many, many ways for there are many ways to perceive the creation about one and within one, and when one has perceived clearly enough, there is nothing but the Creator.

Is there a further query, my sister?

C: No, thank you.

Questioner: I have a question.

We would welcome your query, my brother.

Questioner: As those of us who are gathered today depart and return to our homes, there may be a desire to meditate at times in ways that we can tap into the collective energy that we have been generating here this weekend. Might there be a particular exercise or focus or suggestion that you could offer that many of us could use at any given time to tap into the collective energy so that our meditations are more of an experience of communion rather than solitary exercise?

I am Q'uo, and am aware of your query, my brother.

(Tape ends.)

L/L Research

Sunday Meditation
October 4, 1998

Group question: We would like Q'uo to give us information as to how we can determine what our true heart's desire is, that which is more central to the evolution of our soul rather than what we think we want as we go through our daily lives. We are wondering what you can tell us about determining and discovering what our true desire is.

(Carla channeling)

I am of those known to you as the principle of Q'uo. We greet you in the love and the light of the one infinite Creator, in whose service we are. We bless and thank you for calling us to your circle on this autumn day. The creation of your illusion is most beautiful at this harvest time of year, and we have enjoyed the glimpses that are within your minds of the beauty of these past days. Truly, yours is a lovely plane of illusion, and we greatly enjoy blending our vibrations with yours at this time. As always, we would ask that you listen to our words, not as words of authority, but as opinion from fellow pilgrims along a dusty road. It is often that those who walk upon this road may be the hands and the voice of the Creator for others upon that road also. For each of you is most definitely a receiver and transmitter of energy.

You ask this afternoon concerning energy, for that is the very heart of desire. The energy of desire [fills] the universe in which each entity lives for that entity. The human body takes a certain kind of nourishment, craves a certain kind of liquid to quench the thirst of activity and work done. And just so the desires of the heart, both those known and those unknown, have tremendous power to shape circumstance in order that opportunities might be offered to learn more concerning those desires.

Let us talk for a moment about desire and energy. When we speak to you using this instrument's voice, the sound you are hearing is a vibratory energy. The bodies which you enjoy the use of during this experience are made of overlapping and cooperating fields of energy. As a unique citizen of eternity you have a core vibration which is a distortion of the great original Thought which is Love. Each of you distorts that core vibration of love in such and such a way, creating for yourselves a signature that is as unmistakable as the name and certainly more rich in information offered about the self in comparison to the naming. So your very nature is vibration and, indeed, the nature of all manifest and created things is energetic. All things are vibratory energy fields.

Those upon your level appear solid and real and yet they are tremendously vulnerable to that entity who knows the higher road, who is able to work with that level of self which overarches the current incarnation. And as each of you has evolved you have had these times of realization of the great effect which your desires can have upon experience itself, and as this instrument is often known to say, you must be careful of what you desire for you will get it. For this is the nature of this experience. The whole human nature is geared towards the satisfying of desires. The heritage from your second-density body is a heritage of instinct to breathe, to eat, to procreate, and to survive. These are instinctual desires, but no more powerful than the desires that your consciousness had as it evolves.

Now let us look at how entities desire, how they may go about determining what their desire truly is. On the surface level, on that level which most entities of your density skate upon, not knowing that there is a universe under that skin of ice which is full of life and water and magic, desire is a very plain and simple thing: when the personality says, "I want this." The response is according to its personality: the acquisitive person shall go and get that which is desired straight away and figure out how to pay for it later; the more chary conserver of the nest-egg will take the same desire but will carefully set aside that energy that is needed to achieve the desire. For most of those walking upon the skin of life and not into the ocean of it, the desires are fairly simple and are in the physical world. But something happens which turns the surface skater into a swimmer that can swim to the depths. A spiritual awakening occurs as surely as an alarm clock goes off and it is time to wake up. And, as each has found in this process of awakening to the metaphysical side of life, the desires of the heart become much more complicated and much less easy to satisfy. Yet in the way of enculturated humankind it is not unusual to see quite consciously aware entities still approaching the method of achieving desire in the same materialistic way that an entity would save up money to go see a certain movie, or to buy a certain product, or to get, as this instrument is so fond of getting, a new change of clothes.

And the desires of the heart are not commodities. Indeed, the desires of the heart are constantly in evolution just as your whole vibrator nexus of being is constantly in the process of becoming more of that which you truly are. This would seem to be difficult news to bear, for truly we do wish to satisfy our desires, once they are known. But because life for the seeker has become metaphysical, not to the exclusion of physicality but in the sense that the metaphysical universe is known to overarch and to order the manifested illusion, it would indeed seem that there may be better ways of approaching the question of what does one desire than simply to take the opinion off the top of the consciousness and start to try to figure out ways of achieving this conceived desire.

And indeed there are. Moving into a more skillful way of examining self and the self's milieu is quite possible and not particularly difficult for the one who is moving to be silent and to allow unknowing to remain as it is until it will change. Let us think along the lines of computers for a moment as we often find that such an allegorical comparison is helpful when talking about the structure of the mind or the structure of consciousness. In the software of the computer there are bells and whistles to help you do that which you wish to do upon the computer, but they are not all of the same level. And hidden in many programs are many powerful subprograms that are not seen by the casual observer and are simply ignored with that ignorance that is bliss. They know not that deeper programs exist and they know not what use they would be. They are still [skating] on the surface. They are still asleep. And each of you as seekers have plunged into those infinite waters of consciousness and you have become aware of those deep voices within the mind, those presences, those principles that are personal and yet impersonal, that are the self and yet the oversoul of the self. And in the silence you can put the question: "What do I truly desire?" and then you can listen. Listening to that graceful and yet muscular silence is a discipline of the personality that will never disappoint the persistent listener. Simply allowing the distortions of the moment, the confusions of the day to slip away can put one into the heart's sanctum sanctorum, that inner sacristy of silence and prayer where the Creator waits infinitely and patiently. The Creator awaits each of you within your own heart, within that deep silence that is within that room within the heart, for truly the holy of holies is within you, and within you are not only all of the instructions for this life and for this period of learning but, indeed, all of the instructions whatsoever for the you that you are before time was.

There is no end to that which can be sensed by one who is willing to stop and listen and remain without impulse. This instrument is very fond of an old Irish poem, the last verse of which is, "The peace of God it is no peace but strife closed within the sod, so brothers let us pray for one thing, the marvelous peace of God." As you activate this holy of holies within, as you tabernacle with that great Logos which has created all that there is, you free from your deeper self and allow to move into conscious experience that self that is truly surrendered to service, to the service of the one infinite Creator, to the service of learning and expanding and evolving that you have committed yourself to in a personal way during this incarnation. We would not wish to do your work for you. We cannot make choices for you, but we can encourage each to seek for herself an ever deepening awareness of desire. For we feel that each will find that as he moves into that frame of mind that offers a different vantage point on the concerns of the day that in truth each desire that has seemed to have been thwarted has, in fact, simply not been an opportunity that was part of destiny. And why would this occur? Why would the entity desire and desire and try and try to achieve that desire and feel so completely failed when the attempts do not work?

It is because there is this assumption that desire equals the need to fulfill the desire. As before, we would say to a person skating upon the surface of life this is a logical and useful attitude. To those wishing to live a life in faith and service the attitude simply does not encompass the experience that you have set up for yourself as a seeker. Does this then mean that as one has awakened to one's metaphysical identity one ceases to be able to achieve that which one desires? We cannot answer this for you, for some have a very clear idea of the deeper desires and others perhaps not as clear an understanding of their deeper desires. When you reach the bottom of the personal life, the incarnational mind, you find that the universe within is created as though for the first time in such a way that you have connections into the impersonal and Creator-filled realms that guide events within this realm. When you come to the end of your human ability to reason and to understand, you will come to a point of surrender, and this point of surrender is a [peak]. Working with the personality to see into the deeper energies of the self, you open and enable for yourself the underlying desire that feeds all of life. This level of desire is that which wounds in the flower, that which springs from the smile; or from the eyes. Each time you are able to get to the bottom of desire you will find that the base of that desire is the desire to cooperate faithfully and persistently with the destiny that has brought you all which you have so far enjoyed. At the back end of that great long train of desires you will find a little gay caboose that says, "I surrender. Not my will, but Thine."

Perhaps this is bad news for those who wish to affect their lives in such and such a way. But we believe this to be the way things are in the metaphysical realm, for in that realm thoughts are things. Intentions of actions and desire is turned upon its head, blending for the citizen of eternity the desires of the self and the desires of the Creator, and as these two come slowly into synchronization, destiny becomes fluid and one finds oneself more and more easily able to pierce the illusions of desire to move into that heart which desires completely one thing: the opportunity to love and be loved, to have consciousness, to breathe in and to breathe out, and all else will be as it will be.

One last thought concerning desire. The one known as Ken Keyes has done a good deal of work in looking at desire, and this instrument has a good opinion of that which this author says, which is this: that desires in and of themselves are neither bad nor good; they simply are things which create a bias. If one moves too far along that route of desire, the bias becomes an addiction. So, in many ways, the managing of the too rambunctious desires of the somewhat less evolved person may be seen to be of an addictive quality. The feeling is, "If I have this, I will be all right. If I do not have this, I shall not be all right." This author then encourages the addict to downgrade that addiction to preference. One can say, "I prefer that this thing happen in this way, but I am not addicted to it. It is not necessary." This too, in its own way, is a key, for when you look at desire with the conscious mind it is difficult to see what that energy is. But you will find that there are addictions in the personality just as there are in eating foodstuffs, and certainly life becomes a more, shall we say, comfortable illusion when one is able to see clearly one's preferences and yet have the center quality of balance that allows one to surrender.

We would at this time transfer this contact to the one known as Jim. We thank this instrument and leave it in love and in light. We are those of Q'uo.

(Jim channeling)

I am Q'uo, and greet each again in love and in light through this instrument. At this time it is our privilege ourselves in the attempt to speak to any further queries which those present might have for us. Is there another query at this time?

Carla: For several years I have said that I want to write a book about wanderers for wanderers, but [my] time keeps getting caught up in so many other wonderful things to do. I would appreciate your thoughts. This is obviously something I am not addicted to, but I would prefer to finish this book sometime before I leave this incarnation. Any comments on that, Q'uo?

I am Q'uo, and am aware of your query, my sister. And it is our desire to be service in our response without infringing upon the Way of Confusion, that is, upon your free will choices. For there are, indeed, many possibilities which present themselves at this time to your attention for the fulfilling as a means of being of service. That which you have found yourself doing is the reaching out to those who reach first to you, offering advice and opinions much as do we when this circle of seeking has called us as you have called us this day. We would remind you, my sister, that the ability to serve one is the ability to serve all, and there is, in our humble opinion, no necessity for concern upon your part as to how you shall serve, for service and its opportunities shall continue to present themselves to you. You are in the position of being able to choose how you wish to refine, or indeed how you wish to present, your service to those who would seek your advice, your opinion, your suggestion.

If it is indeed your heart's desire that you write the book for wanderers, then you will find a way for this to be accomplished, as you have done so in the past with other projects of the nature of the book. However, if you find that there are other ways in which you wish to serve, these also may be explored without any feeling of that which "must be done," for, as we are familiar with it, there is the saying from the one known to this instrument as John Lennon that, "Life is what happens to you while you are busy making other plans," and this is indeed true for most entities who seek to be of service. The seeking to serve [is that] which is of primary importance. It is that which draws to you opportunities to serve. The opportunity which you choose, the avenue which you go down, is that which is right for you, for you have chosen it, and it has chosen you.

We realize that we have not added a great deal of insight to your understanding of this situation, but we wish to remain within the bounds of free will in our response.

Is there any further query, my sister?

Carla: No. I appreciate your not wanting to infringe upon free will, and I wouldn't want you to either. I appreciate what you said, and I think it is in my nature to write to one person who is asking the question, and put my whole heart into that, than to sit down and write for the unknown people who would read my book. I know that if I gathered up all that I have written to various wanderers I would have a book. So I guess I can rest easy. Do you have any comment?

I am Q'uo, and am aware of your query and would simply respond by suggesting that to serve one is to serve all.

Carla: Thank you. That gives me peace.

I am Q'uo, and we thank you again, my sister. Is there another query at this time?

A: How does one distinguish between answers that come from the higher self without filtering from the ego?

I am Q'uo, and believe that we understand your query, my brother. The messages that one receives in the meditative state, the prayerful state, the contemplative state, the inspiration that strikes one in the midst of the day, these sources and means of receiving information may be examined again in the meditative state for the depth of purity. For there is within each entity the tree of mind, which moves ever more deeply to make contact with the deepest resources available to one. Whether this is the higher self, the guide, the teacher, or whatever source of inspiration one has sought, it is within the meditative state that one determines the relative purity of or use for this information. For there is within your illusion no clear and certain means to know at each communication what is, shall we say, flavored with the interpretation of what you have called the ego and what we would call the personality structure. Indeed, in some instances it is helpful for this flavoring to occur, for it aids the entity in moving in such and such a fashion. When there is the necessity for a message to be imparted with relative purity one may trust and have faith that this will be done by that source which one seeks, be it the higher self or other sources, and that one may look at this information when it is perceived—in the meditative state—and determine that this is from the higher self.

There are opportunities for each entity to feel that information is more or less helpful according to the origination, the source of the information. We encourage each seeker of truth to use a healthy dose of discrimination on whatever information comes before your notice. We would further add that we would also suggest that all information that comes before one has a value to the entity that notices it. Whether this value is to take the information literally or whether to interpret it with the flavor of the personality structure, is for each entity to determine. For, indeed, all that speaks to one is the one Creator. Each message can have value if followed to its ultimate source. All information can be helpful, and all information can be discriminated, can be evaluated by means of the meditation, the contemplation, and the prayer.

Again, my brother, we realize that we have not biased you in one way or another or given a technique by which information may be discarded or retained unerringly. This is always within the bounds of one's free will. We wish both to emphasize the value of discrimination and the value of the many voices of the one Creator about each seeker of truth.

Is there a further query, my brother?

A: Is it reasonable for me to ask over the last few years what [is the] percentile of accuracy of determining my higher self's messages to me?

I am Q'uo, and am aware of your query, my brother. And we must refrain from giving such a percentile, for we do not wish to seem to judge, and we are aware that each seeker such as yourself must needs make these choices for himself or herself. We again would reiterate that it is as important for each seeker to determine the framework for seeking, that upon which it shall build its metaphysical personality, as it is for a seeker to receive information from any source other than itself that might aid in the building of this structure. What we mean to say here is that your choices, made with consideration, with love, with consideration for the harmony and unity of all things, these choices are as important to you as any information you shall receive. How you choose, what you choose … you can construct the basic foundation out of the desire to know the truth and the faith that it will come to you as certainly as can any structure be builded by any discarnate entity with information to share.

Is there any further query, my brother?

A: No.

I am Q'uo, and again we thank you, my brother. Is there any other query at this time?

R: I just want to thank you for the inspiration such as you provide. I find it very useful. I guess it's my desire to say it again.

I am Q'uo, and we appreciate your heartfelt sentiments, my brother. We seek to serve those such as yourself and those in this circle of seeking in the most helpful way that we can. As you discussed previous to this session, the desire to serve is that which propels entities who wish to seek the light and the love of the one Creator. The means by which the service is rendered is not often easily determined and is, indeed, a delicate process, one which challenges the imagination of all true seekers.

Is there another query at this time?

A: One more. When one is at a higher level of consciousness, as opposed to those of us in third density, the third-density person must operate without clear sight. Can we still give advice in this condition and not get carried away with error? How are we doing?

I am Q'uo, and am aware of your query, my brother. Again, we would remind each that there are no mistakes for any portion of the one Creator which seeks its source and its unity with all. There is in this illusion that you now inhabit the great desire to seek, to love, and to be loved, for this is the lesson before you. The ability to know whether or not one has served well is not a portion of this illusion, for it is that which partakes of wisdom. In this illusion one cannot know anything for certain. One can seek. One can desire. One can build the framework, the foundation for the metaphysical self, and build this foundation securely without knowing anything in detail or in particular. For there is in this illusion the great interplay and interchange of energies as each relates in one form of relationship to each other entity within the illusion. The many steps forward, backward, sideways, missteps, bumped feelings and knees, all of this great cacophony of experience is that which eventually informs each entity precisely as that entity needs be informed. It is a great dance of the one Creator and Its many portions with Itself and though there seem to be many missteps and paths traveled that one may not wish to travel beforehand by entities, indeed, each step is taken with perfection. The ability to learn from what you call the mistake is oftentimes more valuable than avoiding the mistake, as it is called, originally. We are aware that there are forces, subconscious energies, in each entity. There are teachers of an unseen nature for each entity. All work in this great musical effort, this great dance that all participate in that allows each to exchange energies with others that are necessary to be exchanged. We applaud each entity's desire to move in a certain direction, metaphysically speaking. However, it is not so much the direction that is important as it is the desire that is important, the faith that such movement is possible, the faith that it occurs though one may not see it or measure it in any knowable degree. However, the faith that such movement is possible and the desire to move in the direction of love and light is that which is of importance.

Is there a final query at this time?

(No further queries.)

I am Q'uo, and we would take this opportunity once again [to thank you] for inviting our presence to your circle of seeking this day. We would again assure each entity that each walks with many companions upon this unseen and dusty trail of seeking the truth. There are with you many who have traveled this trail before and now return to walk again to aid you in some small way that you may perhaps find the right person, the right book, the right roadmap for that moment. In your quiet moments, give thanks and praise for each entity, for they are indeed an angelic company who walk with you at this time. They have walked with you since before time and shall walk with you through all time. We are known to you as those of Q'uo. We leave each at this time in the love and in the light of the one infinite Creator. Adonai, my friends. Adonai. ✿

L/L Research

L/L Research is a subsidiary of Rock Creek Research & Development Laboratories, Inc.

P.O. Box 5195
Louisville, KY 40255-0195

www.llresearch.org

Rock Creek is a non-profit corporation dedicated to discovering and sharing information which may aid in the spiritual evolution of humankind.

ABOUT THE CONTENTS OF THIS TRANSCRIPT: This telepathic channeling has been taken from transcriptions of the weekly study and meditation meetings of the Rock Creek Research & Development Laboratories and L/L Research. It is offered in the hope that it may be useful to you. As the Confederation entities always make a point of saying, please use your discrimination and judgment in assessing this material. If something rings true to you, fine. If something does not resonate, please leave it behind, for neither we nor those of the Confederation would wish to be a stumbling block for any.

CAVEAT: This transcript is being published by L/L Research in a not yet final form. It has, however, been edited and any obvious errors have been corrected. When it is in a final form, this caveat will be removed.

© 2009 L/L Research

Sunday Meditation
October 18, 1998

Group question: The question this week has to do with the changing seasons in our spiritual life. We all have desires as spiritual seekers to do a certain spiritual practice: to meditate more frequently, to live more peacefully, to be more aware of what we are doing. We have a lot of different desires that we would like to see fulfilled, but it takes us a lot of effort and a long time to make our desires into the rituals and patterns of our lives. As we go on for a while with a pattern, it seems that at some point we need to make a change and a choice, and our further spiritual growth has to do with making new patterns. A part of us dies and a part is reborn. Would Q'uo talk to us about how these changing seasons come about? We would like to work in harmony with them and to have a better understanding as to how change happens in our lives. Is it really due to our desires and to our efforts and to the past that comes before the change, or does the change come because it is time for it to come, and it comes no matter what?

(Carla channeling)

We are those of the principle known to you as Q'uo, and we greet you in the love and in the light of the one infinite Creator. As always, we are most grateful that you have gathered in this circle of seeking and that you have called us to your group. We are honored and blessed, and we bless each of you and thank you for the privilege of being able to share our thoughts. We would ask that these thoughts and, indeed, all thoughts that come before you be subjected to your own powers of discrimination, for you truly shall feel the resonance of that truth that is your own and those resources that will be helpful to you. If that resonance is not there, we would encourage you to move on. For that sometimes very subtle resonance of recognition is a key to wending your way through an incarnation lived in your present third density with its heavy illusion. Much that occurs is not what it seems. Indeed, that is the very nature of illusion.

This day you ask us concerning changes, how to bend with the wind and turn to the sun, how to respond to those biddings and desires of the heart that are hopeful and delicate. The nature of the incarnational experience is change upon change upon change. And this you have seen again and again in your life already. There are many ways to look at the cycles that seem to influence the mind, the emotions, and so forth. There is the cycle of the adept, that this instrument keeps watch over to see when the strong and the weak times are for work in consciousness. There are the various rhythms, known to this instrument as biorhythms, which are very helpful in giving information to the person who wishes to know more about herself, when it would be a good time to do this, when it would not be a good time, and so forth.

There are the divisions of time that your culture has made, splitting the days into years and months and weeks so that there is a definite feeling about each day which is cultural rather than natural. Look at the work cycle, the Monday through Friday that so many among your peoples simply assume as the work week, not thinking that before the days were named they were all Sabbath days, one as holy as the next.

The ways that change comes are sometimes natural and sometimes brought upon one by the culture in which one lives. The changes that are natural are the changes of an organism which is expressing a pattern. The natural run of energy from youth to maturity to the prime of life, to the middle and older ages, these are natural. There is, in any culture, a variety of ways for a person to think of herself as she goes through youth and maturity and old age. And although each entity will predictably have difficulties accepting the natural changes having to do with the physical vehicle and the energies of the physicality of the self, it is generally a relatively, as this instrument would say, doable thing to see where cooperation with nature will help. Perhaps in some entities who do not want to accept the passage of time, do not want to get old, do not want to look old, there are difficulties. But normally it is not at this level that the difficulties which are upon the minds of those within the circle this day come from.

The difficulties in changing that each of you is more aware of have to do rather with the process of desire in fulfillment that characterizes the life of, shall we say, the spiritual appetite. Once an entity has become aware of herself as a citizen of eternity there is no longer the simple feeling of content with accomplishing the necessary chores of the day. The actuality of spirit works upon the seeking entity encouraging the conceiving of desire to be ever more spiritually opening and transforming. It is difficult to talk about this process with those who are not themselves going through it, and once an entity has awakened to her spiritual identity it seems as though a portion of the population were simply asleep. It is a situation which can be alienating, isolating, and even fragmenting. For as the spiritual self emerges one becomes aware of the power of that energy that is within. One wishes to accommodate and encourage these stirrings of desire. And the appetite for transformation can become very keen.

There is a kind of pressure that one can put upon oneself to do more, to be better, to seek harder, to meditate more, to contemplate more, to hew to a practice of life that the intellect can see as the appropriate and desirable way of life that a persons wishes sincerely to follow, never quite acknowledging the various promptings suggesting that perhaps it might be good to slow down, to take it easier. For the seeker intent upon the path, the process is experienced as harmonious and positive usually only when one sees oneself as conforming to those spiritual ambitions of more and better and deeper.

And yet, interestingly enough, often this continuing desire and continuing pressure from the self to do more, do it better, go deeper, and so forth does not satisfy; that is, the person does not fulfill those ambitions, does not meditate more, does not go deeper, and thusly the person is simply frustrated and irritated at the self for not conforming to those spiritual ambitions. This instrument has said several times that although it seems that spiritual evolution would be a process of addition, that it seems many times in fact like a process of subtraction. And we would agree with this instrument in that often the bounty of deepened desire and that feeling of centeredness that spiritual ambition hopes for is contained not by adding activities or doing things different in some way that is measurable physically but, rather, in moving fully into the present moment and becoming able to take the bounty of that moment as it passes. For each moment is itself, whole and perfect. When one is in the moment, one is not in time. When one becomes even a bit aware of the timeless aspect of the moment there is an almost automatic resonance and a feeling of coming home. And this is accomplished not by adding more focus or adding more attention or finding better ways to meditate, but, rather, it is allowed by the seeker who relaxes into the magic of the timeless present moment. If you are within that present moment you are in meditation, aware of who you are, aware of why you are here.

Many other things go out the window: where you are on planet Earth, what time it is, what you have to do in the world. This instrument can give you chapter and verse about being lost in the present moment, and yet this instrument does not give itself the credit it should have for the ability to get lost. For it is in that abandon, that relaxation into the utter present, that the amazing volume of spiritual information can come fully and completely.

We are not suggesting in any way that it is no longer a good idea to meditate, or to ask yourself to meditate. We always encourage spiritual seekers to that activity, for it truly is a powerful, powerful tool. But a little meditation goes a long way, and it is possible that when the seeker does not find itself able to meditate regularly that the seeker may need to ask herself what it is that seems to be changing so quickly that is actually stuck. For many times the wisdom of the self pulls the self away from meditation because the organism instinctively is aware that it cannot handle more change right now. For that is what meditation actually offers, an enhanced vulnerability to change. Perhaps for those who are having difficulty in setting up daily meditation schedules that would be one concern: what issues am I stuck on?

Another question that the seeker may ask herself when it does not seem possible to get a good schedule going is, "How am I not conforming to the needs of my bodily organism?" This group earlier was speaking of the ways that the culture gets us up and shoots us out into jobs and drops us off in the twilight to watch television until too late and that this scheduling is not conducive to the natural way of life. This [is] certainly food we would recommend for your thought. How can you better treat the physical vehicle that carries you through the incarnation? Are there ways in which you could be kinder to the body that carries your consciousness about? Are there ways creatively to adjust when you do things and how you do the things that you need to do so as to bring them more in line with a natural or flowing rhythm?

For many the only time that is truly theirs is that first block of time upon opening the eyes when one wakes up. And it is for this reason that many plan for meditation time the first thing in the morning. And, indeed, that is a natural and deeply resonant time for spiritual work in terms of the energies of your physical body and the energies of your being as a totality. However, any point during the day that seems to be more appropriate is just as highly recommended by us, for the important thing is not to do it a certain way but to have that point in the schedule where there is a formal return to the center of the soul. We encourage you to play with your schedule, to have fun with it, to vary the ways in which you meditate, to bend those stiff necks that say it should be done this way. And play the music of ragtime where anything goes in your head, and find new ways, new times, new practices, if you are unsatisfied on a continuing basis with those that you have now.

More than anything else we could offer, we would simply offer the thought that most spiritual seekers have a tendency to become heavy with their seeking. And certainly that which penetrates to the very heart of self is a weight, a gravity of importance, and yet it is also dancing in the wind, light as a feather. So more than anything else we do encourage the light touch, the forgiving judgment of self, not because you no longer care to do a good job of attempting to aid your own spiritual evolution, but because you trust yourself to be doing all that you can. We ask you each to be gentle with yourselves, for you have hungered and thirsted after the truth, and that truth has lead you on a merry chase and continues to disappear into the mystery. All that you learn seems only to move you into a point into which all dissolves into mystery. To our knowledge, this is a continuing experience, one we share with you.

But while you have the gift of time and space, while you have the illusion of sequence and accomplishment, we encourage you to treasure it, seek to honor it, but do so with a light heart and a conscience free of what this instrument would call the "shouldacouldawouldas." Whatever it is that you felt to do this day, that was the right thing for you. Whatever you shall feel tomorrow, that shall be the right thing then, and you will be inspired. You will become aware by and of those things that are there for you to see. And if you do not see one, another shall come soon. So while you are watching and learning and attempting always to seek along the path as best as you can, relax in the knowledge that there is an unseen hand guiding and taking care that nothing that you need is lost. If you miss one experience you shall have an equivalent. That which you need will come to you. And beyond all the questions of "When should I meditate?" or "How long should I meditate?" we encourage you always to focus on the present, on what is happening at this very moment and on love, for beyond all telling you are love. And you came to bear witness to that love. And you are here, and this is a very precious time for each of you.

Lay your concerns down. Relax into this present moment. See the Earth grow small and disappear. See the solar system becoming a thing of stars. Move further and further into the infinity of creation and yet you still are you, and this is still the present moment. And you are safe. Love reflected in love.

We would speak further through the instrument known as Jim. We leave this instrument in love and light. We are those of Q'uo.

(Jim channeling)

I am Q'uo, and greet each again in love and in light through this instrument. We would offer ourselves at this time to the speaking to further queries if there are any remaining upon the minds of those present. Is there a further query at this time?

Carla: Is there any difference in meditating with a candle with the eyes open and meditating with the eyes shut?

I am Q'uo, and am aware of your query, my sister. The use of the candle is most helpful for those who are beginning the practice of focusing the concentration with the hope of entering into the meditative state during which time the experience is continually focused upon one concept, one thought, or simply the absence of thought or concept. The one-pointed mind is the desired product of the focusing upon the candle. As an entity becomes more familiar with the process of entraining the mind to focus in this unified manner such devices as the candle or the mantra become less necessary. Thus, we would leave it to the entity to determine whether or not the use of the candle or other devices would be helpful in its meditative practice. As we mentioned before, to those who are less practiced, these aids are helpful.

Is there a further query, my sister?

Carla: No. Thank you.

I am Q'uo, and we thank you once again, my sister. Is there another query at this time?

Carla: Here's another question. Say you are having trouble getting yourself to meditate the first thing in the morning, but you are too tired at the end of the day. Are there ways that you can meditate tired?

I am Q'uo, and am aware of your query, my sister. To the entity who must choose between meditating when it is tired or not meditating, we would recommend the meditation when tired, for the meditation then will become the avenue through which the needed sleep may be expressed. The travel to the state of sleep, however, will be helpful in that the entity will be engaging in the practice of focusing its attention upon one point. There will eventually come, for the entity, the ability to remain awake and alert within the meditative state. That shall endure for as long as the entity wishes before it then desires to enter sleep. For those who wish to begin the practice of meditation we recommend the use of any portion of the day which offers itself most beneficially for the regularity of the practice, even if only for the moment or two. As the entity finds a quiet solidarity moment then it may engage in the focus of the mind for as long as time allows. Each effort spent in practicing meditation builds the momentum for the next and so forth until there is a regularization of behavior in this regard; that is, the establishing of the meditative practice.

Is there a further query, my sister?

Carla: Is it possible that if you went to sleep while meditating that your dreams would be clearer?

I am Q'uo, and am aware of your query, my sister. Indeed, it is possible, especially if the desire of the meditator is that such be so. The suggestion given to the subconscious mind within the meditative state is far stronger than the suggestion given in the conscious state. Thus, the entity may program, shall we say, the clarity and the subject matter of the dream.

Is there a further query, my sister?

Carla: No. Thank you.

I am Q'uo, and we thank you once again, my sister. Is there another query at this time?

R: I have a question about feeling various amounts of energy in my body during the month. I have noticed that when there is a full moon I don't seem to need much sleep, and it's difficult to fall asleep, and at other times it is the opposite. Is energy more available at some times more than at others?

I am Q'uo, and am aware of your query, my brother. We believe that we grasp your query and would respond by saying that, indeed, the mind/body/spirit complex and its emotional attachment is a series of energy patterns which move in a rhythmic fashion, as does all of the creation. As these patterns of energy blend and intertwine each with the other and with the rhythms of the planetary entity itself there are those opportunities that are presented as energies harmonize, one with another, that will allow the entity to be able to express more of these energies and to feel the movement of these energies through its vehicle, the mind, the body, and the spirit, as well as the emotional aspect that responds to and energizes the entity in its movement in the daily round of activities. Thus, there are the biorhythms, that you have mentioned, that can be charted and there are those subtler energies which are not currently able to be charted within your third-density illusion but which also add their influence to those energies which can be charted.

Is there another query, my brother?

R: Not on this topic. Of all the questions that I have asked over time I have always seemed to be asking how to do things. Why is that? Being rather than doing?

I am Q'uo, and am aware of your query, my brother. The asking of an inspirational source as to the means of doing is perhaps a paradox, as you have discovered within your own thinking. However, within the third-density illusion the means of existing are composed of a series of those things which are done within the outer illusion. As one begins to penetrate the nature of not only the third-density illusion, but of one's own being and purpose within the illusion, there becomes a more finely honed focus upon how one may be. Yet the transition to being is often made with the concept of how to do that which is necessary to be. This is a transition which is natural for each entity within the third-density illusion, for there must be, within the logical mind, a bridge between doing and being. At some point the seeker will discover that there is a greater Self which is always able to be and which lovingly welcomes home the pilgrim which has done much upon his journey of seeking. And one of its greatest efforts is to return home within the mind of the self so that there is the recognition of that which always has been and always will be by the who does much and seeks its own being. Is there a further query, my brother?

R: No. Thank you.

I am Q'uo, and again we thank you, my brother. Is there another query at this time?

(No further queries.)

I am Q'uo, and as it appears that we have, for the nonce, exhausted the queries for this session of working we would again thank each present for inviting us to join you this day. We are always filled with joy at the opportunity of blending our vibrations with yours. We walk with each most closely and joyfully at this time. We shall take our leave of this instrument and this group, leaving each, as always, in the love and in the light of the one infinite Creator. We are known to you as those of Q'uo. Adonai, my friends. Adonai. ☥

L/L Research

L/L Research is a subsidiary of Rock Creek Research & Development Laboratories, Inc.

P.O. Box 5195
Louisville, KY 40255-0195

www.llresearch.org

Rock Creek is a non-profit corporation dedicated to discovering and sharing information which may aid in the spiritual evolution of humankind.

ABOUT THE CONTENTS OF THIS TRANSCRIPT: This telepathic channeling has been taken from transcriptions of the weekly study and meditation meetings of the Rock Creek Research & Development Laboratories and L/L Research. It is offered in the hope that it may be useful to you. As the Confederation entities always make a point of saying, please use your discrimination and judgment in assessing this material. If something rings true to you, fine. If something does not resonate, please leave it behind, for neither we nor those of the Confederation would wish to be a stumbling block for any.

CAVEAT: This transcript is being published by L/L Research in a not yet final form. It has, however, been edited and any obvious errors have been corrected. When it is in a final form, this caveat will be removed.

© 2009 L/L Research

Sunday Meditation
November 1, 1998

Group question: No group question today. Potluck.

(Carla channeling)

We are those of the principle known to you as Q'uo. Greetings in the love and in the light of the one infinite Creator. We thank you for calling us to your circle this day, and we send you abundant blessings that cannot match the blessing that you give to us to meditate with you and share thoughts with you. As always, we ask that these words be taken as opinion and not facts, for we have thoughts and views but would not wish to be an authority. Rather, we ask that your authority be your own discrimination, for each of you does have these powers to know your own truth.

You have opened to us a vast array of things to speak about by requesting pot luck. We would, however, find all possible threads of thought and concept harmonizing into information concerning love. When we had not been so long among your peoples we offered less richly detailed information. At this point, we and your peoples have a long history of speaking together, and so we have found an increasing number of ways to talk about the love and the light of the one infinite Creator. And yet that basic message remains utterly simply and infinitely profound to us. The simplicity of oneness, of Creator and created, the richness provided by free will which has showered the manifested universe with countless worlds, countless civilizations, and infinite motion and energy and thought. As you gaze up into the night sky and see the stars sprinkled like sand across the blackness of the ether know that there are more ways than you can see stars on the clearest night to speak of love. And yet all speaking and manifestations end in one thing: that same Love that created all that there is.

This instrument finds turmoil within as she views the chasm that exists between the perceptions that some others have of her and perceptions that she has of herself. To the ones to whom she is offering a listening ear and the sharing of opinion she appears as a finished creature, and this instrument has had many fulsome compliments to satisfy her ego. And yet this instrument is not swayed by all of these opinions, for within the instrument's own judgment, she holds herself unworthy. And we would point out that this will undoubtedly be true of each person, that each entity is both deeply flawed and utterly perfect. This is another seemingly contradictory situation, for how can one be both perfect and imperfect? And yet that is what each of you is. Within the illusion one may be seen to be both the giver and the taker, the wise one and the fool. And both estimates are correct. And in the end no estimate is correct, for there is within the illusion no substance of righteousness, no infinite quality. Each of you has the feeling of being in two worlds at once.

The outer world of form and kind and sequence and the inner world of infinity and eternity. The citizenship that you hold as humans within incarnation is limited. The citizenship that each entity has within eternity is infinite.

The concept of infinity first fascinated this particular instrument at a very young age, for it was awakening within its infanthood. For most entities within this particular illusion, however, the awakening comes perhaps later in the teenage years or even beyond. Before waking up, though the illusion may give hints of its theatricality, it is, for the most part, entirely believable. However, once the seeker has awakened to the citizenship that it holds in eternity there is a reorientation of point of view that is profound. Further, it is as the chemical reaction that one cannot reverse. Once one has awakened, one must remain awake. Those who attempt to shut down those organs of perception within the metaphysical part of self find that it is now impossible to close the gate, for the point of view has shifted, and the creation has become new. We would encourage each of you to spend time feeling the newness of life, being aware of each beginning, each sunrise, each relationship, each project and hope, each dream and ambition. Allow the stale air of old opinion to be vented, released and allowed to fall away, for that which is needed this day is a creature of today and not the offspring of old thought.

We find within this instrument a strain of sadness, for she looks behind her at those companions that are no more: family, friends, mate. Banished from the illusion of time and space, disappearing from sight. And yet each of these entities seemingly lost is experiencing newness this day within the illusion that each of them enjoys this day. The one known as R was speaking of holding on to things. And letting go. There is that instinct to clasp to oneself that which one holds dear. Indeed, there is solid instinct and good reason behind that impulse to control one's environment, and yet how can one control novelty? How can one discipline that which is as yet unexpressed? The fear which the one known as R spoke of which causes one to cling and to create the small space within which one huddles is an impulse of self-preservation, the self feeling that it must be defended. Yet, as a citizen of eternity, the entire creation which you presently enjoy is but a moment, a moment in which there is the opportunity to stand in the light, to serve the light, and to allow the light to flow through. That light which is new every day and every moment. As the autumn showers its leaves and creates the golden carpet that crunches and blows with the wind as one walks, [this] may seem to indicate the deadness of the season that is to come and yet at this time as much as at any other all things are made new each day.

We give to this instrument the image of a traveler. The traveler moves across the desert landscape gazing intently, even feverishly, for a source of water. At the same time this entity is, metaphysically speaking, in a world made of water, that which this instrument refers to as water consciousness. As a citizen of eternity one may consider oneself cast upon the shore of an inhospitable environment, the desert land which offers learning opportunity for service and challenges that teach and create the potential for transformation. When you feel that you are truly in the desert, that all is dry and lifeless and without hope, we encourage you to practice knowing by faith the watery environment of the human spirit, for that which seems upon the surface to be dry and dusty and difficult is, in metaphysical terms, wondrous, a treasure, that which is to be prized, a canvas upon which to paint a self in love with the beauty and the majesty of the infinite Creator. When the mouth is parched for something to drink, when the stomach grumbles for food, remember that you are a citizen of eternity and that you have meat and drink that the world does not know of. And allow the desert to become the ocean, life-giving and new with every tide.

We would finish this transmission through the one known as Jim. We are those of Q'uo, and we would leave this instrument in love and in light. We transfer.

(Jim channeling)

I am Q'uo, and greet each again in love and in light through this instrument. We would ask if there may be further queries to which we may speak as this is our habit, to ask for addition queries after we have given the primary message. Is there another query for us at this time?

R: Would you speak to us of how to love the self for those who are on the service-to-others path? How to love yourself so that you do not gain power or control but to prepare yourself for service?

I am Q'uo, and am aware of your query, my brother. We find that the practice of the daily meditation in which one is able to review the experiences of the self is most helpful in coming to know, accept and love this self. At the end of the day is the most efficacious time during which to conduct this review, for the day's activities have made their mark, and the conscious mind is fresh in remembering the experiences which have moved the emotions from one aspect to another; that is, in both directions of the positive affirming emotions and the more judgmental and separative emotions where one has accepted or not accepted the self. To look upon the self in its activities in mediation is to experience that which the self has been able to manifest during the day, the fruits of the day, the fruits of the labors, shall we say. At this time one is able to allow the self to move as it did during the day and to see how one was able to accept or not able to accept the self during these movements. Then, after a period of sitting with the self and experiencing once again that which the self experienced, the entity is able to allow the full range of abilities of the self to express themselves in the meditative state.

That is a simplified form of the balancing exercises which this group is familiar with. The experience of the self, the ramifications of the experience and then the conscious desire and effort to accept the self for having each of these aspects available for the Creator to know Itself. It is within this meditative state that work may be done, whether this work is to accept the self, to know the self, or to simply sit in the silence with the self as a friend.

Is there a further query, my brother?

R: You are saying that the work can be done efficiently by allowing and accepting and just sharing the experience at the end of the day during the meditation? No actual doing is required?

I am Q'uo, and the doing, my brother, is that which is accomplished in the daily round of activities in a spontaneous and natural fashion. This doing then is reviewed in the meditative state at the end of the day, and a conscious effort is made at this time to accept the self for its full range of expression, that which was not at first accepted or that which was accepted. However the conscious effort to accept the self during the meditative state is that which is helpful in actually accepting the self.

Is there a further query, my brother?

R: And so we have a balance between being and doing. Right?

I am Q'uo, and this is so. Is there a further query?

R: No. Thank you. Thank you for the loving words during the first portion of this sitting.

I am Q'uo, and again we thank you, my brother. Is there another query at this time?

(No further queries.)

I am Q'uo, and we are most grateful to each of you as well for inviting us to join you and to speak our humble words of experience, of inspiration, and of information. We are always glad to do so. We find that the energies within this group are somewhat low at this time. Therefore, it would be a propitious time for us to take our leave of this instrument and this group. As always, we leave each in the love and in the light of the one infinite Creator. We are known to you as those of Q'uo. Adonai, my friends. Adonai. ☥

L/L Research

L/L Research is a subsidiary of Rock Creek Research & Development Laboratories, Inc.

P.O. Box 5195
Louisville, KY 40255-0195

www.llresearch.org

Rock Creek is a non-profit corporation dedicated to discovering and sharing information which may aid in the spiritual evolution of humankind.

ABOUT THE CONTENTS OF THIS TRANSCRIPT: This telepathic channeling has been taken from transcriptions of the weekly study and meditation meetings of the Rock Creek Research & Development Laboratories and L/L Research. It is offered in the hope that it may be useful to you. As the Confederation entities always make a point of saying, please use your discrimination and judgment in assessing this material. If something rings true to you, fine. If something does not resonate, please leave it behind, for neither we nor those of the Confederation would wish to be a stumbling block for any.

CAVEAT: This transcript is being published by L/L Research in a not yet final form. It has, however, been edited and any obvious errors have been corrected. When it is in a final form, this caveat will be removed.

© 2009 L/L Research

Sunday Meditation
November 15, 1998

Group question: The question today concerns anger and frustration which we feel for ourselves, and we would like Q'uo to tell us how we can use these feelings to lead us along the path towards compassion for ourselves. Is there hope that we can change ourselves, or should we concentrate on accepting ourselves with the anger and all?

(Carla channeling)

We are those known to you as Q'uo. We greet you in the love and in the light of the one infinite Creator. It is in the service of the One that we come to you, and we are, as always, most grateful that you have called us to your session of working. It is a great blessing to us to be able to have the opportunity to share your meditation and to share our opinions with you. We would ask that each who seeks use the discrimination that is each seeker's gift, that inner voice that says, "This is for me, and that is not." We would not wish for you to take our word as gospel, for we are but fallible servants of the light. We can be wrong, and we only offer our opinion in the hope that it may prove to be a resource for you as it has been for us. But always trust your own discrimination whether listening to our voice or to any voice, for it is given to each seeker to sense truth when it comes.

Your query this day is most interesting, for it moves into the heat of that which is perceived as a battle, that running of the good race, as this instrument would put it, from the words of St. Paul. It is in the midst of the illusion that each of you wished to come before embarking upon this incarnation. It is precisely into this self-perceived cauldron of confusion and negative emotional processes that you genuinely wished to enter. You think to yourself, "Now, why would I want to do such a thing?" "Why would I wish to swim in this sea of confusion?" Yet, you must remember the great difference betwixt the place whereon you were standing when you gazed into the possibilities that such an incarnation could offer you. You were not within the veil of confusion and forgetting and illusion. Rather, when you chose to make this particular pilgrimage at this particular time you were gazing at the opportunity to express faith.

The expression of faith is that expression which claims a harmony and balance that is completely unseen. Before you entered upon this incarnation it was not necessary for you to call upon faith, for the truth was evident. Dwelling within the finer bodies of self, gazing upon the possibilities of service and learning that [they] were before you, each of you felt inspired and strengthened in this desire to move into this heavy illusion, to enter into the sea of confusion completely, accepting the forgetting of those simple truths that are self-evident within the realms of spirit, and taking hold of the opportunity to live a life that was a testament and an anthem of faith and love and joy, for these feelings, these pure emotions well up within you, and you yearned to express them with ever more purity.

Indeed, each of you had to wait and hope for the opportunity to take incarnation at this time because there were so many souls desiring to lend their faith and love and devotion to the Earth plane at this juncture in time and space, for this particular solar system and galaxy is at this particular time moving through what many have called a birth, an entrance into the next density of learning. And indeed, the Earth plane has much difficulty at this time in moving harmoniously through the changes of magnetic energy and spiritual energy that go along with this particular cusp wherein one era or age ends and another begins. Indeed, this is a critical time for many as many have said to this group, as each has heard many times before. There is a time of harvest at this particular juncture, and there are many who are ready to awaken to their spiritual identity, ready to be harvested into a higher understanding.

And with a full and overflowing heart each of you desired purely and truly to be of service, to be one who went into the fields that were white, to be one of those who helped with the harvest of planet Earth. And may we say that each of you is helping. Each of you does express a level of love and faith and devotion that is marked at times. Each of you has been able, to some extent, to intensify that polarity with which you seek to do the service for which you came.

And so if you are doing what you came to do, then why do you have these feelings of frustration and anger? Let us look at this. There are many who have no trouble expressing anger, frustration or other negative emotions, nor have they any trouble assigning the blame and responsibility for these emotions to forces outside themselves. However, each of you has become aware that nothing is truly outside of you, that you cannot impute responsibility for your feelings to other people, to outside forces of any kind. More and more, each of you has begun to take spiritual responsibility for yourself, and so when these emotions occur they are turned inward. This is actually, in terms of metaphysical work, a significant advance to imputing responsibility to forces outside the self.

When you are engaged in chastising the self you are consumed with the desire to be better. This in itself, as we said, is a step forward, a great step forward in the process of balancing these emotions. The one known as J remarked earlier that she felt that of herself she could do nothing, and this was a free quotation from that known to you as your Holy Bible. The one known as St. Paul discussed this further[23], saying that works without love did not have virtue. That if one did all things taught, shared all things, knew all things, and yet had not love, such a person was as a banging gong, a loud noise that signified nothing. This is a key for each of you, we feel; that is, the realization that of yourself you can do nothing, that things done from the self, things done without inspiration, will not have that virtue which you so desired to come and share with your brethren upon planet Earth.

How difficult it is to see that actions without love are not useful! Why [is it] so difficult? Very simply within your culture there is little attention given to the value of being. Rather, there is the almost maniacal focus upon doing, accomplishing things in the illusion, things that you can point to that have an objective referent that are actions. It is the actions that seem to be valuable, and yet in the metaphysical sense it is the love with which these actions are taken that is valuable, rather than the actions themselves. From the standpoint of spiritual work it is the love with which you do or do not do or contemplate things that is your essence and your gift and, indeed, your vocation within the Earth plane.

And this is a difficult thing even to comprehend because of the enculturation, that work ethic that has come down from so many sources and is the lifeblood of your culture at this time. When entities meet each other, what do they ask in order to establish rapport? Very commonly they will ask, "What do you do?" Can you see how far from the heart such a question may take one, for when that is asked there is not even the general intention to ask what are your interests, for it is assumed that there

---

[23] *Holy Bible*, Corinthians 13:1-3: "If I speak the languages of men and of angels, but do not have love, I am a sounding gong or a clanging cymbal. If I have the gift of prophecy, and understand all mysteries and all knowledge, and if I have all faith, so that I can move mountains, but do not have love, I am nothing. And if I donate all my goods to feed the poor, and if I give my body to be burned, but do not have love, I gain nothing."

will be an employment of some kind by which you identity and justify your existence. "I am a librarian. I am a teacher. I am a nurse. I am a researcher." This is the way you are taught to relate to other souls. And yet each of you has a life within that is compelling, fascinating, fruitful and active. Each of you has the dynamic tension between the various portions of self that have revealed themselves to you as you have done spiritual work. Realization after realization have come to you through the years concerning intimate and profound processes within the spiritual evolution which each of you is attempting with a full heart to accelerate, to cooperate with and to intensify.

The sharing of this level of self must usually be done completely without words. Rather, it is usually done simply by that quality of being with someone which the other senses cannot precisely articulate. Yet we know that each of you has those who come to you for counsel because they sense the presence of this inner life and because they trust that being that they sense without words. This is the heart of your gift. This is the heart of your incarnation. To be yourself. To meet the moment with yourself, your full, open, loving self. How infinitely difficult this is upon a daily basis. As the one known as R said, "If I forget to pay attention for just a moment, it all comes back, and I am back where I started, seeming to fight the difficulties of daily living."

How infinitely delicate a job it is to move into your daily behavior with an eye to finding yourself and those gifts that lie deepest within your heart. When faced with what seems to be exigent and continuous demands for action from the outside world we do not know a simple or foolproof way for you to move from those self-perceived frustrations into that deeper self within where love always remains. Each of you has an innermost heart where this is true. But how difficult it is to go there. How little your outer education has prepared you even to attempt to honor the being before the doing, the love before the action. If you demand of yourself that you only do those things which you can do with love, then you shall perhaps find yourself doing little until you get your feet under you. For it is true that the illusion of third density which you now enjoy is specifically designed to frustrate and baffle the intellect, to knock you off balance mentally and emotionally, to destroy safe and controlled places so that the journey of incarnation may more and more be undertaken from the heart.

We have many times recommended meditation. That still, small voice of silence that speaks in meditation is most eloquent. It is as though each of you has within you the Creator, that one great original Thought that created all that there is. That Love creates and destroys and is a principle that has created all of the manifested worlds. It is a difficult thing to find one's way to the Creator within. Every energy of the illusion will attempt to distract your attention from that goal of moving into the heart.

Fortunately, there is that memory, that awareness that abides through all illusion, that star within, that presence within that each of you may forget often, but occasionally each has had the galvanizing and orienting experiencing of being at one with that heart of hearts, that Creator within. And just an instant of such a union gives the seeker a tremendous strength of conviction and a renewed desire to try again to persist in seeking that way of being that will most deeply satisfy the yearning to be of service that each feels so truly.

We can reliably say that none of you grasped just how difficult it would be to express faith in such a heavy and convincing illusion. It is safe to say that each felt more confident before incarnation than now, within incarnation, feeling battered and travel-weary with the dust of the spiritual road. Yet, this road, dusty and in the desert so often, nevertheless feels right, and there is companionship upon this road as each meets others who have similar desires and yearn for similar service and learning.

And so we say to each of you, you do have the power to alter your perceptions, to alter your state of mind. And yet, this is not a power that is expressed through intellect or through great works but, rather, through very small realizations that come again and again throughout the day as each, indeed, has noticed. The voice of spirit seems to speak in so many ways to one who is listening, and the more one begins to attend to coincidences and synchronicities the more one begins to get a feeling of spirit talking back to you, being that unseen companion that is willing to place within the consciousness alternate ways of being. This is work for the persistent, for, indeed, it is the work of the incarnation, not a work done in a day, or a year, or a decade, but rather that goal of self-awareness and self-choice that is as the star that each follows.

We are aware that, from the inside out, each may feel that she has perhaps failed or is failing on this day at this time in such and such a way. And yet this is only true within the illusion. The work in consciousness that each is doing is only tangential to the events to which you are conscious. And so our best advice to those who wish to have ever more control of their own attitudes and feelings is to persist. Certainly we encourage each to persist with humor, with grace, with style, with panache and verve, as Merv Griffin might say. But we say it is all right to be ungraceful. It is all right to be awkward, to be behind hand, to be half there and half not. This does not matter. What matters is that there is a continuation of simple attention and effort to be the best that you can, to do the best that you can, and then to let the devil take the hindmost, as this instrument would say.

What a wonderful gift it is to yourself simply to let it all go. And this is something that we would emphasize. Look at the way the intellect functions. It is a tool designed for making distinctions. You may say to yourself, "Thou shalt not judge," but your intellect knows not how to do anything other. Consequently, no matter how much you are aware that you should not judge yourself, you will judge yourself, for that is the way the mind works. We can only encourage you not to take it too seriously, for it—that is, the mind, the intellect—is a portion of the illusion. The intellect is not the same as consciousness. You have consciousness as a being, as a citizen of eternity. You have an intellect as a function of the illusion. It is enough that you can separate consciousness from intellect in the abstract.

We are not suggesting that you spurn the intellect or cease using it. There is much within your incarnation that the intellect handles very, very well. We would not wish to rob you of that tool that you need to do those things that you do in order to be responsible for the self. We simply ask that you persist in remembering that the consciousness that you are is a mystery that contains deity, that ends in an identity betwixt you and the Creator of all that there is. This portion of yourself would overwhelm completely the incarnative illusion were the veil to lift even for a second. And this does occur with entities, often with disastrous results, within the illusion. But when you sense yourself moving into these negative processes perhaps we might suggest that you could take just the moment to acknowledge that your consciousness is not a portion of this tangle but, rather, is an agent that remains free to be love. Just allowing the breath to move in and the breath to move out while identifying with the consciousness that endures may bring fresh air into the muddle that life often seems to be.

As we said, this is indeed an interesting subject, and this instrument tells us that we have gone on too long discussing it. We apologize. We would at this time like to transfer this contact to the one known as Jim. We leave this instrument in love and in light and in thanks. We are those of Q'uo.

(Jim channeling)

I am Q'uo, and I greet each of you again in love and in light through this instrument. At this time we would welcome any further queries which those present might have for us. Is there another query at this time?

R: It is well to examine what one does to see if it is done with love. If it is not done with love it is OK to let it go because of the potential for learning inherent in that letting go. Can you comment on that?

I am Q'uo, and am aware of your query, my brother. To look at that which one has accomplished and to see if there was love contained in that moment is well, for this is the way in which one becomes familiar with the workings of the incarnation, shall we say. Whatever the amount or lack of love contained it is well to accept the self for the effort made. For in the truth of the incarnation and the experience of each entity within the incarnation, each movement made is a step of the Creator and by the Creator in Its process of discovering Itself within your experience and of you discovering the Creator in your experience. That this journey might occasionally be uneven, filled with confusion and anger, is the inevitable product of forgetting the harmony of all that is and moving within the illusion that you now inhabit. To accept the self as it now is is to bless this process of experience, of discovery, of movement not only towards love but a movement within love that has yet to be perceived. For all about you, my brother, is filled with love. When one is able to speak from love one is able then also to speak to love. If it is necessary to stop the activity, retire to meditation, contemplation or prayer in order to find even the slightest iota of love within a situation that seems devoid of any possibility of love, this is well to do. However, we encourage you always to value the self, its activity, and the direction in which you move at all times.

Is there another query, my brother?

R: Not at this time. You answered my question in more ways than one and it was very inspirational. Thank you.

I am Q'uo, and we thank you, my brother. Is there another query at this time?

Carla: I feel confused about the being versus the doing. It seems like it's worth something to do good works, and I think it's really hard to order yourself so that you ask of yourself that you be loving before you ask of yourself that you be productive.

I am Q'uo, and am aware of your confusion, my sister. The movement into productivity, as is so the custom of this illusion, is that movement which is more or less informed by love. If love is the foundation upon which you build the structure of your daily life of doing, then it is far more likely to contain the colorful and harmonious moments of inspiration as well as providing the framework for action. To move into action without the quality in some degree is to, shall we say, remove the color from the picture so that there is less variety and possibility for inspiration or synchronically for the movement in harmony with those about you. The quality of love is that which enhances the experience to the degree that that which you may call magic occurs, the changing of consciousness in an instant. The ingredient of love and its addition to your activities is that which allows the magic of the moment to occur, the rising of the bread of life, shall we say. The desire to serve is a good and valuable desire. The intention to be of service is that which stands on its own. To imbue it with love is to add to its efficacy. Thus, that which is called love and is so poorly understood by those within the illusion, by the very nature of the illusion is that which has the ability to change the consciousness of those expressing it and those about such an entity in an instant. Thus it is that quality which heals, which informs, which makes whole that which has been broken, and is that which causes the service, the productivity, of an entity to be enhanced in such a way which is quite beyond the description of words but which moves one's being from, shall we say, the inside. Thus, one who has love is co-Creator and is able to share this quality with others.

Is there a further query, my sister?

Carla: Just a tangential one. I just noticed that we all seem to have a tremendous ability to encourage each other, not so much ourselves. It seems harder to love yourself. I guess that's the way it is, huh?

I am Q'uo, and am aware of your query, my sister. And, indeed, within this third-density illusion where so much is hidden from the consciousness of each entity within it, it is most helpful to have those about one who feel the quality of love for one that allows the free sharing of observations that may escape the entity itself while it is moving so diligently along the path of self-discovery, pushing the self to move ever more quickly and surely upon this pilgrim's path. Thus, each reflects to the other the picture more objectively seen so that one may be informed by each other-self as to the qualities of the self that are quite full of love and deserving of love. Thus, each teaches each. It has been well said that those who of like mind together seek shall far more surely find.

Is there another query, my sister?

Carla: No. I think that is very good. Each of us is good support for others.

I am Q'uo, and again we thank you, my sister. Is there another query at this time?

(No further queries.)

I am Q'uo, and as it appears that we have, for the nonce, exhausted the queries within this circle of seeking, we shall take this opportunity to thank each entity present for inviting our presence to your meditation this day. It is a great joy and honor for us to join you here. We remind each that each has a company of angels that joins you in your seeking and walks with you on your path. Retire, then, in meditation whenever possible that you might become more aware of all this host of angelic presences about you that support your every desire to seek and to serve and rejoices at every experience of love that you encounter. We shall take our leave of this instrument and this group at this time, leaving each in the love and in the light of the one infinite Creator. We are known to you as those of Q'uo. Adonai, my friends. Adonai. ☙

Sunday Meditation
November 29, 1998

Group question: What kind of souls are incarnating into the Earth plane now? Ra said there were those with third and fourth-density bodies activated and wanderers as well as those who would like to make the fourth-density graduation. Could you tell us something about the souls being born today?

(Carla channeling)

We are those of the principle known to you as Q'uo, and we greet you in the love and in the light of the one infinite Creator whom we adore and in whose service we are proud to be. We thank you for calling us to your circle of seeking. We acknowledge the great blessing that you give us by inviting us to share our humble opinions, and we send each blessings of thanks for this privilege. As always, we would ask that those things that we say be listened to with discrimination, for each entity has unique needs and deserves nothing less than the personal and highly individualistic truth that is personal truth. For there are many truths and there are many progressions of truths, and each entity which seeks takes a slightly different journey even though the territory is the same.

And this is what we would ask that you think of our words and other opinions into which you might run in your investigations. Select just as you would the flowers that you would put upon your table those thoughts which you wish to bloom within the house that thought furnishes and builds.

This day you would wish to know more about the current population of your planetary sphere and who is coming through as babies in these days. Within your query you pointed out two of the three basic groups that are here within your worlds at this time. It is accurate to say that those third-density entities that are hoping to graduate within the next lifetime make up the bulk of those upon your planet at this time. By and large, you still shall find perhaps two out of three entities born being, shall we say, the old style of physical vehicle where the third-density body is activated and the fourth, fifth, sixth and so forth are in potentiation only. The hope is, of course, that one last lifetime as the planetary sphere itself is ending the third-density cycle might effectuate enough growth and maturity of spirit to create that integrity of spirit that welcomes fuller light.

There are also increasing numbers of newborn infants which are the pioneers of fourth density upon your sphere, those with the third-density and fourth-density bodies activated. Often such children will have unusually mature thought processes and an enhanced ability to learn, to create, to enumerate with joy those things that are found to be beautiful treasures.

The third type of entity which is being born to your peoples at this time is that general term of wanderer. Wanderers have streamed in large numbers to your planetary sphere in the last generation and much of the strong spiritual support in the arts that many have noted during these years has come from such wanderers as these. These entities have much more in common with the third-density Earth native than with the entities with double activated bodies in that they are fully under the veil of forgetting. The differences between wanderers and third-density graduation hopefuls is within the area of faith and intuition. The wanderer has more of an instinctive belief or faith in spiritual coincidence, in the aliveness of all things to the molding of a structure of information communication which moves across all lines of language and culture.

These three types of entities are not homogenous as Earth itself has not had a pure or easy history with third density. Rather, your native sphere is one which has welcomed many, many different populations of those who have not graduated from a previous third-density cycle elsewhere. Your planet is then a highly various group of people. There are several pointedly different archetypical structures that have been passed down in what this instrument would call the equivalent of the genetic code in the time/space universe. Your planet, then, is one characterized by various levels of confusion which has not always been the case in third-density cycles. It is as though your plane of existence is in a class filled with those whom other teachers and other cultures have so far failed to inspire.

We feel that the point of interest for us in discussing your planetary population is not in all of these differences, nor yet in those things which are common amongst all, but, rather, we would point up the unusual vividness and strength of various distortions among your peoples. We compliment your peoples on the intensity and dedication with which ideas are found and held. Yours is a planetary sphere full of tremendous energy, full of great power. This power is most often trapped within the entities' confusion, and our point of interest is in finding ways to discuss love. For it is this simple passage which we always come to give. Yet, to your unruly and various peoples one way of giving shall never be sufficient, nor two, nor three, nor a hundred, nor a thousand. We celebrate this peculiarly vivid energy of your peoples. Indeed, the energies are in some disarray, yet how beautiful and how powerful the potential. There are so many entities just on the threshold of that level of awareness that shakes down the entire organism and rearranges it. And your peoples thirst for this with great energy.

And they are thirsting for that which they are but cannot see within themselves. They are searching for their Creator. They are searching for love. Intelligent infinity rests. Intelligent energy asks, "What not?" And betwixt the rest and the question lies the mortal universe in space and time that supports that universe.

We encourage all souls within the Earth plane to focus upon the young ones, for, as always, it is to those born in innocence and full of expectations that information needs to be most lovingly considered in giving. Whenever there is the opportunity to interact with the children about you, we encourage each in her own way to look into the children's eyes, to make contact with spirit there. For in each of the three cases, the entity is an old soul. The entity has much experience. The entity is full of potential, for each connection with a young one strengthens and bolsters that child's gifts of faith and will. If kindness comes not so easily to you, then let your kindness be for children. Let the heart open for the young ones, for much teaching shall be given in that manner.

Know that when you come in contact with all entities each is teaching each, and to the extent that you can attempt to open the heart without fear as entities are met. For although as children grow into adults they lose some of that faith and perhaps pervert some of that will, yet there is no spirit in incarnation that is more than a few steps away from understanding. You never know, therefore, what you might say or do or express by your presence that might be salvation or realization to another.

We would encourage entities concerned with the caring for children to focus repeatedly, daily if possible, upon the metaphysical needs that you yourself feel and those children who are with you feel. Find ways to practice devotion to the Creator. And share this as a normal and everyday part of living. This shall reassure and orient young entities in ways that go too deep for words. Some keep an altar. Some light a candle and meditate. Some interact with nature, walking amongst the blooms or the dry leaves or the wintry grasses. Some watching the birds or finding ways to take pictures of the animals in their natural habitat. There are so many, many avenues where the spiritual can be taught to children without heaviness or pretension.

Most of all, we encourage each simply to be themselves, for this teaches more than anything else. Entities who are moving from their core outward, being as true to their feelings and sensings as possible, shall always have a head start in communicating with those called children. For as they are simpler and less devious, so are their ways of seeing. And they shall appreciate an entity who is herself far more than an entity, no matter how exciting that is a mask rather than the person herself.

We feel that we have come to a natural stopping point, but before we transfer to the one known as Jim, we would ask if there are any further queries upon this subject. We shall pause.

(No further queries.)

We are those of Q'uo, and since there is no request for related information upon this subject we shall relinquish the contact with the one known as Carla and transfer to the one known as Jim. We thank this instrument and leave it in love and in light. We are those of Q'uo.

(Jim channeling)

I am Q'uo, and greet each again in the love and light through this instrument. At this time it is our honor to offer ourselves to the potential of further queries. If there are any upon other topics of importance to those gathered, we would be most happy to attempt to speak to them.

Is there another query at this time?

J: How much of an idea of what lies ahead in third density does a soul who is incarnating into this illusion have?

I am Q'uo, and believe that we grasp your query. We shall respond to that which we grasp and ask you to query further if we have not covered the topic as you would wish.

Those who now move into incarnation within this planetary sphere's third-density illusion are aware that this is the time of graduation, that this particular planet is having somewhat of a difficult birthing for the fourth-density population that is to inhabit this planetary sphere. The difficulties of blending vibrations, of seeking in unity, and of recognizing the Creator in all are significant enough that there are, as you are well aware, many wars, misunderstandings, miscommunications and other difficulties that make this illusion one filled with confusion and that which seems to be a turmoil of significant degree. This is seen as a kind of chaotic expression of energy by those awaiting incarnation. Yet it is not seen as that which deters the desire to move into the third-density illusion in this planetary influence and to experience the opportunities that await those who seek their own graduation and the graduation of those of their vibration. Rather, the difficulties that are perceived are seen as further opportunities for service as those challenges which enhance the incarnational abilities to learn the lessons of love and to serve the light of the one Creator. The chaotic expression of energy is seen as that which offers the opportunity to enhance one's own expression of energy as one is able to move in harmony through the difficult times and experiences that lie ahead. For previous to incarnation each entity is far more aware that it is a portion of the one Creator and all those about it are the same, as are those with whom it shall spend its third-density days. Thus, the entity awaiting the incarnation sees with clearer eyes that which lies ahead and is far less liable to shy away from such difficulties but is far more likely to embrace them as the opportunities to serve and to learn.

Is there a further query, my sister?

J: No. Thank you.

I am Q'uo, and we thank you, my sister. Is there another query at this time?

Carla: May I ask a question about an experience?

I am Q'uo, and we are happy to entertain whatever query you would have to ask.

Carla: Thank you. When I was channeling earlier in this meeting, I could feel an energy start up at the end. If I closed my eyes I was dizzy, a rush of wind, not chaotic. Just a different energy than I have ever experienced. Could you shed any light on that experience? Is it another contact that wants to speak? Could it be a gift of energy that was being given to me? I couldn't even name it. It felt like it was occurring throughout the top of my brow and head and within my mind.

I am Q'uo, and am aware of your query, my sister. As we scan for the experience which you have described we are aware that there is within your physical vehicle at this time some difficulties that have been of concern to you during this past week as you have measured this cycle of time. And there are those entities within the Confederation of Planets in the Service of the Infinite Creator who move to the need for the healing in their own ways. These you have known in your past as those of Nona. This entity has, in this experience which you have described, offered itself in the attempt to lend an energy exchange to your auric field that has been perceived by you in the manner that you described.

Is there a further query, my sister?

Carla: If I wish to accept Nona's gift, then all I need to do is say "thank you" to her. Is this correct?

I am Q'uo, and this is correct, my sister.

Carla: Thank you, Nona. Thank you Q'uo.

I am Q'uo, and again we thank you, my sister. Is there another query at this time?

(No further queries.)

I am Q'uo, and we would thank each present this day for inviting us to join your circle of seeking. We are gratified that we have been able to offer our humble opinions in those areas which have been expressed as those of concern for you. We would ask that you take those words which we have given which have the ring of truth to you and use them as you will, leaving behind all others without a second thought. At this time we shall take our leave of this instrument and this group, leaving each in the love and in the light of the one infinite Creator. We are know to you as those of Q'uo. Adonai, my friends. Adonai.

L/L Research

L/L Research is a subsidiary of Rock Creek Research & Development Laboratories, Inc.

P.O. Box 5195
Louisville, KY 40255-0195

www.llresearch.org

Rock Creek is a non-profit corporation dedicated to discovering and sharing information which may aid in the spiritual evolution of humankind.

ABOUT THE CONTENTS OF THIS TRANSCRIPT: This telepathic channeling has been taken from transcriptions of the weekly study and meditation meetings of the Rock Creek Research & Development Laboratories and L/L Research. It is offered in the hope that it may be useful to you. As the Confederation entities always make a point of saying, please use your discrimination and judgment in assessing this material. If something rings true to you, fine. If something does not resonate, please leave it behind, for neither we nor those of the Confederation would wish to be a stumbling block for any.

CAVEAT: This transcript is being published by L/L Research in a not yet final form. It has, however, been edited and any obvious errors have been corrected. When it is in a final form, this caveat will be removed.

© 2009 L/L Research

Sunday Meditation
December 20, 1998

Group question: What is the entity, Jesus, doing now, and how can we benefit in our devotional lives from his teachings?

(Carla channeling)

We are those of the principle known to you as Q'uo, and we greet you in the love and in the light of the one infinite Creator whose servants we are. As the shadows lengthen on your winter's afternoon we extend our gratitude and our blessing to you who sit quietly in a circle of working humbly asking for truth, for hope, for resources and tools with which to carry on the seeking of the mystery of love and of deity. We thank you and we bless you, and we give thanks for you. For it is that stubborn and persistent seeker that lights the way for those who follow, that plants the seeds that others shall gather. It does not seem to each who sits in this circle that there is anything out of the ordinary in each life, and yet each has been as a beacon to others in ways that each cannot possibly know. We, too, hope that we may learn and grow as persistently as this group, and we hope that we may share from our experience the opinions and concepts that have been helpful to us. As always, however, we ask that each who hears these words respond only to those ideas that delight and find a home within. Any thoughts that we may offer that may seem disharmonious to you, we would ask that you leave behind, for we do not wish to create problems for you. We only wish to share our thoughts and to share the energy of meditation that blesses us as we hope our presence blesses you.

You have asked this day concerning the entity known to you as Jesus of Nazareth, what he is doing now and what this entity may continue to symbolize and suggest to those who seek the truth. At this level of contact, that is, the light trance of what this instrument calls conscious channeling, we do not wish to attempt to indicate, using this instrument, precisely what planetary sphere or what precise work this particular entity is now doing. We would, however, express our feeling that this entity was one of a social memory complex that was at a stage of graduation to fifth density. This entity and the social memory complex of which it was a part had in common a full consciousness of love and compassion. A love that creates. A love that destroys. A love that transforms. A love that is all that there is. This love was not informed or balanced with wisdom. This state of love of this social memory complex thusly was, if not absolutely perfect, at a very high level of near perfection. And as such, this group was exquisitely poised at the appropriate nexus when the opportunity came for incarnation using Christ consciousness within the Earth plane in third density.

This social memory complex is now, and has been for some of your time, studying the ways of wisdom and progressing in fifth density. However, the state of consciousness of Jesus the Christ and that social memory complex is alive and well within your inner planes where many teachers who have experienced this state of consciousness await the work of what this instrument would call the Holy Spirit. Thusly, the Earth plane has never been without Christ, nor shall it ever be without Christ. For as the Christ came into incarnation it was perhaps, in some part, a personality, but so filled with the Holy Spirit, the identity of self with what the one known as Jesus called the Father, that there was not sufficient personality clinging to this Christed being [for him] to retain a personality shell after the departure of this entity from the inner planes of your Earth.

Thusly, without taking anything away from the accomplishment of the individual who carried Christ's consciousness within the Earth plane we may say that that energy that you know of as Jesus is not owned by an individual, nor was it owned by an individual while that individual was in incarnation. Rather, the one known as Jesus always and persistently stated, "When you hear me, you do not hear me but my Father." This entity found itself completely lost to its Earthly personality experiencing the glory of oneness with the Creator, with the creation of nature with the world around it and with each and every seemingly imperfect human being that seemingly presented itself to this entity. This Christed quality of love is so much a redeemer and a savior of third-density awareness and of fourth-density work that we find it extremely easy to state that Jesus is Lord, as this instrument requires us to do before we may speak. We are not at that time celebrating the individual but stating the Lordship that this individual carried as its identity, eschewing and forgoing the normal ramifications of the ego-driven personality.

Perhaps you may see, then, that each of you has the potential to begin to learn how to carry the consciousness of Christ within the self. For you see, as you consider yourself it is crucial what angle you view the self from. In the eyes of your culture, you are taught to view the self within the nexus of the social arrangement that enables society to live peaceably together. The self then is seen as personality, with characteristics of the personality, with a certain kind of mental ability, with certain culturally conditioned and educated biases, with certain physical work that is done, with certain hobbies and interests and the whole gamut of human identity.

However, each who has awakened spiritually knows well that that is only the surface of self and all of society and its biases, that all of the social arrangements, economic plans and schemes for attaining and maintaining comfort and health and happiness do not identify the self or exhaust its beingness. As spiritual seekers move more and more into consideration of the self as a spiritual being there grows an awareness that the self within is not even a person, that the personality is truly a shell but that what it holds is infinite. There is no bottom to the roots of consciousness. The roots move into infinity. There is no limitation upon the self, the "I" that lives within, and that is one key that the one known as Jesus of Nazareth offers: the redefinition of self, that movement from the "I" of the personality to the "I" of "When you hear me speak, you hear not me but the Father who sent me." For each of us was sent into this illusion. Each of us, indeed, has sent itself into the illusion to serve as the lighthouse for the source of light moving into the Earth plane. It is not that the "I" of self has the fuel to burn an infinite light eternally. Rather, the spiritually awakened self becomes more and more aware that the "I" that is truly the self is simply moving through the vehicle of personality in infinite energy. What the "I" of personality may do to express the true "I-ness" of the Creator within is to allow and bless the energy that moves through the being. For each of you is as a receiver and a sender of energy. Each of you receives infinite light and love in a steady and continual basis, both from the Earth energy itself moving up through the vehicle and from those sources of inspiration which each calls to herself from time to time that move down into the self from above.

All of this energy can be held, or it can be allowed to flow. And each serves by allowing that energy to flow through with as little distortion as possible. And not simply allowing but blessing it on its way. Each has outer gifts, and these gifts are there for each to share. However, the one known as Jesus is that perfect example of one who laid all gifts before the Creator and simply said, "What is your will for me?"

At this time where the world experiences the shortest of days and the longest of nights, at your Christmastide, your light festival, know that the baby that lies within the manger in the story in your

Bible is alive and lying in the manger in your heart. Know that that consciousness of Christ that the one known as Jesus carried is carried by others as well. That there are always Christs within your inner planes, those who dwell in that state of consciousness that is so fruitful and helpful for those within the Earth planes, but know most of all that the savior and redeemer of the world lies within the single unified heart. For each of you has in perfect accomplishment the awareness and the ability to be Christed. And as destiny rules, each of you shall be given your times to express perfect love.

This instrument asks us, mentally, and we repeat it that we may answer for each of you, "How can you say that Jesus is Lord if you say that Jesus can be replaced with another of the same consciousness?" and we say to you that it is our experience that selfhood is far less personal than it seems within third density. It is a matter of breadth of experience, of seeing into the illusion which within your incarnational experiences is such a perfect and complete illusion. Jesus, indeed, is Lord. Christ, indeed, is the highest and most pure and perfect love, that love that destroys only to transform, that kills only to raise and move onward. Whereever we see the Christ within incarnation that consciousness held by that entity is Lord. One recognizes it as one would recognize an oak tree or a brand of food in your marketplace. It is distinctive. It is perfect of its own kind. And it is a deeply impersonal, infinitely true consciousness in metaphysical location of quality and essence that transcends personality and reidentifies the individual as love.

This state of consciousness lies within your awareness even in incarnation, in potentiation, and the thirst for that state of consciousness draws you onward. May we say to you, value and treasure that thirst and follow it faithfully, for it is a true thirst, a thirst that will still be there a hundred millennia from now, only more intense, more single-minded, because you will have found out more, experienced more, been more within the changing and shifting illusions of space/time.

We do not want to turn our backs upon history. We are aware that it is important to this instrument and to others whether the one known as Jesus the Christ was an historical figure. Indeed, this entity did exist and did express as Christ. There have been others who have expressed this consciousness within your Earth plane but certainly less distorted in expression of this gift than the one known as Jesus. We see and believe in the Christ in each of you and in ourselves. Indeed, we have been at that state of consciousness and have shared in expressing Christhood in our service as you shall do in your turn. Beyond all considerations of time and place and history, however, there lies a level of truth that goes quite beyond the personal and moves into essences and qualities of consciousness that open doors within the deep mind and create the possibility for further spiritual evolution.

We wish you light and love on that journey that each of you takes as each pursues the questions of identity and ambition. Who am I? Why am I here? What is my service? Whither do I go? These are the questions that stir life and aid in acceleration of evolution. Move ever deeper into questions of who you really are, what service you truly came to offer. Know that these potentials for transformation and evolution are real, and know that we do not find any consideration more interesting than the pursuit of self into the deeper mind and beyond the local personality shell with which you have equipped yourselves in order to experience this illusion. Know that you are redeemed, loved, cherished and treasured by the Christ that was Jesus, by Christ consciousness wherever it is, and by us. Know that you are part of a great Self, and that as you pursue your selfhood you also pursue the selfhood of the creation and the Creator.

We would finish this transmission through the instrument known as Jim. We thank this instrument and would leave it in love and in light. We are those of the principle known to you as Q'uo.

(Jim channeling)

I am Q'uo, and greet you once again in love and in light through this instrument. It has been our great privilege to speak on this topic this day, and we would offer ourselves in the attempt to speak to any further queries which those present might have for us at this time. Is there another query at this time?

Carla: Are you suggesting that each of us will at some point be given the opportunity to incarnate as a Christ?

I am Q'uo, and am aware of your query, my sister. Though this possibility is also one which is viable, the more likely opportunity is that of moving as does the Christ move within your own incarnation. For at some point in your experience of the third-density illusion, there is the illumination of the mind/body/spirit complex through its own efforts that is signified by the moving into the, shall we say, office of the Christ, the position of the entity which is fully enlightened as to the third-density experience.

Is there a further query, my sister?

Carla: Not just now. Thank you. I'll think about that.

I am Q'uo. We thank you once again, my sister. Is there another query at this time?

J: Can you tell us what was the preincarnative plan of the one known as Paul in the lifetime shortly following Jesus' death?

I am Q'uo, and though we believe that we understand your query, my sister, we are unable to respond to it in the manner in which you had hoped due to our inability to utilize this instrument or this contact in the level of trance, as you would call it, that would be necessary to retrieve this information. Thus, we are unable to respond in a manner other than suggesting that each entity incarnates with the desire to be of service and to utilize the life experience as a means of glorifying the one Creator.

Is there any further query, my sister?

J: No. Thanks.

I am Q'uo, and we thank you, my sister. Is there another query at this time?

Carla: I was thinking about Christ consciousness and I thought about a guy that saved a lot of people and lost his own life in so doing. I thought that was a very Christ-like impulse. Do such people move into this Christ consciousness in so doing, or is Christ consciousness simply a state of mind that is Christhood?

I am Q'uo, and am aware of your query, my sister. As you have described, there is a variety of ways in which an entity may move into a situation of that of a Christ; that is, one who would give his or her life for another. Your allusion provides numerous ways in which this may be done, either as a product of an attitude, as you have surmised, or as the product of the opportunity being presented in an instant and accepted in an instant. In either case, there is the, shall we say, previous decision made by the entity previous to incarnation, perhaps in agreement with the higher self, so that this entity shall be given the opportunity to—"prove its mettle" is the phrase we give this instrument—to be put to the test so that what has been learned previously, as you would measure the experience of time, can be offered as the foundation upon which shall be built the Christed consciousness that is the culmination of the experience in this third-density illusion.

In many instances the entity itself is not consciously aware that this is the process in which it partakes. But this is also a part of the nature of the third-density illusion in that there is a great deal more beneath the surface of events, as you would say, than appears at first glance. For each entity and each entity's experience is layered with vibrations of experience or meaning, each of which is able to add to the total experience so that an entity may become a participant in the event which you described and be moving into that position of the Christ in consciousness by the actions in which its own life is offered in favor of others. When the entity passes through those doors which you have described as larger life or death, the entity then has the remembrance of that which it was to attempt returned to it and is at that moment illuminated in the manner in which the consciousness is placed in the Christed being, shall we say.

Is there a further query, my sister?

Carla: No. Thank you.

I am Q'uo, and we are very honored to have been asked to join your circle at this time. We would again [like] to suggest that you take only that which we say that rings of truth to you, leaving behind all others. We offer our opinions and thoughts to you as freely as is given the breath of life, the energy of the one Creator, the light of the sun, as a blessing. We are hopeful that each will find some value therein.

At this time we shall take our leave of this instrument and this group, leaving each in the love and in the light of the one infinite Creator. We are known to you as those of Q'uo. Adonai, my friends. Adonai. ✸

www.ingramcontent.com/pod-product-compliance
Lightning Source LLC
Chambersburg PA
CBHW080420230426
43662CB00015B/2158